DOCUMENTATION ENCYCLOPAEDIA
OF
UNESCO AND EDUCATION

CONCEPTS IN COMMUNICATION, INFORMATICS & LIBRARIANSHIP (CICIL)

General Editor: S.P. AGRAWAL

CICIL-1	Development of Library Services in India: Social Science Information **S.P. Agrawal**	Rs. 150
CICIL-2	Development of Documentation in India: Social Science Information **S.P. Agrawal**	Rs. 250
CICIL-3	UNESCO and Social Sciences: Retrospect and Prospect **S.P. Agrawal** and **J.C. Aggarwal**	Rs. 250
CICIL-4	INDIANA : A Bibliography of Bibliographical Sources **M.K. Jain**	Rs. 200
CICIL-5	Dimensions of Library and Information Science: Kaula Festschrift **V. Venkatappaiah** (Eds.)	Rs. 600
CICIL-6	Book Numbers: Some Indian Methods **M.P. Satija** and **S.P. Agrawal**	Rs. 100
CICIL-7	National Policy for University Libraries in India: Problems and Perspectives **N.B. Inamdar** and **L.S. Ramaiah** (Ed.)	Rs. 250
CICIL-8	Media Utilisation for the Development of Women and Children **B.S. Thakur** and **Binod C. Agrawal**	Rs. 150
CICIL-9	Terrorism: An Annotated Bibliography **Susheela Bhan** (Ed.)	Rs. 275
CICIL-10	Transnational Library Relations: The Indo-American Experience **M.B. Konnur**	Rs. 175
CICIL-11	Geography of Marketing and Commercial Activities in India (Documentation on Research Information) **R.S. Dixit**	Rs. 130
CICIL-12	Information India 1988: Global View **S.P. Agrawal** and **J.C. Aggarwal**	Rs. 200
CICIL-13	Women's Education in India: Historical Review, Present Status and Perspective Plan **S.P. Agrawal** and **J.C. Aggarwal**	(in press)
CICIL-14	Cultural Communication in India: Role and Impact of Phonograms **J.M. Ojha**	(in press)
CICIL-15	Second Historical Survey of Educational Development in India: Select Documents 1985-1989 **S.P. Agrawal** and **J.C. Aggarwal**	(in press)
CICIL-16	Documentation Encyclopaedia of UNESCO and Education **J.C. Aggarwal** and **S.P. Agrawal**	(in press)
CICIL-17	Attitude Towards Information: A Study of Post-Graduate Teachers and Researchers in Social Sciences **N.G. Satish**	(in press)
CICIL-18	Librarianship and Bureaucratic Organisation: A Study in the Sociology of Library Profession in India **P.K. Jayaswal**	Rs. 175
CICIL-19	Literature Search **K.A. Isaac**	Rs. 150
CICIL-20	Child Education in India: Index to Scholarly Writings in Indian Educational Journals and Newspapers since independence **S.P. Agrawal** and **Naresh Kanta**	Rs. 100
CICIL-21	Lok Sabha and Vidhan Sabha Elections in India 1989 & 1990: Process and Results with Comparative Study of Manifestos **S.P. Agrawal** and **J.C. Aggarwal**	Rs. 250
CICIL-22	Islamic Studies in India: A Survey of Human, Institutional and Documentary Sources **Mohamed Taher**	(in press)
CICIL-23	Panchayati Raj: An Annotated Bibliography **N.B. Inamdar, N.G. Satish** and **Anil Takalkar**	(in press)
CICIL-24	Information India 1989-90: Global View **S.P. Agrawal** and **J.C. Aggarwal**	Rs. 500
CICIL-25	First Handbook of Psychological and Social Instruments **Udai Pareek** and **T. Venkateswara Rao**	(in press)

Concepts in Communication Informatics & Librarianship - 16

General Editor: S.P. AGRAWAL

DOCUMENTATION ENCYCLOPAEDIA OF UNESCO AND EDUCATION

PART ONE

J. C. AGGARWAL
S. P. AGRAWAL

CONCEPT PUBLISHING COMPANY, NEW DELHI 110059

ISBN 81-7022-329-6

First Published 1991

Published and Printed by
Ashok Kumar Mittal
Concept Publishing Company
A/15-16, Commercial Block, Mohan Garden
NEW DELHI 110059 (India)

Lasertypeset by
Microtech Advance Printing Systems (Pvt.) Ltd.
H-13, Bali Nagar
NEW DELHI-110015

General Editor's Introduction

The present publication in CICIL series is in the format of a reference volume which can be consulted conveniently by the interested and by those looking up for information about UNESCO and what it has done to promote education during the last four decades or so of its existence, as also by somebody trying to ascertain what the meeting of minds from various nations produced at various conferences, seminars and workshops held under its aegis.

In the recent past, the august organisation saw much display of dissatisfaction by a few countries with its administrative functioning. It is to be hoped that UNESCO will be judged by the statesmen on its overall record, and while some corrective measures may be necessary, UNESCO will continue to get the support of the developed nations for the betterment of a large underprivileged world.

S.P. AGRAWAL

Contents

SECTION II
OVERVIEW OF UNESCO'S ROLE IN EDUCATION

SECTION III
FACETS OF UNESCO'S EDUCATION PROGRAMMES
(Reports)

SECTION I

UNESCO AND ITS MISSION

1

UNESCO: Its Ideal and Functioning

November 4, 1946, is a landmark in the history of the world as the United Nations Educational, Scientific and Cultural Organisation (popularly abbreviated as UNESCO) came into being on this day when 20 States ratified the Constitution which had been drawn up at the London Conference a year earlier.

IDEAL OF UNESCO

The remark, made by Paul Valery between the two world wars that *"A Society of minds is the prerequisite for a Society of Nations"* was a source of inspiration to thinkers and politicians alike when, to strengthen the action of the League of Nations, they undertook to create the first international bodies[1] for intellectual co-operation in Geneva and Paris.

This humanist ideal was part of the body of ideas formed at a crucial moment during the Second World War by those who from 1942 onwards were to found the United Nations, whose network of institutions includes UNESCO.[2]

---

1. The *International Committee on Intellectual Co-operation* founded in 1922 as part of the League of Nations in Geneva, which in 1931 became the *Organization of Intellectual Co-operation*; and the *International Institute on Intellectual Co-operation* offered by France to the League of Nations in 1924, with its headquarters in Paris.

2. In the *Declaration by the United Nations* (1-1-1942), 26 governments pledged to continue fighting together against the Axis Powers. The *UN Charter* was signed in San Francisco on 26th June, 1945 by the representatives of 50 governments. The *UN* was officially established on 24th October of the same year, with 51 founding members. UNESCO officially came into being almost one year later on 4th November, 1946.

The immense scale of this conflict and the barbarity it unleashed loomed large in the minds of the founding fathers, who were as influenced by the spectre of war and the dangers of fanaticism as they were by the philosophy of enlightenment and the ideology of human rights.

Their goal was simple: peace based on respect for human rights. Such was the sole objective of these newly formed institutions. On the one hand, it was up to the United Nations and its highly political organs – the General Assembly and the Security Council – to uphold the peace in their dual role as diplomats and policemen. On the other hand, it was up to other, more "idealistic" institutions, UNESCO foremost among them, to further this peace using the instruments of education, science and culture.

At the preparatory conference convened in London by Great Britain and France, the head of the French delegation, Leon Blum, declared that the aim of the future organization would be *"to create the spirit of peace throughout the world"*. Ellen Wilkinson, Minister of Education for England and Wales, concurred in this belief by saying: *"Our watchword is educate so that the minds of the peoples shall be attuned to peace."*

This philosophy is spectacularly summed up in the opening paragraph of UNESCO's Constitution: *". . . since wars begin in the minds of men, it is in the minds of men that the defences of peace must be constructed."* This concept, which owes its force and success to the succinctness of its formulation, was put into words by the American poet Archibald MacLeish and the British Labour Prime Minister Clement Attlee.

The Preamble and Article I of the Constitution go on to develop this initial postulate. Therein, UNESCO's founders declare:

> ". . . the great and terrible war which has now ended was a war made possible by the denial of the democratic principles of the dignity, equality and mutual respect of men, and by the propagation, in their place, through ignorance and prejudice, of the doctrine of the inequality of men and races (. . .) a peace based exclusively upon the political and economic arrangements of governments would not be a peace which could secure the unanimous, lasting and sincere support of the peoples of the world (. . .) the peace must therefore be founded, if it is not to fail, upon the intellectual and moral solidarity of mankind."

Heritage, and non-intervention in matters within the domestic jurisdiction of States are the key concepts of this Constitution, of which no fundamental clause has been changed in forty years.

This text, both in letter and in spirit, is evidence that UNESCO's mission was essentially intended to be an ethical one, and that unlike other specialized United Nations agencies, it was first entrusted with the task of ensuring the intellectual and moral development of mankind before attempting to influence its material development.

The Mexican Jaime Torres Bodet, who succeeded Huxley as Director-General, saw UNESCO as the "conscience of the United Nations". The Indian Prime Minister Jawaharlal Nehru, on the other hand, spoke of "the conscience of mankind".

HOW UNESCO CAME INTO BEING?

The immediate ancestor of UNESCO was a war-time conference of Allied Ministers of Education which had the limited aim of planning ahead for the reconstruction after the war. This conference was held in London in November 1942. Within one year the conference moved towards setting up a truly international organization. The United States of America and the USSR sent observers to the meeting of the Allied Ministers of Education. Australia, Canada, China, India, Luxembourg, New Zealand and South Africa became members.

The conference examined a proposal by a committee headed by the British scholar Gilbert Murray calling for a permanent organization for education and better understanding and agreed that all members of the United Nations should be asked to join. It also set up an executive Bureau to consider the long-term project of a United Nations Bureau of Education. The British and French Governments invited all United Nations Member States to a conference in London in November 1945, which decided on the creation of an educational and cultural organization of the United Nations. Science which had lately produced the atom bomb was also to be a major concern along with education and culture.

The Constitution adopted at the 1945 Conference took effect a year later when Greece, as the 20th State to do so, deposited the instrument of ratification in London. The organization thus began its official life on November 4, 1946. A Preparatory Commission with which the Secretariat had moved into Hotel Majestic on the Avenue Kleber in Paris became UNESCO, with the British biologist Julian Huxley as its first Director-General.

UNESCO is a specialized agency of the United Nations but both constitutionally and financially are independent though its work is coordinated with the United Nations and other specialized agencies through the United Nations Economic and Social Council.

The organization's headquarters are in Paris where the General Conference and Executive Board meet periodically, and where its general directorate and the Directors of various Departments, Bureaus and Services have their offices. Yet a significant proportion of the Secretariat is not stationed in Paris. It is scattered all over the world.

Today UNESCO is a group of 158 member States with two Associate Member States, ranging round the world from the vastness of China to the tiny San Marine. All the sovereign States together voting with equal rights in UNESCO's General Conference, decide the organization's programme and pay for its implementation. Many of these are young nations that cast off the colonial yoke only recently and are set to determine their own destinies. The past three decades have seen the birth of many new nations, principally in Africa, the Middle East and Asia. These nations want a higher standard of living for themselves and their children. This "revolution of rising expectations", as it has been called, has had a profound effect on the evolution of the work of UNESCO and the whole United Family in recent years.

The first session was held in Paris in November 1946. Until 1952, it met every year; since then sessions have been held every two years. For 12 years it met either in Paris or in other cities upon the invitation of Member States. With the completion of permanent buildings at Place de Fontenoy at Paris (1958), this practice was discontinued and ever since sessions of the General Conference have been held at UNESCO's headquarters at Paris.

FUNCTIONING OF UNESCO

UNESCO as the Agency of the United Nations System

UNESCO, (the United Nations Educational, Scientific and Cultural Organization) is an association of States as opposed to a government-subsidized foundation as was the International Institute of Intellectual Co-operation (which was associated with the League of Nations and sponsored by France) from 1924 to 1940, and is a Specialized Agency of the United Nations system.

French philosopher Etienme Gibson called UNESCO "the soul" of the United Nations body. Endowed with special competence in its designated fields, UNESCO at the same time has a much broader and clearly political function: that of contributing to peace, specifically by taking action in the fields of education, science, culture and communication.

This dual mission, which makes UNESCO a political auxiliary of the United Nations, is also a sign of its originality – and ambiguity. Its founders, who were determined to avert the possibility of a third world war, had intentionally designed it this way. They dwelt on this subject at length in the Preamble and Article I of the Constitution. In the Preamble alone, the word "war" appears three times, and "peace" five times.

Its whole rationale is further summed up in the very first paragraph of Article I, which states: "*The purpose of the Organization is to contribute to peace and security by promoting collaboration among the nations through education: science and culture in order to further universal respect for justice, for the rule of law and for the human rights and fundamental freedoms which are affirmed for the peoples of the world, without distinction of race, sex, language or religion, by the Charter of the United Nations.*"

Structure

UNESCO's Constitution provides for three structural organs: an assembly called the "General Conference", which is the ultimate authority in all matters, a smaller body called the "Executive Board", which represents the General Conference between its sessions, and an administrative body, the "Secretariat", which is placed under the authority of a Director-General.

General Conference

The General Conference is the supreme body of UNESCO, the other two structural components being the Executive Board and the Secretariat, which is headed by the Director-General. This General Çonference is made up of the representatives of all the Member States of UNESCO.

The General Conference meets in ordinary session every two years for a period of approximately five weeks, either at Paris headquarters of the Organization or in a capital city of its choice. It may meet in extraordinary session if it decides to do so itself, if summoned by the Executive Board, or at the request of at least one-third of the Member States.

As defined by UNESCO's Constitution (Article IV), the General Conference is the supreme decision-making and supervisory body of the Organization. Its main task is to frame UNESCO's policy, adopt its programme and vote on the biennial budget. It elects the members of the Executive Board and appoints the Director-General. In the association of States making up UNESCO, it serves as a general assembly of Member States, the Executive Board acting as a kind of Board of Directors, monitoring the execution of UNESCO's programme by the Director-General, who is appointed for a six-year term of office.

The Constitution also stipulates that the General Conference can take on other functions as well, such as summoning international conferences of States, adopting recommendations (by a simple majority) or international conventions to submit to Member States (by a two-thirds majority), advising the United Nations on questions of concern to it within the fields of competence of UNESCO, and finally, considering the reports sent to the Organization by Member States on the action taken upon recommendations and conventions.

Executive Board

The Executive Board is the pivot between the General Conference, which is the sovereign legislative body, and the Secretariat, which executes the programme, deriving its authority from the General Conference which chooses Board members from among its delegates. The Board supervises all the operations of UNESCO, either by following instructions received from the Conference or by acting on its own initiative, in which case it is accountable to the higher body.

Its role is similar to that of the Board of Directors of a large company in between general meetings of shareholders.

In the period up until 1952, when UNESCO comprised a mere 50 States, the Board was made up of 18 members. Since then, its composition has been modified on several occasions to account for numerical and geographical changes in the Organization's membership. A decision taken by the 1980 General Conference has brought the number of seats up to fifty-one.

The General Conference elects Board members for a four-year term of office from among delegates appointed by governments. In doing so it also seeks to comply with the principle of "equitable geographical distribution". The Member States are accordingly divided into groups based on mainly geographical criteria for the purpose of electing members of the Executive Board: Group I (European countries, including Turkey, plus Israel and Canada) has ten seats. Group II (East European countries, including Yugoslavia and Albania, but also the Ukraine and Byelorussia) has four seats. Group III (Latin American and Caribbean countries) has nine seats. Group IV (countries from Asia and the Pacific) has eight seats. Group V (African and Arab countries) has twenty seats. Negotiations therefore take place within each regional group to decide on candidates to be formally submitted to the General Conference for election. Members are not re-eligible for consecutive terms. At no time may more than one member from any one State sit on the Board.

Article V of the Constitution requires that the Conference "*shall endeavour to include persons competent in the arts, the humanities, the sciences, education and the diffusion of ideas*", and, the Article adds, "*qualified by their experience and capacity to fulfil the administrative and executive duties of the Board*".

The founding fathers had anticipated that the members of the Board would speak in their personal capacity, deriving their authority from their own personal experience in educational, scientific or cultural activities. However, in 1954 in Montevideo (Uruguay), the General Conference departed from this provision, deciding that henceforth each member of the Board would represent the State of which he or she was a national. In addition, since 1976, a Member State may, on grounds of "*exceptional circumstances*", request the replacement of a representative while still in office, regardless of the member's personal wishes.

On average, the Board meets for approximately eighteen weeks in General Conference years (it remains in session for the duration of the Conference and must also have time to examine the draft programme and budget for the forthcoming biennium to be submitted to the Conference), and for about twelve weeks in non-Conference years. The sessions are held in the spring and autumn. At the close of the ordinary session of the General Conference, it also meets briefly to elect its Bureau.

A special session of the Board may be called by the Chairman acting on his own initiative or at the request of six of its members.

Bureau, Commissions, Committees and Groups:

Although the Board conducts much of its work in plenary, it also has various subsidiary bodies to ease its workload:

1. The Bureau, composed of the Chairman and six Vice-Chairmen of the Board, plus the five Commission and Committee Chairmen. The Bureau therefore has a membership of twelve, with two members from each geographical region. The Chairman of the Board – since 1985 Ivo Margan of Yugoslavia – has no statutory duties other than those naturally attributable to his position, but this does confer on him a significant degree of moral authority which he can exert behind the scenes, for instance in negotiations on thorny issues or when selecting candidates to be proposed by the Board for various posts.
2. Five "Permanent subsidiary bodies", which in fact meet at the same time, or just before, the Board itself:
   - Two commissions, of which all Board members are automatically members, one in charge of the programme and external relations and the other handling financial and administrative affairs;
   - A "Special Committee", which was first set up in 1956 and, in one form or another, has on several occasions been given the responsibility of studying the functioning of the Organization and its working methods for the Board. In 1986, it was assigned the task of monitoring the implementation of reforms aimed at improving the functioning of UNESCO, and was reorganized and restructured for this purpose. For reasons of efficiency, the Special Committee (under the chairmanship of Jose Israel Vargas of Brazil) is now made up of only 18 members, three for each geographical region, as against 33 in the previous one.
   - Two other committees, one on conventions and recommendations and the other on non-governmental organizations (NGOs).
3. Working groups, set up on an *ad hoc* basis, as the agenda or particular circumstances may require.

An offshoot of the General Conference, the Executive Board is first responsible for preparing the agenda for the Conference. It examines all the programmes and budget proposals submitted to it by the Director-General. It is responsible to the Conference for the execution of the programmes adopted by the Conference, and is required to take "*all necessary measures to ensure the effective and rational execution of the programme by the Director-General*" [Constitution, Art. V, para 5(b)]. Finally, it nominates the candidate which the General Conference may appoint to the post of Director-General.

Secretariat

The Secretariat is organized and directed by the Director-General and is the executive body responsible for Unesco's formal functioning and for the application of decisions taken by the General Conference and the Executive Board, particularly in carrying out the programme. Responsible for an international task the Secretariat itself is international in its composition and status. Its members are recruited on as wide a geographical basis as possible, subject to the paramount consideration of securing the highest standards of integrity, efficiency and technical competence. Their status, similar to that of all secretariats in the United Nations system, gives these officials certain privileges and immunities similar to those granted to diplomats. But it carries with it strict obligations of objectivity and impartiality along with the discretion and tact indispensable for international service. In particular, they are expected neither to seek nor accept instructions from any authority – governmental or otherwise – outside the organization. Seventy five per cent of staff is based at headquarters in Paris and the remainder in the field where UNESCO has many offices: 11 Regional Offices, 19 Regional Advisers or Sub-regional Advisers and 29 representatives.

GENERAL DETAILS

Permanent Delegations

Many Member States have set up permanent delegations to UNESCO. They have their offices in Paris. These offices act as direct liaison agencies between UNESCO and the representative governments and are responsible for maintaining day-to-day contact. There are at present 124 permanent delegations, six Liaison Officers and six Observers.

National Commissions

Article VII of the Constitution of UNESCO requires that "Each Member State shall make such arrangements as suit its particular conditions for the purpose of associating its principal bodies interested in educational, scientific and cultural matters with the work of the organization, preferably by the formation of National Commission broadly representative of the Government and such bodies", and that "National Commissions or National Cooperating Bodies, where they exist, shall act in an advisory capacity to their representative delegations to the General Conferences and to their governments in matters relating to the organization and shall function as agencies of liaison in all matters of interest to it."

In fulfilment of the requirements of the Constitution of UNESCO and with a view to ensuring active participation of the people. Member States have set up National Commissions. These para-governmental National Commissions which are a distinctive feature of UNESCO's constitutional structure have become valuable liaison agents with the international secretariat. In this role, the National Commissions tend increasingly to fill an executive as well as an advisory function both for their governments and for UNESCO, and within countries they serve as a link between the organized State and free culture and they prepare the material which is given purpose and legal form by the session of the General Conference.

Regional Conferences are held at regular intervals to stimulate cooperation among National Commissions.

153 Member States of the Organization have set up a National Commission, the most recent being that of Antigua and Barbuda, established in 1988 following: five countries do not have National Commissions are Namibia in Africa, Fiji and Samoa in the Asia and the Pacific region, the Bahamas and Saint Christopher and Navis in the Latin America and the Caribbean region. The members of the Commission include representatives of Ministries and of the main groups (educators, scientists, artists, researchers, journalists, etc.). Of all the National Commissions, the French Commission is one of the oldest and the largest. (see also Appendix E).

National Commissions have turned out to be the natural defenders of UNESCO's cause and its most powerful advocates in their respective countries. This was particularly evident when the United States withdrew from the Organization in December 1984 and then Great Britain in December 1985: the American National Commission dissociated itself from its government's decision. The American John Fobes, Deputy Director-General under Rene Maheu and subsequently under Amadou-Mahtar M'Bow, founded the association "*Americans for University*" which is working for the return of the United States to UNESCO.

Similarly, David Church, Secretary-General of the British Commission, was one of the founders of the "*Friends of UNESCO*" association which is actively engaged in securing Great Britain's return to an organization which it has so largely helped to make what it is today.

Working Languages

Working languages in the Secretariat are English and French, the languages of the General Conference and the Executive Board are English, French, Russian and Spanish. The General Conference has since its 15th session, provided interpretation into and from Arabic for its plenary sessions and the meetings of its two Principal Commissions and also the translation into Arabic of its more important documents. Arabic was used for the first time during the 16th General Conference in 1970.

Principal Sectors of UNESCO

1. *Education Sector*

(a) Division of Educational Policy and Planning.
(b) Division of Financing of Education.
(c) Division of Equality of Educational Opportunity and Special Programme.
(d) Division of Educational Sciences, Contents and Methods of Education.
(e) Division of Science, Technical and Environmental Education.
(f) Division of Higher Education and of Training of Educational Personnel.
(g) Division of Primary Education, Literacy and Adult Education and Rural Areas.

Activities of the Education Sector are supplemented by the following institutions:

(i) International Bureau of Education (IBE), Geneva.
(ii) European Centre for Higher Education (CEPES), Bucharest.
(iii) International Institute of Educational Planning (IEP), Paris.

2. *Natural Science Sector*

(a) Division of Ecological Sciences.
(b) Division of Science and Technology Policies.
(c) Division of Scientific Research and Higher Education.
(d) Division of Water Sciences.
(e) Division of Earth Sciences.
(f) Division of Technological Research and Higher Education.
(g) Division of Marine Sciences.
(h) Secretariat of the International Oceanographic Commission.

3. *Social and Human Sciences Sector*

(a) Economic and Social Science Division.
(b) Division of Philosophy and Human Sciences.
(c) Division of Human Rights and Peace.
(d) Population Division.
(e) Youth Division.

4. *Culture Sector*

(a) Division of Cultural Heritage.
(b) Division of Studies and Dissemination of Cultures.
(c) Division of Cultural Development and Artistic Creation.

Liaison Office is at Venic, Italy.

5. *Communication Sector*

(a) Division of Free Flow of Information and Communication Policies.
(b) Division of Development of Means of Communication.
(c) International Programme for the Development of Com-

munication.

(d) Division of Book Promotion, Audio-Visual and International Exchanges.

6. *External Relations and Information Sector*

(a) Office for External Relations:

(i) Africa Division.
(ii) Asia and Pacific Division.
(iii) Arab States Division.
(iv) Europe Division.
(v) Latin America and Caribbean Division.
(vi) National Commissions and UNESCO Clubs Division.
(vii) International Organizations and Foundation Division.
(viii) Public Relations Division.

(b) Office of Public Information:

(i) Press Division.
(ii) Division of Audio-Visual Information.
(iii) Division of Production, Distribution and Pooling of Basic Information and Documentation Material

Liaison Offices are at Geneva and New York and Information Services at Washington and Vienna.

7. *General Programmes and Programme Support Sector*

(a) Division of Copyright.
(b) Office of Statistics.
(c) UNESCO Courier and Periodical Division.
(d) Division of the General Information Programme.
(e) UNESCO Library Archives and Documentation Services Division.
(f) Office of the Unesco Press.
(g) Office of Conferences, Languages and Documents.

8. *General Administration Sector*

(a) Bureau of the Comptroller.

(b) Bureau of Personnel.
(c) Bureau of Data Processing Services.
(d) Bureau of General Services.

In addition there are the secretariat of the General Conference, Secretariat of the Executive Board, Office of International Standards and Legal Affairs, four Regional Coordinators (Africa, Arab States, Asia and the Pacific, Latin America and The Caribbean), Inspectorate General, Office of Mediator, Bureau of Studies and Programming, Bureau of the Budget and Central Evaluation Unit.

THE BUDGET

The adoption of UNESCO's budget is the responsibility of the General Conference, and is in fact one of the most important tasks it has to deal with at its ordinary biennial sessions.

Income

At the opening of each session, the General Conference is presented with the Draft Programme and Budget of the Organization which outlines the resources needed to carry out UNESCO's activities over the forthcoming financial period.

The largest contributions, going down the scale are made by: Japan (10.71%), the USSR (10.08%), the Federal Republic of Germany (8.16%), France (6.29%), Italy (3.74%), Canada (3.02%), Spain (2.00%), The Netherlands (1.72%), Australia (1.64%), Brazil (1.38%), the German Democratic Republic (1.31%), the Ukrainian Soviet Socialist Republic (1.26%), Sweden (1.24%), Belgium (1.17%) and Switzerland (1.11%), all other contributions falling into the under 1% category. At the opposite end of the spectrum, in the scale of assessment of contributions there is a minimum rate of 0.01% which is applied to 77 Member States and 2 Associate Members, the vast majority of which are developing countries. Before it withdrew from the Organization, the United States contribution represented 25% of mandatory contributions; the United Kingdom's, 4.80%, and Singapore's, 0.10%, making a total of 29.90%.

Briefly, this income is derived from two sources:

1. the statutory contributions of Member States, which make up the

bulk of the Organization's "regular" budget and cover the expenses of its regular programme. These contributions, which are something like a membership fee paid in order to belong to UNESCO, are calculated according to a scale of assessments used throughout the United Nations system, based primarily on the GNP and number of inhabitants of each Member State.

2. "extra-budgetary" resources, which for the most part are used to implement operational projects in the fields of education, science and culture. These resources are contributed mainly by other United Nations agencies (particularly the United Nations Development Programme, UNDP), but they can also come from banks and regional institutions (such as AGFUND, the Arab Gulf Programme for the United Nations Development Organizations) and voluntary contributions by Member States, institutions or even private individuals.

Expenditure

The position of the General Conference differs according to whether the programme in question is financed through regular or extra-budgetary funds. In the first case, it has sovereign power to decide how resources are to be allocated. It approves – after amendment if necessary – the draft programme submitted to it, which includes the budgets for each Major Programme, miscellaneous services (management, administrative services, etc.) and posts assigned to them.

On the other hand, even though the operational programmes financed from extra-budgetary resources are part of the Organization's programmes, the amount of these resources and the purposes for which they are allocated are submitted to the General Conference for information only. The donor organizations alone decide how they are to be used.

UNESCO's role here is that of an executing agency for projects falling within its fields of competence. Such is the case for "funds-in-trust", an arrangement whereby one or more Member States make voluntary contributions in order to finance a specific project in an area relevant to UNESCO's mandate, for which one or several other Member States have requested its assistance. The Organization generally takes a percentage of these extra-budgetary resources – usually 13% – to cover its overhead costs.

Notional Currency Value

UNESCO pays roughly two-thirds of its expenses in French francs (its headquarters is in Paris) and in Swiss francs. Its budget, however, is calculated in American dollars, as it is throughout the United Nations system. Exchange rates being neither fixed nor predictable, the budget is worked out in "constant" dollars whose value is fixed in relation to the French and Swiss francs.

For this reason, a provision is set aside to cover currency fluctuations. This provision can be either positive or negative, depending on the foreseeable fluctuation in the value of the American dollar, and its amount is established on the basis of the difference between the constant dollar rates and the actual exchange rates prevailing in the month preceding the General Conference. Thus, for current expenditure in dollars, the budget will be debited with the exact sum in dollars, whereas for any expenditure in French or Swiss francs the budget will be debited or credited with a sum calculated on the basis of the theoretical exchange rates of the constant dollar, and the provision in Part VIII will be debited or credited with a sum corresponding to the difference between the actual current exchange rate and the theoretical rate set for the constant dollar.

The budget also features an "appropriation" reserve to cover the impact of inflation on the costs incurred by UNESCO during the biennium.

In accordance with the Financial Regulations, at the close of the financial period, any unspent regular budget resources are refunded to the Member States according to the same rates of assessment as are used to calculate their contributions. Such "refunds" have mainly been the result of the surplus in the reserve for currency fluctuations (Part VIII) over the past few years. Under this system, over $ 150 million was refunded to Member States for the period 1981-1983.

Items of Expenditure

In the execution of the regular programme, some 55% of resources go to staff costs in 1988-89, a percentage that has been decreasing steadily over the past 10 years. Staff costs include not only the salaries of the people in charge of its programmes, but also those of the experts, specialists and consultants. The expenses devoted to the Major Programmes are distributed as follows, depending on their functions:

35.7% for training, 24.4% for collection, dissemination and exchange of information, 12.6% for participation in the implementation of activities in Member States, 10.8% for advance of knowledge, 10.4% for policy-making planning and project identification, etc.

The "External Auditor" (currently the External Auditor of the International Labour Office, who is also the Comptroller and Auditor-General of the United Kingdom) certifies the accuracy of UNESCO's accounts and financial statements. His report is submitted to and approved by each session of the General Conference.

FIGURES FOR 1988-89

Regular budget: $ 348,833,000, including $ 9,420,000 for the appropriation reserve (inflation, Part VII), with a positive provision of $ 13,711,000 for covering currency fluctuation (Part VIII).

In addition, UNESCO expects to receive $ 207 million in extra-budgetary resources, including $ 76 million in funding from UNDP and $ 39 million from funds-in-trust.

TABLE 1.1: Extra-budgetary resources/field of activity, 1984-1989

(in million $)

Project programmes	Total	for Less Developed Countries
Literacy, primary education, adult education	48.7	16.1
Policies, planning and management of education	31.1	8.8
Population education	29.8	7.3
Training of education personnel	23.2	17.8
Research in education and its application	22.4	7.8
Technical and vocational education	16.5	9.3
Educational infrastructures, equipment and materials	15.5	9.1
Science and technology education	12.2	3.6
Higher education and training	7.3	1
Environment education and information	2.6	—
Others (preventive education, etc.)	1.8	—
Extra-budgetary resources utilized	211.2	80.8
Number of projects	755	248
Number of countries concerned	125	42

UNESCO COUPONS SCHEME

UNESCO issues international coupons in US dollars as a means of payment permitting research workers and students form countries with a weak currency to purchase publications, films, textbooks, audio-visual materials, scientific equipment and products, machine tools, measuring instruments, etc. intended for educational, scientific and cultural purposes.

TABLE 1.2: Total Resources Foreseen, 1990-91

(in million $)

Resources	Amount
Expected extra-budgetary resources	190 (34%)
Resources approved by the twenty-fifth session of the General Conference of UNESCO	380 (66%)
Total	570 (100%)

Note: UNESCO's own budget includes resources provided to Member States for national and regional activities which strengthen the Organization's action (Participation Programme). Extra-budgetary resources are provided by various international and bilateral financing agencies.

TABLE 1.3: Distribution of Programme Allocations by Major Fields, 1990-91

Fields	Percentage of Amount
Education	39
Natural Sciences	29
Culture	15
Human & Social Sciences	11
Communication	6
Total	100

Note: The allocations to education represent 39 per cent of the total. Within education about 35 per cent are foreseen for activities concerning *Basic Education for All.* Furthermore many of the activities in other parts of the Programme and in UNESCO's specialized institutes are also directed to this goal.

The scheme has continued to grow, due mainly to the accession of several new Member States; at present, nearly 100 Member States benefit from its various advantages either as users or as suppliers. The value of UNESCO coupons, which had not exceeded an annual average of 500,000 dollars during the first three years, has reached an annual average 14 million dollars over the past five years. The scheme's master file groups the names and addresses of more than 10,000 publishers, booksellers and suppliers of educational and scientific material and more than 2,000 addresses of national and international institutions, scientific societies and associations and non-governmental organisations from all over the world, all of them regular users of UNESCO coupons.

This is how the programme functions. The coupons, whose value is expressed in United States dollars, are issued by the Organisation in the fcllowing denominations: 1000, 100, 30, 10, 3, and 1 dollar, "Blank" coupons which can be made out for the sum of 1 to 99 cents are also available. The coupons are a real means of payment, permitting educators, research, workers and students from countries with a "weak" currency to purchase publications, films and materials intended for educational, scientific and cultural purposes. This includes school textbooks copies of courses, reproductions of works of art and sheet music. It also includes raw film, developing material, radio and television sets, tape-recorders, exercise books, pencils, typewriters and musical instruments, as well as scientific equipment, chemical products, machine, tools and measuring instruments.

In some cases, the coupons have been used to fit up and furnish schools and universities and fully equip research laboratories and hospital services where future doctors are trained. UNESCO coupons can also be used to pay for subscriptions to institutions of an educational, scientific for cultural nature, and for university registration fees and copyright dues.

In every user country there is a body – often the National Commission for UNESCO – which is responsible for the sale of the coupons, and which supplies information concerning their purchase. In case where it has only a limited allocation of coupons, this body decides on an order of priority for the various requests received.

The user countries form three distinct groups according to the possibilities of payment to the Organisation.

Firstly, Member States whose local currencies are convertible internationally or who are able to make their payments in one of the convertible currencies used regularly by the Organisation. For these countries, there are no limits on the use of UNESCO coupons.

Secondly, Member States with local currencies which are non-convertible internationally and which are not used by the Organisation. These countries can obtain coupons under agreement with the United Nations Development Programme, reached through the Comptroller, and subject to the needs of UNDP for each of the currencies in question. The agreements are concluded for a given period and for a sum in dollars fixed in advance.

Lastly, Member States with internationally nonconvertible local currencies not used by the Organisation, UNDP or the other specialised Agencies of the United Nations, have the possibility of obtaining small allocations of UNESCO coupons under the Revolving Fund to assist member States in acquiring educational and scientific material necessary for technological development.

UNESCO FELLOWSHIPS

The UNESCO Training Abroad Programme, which originated initially in the exchange of personnel service in 1947, offers fellowships and travel grants to mature persons already engaged in careers to improve their academic and professional competence. In many development-oriented projects, fellowships equip persons already intimately connected with the project to take over as counterparts of outside experts upon return. In some cases, fellowships go to promising young candidates to provide career training in vital areas for which study abroad is required, for example, in documentation, librarianship and the use of visual aids in education.

These UNESCO fellowships are available to nationals of all Member States, Associate Member States and Trusts and Non-Self-governing territories. Prospective fellows may apply to their own Governments which forward lists of most promising candidates to UNESCO for consideration and choice. UNESCO fellowships are available for study in fields falling within the domain of UNESCO's overall programme; education, natural sciences, social sciences, human sciences, culture and mass communication.

The different categories of fellowships offered by UNESCO are financed out of the funds provided or made available to UNESCO under a regular programme, a Participation Programme, Technical Assistance and Special Fund (the last two were amalgamated in 1960 under the United Nations Development Programme). Funds-in-Trust, Voluntary Contributions and assistance from the International Bank for

Reconstruction and Development (IBRD). In addition, the sponsored fellowships are paid for by the donating countries or organizations.

Generally speaking, all UNESCO fellowships provide for study outside the holder's own country; the rare exception is a fellowship given for study at an institute established to serve an entire region (for example, in Latin America) which happens to be located in the fellow's own country.

Fellowships under the Regular Programme are created by the General Conference when it decides on the Organization's biennial programme; these are offered either to specific nations or in open competition. Fellowships under the Participation Programme first awarded in 1955, are initiated by Member States in agreement with the Director General in fields of study selected by the General Conference. Education Assistance Fellowships, first awarded in 1951 were created at the request of Member States with a view to promoting their economic and social development and often as an integral part of the Education Assistance Project Fellowships financed from the Special Fund, first awarded in 1960, are always an integral part of a project initiated by a Member State; they are included in the Plan of Operation for the project which usually covers a period of several years. Sponsored fellowships are negotiated between the donor and UNESCO.

Study and travel programmes for fellowship holders are worked out in the UNESCO Secretariat with the advice of specialists in the relevant programme departments as well as of the administering agency in the host country. It is concerned with the implementation of the fellow's study programme. An academic Supervisor is appointed when considered essential.

Extension of the duration of a fellowship is granted only at the request of the fellow's Government and the United Nations Agency concerned, on the basis of recommendations made by the academic Supervisor and the administering agency.

UNESCO fellows are required to submit a report of their work upon completion of their fellowship.

UNESCO INDIVIDUAL GRANTS

Individual grants were first awarded to youth and student leaders in 1952 and are given every year since. The first individual grants for workers were awarded between 1955 and 1958, under a long term workers' exchange programme.

UNESCO TRAVEL GRANTS

UNESCO travel grants are awarded to groups and individuals.

Travel grants were first awarded to European workers for study tours lasting from 10 to 15 days in European countries not their own. In 1955, a similar inter-regional programme was begun in Latin America, Asia and Africa.

UNESCO'S INTERNATIONAL CONFERENCE CENTRE

Open 366 days in 1988. UNESCO's buildings hosted more than 1,200 meetings or events in the course of the year. UNESCO has 17 conference rooms with a total capacity of 3,700. Fourteen of these rooms are equipped for the interpretation and recording of debates (one room in seven languages, eight in six languages, two in five languages, one in four languages, one in three languages and one in two languages). Nine of these rooms are equipped with fixed screens and 16mm and 35mm films can be screened in three of them. UNESCO can also house exhibitions in ten different hall-way areas. In addition, an array of facilities are available to users: checking-in counters, areas for the production and distribution of documents, offices, lounge.

In 1988 the Headquarters hosted 63 meetings coming under the UNESCO programme, 53 unofficial meetings, 735 Secretariat meetings, 193 meetings organized by outside bodies, 38 Secretariat exhibitions, 22 other exhibitions, 53 evenings organized by the Secretariat and 33 by outside bodies.

Journalists have at their disposal a press-room, a photo library and three recording studios (two radio studios with transmission lines and telephone feeds and a video studio with Pal/Secam/NTSC transcoding equipment).

UNESCO also has a restaurant catering for 300 people, three cafeterias catering respectively for 72, for 330 and 400 and three bars. In 1988 some 6,700 outside users availed themselves of these facilities for cocktails and receptions.

A special service is responsible for receiving groups and individuals desirous of visiting the Headquarters buildings. In 1988 some 250 groups (10,000 persons) and 7,500 individual visitors were received.

A library and an archives reading room are available to the public on appointment. The library, which holds 150,000 volumes, 1,500 periodicals and 60,000 microfiches, received 12,500 visitors and the archives 2,600 visitors. The bookshop, open to all, sells 1,700 titles in the six working languages. The *UNESCO Courier* in 35 languages, more than 200 scientific maps and also sound recordings.

Other services such as a bank, a travel agency, a newspaper stand, a gift counter (medals, posters, stamps for collectors, greeting cards) are open to all.

Lastly, 58 art works offered by their authors or by Member States are placed in different parts of the Headquarters buildings. They include works by Calder, Giacometti Moore, Picasso, Tamayo, Vasarely, Matta, Arp and Miro.

UNESCO hosts meetings organized by governments non-governmental organisations, institutes, associations, foundations, etc. provided that the themes dealt with are consonant with the objectives of the Organization's programme and are not likely to impair the image or reputation of UNESCO or its Member States. Requests, constantly on the increase in recent years, concern meetings or conferences and exhibitions, gala evenings or concerts. In 1988 some 248 events took place in the Headquarters buildings, drawing thousands of delegates, spectators or visitors. Some examples are:

* General Assembly of the International Radio and Television University;
* Congress of the International League of Antiquarian Booksellers;
* Congress on Ultra-sounds organized by the French Association for the application of ultra-sounds to medicine;
* International Conference on Buddhism in Western Culture organized by the Permanent Delegation of Sri Lanka;
* First 'Journees Prospectives' of the newspaper *Le Monde*;
* Symposium on Disabled Persons and Museums, organized by the Fondation de France.

INFORMATICS PLAN

UNESCO's activities, of whatever nature, imply gathering, processing, producing and distributing information relating to its spheres of competence throughout the world, in all forms.

These activities still involve many repetitive tasks which are time-consuming at various levels of responsibility. Computer technology, first applied to centralized administration, has gradually been introduced into the individual work environment through training and recourse to microcomputers. Much remains to be done, however. In so far as computerized communication is concerned, the recent introduction of electronic mail marks a significant stage in the modernization of the services; as does the linking up of UNESCO with the EARN network and the United Nations International Computing Centre ir Geneva, which is under way.

In 1988, UNESCO also started on the preparation of the Informatics Plan, which will run parallel to the third Medium-Term Plan. Its main purposes are to increase significantly both individual and housewide efficiency and productivity, and to open UNESCO more widely to the outside world on a two-way basis.

Beyond the old automated management systems, the Organization is turning towards data-based informatics with synthesized data to make decision-making easier and to enhance its outreach.

By encouraging the use of high-performance, cogent computation equipment and productivity and initiative-oriented personal computer systems, as well as by linking up with international communication networks. UNESCO is seeking to improve its management, optimize its operations and consolidate its universality through the use of technology that is already shaping the world of the future.

UNESCO: THE DISSEMINATOR

UNESCO's publications rapidly gained worldwide recognition. Within the Organization, professionals from many horizons work in close collaboration with institutions, specialists, publishers and printers all round the world. To-date, over 8,000 titles have been published or co-published in the six official languages (English, French, Spanish, Russian, Arabic and Chinese) and translations of its works have been brought out in some eighty countries.

Recently, with the aim of turning UNESCO into a genuine 'university-type' publishing house. the publications policy has been given added impetus, to be reflected notably in the preparation and implementation of a publication plan for general public and prestige works.

The UNESCO Courier is doubtless UNESCO's best-known publication issued in thirty-five languages and in Braille (French, English, Spanish and Korean), this monthly provides its readership with a wide range of articles with information and ideas on such varied subjects as the history of civilizations, the arts, literature, human rights, ecology and development.

UNESCO's reference works have also become 'classics' for libraries the world over. *The Statistical Yearbook* and its shorter edition, the *Statistical Digest*, are 'a world in figures' about education, the sciences, culture and communication. *Index Translationum* is considered to be the 'bible' of translations published each year in the world *Study abroad*, which now has 26 editions to its name, offers thousands of opportunities for studies, fellowships and training courses in around a hundred countries.

The extent of UNESCO's education programmes is reflected in the number of subjects dealt with in its publications: staff training, teaching innovations, literacy training, new methods and technologies. . . *Learning to be* translated into 21 languages, will remain a classic in literacy education. *The New UNESCO Manual for Science Teaching* has become a best-seller in 27 languages. The publications of the *Education Sciences* collection prepared by the International Bureau of Education and of the series *Principles of Educational Planning*, produced by the International Institute for Educational Planning (IIEP), as well as studies on post-literacy and continuing education, have been welcomed by specialists in many countries. The review *Prospects* shares the experience of educationists and institutions in some 150 countries with its readers.

UNESCO's science activities include research and training programmes in precise areas such as hydrology, earth science, oceanography or ecology, which have been the subject of a large number of technical publications that have been appreciated by specialists and others.

Recent works that attracted public attention are *Feeding tomorrow's world*, *Women in engineering education* and *Science and Scientific researchers in modern Society*. Two quarterlies: *Impact of Science on Society* and *Nature and Resources* – an review on UNESCO's oceanography, hydrology, geology and ecology programmes – are distributed internationally.

The development of social sciences involves a vast programme of multi-disciplinary research: human rights, socio-economic development, population, status of women, youth. Among the recent publications, *Strategies for Endogenous Dévelopment*, *Famille, enfant et developpement en Afrique*, *Quels emplois pour les jeunes*? and *La Tolerance* (so far published in French only), were favourably reviewed by the press. Moreover, the *International Social Science Journal* is a regular forum for interdisciplinary exchange.

Among its publications in the field of culture, apart from the significant eight-volume *General History of Africa*, UNESCO publishes technical works on the preservation of monuments that are in heavy demand, as well as the quarterly *Museum*, which highlights the latest trends in museology. Ongoing projects include a set of publications on the Silk Roads and collection of the world heritage specially designed for younger readers.

UNESCO publishes many studies on communication planning and development, book promotion, the press and the media. Examples are the *ABC of Copyright*, which has become a reference must for publishing specialists and the *Copyright Bulletin*, which informs readers on agreements, legislation and the protection of literary, artistic and scientific work.

In the audiovisual field, UNESCO has issued slides on art and art teaching, special education and a series illustrating the ecological problems of today's world. UNESCO's films, brought out as video cassettes or 16 mm films, are distributed in over 100 countries. Furthermore, the photos and slides from its collection have been reproduced in the press the world over.

Since 1975, internationally famous artists have been working on a series of posters underlining their support for UNESCO's cause, in co-operation with the International Association of Art (AIAP). UNESCO also produces many posters illustrating its main programme activities.

It also edits two sets of medals: the first illustrates the monuments and sites on the World Heritage List and the second commemorates anniversaries of distinguished personalities and important historical events. Lastly, since 1960, the philately programme has produced several series of postage stamps with themes such as literacy, the Universal Declaration of Human Rights, environment and cultural heritage.

In order to encourage access to its publications by the public at large, UNESCO has set up a vast distribution network. On the one hand, the Organization makes available to the public all its library, research and information resources relating to UNESCO's action. Second, the UNESCO bookshop sells books, periodicals, scientific magazines and records, and the Office of Public Information (OPI) has audio-visual facilities, and stocks of medals, stamps, posters, brochures and newsletters, as well as a pressroom.

UNESCO's field units, the National Commissions, the depository libraries in 144 countries, and an international sales network, are all outlets scattered around the world for the distribution of its publications.

UNESCO Office of Public Information offers to the press and to the public the following services:

Press-room. UNESCO's Pressroom in Paris is open from 9.00 to 12.30 and from 14.30 to 18.00. Press services are also available in UNESCO's regional offices.

Video and Films. UNESCO distributes around the world films and documentaries concerning its activities. A catalogue of the material available and the addresses where material can be obtained regionally, is maintained at Headquarters.

Photolibrary and services. More than 200,000 slides and photographs on UNESCO's activities and programmes are available from UNESCO's photolibrary. These resources are available in Paris.

Documentation Centre. Answers all general information enquiries addressed to UNESCO.

UNESCO's GENERAL INFORMATION PROGRAMME

UNESCO and Information

UNESCO has been concerned with information matters since its foundation in 1946. Under its Constitution, it has a duty to maintain, increase and diffuse knowledge by:

* protecting the world's inheritance of books
* encouraging the exchange of information materials
* initiating international co-operative efforts to give the people of all countries access to the publications produced by any one of them.

It is of prime importance to strengthen the capacity of Member States to exchange, store and use information in support of their economic and social development. It is also necessary to reduce disparities among countries in the field of information, facilitate access to it by all and remove obstacles to its dissemination.

The General Information Programme (PGI) was established in 1976 to provide a focus for UNESCO's activities in specialized information, documentation, libraries and archives. It is the programme within which activities undertaken under UNISIST are carried out – UNISIST comprising the internationally developed methods, norms, standards, principles and techniques governing the processing and transfer of information, particularly through the use of modern computer and telecommunication technologies and their application to the development of compatible information systems. PGI also aims at strengthening national capabilities for handling information through the development of national information systems.

Activities

PGI is responsible (under the terms of the Medium-Term Plan 1984-1989) for most of the tasks carried out under Major Programme VII "Information Systems and Access to Knowledge". These tasks are divided into programmes and sub-programmes as follows:

1. Improvement of Access to Information: Modern Technologies, Standardization and Interconnection of Information Systems.

    * development of tools for the processing and transfer of information
    * development and use of databases through the application of modern technologies and normative tools
    * exchange and flow of information; regional and international co-operation among Member States and with the organizations of the United Nations system

2. Infrastructures, Policies and Training required for the Processing and Dissemination of Specialized Information.

    * national information policies and infrastructures
    * training of information personnel and information users

3. UNESCO Information and Documentation Systems and Services.

    * development of the specialized information services of UNESCO

Priorities

The highest priority among the above tasks is given to those relating to the development of information infrastructures and the training of information personnel and users. Activities aimed at promoting the formulation of policies and plans, promoting and disseminating methods, norms and standards, encouraging the adoption of modern technologies and contributing to the development of specialized information systems are prerequisites for coherent action intended to facilitate the exchange and transfer of information. In respect of each programme, special attention is paid to

* the needs of information users and potential users
* developing user-oriented information systems
* the needs of the least developed countries
* the importance of improving and encouraging

  the flow of and access to information
  creativity and innovation
  the production and use of local information

* the applications of information technology
* the need to evaluate the activities undertaken

Organization

An Intergovernmental Council of 30 members, elected by the General Conference, is responsible for guiding the conception and planning of the Programme. Its administration is the responsibility of the Division of the General Information Programme, whose Director reports to the Assistant Director-General for Studies and Programming.

Role and Functions

The primary role of PGI is to act as a catalyst in promoting and co-ordinating action to improve the provision and use of information throughout the world. It performs this role through consultation and collaboration with a variety of organizations including

* other UNESCO programmes

* Member States
* United Nations and its agencies
* intergovernmental and non-governmental organizations
* individual information specialists.

These relationships are illustrated in Fig. 1.1.

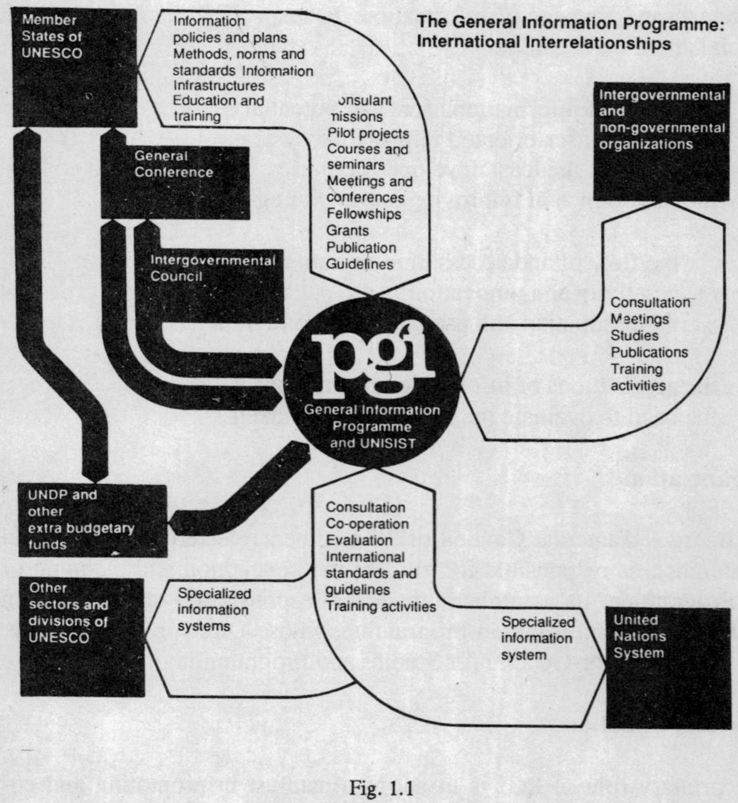

Fig. 1.1

PGI fulfils its role by promoting, sponsoring and supporting such activities as:

* meetings, consultations and conferences

* education and training courses and seminars
* pilot projects and consultancy missions
* study fellowships and equipment grants
* research, studies and publications

Finance

The work of PGI is financed from a variety of sources including the Regular Programme, the Participation Programme, Funds-in-Trust Agreements, Development banks, the United Nations Financing System for Science and Technology for Development and the United Nations Development Programme (UNDP). Its total budget from all sources for 1984-85 was approximately US $ 16 million.

Information Policies

PGI provides guidance to Member States on formulating and implementing national information policies and plans as part of overall national development plans. It also aims to promote regional co-operation in this field and to study obstacles to the flow of information. It stimulates greater participation in PGI activities by Member States, particularly through establishing links with national focal points and national committees.

National Information Policies

Guidelines on formulating and implementing national information policies were revised for publication in 1985. They are intended to help Member States to lay firm foundations for planning information provision in accordance with local needs.

Regional Co-operation

Regional meetings of experts are convened to advise on the harmonization of information activities in the regions through the selection of joint projects in priority areas.

Research and Studies

Several studies on aspects of information policy and plans and the collection of data for planning have been undertaken. One of the most important is a study of the development of an index of information Utilization Potential as a quantitative measure of information activity within a country. This will not only provide a basis for national planning of information provision but also facilitate comparisons of the ability of different countries to make effective use of information.

National Focal Points and Committees

The establishment of national focal points for information activities in Member States and of national committees to advise them on their links with PGI was initiated under UNISIST in 1973. By 1984, 57 Member States had established national focal points and 52 had established national committees. Seminars for the exchange of experience between these bodies are organized from time to time and renewed efforts are being made to establish regular communication with them.

Methods, Norms and Standards

The promotion and development of international methods, norms, standards, guidelines and other normative tools applicable to all processes of the information transfer chain are essential as a basis for establishing compatible systems to facilitate the exchange of information. A Working Group on Methods, Norms and Standards composed of specialists from developed and developing countries advises PGI on the implementation of the UNISIST standardization programme. PGI also works closely with the International Organization for Standardization (ISO) and other professional organizations and the results of its efforts are reflected mainly in guidelines and technical studies and in seminars intended to promote an awareness of the importance of standards in information work.

Guide to Standards

The *UNISIST Guide to Standards for Information Handling*, which explains existing standards and guidelines, is one of the major achievements in this field.

PGI has also worked in close collaboration with ISO in producing a revised and enlarged edition of the *ISO Standards Handbook 1: Information Transfer*, which contains the full text of all ISO standards on information.

Bibliographic and Terminological Control

The *UNISIST Reference Manual for Machine-Readable Bibliographic Descriptions*, (second edition, 1982) is designed for any type of information service involved in creating and managing bibliographic databases.

The Common Communication Format (CCF) is designed to facilitate the transfer of bibliographic records between systems using different formats which at present are incompatible.

The *ASCOBIC Manual on Bibliographic Control in Africa* has been revised and developed with the help of appropriate non-governmental organizations such as the Universal Bibliographic Control (UBC) office of the International Federation of Library Associations and Institutions (IFLA).

PGI was closely involved in the development of the International Serials Data System (ISDS) and the establishment of the International Information Centre for Terminology (Infoterm) and its associated international terminological data network, Term Net.

Subject Organization

PGI has worked closely with the International Federation for Information and Documentation (FID) in developing the general subject classification scheme known as the Broad System of Ordering (BSO). In collaboration with ISO, separate guidelines on the creation of monolingual and multilingual thesauri have also been produced.

Data Bases and Modern Technologies

PGI promotes the development and use in Member States of portable software packages for micro-computers for setting up specialized bibliographic and numerical data bases; it collaborates with Member States in launching integrated library and information service projects leading to the creation of local data bases, the exploitation of internationally available data bases, the establishment of linkages with host centres and the adoption of modern technologies.

Regional and International Networks

PGI collaborates with Member States and organizations of the United

Nations system in promoting the development of compatible specialized information networks at the regional and international levels, with a view to the gradual establishment of a Global Network of Scientific and Technological Information.

At present, the Regional Network for the Exchange of Information and Experience in Science and Technology in Asia and the Pacific (ASTINFO) is being developed. Similar projects are being promoted in Africa, the Arab states and Latin America and the Caribbean. Asia-Pacific Information Network in Social Sciences (APINESS) had also been launched in 1986.

Information Infrastructures

PGI promotes the creation and development of libraries, archives and information services, as well as the establishment of units performing referral, analysis, consolidation and repackaging of information, data compilation and information on on-going research and other functions which support the flow of information from the source to the user.

It promotes, in collaboration with IFLA, the concept of the Universal Availability of Publications (UAP), which aims at ensuring user access to published materials of all types whenever and wherever required.

Information Institutions and Networks

Support is provided through consultant missions, pilot projects and meetings to the development of information systems and networks in all parts of the world. The introduction of new technologies for information handling is encouraged as well as access to and interconnection of existing systems. Current projects are concerned with developing rural public libraries to support adult literacy programmes, promoting community use of university libraries and developing school library networks and library services to the handicapped.

Records and Archives Management Programme (RAMP)

This programme, which is implemented in consultation with the International Council on Archives (ICA), covers policies, norms and standards, infrastructures, training, research and other aspects of national, regional and international archival development.

New Information Technology

Activities in this field include the compilation of an inventory of software packages for information work, the development of a portable microcomputer package for bibliographic work and studies of the use of satellites and other telecommunications facilities in information transfer.

Education and Training

PGI promotes the training of information personnel and users. It is advised by an *Ad Hoc* Committee on Education and Training Policy and Programme.

Harmonization

The problems of harmonizing and co-ordinating education and training programmes in librarianship, information science and archival studies are dealt with by organizing expert meetings and symposia and by issuing guidelines on the subject.

Training Programmes

PGI has helped to establish permanent regional education and training facilities in several regions and supports national education and training programmes in many countries.

In addition, PGI each year sponsors ten to fifteen international or regional courses of seminars on various aspects of information work at various levels and supports the publication by FID of a quarterly newsletter on education and training programmes in the information field.

Teaching Materials

The needs of developing countries for suitable teaching materials in the field of information work have been studied, and a serious shortage of such materials in Arabic, French and Spanish was revealed. Support is provided to the FID International Clearing House for Information Education and Training Materials which collects teaching and training materials and makes them available to interested institutions. Teaching material prepared includes curricula, guidelines, textbooks and teaching packages.

Training of Information Users

The education and training of information users is a wide field in which only limited resources can be deployed. Guidelines for preparing and implementing a national plan for user education and a teachers' guide to the education and training of users of scientific and technical information have been published.

Programme Promotion and Support

PGI strives to promote a wider knowledge of the aims of its programme and to enhance the participation of Member States in its activities through exhibitions, audio-visual presentations, seminars and distribution of information files to focal points and national committees. It provides documentation support to PGI staff, consultants and experts and to Member States, and supplies copies of PGI documents and publications to the international community of users. It collaborates with UNESCO's Computerized Documentation Section in producing lists of UNESCO documents and publications on information matters and publishes the *PGI-UNISIST Newsletter* in Arabic, English, French, Russian and Spanish, distributed to some 7,000 selected institutions and specialists throughout the world.

Operations

PGI is concerned with the implementation in Member States of projects financed by UNDP or Funds-in-Trust Agreements and development banks as well as dealing with requests for assistance approved under the Participation Programme. It evaluates project proposals and helps Member States to prepare them. It undertakes the selection, recruitment and briefing of consultants and experts assigned to PGI missions and projects and ensures that reports on their work are produced. It also co-operates with the Fellowships and Equipment Division of UNESCO in allocating training fellowships and purchasing equipment for these projects. Major fields supported by extra-budgetary funds are infrastructure development in the fields of libraries, archives and specialized information, at regional and national level, and the training of information specialists. PGI, looking especially to the future, is giving particular support to the adoption of new technologies in information processing.

Specialized Information Systems

PGI promotes the application of the UNISIST normative tools in the development and running of UNESCO's information and documentation systems and services in the fields of education, the natural and social sciences, culture and communication.

The Intersectoral Committee for the Co-ordination of Activities in the field of Information, chaired by PGI, was set up in 1977 to monitor UNESCO's information activities and thus to allow for the harmonized planning and implementation of projects in this field among all sectors, including PGI, especially with regard to the development of sectoral information systems and services.

ADMINISTRATION

The reorganization at UNESCO since 1988 has been based on two complementary principles laid down by the Director-General at the beginning of 1988:

* Management of available resources in terms of objectives. Those in charge of each programme are therefore responsible, in particular for ensuring that the activities undertaken and the ways used to implement them are the most effective for attaining the specific objectives set by the General Conference.
* Attributing to each staff member the real responsibilities attaching to their function and the means of assuming them.

For this purpose the Director-General on 4th February, 1988, delegated a large part of his authority to the Assistant Directors-General, who in turn hand it down through all levels of the Secretariat. This delegation of authority implies real transparency in the way in which one and all give an account of their work.

The implementation of these principles has important implications for the whole operation of the Organization:

* *Evolving of the competency profiles.* The development of

efficiency calls for new competencies (e.g., to manage people or ability to work efficiently in a team and to work independently, to manage resources, to make decisions and to get others to participate). To enable staff members to acquire these competencies a management training programme was launched in 1989.

* *Evolving of working methods.* Introduction of new management tools: programme management chart, increased use of office equipment, development of effective formal and informal communication and cross-sectional methods of organization, intersectoral committees, idea groups, task forces.
* *Evolving style of management at all levels of Organization.* A new style of management is gradually being introduced reflecting the delegation of authority. Based on more confident working relations, it is aimed at ensuring that staff members are properly informed and can genuinely participate in decisions concerning them and at encouraging individual initiative to improve the efficiency of the Organization.
* *Evolving structures.* The new structures are designed to allow this new efficiency to develop fully.

Efforts are being centred on encouraging the formation of small integrated units, adapted to the methods of management by objectives and to fuller individual responsibility. In 1988 and 1989 priority was being given to the central and support services, that is, to all those services which enable the sectors to carry out the programme. During the second stage in 1990, efforts will be made to reorganize the other units of the Secretariat, which must adapt to the lines of emphasis of the third Medium-Term Plan, as approved by the General Conference.

The importance attached to management has also led to a reorganization of the Directorate, to the appointment of two Deputy Directors-General, one responsible for the implementation of the Programme and the strengthening of intersectoral co-operation, the other for the management of the Organization, and to the creation of the Office for Planning, Budgeting and Evaluation (PBE). The General Programmes and Programme Support Sector (PRS) and the Office of Public Information (OPI) have also been restructured along the same lines.

The strengthening of the Organization's advisory activities in its different spheres of competence – redefining of financing priorities in education, rational development of the science and technology potential, etc. – calls for a more developed 'systems analysis' approach to development problems than heretofore. UNESCO's operational action are therefore to be organized as follows:

* Closer co-operation between UNESCO and the resident co-ordinators of the United Nations system and the UNDP, which contributes 60 per cent of the funds for UNESCO's operational projects.
* At Headquarters, a Bureau for the co-ordination of operational activities to work out timeframes for the analysis of needs and for the formulation of the strategy of each sector.
* The programme sectors to strengthen their analytical functions and operational follow-up.

  The decentralized units in the field to direct their efforts more towards supporting development in UNESCO's spheres of competence and strengthening international co-operation in response to national and regional needs. Their staff will represent the entire organization and all its activities.

CONSTRAINTS

UNESCO faces the following constraints:

* As a result of world economic trends since 1973, all countries attach new importance to more rigorous management of their resources. Despite recognition of their efforts the agencies of the United Nations system, and UNESCO in particular have still to contend with considerable budgetary restrictions.
* The withdrawal of the United States, the United Kingdom and Singapore, in 1984 and 1985, not only deprives UNESCO of 30 per cent of its resources but also limits the contributions of these countries to the Organization's work.
* The effectiveness of an organization such as UNESCO depends in the first place on the existence of a strong consensus between the Member States concerning the goals to be attained and a will to go forward on the part of all the Organization's partners. The year 1988 was clearly marked by progress in this respect.
* UNESCO's staff is made up of nationals of more than 130 different countries who contribute the wealth of their cultures and

experience but add to the complexity of administration.

* Finally, UNESCO has to adapt its methods of evaluation, management and follow-up in order to remain competitive and meet the exigencies of its financial partners, on whom many of its activities in the developing countries depend.

2

UNESCO'S MISSION FOR 1990s

GENESIS

UNESCO's task within the United Nations System is to build the defences of peace in the minds of men as the foundation of development and international co-operation with primary emphasis being laid on education.

UNESCO Director-General Federico Mayor has recently observed[1] by way of comments which aptly define the parameters of UNESCO Mission.

> "UNESCO is not just a building in Paris. Its work involves real people with real problems all over the world. Children who may never see the inside of a schoolroom or a textbook. Teachers in need of training and advice. Scientists with inadequate equipment and little access to colleagues abroad. Decision-makers who do not have enough help to make better decisions. Rural communities cut off from the rest of their country. Men, women and children the world over as misunderstood as are their unique cultures, who remain wary of languages and lifestyles they cannot easily fathom by themselves. These are among the challenges facing UNESCO.
>
> In November 1987, the General Conference of UNESCO, concerned about the Organization future, called for reform, new programmes, a concentration on priority issues and a reinvigorated Secretariat, and chose the undersigned to spearhead this task. The Organization had to be in closer touch with its natural partners, to

1. Foreword to *1988 at UNESCO: New openings*, Paris, UNESCO, 1989.

be more present in the field, which is where it is most needed to help decision-makers, steer projects and prepare good new ideas. Furthermore, its specificity and credibility had to be enhanced.

UNESCO is not big enough to do everything by itself, with our relatively small budget, we could not possibly put everything right ourselves. That is why I so firmly emphasize our catalytic role. 'Ours is not to supply the bread, but the yeast' is, for some, a phrase I use too often. But I can find no better or simpler way of expressing my ideas about the part this Organization should play in development in the years to come. I shall, therefore, not tire of repeating it.

It will also be seen that we have begun to concentrate our programmes more, to 'do less, in order to do better'. The year 1988 has been one of 'openings', of transition, as we near completion of one six-year programming cycle and prepare a new one, searching for innovative approaches, better service and greater cost-effectiveness.

The preparation of the Organization's next Medium-Term Plan has taken up a lot of our time. When it comes into force on 1st January, 1990, UNESCO must be ready to act. And to do that fully means that universal membership must continue to be a fundamental objective.

Universality is not just a word or an ideal, it is a state of mind that deeply influenced the Organization's founders. Commitment to UNESCO must be as global, as universal, as are its goals.

Otherwise, UNESCO is not UNESCO."

1990-1995 PRIORITIES

In its overall programmes for the period 1990-1995, UNESCO has set itself three priority missions which pervade all its fields of action:

1. The construction of peace
2. The furtherance of soliditary and sustainable development
3. The reconciliation of man with nature.

PROCEDURES AND MEANS

The founders of the Organization were pragmatists. As far back as 1945, they considered that while political and economic agreements were essential, they were not enough to guarantee a lasting, universal peace. Other foundations had to be laid, of a spiritual kind — respect for human dignity, human rights and fundamental freedoms at all levels of existence and society; recognition of the equal dignity of all cultures and of their diversity, and individual and collective solidarity for worldwide development, again on both an individual and a collective basis. Dogmatism was unmasked as a form of fantasy, spawned by ignorance and the fear of what is different.

In 1988, UNESCO, after 40 years' existence during which it had made a major contribution to the world, needed to go back to its sources. The values it represented had lost none of their vitality or universality, but the structures, procedures and means available to it had become blunted or obsolete. There was an obvious need for renewal. The world had changed considerably but needed UNESCO just as much as before.

Communication is instantaneous, borders can be crossed, people are constantly on the move. In this global village the foremost concern is to reduce the unacceptable gap between industrialized countries and developing countries and the inequalities that persist today. More than even, the illiterates, the unemployed and the sick are neighbours. Their exclusion condemns everyone as does the lack of prospects for the young, who do not know which way to turn to find either themselves or their place in society and who are in danger of falling prey to drugs or to violence. Disease knows no frontiers. One country's pollution becomes another's, affecting 'its' clouds and 'its' rains river-borne waste travels from one country to another and into the oceans they share. The Amazonian rain forest, the ozone layer and the greenhouse effect are reminders of the interdependence of human beings, irrespective of their country, religion or political system.

The tasks assigned to UNESCO, which is the only intergovernmental organization of universal scope entrusted with such responsibilities, far exceed the resources granted to it, consisting as they do in promoting education for all and the worldwide spread and proper use of scientific and technological knowledge and facilitating the mutual enrichment of cultures and the flow of written and audio-visual information among all nations.

UNESCO can and must first make every effort to analyse and make known the state of development of the world within its fields of competence. This is an essential role if there is to be more effective planning, thereby making it possible to help organize the international drive to tackle the most urgent and inadmissible forms of underdevelopment.

UNESCO must then assist in working out development policies and strategies and propose well-designed pilot projects chosen to have a considerable spillover effect or make for the development of new approaches. These efforts must centre on human beings and on the development of human resources. As the raw material of all real, vital growth, their creativity, their skills, their capacity for commitment, initiative and management the tapping of all their potential in the form of intelligence, energy and talents – are the basis of collective development. A development which must go hand in hand with a rational use of the environment if it is to be sustainable, and be rooted in cultural realities if it is to be authentic. Science and technology may have been instrumental in widening the gap between industrialized countries and developing countries, but they may also be instrumental in reversing the trend.

UNESCO must also strengthen its co-operation with the United Nations system. It is already working with UNICEF, the United Nations Development Programme, the World Bank and other partners in strengthening education systems; facilitating exchanges among scholars and researchers; helping to develop press and radio; and preserving and promoting knowledge of cultural resources.

If UNESCO is to be able to perform all these tasks, it must make better use of its human and financial resources, optimize the ways in which it operates and enhance its presence in the Field, reaching out to decision-makers, to all its partners and especially to its end-users, increasing the quality of its services, its expertise and its activities: this is where the challenge lies.

If it is met, UNESCO will have demonstrated, forty years after the founding of the United Nations system, that an international body does not necessarily have to get caught up in a morass of red tape: that international civil servants do indeed have the qualities of professionalism, integrity, competence and efficiency; that modern methods of management are not the preserve of private firms; that international solidarity may enlist powerful, efficient organizations in its service. And that human beings and the development of their spirit and their abilities are the safest investment for the future.

3

UNESCO'S MEDIUM-TERM PLAN (1990-1995)

UNESCO adopted medium-term planning in 1977 after several trial runs since 1970. UNESCO's medium-term plans follow a very different pattern from those adopted by many States for the purposes of national development and by a number of public or private industrial groups.

NEED

As in most of the organizations of the United Nations system, it was gradually realized that there was a need to engage in the medium-term planning of activities. It became clear that the basic, permanent tasks of UNESCO, as set out in the Constitution, had to tie in more closely with the biennial programmes and budgets adopted by the General Conference of the Organization.

The Plan therefore serves as a link between the general aims of UNESCO and its more detailed programmes of activities, which have a two-year time-frame. In addition, the preparation of the Medium-Term Plan provides an opportunity to take a hard look at UNESCO's prospects for action.

Medium-term planning also provides a safeguard against dispersal. It serves as an appropriate framework within which to make strategic choices and discuss priorities, in a word, to achieve the necessary programme concentration, in the light of essential lines of emphasis, the most urgent needs of Member States and the international community, and the limited nature of resources. Furthermore, medium-term planning is a means of promoting interdisciplinarity in the programme, which is particularly necessary at UNESCO owing to the multiplicity and interdependence of its fields of competence education, natural sciences, culture, social and human sciences, and communication.

UNESCO's Medium-Term Plan represents – and this is what distinguishes it from similar plans adopted by State agencies – a programme agreement concluded for a period of six years, representing a shared vision among Member States that serves as a means of charting the course that UNESCO should follow over three successive biennial programmes and budgets.

In a nutshell, once approved, the common basis for action symbolized by the Plan serves to map out the future of the Organization.

In addition, it should enable UNESCO to give sufficient thought to the future, but also to contribute in a flexible, effective manner to the development of Member States in the Field by means of multilateral co-operation and operational action within the areas defined by its Constitution.

PREPARATION

The first Medium-Term Plan (1977-1982) was set out by objectives, distributed among sectoral chapters. The second Medium-Term Plan (1984-1989), which will be completed in less than a year's time, was based on an analysis of world problems. It comprises 14 major programmes and has already, during the last two biennial periods, undergone some concentration. Moreover, the present programme and budget (1988-1989) is being implemented in the new spirit of open-mindedness, flexibility and innovation which characterizes the preparation of the third plan.

Consultation and co-ordination play a crucial role in the preparation of the future Plan. Like any work that needs fundamental endorsement by a large number of contributing parties, the third Plan will be the fruit of active and indeed attractive participation by all UNESCO's partners: governments, National Commissions, the United Nations and the sister organizations of the system, professional and scientific communities and international governmental and non-governmental organizations. The third Plan is thus a collective, ongoing undertaking, whose success depends on the contribution of everyone and on the co-ordination of effort and imagination from all quarters. It must be based on a dynamic balance between continuity and innovation.

In addition, UNESCO's partners unanimously expressed the wish that the third Plan facilitate concentration in the Organization's programmes so that activities had the right critical mass with which to produce the right impact with the right amount of visibility.

ACTION

The aim is to do less in order to do better. Consequently, the number of programmes had to be considerably reduced. The second Plan comprised 14 major programmes. The future Plan will comprise seven major programme areas. While there were 54 programmes in the second Plan, the new one will include no more than 17. In the interests of concentration it is also necessary for the draft Plan submitted to the Executive Board in May-June 1989 and to the General Conference next autumn to be based on the careful selection of priorities. Far from signifying a shrinking or involution of UNESCO's role, concentration will make for better selection of activities and more finely defined lines of action. UNESCO's impact on reality and its influence in its spheres of competence will thus be enhanced.

It is indeed by doing less and better that UNESCO will be able to do more for its Member States. If its action is based on genuine co-operation among Member States, funding sources and scientific and intellectual communities, if it wagers on the richness of the potential of peoples and on the fruitfulness of their cultural diversity, viewed as a leaven of progress and not as a limit to development, the sum of UNESCO's future achievements may far exceed the simple total of its activities taken in isolation.

The third Plan will define the framework that will make it possible to enhance UNESCO's efficiency, its 'catalytic' role and the quality of the work specifically entrusted to it. Intensifying the Organization's presence in the Field, increasing its influence on decision-makers, encouraging technical and intellectual co-operation among developing countries, as well as regional and interregional co-operation, strengthening UNESCO's role as a clearing-house and stepping up its collaboration with the world scientific and intellectual community and activating the synergic effects of the United Nations system – these are some of the principles that are at present serving as guidelines in the preparation of the third Plan.

Efficiency, which is not an end in itself but a criterion of action, has meaning only if UNESCO achieves agreement in respect of strategic choices when it comes to adopt its future Plan. The annotated outline of the draft Plan submitted to the Executive Board in October 1988 was the subject of thorough-going debate, at the end of which a broad consensus emerged. Interdisciplinarity will be an essential feature of the third Plan and will be achieved by means of appropriate co-ordinating structures, the interweaving in the 'fabric' of programmes of cross-sector activities and transverse themes, and proposals for 'mobilizing projects' relating in particular to literacy, youth, the environment and cities.

Seven major programme areas will constitute the pillars of the third Plan. 'Education and the future' will be the first, with absolute priority being given to literacy teaching and the prevention of functional illiteracy. The other major programme areas will concern "Science for progress and the environment', "Culture-past, present and future', 'Communication in the service of humanity', 'Man and society in a changing world', 'UNESCO's contribution to future-oriented studies and to strategies for development' and 'UNESCO's contribution to peace, human rights and the elimination of all forms of discrimination.

These 'specifications' to be proposed by the third Plan will naturally be set in the context of the world situation, in the light of which UNESCO's tasks and objectives for the period 1990-1995 need to be spelled out. The third Plan will accordingly indicate the main strategy lines whereby UNESCO may, within its fields of competence, be instrumental in taking up the three major challenges of the present day represented by peace, development and environmental protection, in particular by reducing the gap between the industrialized countries and the developing countries. It is for this reason that the annotated outline of the draft highlighted the main lines of emphasis emerging from the consultation of Member States themselves promotion of human rights and peace among nations, the search for greater equity and more active solidarity in North-South relations, and the improvement of relations between man and nature.

BIBLIOGRAPHY

UNESCO DOCUMENTS AND PUBLIICATIONS*

General Reference Books

1. *Index translationum*: International bibliography of translations,

* Listing to illustrate the range of UNESCO documents and publications.

Vol. 36:1983, 1120 p., Trilingual: English/French/Spanish.
This bibliographical catalogue contains more than 50,000 entries for translated books published in 58 countries. An indispensable reference work for libraries, archives, documentation and research centres, publishing houses and information offices.

2. *International yearbook of education.* Vol. XL, 1988, *Education in the world* by Abdulatif Hussein Faraj, UNESCO/IBE; 1988, 159 p.
   Describes the education systems and presents recent developments in a selected sample of countries from different regions of the world.
3. *Study abroad*: International scholarships. International courses, Vol. xxvi, 1989-1990-1991, Trilingual: English/French/Spanish
   More than 3,000 opportunities for further study and training in all academic and professional fields offered by international organizations, governments, private and public foundations, universities and other institutions in more than 120 countries.
4. *UNESCO statistical digest 1988:* A statistical summary of data on education, science and technology, culture and communication by country, xxiv + 335 pp., tables, Trilingual: English/French/ Spanish
   While the *UNESCO Statistical Yearbook* contains a greater number of data series, presented subject-by-subject in some 100 tables covering over 200 countries and territories, the *Statistical Digest* enables the reader to obtain an overview of the basic statistics available on a country-by-country basis in the fields of education, science and technology, and culture and communication.
5. *UNESCO statistical yearbook 1988*: 1988, (25th ed.), 1182 p., tables, Trilingual: English/French/Spanish. Introductory texts in Russian and Arabic
   The 25th edition contains data on population, education, science, technology, culture and communication in more than 200 countries and territories. For the first time, it includes Russian translations for the introductory texts to chapters and tables.

BIBLIOGRAPHIES/CATALOGUES

1. *Aesthetic education*, Bulletin of the IBE. Educational documentation and information. UNESCO/ IBE, 1978, 84 p.
2. *Annotated bibliography of recent literature on "employment and*

education in the informal urban sector", Paris, UNESCO, 1977, 28 p.

3. *Annotated bibliography of selected UNESCO publications and documents selective to training and research.* Paris, UNESCO, 1986, 44 p. (Papers on higher education No. 15).
4. *Annotated bibliography on practice and research in educational administration and management*, by Anne Basile, Paris, UNESCO, 1979, 130 p.
5. *Bibliography of books for handicapped children*, Part I and II, compiled by the International Youth Library, Munich. Paris, UNESCO, 1982, 103 p. (Studies on books and reading No. 11).
6. *Bibliography of chemical education journals*, by J.N. Lezomby, Waddington, D.J., University of York, 1981.
7. *Bibliography of major decisions, meetings and documents related to UNESCO's activities in the domain of mother tongue instruction and languages.* Paris, UNESCO, 1981, 72 p. ED-81/CONF.601/4.
8. *Books for language-retarted children*, an annotated bibliography compiled by the International Board on Books for Young Children. Paris, UNESCO, 1985.
9. *Co-ordinating the forecasts and policies of technological, employment and educational development experiences in Poland* (*A synthesis of research and practical experiences and a selected annotated bibliography*) by Karol I. Pelc. Paris, UNESCO, 1986, 39 p.
10. *The Coordination of education policies and the integration of education plans with those for science, technology, culture and communication* (*Reflections on method and an annotated bibliography*) by Hans Reiff and Qutub Khan. Paris, UNESCO, 1986, 79 p.
11. *The (ordination of education policy and planning and employment policy and planning.* Vol. II: *An annotated bibliography* by Angela Little and Audrey Nunn. Paris, UNESCO, 1984, 126 p.
12. *Current bibliographical sources in education*, 3rd ed., Bulletin of the IBE, Educational documentation and information, 1989, UNESCO/IBE, 1989, 89 p.
13. *Documents of the international conferences on education, 1979-1986: cumulative catalogue*, UNESCO/IBE, 1988, xiv + 147 p. (IBEDATA series).
14. *Education and employment.* Bulletin of the IBE. Educational documentation and information. Paris, UNESCO/IBE, 1986,

183 p.

15. *Ergonomics in school and within the educational system.* Annotated bibliography by G. Lambert and R. Pascal. Paris, UNESCO, 1983.
16. *The Future of education.* Bulletin of the IBE. Educational documentation and information. UNESCO/IBE, 1981, 69 p.
17. *Health education intervention: annotated bibliography.* Paris, UNESCO, 1986, 103 p. (Nutrition education document series (NEDS No. 13) ED-86/WS/83.
18. *The Interaction between education and productive work.* Bulletin of the IBE. Educational documentation and information, UNESCO/IBE, 1982, 112 p.
19. *International annotated bibliography on technical teacher education.* Paris, UNESCO, 1986, 102 p.
20. *Lifelong education and the school* prepared by R.H. Dave and N. Stiemerling, UNESCO/UIE, 1973, 154 p.
21. *Lifelong education bibliography* compiled by Ursula Giere, UNESCO/UIE, 1986, 5 p.
22. *Media education in the United Kingdom: an annotated bibliography* by L. Masterman, Paris, UNESCO, 1983, 72 p.
23. *Media education materials: an annotated bibliography* by Jung Sook Lee et al. Paris, UNESCO, 1982, 40 p.
24. *Printed technical learning materials,* Paris, UNESCO, 1989, (Info TUE series No. 7).
25. *Publications 1987-1988*, UNESCO/PROAP, 1988.
26. *Recent experiences in the coordination of education, employment and technology in Latin America and the Caribbean: A state of the art review and annotated bibliography* by Noel McGinn, Nancy Barra, Christopher Harris. Paris, UNESCO, 1985, 105 p.
27. *Reflection on the future development of education: a selective and annotated bibliography*, Part I by U. Von Haumeder. Paris, UNESCO, 1979, 35 p. Part II by R. Di Carlo. Paris, UNESCO, 1980, 70 p.
28. *School buildings*, Bulletin of the IBE, Educational documentation and information 1978, UNESCO/IBE, 1978, 71 p.
29. *Special education*, Bulletin of the IBE, Educational documentation and information. UNESCO/IBE, 1983.

DIRECTORIES

1. *Directory of adult education periodicals.* Paris, UNESCO, 1985,

151 p. ED-85/WS/55.

2. *Directory of adult education training and research institutions.* 3rd. ed. Paris, UNESCO, 1984, 287 p. (IBEDATA series).
3. *Directory of educational documentation and information services.* 5th ed., UNESCO/IBE, 1988, x + 114 p. (IBEDATA Series).
4. *Directory of educational research institutions.* Paris, UNESCO, 1985, 208 p. (IBEDATA series)
5. *Directory of governmental bodies and institutions dealing with educational planning and administration.* Paris, UNESCO, 1980, 337 p.
6. *Directory of innovative institutions preparing educational personnel.* UNESCO/IBE, 1979, 100 p. ED-80/WS/20.
7. *Directory of national adult education co-ordinating bodies.* Paris, UNESCO, 1984, 167 p. ED-84/WS/34.
8. *Directory of participating institutions.* International Network for Information in Science and Technology Education (INISTE). Paris, UNESCO, 1985. ED-85/WS/59.
9. *Directory of special education.* Paris, UNESCO, 1986, 106 p. (IBEDATA Series).
10. *Directory of teacher training institutions in Africa* (first elements). Paris, UNESCO, 1978, 51 p. ED-79/WS/7.
11. *Directory of teacher training institutions in the Arab States* (first elements), Paris, UNESCO, 1979, 63 p.
12. *Directory of writers on lifelong education* prepared by Ursula Giere and Yasushi Maehira, UNESCO/UIE, 1980, 62 p.
13. *First world directory of services in the field of educational buildings and furniture (Provisional)*, Paris, UNESCO, 1988, 53 p.
14. *International directory of individuals active in the field of environmental education*, Paris, UNESCO, 1977, 126 p. ED-77/WS/121.
15. *International directory of institutions active in the field of environmental education*, revised and enlarged edition, Paris, UNESCO, 1981. ED-81/WS/86.
16. *International directory of research institutions on higher education*, 2nd revised edition, Prepared by the European Centre for Higher Education with an Introduction by Robert Cowen. UNESCO/IBE, 1988, xv + 134 p. (IBEDATA series).
17. *TEP atlas – 5.5 atlas of teacher training projects*, Paris, UNESCO, 1978. ED-78/WS/16.
18. *World directory of selected research and teacher training institu-*

tions in the field of technical and vocational education, revised edition, Paris, UNESCO, 1986.

19. *World-wide inventory of non-traditional post-secondary institutions*. Paris, UNESCO, 1989.

GLOSSARIES, TERMINOLOGIES, THESAURI

1. *Educational administration terminology* by E. Ortiz and A. Basile. Paris, UNESCO, 1982, 354 p.
2. *Educational facilities thesaurus, Descriptor list*, Paris, UNESCO, 1981, 80 p.
3. *Glossary of educational technology terms*, 2nd edition, revised and enlarged, Prepared by the Division of Educational Sciences, Contents and Methods of Education, UNESCO, for the International Bureau of Education, UNESCO/IBE, 1988, 268 p. (IBEDATA series).
4. *Glossary of environmental education terms*, UNESCO, 1983, 67 p.
5. *Glossary of terms used in science and technology education*. Paris, UNESCO, 1981 (Science and technology education document series, (STEDS No. 1) ED-84/WS/68.
6. *Terminology of adult education*, UNESCO/IBE, 1985. (IBEDATA series).
7. *Terminology of special education*, 3rd. ed., A revised edition of quadrilingual publication providing clusters and glossary of terms used in special education, in four languages: English, French, Russian and Spanish, UNESCO/IBE, 1983, 167 p. (IBEDATA series).
8. *Terminology of technical and vocational education*, UNESCO/IBE, 1984. (IBEDATA series).
9. *UNESCO: IBE education theasaurus*, 4th. ed., UNESCO/IBE, 1984, 4 Vols. (IBEDATA series).

PERIODICALS

Published by Headquarters

Copyright Bulletin
A quarterly to meet the needs not only of specialists in the field, but authors, librarians, publishers, editors, record producers, broadcasters, film makers, scientific researchers and lawyers.

Impact of Science on Society
An interdisciplinary quarterly devoted to the effect of science in our lives in an effort not only to document but to analyse change stimulated by science and technology.

Subscription: Taylor and Francis Ltd., Rankine Road, Basingstoke, Hants., RG24 OPR, United Kingdom.

International Social Science Journal
A quarterly interdisciplinary forum for the international spectrum of today's social scientists, with a worldwide network of correspondents.

Subscription: Basil Blackwell Ltd., 108 Cowley Road, Oxford, OX4 1JF, United Kingdom.

Museum
The sole international journal that presents museological evolution and its multiple facets around the world, from security to cultural policies and curating.

Nature and Resources
Provides international news and information about UNESCO programmes concerning environmental activities, natural resources research and conservation.

Prospects
A quarterly review of education which benefits from the direct collaboration of institutions and academics from more than 150 countries. For specialists and all those interested in education in all its socio-economic and cultural contexts.

The UNESCO Courier
Directed towards the general public, it deals in an intercultural perspective with all UNESCO's fields of activity. Its publication in 34 languages (plus braille) makes this a precious teaching aid.

Published by Regional Offices and/or Specialized Institutes

Bulletin of the International Bureau of Education
Educational documentation and information. (Quarterly) Intended for specialists and documentalists. Each issue deals with a specific theme and contains a selected annotated bibliography on works published

throughout the world.

Bulletin of the Major Project in the Field of Education in the Latin American and Caribbean Region
Published three issues per year by the UNESCO Regional Office for Education in Latin America and the Caribbean (OREALC),
P.O. Box 3187, Santiago de Chile, Chile.

Bulletin of the UNESCO Principal Regional Office for Asia and the Pacific
Published one issue per year by the UNESCO Principal Regional Office for Asia and the Pacific (PROAP).
G.P.O. Box 967, Bangkok 10110, Thailand.

Educafrica
Published one issue per year by the UNESCO Regional Office for Education in Africa (BREDA).
B.P. 3311, Dakar, Senegal.

L'Education nouvelle
Published three issues per year by the UNESCO Regional Office for Education in the Arab States (UNEDBAS). In Arabic, with summaries in French.
P.O. Box 950492, Wadi Saqra, Amman, Jordan.

Higher Education
Published two issues per year by the UNESCO Regional Centre for Higher Education in Latin America and the Caribbean (CRESALC).
Apartado postal 68394, Caracas 1062-A, Venezuela.

Higher Education in Europe
Published four issues per year by the European Centre for Higher Education (CEPES).
Subscription: The Romanian Bank for Foreign Trade (BRCE), Telex No. 11235, ebank r, 22-24 Calea Victoriei, Bucharest, Romania, Account No. 47 11 159.300-4.

International Review of Education
Published quarterly by the UNESCO Institute for Education, Hamburg. Original articles and resumes in English, French or German.

Subscription: Kluwer Academic Publisher Group, Distribution Centre. P.O. Box 322, 3300AH, Dordrecht, The Netherlands.

Selective List of Information Notes and Newsletters

Adult Education Information Notes
Quarterly.

Connect
Quarterly. UNESCO/UNEP Environmental Education Newsletter.

IIEP Newsletter
Published quarterly by the International Institute for Educational Planning.
7-9 rue Eugene-Delacroix – 75016 Paris, France.

Information Note
Quarterly. International Network for Information in Science and Technology Education (INISTE).

International Understanding at School
Twice yearly. Published for the UNESCO Associated Schools Projects.
PGI-UNISIST Newsletter
Quarterly.

Technical and Vocational Education
A bi-annual international information bulletin on technical and vocational education.
UNESCO Sources
Published since February 1989.

UNESCO SERIES ON EDUCATION

Education

African research monographs (UNESCO:IIEP)

The development of higher education in Africa
Higher education and development in South East Asia

Lifelong education and university resources
New trends and new responsibilities for universities in Latin America
Present problems in the democratization of secondary and higher education
Teaching and learning. An introduction to new methods and resources in higher education
The teaching of sciences in African universities. Report of the Rabat Seminar, December 1962.
Towards lifelong education: a new role for higher education institutions
Training university administrators: a programme guide
Universities and environmental education

Education and rural development

Agriculture and the development process. Tentative guidelines for teaching.
Education in a rural environment (2nd edn. 1980)

Education on the move

Curricula and lifelong education
Educational reforms: experiences and prospects
Environmental education in the light of the Tbilisi Conference

Educational buildings and equipment

Building community schools: an analysis of experiences
Planning buildings and facilities for higher education
Planning standards for higher education facilities
School furniture handbook
School buildings and natural disasters

Educational methods and techniques

The economics of new educational media
Vol. 1. Present status of research and trends
Vol. 2. Cost and effectiveness
Vol. 3. Cost and effectiveness overview and synthesis
The multilateral exchange of educational audio-visual materials:

existing mechanisms and suggestions for the future

Educational sciences

Empirical research in education
The theory of curriculum content in the USSR
Teaching methods in the Soviet school
The history of education today
Cultural Anthropology and education
The language sciences: an educational challenge?
Introduction to the educational sciences
Education and bilingualism
Music and education: a composer writes about musical education

Educational studies and documents (new series)

Education in the Arab region viewed from the 1970 Marrakesh Conference
Agriculture and general education
Teachers and educational policy
Comparative study of secondary school building costs
Literacy for working: functional literacy in rural Tanzania
Rights and responsibilities of youth
Growth and change: perspectives of education in Asia
Sports facilities for schools in developing countries. An inventory of experience and proposals for future projects
Possibilities and limitations of functional literacy: the Iranian experiment
Functional literacy in Mali: training for development
Anthropology and language science in educational development
Towards a conceptual model of life-long education
Curriculum planning and some current health problems
ALSED directory of specialists and research institutions
MOBRAL – the Brazilian adult literacy experiment
School furniture development: an evaluation
An experience-centred curriculum: exercises in perception, communication and action
Nutrition education curricula: relevance, design and the problem of change
World survey of pre-school education

The operational seminar: a pioneering method of training for development
The aspirations of young migrant workers in Western Europe
Guide for the conversion of school libraries into media centres
Youth institutions and services: present state and development
Group techniques in education
Education in Africa in the light of the Lagos Conference (1976)
Buildings for school and community use: five case-studies
The education of migrant workers and their families
Population education. A contemporary concern
Experiments in popular education in Portugal (1974-1976)
Techniques for improving educational radio programmes
Methods and techniques in post-secondary education
National languages and teacher training in Africa
Educational systems regulation: a methodological guide
The child and play
Non-formal education and education policy in Ghana and Senegal
Education in the Arab States in the light of the Abu Dhabi Conference 1977
The child's first learning environment
Education in Asia and Oceania: a challenge for the 1980s
Self-management in educational systems
Impact of educational television on young children
World problems in the classroom
Literacy and illiteracy
The training of teacher educators
Recognition of studies and competence: implementation of conventions drawn up under the aegis of UNESCO
The outflow of professionals with higher education from and among States Parties to the Regional Convention on the Recognition of Studies, Diplomas and Degrees in Higher Education in Latin America and the Caribbean
National languages and teacher training in Africa II: a methodological guide for the use of teacher trainers in Africa
Technical and economic criteria for media selection and planning in educational institutions
Reflections on the future development of education
Education in Africa in the light of the Harare Conference (1982)
Senior educational personnel: new functions and training, Vol. 1
Senior educational personnel: new functions and training, Vol. 2

Experiments and innovations in education (UNESCO: IBE)

The TEVEC case
The school readiness project
Innovation in reading in Britain
Understanding change in education: an introduction
Changes in secondary education and their implications for continuing education in Canada
A community school in Yugoslavia
The basic secondary school in the countryside: an educational innovation in Cuba
An experiment in the ruralization of education: IPAR and the Cameroonian reform
Educational innovation in Singapore
Educational innovation in Iran
Educational innovation in India
Educational innovation in the Republic of Korea
Educational innovation in Indonesia
Experimental period of the International Baccalaureate: objectives and results
Radio study group campaigns in the United Republic of Tanzania
Educational reform in Peru
Establishing an institution teaching by correspondence
Youth participation in the development process: a case-study in Panama
Mostaganem Institute of Agricultural Technology: an educational innovation
Postgraduate teacher training: a Nigerian alternative
Innovation in Upper Volta: rural education and primary schooling
The Peruvian model of innovation the reform of basic education
In-service training of teachers in Sri Lanka
Examination reforms in Sri Lanka
Management of educational reforms in Sri Lanka
Integrated approach to curriculum development in primary education in Sri Lanka
Integrated science in the junior secondary school in Sri Lanka
Pre-vocational education in Sri Lanka
An alternative pattern of basic education: Radio Santa Maria
The Spanish educational reform and lifelong education
The Caribbean Mathematics Project: training the teacher as the agent

of reform
Educational innovations in Switzerland: traits and trends
Educational reforms and innovations in Africa
Basic services for children: a continuing search for learning priorities, Part I
Basic services for children: a continuing search for learning priorities, Part II
Institutional leadership for educational reform: the Atlantic Institute of Education
Caribbean co-operation for curriculum development and reform in teacher training
Outdoor primary education in Bangladesh
Examination reforms in India
Education and work in the Spanish educational reform
The Hungarian experience of OOK: an instrument for the development of educational technology

Fundamentals of ducational planning (UNESCO: IIEP)

What is educational planning?
The relation of educational plans to economic and social planning
Educational planning and human resource development
Planning and the educational administrator
The social context of educational planning
The costing of educational plans
The problems of rural education
Educational planning: the adviser's role
Demographic aspects of educational planning
The analysis of educational costs and expenditure
The professional identity of the educational planner
The conditions for success in educational planning
Cost-benefit analysis in educational planning
Educational planning and unemployed youth
The politics of educational planning in developing countries
Planning education for a plural society
Planning the primary school curriculum in developing countries
Planning educational assistance for the Second Development Decade
Study abroad and educational development
Realistic educational planning
Planning education in relation to rural development

Alternatives and decisions in educational planning
Planning the school curriculum
Cost factors in planning educational technology systems
The planner and lifelong education
Education and employment: a critical appraisal
Planning teacher demand and supply
Planning early childhood care and education in developing countries
Communication media in education for low-income countries
The planning of non-formal education
Education, training and the traditional sector
Higher education and employment: the IIEP experience in five less developed countries
Educational planning as a social process
Higher education and social stratification: an international comparative study
A conceptual framework for the development of lifelong education in the U.S.S.R.
Educational in austerity: options for planners

IBEDATA (UNESCO: IBE)

Bibliography: educational and vocational guidance for girls and women
Bibliography: reports from the International Conference on Education, 1975
Current bibliographical sources in education
Directory of adult education documentation and information services
Directory of educational documentation and information services
Directory of educational research institutions
Glossary of educational technology terms
International directory of higher education research institutions
International guide to education systems
A statistical study of wastage at school
Systems and policy: the function of information in improving education systems
Terminology of adult education
Terminology of special education
Terminology of technical and vocational education
UNESCO: IBE education thesaurus

International studies in education
(UNESCO Institute for education, Hamburg)

Educational achievements of thirteen-year olds in twelve countries
Education for international understanding
Educational reform in the Federal Republic of Germany
The further training of mathematics teachers at secondary level. Report of the Hamburg meeting, October 1968
Community schools in developing countries
Current problems of teacher education
Correspondence courses for in-service teacher training at primary level in developing countries
Mother-tongue teaching
Relevant methods in comparative education. Report of a meeting of international experts.
Youth and the changing secondary school
Educational research in Europe: a new look at the relationship between school education and work

Monographs on education

Adult education in Yugoslavia
Polytechnical education in the U.S.S.R.
The psychology of the use of audio-visual aids in primary education
The theory and practice of programmed instruction
Technical and vocational teacher education and training
Some aspects of professional freedom of teachers
Museums and children
The school education of girls

Special education

Case studies in special education, Cuba, Japan, Kenya, Sweden
Economic aspects of special education: Czechoslovakia, New Zealand, United States
Integration of technical and vocational education into special education
The present situation and trends of research in the field of special education. Four studies: Sweden and other Scandinavian countries, Union of Soviet Socialist Republics, United States of America and Uruguay

Structure and terminology of agricultural education

Elements of the structure and terminology of agricultural education in Japan
Elements of the structure of agricultural education in the Philippines
Elements of the structure and terminology of agricultural education in India
Elements of the structure of agricultural education in the United States
Elements of the structure and terminology of agricultural education in Poland

Studies and surveys in comparative education (UNESCO: IBE)

The changing role of the teacher
Constructive education for adolescents
Constructive education for children
Constructive education for special groups: handicapped and deviant children
Educational goals
Education today for the world of tomorrow
Initiatives in education: a world profile for 1971-1972
The place of information in educational development
The right to education: what kind of management?
The role of information in educational development
Solving education problems: the theory and reality of innovation in development countries
A statistical study of wastage at school
Wastage in education: a world problem
World problems in education: a brief analytical study
Educational and the world of work
Science and technology education in the primary school of tomorrow

Studies on international equivalences of degrees

Comparability of degrees and diplomas in international law
Comparability of engineering courses and degrees
From equivalence of degrees to evaluation of competence
International equivalences in access to higher education
Methods of establishing equivalences between degrees and diplomas

Studies on the evaluation of qualifications at the higher education level

The education of primary and secondary school teachers
World guide to higher education

The teaching of basic sciences

Mathematics applied to physics
New trends in biology teaching, Vols. 1, 2, 3, 4, 5
New trends in chemistry teaching, Vols. 1, 2, 3, 4, 5
New trends in home economics education, Vol. 1
New trends in integrated science teaching, Vols. 1, 2, 3, 4, 5
New trends in mathematics teaching, Vols. 1, 2, 3, 4
New trends in physics teaching, Vols. 1, 2, 3, 4
New trends in primary school science education, Vol. 1
Studies in mathematics education, Vols. 1, 2, 3, 4, 5, 6

Trends and issues in technical and vocational training

Developments in technical and vocational education: a comparative study
The transition from technical and vocational schools to work
The integration of general and technical and vocational education
Policy, planning and management in technical and vocational education: a comparative study

UNESCO source books on curricula and methods

African geography for schools. A handbook for teachers
English in Africa
French in Africa
New UNESCO source book for science teaching
New UNESCO source book for geography teaching
Planning for health education in schools
The teaching of reading
Teaching school mathematics
Teaching school physics
UNESCO source book for geography teaching
UNESCO handbook for science teachers

UIE case studies (UNESCO Institute for Education, Hamburg)

Integrating vocational and general education: a Rudolf Steiner School
The Forsoksgymnaset, Oslo, Norway, in the perspective of lifelong education
Functional illiteracy and literacy provision in developed countries: the case of the Federal Republic of Germany

UIE monographs (UNESCO Institute for Education, Hamburg)

Lifelong education and school curriculum
Lifelong education and the school: abstract and bibliography
Reflections on lifelong education and the school
Lifelong education, schools and curricula in developing countries
Lifelong education and the preparation of educational personnel
Basic education in the Sahel countries
Lifelong education and community learning: three case studies in India
Lifelong education: a stocktaking
School curriculum in the context of lifelong learning
Lifelong teacher education and the community school
Evaluation of nonformal education programmes: the applicability and utility of the criterion sampling approach
Child-to-child. Another path to learning

UIE studies on post-literacy and continuing education

Learning strategies for post-literacy and continuing education: a cross-nations perspective
Learning strategies for post-literacy and continuing education in Mali, Niger, Senegal and Upper Volta
Learning strategies for post-literacy and continuing education in Kenya, Nigeria, Tanzania and the United Kingdom
Learning strategies for post-literacy and continuing education in China, India, Indonesia, Nepal, Thailand and Vietnam
Learning strategies for post-literacy and continuing education in Brazil, Colombia, Jamaica and Venezuela
Learning strategies for post-literacy and continuing education in Algeria, Egypt and Kuwait

Interdisciplinary

Insights

Suicide or survival?
Biology and ethics
Apartheid: power and historical falsification
Violence and its causes
Domination or sharing? Endogenous development and the transfer of knowledge
Harvesting ocean energy
Obstacles to disarmament an ways of overcoming them
Racism, science and pseudo-science

Sextant

More than enough? An optimistic assessment of world energy
Biotechnologies: challenges and promises

SECTION II

OVERVIEW OF UNESCO'S ROLE IN EDUCATION

4

HIGHLIGHTS OF UNESCO'S EDUCATION PROGRAMMES

LITERACY

With just over a decade to go before the year 2000, one quarter of the adult population of the world is illiterate; that means eight hundred and eighty-nine million individual human beings (in 1985) cannot read, write or count. Over one hundred million children of primary school age are not even enrolled in school, let alone in regular attendance. The majority of adult illiterate are women, with the direct and detrimental effect that has on the education and well-being of children.

As UNESCO, in its role as lead agency for 1990 international Literacy Year, prepares its strategies for that year and beyond, the above picture represents for the Organization, and for the entire world, a summons to action.

Access to learning and to skills for all, according to the context in which each person lives, is the basis for UNESCO's plans. To achieve this target means not only a well drawn-up programme, not only the devotion of many governmental and non governmental organizations, not only the firm resolve of political leaders and government authorities, not only the concern and involvement of teachers and intellectuals, although all these are important. It means much more this world-wide priority, which affects every country, developing, newly industrialized and economically developed, requires world-wide mobilization. It is a question of eradicating, or at the very least massively reducing illiteracy from the planet by the end of the century.

In the Organization's next Medium Term Plan the absolute priority is thus being placed on Basic Education for All a programme to be launched in conjunction with UNICEF the World Bank and the United Nations Development Programme and with the support of hundreds of organizations and institutions around the world. Our strategy for literacy and basic education reposes on four action principles. First is the recognition of the primacy of national responsibility for promoting literacy UNESCO's role will be to support activities in Member States that are critical for the success of national action. Second people are not made literate: they make themselves so where they have the motivation and incentive. This means that literacy activities must be supported by post-literacy work. Third is the recognition that particular groups in every society need special support and attention (women and girls in general, and also persons with physical, sensory and mental disabilities). Lastly UNESCO recognizes that its action inter-relates closely with its work in all other areas. This implies focusing on the relevance of curricula to the cultural and physical environment, on the availability of appropriate learning materials and well-trained and committed teachers. It also implies using all the possibilities of modern methods for formal and non-formal education, particularly communications technology.

Living and learning takes skills. . . to read, write and count; to cope with, preserve and improve the environment; protect individual and family health; acquire productive and occupational skills and participate actively in civic life. The provision of these skills is thus the very foundation of individual fulfilment and dignity, and at the heart of UNESCO's task.

EARLY CHILDHOOD CARE AND EDUCATION

The first years of childhood are decisive for the development of a child's mind and personality. For millions of children, the chance to acquire an adequate education is lost long before they reach primary-school age. Ill-health, malnutrition and inadequate stimulation and care permanently stunt their potential to grow and develop. This is why UNESCO sees efforts to improve early childhood care and education as essential to the success of basic education. The approach applied by UNESCO, in conjunction with UNICEF, calls for contributions from many fields and disciplines, educationists, nutritionists, brain researchers and child psychologists.

Specialists from all these disciplines meeting in Stockholm in early 1988 at a UNESCO symposium concluded that programmes for children of pre-school age need to combine health care, early detection and treatment of handicaps, food supplements and psycho-social stimulation. In many poor developing countries, pregnant women are nutritionally at risk and up to two-thirds of all newborns may have insufficient birthweight. Proper stimulation and education during the early years of life can, however, compensate for such nutritional deficiencies to a significant degree, restoring and developing the child's innate ability to learn.

No amount of teacher-training or improvement in physical facilities will produce results when children are hungry and unable to concentrate, suffering from shortage of Vitamin A or other micronutrients, or victims of diarrhoea, intestinal parasites, or other diseases.

For these reasons, an important programme of the next Medium-Term Plan will be devoted, in co-operation with UNICEF and WHO, to early childhood education.

PRIMARY EDUCATION

The primary school is the main vehicle for acquiring basic education and for diffusing literacy throughout societies. Yet, in many developing nations, the rapid growth in primary enrolment has ended and, in some, enrolments have even begun to decline. Progress towards universal primary education can no longer be taken for granted.

This is one of several alarming findings which a UNESCO study, completed in 1988, has brought to light. Data covering the first half of the 1980s suggest that dropout and grade repetition in primary schools continue on a massive scale particularly for girls; teachers' real income has dropped dramatically in a majority of the world's developing countries; resources to print and distribute textbooks, to equip classrooms and to ensure regular supervision are frequently minimal.

However, maintaining educational quality even in remote, poorly staffed and ill-equipped primary schools is possible. UNESCO case-studies of rural multi-grade schools in such countries as Bolivia, Mali or Zaire tend to demonstrate this point. Given proper training, teachers and headmasters can learn to mobilize local communities in support of their schools, practise peer-teaching, ability-grouping of pupils and other pedagogical methods, and manage the meagre resources at their disposal to maximum effect.

The problems of basic education are, for the main part, bound up with the poverty of rural areas in the Third World. UNESCO's programmes, therefore, give special attention to the links between education and rural development.

Experience shows that legal and administrative obstacles often need to be cleared away and many innovations introduced, if access of rural people, especially women, to basic education is to be achieved.

Educational innovation, meant to overcome institutional inertia and the constraints of material scarcity, is the chief concern of the five educational innovation networks which countries have at UNESCO's be hest, formed in different regions of the world. The problems of basic education whether in school or in programmes meant for adult learners, have occupied a top spot on the 1988 agenda of these networks.

The industrialized countries, too, are experiencing problems of failure and low achievement in primary education. The seeds of functional illiteracy among adults are often planted in the primary school itself. At the 1988 Conference of Ministers of Education of Member States of the Europe Region, convened by UNESCO in Paris, these problems were a key issue of discussion.

ADULT EDUCATION

The education of adults encompasses literacy but goes beyond it if life-long learning is to become a reality, especially for those who wish to broaden and deepen their literacy skills, then adult education is a must. The rapid advances of sciences and technology make it vital to allow citizens to update and constantly improve their knowledge and skills. This is indeed, one of the points most forcefully made by developing Member States in their identification of priority needs for the coming years.

To facilitate the spread of adult education in Member States, an international handbook is being prepared for publication, an inventory of adult education and research institutions is being brought up to date and a study of innovating methods for the training of adult educators has been completed by the International Council of Adult Education.

Expert panels were convened to discuss the principal themes which adult education programmes need to address: teaching about human rights, people and the environment, the use of mass media, and the exercise of civic rights and responsibilities.

GIRLS' EDUCATION

To stimulate initiatives and promote equality of opportunity or girls in scientific, technical and vocational education. UNESCO sponsored studies in four countries (the German Democratic Republic, the Netherlands, New Zealand and Sweden) and distributed their reports widely. In co-operation with Gūyana and Tunisia, UNESCO is now conducting two pilot projects, each involving two secondary schools. The aim is to improve girls' participation in technical and vocational education at the secondary level in terms of diversity, quality and quantity. The achievements so far recorded show that significant progress has already been made.

A manual on educational and vocational guidance for girls and women is being prepared for wide distribution. A joint research-action programme is also be undertaken in Europe with a view to improving the access of girls and women to scientific, technological and vocational education.

SCIENCE EDUCATION

The challenges of new and unprecedented scientific, technological and social developments which are so rapidly transforming peoples' lives in all parts of the world require an updating of science, mathematics and technology education and an interdisciplinary approach.

Countries are becoming increasingly concerned about social, ethical, and environmental implications of science and technology. Programmes in science, mathematics and technology education must prepare both adults and children to cope with these challenges. Mental skills such as how to find data, how to solve problems, how to respond to new situations, how to learn, must take precedence over factual learning, and practical skills related to the use of new information and communication technologies must receive greater emphasis.

UNESCO's co-operation with the Member States includes programmes for education in science at all levels to contribute to rapid economic growth, as well as to create a scientific understanding in the general public. Special efforts are made to encourage girls to take up scientific and technical careers and, more generally, careers in which they are numerically under-represented.

Many other activities are helping to stimulate and promote renovation and improvement of programmes, including a series of experimental and pilot projects on the application of calculators and microcomputers to mathematics and science teaching; science and technology education in rural areas, in-service training for science teachers using the media and other innovative techniques; technology and general education; science and technology education in productive work; science and technology education in an inter-disciplinary context; educational games and toys in teaching science to children; and continuity between school and out-of-school education.

The provision of low-cost school science equipment constitutes a very serious problem, particularly for many developing countries. The centre for the production of school science equipment launched in Zambia in 1988 with UNDP funding of $2 million is but one supported by UNESCO to help remedy this situation. It will design and make simple science equipment from local materials in sufficient qualities for distribution throughout the country and provide in-service training in modern methods and content for science teachers.

The development of teaching and learning resource materials is yet another important area of activity. It covers the fields of physics, chemistry, biology and mathematics education; special emphasis is being placed or the development of resources in newer content areas such as electronics, biotechnology and marine science. At the same time, attention is also being focused on integrated or unified courses, notably within the framework of 'Science Education for All' programmes. UNESCO publications play their part in communicating ideas and experience. Innovations in Science and Technology Education, for example, is produced biennially. A second biennial title covering recent trends and developments, is Studies in Mathematics Education.

Another way in which UNESCO is actively facilitating exchanges is through its International Network for Information in Science and Technology Education (INISTE) with its 185 member institutions in 135 Member States, some 20 inter-governmental and non-governmental organizations, and its own quarterly *Information Note.*

TECHNICAL AND VOCATIONAL EDUCATION

UNESCO's current activities to improve and develop secondary education are run in the perspective of lifelong education bringing more closely together general education with technical and vocational education, providing opportunities for re-entry into secondary education for those who left it early or entry for those who may never before have had the chance to do so.

UNESCO is today running some twenty-five projects in different regions to develop and improve technical and vocational training. One example is a four-year Technical Education Project launched in Egypt in 1988 with $2 million funding from the United Nations Development Programme (UNDP).

Secondary-level technical teachers are also in short supply throughout the world. Many of UNESCO's projects are concerned with improving this situation. Preparations are for example, being made for an international convention on technical and vocational education.

SPORTS AND PHYSICAL EDUCATION

UNESCO aims to make known and to give effect to the International Charter of Physical Education and Sport, adopted in 1978, which recognizes that every human being has a fundamental right to physical education and sport endeavouring thereby to promote the educational, ethical and cultural values of sport. To this end, the Organization has machinery for co-operation at its disposal but not yet enough funds.

However, the gap between the industrialized countries and the developing countries is widening: 80 per cent of school children in the Third World do not receive physical education, whereas in the industrialized countries the proportions are reversed. Sport is an expanding market, but the money earned from sport is not channelled into school or university sport, nor into sport for all. The marriage between sport and money often means a divorce between sport and the sporting spirit.

Fresh ways need to be found of advancing the cause of sport, involving the partnership of all the protagonists and decision-makers in the world of sport - public and private sectors, industry, the media and sports organizations.

The Conference of Minister of Physical Education and Sport (MINEPS II), organized by UNESCO in Moscow in November 1988, recommended that the role and prestige of physical and sports education be enhanced at school and in society.

As for the problem of doping the Conference recommended comprehensive action and the development of international instruments to combat this phenomenon. In addition, UNESCO and the Olympic Movement decided to unite their efforts to reduce the gaps between countries, uphold the sporting ethic and ensure the universality of the Olympic Games.

INTERNATIONAL EDUCATION

The major objective in this field is to promote education for international understanding, co-operation and peace, and education relating to human rights and fundamental freedoms.

UNESCO has initiated a permanent system of reporting by the Member States on the extent to which the Recommendation of the General Conference of UNESCO (1974) on this subject has been applied, and on the problems encountered. The synthesis of the reports provides UNESCO and Member States with valuable guidance for international action

Another UNESCO contribution to international understanding through education was the Fourth Conference of Ministers of Education of Member States of the Europe region, which met at UNESCO Headquarters in September 1988. Topics on the agenda included international education and broader humanistic and cultural dimensions of education. Special attention was given to information technologies and the role they should play in education from now on. The Conference highlighted UNESCO's position as the only organization within which all the states of the European region (that is, Eastern and Western Europe, North America and Israel) can co-operate in the field of education.

Other significant meetings were held in 1988 on teacher-training (Indonesia), on the study of major problems of humankind and their presentation in curricula and text-books (Federal Republic of Germany) and on the revision of school history and geography text-books used in the Balkan countries (Greece).

ASSOCIATED SCHOOLS PROJECT

This project aims to harness the natural goodwill, curiosity and tolerance of young people in the development of international dialogue and understanding. Participating primary and secondary schools and teacher training colleges are encouraged to organize special education programmes on international co-operation, the study of other people and cultures, human rights and the environment.

In many countries Associate Schools act as a testing ground to introduce UNESCO's ideals and projects in educational methodologies.

During 1988, over 100 institutions joined the Associated School Project (ASP), bringing the total number to 2,246 in 97 countries.

Information about ASP activities are regularly made available through the circular newsletter. A Glimpse of Associated School Project and the bulletin International Understanding at school.

Among the 1988 events: an inter-regional action launched to increase the Project's multiplier effect was the subject of an international consultation in Bangkok (December 1988) a photographic exhibit entitled 'Associated Schools Project Alphabet of Ingredients for Human Rights Education', and the production guidelines for the preparation of teaching material on peoples own countries and cultures to be widely distributed by Associated School throughout the newly launched World Decade for Cultural Development.

HIGHER EDUCATION

Most of the Organization's programmes have direct links with universities or systems of higher education.

Issues at stake for the future of higher education and of concern to UNESCO include the following: higher education and the world of work, the integration of training and research in the teaching/learning process, the problem of interdisciplinarity and the participation of women in higher education.

(a) **Innovative Channels for Cooperation**

During 1988 UNESCO has sought innovative channels of cooperation, particularly with universities and non-governmental organizations. Thus, a successful first collective consultation of non-governmental organizations on 'Higher Education: Problems and Challenges, for What Future?' and a round-table on the problems of women and higher education were organized. The year 1988 also saw the launching of a joint project with the United Nations University on the role of Third World universities in scientific and technological development.

(b) **Academic Mobility**

Academic mobility is an excellent way of encouraging the meeting of cultures. UNESCO has long had activities in this area, in particular through agreements on the mutual recognition of higher education studies and diplomas. Six regional conventions are now in force covering the whole world. Under these conventions, regular meetings have generated a number of publications designed to facilitate information exchange and mobility: a guide to national bodies working in the field of recognition, and a comparative survey describing of the structure of national higher education systems and degrees.

(c) **Life-Long Education**

The need for lifelong education for higher education personnel is the main concern of the interuniversity co-operation networks in the University of Latin America and the Caribbean (REDESLAC) and Europe (Network for Staff Development)

In 1988 the REDESLAC Network held its Third International Workshop at the University of Havana, Cuba and outlined five joint educational research projects for 1988-91 to be co-financed by UNESCO and member universities.

1988 also saw the establishment of a consortium of Latin American Universities in the countries in and surrounding the Amazon region (UNAMAZ) to work on training and research related to development and environmental preservation of the Amazon basin. This major new project is innovative in its transdisciplinary approach.

(d) **Distance Learning**

With the rising demand and decreasing funds for higher education, the need or increased cost-effectiveness makes it essential to use the latest educational technologies in 1988. UNESCO created an international institute for distance learning, the International Technological University (UIT), through a funds-in-trust contract from a private foundation, the International Centre for Technical Research, to produce low cost distance learning packages for institutes of education in Member States.

UNESCO and Deakin University (Australia) co-published the proceedings, including case-studies from fifteen countries of an international meeting of high-level distance education held at the University in September 1987.

Associated with these development plans proceed for the creation of number of externally financed UNESCO Chairs for eminent visiting professors, one of the firsts of which will be in distance learning.

(e) **University Science Teaching**

Mathematics, physics, chemistry and biology form the very basis of all studies leading to professional careers in science, engineering, health, agriculture and industry. These 'basic sciences' are the first subjects the future professional counters upon entering university and it is of particular importance that they are taught in courses of high quality which take into account the cultural and educational background of students as well as the development needs and aspirations of the country.

Worldwide, there is today an increasing awareness that science teaching at the early university level needs to be updated and modernized in both content and approach, and UNESCO is responding to this challenge by strengthening its co-operation with international and regional scientific organizations.

In collaboration with the International Council of Scientific Unions (ICSU) and the regional networks in chemistry and physics, a major effort was undertaken to launch two government-sponsored pilot projects on university science teaching, one in Thailand (chemistry, physics and biology), the other in the Philippines (Chemistry and Physics) which will develop flexible teaching packages stressing experimentation and adaptable to the science faculties of rural universities.

DRUG EDUCATION

UNESCO combats drug addiction by means of preventive education. It concerns itself with licit drugs--medicines, tobacco or alcohol – just as much as with illicit drugs. It engages in pilot activities, produces teaching materials and publishes studies. For example, the book 'Educating Against Drug Abuse' was widely distributed in 1988.

A seminar was held in Dakar in 1988 to study the impact of prevention schemes financed by the United Nations Fund for Drug Abuse Control in that region, initiate South-South collaboration in this sphere and extend such schemes to other African countries.

In France, UNESCO is co-operating with advertising agencies and non-governmental organizations in conducting a pilot audio-visual prevention campaign.

In Latin America, it is providing support for non-governmental organizations active in this sphere.

AIDS EDUCATION

The AIDS pandemic has created an emergency situation calling for international action. Failing a vaccine or cure, the most important component of AIDS programmes is information and education. UNESCO has joined the worldwide AIDS prevention effort being coordinated by WHO and, in 1989, will set up an international resource centre, issue a Guide to school-based AIDS education and initiate pilot projects through its regional offices. It will also seek to mobilize communities and young people, adapt information campaigns and deal with the human rights dimension of AIDS.

TEXTBOOKS

Ever since its creation, UNESCO has made efforts to promote textbook production. Its activities in the earlier stages included sending of experts and equipment to develop national publishing industries and train local personnel. In 1970, UNESCO published a book entitled *Preparing Textbook Manuscripts: A Guide for Authors in Developing Countries*. It includes the following chapters:–

1. The textbook as an aid to teaching.
2. Special problems of low-income countries.
3. Planning the textbook.
4. Developing the manuscript.
5. Responsibilities and rights of authors.
6. Problems of printing.
7. Distribution.

The publication also includes a useful bibliography.

HUMAN RIGHTS EDUCATION

A vast co-operation network enables UNESCO to encourage specialists working on matters connected with human rights, racism, violence and peace, and all forms of discrimination including those based on sex.

So that a wider public can be informed, one of UNESCO's essential tasks is to develop human rights teaching. The Organization acts at two levels - in the training of teachers and members of all those professions necessitating a particular sensitivity in regard to human rights and in the preparation of teaching materials. A bi-annual bulletin entitled Human Rights Teaching is published in English and in French.

The year 1988 marked the fortieth anniversary of the Universal Declaration of Human Rights. UNESCO was in duty bound to highlight this anniversary and to seize the opportunity to make world opinion more conscious of the urgent need to protect those rights effectively. A large number of events took place world-wide and the Organization appealed for 10 December to be made a special day in all schools and educational institutions throughout the world so that youth everywhere might feel particularly concerned. Information received from the Member States shows that this initiative met with a considerable response.

The emerging priorities in the human rights field are now focused on problems of application and protection of such rights, rather than on the formulation of new international instruments. Teaching has an important role in such questions.

QUALITY OF EDUCATION AND CURRICULUM REFORM

Education authorities in general curriculum and planners in particular have been showing increased concern for the relevance of the content of school curricula and textbooks. UNESCO advises countries on the role of education in overall policies of socio-economic and cultural development. In 1988, two UNESCO publications, *Interdisciplinarity in General Education*, followed by S. Rassekh and G. Vaideanu's *The Contents of Education* and five regional workshops all dealt with this subject.

While curriculum development tend to be a national preoccupation UNESCO often provides technical advice, especially for institution building. More and more Member States are creating formal curriculum development centres within ministry of education, and UNESCO helps to develop such institutions and to train their personnel. UNESCO acts also as the participating and executing agency for numerous operation projects financed by extra-budgetary sources in the field of curriculum development.

LIFE-LONG EDUCATION

To the minds of UNESCO specialists, lifelong education is first a concept, but can also be a policy, a practice, an Ideal and a process. It can be universal or specific (depending on the historical period and culture concerned), both theoretical and practical. It is something to be taken seriously.

To UNESCO experts, putting practice the principle of life-long education means taking action at all levels of discussion, planning and organization in order that, in addition to education provided by the school system, the education received individually or collectively - voluntarily or not - by children, young people, adults and the elderly in their personal, family, professionals or community lives, be recognized and integrated into the overall educational process.

Lifelong education thus has obvious applications in - for example - the post-literacy and continuing education programmes that the Organization prepares when asked to do so by the developing countries.

How can newly literate adults - or young people who have just left school (sometimes prematurely) - be helped to at least retain the skills they have acquired? This problem concerns the future of some hundreds of millions of people throughout the world. For this reason, specialists have established the following three goals:

- retention and consolidation of knowledge acquired;
- continuation of learning;
- implementation of programmes designed to improve personal, social and professional life.

In UNESCO's Second Medium-Term Plan (1984-1989) adopted by the General Conference at its extraordinary session held in Paris from 23 November to 3 December 1982, several explicit references to lifelong education may be found:

- in the discussion of world problems and the lines of emphasis of the Plan by the Director-General, Amadou-Mahtar M'Bow;
- in Major Programme II, "Education for All", which proposes, among other things, "to foster better understanding among the public and decision-makers, planners and educational personnel – teachers and administrators – of the reasons underlying the adoption, as a matter of urgency, of the principle of lifelong education."

EMERGENCY ACTION

At least once a month UNESCO's aid is requested by a country that has been struck by disaster. In cases where educational and scientific institutions or the cultural heritage have been damaged, the Organization endeavours to provide technical or financial assistance, alone or in the context of the relief organized by the United Nations system.

Unless rapid action is taken, there is a risk of situations remaining unchanged or indeed of becoming irreversible: schools rebuilt too slowly, libraries destroyed and collections needing to be restored, monuments and works of art lost for ever.

UNESCO dispatches experts on the spot to assess the damage caused, to offer advice and expertise for reconstruction or restoration. It assists in the rebuilding of schools, the purchase of educational equipments or in the organization of specific training.

A fund has been established on the initiative of the Director-General, which will be financed exclusively through voluntary contributions. As from 1988, UNESCO offered initial assistance to some ten countries financed by the regular budget.

AID OPERATIONS IN 1988

Afghanistan. UNESCO allocated $200,000 for the planning of its action and sent an educational adviser on secondment to the Coordinator for United Nations Humanitarian and Economic Assistance Programmes relating to Afghanistan.

Bangladesh. Disastrous floods; mission organized by the United Nations with UNESCO participation, Initial UNESCO aid: $100,000 for the rebuilding of educational establishments.

Jamaica. Initial UNESCO aid of $50,000 to study the rebuilding of schools and cultural institutions destroyed or damaged by the hurricane.

USSR: Leningrad. Fire in the library of the Soviet Academy of Sciences (February 1988): 400,000 books destroyed. A mission of experts assessed the damage and examined the question of the international aid needed to restore and replace the collections. UNESCO organized study tours in various countries for four specialists with a view to setting up a conservation laboratory.

Mozambique. Populations flee the areas affected by civil war; UNESCO will finance education projects ($200,000).

Nepal. Joint mission by UNESCO and the United States Geological Service: three experts investigated *in situ* the causes of the earthquake of 21 August. Initial rebuilding of school buildings: $100,000.

Nicaragua and Costa Rica. December: Two UNESCO experts went to Costa Rica and Nicaragua to study the question of UNESCO aid to repair or rebuild the educational establishments damaged in October by hurricane Joan and to identify the necessary funding sources.

EDUCATIONAL POLICY, PLANNING AND SERVICES

Each Member State has its own needs, strategies and objectives in the field of education and thus sets, by definition, its own course of action. UNESCO helps by suggesting educational methods best suited to prepare the children of the world for the responsibilities of freedom; providing access to information on educational experiments, policies, achievements and failures around the world, as well as advice on how such data could be applied to national planning and policy formulation. UNESCO, therefore, plays a catalytic role of conceptual stimulation, clarification and enrichment in an area in which the interactions between education, culture, science, technology and society are essential.

RECOVERY AND EDUCATION

Education policy formulation in sub-Saharan Africa has been seriously affected by economic and financial constraints. UNESCO provides some response to this crucial question in Education and Training Policies in sub-Saharan Africa; Problems Guidelines and Prospects prepared by its Regional Office for Education in Africa (BREDA). This contribution to the Programme of Action of the United Nations for the Economic Recovery and Development of Africa (1986-90) has been widely distributed and used.

EDUCATIONAL STATISTICS (EDSTATS)

As part of its programme of assistance to Member States for the collection and analysis of statistical data on education, the Office of Statistics has recently produced a software package intended to facilitate the calculation and analysis of such data. The package, entitled EDSTATS (EDucation STATistics) was developed with financial assistance from the Swedish International Development Authority (SIDA), and provides a broad range of statistical measures for the analysis of education data at the national level or at local levels.

The development of this system, and of those which are now in the planning stage, has been made feasible by the increasingly large-scale introduction of microcomputers throughout the world. These machines are accessible to persons having no experience or training in informatics and can significantly reduce the burden of time-consuming calculations, thus allowing both flexibility and adaptability in meeting the needs of users.

The EDSTATS package will be provided to statistical services in Member States at no cost; it is hoped that it will significantly facilitate the analysis and assessment of the quantitative development and efficiency of education systems.

EDUCATIONAL INFORMATION CENTRE

UNESCO relies on the circulation and use of information produced and accumulated in the course of programme implementation. This information is carefully targeted to reach its various 'users', who range from schoolteachers in rural areas to major national or regional institutions.

UNESCO has thus:

- established a sub-network linking the documentation centre at Headquarters to all the centres away from Headquarters, including those of associated institutions;
- strengthened the INED network.
- given support to national documentation centres (seminars and missions: provision of microcomputer equipment and MICRO-ISIS software packages);
- circulated UNESCO's education catalogue, documents and publications to more than 3000 institutions, as well as to 340 ongoing extra-budgetary projects.
- distributed the half-yearly catalogue of acquisitions of the IBE's

documentation centre to some 1000 institutions.

- replied to more than 5,200 requests for documentation;
- distributed some 30,000 documents and publications;
- assisted more than 4,700 visitors in seeking information.

5

UNESCO'S MAJOR ACTIVITIES IN THE FIELD OF EDUCATION

OVERVIEW

Priorities for 1990-1995

UNESCO recognises that collective development depends upon the education of each individual human being and gives top priority to the promotion of literacy.

The approach is two-pronged:

* stemming illiteracy at its source by making primary education available to all children;
* providing literacy training and basic education for adults and young people who are not attending school.

UNESCO attaches particular importance to the education of underprivileged sectors of the population:

* women and girls, accounting for over one half of the entire human race;
* young people in rural areas and isolated regions;
* handicapped children and young people;
* other disadvantaged groups.

Preparing for the twenty-first century is the other priority. The Organization's efforts are directed towards ensuring:

* due regard for the humanistic, cultural and international dimensions of education and improvement of the quality of life, with particular emphasis on the environment, physical fitness and health;
* mastery of science and technology;
* the promotion of technical and vocational education and the acquisition of experience of productive work within the framework of general education;
* the quality and relevance of higher education.

UNESCO is particularly concerned with the training of educational personnel and the development of new forms and methods of education making use of all available technologies.

ACTIVITIES

Right to Education

(i) UNESCO promotes activities related to the implementation of the convention and recommendation against discrimination.
(ii) UNESCO initiates studies on the democratization of education.
(iii) UNESCO encourages activities designed to increase educational opportunities for girls and women within the framework of UNESCO's Long-term action for their equal access to education, science and culture.
(iv) UNESCO initiates programmes for the promotion of the education of the handicapped children and youth.

Education for Refugees

(i) UNESCO co-operates with the United Nations Relief and Works Agency for Palestine Refugees (UNRWA) in assuming technical responsibility for the planning, execution and supervision of education programme for the Arab refugees from Palestine.
(ii) UNESCO co-operates with the Secretary-General of the United Nations and the United Nations High Commissioner for Refugees from Southern Africa by providing the necessary technical advice on study programmes and by collaborating with the Bureau of Placement and Education of the Organization of African Unity.

Life-Long Education

UNESCO undertakes studies and fosters experimental activities in Member States based in particular on information gained through the International Education Year, with a view to assisting in further clarifying the concept of life-long education.

Developing Strategies for Education

(i) UNESCO makes studies and issues publications on the main trends of educational development in the world.
(ii) UNESCO provides assistance to the UNESCO Institute of Education in Hamburg, which has extensive contacts with educational research institutions.

Conferences

UNESCO organizes regional conferences at the ministerial level to help Member States formulate policies and strategies orientated toward the advancement of education in close connection with scientific, technological and economic development.

Training Abroad

(i) UNESCO assists Members States to develop national policies and programmes for training abroad in the light of perspective national educational development and reform.
(ii) UNESCO promotes increasing international use of key national training facilities.
(iii) UNESCO administers fellowships and group training schemes.

Co-operation with International Non-Governmental Organizations

UNESCO associates international non-governmental organisations in the field of education with its programmes and provides selected organizations with subventions.

Curriculum

(i) UNESCO gives particular attention to the development of institutions for educational research and for curriculum development.

(ii) UNESCO undertakes activities for the improvement of integrated curriculum planning and the encouragement of curriculum development in such fields as social studies, languages, home economics, health, nutrition and population education.

(iii) UNESCO encourages activities for the strengthening of moral and civic education with emphasis on its contribution to education for international understanding and co-operation, respect for human rights and the ideals of peace.

Educational Methods, Materials and Techniques

(i) UNESCO promotes and assists the development and improvement of educational materials, methods and techniques, including new forms of printed materials, audio-visual media, correspondence education, scientific organization of the learning process, team teaching, group dynamics.

(ii) UNESCO undertakes activities for the adoption to the needs of Member States of advanced educational technology such as combined media, space communication for education, computer-assisted instruction and related approaches taking into account recent developments in educational psychology, sociology, communication and cybernetics.

(iii) UNESCO assists in the development and maintenance, on a regional basis, of institutions and services designed to support national efforts concerned with the improvement of educational media, methods and techniques.

(iv) UNESCO participates in the activities of Member States which are in pursuit of the above objectives.

Educational Structures

(i) UNESCO promotes and assists the development and improvement of educational structures suitably adapted to the requirements of life-long education.

(ii) UNESCO fosters the reform of secondary education, both general and technical, with a view to meet the needs of the community and the requirements of individual fulfilment.

Programmes for Teachers

(i) UNESCO renders services to Member States for the planning and execution of their programmes in teacher education for primary, secondary and technical schools.
(ii) UNESCO promotes the introduction of interdisciplinary approaches and of new methods and techniques in teacher preparation.
(iii) UNESCO develops new models for the life-long education of teachers, teacher educators, inspectors, supervisors and administrators.
(iv) UNESCO develops regional institutions and services designed to support national programmes for pre-service training and in-service training of teacher-educators and supervisors for primary and secondary schools.
(v) UNESCO provides technical assistance to Member States for the expansion and improvement of pre-service and in-service education of teachers for all levels of school education.

Higher Education

(i) UNESCO undertakes studies of major organizational pedagogical and institutional problems in the field.
(ii) UNESCO promotes inter-university dialogue by providing opportunities for discussion.
(iii) UNESCO stimulates experimentation with alternative models of higher educational systems.
(iv) UNESCO diffuses information, particularly through collaboration with competent international governmental, non-governmental and inter-university organizations.
(v) UNESCO pursues activities designed to extend the comparability and equivalence of certificates, diplomas and degrees in higher education.

Out-of-School Education

(i) UNESCO organizes conferences on adult education.
(ii) UNESCO assists Member States in promoting and improving their adult education institutions and practices through a fuller utilization of advanced methods and techniques including the

mass media and space communication, and in the training of specialized personnel.

(iii) UNESCO strengthens and supports adult education activities related to development objectives.

(iv) UNESCO supports the development and study of leisure-time activities, especially by assisting the European Centre for Leisure and Education in Prague.

Programmes for Youth

(i) UNESCO promotes better knowledge of the problems and attitudes of youth.

(ii) UNESCO assists Member States and non-governmental organizations in developing ways and means for increased youth participation in (a) the renewal of education, (b) the promotion and dissemination of science and (c) cultural development.

(iii) UNESCO encourages youth participation in social and economic development.

(iv) UNESCO undertakes activities to analyse problems of the less privileged among youth and assists Member States in searching for appropriate solutions to these problems.

(v) UNESCO seeks increased youth participation in its work.

Literacy Programmes

(i) UNESCO supports the International Institute for Adult Literacy Methods, Teheran.

(ii) UNESCO develops systematic dissemination of information concerning the experiences gained in functional literacy by governmental and non-governmental organizations, public and private enterprises, regional and international organizations.

(iii) UNESCO develops experimental World Literacy Programmes.

(iv) UNESCO promotes research on various aspects of adult literacy.

(v) UNESCO increases the provision of the training facilities necessary for the implementation both of mass literacy programmes and experimental functions literacy projects by way, in particular, of (a) organizing seminars, workshops and courses, (b) arranging contracts for special training with universities and other appropriate institutions, (c) promoting the use of mass media for such training purposes, and (d) supporting regional training centres and especially the regional rural functional literacy centres for Arab States (ASFEC) and Latin America (CFEFAL).

Planning and Financing of Education

UNESCO assists Member States in the definition of long-term educational plans and strategies within the framework of their national, social and economic policies and of internationally agreed goals in the development of education, in the formulation of integrated programmes: and in the identification, analysis and preparation of projects.

Long-Term Planning and Management of Education and Elaboration of National Strategies

(i) UNESCO promotes, co-ordinates and conducts studies contributing to changes in the total education process through advancement in the practice of educational planning and administration, particular attention being given to improved governance, management and effectiveness of education systems.
(ii) UNESCO provides advisory services to Member States for promoting planning focused on life-long education and for the elaboration of national strategies of integrated educational development.

Research and Training in Education, Planning and Administration

(i) UNESCO supports the International Institute of Educational Planning (IIEP) Paris with a grant-in-aid and services.
(ii) UNESCO supports the Arab States Centres for Educational Planning and Administration (Beirut) with a grant-in-aid and services.
(iii) UNESCO supports the Asian Institute of Educational Planning and Administration (New Delhi) with a grant-in-aid and services. (Now a unit of National Staff College, for Educational Planners and Administrators, New Delhi).
(iv) UNESCO maintains the planning sections of the Regional Offices for Education in Africa (Dakar) and in Latin America and the Caribbean (Santiago).

(v) UNESCO assists Member States in the development of national institutions for training and research.

Educational Buildings

(i) UNESCO promotes research and develops information services that helps Member States to plan and implement Educational Buildings Programmes to provide facilities for accommodating educational growth and change.
(ii) UNESCO promotes regional activities for research, training and development group work in the field of educational building.
(iii) UNESCO provides grant-in-aid and services to the Regional Educational Building Institute for Africa, Khartoum.
(iv) UNESCO provides grant-in-aid and services to the Regional School Building Centre for Latin America and the Caribbean, Mexico city.
(v) UNESCO provides grant-in-aid and services to the Asian Regional Institute for School Building Research, Colombo.
(vi) UNESCO provides advisory services to Arab Member States.
(vii) UNESCO provides technical assistance to Member States for the planning and implementation of their educational building programmes.

Project Development and Capital Aid

(i) UNESCO co-operates with the International Bank for Reconstruction and Development (IBRD) and its affiliate, the International Development Association (IDA), in a programme designed to assist governments' in making their national systems of education more productive and efficient.
(ii) UNESCO co-operates with the Inter-American Development Bank (IDB) and the African Development Bank (ADB) and Asian Development Bank and other sources of financing educational development.
(iii) UNESCO promotes research on educational and financing problems that are of common interest to Member States.

Science Teaching

(i) UNESCO promotes the international exchange of ideas on

science education.

(ii) UNESCO assists the Member States in the development of programmes of science education improvement.

(iii) UNESCO acts as executing agency for United Nations Development Programme Projects in the field.

Communication

(i) UNESCO promotes free flow of information and international exchange.

(ii) UNESCO conducts research and studies in mass communication.

(iii) UNESCO trains information personnel.

(iv) UNESCO develops mass media.

(v) UNESCO promotes book production and distribution.

(iv) UNESCO promotes research and international co-operation in documentation.

(vii) UNESCO develops documentation, Library and archives services.

(viii) UNESCO collects, compiles and analyses statistical data.

Associated School Project

The promotion of international understanding and peace through school education has from the outset been one of UNESCO's basic aims and UNESCO's General Conference, at each of its sessions, has adopted resolutions to this end. The Associated Schools Project has served for more than 37 years as an effective means of extending to educational institutions in many different countries the Organization's education activity for international understanding and peace.

The Associated Schools Project in education for international co-operation and peace was launched with a planning meeting held in November 1953, as the logical next step in UNESCO's action to promote education in schools for international understanding and co-operation. The main purpose is to encourage primary and secondary schools and teacher-training institutions selected by their UNESCO National Commissions to organize special programmes designed to increase knowledge of world problems and international co-operation, to develop international understanding through the study of other peoples and cultures and to strengthen understanding and observance of the principles of human rights. The ultimate aim is to promote the general development of education for international understanding through the work of a widespread network of institutions.

At the first Associated Schools meeting held in Paris, there were 21 participants representing a total of 33 schools in 15 Member States. There are now over 1,000 participating schools and 200 teacher Training Institutions in 73 Member States. Member institutions are to be found in Africa, Asia, Oceania, the Middle East, Europe, Latin America and North America, in countries representing not only different cultural traditions and different stages of development, but also different economic and social systems.

The International Institute for Educational Planning, Paris

The International Institute for Educational Planning (IIEP), since its foundation in 1963 has played a key role in developing educational planning to what it is today. As an international centre for advanced training and research in the field of educational planning, the Institute is in a unique position to play a leading part in coping with the new challenges facing educational planning now.

While an integral part of UNESCO, the Institute's special statues ensure its intellectual autonomy: the IIEP's own Governing Board determines the overall direction of the Institute's research and training activities and approves the annual budget.

UNESCO Institute for Education, Hamburg

UNESCO Institute for Education (UIE) is a centre established by UNESCO in Hamburg (Federal Republic of Germany) in 1951 to serve as a centre for contact between educators of different countries so as to enable them to compare and exchange without national, racial of cultural prejudice, their knowledge and experience in the various fields of education.

"*The International Review*' is the Institute's quarterly journal published in English, French and German.

International Bureau of Education, Geneva

The International Bureau of Education (IBE) was established in 1952 as an international non-governmental organization. Its functions are to "act as an international centre of information and educational research and provide for a wide exchange of data so that each country may be encouraged to profit by the experience of others". IBE is financed principally from contributions of Member Governments. Its activities are governed by a council which consists of all Member governments, and an executive committee.

An International Conference on Public Education is held jointly with UNESCO. Topics for discussion are selected in advance by the Joint Committee of UNESCO and the International Bureau of Education and questionnaires on the subject chosen are circulated to the ministries of education and Member Governments. Material furnished by the replies is published each year. Further, the study of each of these topics provides the basis for preparing recommendations which are subsequently widely distributed.

6

UNESCO'S COLLABORATION IN THE FIELD OF EDUCATION

UNESCO AND UNEPTA

The year 1950 seems to have marked the beginning of what is today a major part of UNESCO's work. It was in that year that UNESCO was first able to send experts to Member States, paid for under the United Nations Expanded Programme of Technical Assistance (UNEPTA), the purpose of which was to assist countries, at their request, 'to strengthen their national economy through the development of their industries and agriculture with a view to strengthening their economic and political independence in the spirit of the Charter of the United Nations and to ensure the attainment of higher levels of economic and social welfare for their entire populations'.

By 1965, UNESCO had given assistance to a hundred countries, mainly in the fields of education and natural sciences. Many expert missions for periods ranging from months to several years and more than 4,000 fellowships had been provided under this programme. Hundreds of experts and fellowships had also been provided under UNESCO's Regular Budget.

In its initial years, UNESCO's main educational efforts had been directed at helping the war-stricken countries of Europe to repair the ravages of the Second World War by providing books and equipment for schools and libraries and generally aiding in the vast task of post-war reconstruction. In the ensuing years special terms were formed to aid UNESCO member countries in other parts of the world to expand and reorganize their education systems. This was the period during which UNESCO laid special emphasis on what came to be known as 'fundamental education centres'—pilot schemes for training rural teachers and leaders. The first centre of this kind was opened for men and women from sixteen Latin American countries of Patzcuaro (Mexico) in 1951. The second, serving the Arab world, opened at Sirs-el-Layyan (U.A.R.) in 1953.

UNESCO AND UNSF

The year 1960 marked another milestone in the history of UNESCO's work in education. This was the year that saw the creation of the United Nations Special Fund (UNSF) which together with Technical Assistance funds enabled UNESCO to give far greater emphasis to operational assistance. At its eleventh session that year, UNESCO's General Conference decided that priority should be accorded to education in the programmes of the Organization, and urged that increased aid be made available to Member States in their efforts to develop education at all levels and to eliminate illiteracy. The General Conference affirmed that educational development was a pre-requisite to the economic, social and political development of all countries, and was a means by which each nation could make a fuller contribution to international understanding and to world peace.

The same session of the General Conference adopted a convention and a recommendation against discrimination in education. These measures were aimed not only at eliminating national statutory provisions or administrative practices involving discrimination, but also at promoting national policies to give equal educational opportunities to all and translate the right to education into a reality.

UNESCO AND UNDP

By 1966, when the Special Fund and United Nations Expanded Programme of Technical Assistance were merged to form the United Nations Development Programme, (UNDP) UNESCO was responsible, as the executing agency, for financial assistance to ninety-eight projects in fifty-eight countries. Almost all of the projects, which originate in and call for large expenditure by the countries concerned, deal with higher technical and technological training, with science education and with the training of teachers for secondary and higher education. Experimental literacy projects were started in many countries.

UNESCO AND UNICEF

UNESCO and UNICEF—the United Nations Children's Fund—have for many years been combining their financial resources and professional expertise to develop, expand, often even to help to create, education projects in countries all over the world, especially in developing countries. During 1968-69 and 1969-70 together, their joint efforts were supporting some seventy projects in some seventy countries, from Peru to Pakistan, Morocco to Madagascar, Yugoslavia to Yemen. Most of these projects were concerned with training teachers for rural, primary and secondary schools, pre-vocational education and training. Instruction in science, and training in health, nutrition, home economics and general community development have been often added to the traditional teaching of the three R's

Projects vary widely, from the education of blind and handicapped children, as in Thailand, or science teaching for primary school children in Malawi to the creation of one teacher, one room schools in Guatemala.

In the joint UNESCO-UNICEF projects, UNICEF provides material assistance in the form of supplies and teaching equipment, such as 1,000 mobile science carts containing the essentials for 100 simple experiments which could be wheeled from one classroom to another. Equipment and material are also supplied for the teaching of home economics, nutrition, manual arts, physical training. Stipends, honoraria, sometimes even travel allowances, are provided for trainees and instructors in teacher training courses. Sometimes the cost of providing educational experts have also been borne by UNICEF for a limited period, until these could be taken over by the local authorities or financed for a further period by arrangement between UNESCO and the United Nations Development Programme.

UNESCO provides guidance and technical supervision of projects, educational experts and fellowships. It advises and helps countries in drawing up plans, establishing estimates of needs and in framing requests for international staff.

The Thailand-UNESCO Rural Teacher Educational Project (TURTEP), at Ubol in Thailand may be regarded as the opening phase of UNESCO-UNICEF cooperation. UNESCO gave assistance to this project from its inception in 1956 and UNICEF aid started in 1960.

UNESCO AND WORLD BANK

Under the 1965 agreement, UNESCO was mainly responsible for identifying projects considered eligible for assistance from the World Bank, and for helping Member States in the preparation of their requests for loans. The agreement in fact confirmed the close collaboration which had already existed between the two organizations for several years, making possible the allocation of loans to Pakistan, the Philippines, Tanzania and Tunisia.

Within UNESCO the operational responsibility for the cooperative programme lies with the Educational Financing Division of the Department of Planning and Financing of Education. In the Bank, these responsibilities are dealt with by the Educational Projects Department.

The co-operative programme is designed to assist governments in expanding and improving their education systems in the framework of national economic development programmes. In the first instance, systems of education are studied as a whole, though in later stages, priority may be given to the development of particular sectors (general education, agricultural, industrial, technical, commercial or teacher training). In general, the decision to give assistance to one or more of these sectors is made in the context of a study of the entire system. In granting loans and credits, emphasis placed on the economic aspects of education does not imply that the World Bank regards other objectives as less important. This policy conforms with its mandate to foster economic progress by various means, and with UNESCO's programme to promote education as part of overall development, including economic development. In this connection it is important to make a clear distinction between fundamental needs which, particularly in the developing countries, greatly exceed the resources available, and priorities which must be determined within the framework of a plan, or at least of a policy, for education.

The implications of this economic approach to educational problems are two-fold. Firstly, the requirements in qualified personnel are generally assessed on the basis of analyses of the labour market and in the light of other economic indicators. Whatever the method applied, projects financed by the World Bank must result in an increased output of the education system. In addition, it is essential that suitable conditions exist to ensure the internal efficiency of the entire system, not merely those sectors benefiting from financial aid from the Bank and the IDA.

To sum up, the co-operation programme was not conceived purely and simply to facilitate the allocation of funds. This aid must serve a definite purpose : that of implementing national systems of education and, more specifically, of increasing their output and efficiency.

Types of Assistance

International assistance given for the purpose of increasing a country's existing resources is mainly of two types : technical assistance and capital aid. UNESCO has been providing technical assistance, mainly from funds allocated under the United Nations Development Programme (UNDP), for the training of teachers, missions by expert advisers on curriculum reform and on the development of new teaching methods, granting of fellowships for training administrators, etc. But financial aid is also allocated for material needs – school buildings and equipment, teaching aids and so on. The World Bank is the sole institution in the United Nations system which provides this kind of aid on so large a scale. Its policy is to supply aid in the form of loans or credits (not, for example, through grants-in-aid). Loans are made on the basis of an interest rate of 6.5%, repayable over a period of about 25 years, beginning after five to 10 years. Credits, on the other hand, are granted interest free by the IDA, with a service charge of 0.75%, and are repayable over 50 years, with a 10-year period of grace. In some cases, loans and credits are made available simultaneously, but generally the decision whether to grant a loan or a credit depends on the economic situation of the country and not on the type of project (education, roads, power, etc.).

Technical assistance and financial aid are often – but not always – complementary. The real interrelationship is between the various categories of inputs, as an inadequacy in any one of them may have repercussions on the quality or quantity of the outputs. It is therefore necessary to examine all categories of inputs before deciding which of them need strengthening and how this can best be achieved. This again underlines the paramount importance of educational planning as a tool for development.

The Bank only allocates financial aid to well defined projects designed to meet urgent and vital needs for educational development at a reasonable cost. A project might, for example, include the building and equipment of a number of comprehensive secondary schools and higher teacher training establishments or the provision of physical plant for putting into effect a new curriculum of improved teaching methods, but technical assistance will be earmarked for specific institutions.

UNESCO AND OTHER U.N. ORGANIZATIONS

UNESCO has been called "the latest specialized of the specialized agencies". As a specialized agency of the United Nations. UNESCO collaborates closely with other agencies. Agreements have been concluded with the Food and Agriculture Organization (FAO), International Atomic Energy Agency Development (IAEAD), International Development Association (IDA), International Labour Organization (ILO), United Nations High Commissioner for Refugees (UNHCR), United Nations Industrial Organization (UNIDO), World Health Organization (WHO), etc. UNESCO also works closely with the United Nations Regional Economic Commission.

UNESCO AND SWEDISH FUNDS-IN-TRUST PROGRAMME

Since 1963, voluntary contributions have been deposited in Sweden's Funds-in-Trust at UNESCO. These funds have been used to finance a number of different projects for education in Africa, particularly education of girls. The Primary Teacher Training College in Francistown (Botswana) was started in the Swedish programme, and executed by UNESCO. UNESCO provided experts. Equipment was supplied through the combined efforts of UNICEF, Sweden and the Government of Botswana; fellowships in correspondence education were given by the government of Sweden on a bilateral basis.

With the opening of the College in Francistown the Swedish Funds-in-Trust Programme began operating in seven African countries. It has financed the construction of a primary teacher training college for girls in Sierra Leone and a secondary school for girls in Tanzania, and the costs for running both of them for five years. Three bookmobiles – and funds to operate them for three years – have been made available for Tanzania, Kenya and Uganda with a wide range of educational and general reading material – of special help to new literates. A mobile cinema has been supplied to Sierra Leone and is being used for local and national health campaigns as well as health education in schools.

In Ghana, many secondary schools have received science teaching equipment for secondary and advanced levels, and many girls were awarded scholarships to secondary schools for four years. Many African women received fellowships for courses in adult education and literacy teaching under the Swedish Funds-in-Trust Programme and undertook their training at the Mount Carmel International Training Centre for Community Services in Israel. A secondary girls boarding school has been completed in Sfax, Tunisia.

UNESCO AND NON-GOVERNMENTAL ORGANIZATIONS

From the beginning UNESCO has worked closely with various non-governmental organizations known as NGOs, each one bringing together on an international level specialists from disciplines within its competence or endeavouring to give direction to the interests and loyalties evoked by certain aspects or goals of UNESCO's work, within specific social groups or sectors of public opinion. UNESCO maintains official relations with these organizations and some of them have consultative status. No other agency in the United Nations has built up so extensive a network of international cooperation on a non-governmental lead. There are at present more than 1000 non-governmental organizations around the globe with whom UNESCO is working, 557 of them on an official basis.

UNESCO's reasons for cooperating with NGOs stem directly from its constitution. This document's preamble affirms "That a peace based exclusively on the political and economic arrangements of governments would not be a peace which would secure the unanimous, lasting and sincere support of the peoples of the world, and that the peace must therefore by founded, if it is not to fail, upon the intellectual and moral solidarity of mankind."

Four complementary conclusions may be drawn from this affirmation. First, that the "support of the peoples of the world" must be secured without which peace is not possible. Second, that to create conditions in which peace is possible. UNESCO must work to forge "intellectual and moral solidarity" among "the peoples of the world". Third, both these things must be done outside as well as through governments. Fourth, as the foregoing preconditions, an extra-governmental channel of communication and action must be opened between UNESCO and "the peoples of the world".

So vital are NGOs to UNESCO's activities that it has helped to create several non-governmental partners. Broadly interpreting its constitutional mandate to "invite them to undertake specific tasks". UNESCO has played an instrumental part in founding certain NGOs in fields where no representative international body existed before UNESCO also has encouraged union or federation of similar NGOs and strengthened those already in existence. Among these are the International Association of Universities, International Music Council, International Council of Museums and International Council for Philosophy and Humanistic Studies.

Generally "the specific tasks" that UNESCO helps an NGO to undertake are rather more specific than its own creation. In some cases, substantial aid is provided on a long-term basis to subsidize an NGO fulfilling some basic function in its field of competence such as running a documentation centre or sponsoring a series of meetings. In other instances, limited help is provided under contract on a short-term basis to enable an NGO to carry out a single project, e.g. execution of a study or organization of a symposium.

UNESCO AND EXPERIMENTAL LITERACY PROJECTS

Algeria	:	Work-Oriented Adult Literacy Pilot Project (1967-72).
Ecuador	:	Proyecto Piloto de Alfabetizacion Functional de Adultos (1967-72).
Ethiopia	:	Work-Oriented Adult Literacy Project (1968-73).
Guinea	:	Project Pilote d'alphabetisation fonctionnelle des adultes (1968-73).
Iran	:	Work-Oriented Adult Literacy Pilot Project (1967-1971).
Madagascar	:	Project Pilote d'alphabetisation fonctionnelle des adultes (1968-72).
Mali	:	Project Pilote d'alphabetisation fonctionnelle des adultes (1967-72).
Sudan	:	Work-Oriented Adult Literacy Project (1969-72).
Tanzania	:	Work-Oriented Adult Literacy Project (1968-72).
India	:	Farmer's Education and Functional Literacy (1969-72).
Syria	:	Agricultural Development of the Ghab Region Phase II (1969-72).
Venezuela	:	Proyecto Piloto Experimental de Alfabetizacion Funcionaly Educacion de Adultos (1968-73).

UNESCO'S REGIONAL OFFICES AND OTHER ORGANIZATIONS

Regional Offices for education

The Regional Offices constitute the principal executive arms for the Organization's programme at the regional level. The basic purpose of the Regional Offices for Education is to promote and strengthen co-operation among the Member States of one and the same region with the aim of developing education. Within this general framework, they assume the following main functions:

(a) Studies and research to analyse educational situations and new trends with a view to highlighting conceptions, needs and pre-occupations of Member States;
(b) advisory services for the study of individual or sectoral problems, intended to assist Member States in their efforts to renew their educational systems;
(c) training of educational personnel;
(d) information and documentation, the aim being to collect and circulate to Member States information and documentation on education and to publish reviews or newsletters;
(e) support for operational programmes in the form of technical assistance to the experts responsible for implementing operational projects and of participation in country programming, execution and evaluation activities in regard to projects concerning education in the particular region.

In carrying out their various functions, the Regional Offices co-operate with regional institutions of the United Nations system.

These are of two types:

(i) Regional Offices or Centres which are integral parts of the Secretariat, and
(ii) Regional Institutes, which have been established on behalf of all Member States, by a Member State or States with UNESCO aid.

In Asia the First Group comprises the following:

(i) Regional Office for Education in Asia and the Pacific, Bangkok, Thailand.

(ii) Field Science Office for South Asia, New Delhi, India.
(iii) Field Science Office for South-East Asia, Djakarta, Indonesia.
(iv) Regional Centre for Book Development in Asia, Karachi, Pakistan.

The Regional offices in other countries include: Regional Office for Education in Africa, Dakar, Africa: Regional Centre in the Centre in the Western Hemisphere, Havana, Cuba.

The Second Group is composed of:

(i) The Asian Institute of Educational Planning and Administration, New Delhi, India (Now a wing of National Institute of Educational Planning and Administration, New Delhi).
(ii) The Asian Institute for Teacher Educators, Quezon City, Philippines, and
(iii) The Asian Regional Institute for School Building Research, Colombo, Ceylon.
The centres created by UNESCO in other countries include : African Training and Research Centre in Administration for Development (CAFRAD), Tangiers (Morocco); Arab State Centre for Educational Planning and Administration (ASCATEP), Beirut, (Lebanon); Regional Centre for Functional Literacy in Rural Areas for Latin America (CREFAL), Patzcurao, (Mexico); European Co-ordination Centre for Research and Documentation in the Social Sciences, Vienna (Austria).

Regional Office for Education in Asia, and the Pacific, Bangkok, Thailand

The Regional Office for Education in Asia and the Pacific (ROEAP) was established in Bangkok in 1962 and merged into a single unit later in that year with the Regional Centre for Educational Information and Studies. It is a Regional Office created by UNESCO as an integral part of the Secretariat. The Government of Thailand contributes the premises where the office is housed and makes a fixed cash contribution towards the cost of local staff.

It assists all Asian Member States at the regional level in the implementation of the Karachi Plan for universal, free and compulsory primary education as extended at the Tokyo Conference of Asian Education Ministers.

The Office is responsible for implementing regional educational programmes in Asia and for developing and providing clearing house services in education to Member States in the region. The regional educational Programmes in Asia are carried out through Regional Institutes and are designed to provide training facilities for key personnel from Member States in the region. The research and training programmes of the Institute are co-ordinated and guided by the office.

The functions of the Regional Office and the services that it seeks to provide, cover the following main education areas:

1. to play a substantive role in the preparation, organization and follow up of the regional conferences of ministers of Education,
2. to provide documentary and information services to Member-States and to UNESCO field experts in the regions,
3. to assist Member-States in developing and maintaining their own documentation, information, statistical and research services for use in continuous planning of educational development,
4. to provide supervision and guidance for the activities of the regional education institutes assisted by UNESCO in Asia, mentioned above, and
5. to collaborate with the United Nations Economic Commission for Asia and the Far East (ECAFE) and with the regional offices of the other Specialized Agencies.

Upon the recommendation of the Evaluation Commission of 1965, it was decided to establish for the Regional Office an advisory organ composed of nine leading Asian educators at the level of permanent secretaries and serving in a personal capacity with the Director of the Regional Office serving as Secretary, to advise the Director-General of UNESCO and to assist in co-ordinating regional programmes in the field of education. The Director-General further decided that to the meeting of the advisory organ will be invited not only the Directors of the three regional institutes, but also the Directors concerned and Heads of all related regional centres and programmes in Asia.

Regional Centre for Book Development in Asia, Karachi, Pakistan

The Karachi Centre, which was established to serve the "Project for the Provision of Reading Materials", in 1958, was reoriented in January 1969 to serve as the field instrument for Asia of UNESCO's Book

Development Programme, adopted by the General Conference at its fourteenth session.

The Centre is responsible for the implementation of this programme including all its aspects such as writing, publishing, printing and the relevant training components. Assistance from or through the Centre is mainly provided upon the request of Member-States, for national and regional training course in the above-mentioned areas, and through expert missions by the Centre's staff.

The Centre operates in close contact with the Tokyo Book Development Centre whose regional training courses in publishing techniques are financially assisted by UNESCO.

The Centre publishes its quarterly *Newsletter* in English. The *Newsletter* serves as a forum for the exchange of practical experience in the region and depends largely on the co-operation of experts of the Member-States.

The Centre provides a Documentation Section for the benefit of interested bodies and individuals from Member-States.

Asian Institute of Educational Planning and Administration, New Delhi, India (Now a wing of *National Institute of Educational Planning and Administration, New Delhi*).

The General Conference of UNESCO at its eleventh session authorised the establishment of a Regional Centre for the Training of Educational Planners, Administrators and Supervisors in Asia to help Member-States in preparing the key personnel need for implementing the Karachi Plan. The Centre was set up under an agreement with the Government of India and began to function in New Delhi from February 1962. It was redesignated as the Asian Institute of Educational Planning and Administration with effect from April 1, 1965. A new agreement was signed between UNESCO and the Government of India on August 26, 1970. The Institute functioned under the legal and constitutional framework of the Government of India.

The functions of the Institute are:

(a) To provide short in-service training courses for the officers of the various Ministries or Departments of Education of participating Asian Member States and Associate Members of UNESCO.
(b) To undertake and promote research in the techniques of educational planning, administration and supervision and to place the

results at the disposal of such States.

(c) To assist such States, upon request, in organizing educational planning services and in holding national training courses.

The agreement signed by the Government of India and UNESCO for the establishment of this Institute, stipulated that UNESCO's assistance would terminate at the close of 1972. The Government of India established National Staff College for Educational Planners and Administrators with effect from April 1, 1971. The National Staff College has established an Asian Wing which continues the existing programmes of the Asian Institute. The Staff College has been renamed as the National Institute of Educational Planning and Administration, New Delhi.

Asian Institute for Teacher Educators, Quezon City, Philippines

The Karachi Meeting of Representatives of Asian Member States, convened by UNESCO in 1960, recommended that in order to raise the quality of teacher training in Asia, a regional institute for the training of teacher educators should be established with the assistance of UNESCO. In pursuance of this recommendation and a programme approved by the eleventh session of the General Conference of UNESCO, an agreement was concluded (28 March, 1962) with the Government of the Philippines to set up a Regional Centre for the Training of Teacher Educators in the University of the Philippines. At the thirteenth session of the General Conference in 1964, the name was changed to Asian Institute for Teacher Educators.

On the recommendation of the Evaluation Commission, it was decided in 1967 that the Institute would in future offer short training courses for high-level personnel in teacher education and the University of the Philippines agreed to institute a post-graduate course in teacher training leading to a Master's degree.

Following the above recommendation of the Evaluation Commission, the functions of the Institute were also redefined and now stand as follows:

> The purpose of the Institute shall be to provide a forum and focal point for those responsible for teacher education in Asia, in order to enable the following categories of personnel to meet and exchange experiences, discuss programmes, develop common stan-

dards and draw up plans for the development and upgrading of teacher education in Asia:

(a) heads of teacher training programmes in Ministries of Education;
(b) principals of teacher training institutions; and
(c) those responsible for the organization of in-service teacher training.

With this purpose in view, the main functions of the Institute shall be:

(a) to provide short courses for the personnel referred to above;
(b) to undertake and promote studies and research on priority problems in teacher education, with particular reference to the techniques of teacher training and teaching methods;
(c) to organize periodically high-level symposia to review the substantive aspects of the Institute's training and/or research programmes and assist in the coordination of programmes in this field;
(d) to promote the development and to service through exchange of information and advice, a network of national teacher education centre, as well as a scheme of associated teacher colleges, teacher training institutions and service.

Asian Regional Institute for School Building Research, Colombo, Ceylon

The Regional Meeting of Representatives of Asian Member States on primary and compulsory education, convened in Karachi by UNESCO from 28 December, 1959 to 9 January, 1960, adopted a working plan for the provision of universal, compulsory and free primary education in Asia. Realizing the magnitude of the task, in that provision had to be found for the education of a tremendously large school-going population, spread over a vast region with much diversity of culture, climatic conditions and per capita income, the Regional Meeting recommended that UNESCO Regional Programmes should include a centre for school building research. Accordingly in 1962, UNESCO sponsored the establishment of an Asian Regional Institute for School Building Research in Indonesia.

The Institute opened in a building, provided by the Government of Indonesia, at Bandung in 1962. The Government also provided staff, housing and local staff including a Joint Director, architect, draughtsmen and other office personnel. UNESCO, at this stage, provided a staff of three experts and an administrative officer. The Institute functioned in Indonesia until the end of 1964, producing eleven Occasional Papers and conducting a two months' training course.

Following the temporary withdrawal of Indonesia from UNESCO, the Institutes's international staff was transferred to Bangkok where the programme was continued for 15 months. During this period work progressed with development groups in the Region, with preparation for a major cost study in collaboration with sister Institutes in Africa and Latin America, the publication of a primary School Design Work Book and a School Building Seminar in the Republic of China. During this period too, on the occasion of a meeting at Islamabad between the then Secretary for Education, Pakistan, and UNESCO's former Deputy Director General, Dr. Adiseshiah, the Institute was requested to start work on the problems of cyclone resistant school building design for East Pakistan.

The agreement between UNESCO and the Government of Ceylon to establish the Institute on its territory was signed in May 1966 and the Institute's permanent home in Colombo was declared on 26 January, 1967.

The Ministers of Education of the Asian Member States of UNESCO who met in Tokyo in 1962 decided that the Karachi Plan should be extended to all levels of education. In keeping with this, the functions of the Institute now cover all levels of education and are:

(a) to promote, contract for and undertake research and comparative studies relating to the planning, designing, costing, construction, furnishing and maintenance of educational buildings at all educational levels;

(b) to promote experimentation through encouraging Member States of the Region to establish school building development groups and to provide these groups with technical guidance and information;

(c) to conduct seminars and training courses at regional and international levels, both for members of the development groups, mentioned above, and for government officials who are responsible for planning, designing, costing of school buildings or for the administration of national construction programmes in this field.

(d) to collect, classify, index and disseminate to Member States of the Region information relating to educational buildings.

(e) to serve as a briefing centre for international experts in educational buildings who are working in the region;

(f) to provide consultant services, when requested by the Secretariat of UNESCO, for the identification, preparation and approval of school building programmes involving international assistance.

Regional Office for Education in Africa, Dakar, Africa

The Regional Office for Education in Africa (BREDA) was officially inaugurated by the Director-General of UNESCO in Dakar on March 11, 1970.

The staff of the Regional Centre for Educational Planning and Administration in Africa, which was set up in Dakar in March 1964 as the educational planning section of the African Institute for Economic Development and Planning and which, since April 1965, has been administered entirely by UNESCO, formed the initial core of the new office.

The functions of the office with regard to education are as follows:

(i) to carry out regional pre-service and in-service training activities by organising courses and seminars;

(ii) to provide technical support for the regional institutes and centres set up or aided by the Organization and for the preparation of regional conferences convened by UNESCO and

(iii) to help Headquarters with the country programming of the Organization's co-operation with each of the Member States in the region.

So far as courses and seminars are concerned, it will continue the work hitherto carried out by the centre from which it is now taking over the Dakar Centre already mentioned, which was responsible for the pre-service and in-service training of African Educational planners and administrators.

Regional Centre in the Western Hemisphere, Havana, Cuba

The Regional Centre in the Western Hemisphere was created in fulfilment of a resolution adopted by the General Conference of the organisation held in Beirut. The opening ceremonies took place in Havana on February 24, 1950. The Centre was created for the purpose of co-operating in the execution of the Organisation's programmes in this part of the world. In 1966 the Regional Centre was given the additional character of the UNESCO Mission in the Republic of Cuba, charged with co-operating in the ever-growing activities of the UNESCO/UNDP, UNESCO/UNICEF projects and the regular UNESCO programme being carried out in Cuba.

The Centre is specifically in charge of :

1. Developing the activity of the national commissions in the region.
2. Collaborating in the execution of the UNESCO programme in the region, especially that part related to social sciences and cultural activities.
3. Collaborating through the services of the Pedagogical Documentation Centre attached to the Regional Centre, in educational activities and the improvement of pedagogical information in the Hemisphere. To that purpose it publishes and circulates the Quarterly "Informaciones Trimestrales", the organ of the Documentation Centre.

The Ninth Meeting of the General Conference, held in New Delhi, entrusted the Centre with co-ordinating the Major Project on the Extension and improvement of primary Education in Latin America until it was transferred to Santiago, Chile in 1961.

One of the Centre's important functions, which is stimulating the work of national commissions, is performed: (1) by means of frequent contact with them; (2) by strengthening active participation of the national commissions in carrying out the UNESCO programme; (3) by co-operating as far as possible with national commissions and the ministries of the countries so as to organise them in such a way that their functions will be properly carried out; (4) by co-operating in the organisation of regional and sub-regional conferences of national commissions as resolved by the General Conference.

The Centre keeps in contact with international organizations, both governmental and non-governmental for carrying out UNESCO programmes in the region. Also it fosters the creation in Hemisphere countries of associations affiliated with international non-governmental organisations in the educational and cultural fields.

Asian Programme of Educational Innovation for Development

The Third Regional Conference of Ministers of Education and those Responsible for Economic Planning in Asia (Singapore, May-June 1971) recommended the establishment of a regional mechanism through which national efforts in educational reform and innovation could be promoted. Accordingly, the Asian programme of Educational Innovation for Development has been initiated, following the authorization of the General Conference of UNESCO at its seventeenth session.

The Asian Programme of Educational Innovation for Development (APEID) has two institutional components: an Asian Centre of Educational Innovation for Development (ACEID), and a network of Associated Centres which are offered by some of the Member States to work cooperatively with ACEID, each Associated Centre being generally concerned with a specific programme area. It has been established in Bangkok as an integral part of the UNESCO Regional Office for Education in Asia. The Associated Centres are identified on the basis of offers received from the Member States.

The main objectives of APEID are:

(i) To promote awareness to the need for educational innovation;
(ii) to promote understanding of innovative practices, and to encourage experimentation and adoption of educational innovations;
(iii) to help strengthen national capabilities for the creation and use of educational innovations;
(iv) to identify and stimulate innovative activities and co-operative action among Member States; and
(v) to promote the transfer of experiences.

AFRICAN BUREAU OF EDUCATIONAL SCIENCES

The foundation of African Bureau of Educational Sciences (BASE) was decided during the Sixth Congress of the International Association for the Advancement of Educational Research (September 1973, Paris).

BASE aims at fulfilling the function of liaison centre of the International Association for the Advancement of Educational Research an executive organ of the African Scientific and Pedagogical Council

(CSPA); it intends to promote African interuniversity co-operation. By its action, it associates itself to the general action of international organisms such as UNESCO, IBE, CAMES, AAU, etc.

To reach its aim, BASE uses, on a smaller scale, the structures of many other establishments in charge of similar programmes.

BASE has a Scientific and Pedagogical Council (CSP). This Council determines the main orientation of BASE. It is composed of all African members of AISE, one or two members from each faculty of sciences of education, some representatives from out-of-school educational organizations, as well as some parents and teachers. The chairman can invite some other personalities with the consent of the Bureau. The Council meets every two years.

The bureau prepares and executes the decisions from CSP. Its immediate objectives are the written and oral diffusion of on-going research, the easing of contacts that could help to identify research areas, and the definition of the mechanisms of innovation and the value of the educational process.

UNITED NATIONS UNIVERSITY

The late Mr. U. Thant, former Secretary-General of the United Nations, proposed in 1969 a United Nations University (UNU) that would be "truely International and devoted to the Charter objectives of peace and progress". After world-wide consultation, a UN-appointed committee recommended that, to promote international scholarly and scientific co-operation, a new kind of university was needed. The concept was enshrined in the UNU Charter* adopted by the UN General Assembly in 1973 and the University began work in 1975.

UNU Organisation

The University operates through global network of individuals and institutions, and is organised with the following component parts: (i) The University Centre in Tokyo – main programming and coordinating body; (ii) Research and training facilities are created by the UNU itself in various parts of the world to focus on specific long-term problems not sufficiently addressed elsewhere; and (iii) Linkages with existing

* Resolution 3081 (XXVIII), December 6, 1973.

universities, national research centres, etc., located mainly in developing countries – to help carry out research and training and denote the UNU's global mandate.

These interacting elements form a flexible and organic university as a whole.

In addition to the networks of existing institutions – universities, research organizations and the like – participating in the work, the UNU also establishes its own research and training centres to deal with long-term problems that are not sufficiently being addressed elsewhere.

The first such centre is the UNU World Institute for Development Economics Research (WIDER) in Helsinki, Finland. Its principal purpose is to help identify and meet the need for policy-oriented socio-economic research on pressing global and development problems.

Another centre the UNU Institute for Natural Resources in Africa (INRA), which will be located in Yamoussoukro, Cote d'lvoire, with a mineral resources unit in Lusaka, Zambia will begin work soon. It is designed to mobilize the African scientific community in evolving better use of the continent's rich natural resource base. A third centre, the UNU Institute for New Technologies (INTECH), in Maastricht, The Netherlands, will start work on various aspects of new technologies and their economic and social implications, particularly in relation to developing countries. A fourth centre to be located in Macau, is the UNU Institute for Software Technology (UNUIST) which will undertake research, advanced training and dissemination of knowledge on the development and adaptation of advanced computer software to meet the needs and strengthen the capabilities of developing countries. An Institute of Advanced Studies is expected to be established as part of the University headquarters complex in Tokyo. A programme on biotechnology in Latin America and the Caribbean, with a programme office in Caracas, Venezuela, has also been launched.

Other UNU centres and programmes, now at different planning stages, will be in the areas of governance, environment and health, and outer space and society.

UNU Activities

In 1988-89, UNU concentrated on following eight programme areas relative to contemporary inter-locking global concern: (i) Peace, culture and governance; (ii) Global economy and development; (iii)

Global life-support systems; (iv) Alternative rural-urban configurations; (v) Science, technology and society; (vi) Food, nutrition and biotechnology; (vii) Human and social development; (viii) Global learning and informatics.

UNU in the 1990s

The University's Second Medium-Term Perspective (MTP II) defines the essential thrust of the UNU work in the 1990s. The work is motivated by the heightened awareness that human activities are now capable of altering out world in unprecedented and often frightening fashion. Human striving for social and material progress is bringing about marked changes in the systems that support life on Earth.

MTP II defines five major clusters of interrelated problems and trends:

* *Universal human value and global responsibilities* – consideration of the clashing human values in our time that can cause conflict and tension and impede the ability of societies to equitably manage and govern the affairs of their members.
* *New directions for the world economy* – fragmentation and disarray pose new sets of concerns about the world economy, including the recognition that the planet's biological and geophysical systems are important components of modern economic impulses.
* *Sustaining global life-support systems* – environmental problems have gone from largely localized disruptions of long-term, potentially catastrophic repercussions that could threaten all life on Earth.
* *Advances in science and technology* – the consequences of technological changes at the frontiers of knowledge – robotics, informatics, new materials technology – that are reweaving the fabric of the global society.
* *Population dynamics and human welfare* – coping with demographic forces that are creating huge and unmanageable cities, with particular emphasis on nutrition and health problems.

A number of specific programmes within these five major clusters have been developed for implementation during the six-year MTP II, beginning in 1990.

SECTION III

FACETS OF UNESCO'S EDUCATION PROGRAMMES
(Reports)

7

RIGHT TO EDUCATION

CONVENTION AGAINST DISCRIMINATION IN EDUCATION, 1960

The General Conference of the United Nations Educational, Scientific and Cultural Organisation, meeting in Paris from 14 November to 15 December 1960, at its eleventh session.

Recalling that the Universal Declaration of Human Rights asserts the principle of non-discrimination and proclaims that every person has the right to education,

Considering that discrimination in education is a violation of rights enunciated in that Declaration, the United Nations Educational, Scientific and Cultural Organisation has the purpose of instituting collaboration among the nations with a view to furthering for all universal respect for human rights and equality of educational opportunity,

Recognising that consequently, the United Nations Educational, Scientific and Cultural Organisation, while respecting the diversity of national educational systems, has the duty not only to prescribe any from of discrimination in education but also to promote equality of opportunity and treatment for all in education,

Having before it proposals concerning the different aspects of discrimination in education, constituting item 17.1.4 of the agenda of the session,

Having decided at its tenth session that this question should be made the subject of an international convention as well as to recommendations to Member States,

Adopts this Convention on the fourteenth day of December 1960.

Article 1

1. For the purpose of this Convention, the term "discrimination includes any distinction, exclusion, limitation or preference which, being based on race, colour, sex, language, religion, political or other opinion, national or social origin, economic condition or birth, has the purpose or effect of nullifying impairing equality of treatment in education and in particular:

(a) Of depriving any person or group of persons of access to education of any type or at any level;
(b) Of limiting any person or group of persons to education of any inferior standard;
(c) Subject to the provisions of Article 2 of this Convention, of establishing or maintaining separate educational systems or institutions for persons or groups of persons; or
(d) Of inflicting on any person or group of persons conditions which are incompatible with the dignity of man.

2. For the purposes of this Convention, the term "education" refers to all types and levels of education, and includes access to education, the standard and quality of education, and the conditions under which it is given.

Article 2

When permitted in a State, the following situations shall not be deemed to constitute discrimination, within the meaning of Article 1 of this Convention:

(a) The establishment or maintenance of separate educational systems or institutions for pupils of the two sexes, if these systems or institutions offer equivalent access to education, provide a teaching staff with qualifications of the same standard as well as school premises and equipment of the same quality, and afford the opportunity to take the same or equivalent courses of study;
(b) The establishment or maintenance for religious or linguistic reasons, of separate educational systems or institutions offering an education which is in keeping with the wishes of the pupil's parents or legal guardians, if participation in such systems or at-

tendance at such institutions is optional and if the education provided conforms to such standard as may be laid down or approved by the competent authorities, in particular for education of the same level;

(c) The establishment or maintenance of private educational institutions, if the object of the institutions is not to secure the exclusion of any group but to provide educational facilities in addition to those provided by the public authorities, if the institutions are conducted in accordance with that object, and if the education provided conforms with such standards as may be laid down or approved by the competent authorities, in particular for education of the same level.

Article 3

In order to eliminate and prevent discrimination within the meaning of this Convention, the States Parties thereto undertake:

(a) To abrogate any statutory provisions and any administrative instructions and to discontinue any administrative practices which involve discrimination in education;

(b) To ensure, by legislation where necessary, that there is no discrimination in the admission of pupils to educational institutions;

(c) Not to allow any differences of treatment by the public authorities between nationals, except on the basis of merit or need, in the matter of school fees and the grant of scholarships or other forms of assistance to pupils and permits necessary facilities for the pursuit of studies in foreign countries;

(d) Not to allow, in any form of assistance granted by the public authorities to educational institutions, any restrictions or preference based solely on the ground that pupils belong to a particular group;

(e) To give foreign national residents within their territory the same access to education as that given to their own nationals.

Article 4

The States Parties to this Convention undertake furthermore to formulate, develop and apply a national policy, which, by methods appropriate to the circumstances and to national usage, will tend to promote equality of treatment in the matter of education and in particular:

(a) To make primary education free and compulsory; make secondary education in its different forms generally available and accessible to all; make higher education equally accessible to all on the basis of individual capacity; assure compliance by all with the obligation to attend school prescribed by law;
(b) To encourage and intensify by appropriate methods the education of persons who have not completed the entire primary education course and the continuation of their education on the basis of individual capacity;
(c) To provide training for the teaching profession without discrimination.

Article 5

1. The States Parties to this convention agree that:

(a) Education shall be directed to the full development of the human personality and to the strengthening of respect for human rights and fundamental freedoms; it shall promote understanding, tolerance and friendship among all nations, racial or religious groups, and shall further the activities of the United Nations for the maintenance of peace;
(b) It is essential to respect the liberty of parents and, where applicable, of legal guardians, firstly to choose for their children institutions other than those maintained by the public authorities but conforming to such minimum educational standards as may be laid down or approved by the competent authorities and secondly, to ensure in a manner consistent with the procedures followed in the State for the application of its legislation, the religious and moral education of the children in conformity with their own convictions; and no person or group of persons should be compelled to receive religious instruction inconsistent with his or their convictions;
(c) It is essential to recognize the right of members of national minorities to carry on their own educational activities, including the maintenance of schools and, depending on the educational policy of each State, the use or the teaching of their

own language, provided however:

(i) That this right is not exercised in a manner which prevents the members of these minorities from understanding the culture and language of the community as a whole and from participating in its activities, or which prejudices national sovereignty;

(ii) That the standard of education is not lower than the general standard laid down or approved by the competent authorities; and

(iii) That attendance at such schools is optional.

2. The States Parties to this Convention undertake to take all necessary measures to ensure the application of the principles enunciated in paragraph 1 of this Article.

Article 6

In the application of this Convention, the States Parties undertake to pay the greatest attention to any recommendations hereafter adopted by the General Conference of the United Nations Education, Scientific and Cultural Organization defining the measures to be taken against different forms of discrimination in education and for the purpose of ensuring equality of opportunity and treatment in education.

Article 7

The States Parties to this Convention shall in their periodic reports submitted to the General Conference of the United Nations Educational, Scientific and Cultural Organization on dates and in a manner to be determined by it, give information on the legislative and administrative provisions which they have adopted and other action which they have taken for the application of this Convention, including that taken for the formulation and the development of the national policy defined in Article 4 as well as the results achieved and the abstracts encountered in the application of that policy.

Article 8

Any dispute which may arise between any two or more States Parties to this Convention concerning the interpretation or application of this Convention, which is not settled by negotiation shall at the request of the parties to the dispute be referred, failing other means of settling the dispute, to the International Court of Justice for decision.

Article 9

Reservations to this Convention shall not be permitted.

See also *International Conference on Education Recommendation Concerning the Improvement of the Organisation and Management of Education Systems as a Means of Raising Efficiency in order to Extend the Right to Education (Chapter Number 12).*

BIBLIOGRAPHY

UNESCO DOCUMENTS AND PUBLICATIONS*

1. *Analysis of some aspects of the action undertaken since 1975 by the section of equality of educational opportunity for girls and women to promote equality of educational opportunity for girls and women.* Paris, UNESCO, 1985, 51 p. ED-85/WS/24.
2. *The Child's right to education* ed. by Gaston Mialaret, Paris, UNESCO, 1979, 258 p.
3. *Equality of educational opportunity for girls and women*, Paris, UNESCO, 1983, 62 p. ED-83/WS/55.
4. *International symposium on the right of women to education with a view to their access to employment*, Paris, UNESCO, 14-18 September 1987. *Final report*, Paris, UNESCO, 1987, 20p. ED-87/CONF 809/*Reference document No. 1.* Paris, UNESCO, 1987, 50 p. ED-87/CONF, 809/COL.2
5. *A Long Way ... : a study of some activities implemented in the Netherlands to promote equality of opportunity for girls and women in scientific, technical and vocational education* by Ria Jaarsma, Paris, UNESCO, 1987, 95 p. ED - 87/WS/C/L.
6. *Measures to provide the access of girls and women to secondary*

* Listing to illustrate the range of UNESCO documents and publications.

technical and vocational education in New Zealand A report on policies and selected activities by Doris MacDonald. Paris, UNESCO, 1987, 47 p. + annexes ED-87/WS/C/O.

7. *The Protection of the rights of disabled persons afforded under various international instruments* by Maurice Torrelli, University of Nice, 1980. Paris, UNESCO, 1981, 21 p. 55-81/WS/43.
8. *Study on access of women to science education and training and associated careers in Malaysia.* Paris, UNESCO, 1983, 77 p. ED-83/WS/107.
9. *Women's right to education* by F. Best *Reference document No.* 2, Paris, UNESCO, 1987, 40 p. ED-87/CONF 809/COL1.

8

EDUCATION, ROLE, SERVICE CONDITIONS AND STATUS OF TEACHERS

SPECIAL INTER-GOVERNMENTAL CONFERENCE ON THE STATUS OF TEACHERS, 1966

Organisation of the Conference

The Conference convened in implementation of a decision taken by the Executive Board of UNESCO at its 772nd Session, met in Paris from 21 September to 5 October 1966. It was attended by delegates of 75 Member States and one Associated Member; by representatives of the United Nations and the International Labour Organization; and by observers from four Member States, one non-Member State, five inter-governmental organizations.

Terms of Reference

The terms of reference of the Conference were to draw up and adopt recommendation concerning the Status of a teacher.

Background of the Recommendation

The Special Inter-governmental Conference on the Status of Teachers, recalling that the right to education is a fundamental human right,

Conscious of the responsibility of the States for the provision of proper education for all in fulfilment of Article 26 of the Universal Declaration of Human Rights, of Principles 5, 7 and 10 of the Declaration of the Rights of the Child and of the United Nations Declaration concerning the Promotion among Youth of the Ideals of Peace, Mutual Respect and Understanding between peoples,

Aware of the need for more extensive and widespread general and technical and vocational education, with a view to making full use of all the talent and intelligence available as an essential contribution to continued moral and cultural progress and economic and social advancement,

Recognizing the essential role of teachers in educational advancement and the importance of their contribution to the development of man and modern society,

Concerned to ensure that teachers enjoy the status commensurate with this role,

Taking into account the great diversity of the laws, regulations and customs which, in different countries, determine the patterns and organization of education,

Taking also into account the diversity of the arrangements which in different countries apply to teaching staff, in particular according to whether the regulations concerning the public service apply to them,

Convinced that in spite of these differences similar questions arise in all countries with regard to the status of teachers and that these questions call for the application of a set of common standards and measures, which it is the purpose of this Recommendation to set out,

Noting the terms of existing international conventions which are applicable to teachers, and in particular of instruments concerned with basic human rights such as the Freedom of Association and Protection of the Right to Organize Convention, 1948, the Right to organize and Collective Bargaining Convention, 1949, the Equal Remuneration Convention, 1951, and the Discrimination (Employment and Occupation) Convention, 1958, adopted by the General Conference of the International Labour Organization and the Convention against Discrimination in Education, 1960, adopted by the General Conference of the United Nations Educational, Scientific and Cultural Organization,

Noting also the recommendations on various aspects of the preparation and the status of teachers in primary and secondary schools adopted by the International Conference on Public Education convened jointly by the United Nations Educational, Scientific and Cultural Organization and the International Bureau of Education, and the Recommendation concerning Technical and Vocational Education, 1962, adopted by the General Conference of the United Nations Educational, Scientific and Cultural Organization,

Desiring to supplement existing standards by provisions relating to problems of peculiar concern to teachers and to remedy the problems of teacher shortage has adopted this Recommendation:

Recommendations

I. Definitions

1. For the purpose of the Recommendation

(a) the word 'teacher' covers all those persons in schools who are responsible for the education of pupils;
(b) the expression 'status' as used in relation to teachers means both the standing or regard accorded them as evidenced by the level of appreciation of the importance of their function and of their competence in performing it, and the working conditions, remuneration and other material benefits accorded them relative to other professional groups.

II. Scope

2. This recommendation applies to all teachers in both public and private schools up to the completion of the secondary stage of education whether nursery, kindergarten, primary, intermediate or secondary, including those providing technical, vocational, or art education.

III. Guiding Principles

3. Education from the earliest school years should be directed to the all-round development of the human personality and to the spiritual, moral, social, cultural and economic progress of the community, as well as to the inculcation of deep respect of human rights and fundamental freedoms; within the framework of these values the utmost importance should be attached to the contribution to be made by education to peace and to understanding, tolerance and friendship among all nations and among racial or religious groups.
4. It should be recognized that advance in education depends largely on the qualifications and ability of the teaching staff in general

and on the human, pedagogical and technical qualities of the individual teachers.

5. The status of teachers should be commensurate with the needs of education as assessed in the light of educational aims and objectives; it should be recognized that the proper status of teachers and due public regard for the profession of teaching are of major importance for the full realization of these aims and objectives.
6. Teaching should be regarded as a profession: it is a form of public service which requires of teachers expert knowledge and specialized skills, acquired and maintained through rigorous and continuing study; it calls also for a sense of personal and corporate responsibility for education and welfare of the pupils in their charge.
7. All aspects of the preparation and employment of teachers should be free from any form of discrimination on grounds of race, colour, sex, religion, political opinion, national or social origin, or economic condition.
8. Working conditions for teachers should be such as will best promote effective learning and enable teachers to concentrate on their professional tasks.
9. Teacher's organizations should be recognized as a force which can contribute greatly to educational advance and which, therefore should be associated with the determination of educational policy.

IV. Educational Objectives and Policies

10. Appropriate measures should be taken in each country to the extent necessary to formulate comprehensive educational policies consistent with the guiding principles, drawing on all available resources, human and otherwise. In so doing, the competent authorities should take a account of the consequences for teachers of the following principles and objectives:

    (a) it is the fundamental right of every child to be provided with the fullest possible educational opportunities; due to attention should be paid to children requiring special educational treatment;
    (b) all facilities should be made available equally to enable every person to enjoy his right to education without discrimination

on grounds of sex, race, colour, religion, political opinion, national or social origin, or economic condition;

(c) since education is a service of fundamental importance in the general public interest, it should be recognized as a responsibility of the State, which should provide an adequate network of schools, free education in these schools and material assistance to needy pupils; this should not be constructed so as to interfere with the liberty of the parents and, when applicable, legal guardians to choose for their children schools other than those established by the State, or so to interfere with the liberty of individuals and bodies to establish and direct educational institutions which conform to such minimum educational standards as may be laid down or approved by the State;

(d) since education is an essential factor in economic growth, educational planning should form an integral part of the total economic and social planning undertaken to improve living conditions;

(e) since education is a continuous progress the various branches of the teaching service should be so co-ordinated as both to improve the quality of education for all pupils and to enhance the status of teachers;

(f) there should be free access to a flexible system of schools, properly interrelated, so that nothing restricts the opportunities for each child to progress to any level in any type of education;

(g) as an educational objective, no State should be satisfied with mere quantity, but should seek also to improve quality;

(h) in education both long-term and short-term planning and programming are necessary: the efficient integration in the community of today's pupils will depend more on future needs than on present requirements:

(i) all educational planning should include at each stage early provision for the training, and the further training of sufficient numbers of fully competent and qualified teachers of the country concerned who are familiar with the life of their people and able to teach in the mother tongue;

(j) co-ordinated systematic and continuing research and action in the field of teacher preparation and in-service training and potential, including, at the international level, co-operative projects and the exchange of research findings;

(k) there should be close co-operation between the competent authorities, organizations of teachers, of employers and workers, and of parents as well as cultural organizations and institutions of learning and research, for the purpose of defining educational policy and its precise objectives;

(l) as the achievement of the aims and objective of education largely depends on the financial means made available to it, high priority should be given, in all countries, to setting aside, within the national budgets, an adequate proportion of the national income for the development of education.

V. Preparation for the Profession

11. Policy governing entry into preparation for teaching should rest on the need to provide society with an adequate supply of teachers who possess the necessary moral, intellectual and physical qualities and who have the required professional knowledge and skills.
12. To meet this need, educational authorities should provide adequate inducements to prepare for teaching and sufficient places in appropriate institutions.
13. Completion of an approved course in an appropriate teacher/preparation institution should be required of all persons entering the profession.
14. Admission to teacher preparation should be based on the completion of appropriate secondary education, and the evidence of the possession of personal qualities likely to help the persons concerned to become worthy members of the profession.
15. While the general standards for admission to teacher preparation should be maintained, persons who may lack some of the formal academic requirements for admission, but who possess valuable experience, particularly in technical and vocational fields, may be admitted.
16. Adequate grants or financial assistance should be available to stu-

dents preparing for teaching to enable them to follow the courses provided and to live decently; as far as possible, the competent authorities should seek to establish a system of free teacher-preparation institutions.

17. Information concerning the opportunities and the grants or financial assistance for teacher preparation should be readily available to student and other persons who may wish to prepare for teaching.
18. (a) Fair consideration should be given to the value of teacher-preparation programmes completed in other countries as establishing in whole or in part the right to practise teaching.
    (b) Steps should be taken with a view to achieving international recognition of teaching credentials conferring professional status in terms of standards agreed to internationally.

Teacher-preparation Programmes

19. The purpose of a teacher preparation programme should be to develop in each student his general education and personal culture, his ability to teach and educate others, an awareness of the principles which underlie good human relations, within and across national boundaries, and a sense of responsibility to contribute both by teaching and by example to social, cultural, and economic progress.
20. Fundamentally, a teacher preparation programme should include:
    (a) general studies;
    (b) study of the main elements of philosophy, psychology, sociology as applied to education, the theory and history of education, and of comparative education, experimental pedagogy, school administration and methods of teaching the various subjects;
    (c) studies related to the student's intended field of teaching;
    (d) practice in teaching and in conducting extra-curricular activities under the guidance of fully qualified teachers.
21. (i) All teachers should be prepared in general, special and pedagogical subjects in universities, or in institutions on a level comparable to universities, or else in special institutions for the preparation of teacher.

(ii) The content of teacher-preparation programmes may reasonably vary according to the tasks the teachers are required to perform in different types of schools, such as establishments for handicapped children or technical and vocational schools. In the latter case, the programmes might include some practical experience to be acquired in industry, commerce or agriculture.

22. A teacher-preparation programme may provide for a professional course either concurrently with or subsequent to a course of personal academic or specialized education or skill cultivation.
23. Education for teaching should normally be full time; special arrangements may be made for older entrants to the profession and persons in other exceptional categories to undertake all or part of their course on a part-time basis, on condition that the content of such courses and the standards of attainment are on the same level as those of the full-time courses.
24. Consideration should be given to the desirability of providing for the education of different types of teachers, whether primary, secondary, technical, specialist or vocational teachers, in institutions organically related or geographically adjacent to one another.

Teacher-preparation Institutions

25. The staff of teacher-preparation institutions should be qualified to teach in their own discipline at a level equivalent to that of higher education. The staff teaching pedagogical subjects should have had experience of teaching in schools and wherever possible should have this experience periodically refreshed by secondment to teaching duties in schools.
26. Research and experimentation in education and in the teaching of particular subjects should be promoted through the provision of research facilities in teacher-preparation institutions and research work by their staff and students. All staff concerned with teacher education should be aware of the findings of research in the field with which they are concerned and endeavour to pass on its results to students.
27. Students as well as staff should have the opportunity of expressing their views on the arrangements governing the life, work and discipline of a teacher preparation institution.

28. Teacher-preparation institutions should form a focus of development in the education service, both keeping schools abreast of the results of research and methodological progress, and reflecting in their own work the experience of schools and teachers.
29. The teacher-preparation institutions should, either severally or jointly, and in collaboration with another institution of higher education or with the competent education authorities, or not, be responsible for certifying that the student has satisfactorily completed the course.
30. School authorities, in cooperation with teacher-preparation institutions, should take appropriate measures to provide the newly trained teachers with an employment in keeping with their preparation, and individual wishes and circumstance.

VI. Further Education for Teachers

31. Authorities and teachers should recognize the importance of in-service education designed to secure a systematic improvement of the quality and content of education and of teaching techniques.
32. Authorities, in consultation with teachers' organizations, should promote the establishment of a wide system of in-service education, available free to all teachers. Such a system should provide a variety of arrangements and should involve the participation of teacher-preparation institutions, scientific and cultural institutions, and teachers' organizations. Refresher courses should be provided, especially for teachers returning to teaching after a break in service.
33. (i) Courses and other appropriate facilities should be so designed as to enable teachers to improve their qualifications, to alter or enlarge the scope of their work or seek promotion and to keep up to date with their subject and field of education as regards both content and method.
    (ii) Measures should be taken to make books and other material available to teachers to improve their general education and professional qualifications.
34. Teachers should be given both the opportunities and the incentives to participate in courses and facilities and should take full advantage of them.
35. School authorities should make every endeavour to ensure that schools can apply relevant research findings both in the subjects

of study and in teaching methods.

36. Authorities should encourage and, as far as possible, assist teachers to travel in their own country and abroad, either in groups or individually, with a view to their further education.
37. It would be desirable that measures taken for the preparation and further education of teachers should be developed and supplemented by financial and technical cooperation on an international or regional basis.

VII. Employment and Career

Entry into the teaching profession

38. In collaboration with teachers' organizations, policy governing recruitment into employment should be clearly defined at the appropriate level and rules should be established laying down the teachers' obligations and rights.
39. A probationary period on entry to teaching should be recognized both by teachers and by employers as the opportunity for the encouragement and helpful initiation of the entrant and for the establishment and maintenance of proper professional standards as well as the teacher's own development of his practical teaching proficiency. The normal duration of probation should be known in advance and the conditions for its satisfactory completion should be strictly related to professional competence. If the teacher is failing to complete his probation satisfactorily, he should be informed of the reasons and should have the right to make representations.

Advancement and Promotion

40. Teachers should be able, subject to their having the necessary qualifications, to move from one type or level of school to another within the education service.
41. The organization and structure of an education service, including that of individual schools, should provide adequate opportunities for and recognition of additional responsibilities to be exercised by individual teachers, on condition and those responsibilities are not deterimental to the quality or regularity of their teaching work.

42. Consideration should be given to the advantages of schools sufficiently large for pupils to have the benefits and staff the opportunities to be derived from a range of responsibilities being carried by different teachers.
43. Posts of responsibility in education, such as that of inspector, educational administrator, director of education or other posts of special responsibility, should be given as far as possible to experienced teachers.
44. Promotion should be based on an objective assessment of the teacher's qualifications for the new post, by reference to strictly professional criteria laid down in consultation with teacher's organizations.

Security of Tenure

45. Stability of employment and security of tenure in the profession are essential in the interests of education as well as in that of the teacher and should be safeguarded even when changes in the organization of or within a school system are made.
46. Teachers should be adequately protected against arbitrary action affecting their professional standing or career.

Disciplinary Procedures Related to Breaches of Professional Conduct

47. Disciplinary measures applicable to teachers guilty of breaches of professional conduct should be clearly defined. The proceedings and any resulting action should only be made public if the teacher so requests, except where prohibition from teaching is involved or the protection or well-being of the pupils so requires.
48. The authorities or bodies competent to propose or apply sanctions and penalties should be clearly designated.
49. Teachers' organizations should be consulted when the machinery to deal with disciplinary matters is established.
50. Every teacher should enjoy equitable safeguards at each stage of any disciplinary procedure, and in particular:

    (a) the right to be informed in writing of the allegations and the grounds for them;
    (b) the right to full access to the evidence in the case;

(c) the right to defend himself and to be defended by a representative of his choice, adequate time being given to the teacher for the preparation of his defence;
(d) the right to be informed in writing of the decisions reached and the reasons for them;
(e) the right to appeal to clearly designated competent authorities or bodies.

51. Authorities should recognize that effectiveness of disciplinary safeguards as well as discipline itself would be greatly enhanced if the teachers were judged with the participation of their peers.
52. The provisions of the foregoing paragraphs 47-51 do not in any way affect the procedures normally applicable under national laws or regulations to acts punishable under criminal laws.

Medical Examinations

53. Teachers should be required to undergo periodical medical examinations, which should be provided free.

Women Teachers with Family Responsibilities

54. Marriage should not be considered a bar to the appointment or to the continued employment of women teachers, nor should it affect remuneration or other conditions of work.
55. Employers should be prohibited from terminating contracts of service for reasons of pregnancy and maternity leave.
56. Arrangements such as creches or nurseries should be considered where desirable to take care of the children of teachers with family responsibilities.
57. Measures should be taken to permit women teachers with family responsibilities to obtain teaching posts in the locality of their homes and to enable married couples, both of whom are teachers, to teach in the same general neighbourhood or in one and the same school.
58. In appropriate circumstances women teachers with family responsibilities who have left the profession before retirement age should be encouraged to return to teaching.

Part-time Service

59. Authorities and schools should recognize the value of part-time service given, in case of need, by qualified teachers who for some reason cannot give full-time service.
60. Teachers employed regularly on a part-time basis should:

    (a) receive proportionately the same remuneration and enjoy the same basic conditions of employment as teachers employed on a fulltime basis;
    (b) be granted rights corresponding to those of teachers employed on a full-time basis as regards holidays with pay, sick leave and maternity leave, subject to the same eligibility requirements; and
    (c) be entitled to adequate and appropriate social security, protection, including coverage under employers' pension schemes.

VIII. The Rights and Responsibilities of Teachers Professional Freedom

61. The teaching profession should enjoy academic freedom in the discharge of professional duties. Since teachers are particularly qualified to judge the teaching aids and methods most suitable for their pupils, they should be given the essential role in the choice and the adaptation of teaching material, the selection of textbooks and the application of teaching methods, within the framework of approved programmes, and with the assistance of the educational authorities.
62. Teachers and their organizations should participate in the development of new courses, textbooks and teaching aids.
63. Any systems of inspection or supervision should be designed to encourage and help teachers in the performance of their professional tasks and should be such as not to diminish the freedom, initiative and responsibility of teachers.
64. (i) Where any kind of direct assessment of the teacher's work is required, such assessment should be objective and should be made known to the teacher.
    (ii) Teachers should have a right to appeal against assessments which they deem to be unjustified.
65. Teachers should be free to make use of such evaluation tech-

niques as they may deem useful for the appraisal of pupils' progress, but should ensure that no unfairness to individual pupil results.

66. The authorities should give due weight to the recommendations of teachers regarding the suitability of individual pupil for courses and further education of different kinds.
67. Every possible effort should be made to promote close cooperation between teachers and parents in the interests of pupils, but teachers should be protected against unfair or unwarranted interference by parents in matters which are essentially the teacher's professional responsibility.
68. (a) Parents having a complaint against a school or teacher should be given the opportunity of discussing it in the first instance with the school principal and the teacher concerned. Any complaint subsequently addressed to higher authorities should be put in writing and a copy should be supplied to the teacher.
    (b) Investigations of complaints should be so conducted that the teachers are given a fair opportunity to defend themselves and that no publicity is given to the proceedings.
69. While teachers should exercise the utmost care to avoid accidents to pupils, employers of teachers should safeguard them against the risk of having damages assessed against them in the event of injury to pupils occurring at school or in school activities away from the school premises or groups.

Responsibilities of Teachers

70. Recognizing that the status of their profession depends to considerable extent upon teachers themselves, all teachers should seek to achieve the highest possible standards in all their professional work.
71. Professional standards relating to teacher performance should be defined and maintained with the participation of the teachers' organizations.
72. Teachers and teacher's organizations should seek to co-operate fully with authorities in the interests of pupils of the education service and of society generally.
73. Codes or ethics or of conduct should be established by the teachers' organizations, since such codes greatly contribute to ensuring the prestige of the profession and the exercise of profes-

sional duties in accordance with agreed principles.

74. Teachers should be prepared to take their part in extra-curricular activities for the benefit of pupils and adults.

Relations between Teachers and the Education Service as a Whole

75. In order that teachers may discharge their responsibilities authorities should establish and regularly use recognized means of consultation with teachers' organizations on such matters as educational policy, school organizations and new developments in the education service.
76. Authorities and teachers should recognize the importance of the participation of teachers, through their organizations and in other ways, in steps designed to improve the quality of the education service, in educational research, and in the development and dissemination of new improved methods.
77. Authorities should facilitate the establishment and the work of panels designed, within a school or within a broader framework, to promote the co-operation of teachers of the same subject and should take due account of the opinion and suggestions of such panels.

Right of Teachers

78. The participation of teachers in social and public life should be encouraged in the interests of the teacher's personal development, of the education service and of society as a whole.
79. Teachers should be free to exercise all civic rights generally enjoyed by citizens and should be eligible for public office.
80. Where the requirements of public office are such that the teacher has to relinquish his teaching duties, he should be retained in the profession for seniority and pension purposes and should be able to return to his previous post or to an equivalent post after his term of public office has expired.
81. Both salaries and working conditions for teachers should be determined through the process of negotiation between teachers' organizations and the employers of teachers.
82. Statutory or voluntary machinery should be established whereby the right of teachers to negotiate through their organizations with their employers, either public or private, is assured.

83. Appropriate joint machinery should be set up to deal with the settlement of disputes between the teachers and their employers arising out to terms and conditions of employment. If the means and procedures established for these purposes should be exhausted or if there should be a breakdown in negotiations between the parties, teachers' organizations should have the right to take such other steps as are normally open to other organizations in the defence of their legitimate interests.

IX. Conditions for effective teaching and learning

84. Since the teacher is a valuable specialist, his work should be so organized and assisted as to avoid waste of his time and energy.

Class Size

85. Class size should be such to permit the teacher to give the pupils individual attention. From time to time provision may be made for small group or even individual instruction for such purposes as remedial work, and on occasion for large groups instruction employing audio-visual aids.

Ancillary Staff

86. With a view to enabling teachers to concentrate on their professional tasks, schools should be provided with ancillary staff to perform non-teaching duties.

Teaching Aids

87. (i) Authorities should provide teachers and pupils with modern aids to teaching. Such aids should not be regarded as substitute for the teacher but as a means of improving the quality of teaching and extending to a larger number of pupils the benefits of education.

(ii) Authorities should promote research into the use of such aids and encourage teachers to participate actively in such research.

Hours of Work

88. The hours teachers are required to work per day and per week should be established in consultation with teachers' organizations.
89. In fixing hours of teaching account should be taken of all factors which are relevant to the teacher's work load, such as:

    (a) the number of pupils with whom the teacher is required to work per day and per week;
    (b) the necessity to provide time for adequate planning and preparation of lessons and for evaluation of work;
    (c) the number of different lessons assigned to be taught each day;
    (d) the demands upon the time of the teacher imposed by participation in research, in co-curricular and extra-curricular activities, in supervisory duties and in counselling of pupils;
    (e) the desirability of providing time in which teachers may report to and consult with parents regarding pupil progress.

90. Teachers should be provided time necessary for taking part in in-service training programmes.
91. Participation of teachers in extra-curricular activities should not constitute an excessive burden and should not interfere with the fulfilment of the main duties of the teacher.
92. Teachers assigned special educational responsibilities in addition to classroom instruction should have their normal hours of teaching reduced correspondingly.

Annual Holidays with Pay

93. All teachers should enjoy a right to adequate annual vacation with full pay.

Study Leave

94. (a) Teachers should be granted study leave on full or partial pay at intervals.
    (b) The period of study leave should be counted for seniority and pension purposes.
    (c) Teachers in areas which are remote from population centres

and are recognized as such by the public authorities should be given study leave more frequently.

Special Leave

95. Leave of absence granted within the framework of bilateral and multilateral cultural exchanges should be considered as service.
96. Teachers attached to technical assistance projects should be granted leave of absence and their seniority, eligibility for promotion should be safeguarded. In addition special arrangements should be made to cover their extraordinary expenses.
97. Foreign guest teachers should similarly be given leave of absence by their home countries and have their seniority and pension safeguarded.
98. (a) Teachers should be granted occasional leave of absence with full pay to enable them to participate in the activities of their organizations.
    (b) Teachers should have the right to take up office in their organizations; in such case their entitlements should be similar to those of teachers holding public office.
99. Teachers should be granted leave of absence with full pay for adequate personal reasons under arrangements specified in advance of employment.

Sick Leave and Maternity Leave

100. (a) Teachers should be entitled to sick leave with pay.
     (b) In determining the period during which full or partial pay shall be payable, account should be taken of cases in which it is necessary for teachers to be isolated from pupils for long periods.

101. Effect should be given to the standards laid down by the International Labour Organisation, in the field of maternity protection, and in particular the Maternity Protection Convention, 1919, and the Maternity Protection Convention (Revised), 1952, as well as to the standards referred to in paragraph 126 of this Recommendation.
102. Women teachers with children should be encouraged to remain in the service by such measures as enabling them, at their request, to

take additional unpaid leave of up to one year after childbirth without loss of employment, all rights resulting from employment being fully safeguarded.

Teacher Exchange

103. Authorities should recognize the value both to the education service and to teachers themselves of professional and cultural exchanges between countries and of travel abroad on the part of teachers; they should seek to extend such opportunities and take account of the experience acquired abroad by individual teachers.
104. Recruitment for such exchanges should be arranged without any discrimination, and the persons concerned should not be considered as representing any particular political view.
105. Teachers who travel in order to study and work abroad should be given adequate facilities to do so and proper safeguards of their posts and status.
106. Teachers should be encouraged to share teaching experience gained abroad with other members of the profession.

School Buildings

107. School buildings should be safe and attractive in overall design and functional in layout; they should lend themselves to effective teaching, and to use for extra-curricular activities and especially in rural areas, as a community centre; they should be constructed in accordance with established sanitary standards and with a view to durability, adaptability and easy, economic maintenance.
108. Authorities should ensure that school premises are properly maintained, so as not to threaten in any way the health and safety of pupils and teachers.
109. In the planning of new schools representative teacher opinion should be consulted. In providing new or additional accommodation for an existing school the staff of the school concerned should be consulted.

Special Provisions for Teachers in Rural or Remote Areas

110. (a) Decent housing, preferably free or at a subsidized rental, should be provided for teachers and their families in areas

remote from population centres and recognized as such by the public authorities.

(b) In countries where teachers, in addition to their normal teaching duties, are expected to promote and stimulate community activities, development plans and programmes should include provision for appropriate accommodation for teachers.

111. (a) On appointment or transfer to schools in remote areas, teachers should be paid removal and travel expenses for themselves and their families.

(b) Teachers in such areas should, where necessary, be given special travel facilities to enable them to maintain their professional standards.

(c) Teachers transferred to remote areas should, as an inducement, be reimbursed their travel expenses from their place of work to their home town once a year when they go on leave.

112. Whenever teachers are exposed to particular hardships, they should be compensated by the payment of special hardship allowances which should be included in earnings taken into account for pension purposes.

X. Teachers' Salaries

113. Amongst the various factors which affect the status of teachers, particular importance should be attached to salary, seeing that in present world conditions other factors, such as the standing or regard accorded them and the level of appreciation of the importance of their function, are largely dependent, as in other comparable professions, on the economic position in which they are placed.

114. Teacher's salaries should:

(a) reflect the importance to society of the teaching function and hence the importance of teachers as well as the responsibilities of all kinds which fall upon them from the time of their entry into the service;

(b) compare favourably with salaries paid in other occupations requiring similar or equivalent qualifications;

(c) provide teachers with the means to ensure a reasonable standard of living for themselves and their families as well as to invest in further education or in the pursuit of cultural activities, thus enhancing their professional qualifications;

(d) take account of the fact that certain posts require higher qualifications and experience and carry greater responsibilities.

115. Teachers should be paid on the basis of salary scales established in agreement with the teachers' organizations. In no circumstances should qualified teachers during a probationary period or if employed on a temporary basis be paid on a lower salary scale than that laid down for established teachers.

116. The salary structure should be planned so as not to give rise to injustices or anomalies tending to lead to friction between different groups of teachers.

117. Where a maximum number of class contact hours is laid down, a teacher whose regular schedule exceeds the normal maximum should receive additional remuneration on an approved scale.

118. Salary differentials should be based on objective criteria such as levels of qualification, years of experience or degrees or responsibility but the relationship between the lowest and the highest salary should be of a reasonable order.

119. In establishing the placement on a basic salary scale of a teacher of vocational or technical subjects who may have no academic degree, allowance should be made for the value of his practical training and experience.

120. Teachers' salaries should be calculated on an annual basis.

121. (a) Advancement within the grade through salary increments granted at regular, preferably annual, intervals should be provided.

(b) The progression from the minimum to the maximum of the basic salary scale should not extend over a period longer than ten to fifteen years.

(c) Teachers should be granted salary increments for service performed during periods of probationary or temporary appointment.

122. (a) Salary scales for teachers should be revised periodically to take into account such factors as a rise in the cost of living, increased productivity leading to higher standards of living in the country or a general upward movement in wage or salary levels.

(b) Where a system of salary adjustments automatically following a cost-of-living index has been adopted, the choice of index should be determined with the participation of the teachers' organizations and any cost-of-living allowance granted should be regarded as an integral part of earnings taken into account for pension purposes.

123. No merit rating system for purposes of salary determination should be introduced or applied without prior consultation with and acceptance by the teachers' organizations concerned.

XI. Social Security

124. All teachers, regardless of the type of school in which they serve, should enjoy the same or similar social security protection. Protection should be extended to periods of probation and of training for those who are regularly employed as teachers.

125. (a) Teachers should be protected by social security measures in respect of all the contingencies included in the International Labour Organization Social Security (Minimum Standards) Convention, 1952, namely by medical care, sickness benefit, unemployment benefit, old-age benefit, employment injury benefit, family benefit, maternity benefit, invalidity benefit and survivors' benefit.

(b) The standards of social security provided for teachers should be at least as favourable as those set out in the relevant instruments of the International Labour Organization and in particular the Social Security (Minimum Standards) Convention, 1952.

(c) Social security benefits for teachers should be granted as a matter of right.

126. The social security protection of teachers should take account of their particular conditions of employment, as indicated in paragraphs 128-140.

Medical Care

127. In regions where there is scarcity of medical facilities teachers should be paid travelling expenses necessary to obtain appropriate medical care.

Sickness Benefit

128. (a) Sickness benefit should be granted throughout any period of

incapacity for work involving suspension of earnings.

(b) It should be paid from the first day in each case of suspension of earnings.

(c) Where the duration of sickness benefit is limited to a specified period, provisions should be made for extensions in cases in which it is necessary for teachers to be isolated from pupils.

Employment Injury Benefit

129. Teachers should be protected against the consequences of injuries suffered not only during teaching at school but also when engaged in school activities away from the school premises or grounds.

130. Certain infectious diseases prevalent among children should be regarded as occupational diseases when contracted by teachers who have been exposed to them by virtue of their contact with pupils.

Old-age Benefit

131. Pension credits earned by a teacher under any education authority within a country should be portable on the teacher's transfer to employment under any other authority within that country.

132. Taking account of national regulations, teachers who, in case of a duly recognized teacher shortage, continue in service after qualifying for a pension should either receive credit in the calculation of the pension for the additional years of service or be able to gain a supplementary pension through an appropriate agency.

133. Old-age benefit should be so related to final earnings that the teacher may continue to maintain an adequate living standard.

Invalidity Benefit

134. Invalidity benefit should be payable to teachers who are forced to discontinue teaching because of physical or mental disability. Provision should be made for the granting of pensions where the contingency is not covered by extended sickness benefit or other means.

135. Where disability is only partial in that the teacher is able to teach

part time, partial invalidity benefit should be payable.

136. (a) Invalidity benefit should be so related to final earnings that the teacher may continue to maintain an adequate living standard.

(b) Provision should be made for medical care and allied benefits with a view to restoring or, where this is not possible, improving the health of disabled teachers, as well as for rehabilitation services designed to prepare disabled teachers, wherever possible, for the resumption of their previous activity.

Survivour' Benefit

137. The conditions of eligibility for survivors' benefit and the amount of such benefit should be such as to enable survivors to maintain an adequate standard of living and as to secure the welfare and education of surviving dependent children.

Means of Providing Social Security for Teachers

138. (a) The social security protection of teachers should be assured as far as possible through a general scheme applicable to employed persons in the public sector or in the private sector as appropriate.

(b) Where no general scheme is in existence for one or more of the contingencies to be covered, special schemes, statutory or non-statutory, should be established.

(c) Where the level of benefits under a general scheme is below that provided for in this Recommendation, it should be brought up to the recommended standard by means of supplementary schemes.

139. Consideration should be given to the possibility of associating representatives of teachers' organizations with the administration of special and supplementary schemes, including the investment of their funds.

XII. The Teacher Shortage

140. (a) It should be a guiding principle that any severe supply problem should be dealt with by measures which are recognized as exceptional, which do not detract from or endanger in

any way professional standards already established or to be established and which minimize educational loss to pupils.

(b) Recognizing that certain expedients designed to deal with the shortage of teachers, such as over-large classes and the unreasonable extension of hours of teaching duty are incompatible with the aims and objectives of education and are detrimental to the pupils, the competent authorities as a matter of urgency should take steps to render these expedients unnecessary and to discontinue them.

141. In developing countries, where supply considerations may necessitate short-term intensive emergency preparation programmes for teachers, a fully professional, extensive programme should be available in order to produce corps of professionally prepared teachers competent to guide and direct the educational enterprise.

142. (a) Students admitted to training in short-term, emergency programmes should be selected in terms of the standards applying to admission to the normal professional programme, or even higher ones, to ensure that they will be capable of subsequently completing the requirements of the full programme.

(b) Arrangements and special facilities, including extra study leave on full pay, should enable such students to complete their qualifications in service.

143. (a) As far as possible, unqualified personnel should be required to work under the close supervision and direction of professionally qualified teachers.

(b) As a condition of continued employment such persons should be required to obtain or complete their qualifications.

144. Authorities should recognize that improvements in the social and economic status of teachers, their living and working conditions, their terms of employment and their career prospects and the best means of overcoming any existing shortage of competent and experienced teachers, and of attracting to and retaining in the teaching profession substantial numbers of fully qualified persons.

XIII. Final Provision

145. Where teachers enjoy a status which is, in certain respects, more favourable than that provided for in this Recommendation, its terms should not be invoked to diminish the status already granted.

Dissemination of the Principles of the Recommendation

As soon as the final text of the recommendation was adopted, the two sponsoring agencies made a systematic effort to publicize its content. Copies of the recommendation in four working languages have been put at the disposal of governments and their appropriate public services, National Commissions, UNESCO and ILO experts in the field, numerous teacher training institutions and teachers' organizations. In addition to this free distribution, organizations wishing to distribute large quantities of the recommendation have been offered the possibility of obtaining copies at a nominal price. The total number of UNESCO printed copies distributed up to October 1968 exceeded 12,000. Several teachers' organizations reprinted the recommendation in their national periodicals, some of which have impressive circulation figures: for example, "The Teacher" (U.K.), over 200,000, and "L'enseignement" (Canada), 80,000. Two years after its adoption in four languages, the recommendation was translated into seventeen other languages : Arabic, Chinese, Czech, Danish, Finnish, Flemish, German, Hebrew, Hungarian, Indonesian, Japanese, Korean, Portuguese, Serbo-Croatian, Swedish, Thai, Urdu. It appears that more than one translation was made into German, Flemish and Italian. In one country, the Ministry of Education addressed the full text of the recommendation to all local educational authorities.

In October 1967, a pamphlet entitled *Status of Teachers* was published jointly by ILO and UNESCO. The publication describes the origin and the significance of the recommendation, and in addition to the text of the instrument, gives pertinent quotations from other international declarations and instruments applying to teachers and referred to in the recommendation [the Declaration of the Rights of the Child, Freedom of Association and Protection of the Right to Organize Conventions (ILO), Convention against Discrimination in Education (UNESCO), etc.]. The pamphlet also reprints the report of the Special Intergovernmental Conference and a list of relevant recommendations adopted by the International Conference on Public Education (UNESCO/IBE).

In order to explain to the general public the main issues underlying the objectives and main provisions of the recommendation, Professor Jean Thomas (France), President of the Special Intergovernmental Conference on the Status of Teachers, wrote a booklet at the request of UNESCO entitled *Teachers for the Schools of Tomorrow*, available in

French, English and Spanish.

There is no doubt that the wide dissemination of the principles of the recommendation is the first step towards achieving its objectives. At their meeting held in April 1968 at UNESCO House, international teachers' organizations rightly emphasized this point of view and expressed their determination to continue the work of dissemination, in co-operation with other groups of organised public opinion, especially at provincial and local levels, so as to make the recommendation known and understood not only by individual practising and student teachers and all parents, but generally by all those concerned with progress and the quality of education.

Studies and Enquiries

Although the principal provisions of the recommendation are based on trends observable in all regions of the world, the extent to which these trends are manifest in individual countries varies considerably according to socio-economic and cultural differences, and according to the patterns and organizations of educational systems. For this reason, the Secretariat of UNESCO has initiated international surveys and comparative studies on the manner in which the common standards set out in the recommendation are understood and applied in a selected number of countries. It is hoped that the results of these studies, when published, will provide stimulation and guidance for improving the status of teachers, and promote progressive educational policies in other countries. In 1968, an enquiry on the participation of teachers in the elaboration of educational policy and in the improvement of education, was carried out in co-operation with four international teachers' organizations (World Confederation of Organizations of the Teaching Profession. World Federation of Teachers' Unions, International Federation of Free Teachers' Unions, World Union of Catholic Teachers). The enquiry covered 33 countries : Austria, Belgium, Canada, Ceylon, Chile, Republic of the Congo, Democratic Republic of the Congo, Cuba, Denmark, France, Federal Republic of Germany, Ghana, Hungary, India, Israel, Italy, Japan, Republic of Korea, Netherlands, New Zealand, Nicaragua, Peru, Philippines, Sudan, Sweden, Tanzania, Thailand, Trinidad and Tobago, Tunisia, USA, USSR, Uruguay, Yugoslavia.

In 1967-68, each of the international teachers' organizations selected one or more major chapters of the recommendation as a subject of study for their international or regional conferences. The discussions were based on reports of national associations on problems relating to the implementation of the recommendation. Thus the World Confederation of Organizations of the Teaching Profession chose as the theme of its conference in Vancouver (Canada) 1967, "Professional responsibility of teachers", and discussed the content and implications of the recommendation at regional seminars in Latin America (Bogota, 1966), Africa (Tunis, 1967) and Asia (Tokyo, 1967). "Conditions for effective teaching and learning" was the theme discussed by the International Federation of Teachers' Associations and the Federation of Secondary Teachers' Associations in Copenhagen in 1967. The conference of the Confederation de Educadores Americanos in Mexico, 1967, was devoted to the theme "Improvement of the status of teachers in Latin America", while the World Federation of Teachers' Union examined "The scope and limits of the recommendation concerning the status of teachers" in Leipzig in the same year. The World Union of Catholic Teachers analysed the "Main features of the recommendation" in Berlin, 1967, and the theme selected by the International Federation of Teachers' Associations for its conference in Dublin in 1968 was "Teachers Rights". Lastly, the International Federation of Free Teachers' Union has undertaken a systematic analysis of international conventions and recommendations adopted by ILO and applicable to teachers.

The provisions of the recommendation concerning the pre-service preparation of teachers served as a frame of reference for a committee of experts convened by UNESCO in December 1967 to review trends and problems in teacher education. The committee, whose composition reflected the diversity of educational systems and the main geographical and cultural regions of the world, examined the present needs and changes in the organization and content of teacher education in both developed and developing countries. Its conclusions, while in harmony with the general principles of the recommendation, offer more explicit guidance for future planning and action in the field of teacher preparation and, in addition, include an inventory of urgent problems which deserve further study.

The development of systematic measures for further education of teachers in service is a task upon which the recommendation places strong emphasis. The recent meeting of international teachers' organizations convened by UNESCO revealed that most national professional associations consider the strengthening of measures in this field, with the active participation of the organized teaching profession, as a top priority activity for the improvement of the status of teachers. Assistance to national and regional schemes of further education of teachers has been a standing feature of UNESCO's educational programmes for many years.

Novelty of Recommondation

The novelty of the recommendation elaborated jointly by UNESCO and the International Labour Organization, in co-operation with teaching organizations is three-fold. First, it is based on all the previous work in this field, enriched and updated by regional international surveys and meetings for experts devoted to these issues, organized under the auspices of ILO and UNESCO during the period 1958-1966. It is therefore more comprehensive and more systematic than any previous "charter". Secondly, the provisions of the recommendation aimed at the improvement of the academic, professional, economic and social status of teachers are conceived in terms of an overall educational planning and policy and organically related to the quantitative and qualitative progress of education. Thirdly — and most important — the recommendation was adopted by governments, which means on the one hand that, in its final version, due account was taken of the diversity of educational systems and socio-economic conditions in different parts of the world, and on the other, that the governments of Member-States of UNESCO and ILO are morally bound by this instrument and, by virtue of the constitutional provisions of the two organizations, responsible for its implementation.

Instrument of Educational Progress

There is evidence that the impact of the recommendation is being felt in educational circles in many parts of the world. Whenever national teachers' organizations discuss their professional problems with educational authorities, they are now in a position to refer to the provisions of an official international instrument which clearly defines their rights. These provisions affirm not only the rights of teachers to negotiate with their employers the employment and working conditions commensurate with the importance of the teacher's social function, but also the right to be associated in the determination of educational policy. This right implies new responsibilities for teachers, in addition to their current classroom duties. They are expected, through their organizations or by other means, to collaborate with educational authorities in such matters as the preparation of educational reforms, the revision of curricula and the development of new educational methods. There are signs all over the world that teachers are increasingly aware of these responsibilities which require a serious effort on their part to keep abreast of new educational developments. Through its programme of international studies on the new responsibilities of teachers, its regular consultations and active co-operation with teachers' organizations, UNESCO intends to stimulate this process aimed at developing a fruitful partnership between teachers and educational authorities for the improvement of education.

INTERNATIONAL CONFERENCE OF EDUCATION RECOMMENDATION CONCERNING CHANGING ROLE OF THE TEACHERS AND ITS INFLUENCE ON PREFPARATION FOR THE ROFESSION AND ON IN-SERVICE TRAINING, 1975

Preamble

The conference convened by the UNESCO meeting in Geneva, at its thirty-fifth session, held from the twenty-seventh of August to the fourth of September, nineteen hundred and seventy-five.

Having regard to the relevant conventions, recommendations and declarations adopted at the international level, which are applicable to educational personnel, and more particularly to the Recommendation concerning the Status of Teachers, adopted by the special Intergovernmental Conference (1966) and the Revised Recommendation concerning Technical and Vocational Education, adopted by the General Conference of UNESCO at its eighteenth session (1974).

Considering the rapid changes brought about by economic, scientific, technological, social and cultural progress in the modern societies as well as national aspirations,

Recognizing that changes in the teacher's role resulting from changes in society and in education have an effect on initial and on in-service education of various categories of teachers, and other personnel in education, as well as on their status and conditions of work,

The International Conference of Education. *adopts* on the 3rd September, 1975, and submits for consideration by the Ministers responsible for education and the competent authorities and agencies in the various States and appropriate international bodies, the following recommendations.

A. Underlying Principles of Recommendation

1. Coherent policy and action in the field of teacher education and in the field of their employment and conditions of work should be based on the following principles:

   (a) Whatever are or will be the changes in the education system, the teacher-learner relationship will remain at the centre of the educational process and therefore better preparation of educational personnel constitutes one of the essential factors of educational development and an important condition for any renovation in education.
   (b) To improve the contribution that education makes to international, national, social, economic and cultural development, fresh efforts in teacher education are required but these presuppose that education authorities in Member-States take account of the directions of change in the role of the teacher and the factors involved.
   (c) All appropriate forces of the society should be involved in the definition of the aims and objectives of education and consequently of teacher education. In this definition of purposes and objectives, teachers should take a responsible part, together with their professional associations or groups.
   (d) All aspects of teacher education, including access thereto, should be free from any form of discrimination on grounds of race, colour, sex, religion, political origin, economic condition etc.
   (e) Specialists from other professions and other people from the community should be appropriately involved in the process of education.

B. The Role of the Teacher

2. Teachers and administrators of all categories and levels should be aware of the roles played by them in the present state and

development of education. They should understand that their roles and functions are not fixed unchangeable categories, but are evolving under the influence of changes taking place in society and in the education system itself.

3. Despite the diversity of education systems and of arrangements for teacher education throughout the world there is a general need for fresh national scrutiny, in a realistic manner, of the teachers' specific tasks and functions in terms of national policies and legislation. Such national analyses, with the participation of teachers themselves, should lead to the establishment of professional profiles for all categories of teachers and other educational personnel with clear definitions of the roles and functions assigned to them by the society.
4. Measures should be taken to ensure that conditions exist for serving teachers and future teachers to be aware of the changes in the teachers' roles and to be prepared for new roles and functions:

   (a) The teacher is engaged more and more today in the implementation of new educational procedures, taking advantage of all the resources of modern educational devices and methods. He is an educator and a counsellor who tries to develop his pupils' abilities and interests and not merely to serve as a source of information and a transmitter of knowledge; the teacher plays a principal role in providing his pupils with a scientific world outlook.

   (b) Since the role of the school is no longer limited to instruction, the teacher, apart from his instructional duties, has now to assume more responsibility, in collaboration with other educational agents in the community for the preparation of the young for community life, family life, productive activity, etc. The teacher should have more opportunity for involvement in extra-curricular activities and out-of-school also in guiding and counselling the pupils and their parents, and in organizing his pupils' leisure time activities.

   (c) Teachers should be aware of the important role they are called upon to play in the local community as professional and citizens, as agents of development and change and be given the possibility of practising that role.

   (d) It should be recognized that the effectiveness of school education depends largely upon the development of new relationships between the teacher and his pupils, who become more active partners in the education process; between the teacher and his colleagues and other agents who may be called upon to co-operate with him; between the teacher and his pupils' parents and others in the community concerned with the process of education.

C. Other Professionals and Specialists in Education

5. With the development and the continued diversification and enlargement of the function and programmes of educational establishments at various levels, the need may arise to use other professionals and specialists in the education system on a full-time or part-time basis to participate with the teachers in the realisation of the education programme. This practice should be encouraged, taking into account the experience of the Member-States, and be recommended for wider implementation wherever it has produced positive results, provided that educational responsibility remains in the hands of qualified teachers.
6. In each case it is important to analyse the national situation in order to identify the categories of personnel desirable in the educational process apart from regular teachers and at the same time to identify and eliminate administrative or institutional obstacles which may retard or make it difficult for such personnel to participate widely in the education process.
7. The same analyses should be applied to other personnel appointed to assist teachers and school administrators in non-teaching duties, both in the administrative and in the technical sectors, in order to improve the efficiency of the school and of the teacher.
8. Other professionals and specialists engaged on a full-time basis should receive pedagogical training either prior to or during their work at the educational institution.

D. Influence of the Changing Role of Preparation for the Professional and on In-service Education

General Considerations

9. If education is to meet the demands of our time and of the coming decades, the organization, content and methods of teacher educa-

tion must be constantly improved. In particular situations, a search for new educational strategies and concepts should be undertaken, taking into account of the special social and cultural conditions under which the school and the teachers must perform their basic functions.

10. In view of the continuous renovation and development of general and pedagogical knowledge, and of the constant change taking place in education system and the increasingly creative character of pedagogical activities, it does not seem possible to equip the student teacher with knowledge and skills which would be sufficient for his whole professional life. Therefore, the initial preparation for the profession, pre-service education and training, should be considered as a first fundamental stage in the process of the continuous education of teachers.
11. Hence a comprehensive policy is needed to ensure that teacher education is reorganized as a continuous co-ordinated process which begins with pre-service preparation and continues throughout the teacher's professional career. In such a system, pre-service and in-service education should be integrated, fostering the concepts of life-long learning and the need for recurrent education.
12. In-service education should not only permit professional updating but should also ensure the necessary professional mobility by preparing educational personnel to assume new functions and responsibilities.
13. Such a comprehensive policy of teacher education should include provision for pre-service and in-service training of educational personnel of various categories and of various levels, including inspectors, supervisors and other administrators as well as other professionals and specialists engaged in education.
14. At the level of educational policy with regard to in-service education the four principles which it seems most important to apply are:

    (a) continuity designed to keep the teacher continually aware of new developments in the education system and in the field of educational research and to expand his knowledge and skills in his particular subjects;
    (b) comprehensiveness that will involve all those who participate in the education process — various categories of teachers,

school administrators and inspectors, teacher educators and others;

(c) establishment of an organizational framework with appropriate funding and staff provisions, making possible the participation of all educators in various forms of in-service education and the mobilization, in collaboration with all institutions concerned, of all the resources likely to contribute to such training;

(d) involvement of various categories of educational personnel in the definition of in-service teacher education policy, objectives and programmes and their implementation as well as in educational research.

Preparation for the Profession

15. Taking into account the fact that there are, and always will be, changes in all aspects of social, cultural and educational life which will influence the roles and functions of teachers, it is essential to make future teachers aware of these changes and to prepare them for the profession with this in mind. This underlines particularly the importance of the development of the personality of the teacher in the course of his training and the development of his readiness and capacity for further training and self-education.
16. Within the context of existing educational legislation there should be flexibility for adapting rules, regulations, professional status, so as to facilitate progressive changes in the initial and continuing education of teachers, the formation of teacher teams which would include persons performing appropriate educational roles, the provision of incentives in career situations and prospects, etc. Accreditation and certification procedures should be geared to the new roles of teachers.
17. From the point of view of content, initial teacher education should enable the future teacher to acquire the necessary professional preparation for new roles and functions, and should provide a basis for continuing professional development in the framework of life-long education for teachers. The development of the curriculum for teacher education courses should be linked closely with curriculum developments in the schools.
18. Considered from the point of view of general principles and aims, the programmes of initial teacher education should:

(a) Relate closely to roles and functions expected of the teacher today and prepare the future teacher not only for his instructional role but also for the variety of roles and functions demanded for him by the society and the development of education. Teachers are now more and more involved in various extra-curricular and out-of-school activities and should be prepared so that they will be able to combine teaching and upbringing into the single process of developing personality.

(b) Prepare future teachers to use effectively and for the benefit of learners all the facilities and resources offered by the social and cultural environment.

(c) Give an opportunity for student teachers to experience these new roles and functions during the training period, by giving them responsibilities in the administration of teacher education institutions, by establishing closer links with various educational institutions and providing practical training so as to develop the students' initiative, responsiveness, resourcefulness and adaptability to change, and so enable them in the future to assume such new roles and functions as may appear.

(d) Provide for and ensure the student teachers' personal and professional self-development, so that they will be prepared to continue their education and development in the future either by self-education or by seeking to attend courses of in-service training and also prepare them to develop the same aptitudes in their pupils.

(e) Include adequate provision for general and professional, theoretical and practical preparation. The studies of specialization should be up to date and interdisciplinary in character and cover not only the facts but also the fundamental concepts, principles, structures of subjects so that students acquire an interdisciplinary framework within which they can continue to gain new knowledge independently during their professional life, taking account of the latest developments in the field of their specialisation.

(f) Include ample provision for professional development both theoretical and practical including introduction to problems of educational research and its application, to elements of experimental technique in education in order to facilitate teacher participation in educational research and strengthen the links between training and research.

(g) Prepare the teacher for the effective use of educational technology, including the media of mass communication.

In-Service Education

19. Continuing education should be an integral part of the teacher education process and should therefore be arranged on a regular basis for all categories of educational personnel. Procedures should be as flexible as possible and adaptable to teacher's individual needs and to the special features of each region, taking into account developments in the different specialities and the extension of knowledge.
20. The functions of teacher education institutions should be extended not only to provide for the pre-service education of teachers but also to contribute substantially towards their further education; it is thus desirable that these institutions provide pre-service education and continuing education.
21. Special regional centres should also be developed for this purpose and also to provide initial in-service education for those teachers, particularly in developing countries, who did not receive adequate preparation before starting teaching.
22. Teachers' organizations should be encouraged to contribute to the continuing education of teachers by initiating opportunities for teachers to meet and work together on common problems. Conferences, seminars and courses organized by teachers' organizations may represent a significant measure in encouraging teacher development by the profession itself.
23. Self-education of teachers should be considered as an important element in their continuing education. The educational authorities and educational research and documentation centres should help the teachers to organize their individual in-service education by providing guidance, the necessary documentation and literature, library facilities, etc., and by making the necessary time available.
24. In order to make continuing education more effective and to reach educators in remote regions, extensive use should be made of radio, TV and correspondence courses. The combination of short fulltime courses with long periods of multi-media programmes, including radio, TV and correspondence courses may provide one immediate solution of in-service education of

the broad mass of teachers.

25. The strengthening of the continuing education of teachers as required at all levels of the system, from early childhood education to the tertiary level and adult education will require considerable efforts on the part of education authorities. Such efforts include the quantitative analysis of teacher supply and demand in the country and the working out of national or regional plans for the continuing education of teachers.
26. Present rules, regulations and statutes should be so modified as to recognize the importance, necessity and effect of in-service education, to take into account the developments in its organization which have already occurred and to provide a legal right for all educational personal to take part in continuing education.
27. Measures should be taken to give all full-time or part-time, specialists working in education the opportunity for in-service education and at the same time to ensure that their professional experience benefits other teachers.

E. Status of Educational Personnel

28. (a) It should be recognized that the social and economic status of teachers and the level of appreciation of their role are important for the quantitative and qualitative development of education.

    (b) Special attention should be paid to the status of women teachers and their educational opportunities, especially their reintegration into the educational service after absence due to family responsibilities.
29. It is desirable, however, that the improvement and adaptation of the existing administrative and socio-economic status of teachers to new requirements should also permit an enlargement of scope so as to make the education function accessible to a much greater number of competent people available in the community, at least for part-time participation in the educational activities.
30. For this purpose, it is desirable that an administrative, social and economic status should be granted to these specialists consistent with their roles and functions.
31. The Recommendation concerning the Status of Teachers (1966) should also be revised in this sense, and its proper application should be promoted.

F. Participants in the Education of Teachers

32. Whatever may be the intentions to improve or to reform the education of teachers, the practical realization of such intentions will greatly depend on the quality and initiative of those called upon to participate in this activity. In order to prepare future teachers to assume new roles, such persons should in their own turn be competent psychologically, scientifically, academically and practically to educate teachers in this way.
33. Consequently, those responsible for educational policy should give more attention, in general, to the problem of the preparation of those called upon to contribute to the education of teachers. The continuing education of such persons is an essential aspect of educational strategy, which involves, notably, the contribution of universities and specialized institutions. Resources devoted to these purposes are likely to have a maximum multiplier effect.
34. Those responsible for the education of teachers should have at their disposal all the necessary means of keeping abreast of progress achieved in the field of education and of new methodologies and approaches concerning their specific functions.
35. Such persons should be competent to prepare teachers and other personnel for various specializations and functions in education and also for professional mobility, and should be in a position to promote among them the right attitudes towards innovation and towards life-long education.

G. Regional and International Co-operation

36. Co-operation in the field of initial and in-service teacher education should be carried out at bilateral, regional and international levels. The effect of such co-operation will be:

(a) to promote the formulation and to support the application of policies and plans for the pre-service and recurrent education of teachers and other specialists at all levels and for all types of education in order that education systems may better contribute to economic, scientific, technological, social and cultural progress;

(b) to facilitate programmes and activities for the education of teachers, teacher educators and various full-time and part-time specialists required for improving formal and non-formal education at all levels:

(c) to encourage structures, programmes and methods facilitating the introduction of appropriate innovations in initial and continuing education for all those who may be called upon to assume educational responsibilities;

(d) to encourage the Member-States to collect and to disseminate all possible information about their policies and plans concerning teacher education and also, to undertake case study and comparative study of such policies and plans;

(e) to recognize the diversity of situations in the development of education, to work out appropriate strategies in the field of teacher education and to intensify policies of assistance in this respect.

37. Regional organizations and international organizations such as UNESCO, interested in the training of educational personnel, should help to establish a world network of documentation and information centres likely to stimulate and to support renovative action undertaken in various States, fostering the exchange of information on innovations between the institutions and services responsible for initial and continuing training of educational personnel.

38. UNESCO is invited to give priority in its programme to such important aspects of training of educational personnel as are mentioned in this Recommendation: to search for new strategies, roles and functions of various educational personnel, continuing education, wider participation of people other than regular teachers in education, etc. In particular, UNESCO should seek to increase concerted international action to support developing countries in their efforts to provide systems of continuous education for their teachers.

39. It is desirable that UNESCO, in collaboration with the Member-States' competent authorities, should study the possibility of extending the scope of the Recommendation concerning the Status of Teachers (1966) so as to cover various categories of full-time and part-time educational personnel.

BIBLIOGRAPHY

UNESCO DOCUMENTS AND PUBLICATIONS*

Status of Teachers

1. *Conclusions of the final report and relevant decisions taken by UNESCO General Conference at its 19th session.* Nairobi, 1976. Paris, UNESCO, 1977, 28 p. ED-77/WS/61.
2. *Joint ILO/UNESCO committee of experts on the application of the recommendation concerning the status of teachers.* (Third session), Geneva, 8-19 March 1976. *Report.* Genevaa, ILO/UNESCO, 1976, 66 p. CEART/III/1976/10.
3. *Joint ILO/UNESCO committee of experts on the application of the recommendation concerning the status of teachers.* (Special session), Paris, 19-23 November 1979. *Report + annexes.* Paris, UNESCO, 1980 CEART/SR/79/7.
4. *Joint ILO/UNESCO committee of experts on the application of the recommendation concerning the status of teachers.* (Fourth session), Geneva, 29 November-7 December 1982. *Report.* Paris, UNESCO, 1982, 165 p. CEART/IV/82/12.
5. *Joint ILO/UNESCO committee of experts on the application of the recommendation concerning the status of teachers.* (Special session), Paris, 3-10 September 1985. *Report.* Paris, UNESCO, 1985, 46 p. CEART/SP/85/7.
6. *Recommendation concerning the status of teachers adopted by the special intergovernmental conference on the status of teachers.* Paris, UNESCO, 1966, 14 p.
7. *Some aspects of professional freedom of teachers* by Ben Morris. Paris, UNESCO, 1977, 213 p. (Monographs on education No. IX)
8. *The Status of teachers,* Brochure containing the annotated text of the 1966 recommendation. Paris, ILO/UNESCO, 1984, 52 p.
9. *Status of teachers in the Arab region.* UNESCO/UNEDBAS, 1983, 120 p.
10. *Status of teachers.* Paris, UNESCO/ILO, 1967, 35 p. ED/WS/13A.
11. *Surveys on the possible updating of the recommendation concern-*

* Listing to illustrate the range of UNESCO documents and publications.

ing the status of teachers and on the usefulness of the instrument. Paris, ILO/UNESCO, 87 p. CEART/SP/85.

New Trends and New Roles

1. *Computer science in vocational teacher education in Denmark.* Paris, UNESCO, 1986, 69 p. ED-86/WS/3.
2. *Computers in technical teacher education in the United Kingdom.* Paris, UNESCO, 1984, 61 p.
3. *Education in Malta : a look to the future*, Proceedings of a national workshop for further training of educational advisers and school principals in Malta, 12-23 October 1987. Paris, UNESCO, 1988, 184 p. + appendices.
4. *Innovations in technical teacher's training – Ukrainian SSA.* Paris, UNESCO, 50 p. ED-86/WS/72.
5. *Innovations in teacher training in the field of agriculture — Federal Republic of Germany*, Paris, UNESCO, 1986, 118 p. ED-86/WS/118.
6. *Interregional symposium on "integrated policies and plans for the training of educational personnel".* Paris, 1-5 April 1985. *Final Report* by J.C. Pauvert. Paris, UNESCO, 1985, 120 p.
7. *Recommendation No. 69 to the ministries of education concerning the changing role of the teacher and its influence on the preparation for the profession and on in-service training.* Reprinted form the final report of the 35th session of the International Conference on Education, Geneva, 1975, 6 p.
8. *Seminar on the training of teachers by the interdisciplinary system, to use this system in schools.* Bouake, Ivory Coast, 24 March-4 April 1970. *Final Report.* Paris, UNESCO, 1970, 37 p. ED/MD/12.
9. *Social sciences and the training of educational personnel.* Paris, UNESCO, 1979, 21 p.
10. *Teacher education and the production workshop* by J.A. Hendry. Paris, UNESCO, 1979, 38 p.
11. *Teacher training in educational technology* by Lazar Vlasceanu. UNESCO/CODIESEE, Bucharest, 1986, 192 p.
12. *Teachers and educational research.* Paris, UNESCO, 1980, 21 p.
13. *Teachers and out-of-school education.* Paris, UNESCO, 1980, 22 p.
14. *Towards self-instruction in teacher education* by J.A. Hendry.

Paris, UNESCO, 1979, 21 p.

15. *Training needs of educational personnel* by J.C. Pauvert. Paris, UNESCO, 1986, 137 p.

Pre-service and In-service Training of Educational Personnel

1. *Biennial meeting (7th) of national directors and chief technical advisers of teacher training projects.* Paris, 8-19 September 1975. *Report.* Paris, UNESCO, 1976, 95 p. ED-75/CONF. 602/COL.13.
2. *Directory of innovative institutions preparing educational personnel.* UNESCO/IBE, 1979, 100 p. ED-80/WS/20.
3. *Directory of teacher training institutions in Africa* (first elements). Paris, UNESCO, 1978, 51 p. ED-79/WS/7.
4. *Directory of teacher training institutions in the Arab States* (first elements). Paris, UNESCO, 1979, 63 p.
5. *European regional workshop on the implication of the educational integration of disabled children and adolescents into the normal structures of general education for teacher training.* Bologna, Italy, 30 September - 4 October 1985. *Final Report.* Paris, UNESCO, 1985, 11 p. + annexes. ED-86/WS/31.
6. *Further training of educational personnel; the activities of UNESCO* by A. Chiappano. Paris, UNESCO, 1985, 20 p.
7. *General survey of aspects of foreign language teacher training* by Reinhold Freudenstein, Philipps University Marburg, FRG. Paris, UNESCO, 1987, 76 p. ED-87/WS/13.
8. *Guide for the analysis of systems and programmes of in-service training of educational personnel.* Paris, UNESCO, 1981, 13 p.
9. *Helping handicapped pupils in ordinary schools : strategies for teacher training.* Report on a survey of fourteen countries. Paris, UNESCO, 1985. ED-86/WS/88.
10 *In-service education of educational personnel in comparative perspective.* Report of a UNESCO joint study in the field of education ed by Wijnand Hoeben Gravenhage, Netherlands. SVO/UNESCO Netherlands National Commission, 1986, 220 p.
11. *International annotated bibliography on technical teacher education.* Paris, UNESCO, 1980, 107 p. ED-86/WS/108.
12. *International seminar on evaluation in the education of teachers.* Maseru, Lesotho, National Teacher Training College, 27 March-1st April 1978. *Final report,* 56 p.
13. *National languages and teacher training in Africa, A*

methodological guide for the use of teacher training institutes by Joseph Poth. Paris, UNESCO, 1988, 49 p. (Educational studies and documents, 47).

14. *National languages and teacher training in Africa.* Report of seminar held in Kaduna, Nigeria, 19-24 January 1976. Paris, UNESCO, 1976, 46 p. ED-76/CONF. 817/1.
15. *Needs in respect of the training of educational personnel* by J.C. Pauvert. Paris, UNESCO, 1985, 130 p.
16. *Out-of-school activities and influences and the extent to which they are taken into account in the training of teachers* by Jean-Marie Moeckli. Paris, UNESCO, 1980, 51 p.
17. *Practicum in teacher education.* An agenda, prepared by Robert D. Phillips and Howard L. Jones. Paris, UNESCO, 1984, 77 p. ED-84/WS/72.
18. *Preparation of teachers for large classes.* Instruments of observation 1-9 by L. Vandevelde. Paris, UNESCO, 1983, 83 p.
19. *Production units and technical teacher education.* Paris, UNESCO, 1982 (Inf. TVE Series No. 7).
20. *Regional seminar of national directors and chief technical advisors of UNDP/UNESCO operational training projects in Latin America and the Caribbean.* Buenos Aires, 13-24 November 1978. *Final Report.* UNESCO/OREALC, 1979, 37 p.
21. *Regional training seminar for national directors and chief technical advisers of UNDP/UNESCO assisted on-going and completed training projects in the Arab States.* Bahrain, 7-16 October 1978. Paris, UNESCO, 1979, 23 p.
22. *Role of teacher training institutions in the promotion of national languages as teaching languages in Africa* by Arame Fal. Dakar, 1979, 73 p.
23. *School knowledge, media knowledge : media literacy in teacher training and student learning* by Len Masterman. Paris, UNESCO, 1983, 42 p.
24. *Seminar on national languages and teacher training in Africa.* Dar-es-Salaam, Tanzania, 12-16 November 1979. *Content and methodology in African language teacher education. Final Report.* UNESCO, NEIDA, 1980, 52 p.
25. *Status of staff employing modern educational techniques* by J. Leedham and A. Berruer. Paris, UNESCO, 1979, 122 p. ED-79/WS/49.
26. *Study on drug problems and drug education in African schools*

from the point of view of teachers and the teaching profession prepared by the World Confederation of Organizations of the Teaching Profession for regional meeting on education concerning problem connected with the use of drugs in African countries. Lome, Togo, 13-17 September 1976. Paris, UNESCO, 1977, 42 p. EPDAF/3e.

27. *Sub-regional seminar on the elaboration of materials for teacher formation suitable for subsequent use and adaptation by national teams for large classes.* Brazzaville, 1-10 September 1984. Part 1: seminar; Part 2 : workshop. UNESCO/BREDA.
28. *Sub-regional training seminar for teachers of visually handicapped children* Malawi, 2-20 November 1981. *First report.* Paris, UNESCO, 1981, 166.
29. *Sub-regional workshop on teacher training in environmental education to the Arab States.* Bahrain, 25-30 January, 1986, Bahrain, 1986, 100 p.
30. *TEP atlas - 5.5 atlas of teacher training projects.* Paris, UNESCO, 1978 ED-78/WS/16.
31. *Technical teacher education course : a suggested one year curriculum.* Paris, UNESCO, 1978. (Inf. TVE Series No. 5).
32. *Workshop guide on the use by teachers of the mass-media in the educational process.* Paris, UNESCO, 1983, 98 p.
33. *World directory of selected research and teacher training institutions in the field of technical and vocational education.* Revised edition. Paris, UNESCO, 1986.

Training of Teachers (Case Studies)

1. *A Case study of consolidated teacher education in Lesotho* by Zacharias A. Matsela. Paris, UNESCO, 1979, 74 p. ED-79/WS/96.
2. *A Case study of the systems and programmes of in-service training of educational personnel in Sri Lanka* by S.B. Ekanayake. Sri Lanka, 1982, 68 p.
3. *A Case study on the coordination of teacher education programmes (for teachers of primary and secondary schools) in Malaysia* by Awang Had Salleh. Paris, UNESCO, 1979, 56 p. ED-79/WS/97.
4. *Coordinated teacher education. The preparation of teachers for primary and secondary schools in Malta* by Charles Farrugia,

Paris, UNESCO, 1979, 21 p. ED-79/WS/99.

5. *Report on qualitative evaluation in educational training projects (1976-1977).* Paris, UNESCO, 1977, 12 p. ED-77/WS/147.
6. *Social science and teacher education. A case study approach: Guyana and Canada* by Rudolph W. Grant. Paris, UNESCO, 1980, 30 p. ED-80/WS/116.
7. *Synthesis of studies of the consolidation of the training of primary and secondary school teachers* by V. Hercik. 19 p.
8. *Teacher education in Poland, Institutions-programmes-coordination* by J. Myslinski. Paris, UNESCO, 1979, 14 p. ED-79/WS/98.
9. *Teacher training in the field of educational technology. A comparative analysis based on national studies from Bulgaria. Hungary, Romania, Turkey and Yugoslavia* ed. by Lazar Vlasceanu. Department of Education and Psychology, Bucharest, University of Bucharest, 1986, 192 p.

Productive Work and Teacher Training

1. *Guide to the workshop on the introduction of productive work in African schools.* Volume A, B and C. Paris, UNESCO, 1983, 3 fascicules.
2. *The Preparation of teachers for their tasks in polytechnic education and the productive and socially useful work of pupils in the ten-class general and polytechnic secondary education in the German Democratic Republic* by H. Frankiewicz. 37 p.
3. *Regional seminar for directors and specialists from national training institutions on the training of teachers, inspectors and teacher educators for the introduction of productive work into education.* Baghdad, Iraq, 24-28 November 1979:
   (i) *A case study on India* by M.B. Buch and Piloo Buch. Working paper No. 1. Paris, UNESCO, 1979, 25 p. ED-79/CONF.704/COL.1.
   (ii) *A case study on the introduction of practical productive work in the teacher training curriculum in Tanzania.* Working document by A.G.M. Ishumi. Paris, UNESCO, 1979, 17 p. ED-79/CONF.704/COL.3.
   (iii) *Major working document* by Keith Jackson. Paris, UNESCO, 1979, 33 p. ED-79/CONF.704/COL.4.
   (iv) *Report and general trends.* Paris, UNESCO, 1980, 21 p.

ED-79/CONF.704/COL.5.

4. *Regional seminar on the introduction of productive work into education and its implications for the training of educational personnel*. Porto Novo/Come, Benin, 8-12 December 1980.
   (i) *Discussion guide* by I. Beharo-Beri. Paris, UNESCO, 1980, 14 p.
   (ii) ED-80/WS/159 *Final report*. Paris, UNESCO, 1981. 18 p. ED-81/WS/16.
5. *Workshop on productive work and teacher education*. New Delhi, 5-14 April 1982. Sets I-IV. Paris, UNESCO, 1982. ED-82/CONF. 704/COL.4.

Teacher Educators

1. *European regional seminar, University teaching and the training of teachers : the contribution made by innovation in content and method to the further pedagogic training of teacher educators*. Prague, 25-29 November 1985. Working document.
2. *Guidelines for the design and management of teacher education programmes by J.A. Hendry*. Paris, UNESCO, 1978, 114 p.
3. *Lifelong education and the preparation of educational personnel* by James Lynch. UNESCO/UIE, 1977, 123 p.
4. *Lifelong teacher education and the community school* by Linda A. Dove. UNESCO/UIE, 1982, 147 p.
5. *Preparing educators of teachers and inspectors in some countries of Europe*. Report on the consultative meeting held at UNESCO, 3-6 November 1981. Paris, UNESCO, 1983, 166 p. ED-83/WS/26.
6. *Sub-regional seminar for administrators and teacher trainers of special education*. Limuru, Kenya, 10-12 September 1984. *Report of seminar*.
7. *The Training of teacher educators* by R. Lallez. Paris, UNESCO, 1980, 133 p. (Educational studies and documents ESD No. 43).
8. *Training of teacher educators in the use of microcomputers in secondary education on the basis of French and English experiments*, by B. Dubreuil. Paris, UNESCO, 1982, 31 p.
9. *Workshop guide for teacher educators*. Section A, B, C. Paris, UNESCO, 1982, 3 fascicules ED-82/WS/13.

See also (Chapter 13) *Management of Education* (*Bibliography*).

Non-Formal Educational Personnel

1. *The Functions and training of teachers who participate in out-of-school educational activities. A provisional analysis of the available documentation* by Vladimir Hercik. Paris, UNESCO, 1978, 27 p.
2. *Non-Formal education and teacher participation in French-speaking Africa south of the Sahara* by T. Trevisini. Paris, UNESCO, 1975, 75 p. ED-75/WS/20.
3. *Non-formal education and teacher participation in the People's Republic of Benin* by Michel Gomez. Paris, UNESCO, 1977, 29 p. ED-77/WS/149.
4. *Personnel requirements for multi-purpose community education centres in Sierra Leone : the Bunumbu experiment* by F.B.S. Ngegba. Paris, UNESCO, 1977, 26 p. ED-77/WS/119.
5. *Symposium on conditions for effective participation by teachers in non-formal education in Africa.* Dakar, 3-7 May 1976:
   (i) *Report* Paris, UNESCO, 1977, 56 p. ED-76/WS/90. (ii) *Working document* by Richard Quetel. Paris, UNESCO, 1976, 34 p. ED-76/WS/10.
6. *Teacher participation in out-of-school education in Europe.* Paris, UNESCO, 1975, 23 p. ED-75/WS/10.
7. *The Use of general TV programmes in school and community. The linkage between in-school and out-of-school education* by Takashi Sakamoto. Tokyo, Institute of Technology. Paris, UNESCO, 1981, 38 p.

9

EDUCATIONAL PLANNING

SYMPOSIUM ON MANPOWER ASPECTS OF EDUCATIONAL PLANNING, 1966

The symposium held at the International Institute for Educational Planning, Paris was attended by participants coming from diverse professional and cultural backgrounds. Most of them were practising manpower and educational planners or academic students of the subjects. But they were supplemented by general development economists, educators and agricultural experts. Drawn from both developing and developed countries, they had worked in the context of widely different social and economic systems. The symposium identified, examined and classified specific problems emerging on the moving frontier of manpower and educational planning. It highlighted urgent policy questions on that frontier which awaited decisions by policy-makers. It attempted to indicate where the co-operative efforts of men from different intellectual disciplines could help to guide the practical work of manpower and educational planners.

The proceedings of the symposium have been published by UNESCO's International Institute for Educational Planning (IIEP) under the title *'Manpower Aspects of Educational Planning : Problems for the Future'* (1968)

Topics of the symposium were as under:

1. Employment opportunities for the educated. This rapidly growing problem is rather the reverse of the problem of manpower shortages which commanded prime attention only a few years ago.

2. The role of education in rural and agricultural development. Economic development experts and policy-makers have lately come to regard agricultural and rural development as perhaps the number one problem for many developing countries, deserving of a higher priority than it has been getting.
3. The implementation of educational and manpower plans. This includes not only problems of administration and organization but the thorny issue of how prevailing wage structures and other incentives can make or break the best-laid plans.

The publication begins with a foreword by Philip H. Coombs, Director of IIEP and includes

Highlights of the symposium by George Skorov

I. Relationship between education, manpower, and economic growth: evolution of concepts
II. Employment opportunities and their implication for educational planning
III. Modernization of the rural sector and its implication for educational planning
IV. Implementation of educational and manpower plans

A systems analysis approach to human-resource development planning by Frederick Harbison

Human-resource problems in developing economies
Development and utilization of human resources in Nigeria
Conclusion
Colloquy

The absorptive capacity of the economy by George Skorov
Educational output in relation to employment opportunities, with special reference to India by V. K. R. V. Rao
Unemployment among school leavers in an African city by Archibald Callaway

The city of Ibadan
Free primary education in Western Nigeria
Unemployed school leavers
The drive for self-improvement
The dynamics of migration
The employment market: expectations and reality

Investment in basic education
Colloquy

Manpower and educational needs in the traditional sector, with special reference to East Africa, by Guy Hunter
Background of social and economic growth
Problems and strategy
Education and rural development
Finance, acceptability, and training
Ages 12-18: the educational vacuum
Conclusions

African agriculture and its educational requirements by Rene Dumont
The present near-critical situation
Schooling, agricultural progress, and the population explosion
Agriculture's need for improved skills
Higher education: bilingualism and the africanization of research
Tentative conclusions
Colloquy

Implementing a manpower programme in a developing country by Robert L. Thomas
Introduction
Policies
Pre-conditions to implementation
The process of implementation
Administrative and institutional arrangements
Creating a climate of public opinion conducive to plan implementation

Employment, wage levels, and incentives by A.R. Jolly
The background
The dynamics of the situation
Incentives: useful and perverse
Policy implications
Summary and conclusions
Colloquy

Extracts from the proceedings of the symposium are given below:

Overview of Manpower Problems

I would add several other matters that have come to the front over the past five or six years and need to be grasped firmly. For one thing, it had previously escaped our notice that modernization itself – indeed, economic progress – is a generator of unemployment or of under-employment. Like all good things, it has its own particular diseases which must be cured. I am not saying that we should forgo modernization. I am simply saying, to repeat, that modernization generates problems of its own which need to be solved.

There is a second thing we have learned since 1959 or 1960 – though there will be people who will not agree with my conclusion. Where it was once believed that all investments in education were good – and that economic growth was a pure and simple consequence of investment in education – we know now that education can impede economic growth as well as accelerate it. The major question before us now is how to achieve a proper balance within an educational system. It is how to achieve the right types of education rather than simply greater quantities of education.

Third, we used to feel that manpower requirements and educational targets were to be derived from economic-development plans. In that connection, we talked about the need to integrate manpower and educational planning with general economic-development planning. Today, we can still agree that this need is real. But I would here suggest that manpower problems of newly developing societies have become so vast and important that we may have to reverse the earlier view of the case. We may have to adapt economic-development planning to the end of solving the problems of manpower which are being identified.

This applies especially to the newly developing countries where economic progress and modernization generate high levels of unemployment – and where the greater the increase in GNP, as in Venezuela, the greater may be the rate of accumulation of unemployment. If so, we may have to think of the manpower approach as lending a whole new dimension and a whole new set of objectives to general economic-development planning. What I am saying, to sum up, is this. Perhaps manpower planning is not a derivative of general economic-development planning but rather that general economic-development planning now may have to be thought of as a means of helping to solve some of the more critical manpower problems that occur during the process of modernization.

I have several points to make here. First, we should drop the phrase 'economic planning' and substitute for it the phrase 'national planning'. By enlarging the conceptual frame in this way, we could bring in the factors of political and social development as well as economic development.

Secondly, one of the misleading ideas we have to contend with in developmental work is the idea of gross national product. GNP, at best, is subject to guess-work. Yet it gives you a single goal – the rate of growth – and this in turn tends to overshadow other goals. It leads you to equate progress and success with this fictitious figure called GNP. In new countries in particular, progress cannot be equated with GNP. GNP really conceals the wide disparity between the modern and the traditional sector: as I have already said, there can be a tremendous increase in GNP, along with an exceptionally high unemployment rate.

Instead of making GNP a goal, we need to ask: Is a country capable of feeding itself, or are its people starving to death? Is it utilizing its human resources? Is it closing instead of widening the gap between the modern and traditional sectors? Is it improving the conditions of health? If we view all progress made in development economics solely through the lens of GNP, we give a distorted focus to the idea of progress.

I recognize that, once you depart from the concept of GNP, you get into great methodological difficulties and complicate your problems from a planning standpoint. Yet by clinging to it to the exclusion of other considerations, we resemble the case of the drunken man in New York's Central Park, who seemed to be looking for something when he was approached by a policeman. The policeman asked him what he was looking for. 'I lost my watch,' the man said. 'Where?' the policeman asked him. 'Oh,' said the man, 'I lost it two miles from Central Park – but the light is better here.' (F. HARBISON, Director, Industrial Relations Section, Princeton University, Princeton, New Gersey, U.S.A.).

Excerpts from 1966 Symposium

I agree with Harbison's view that primary education can produce unemployment in the sense that it can create an aversion to existing employment opportunities. A person growing up in a village who does not go beyond primary education and who is going to stay in the village can get a type of education which makes him contemptuous of his father's way of life and of the kind of income to be secured from the land.

Incidentally, there is a difference between the position in India and some other countries with which I am familiar. In India, primary-school leavers do not get civil service jobs. This would be more true of college graduates in the arts and humanities. Having been in Uganda, Kenya and Nyasaland, I have a sense that secondary-school leavers in those countries have been given jobs which would normally be taken up in India by university graduates, including those holding master of arts degrees. At the same time, the performance of the people in the African countries, I visited, makes me wonder if we have not over-emphasized academic qualifications in India as a prerequisite for jobs. What has been happening in India is that our own university graduates are now taking up jobs which could be done by a matriculate. We are trying to restrict enrolments in the universities, but, once you have primary education, you set in motion a chain-reaction of pressures. Primary education leads to middle education – which leads to secondary education – which leads to university education. We can only try to have more diversified courses and multi-purpose schools. so that at a given age a young man of 14 or 16 can go off and get a job. We can also try to raise the qualification standards for admission to the universities. Primary education exists in India, not as a passport to employment, but because, under our written constitution, we are pledged to provide universal free compulsory primary education for children up to the age of 14. The question of the cost-benefit ratio, therefore, does not apply. Nor does the question present itself as to whether education leads to employment. The kind of primary education we are giving today will definitely create problems in the countryside. It is possible to change the content of the primary education, and I think it is absolutely essential that this be done by the educationists. But educationists cannot provide all the answers merely by changing the curricula for education and the methods of teaching. We must also have the necessary environmental changes in institutions, social and political climate, and so on. This is important not only for my own country but for the African countries as well, since they are reaching the stage where they are producing more and more secondary graduates and university graduates. To what I have said about the way primary education can contribute to unemployment, I would add that, at higher levels, education can definitely create unemployment when it produces specific skills for which there are no job openings. There are specific skills which society has a right to demand of its educational system. But who is to establish the proportion of the skills that are needed? You cannot expect the educators to decide this question by themselves; they need the indispensable guidance of the manpower planners.

To come more directly to the positive effects of education on employment: education removes manpower bottle-necks that hold back economic growth. After India gained its independence and we set about drawing up a national development plan, we created a committee that was to determine the number of engineers and other technically trained people who would be required. Then, with this information in hand, we spent a great deal of money in deliberately creating a number of new engineering colleges and polytechnical schools. If we had not done this, the plan would have gone completely off the rails. This is because the private capitalist does not create his own engineers or his own diploma people. He just advertises and he gets them. If the trained manpower supply had not been there, a very great bottleneck would have imperiled the plan. There is, therefore, no question in my mind but that education which is linked to manpower planning can do a great deal to increase employment, to increase production, to increase employment opportunities and, above all, to form a proper attitude toward work itself. Finally, I would very strongly agree with a conclusion voiced by Wilson a moment ago, though I disagree with his logic. His logic is that the public sector is unfit or is less fit for doing economic activity than the private sector. I am not prepared to concede this point. I agree with him, however, when he stresses the importance of an educational system that will increase productivity in the self-employed occupations where most of the jobs are to be found – not only in India but in most of the other developing countries. Indeed, education can play a positive role, not only in creating jobs but in increasing the productivity of the jobs held (V.K.R.V. Rao, Member of the Planning Commission, Government of India, New Delhi).

Our discussion of education and employment has shed useful light on several dynamic aspects of development which educational planners and economists should bear in mind.

One significant point brought out in Professor Rao's analysis of India's experience is that, as the supply of educated people improves, the educational equivalents for various jobs tend to rise also. Thus, a particular job is upgraded even though its label remains unchanged.

This same 'upgrading' phenomenon is to be found in the history of more advanced countries, such as Japan and the United States, where positions formerly requiring a high-school diploma now call for a college degree. Upgrading, then, is one of the important forms of adjustment between educational output and the supply of jobs. A second point concerns the dynamic way in which education feeds and multiplies its own demand, quite independently of what national manpower requirements may be, by heightening the educational ambitions of people. When the gates to primary education are flung open to the educationally under-privileged, this inevitably results a few years later in great pressure to broaden secondary educational opportunities and this, in turn, gets reflected in higher education. Individual aspirations have a snowballing effect, and translate into inexorable political pressures and public policy decisions. Educational planners who simply decry or ignore these realities will emerge with statistically tidy plans that never get implemented.

A third and related point, and this foreshadows our discussion of implementation, is the dangerous hidden assumption that in choosing between different types of education and different types of job, people will behave the way the planners wish they would. If, for example, the manpower planners have plotted the long-run manpower requirements for national development and the educators have reshaped the educational system to turn out just the right numbers and proportions of graduates at each level to match this pattern of requirements, is the 'fitness' problem then solved? Has the right balance been achieved? Not at all. The problem remains of persuading people to follow these educational paths and to accept these various employment opportunities in the right numbers.

We know from experience that individual decisions often have a way of defeating the best-laid blueprints of the planners, partly for irrational reasons or out of ignorance, but very often for very rational reasons pertaining to the structure of economic and social incentives. Not infrequently, as has been emphasized here, the prevailing incentive structure works directly against the successful implementation of a seemingly rational plan. But we will come to this matter of incentives later. The main point now is that people who are given expensive training for jobs they do not get – or may not want – constitute in some measure a waste of scarce educational resources, which might otherwise have been used more productively to foster development and to create employment. In this sense, we seem to be agreed, education may actually contribute to unemployment; not because it is education, *per se*, but because it is the wrong education in the circumstances.

But for the most part, we also seem agreed, education is not the perpetrator of unemployment; its main effect in this regard is to make the unemployed and the underemployed more visible and in some cases more frustrated and vocal.

What can education and educators do to help the employment situation? Theoretically, much can be done, we have agreed. We can alter the character and the quality of education, with a view to breaking specific manpower bottle-necks and, more broadly, to inculcating the skills and knowledge, the attitudes and motivation, and the sense of initiative and entrepreneurship required on a vast scale for successful national development. Educational development can be shaped to match manpower requirements; better vocational guidance can be provided; educational administrators can be more realistic about resource scarcities and bend greater effort towards the more efficient and productive use of available educational resources through better management, innovations and otherwise.... (Philip H. Coombs, Director, IIEP, Paris).

Study based on a visit to Tanzania, 1965-66: (main points, Guy Hunter, Member Institute of Race Relations, London)

1. Manpower planning, and in some degree economic planning, has failed to take into account the development and the best use of four-fifths of the potential human resources in such countries as those of East Africa.
2. Even with the maximum feasible programme of industrialization, this development of human resources can be achieved on a large scale only within the rural economy.
3. Resources devoted to formal primary education (and soon, to some proportion of secondary education) are outrunning resources devoted to creating economic opportunities for the school leavers and thus in some degree are wasting a large investment. In consequence, far greater emphasis, in national plans and by aid agencies, should be placed on educative services directed to increasing the productivity of the rural economy (i.e., mainly to adults).
4. All educative services (formal education, agricultural extension, community development, youth service, vocational training) should be regarded as branches of a single educative effort in

which the balance between each branch can and should be adjusted to the changing needs of economic and social growth.

5. Finally, in view of the falling age of primary-school leavers and the decreasing openings for training open to them, urgent action is needed, on educational, social, political and economic grounds, for new and extended educative or training programmes for the age group 12-18.

Education and Rural Development

. . . Throughout this experience I became increasingly convinced of the key role which education and training must play in the whole field of rural transformation. Not only it is necessary to develop satisfactory technical services for agricultural improvement; it is essential to generate within the people themselves – and particularly the rural community – the desire for change, the desire for progress and the willingness of work hard to achieve it, and the desire to grasp the tools of technology for improvement through the medium of education and training.

Perhaps 90-95 per cent of the life and occupation of the people in the developing countries is rural. Agriculture, for these people, represents the central fact of existence. Yet, with certain notable exceptions, like irrigation projects, capital investment in the improvement of the agricultural potential of subsistence land areas in these countries has been practically nil. Indeed, under their current land-use patterns – with fragmented holdings, common land-use and common grazing – the improvement of the land by capital investments in the form of human skill or money is hardly possible. Peasant agriculture might be regarded as the 'depressed industry' of these countries. It means an endless round of toil, suffering the hazards of the weather, and of pests and disease of crops and livestock, to say nothing of unpredictable fluctuations in prices for agricultural products. It means miserably poor returns even in good years. It means an agriculture in which in many places in the last three or four decades – production per acre and per unit of labour have remained static or have actually declined.

Meanwhile, because of population pressures, standards of living – as measured by food per head or cash income per family – have actually decreased in many of the developing countries. We are as Dumont has quite rightly stated, facing an absolutely critical situation. On the one side – to repeat – agriculture is the basic occupation of the developing countries (and of mankind as a whole); upon its development depends the world food supply and much of future progress in all sectors of society. On the other side, in most of the countries we are now talking about, agriculture is looked upon as an occupation in which the poor and the unprogressive will be retrained – and from which the intelligent and the educated must escape. Yet it is precisely this basic industry which is in greatest need of people trained as scientists, technicians, extension workers and more efficient producers.

In this situation, education, by itself, is powerless to do very much. If education is to pay off, the development of modern economic agriculture must be at the forefront of national development policies and plans. It is absolutely useless trying to create among school children a love of the land and an interest in going into farming if agriculture – as in many developing countries - supply is not worth going into. Education for rural development must, of course, go hand in hand with policy change – outside the specific sphere of education. Land reform for example, is an essential prerequisite to an improved agriculture – simply because most forms of modern economic farming cannot take place except in farming units of viable economic size. Besides, there must be created institutions for the supply of farm credit and there must be developed a wide range of other support activities – marketing facilities, transport and access roads, food-processing plants, co-operative, and so on.

The fruits of a determination to create a new agriculture can be seen today when we look at what Israel has done. It can be seen retrospectively when we look back at the Morrill Act of 1862, which set up the land-grant colleges in the United States – at a time when the U.S.A. was, basically, a subsistence farming economy. It can also be seen in the agriculture of Japan and many of the advanced countries. It is only within the context of a determination to create a new agriculture that agricultural education and training can really begin to make a significant contribution to economic and social development.

What sort of agricultural education and training are needed, given this determination? The obvious and simple answer points to an education and training which will lead to positive, substantial and sustained increases in agricultural productivity – and in farm-family income. Within this broad framework, we may identify three types of necessary education and training.

First, there is the training of the farmer, or the potential farmer, and other producer occupations. Incidentally, in some of the countries we are speaking about, there has been a strong shift of emphasis toward training practising farmers – even if they are illiterate – as opposed to spending great sums of money on training potential farmers, most of whom do not in actual practice go into farming.

There is, secondly, the training of the intermediate or skilled technician, manager, or extension worker. The aim here is the acquisition of practical skills and managerial ability backed by a sound basic and technical education. In essence, it is training of an applied, practical kind, geared to the performance of specific jobs.

The third type that is needed is at the professional or university level. It must be geared to the production of scientists, agriculturists, veterinarians, foresters and others for research work, for teaching, for senior administrative posts in the agricultural services; people who can direct the work of agriculture at the policy-making level, and so on.

All three types of training are essential to agricultural progress, but the notion that one is inferior to the other – and hence should be avoided if possible by students – has led to many unfortunate situations in the developing countries. For example, the diploma type of training at the technical level is commonly thought to be something inferior to the training at the professional level of university work which leads to a degree. This is an unfortunate impression. The two types of training are fundamentally different in character. Their aims are different. The types of person produced are meant for different – but essentially complementary – functions. In other words, you cannot get agricultural progress without substantial numbers of both types of personnel, and particularly without a very much larger number of the technician than of the professional, university-trained type. Yet the common impression is that, if you hold a diploma qualification, it is something inferior to the university degree and that you must spend the next few years applying for scholar-ships that will enable you to go on to a university in order to get a full and proper qualification for work.

From the point of view of the developing countries, this kind of wrong thinking is very costly. It is precisely the skilled, practical managerial type of people who are so desperately needed to spur economic growth in the agricultural sector of the developing countries. This fact has been recognized by the East African Council for Agricultural Education, representing the ministries of agriculture and education, the different levels of agricultural training, and the agricultural industry and research. The Council was so convinced of the complementary importance of the diploma and the degree type of approaches to agricultural development that it persuaded the university to sponsor an East African diploma in agriculture awarded by the university. In this way, it was hoped that high standards would be achieved and status accorded to the diploma level of qualifications.

Where does the primary school system fit into the thesis I have been advancing here? I repeat that I see no point whatever in trying to orient the primary school system toward royal life and farming unless agriculture is assigned a very high priority in the development of the national economy. Besides, the primary school is not the place to teach technical agriculture. It is the place to give a basic education to children, naturally geared to the environmental conditions of the countryside, it needs economic development and so on. But this is something quite different from teaching agricultural techniques to small children in schools.

Turning briefly to the question of incentives, here again there is a lot of very loose thinking. It seems to me that the things that really matter to people are first of all their families and the future of their families; secondly, the education of their children; and thirdly, improvement in their living conditions and social amenities in the form of better housing, domestic water supplies, and so on. If this is correctly stated, then it is incredible that we have managed to get so far in this symposium without ever having mentioned women's education. I am not going to open up that subject now. But, having worked just over thirty years in Africa, if I were asked what is the most important single factor in transforming the economies and the life of African countries, I would say women's education. I say this because it is women who are most immediately concerned with the basic 'incentives' that motivate societies.

A final word. It is misleading to adhere to the division usually made between the industrial sector and the traditional agricultural sector – as if they were independent entities. What we need is the industrialization of agriculture. Here is where agriculture and industry must come together. The future of industrial progress, whether in the towns or rural areas, is, in most developing countries, inevitably bound up with raising levels of agricultural productivity and a steady increase in the creation of wealth from the soil. (Fergus B. Wilson, Head Agricultural Education Branch, Rural Institutions and Services Division, Food and Agriculture Organisation, United Nation, Rome).

REGIONAL SYMPOSIUM ON PROMOTING EQUITY, EXCELLENCE AND EFFICIENCY IN HIGHER EDUCATION: IMPLICATIONS FOR POLICY, PLANNING AND MANAGEMENT, 1985

The Symposium was organized at New Delhi from 14 to 23 October, 1985, jointly by the UNESCO Regional Office for education in Asia and the Pacific, Bangkok, the Indian National Commission for Cooperation with UNESCO and the University Grants Commission, New Delhi.

Objectives

(a) to provide a forum for in-depth discussion on aspects of policy, planning and management in relation to Equity, Excellence and Efficiency in higher education;
(b) to share experiences of the countries concerned on the understanding of the problems and policy alternatives for attaining efficiency, excellence and equity under the particular socio-political economic and institutional conditions prevailing;
(c) to make observations and recommendations for programmes and measures with a view to enhancing efficiency, equity and excellence in higher education in the interest of desired socio-economic development;
(d) to promote further bilateral and multilateral co-operation for joint studies, exchange of documentation and sharing of intellectual resources; and
(e) contribute to the generation of documentation on policy, planning and management of higher education to be useful to educators, policy-makers and administrators of higher education.

Conclusion and Recommendations

The symposium has emphasized the importance of equity, excellence and efficiency (EEE) in higher education. The participants have reported on the attempts being made, by the countries concerned, towards greater progress in achieving higher levels in their pursuit of the three E's. Their experiences show that the E's are interrelated, and one cannot be achieved in isolation from the other two. It is a question of balance, of a trade-off and of both a short term and a long term approach. The symposium urged the governments to recognize this inter-relationship in formulating and implementing their policy and programmes for Higher Education.

Resource Allocation

One of the difficulties in promoting equity in higher education arises out of relative lack of equity in primary and secondary education. It is recommended therefore, that every effort should be made to promote equity in primary and secondary education so that the base is wide and strong.

It is recognized that higher education contributes to socio-economic development by providing trained manpower as well as by production of knowledge, specially scientific and technological R and D, which helps developmental transformation for self-reliance and thus augments the resources of a country. Therefore, it is desirable to strengthen higher education, for which a larger allocation of funds is necessary. However, the fact is that there are financial constraints, which retard the progress towards a higher level of equity and excellence, and which may have repercussions on efficiency in higher education. It is, therefore, recommended that every effort should be made to highlight the contributions that higher education might make to development and emphasize the need for a larger allocation of funds. At the same time, every effort should be made to increase the efficiency with which the resources – physical, academic and financial – are utilized.

Relevance and Linkage

In judging the role of higher education in a developing society, the question of relevance is not just theoretical, but much more a reflection of the needs of society, which requires that higher education should not function such as an ivory tower, or an island of culture, but should link up with the plans and programmes of socio-economic and cultural development of a country. It is, therefore, recommended that a deliberate attempt should be made to establish linkages between socio-economic and cultural development policies and plans and higher education. As higher education, through its R and D functions as well as through the supply of manpower, contributes to practically all the facets of development, it is necessary to link higher education with other Ministries/Departments of the Government, through a higher level model agency so that resources can be augmented through the contributions of all Ministries/Departments as well as Education.

Information and Database

In view of the paucity of reliable information on various aspects of higher education in the countries, a need is established for having a database in every institution, and at the national level, so that policy formulation and development of plans and programmes may be guided by adequate and reliable information about inputs, processes, outputs, structures, and so on. It is, therefore, recommended that each country may such as to strengthen and develop a system for reliable statistics, on various aspects of higher education. In order to do this efficiently, standardization of statistics is important. It is recommended that, at the regional level, workshops and seminars, may be organized for the participating countries in order to develop the information system in higher education through a mutual sharing of expertise and experiences.

Equity as Access

Considering the problems of equity in terms of access to higher education in the general context of various constraints, alternatives, such as non-formal education and distance education are being developed in some countries. But these alternatives should also be viewed from the point of view of excellence and efficiency. These should not be an excuse for providing second rate education for the disadvantaged in the name of equity. It is recommended that the possibilities of non-formal education and distance education should be seriously considered, and countries may hold national seminars on modalities and cost effectiveness and develop research on all aspects. At the Regional level, seminars may be useful for developing, models of distance learning systems and their evaluation, and workshops may be held for development of reading materials.

Networking of Institutions

In view of the limited facilities available in many institutions of higher learning, it is recommended that a networking of institutions within the country should be considered so as to share the facilities available and augment the resources, and some of the countries have already taken some steps in this regard. It is recommended that inter-institutional co-operation between countries may be encouraged, and UNESCO may initiate steps towards the development of a regional network of institutions.

Importance of Extension Function

Although it is recognized that a university has research, teaching and extension functions, it is usually research and teaching which attract the utmost attention and extension is neglected. It is, however, recognized that the importance of extension work/field work/social or community work by the students and teachers is very high in shaping the products of higher-education. It is also recognized that extension contributes to learning and to academic work. In view of this it is recommended that a Regional Seminar should be organized on extension in order to improve it where it is already on the ground and help other countries in planning and preparing for it, if they are thinking of it.

Specific Measures to Attain EEE

Studies and Research. There is paucity of research on higher education in the countries of the region, due to which the formulation of policies, plans and management in the countries represented in the symposium do not have the full benefit of studies and research on the three E's in higher education. It is recommended that studies and investigations on educational structures, processes, curriculum development and such other facets of higher education should be maximized so that studies on the three E's are available within a country on a continuing basis.

Information sharing for approach determination. With this end in view, national seminars on the three E's in higher education should be organized within each country involving a large segment of the academic community. National seminars on planning and designing research studies on E's should also be organized and UNESCO may provide some funds for such national level activities.

Regional co-operation is recommended for the development of research studies in higher education. There are various problems for which some data are available but further work needs to be done, such as what is the intake of students in various fields of studies and what does the picture look such regionally and the reasons thereof, or the policy of protective discrimination which is followed in some countries may be studied with reference to student characteristics, outcomes, facilities and so on; or, the problem of the number of contact hours in various subjects at various levels. UNESCO should encourage such activities.

Improvement of Student Evaluation

Considering the problems of equity, excellence and efficiency in respect of the intake of students, procedures of selection on merit have been developed. However, scholastic examination measures only some cognitive abilities. In view of the fact that the products of higher education are required to have qualities which are not restricted to the cognitive domain (and within that too a narrow spectrum of abilities), the procedure of scholastic examination leaves out many potential students. It is, therefore, recommended that within country research should be undertaken to develop suitable methods of evaluation and assessment of the students' abilities, aptitudes, past experience of work and such other characteristics relevant for professional education as well as for higher levels of education in other fields. Likewise, it is important to undertake research on the identification of talent for higher education, within country. Regional seminars and workshops at the level of experts may be organized bilaterally or multi-laterally for designing studies and evaluating research findings and their dissemination.

Employment Perspective

Considering the relationship between higher education and employment and especially the context of efficiency of the system, the aspect of employability of graduates is receiving increasing attention in many countries, and efforts are being made to alter suitably the course structures and the curriculum so as to develop abilities and skills of entrepreneurship and self-employment.

However, it is recommended that systematic research on the subject should be undertaken within countries and experience exchanged. It is recommended that, at the Regional level, workshops and co-operative research projects may be organized in the matter of linkage of higher education with the world of work.

Training

It is recognized that the teacher is a key factor in the pursuit of the three E's. Considering the key role of the teacher, specially for excellence, it is recommended that, within each country, in-service education and pedagogical training of teachers should be organized. In addition to the above, a system of continuing education of the teacher has to be devised within a country.

Evaluation of Faculty Performance

The question of evaluation of performance of teachers has been raised and discussed, and it has been felt that there is need for improvement in evaluation instruments and processes. However, it is recognized that reliable methods have yet to be established and, therefore, it is recommended that a Regional Seminar on the subject should be organized so that a system of evaluation can be put on the ground.

Training in Management

Expansion in higher education at a fairly rapid rate has led, among other things, to academics occupying managerial positions where the tasks of management have posed problems arising out of size and heterogeneity of students and teachers, as well as problems related to other factors. In view of the experiences of the countries, in the matter of educational administration by academics, it is recommended that within country programmes of management training for academics should be organized. It is recommended that at the Regional level, workshops and seminars should be organized in order to develop management training systems, methodologies and training materials, not only for use by teachers but also by other educational administrators in higher education, such as Registrars, Controllers, Finance Officers etc.

Institutional Evaluation

The need for developmental work within country in relation to information/database, staff development, development of teaching/

learning package, development of criteria for evaluation of institutions etc. The project areas may be identified on the basis of recommendations made in this Report. It is recommended that the UNESCO may consider the promotion of such developmental projects on regional/sub-regional basis.

INTERNATIONAL CONFERENCE ON EDUCATION RECOMMENDATION CONCERNING DIVERSIFICATION OF POST-SECONDARY EDUCATION IN RELATION TO EMPLOYMENT, 1989

Preamble

The International Conference on Education convened by the United Nations Educational, Scientific and Cultural Organization, meeting in Geneva at its forty-first session from 9 to 17 January 1989,

Recalling the aims and purposes of UNESCO which are clearly defined in the Constitution, particularly in relation to education and international cultural co-operation,

Recalling 24C/Resolutions 4.1, 4.2 and 4.3 by which the General Conference provided, guidelines for 'the formulation and application of education policies', having regard to specific functions of the International Bureau of Education and of the 41st session of the International Conference on Education in the implementation of UNESCO's programmes in this field,

Taking note of paragraph 15 of decision 4.1 on the third Medium-Term Plan, adopted by the Executive Board at its 130th session, by which it considered that the coherence of the Major Programme Area 'Education and the future' should be strengthened,

Recognizing the value of post-secondary education in the development and application of education for international understanding, co-operation and peace and education relating to human rights and fundamental freedoms,

Noting the great importance of the improvement of the international political climate and the initiatives of Member-States seeking new opportunities for the development of post-secondary education from resources made available as a result of practical moves towards disarmament and the ending of regional conflicts,

Recognizing the role of post-secondary education in enhancing intellectual, practical and creative capabilities at individual and collective levels and its importance as a factor in the promotion and acceleration of cultural, socio-economic, scientific and technological development in all contemporary societies,

Emphasizing that post-secondary education should contribute alike to the all-round development of the individual and to his or her preparation for active life at the cultural, social and economic levels,

Noting that universal recognition of the fact that education is a fundamental right of the individual and a pre-condition of social progress has for the past 40 years brought about an unprecedented development of education throughout the world, including education at the post-secondary level,

Recognizing that the speed of scientific, technological and socio-economic development is creating new challenges which make it necessary both to extend and to improve the quality of post-secondary education, including changes of structure, in order to meet the needs of the individual, the world of work and society as a whole,

Emphasizing the role of post-secondary education in overcoming the global problems of humanity and in the shaping of models of sustainable development as recommended by the World Commission on the Environment and Development,

Noting that post-secondary structures and curricula have for many years been the subject of radical reforms of smaller-scale changes designed not only to enhance the effectiveness of such education, but also to make it more relevant to the demands of new population groups and to diversify its courses and curricula to meet the changing needs of the world of work,

Mindful nevertheless of the imbalance in many countries between the supply of and demand for highly skilled labour, resulting from the rapid expansion of the student body and the fact that their training is not sufficiently adapted to the requirements and to the limited absorption capacity of the economy,

Further noting that in many countries the problems of unemployment and underemployment afflict the entire population,

Bearing in mind, in this regard, the importance of taking additional practical, carefully planned measures designed to ensure that in terms of both quantity and quality, post-secondary education and training are matched more closely to employment requirements,

Acknowledging that the diversification of post-secondary education is an important means of achieving the twofold objective of, on the one hand, producing highly qualified persons with an all-round education and, on the other, satisfying the many different cultural and educational requirements of national communities, professional associations, age-groups, other groups and individuals for the creation of conditions conducive to spiritual development, freedom of self-expression and the humanization and intellectualization of work, social contacts and leisure,

Convinced that the exchange of information and of experience, including the most innovative experiments conducted by Member-States aimed at the improvement and diversification of post-secondary education and bearing in mind the new trends in employment, will contribute considerably to the advancement of ideas and practices in a domain that is vital for the development of all nations,

Considering that the strategies to be adopted in the implementation of the Recommendation will depend on the particular stages and levels of development of individual countries,

Having regard to the relevant conventions, recommendations and declarations adopted at the international level, and more especially by UNESCO,

Adopts on the seventeenth of January, nineteen hundred and eighty-nine, and submits for examination to the ministries responsible for post-secondary education and other competent authorities and bodies of the different Member-States, to the agencies of the United Nations system that have responsibilities in this domain and to the intergovernmental and non-governmental organizations concerned, the present Recommendation:

A. General Principles and Key Concepts

1. Post-secondary education comprises the whole range of formal and non-formal education and training and of research systems provided by both university and non-university establishments and pertaining both to the public and to the private sectors.
2. The diversification of post-secondary education is a necessary consequence of scientific and technological development, of the need to ensure access to this level of education for all, including new population groups, and of the new requirements entailed by the employment situation. Diversification in its turn affects scientific and technological development. It is reflected in the creation

of new institutions, training courses and disciplines, and new structures to cater for student enrolment; it has a profound impact upon objectives, content, learning methods, procedures governing student admission and recognition of studies, and the management and financing of establishments.

3. The diversification of post-secondary education should be guided by the following general principles and "key concepts":

(a) making an active contribution to cultural, socio-economic and technological development, promoting sustainable development, based on scientific foundations, while taking account of specific national features and of the cultural identity of each people;
(b) making a constructive contribution to defining the prospects for the development of post-secondary education and the ways in which it can be diversified in the light of humanity's common interests and of world problems, in the solution of which post-secondary education is able to play a positive role;
(c) ensuring a high standard of teaching, training and research, which should be regarded as a paramount task in the context of the rapid expansion of enrolment in post-secondary education;
(d) ensuring that all those who have the abilities required to accede to this level of education should enjoy equality of opportunity in equipping themselves for life, and more especially for professional life, and in participating in the various activities of society;
(e) promoting the self-fulfilment and harmonious development of the individual by providing the requisite conditions for his or her intellectual, moral, professional, spiritual, physical, aesthetic and social training;
(f) seeking to ensure a better match in both quantity and quality between the education provided and the ever-changing requirements of the employment situation;
(g) associating the different social and economic partners more closely in the effective operation and development of this level of education;
(h) stepping up the contribution of post-secondary education, particularly at university level, to the strengthening and extension of lifelong education;

(i) increasing the contribution of post-secondary education to the development of other levels and forms of education in the context of lifelong education, and particularly to training and research activities designed to bring about a massive reduction in illiteracy;

(j) encouraging universities and other higher education institutions to function also as centres for continuing individualized and distance education;

(k) promoting education for international understanding, co-operation and peace and education relating to human rights and fundamental freedoms;

(l) strengthening the culture and cultural identity of each country;

(m) contributing to the solving of the global problems facing society, and to the promotion of international intellectual co-operation;

(n) promoting teacher and student mobility at the international level.

B. Practical Measures and Programmes at National Level

4. The goals and functions of post-secondary education should be regularly reviewed with regard to their relevance to emerging social, economic and cultural needs and to technological changes. In view of the important changes in the composition of the student body and in order to keep pace with scientific and technological developments and the resulting transformation of the labour market, post-secondary educational institutions should adopt a more flexible and adaptable structure, related among other things to criteria for admission, duration of study, curricula, instructional methods, standards and methods of practical training.
5. Policies for post-secondary education in the 1990s should take into account developments extending into the year 2000 and beyond, which may entail drastic changes in the size and composition of the labour force and therefore have numerous implications for post-secondary education. Appropriate solutions should also be devised to counteract unemployment deriving from the applications of technology and the extensive automation of production and services, by offering wide access to lifelong education and retraining courses.

6. In taking decisions about the allocation of resources for post-secondary education and the distribution of these resources between different fields, sectors and institutions, due consideration should be given to long-term objectives in order to allow this education to respond to changing needs and fulfil its fundamental function in society.
7. At this level of education, it is essential not only to promote a more equitable sharing of education facilities among young people and working adults, but also to promote the extension of educational opportunities to outlying regions, to marginal, minority and disadvantaged groups and to handicapped persons, especially through local development programmes and organizations. Post-secondary education institutions should take the necessary measures to adjust to the increasing inflow of non-traditional students, such as adult part-time students, students of low socio-economic status, and working people in need of stimulation through refresher or upgrading courses or retraining. It is also necessary to respect the right of the populations of those territories still subject to foreign occupation to receive education adapted to their needs and to preserve their national and cultural identity.
8. In the expansion of post-secondary education, priority should be given in both teaching and research to those areas which are undergoing rapid development as a result of advances in science and technology, and to satisfying the labour and other essential needs of society.
9. In the context of national priorities, the orderly development of post-secondary education should be ensured through planning and through efforts at co-ordination and harmonization on the part of the public authorities. The coherence of the post-secondary system as a whole needs to be improved, particularly in so far as the universities and their relationships with the other institutions providing occupational training are concerned, in order to ensure that the different types of post-secondary education complement one another more effectively. For this purpose it may be appropriate to consider the creation of permanent co-ordinating arrangements.
10. Better co-ordination and greater continuity should be sought between secondary and post-secondary education. Measures will also need to be taken to increase the contribution of post-

secondary education to the other levels of education, particularly as regards the training of staff and the development of educational research.

11. The formulation of policies and strategies and the planning of the development of post-secondary education should entail a wide-ranging process of research, evaluation and consultation, involving, in addition to the authorities responsible for this level of education, the representatives of the different sectors of soico-economic life.
12. The planning of post-secondary education should if possible take into consideration forecasts of future labour requirements. It would be desirable to improve the quality of forecasting of highly skilled labour-force requirements; such information should be regularly made available to the authorities in charge of post-secondary education.
13. It is desirable to establish multidimensional criteria for admission to post-secondary education institutions. Such criteria should ensure equity, objectivity, comprehensiveness, and balance between individual interests and societal needs.
14. It is important that aptitudes required by the employment sector, in particular because of the use of computers and information technology, such as versatility and adaptability, a broad general and technological culture, the ability to work in a group, to communicate and co-operate, a sense of responsibility and initiative, an inclination for learning on one's own, and so on, should be developed in the specialists of tomorrow.
15. Curricula, textbooks and teaching and training methods should be regularly evaluated, revised and adjusted and new forms of university teaching explored so that they can be geared to the changes occurring in industrial, agricultural and social processes, and keep pace with the accelerating rate of scientific and technological progress and the resultant new developments in knowledge and know-how. To this end, it will be necessary, *inter alia*, to strike an optimal balance in each course or stream between general, theoretical and practical instruction and training, and to provide students with opportunities for practical training periods in enterprises and alternate periods of study and work. Interdisciplinary and multidisciplinary programmes should be encouraged. It is desirable that theoretical and practical training should be combined as far as possible with an introduction to

research work, and that the new technological options should be used to enable students to acquire knowledge by means of self-directed training.

16. It is important that post-secondary establishments should henceforth organize their courses in liaison with the professional communities. To this end, representatives of the economic and social sectors might be co-opted, as persons of note in the outside world, into the boards of such establishments, the committees of experts responsible for drawing up syllabuses, and if necessary, onto the juries responsible for end-of-course evaluation of students' performance.
17. It is desirable that post-secondary establishments should recruit specialists from the world of work and from research institutions as teachers, and that appropriate legislative measures be taken in order to encourage such an undertaking.
18. While efforts should be made to provide established teachers and trainers at post-secondary institutions, particularly the younger ones, with the best conditions and appropriate resources to carry out their work, opportunities should also be provided for them to retrain, to update their knowledge and to familiarize themselves with scientific and technological progress in the actual conditions prevailing in the production process. For this purpose, training courses should be promoted in enterprises and in research institutions for the benefit of teachers and trainers.
19. In the process of further developing policies and strategies of post-secondary education in general and of setting up new courses and new programmes in this field in particular, serious consideration should be given to the training and further training of teachers, educators and other educational personnel. The establishment of new institutions, courses and curricula should be accompanied by the provision of appropriately qualified teachers and auxiliary staff.
20. In order to ensure the more effective linking and dovetailing of education, training, production and research, appropriate measures should be introduced to facilitate the development of relations of co-operation between post-secondary establishments, enterprises and research institutions, such relations being mutually beneficial, particularly as far as the production, dissemination and utilization of knowledge are concerned. A better linkage should be encouraged between the problems of society

and research topics in higher education.

21. Material and financial resources for the appropriate development of infrastructures, laboratories, specialized facilities and libraries should be provided so that teachers and students remain motivated to promote education that is of a high standard. A larger contribution from the different socio-economic sectors would be desirable in this regard. In addition to the seeking of new sources of financing, particular attention should be given to rationalizing the processes of mustering, earmarking and using the resources that are available, as well as to the strengthening of international and regional co-operation for the production of low-cost equipment and supplies for educational and research institutions. The consolidation and modernization of existing institutions should be given precedence over the proliferation of new institutions.
22. For post-secondary education as a whole, it is important to preserve university autonomy and academic freedom, especially:

    freedom of education and scientific research;
    freedom of expression, association and publication;
    free access to all publications.

    Exercise of these freedoms should be in accordance with the International Covenant on Economic, Social and Cultural Rights and the International Covenant on Civil and Political Rights, adopted on 16 December 1966.
23. Changes in the roles and functions of higher education establishments call for major changes in their management. To this end, it is desirable to modernize the administration of post-secondary institutions in order to increase their effectiveness and their ability to employ new techniques and advanced equipment and methods which enable them to take sound decisions at the proper time. Efforts should be made to step up current research on the ways and means of making the management and administration of post-secondary education more efficient.
24. Diversification of post-secondary education, however welcome and timely, should in no way lead to the lowering of standards in post-secondary education and training. It is necessary, in particular, to be aware of the dangers of excessive fragmentation in the provision of professional training which could result from a

profusion of cheap, substandard courses claiming to meet the 'immediate needs' of career orientation. A warning should also be given about the possible risk of higher education becoming subject to undue pressure from business executives when it seeks financial support from industry.

25. In order effectively to combat unemployment and underemployment among graduates, it is essential that concerted action should be taken by all the partners concerned: government authorities, post-secondary education establishments, public and private enterprises and other bodies.
26. It is of fundamental importance, particularly in developing countries, that projects for industrial investment or other investment projects relating to post-secondary education and using new technology or involving the use of new scientific processes or equipment, should be evaluated carefully, prior to implementation, having particular regard to the conditions for the effective transfer of technology and scientific information, and to the investment programme's implications for training and employment.
27. It is important that the effectiveness of vocational guidance and information services should be improved. In particular, an effort should be made to improve information for students so as to direct them in a positive way towards the various branches of post-secondary education and help them in their choice. It is particularly desirable that specialized services should be organized with responsibility for ensuring that graduates find a place in professional life at the end of their period of training.
28. The rapidity with which knowledge and skills become obsolete demands that post-secondary education should provide various forms of recurrent and refresher education. Post-secondary establishments should offer all those who already possess a basic university diploma or professional qualification an opportunity to undertake refresher courses, specialized training or retraining, without needing to interrupt their professional activities for the purpose. They should give all who have reached the end of their professional career and all adults should have sufficient free time the chance to remain in touch with the world of science, new technologies and culture, so that they may continue to take an active part in the development of their society.
29. It is advisable to certify knowledge acquired in the course of refresher or continuing training so that those who have received it may, without discrimination, have the opportunity to improve

their position and mobility within the employment market on the basis of their new qualifications.

30. It is important that the links between post-secondary education and the community and society it serves should be strengthened, particularly in the following fields: (a) promotion of basic and applied research and consulting services; (b) participation in national development efforts; (c) extension of educational provision for adults in different forms; (d) participation in efforts to achieve the democratization of education, with special attention to disadvantaged groups; (e) improvement of students' practical training in enterprises; (f) the updating and continued improvement of the qualifications of post-secondary teaching staff.
31. At the research level, post-secondary institutions and, in particular, universities have an important role to play, being called upon to make a major contribution to the training of research workers. Since research, and particularly fundamental research, is often extremely costly, such institutions should pool their human and other resources for the purpose of carrying out co-operative projects.
32. Measures should be taken to avoid all forms of discrimination, including any distinction, exclusion, limitation or preference which, being based on race, colour, sex, language, religion, political or other opinion, national or social origin, economic condition or birth, has the purpose or effect of nullifying or impairing equality of treatment in education. To this end, it is essential to take appropriate measures to ensure that eligible students whose economic situation so requires are granted fellowships, loans or other forms of social and financial assistance. Special attention should be given to occupational training for women and girls. The enrolment of girls in scientific and technological courses should accordingly be encouraged. A larger place should also be given to the recruitment of women teachers at post-secondary level.
33. Distance education, correspondence courses and evening classes, as well as other forms of part-time post-secondary education, should be encouraged and diversified in order better to meet the educational and training requirements of the various population groups, in particular those of adult workers. Special attention should be paid to improving the quality of such education.
34. Post-secondary education should be concerned to make students aware of the major problems, both current and future, facing nations and the international community, such as violations of

human rights, the arms race, racism, the deterioration of the physical and natural environment and the cultural heritage, the persistence in a large part of the world of poverty, hunger, malnutrition, illiteracy, etc., and all forms of exploitation, and to stimulate in them the will to contribute effectively to the solution of these problems.

C. Regional and International Co-operation

35. In view of the growing importance of diversifying post-secondary education in response to the new employment situation, socio-economic change and the constant new challenges represented by advances in science and technology, a concerted regional and international approach is essential in order to enable Member-States to perform their task more effectively in developing and improving such education.
36. Member-States should take steps to foster the intellectual climate and material conditions necessary to favour the mobility of teachers, students, researchers and members of the learned professions, and to help overcome difficulties encountered by persons returning to their countries of origin after receiving education abroad.
37. Member-States should continue to strengthen and develop bilateral, regional and international co-operation in order to bring post-secondary education more closely into line with socio-economic requirements, and provide all necessary support to the centres of higher education set up by the United Nations and UNESCO, to the networks of inter-university co-operation for the continuing training of higher education staff and to the regional networks of educational innovation set up by UNESCO, in so far as the latter are concerned with post-secondary education.
38. In view of the diversity of the experience acquired, Member-States should initiate or develop, on a subregional, regional or interregional basis, the institutional co-operation that is essential if forms of diversification that are relevant to the solution of the problems of socio-economic development are to be implemented and strengthened.
39. The various centres of excellence in science and learning should be encouraged to find appropriate instruments for participation in actions aimed at reducing the research-technology gap between countries. The international co-operation of scientists should be

encouraged with a view to solving global human problem. It is imperative that scientists adopt a responsible attitude to their work, to the use of science in general and to enhancing its intrinsic humanistic goals.

40. As an international organization serving as a driving force in the areas of education and science, UNESCO should endeavour to:

(a) provide technical support for the design and implementation of policies and reforms relating to educational structures, courses and curricula, in order to pave the way for the diversification and improvement of the various forms of post-secondary education and, in this domain, to facilitate the exchange of information and experience among the different countries and to enhance educational innovation programmes and support networks in this field;

(b) take special note of the many serious problems facing developing countries in gaining access to science and technology, in introducing them into post-secondary education and training, in widening the spectrum of employment, and in making effective use of new technology;

(c) promote the exchange of administrators, teachers and students in the context of co-operation between Member-States and thereby encourage collaboration in research and training;

(d) encourage the more frequent granting of fellowships for further straining and short-term research courses for the benefit of the developing countries;

(e) take the necessary measures to promote the application of the regional conventions on the recognition of studies, diplomas and degrees in higher education adopted to update under the auspices of UNESCO.

41. UNESCO and, under its aegis, the IBE and the regional centres of higher education set up by the Organization, as well as specialized NGOs, should also endeavour to:

(a) provide all possible assistance, including negotiation of extra-budgetary resources, to enable developing countries to implement the policies and practical recommendations made by this Conference;

(b) increase the exchange, synthesis and dissemination of information and experience on post-secondary education, and promote co-operative projects with relevant partners at the national and regional levels;

(c) promote research and studies aimed at diversifying and improving post-secondary education, particularly with regard to the new procedures for recognition of academic achievement, work out criteria for assessment and create a data bank containing information on educational content at each stage for distribution among Member-States;

(d) within the framework of their documentation programmes give due prominence to post-secondary education, to projects for the reform, improvement and diversification of such education, and to all other relevant information in this field, analyse the data thereby collected and make such data available to Member-States;

(e) carry out activities to follow up the present Conference and advise Member-States, at their request, regarding ways and means of applying this Recommendation, having regard to the particular situation obtaining in each country.

42. The IBE, in co-operation with other UNESCO units, and in particular with the established offices away from Headquarters, especially the regional centres of higher education, and with the intergovernmental and non-governmental organizations concerned, will give even greater prominence to the production and dissemination of information relating to the diversification of post-secondary education systems and to making available the results of national experiments aimed at matching such education more closely to socio-economic needs. In the light of such information, and on the basis of the studies already carried out, the IBE will undertake comparative studies and studies focused on innovative experiments conducted in this field. With a view to improving communication and comparability of statistical information concerning the development of post-secondary education and its growing diversification, there is a need to update the International Standard Classification of Education, especially its third level.

43. The Director-General of UNESCO, when drawing up the third Medium-Term Plan, might study the desirability of including an interdisciplinary plan of action at the international level, possibly incorporating a UNESCO World programme on the development of post-secondary education aimed at improving its quality and

relevance, which would provide for the development of co-operation and for the study and satisfaction of the new demands made on secondary education by post-secondary training, including the creation and introduction of a concept of knowledge that is qualitatively higher, admits of a broader content linking cognitive with cultural aspects and in consonant with the prospects for the development of humanity in the context of the scientific information society now taking shape. UNESCO, with interested Member-States and international organizations, is urged to encourage the establishment of new machinery, structures and programmes of co-operation in the field of post-secondary education (similar to the project for the creation of a university of the peoples of Europe, for which the Fourth Conference of Ministers of Education of Member-States of the of Europe Region recommended that a feasibility study should be carried out) aimed at deepening the understanding of the common historical destiny of humanity and of the intrinsic value of the cultural diversity of peoples, and at pooling efforts to make use of the potential of education, science and post-secondary training in solving global and regional problems.

44. UNESCO, in co-operation with other international organizations, should strengthen activities concerning education for international understanding, co-operation and peace and education relating to human rights and fundamental freedoms, sustainable development and the protection of the environment. It should also promote in Member-States measures of an innovative nature aimed at establishing or redesigning post-secondary programmes for this purpose and at encouraging the revision and updating of textbooks and teaching aids to that end.

BIBLIOGRAPHY

UNESCO DOCUMENTS AND PUBLICATIONS*

Policy, Planning and Administration

1. *Annotated bibliography of recent literature on "employment and*

---

* Listing to illustrate the range of UNESCO documents and publications

education in the informal urban sector". Paris, UNESCO, 1977, 28 p.

2. *An Assessment of educational reform in India and lessons for the future* by J.P. Naik. Paris, UNESCO, 1980, 75 p.
3. *A Comprehensive view of long-term educational planning* by John Wood. Paris, UNESCO, 1986, 120 p.
4. *The Coordination of education policies and the integration of education plans with those for science, technology, culture and communication. (Reflections on method and an annotated bibliography)* by Hans Reiff and Qutub Khan. Paris, UNESCO, 1986, 79 p. (Introduction in French).
5. *The Coordination of education policies and plans with those in the fields of science, technology, culture and communication. A survey of experiences in countries of the Arab region* by Phyllis Kotite. Paris, UNESCO, 1986, 71 p. (Preface in French).
6. *The Coordination of educational policy and planning and employment policy and planning* by A. Little. Paris, UNESCO, 1984. Vol. I : A state of the art review, 48 p. Vol. II : An annotated bibliography, 126 p.
7. *The Democratization of education. Working document and final report* of an international symposium on the democratization of education. Paris, UNESCO, 1986, 48 p.
8. *Determinants and options in the development of higher education in Poland* by A. Josefowicz and J. Klucznski. Paris, UNESCO, 1980, 43 p.
9. *Directions of educational development in the developing countries* by S. Lingappa. Paris, UNESCO, 1979, 35 p.
10. *Directory of governmental bodies and institutions dealing with educational planning and administration*. Preliminary version. Paris, UNESCO, 1980, 337 p.
11. *Education and basic needs : views on concepts and measurement* by R. Carr-Hill. Paris, UNESCO, 1977, 40 p.
12. *Education and training policies in Sub-Saharan Africa*. Problems, guidelines and prospects. Paris, UNESCO, 1987, 120 p. + annexes. ED-87/WS/44.
13. *Education for all* by Wolfgang Mitter. (International yearbook of education), Vol. XXXVI. UNESCO/IBE, 1984, 153 p.
14. *Education in Barbados : development policies problems and prospects* by F.B Scott. Paris, UNESCO, 1980, 34 p.
15. *Education in the least developed countries – problems, priorities*

and programmes by S. Colton. Paris, UNESCO, 1983, 70 p.

16. *Educational development trends* by Brian Holmes. (International yearbook of education), Vol. XXXV. UNESCO/IBE, 1983, 232 p.
17. *Educational developments in Europe and North America since 1960* by D. Kallen and S. Colton. Paris, UNESCO, 1980.
18. *Educational employment: speculations for the future*. Paris, UNESCO, 1978. (Inf TUE series No. 4)
19. *Educational planning methodology for the integrated development of rural areas*. UNESCO/OREALC, 1980, 90 p.
20. *Educational policies and plans in Asia in the 1970's : summaries and synthesis* by EPP and the assistance of Mr. S. Lingappa. Paris, UNESCO, 1977, 87 p.
21. *Educational structures* by Robert Cowen. (International yearbook of education), Vol. XXXIV. UNESCO/IBE, 1982, 159 p.
22. *Fifth regional conference of ministers of education and those responsible for economic planning in Asia and the Pacific*. Bangkok, 4-11 March 1985. *Development of education in Asia and the Pacific*. Paris, UNESCO, 1985, 104 p. ED-85/MINEDAP/3. *Final report* Paris, UNESCO, 1985, 97 p. ED/MD/80.
23. *Fourth conference of ministers of education of Member-States of the Europe region*. Organized by UNESCO with the cooperation of the United Nations Economic Commission for Europe. Paris, 21-27 September 1988. *Prospects and tasks of educational development in Europe at the dawn of a new millennium*. Paris, UNESCO, 1988, 35 p. ED-88/MINEDEUROPE/3.
24. *Higher education and manpower planning – a comparative study of planned and market economies* by O Fulton, A. Gordon and G. Williams. Geneva, UNESCO/CEPES/ILO, 1982, 127 p. (WEP study).
25. *Information : an essential factor in educational planning and policy* by G. Psacharopoulos. Paris, UNESCO, 1980.
26. *Information in educational decision-making in Greece* by K. Kassimati. Paris, UNESCO, 1978, 10 p.
27. *Integrating educational and cultural planning. A synthesis of experiences in the Nordic counties* by Kjell Eide. Paris, UNESCO, 1986, 53 p.
28. *International cooperation in education in countries of Asia and the Pacific : objectives, statistical trends and prospects* by Peter

Herold *et al*. Paris, UNESCO 1983, 53 p.

29. *An Inventory of documents on educational planning and management in Asia and the Pacific* by Mellor Warren. UNESCO; ROEAP, 1984, 229 p.
30. *Investment in skills : a review of the relationship between the structures of small industry in developing countries and prevocational learning systems* by K. King. Paris, UNESCO, 1976, 20 p.
31. *Major quantitative developments in the field of education in the East-European socialist countries in the 1970's* by L.G. Menyalenko. Paris, UNESCO, 1981, 29 p.
32. *Meeting on the least developed countries needs and priorities in regard to education*. Paris, UNESCO, 1982, 74 p. (a. Working paper; b. International co-operation in education : a statistical analysis; c. Final report).
33. *Meeting of the multidisciplinary consultative panel on continued action to give effect to the lines of emphasis set out in the medium term plan*. Paris, UNESCO, 17-21 November 1986. *Final report*. Paris, UNESCO, 12 p. + annexes. ED-87/WS/4.
34. *Meeting of senior officials responsible for education in the Arab States*. Amman, Jordan, 22-26 June 1987. *Final report*. UNESCO/Mineduc Jordan. Paris, UNESCO, 1987, 41 p. ED-87/WS/39.
35. *Methods and techniques for the formulation of interdisciplinary plans and policies and the implementation of integrated programmes and projects in the educational sector* by Roy Carr-Hill. Paris, UNESCO, 1986, 91 p.
36. *Monitoring and the management of educational policy implementation – a theoretical approach* by R. Sack. Paris, UNESCO, 1985, 34 p.
36. *On the coordination of education policies and plans with those for science and technology. Part I : an overview. Part II : an annotated bibliography* by Dr. Thomas G. Whiston. Paris, UNESCO 1987, 156 p. ED-87/WS/3.
37. *Participatory planning in education : testing some concepts* by R. Carr-Hill. Paris, UNESCO, 1976, 117 p.
38. *Planning and management of the integrated development of formal and non-formal education : a review of the possibilities and difficulties* by W. Courtney and G. Kutsh. Paris, 1978, 72 p.
39. *Planning standards for higher education facilities. Examples*

from national practices by Y. Chahrouzi *et al*. Paris, UNESCO, 1979, 328 p.

40. *Policy, planning and administration of technical and vocational education in China*. Paris, UNESCO, 1987, 76 p. (Studies in technical and vocational education No. 29) ED-87/WS/48.
41. *Policy, planning and administration of technical and vocational education in Ghana*. Paris, UNESCO, 1984, 44 p. (Studies in technical and vocational education (STVE No. 4) ED-84/WS/44.
42. *Policy, planning and management of technical and vocational education in the Hashemite Kingdom of Jordon*. Paris, UNESCO, 1986, 121 p. (Studies in technical and vocational education No. 12) ED-86/WS/12.
43. *Policy, planning and administration of technical and vocational education in India*. Paris, UNESCO, 1985, 172 p. (STVE No. 8) ED-85/WS/18.
44. *Policy, planning and administration of technical and vocational education in the Netherlands*. Paris, UNESCO, 1984 (STVE No. 7) ED-84/WS/97.
45. *Policy, planning and management in technical and vocational education : a comparative study*. Paris, UNESCO, 1984 (Trends and issues in technical and vocational education No. 3).
46. *Population dynamics and educational planning (a focus on Asia)* by J.A. Johnston *et al*. Paper presented at the regional seminar of experts on population dynamics and educational planning, Bangkok, September 1973. Paris, UNESCO, 1973, 124 p.
47. *Reflection on the concept and practice of educational planning* by B. Kluchnikov. Paris, UNESCO, 1980, 52 p.
48. *Reflection on the future development of education. Trends and projections of enrolment by level of education and by age. World and regional aggregates 1960-2000*. 1981 assessment (Provisional). Paris, UNESCO, 1981, 45 p. + annexes.
49. *Regional conferences and educational development in Africa, Arab States, Asia and Latin America : Bombay 1952 - Mexico City 1979* by F.L. Bartels. Paris, UNESCO, 1983, 187 p.
50. *Regional conferences and educational development in Africa from the Addis Ababa conference 1961 to the Lagos conference 1976* by F.L. Bartels. Paris, UNESCO, 1983, 93 p.
51. *Red regional REPLAD. Actividades realizadas 1985-1986. Sugerencias sobre evaluacion* por C.R. Velasco B. UNESCO/OREALC, 1986, 119 p.

52. *The Role of information and research in educational decision-making : some questions.* Paper presented at the symposium on future programmes of information and communication in educational policy and planning, UNESCO, Paris, November 1977. Paris, UNESCO, 1977, 22 p.
53. *The Role of information in the decision-making process concerning the development of education in Poland* by J. Kluczynski and S. Kwiatowski. Paris, UNESCO, 1977, 24 p.
54. *School experiments in the Hungarian public education system.* Case study prepared by Eva Zsadon-Mayer. Paris, UNESCO, 1987, 12 p. (CODIESEE Doc. 2/87).
55. *Second meeting of the intergovernmental regional committee for the major project in the field of education in Latin America and the Caribbean.* Bogota, 24-28 March 1987. *Progress made, obstacles encountered and priorities for the future.* Paris, UNESCO, 1987, 60 p. ED-87/PROMEDLAC/3; (ii) Final Report. Paris, UNESCO, 1988, 72 p.
56. *Sixth regional conference of ministers of education and those responsible for economic planning of Member-States in Latin America and the Caribbean.* Bogota, 30 March-4 April 1987. *Education and the demands of socio-economic development, particularly scientific and technological development, in the context of the current economic situation of the region.* Paris, UNESCO, 1987, 45 p. ED-87/MINEDLAC/3.
57. *Socio-economic aspects of the democratization of education* by Traugott Schofthaler. Paris, UNESCO, 1986, 72 p.
58. *A Study of the participation of teachers, unions in educational planning/Etude sur la participation des syndicats d'enseignants a la planification de l'education* by Leslie C. Atherley and Francis L. Bartels. Paris, UNESCO, 1985, 151 p.
59. *A Survey of the evaluation methods and techniques of educational plans, programmes and projects within the framework of the implementation of education policies* by Qutub Uddin Khan. Paris, UNESCO, 1985, 44 p.
60. *Trends of educational policy in socialist countries* by J. Kluczynski. Paris, UNESCO, 1980, 54 p.
61. *The Use of information in the decision-making for educational development – experiences in : Bahrain, Bangladesh, Egypt, Ghana, Mexico* by H. Sylayti *et al.* Paris, UNESCO, 1977, 45 p.

Educational and Employment Planning

1. *Analytical study of the inter-relation between demographic technological and socio-cultural factors in the process of educational and employment planning in the Kazakh SSR* by Evgeny Zhiltsov *et al.* Paris, UNESCO, 1986, 75 p.
2. *Annotated bibliography of recent literature on employment and education in the informal sector.* Paris, UNESCO, 1977, 28 P.
3. *The coordination of educational policy and planning and employment policy and planning* Vol.1: *A State of the art review* by Angela Little. Paris, UNESCO, 1984, 48 p. Vol II: *An annotated bibliography* by Angela Little and Audrey Nunn. Paris, UNESCO, 1984, 126 p.
4. *Education and employment: a methodology for local policy research* by M. Carnoy, Paris, UNESCO, 1979, 31 p.
5. *Suggestions for policy regarding the integration of young people into working life* by William C. Bingham, Paris, UNESCO, 1987, 22 p.
6. *Technological occupational challenge, social transformation and educational response* by Edmund King. UNESCO/IBE, 1985, 366 p.

See also UNESCO series *Fundamentals of Educational Planning (UNESCO/IIEP)* (at the end of Section I)

10

LIFELONG EDUCATION: Learning to Be

INTERNATIONAL COMMISSION ON THE DEVELOPMENT OF EDUCATION, 1972

Introduction

In December 1970, by a resolution adopted at its 16th session, the General Conference of UNESCO authorized the Director-General to establish an International Commission on the Development of Education.

The Director-General appointed the Commission in February 1971, conferring its presidency to Mr Edgar Faure, a former French Prime Minister and Minister of Education, and calling on persons belonging to different cultural regions and particularly qualified by training and experience: Felipe Herrera (Chile), Professor, University of Chile, formerly President of the Inter-American Development Bank and Executive-Director of the International Monetary Fund; Abdul-Razzak Kaddoura (Syrian Arab Republic), visiting scientist at the Nuclear Physics Laboratory, Oxford University, and member of the Board of Governors of the United Nations International Atomic Energy Agency; Henri Lopes (People's Republic of the Congo), the then Minister of Education and thereafter Minister of Foreign Affairs; Arthur Vladmirovitch Petrovsky (USSR), Secretary of the Psychology and Physiology of Growth Section of the Academy of Pedagogical Sciences; Majid Rahnema (Iran), formerly Minister of Higher Education and Sciences and Vice-President of the United Nations Economic and Social Council; Frederick Champion Ward (United States), programme adviser on international education to the Ford Foundation and Former Dean at the University of Chicago.

The Commission submitted its report entitled *Learning to be – The World of, Education To-day and Tomorrow* to the Director-General in May 1972.

Twenty-one Principles and Recommendations

Sl. No.	*Principle*	*Recommendation*
1.	*Guiding principle for educational policies* Every individual must be in a position to keep learning throughout his life. The idea of lifelong education is the keystone of the learning society.	We propose lifelong education as the master concept for educational policies in the years to come for both developed and developing countries.
2.	*Over-all perspective* The dimensions of living experience must be restored to education by redistributing teaching in space and time.	Educational institutions and means must be multiplied, made more accessible, offer the individual a far more diversified choice. Education must assume the proportions of a true mass movement.
3.	*Less formalism in institutions* Education should be dispensed and acquired through a multiplicity of means. The important thing is not the path an individual has followed, but what he has learned or acquired.	Each person should be able to choose his path more freely, in a more flexible framework, without being compelled to give up using educational services for life if he leaves the system.
4.	*Mobility choice* An over-all open education system helps learners to move within it, both horizontally and vertically, and widens the range of choice available to them.	Artificial or outmoded barriers between different educational disciplines, courses and levels, and between formal and non-formal education should be abolished: recurrent education should be gradually introduced and made available in the first place to certain categories of the active population.
5.	*Pre-school education* The education of pre-school-age children is an essential pre-condition to any educational and cultural policy.	The development of education for pre-school-age children must become one of the major objectives for educational strategies in the 1970s.

Sl. No.	*Principle*	*Recommendation*
6.	*Basic education* All children must be guaranteed the practical possibility of receiving basic education, full-time if possible, in other forms if necessary.	Universal basic education, in a variety of forms depending on possibilities and needs, should be the top priority for educational policies in the 1970s.
7.	*Broadening general education* The concept of general education must be markedly broadened, so that it definitely includes general socio-economic, technical and practical knowledge.	Rigid distinctions between different types of teaching — general, scientific, technical and professional — must be dropped, and education, as from primary and secondary levels, must become theoretical, technological, practical and manual at the same time.
8.	*Maximum vocational mobility* Educational action to prepare for work and active life should aim less at training young people to practise a given trade or profession than at equipping them to adapt themselves to a variety of jobs, at developing their capacities continuously, in order to keep pace with developing production methods and working conditions. It should help to achieve optimum mobility in employment and facilitate conversion from one profession or branch of a profession to another.	Professional and technical training colleges must be developed in conjunction with the secondary education system. The instruction they give must be followed by practical training at places of work, all of which must, above all, be completed by recurrent education and vocational training courses.
9.	*Educational role of commerce and industry* Lifelong education, in the full sense of the term, means that business, industrial and agricultural firms will have extensive educational functions.	Efforts must be made to bridge the gap, still found in all too many cases, between educational establishments and business companies, whether privately or publically owned, for the latter constitute key element in the over-all education system. Their role should not be limited to training workers, but extended so far as possible to training technicians and researchers.
10.	*Variety in higher education* Expansion of higher education should lead to broad development of many institutions capable of meeting more	Throughout the post-secondary educational system, structures, subject-matter and student categories must be

Sl. No.	*Principle*	*Recommendation*
	and more individual and community needs.	very broadly diversified.
11.	*Selection criteria* Access to different types of education and professional employment should depend only on each individual's knowledge, capacities and aptitudes, and should not be a consequence of ranking knowledge acquired in school above or below experience gained during the practice of a profession or in private studies.	As educational systems become more diversified and as possibilities for entry, exit and re-entry increase, obtaining university degrees and diplomas should become less and less closely linked to completing a pre-determined course of study. Examinations should serve essentially as a means of comparing skills acquired under varying conditions by individuals of different origins, a mark not of a conclusion but of a starting-point, helping each individual to assess the effectiveness of his own study methods. Evaluation procedures should measure an individual's progress as much as the extent to which he conforms to externally fixed standards.
12.	*Adult education* The normal culmination of the education process is adult education.	Educational strategies in the coming decade should have rapid development of adult education, in school, and out of school, as one of their priority objectives.
13.	*Literacy* Literacy training is only a 'moment', and element, in adult education.	In all areas where there is widespread illiteracy, programmes organized for the adult population must include a strong literacy campaign. Action must be taken in two ways: it must aim firstly at functional literacy among strongly motivated sections of the working population and secondly at mass literacy when conditions are appropriate and, above all, when social development conditions — political, economic and cultural — are suitable for active large scale participation by the people.
14.	*Self-learning* The new educational ethos makes the individual the master and creator of his own cultural progress, self-learning,	Institutions and services of a new kind, intended to help people teach themselves — language laboratories,

Sl. No.	*Principle*	*Recommendation*
	especially assisted self-learning has irreplaceable value in any educational system.	technical training laboratories, information centres, libraries and related services, data banks, programmed and personalized teaching aids, audio-visual aids, etc. — should be integrated into all education systems.
15.	*Educational technology* The accelerating and multiplying effect of new techniques of reproduction and communication is most educational innovation.	1. In the conception and general planning of education systems, allowance must be made for the possible contribution of new techniques with a view to developing a unified process aimed at using available means and resources in the most efficient way. 2. When getting systems with technological support underway, strategies must be differentiated according to different levels of economic development.
16.	*Application of new techniques* Widespread and efficient use of new technologies in education is only possible if sufficient change takes place within the system itself.	1. Modify teacher-training programmes so that teachers are equipped for the different roles and functions imposed by new technologies. 2. Reserve a fixed part of the increase in education budgets for the rational development of sophisticated techniques.
17.	*Status of teachers* The teaching profession will not be in a position to fulfil its role in the future unless it is given, and develops itself, a structure better adapted to modern educational systems.	Legislative, professional, labour union and social action should gradually reduce and finally abolish hierarchical distinctions maintained for no valid reason among the various categories of teachers.
18.	*Teacher training* One of the essential tasks for educators at present is to change the mentalities and qualifications inherent in all professions; thus they should be first to be ready to rethink and change the criteria and basic situation of the teaching profession, in which the job of educating and stimulating students is steadily superseding that of simply giving instructions.	Conditions in which teachers are trained should be profoundly changed so that, essentially they become educators rather than specialists in transmitting pre-established curricula; the principle of a first, accelerated training stage, followed by in-service training cycles, should be adopted.

Sl. No. *Principle*	*Recommendation*
19. *Conventional and non-conventional educators*	
Education is developing continually to the point where it is becoming a function of the entire society; larger and larger sections of the population should therefore take part in it	Auxilliaries and specialists from other professions (workers, technicians, professional and executive personnel) should be called in to work beside professional teachers. Authorities should also enlist the co-operation of pupils and students, in such a way that they teach themselves while instructing others and become imbued with the idea that acquiring an 'intellectual capital' involves its possessor in the duty of sharing it with others.
20. *Learner's place in school life*	
Teaching, contrary to traditional ideas and practice, should adapt itself to the learner; the learner should not have to bow to pre-established rules for teaching.	It should be made a principle to centre educational activity on the learner, to allow him greater and greater freedom, as he matures, to decide for himself what he wants to learn, and how and where he wants to learn it and take his training. Even if the learner has to accept certain pedagogic and socio-cultural obligations as to subject-matter and methods these should still be defined more in terms of free choice, of psychological propensities and drives among learners than hitherto.
21. *Learner's responsibilities*	
Any system according educational services to a passive population and any reform which fails to arouse active personal participation among the mass of learners can achieve at best only marginal success.	All learners, whether young or adult, should be able to play a responsible part not only in their own education but in the entire educational enterprise.

BIBLIOGRAPHY

UNESCO DOCUMENTS AND PUBLICATIONS*

1. *Comprehensive, diversified and flexible educational structures in the context of lifelong education. A comparative analysis of four case studies* by Wolfgang Mitter. Paris, UNESCO, 1982, 89 p.

* Listing to illustrate the range of UNESCO documents and publications.

2. *Democratization and evaluation* by Joseph Nagy. Paris, UNESCO, 1984, 32 p. + references. ED-84/WS/57.
3. *Directory of writers on lifelong education* prepared by Ursula Giere and Yasushi Maehira. UNESCO/UIE, 1980, 62 p.
4. *Education and employment.* Bulletin of the IBE. Educational documentation and information. Paris, UNESCO/IBE, 1986, 183 p.
5. *The Interaction between education and productive work.* Bulletin of the IBE. Educational documentation and information. UNESCO/IBE, 1982, 112 p.
6. *International meeting of experts on the implementation of lifelong education principles in Member-States : statement and prospects*. UNESCO/UIE, 2-6 May 1983, 63 p.
7. *Lifelong education and community learning : three case studies in India* by V. Patel and N.N. Shukla, edited by W. van Vliet. UNESCO/UIE, 1978, 46 p.
8. *Lifelong education and the preparation of educational personnel* by James Lynch. UNESCO/UIE, 1977, 123 p. (UIE monograph No. 5).
9. *Lifelong education and the school* by R.H. Dave and N. Stiemerling. UNESCO/UIE, 1973, 154 p.
10. *Lifelong education and school curriculum* by R.H. Dave. UNESCO/UIE, 1973, 92 p.
11. *Lifelong education bibliography* compiled by Ursula Giere. UNESCO/UIE, 1986, 5 p.
12. *Lifelong education, schools and curricula in developing countries* by H.W.R. Hawes. UNESCO/UIE, 1975, 110 p. (UIE monograph No. 4).
13. *Lifelong education : a stocktaking* edited by A.J. Cropley with contributions by A.J. Cropley, E. Gelpi, P. Lengrand, A. Pfluger, K. Richmond, A.K. Stock and B. Suchodoslki. UNESCO/UIE, 1979, 115 p.
14. *Lifelong teacher education and the community school* by Linda A. Dove. UNESCO/UIE, 1982, 147 p.
15. *Permanent education and creativity* by Bogdan Suchodelski with *Creativity as a practical philosophy* J. Kuczynski. Paris, UNESCO, 1982, 268p. ED-82/WS/16.
16. *Reflections on lifelong education and the school* edited by R.H. Dave. UNESCO/UIE, 1979, 80 p.
17. *School curriculum in the context of lifelong learning* by Uwe Hameyer. UNESCO/UIE, 1979, 112 p.

18. *Spanish educational reform and lifelong education* by R. Diez Hochleitner, J. Tena Artigas and Marcelino Garcia Cuerpo. Paris, UNESCO, 1978, 112 p. (Experiments and innovations in education No. 31, IBE/UIE).
19. *Towards lifelong education : a new role for higher education institutions* by Gareth Williams. Paris, UNESCO, 1977, 188 p. (The development of higher education).
20. *Travail manuel, travail intellectual et education* par Antonio Carbonaro. Paris, UNESCO, 1986. Ed-86/WS/8.

See also UNESCO series *Education on the move; UIE studies on post-literacy and continuing education and UIE monographs* (UNESCO Institute for Education, Hamburg).

11

EDUCATION FOR INTERNATIONAL UNDERSTANDING, PEACE, HUMAN RIGHTS AND FUNDAMENTAL FREEDOMS

UNESCO GENERAL CONFERENCE RECOMMENDATION, 1974

The General Conference of the United Nations Educational, Scientific and Cultural Organization, meeting in Paris from October 17 to November 23, 1974, at its 18th session.

Mindful of the responsibility incumbent on States to achieve through education the aims set forth in the character of the United Nations, the Constitution of UNESCO, the Universal Declaration of Human Rights and the Geneva Conventions for the Protection of Victims of War of August 12, 1949, in order to promote international understanding, co-operation and peace and respect for human rights and fundamental freedoms,

Reaffirming the responsibility which is incumbent on UNESCO to encourage and support in Member-States any activity designed to ensure the education of all for the advancement of justice, freedom, human rights and peace,

Noting nevertheless that the activity of UNESCO and of its Member-States sometimes has an impact only on a small minority of the steadily growing numbers of school children, students, young people and adults continuing their education, and educators, and that the curricula and methods of international education are not always attuned to the needs and aspirations of the participating young people and adults,

Noting moreover that in a number of cases there is still a wide disparity between proclaimed ideals, declared intentions and the actual situation,

Having decided, at its seventeenth session, that this education should be the subject of a recommendation to Member-States,

Adopts this nineteenth day of November 1974, the present recommendation.

The General Conference recommends that Member-States should apply the following provisions by taking whatever legislative or other steps may be required in conformity with the constitutional practice of each State to give effect within their respective territories to the principles set forth in this recommendation.

I. Significance of Terms

1. For the purpose of this recommendation:

(a) The word "education" implies the entire process of social life by means of which individuals and social groups learn to develop consciously within, and for the benefit of the national and international communities, the whole of their personal capacities, attitudes, aptitudes and knowledge. The process is not limited to any specific activity.

(b) The terms "international understanding", "co-operation" and "peace" are to be considered as an indivisible whole based on the principle of friendly relations between peoples and States having different social and political systems and on the respect for human rights and fundamental freedoms. In the context of this recommendation, different connotations of these terms are sometimes gathered together in a concise expression, "international education".

(c) "Human rights" and "fundamental freedoms" are those defined in the United Nations Charter, the Universal Declaration of Human Rights and the International Covenants on Economic, Social and Cultural Rights, and on Civil and Political Rights.

II. Scope

2. This recommendation applies to all stages of education.

III. Guiding Principles

3. Education should be infused with the aims and purposes set forth in the Charter of the United Nations, the Constitution of UNESCO and the Universal Declaration of Human Rights, particularly Article 26, paragraph 2, of the last named, which states: "Education shall be directed to the full development of the human personality and to the strengthening of respect for human rights and fundamental freedoms. It shall promote understanding, tolerance and friendship among all nations, racial or religious groups, and shall further the activities of the United Nations for the maintenance of peace."
4. In order to enable every person to contribute actively to the fulfilment of the aims referred to in paragraph 3, and promote international solidarity and co-operation, which are necessary in solving the world problems affecting the individuals' and communities' life and exercise of fundamental rights and freedoms, the following objectives should be regarded as major guiding principles of educational policy:

   a. an international dimension and a global perspective in education at all levels and in all its forms;
   b. understanding and respect for all peoples, their cultures, civilizations, values and ways of life, including domestic ethnic cultures and cultures of other nations;
   c. awareness of the increasing global interdependence between peoples and nations;
   d. abilities to communicate with others;
   e. awareness not only of the rights but also of the duties incumbent upon individuals, social groups and nations, towards each other;
   f. understanding of the necessity for international solidarity and co-operation;
   g. readiness on the part of the individual to participate in solving the problems of his community, his country and the world at large.
5. Combining learning, training, information and action, international education should further the appropriate intellectual and emotional development of the individual. It should develop a sense of social responsibility and of solidarity with less privileged

groups and should lead to observance of the principles of equality in everyday conduct. It should also help to develop qualities, aptitudes and abilities which enable the individual to acquire a critical understanding of problems at the national and international levels; to understand and explain facts, opinions and ideas to work in a group; to accept and participate in free discussions; to observe the elementary rules of procedures applicable to any discussion; and to base value-judgements and decisions on a rational analysis of relevant facts and figures.

6. Education should stress the inadmissibility of recourse to war for purposes of expansion, aggression and domination, or to the use of force and violence for purposes of repression, and should bring every person to understand and assume his or her responsibilities for the maintenance of peace. It should contribute to international understanding and strengthening of world peace and to the activities in the struggle against colonialism and neo-colonialism in all forms and manifestations, and against all forms and varieties of racialism and apartheid as well as other ideologies which breed national and racial hatred and which are contrary to the purposes of this recommendation.

IV. National Policy, Planning and Administration

7. Each Member-State should formulate and apply national policies aimed at increasing the efficacy of education in all its forms and strengthening its contribution to international understanding and co-operation, to the maintenance and development of a just peace, to the establishment of social justice, to respect for and application of human rights and fundamental freedoms, and to the eradication of the prejudices, misconceptions, inequalities and all forms of injustice which hinder the achievement of these aims.
8. Member States should, in collaboration with the National Commissions for UNESCO, take steps to create co-operation between ministries and departments and co-ordination of their efforts to plan and carry out concerted programmes of action in international education.
9. Member-States should provide, consistent with their constitutional provisions, the financial, administrative, material and moral support necessary to implement this recommendation.

V. Particular Aspects of Learning, Training and Action

Ethical and Civic Aspects

10. Member-States should take appropriate steps to strengthen and develop, in the process of learning and training, attitudes and behaviour based on recognition of the equality and necessary interdependence of the nations and peoples.
11. Member-States should take steps to ensure that the principles of the Universal Declaration of Human Rights and of the International Convention of the Elimination of All Forms of Racial Discrimination become an integral part of the developing person or adult by applying these principles in the daily conduct of education at each level and in all its forms, thus enabling each individual to contribute personally to the regeneration and extension of education in the direction indicated.
12. Member-States should urge educators, in collaboration with pupils, parents, the organizations concerned and the community, to use methods which appeal to the creative imagination of children and adolescents and to their social activities and thereby to prepare them to exercise their rights and freedoms while recognizing and respecting the rights of others and to perform their social duties.
13. Member-States should promote, at every stage of education, an active civic training which will enable every person to gain a knowledge of the method of operation and the work of public institutions, whether local, national or international, to become acquainted with the procedures for solving fundamental problems, and to participate in the cultural life of the community and in public affairs. Where possible, this participation should increasingly link education and action to solve problems at the local, national and international levels.
14. Education should include critical analysis of the historical and contemporary factors of an economic and political nature underlying the contradictions and tensions between countries together with study of ways of overcoming these contradictions, which are the real impediments to understanding, true international cooperation and the development of world peace.
15. Education should emphasize the true interests of peoples and their incompatibility with the interests of monopolistic groups holding

economic and political power, which practise exploitation and foment war.

16. Student participation in the organization of studies and of the educational establishment they are attending should itself be considered in factor a civic education and an important element in international education.

Cultural Aspects

17. Member-States should promote, at various stages and in various types of education, study of different cultures, their reciprocal influences, their perspectives and ways of life, in order to encourage mutual appreciation of the differences between them. Such study should, among other things, give due importance to the teaching of foreign languages, civilizations and cultural heritage as a means of promoting international and inter-cultural understanding.

Study of the Major Problems of Mankind

18. Education should be directed both towards the eradication of conditions which perpetuate and aggravate major problems affecting human survival and well-being, inequality, injustice, international relations based on the use of force and towards measures of international co-operation likely to help solve them. Education which in this respect must necessarily be of an interdisciplinary nature should relate to such problems as:

    a. equality of rights of peoples, and the right of peoples to self-determination;
    b. the maintenance of peace; different types of war and their causes and effects; disarmament; inadmissibility of using science and technology for war-like purposes and their use for the purposes of peace and progress; nature and effect of economic, cultural and political relations between countries; and importance of international law for these relations, particularly for the maintenance of peace;
    c. action to ensure the exercise and observance of human rights, including those of refugees; racialism and its eradication; the fight against discrimination in its various forms;

d. economic growth and social development and their relation to social justice; colonialism and decolonization; ways and means of assisting developing countries; struggle against illiteracy; campaign against disease and famine; fight for a better equality of life and the highest attainable standard of health; population growth and related questions;
e. use, management and conservation of natural resources, pollution of the environment;
f. preservation of the cultural heritage of mankind;
g. role and methods of action of the United Nations as a system in efforts to solve such problems and possibilities for strengthening and furthering its action.

19. Steps should be taken to develop the study of those sciences and disciplines which are directly related to the exercise of the increasingly varied duties and responsibilities involved in international relations.

Other Aspects

20. Member-States should encourage educational authorities and educators to give education, planned in accordance with this recommendation an, interdisciplinary, problem-oriented content adapted to the complexity of the issues involved in the application of human rights and in international co-operation, and in itself illustrating the ideas of reciprocal influence, mutual support and solidarity. Such programmes should be based on adequate research, experimentation and identification of specific educational objectives.
21. Member-States should endeavour to ensure that international educational activity is granted special attention and resources when it is carried out in situations involving particularly delicate or explosive social problems in relations, for example, where there are obvious inequalities in opportunities for access to education.

VI. Action in Various Sectors of Education

22. Increased efforts should be made to develop and infuse an international and inter-cultural dimension at all stages and in all forms

of education.

23. Member States should take advantage of the experience of the Associated Schools which carry out, with UNESCO's help, programmes of international education. Those concerned with Associated Schools in Member-States should strengthen and renew their efforts to extend the programme to other educational institutions and work towards the general application of its results. In other Member-States, similar action should be undertaken as soon as possible. The experience of other educational institutions which have carried out successful programmes of international education should also be studied and disseminated.
24. As pre-school education develops, Member-States should encourage activities which correspond to the purposes of the recommendation because fundamental attitudes, such as for example, attitudes on race, are often formed in the pre-school years, in this respect, the attitude of parents should be deemed to be an essential factor for the education of children, and the adult education referred to in paragraph 30 should pay special attention to the preparation of parents for their role in pre-school education. The first school should be designed and organized as a social environment having its own character and value, in which various situations, including games, will enable children to become aware of their rights, to assert themselves freely while accepting their responsibilities, and to improve and extend through direct experience their sense of belonging to larger and larger communities—the family, the school, then the local, national and world communities.
25. Member-States should urge the authorities concerned, as well as teachers and students, to re-examine periodically how post-secondary and university education should be improved so that it may contribute more fully to the attainment of the objectives of this recommendation.
26. Higher education should comprise civic training and learning activities for all students that will sharpen their knowledge of the major problems which they should help to solve, provide them with possibilities for direct and continuous action aimed at the solution of those problems, and improve their sense of international co-operation.
27. As post-secondary educational establishments, particularly universities, serve growing numbers of people, they should carry

out programmes of international education as part of their broadened function in life-long education and should, in all means of communication available to them, provide opportunities, facilities for learning and activities adapted to people's real interests, problems, and aspirations.

28. In order to develop the study and practice of international co-operation, post-secondary educational establishments should systematically take advantage of the forms of international action inherent in their role, such as visits from foreign professors and students and professional co-operation between professors and experimental work should be carried out on the linguistic, social, emotional and cultural obstacles, tensions, attitudes and actions which affect both foreign students and host establishments.
29. Every stage of specialized vocational training should include training to enable students to understand their role and the role of their professions in developing their society, furthering international co-operation, maintaining and developing peace, and to assume their role actively as early as possible.
30. Whatever the aims and forms of out-of-school education, including adult education, they should be based on the following considerations:

   a. as far as possible a global approach should be applied in all out-of-school education programmes which should comprise the appropriate moral, civic, cultural, scientific and technical elements of international education;
   b. all the parties concerned should combine efforts to adapt and use the mass media of communication, self-education and inter-active learning, and such institutions as museums and public libraries to convey relevant knowledge to the individual to faster in him or her favourable attitudes and a willingness to take positive action, and to spread knowledge and understanding of the educational campaigns and programmes planned in accordance with the objectives of this recommendation;
   c. the parties concerned, whether public or private, should endeavour to take full advantage of favourable situations and opportunities, such as the social and cultural centres, community centres or trade unions, youth gatherings and festivals, sporting events, contacts with foreign visitors, students for

immigrants and exchanges of persons in general.

31. Steps should be taken to assist the establishment and development of such organizations as student and teacher associations for the United Nations, International Relations Clubs and UNESCO Clubs, which should be associated with the preparation and implementation of co-ordinated programmes of international education.
32. Member-States should endeavour to ensure that, at each stage of school and out-of-school education, activities directed towards the objectives of this recommendation be co-ordinated and form a coherent whole within the curricula for the different levels and types of education, learning and training. The principles of co-operation and association which are inherent in this recommendation should be applied in all educational activities.

VII. Teacher Preparation

33. Member-States should constantly improve the ways and means of preparing and certifying teachers and other educational personnel for their role in pursuing the objectives of this recommendation and should, to this end:

   a. provide teachers with motivations for their subsequent work commitment to the ethics of human rights and to the aim of changing society, so that human rights are applied in practice; a grasp of the fundamental unity of mankind; ability to instil appreciation of the riches which the diversity of cultures can bestow on every individual, group or nation;
   b. provide basic interdisciplinary knowledge of world problems and the problems of international co-operation, through, among other means, work to solve these problems;
   c. prepare teachers themselves to take an active part in devising programmes of international education and educational equipment and materials, taking into account the aspirations of pupils and working in close collaboration with them;
   d. comprise experiments in the use of active methods of education and training in at least elementary techniques of evaluation, particularly those applicable to the social behaviour and attitudes of children, adolescents and adults;

e. develop aptitudes and skills such as a desire and ability to make educational innovations and to continue his or her training: experience in teamwork and in interdisciplinary studies; knowledge of group dynamics; and the ability to make educational innovations and to continue his or her training; experience in teamwork and in interdisciplinary studies; knowledge of group dynamics; and the ability to create favourable opportunities and take advantage of them.

f. include the study of experiments in international education, especially innovative experiments carried out in other countries, and provide those concerned, to the fullest possible extent, with opportunities for making direct contact with foreign teachers.

34. Member-States should provide those concerned with direction, supervision or guidance for instance, inspectors, educational advisers, principals of teacher-training colleges and organizers of educational activities for young people and adults—with training, information and advice enabling them to help teachers work towards the objectives of this recommendation, taking into account the aspirations of young people with regard to international problems and new educational methods that are likely to improve prospects for fulfilling these aspirations. For these purposes, seminars or refresher courses relating to international and intercultural education should be organized to bring together authorities and teachers; other seminars or courses might permit supervisory personnel and teachers to meet with other groups concerned such as parents, students, and teachers' associations. Since there must be a gradual but profound change in the role of education, the results of experiments for the remodelling of structures and hierarchical relations in educational establishments should be reflected in training, information and advice.

35. Member-States should endeavour to ensure that any programme of further training for teachers in service or for personnel responsible for direction includes components of international education.

36. Member-States should encourage and facilitate educational study and refresher courses abroad, particularly by awarding fellowships, and should encourage recognition of such courses as part of the regular process of initial training, appointment, refresher

training and promotion of teachers.

37. Member-States should organize or assist bilateral exchange of teachers at all levels of education.

VIII. Educational Equipment and Materials

38. Member-States should increase their efforts to facilitate the renewal, production, dissemination and exchange of equipment and materials for international education, giving special consideration to the fact that in many countries pupils and students receive most of their knowledge about international affairs through the mass media outside the school. To meet the needs expressed by those concerned with international education, efforts should be concentrated on overcoming the lack of teaching aids in improving their quality. Action should be on the following lines:

   a. appropriate and constructive use should be made of the entire range of equipment and aids available, from textbooks to televisions and of the new educational technology;
   b. there should be a component of special mass media education in teaching to help the pupils to select and analyse the information conveyed by mass media;
   c. a global approach, comprising the introduction of international components, serving as a framework for presenting local and national aspects of different subjects and illustrating the scientific and cultural history of mankind, should be employed in textbooks and all other aids to learning, with due regard to the value of the visual arts and music as factors conducive to understanding between different cultures;
   d. written and audio-visual materials of an interdisciplinary nature illustrating the major problems confronting mankind and showing in each case the need for international co-operation, and its practical form should be prepared in the language or languages of instruction of the country with the aid of information supplied by the United Nations, UNESCO and other specialized Agencies;
   e. documents and other materials illustrating the culture and the way of life of each country, the chief problems with which it is faced, and its participation in activities of worldwide concern should be prepared and communicated to other countries.

39. Member-State should promote appropriate measures to ensure that educational aids, especially textbooks, are free from elements liable to give rise to misunderstanding, mistrust, racialist reactions, contempt or hatred with regard to other groups or peoples. Materials should provide a broad background of knowledge which would help learners to evaluate information and ideas disseminated through the mass media that seem to run counter to the aims of this recommendation.
40. According to its needs and possibilities, each Member-State should establish or help to establish one or more documentation centres offering written and audio-visual material devised according to the objectives of this recommendation and adapted to the different forms and stages of education. These centres should be designed to foster the reform of international education, especially by developing and disseminating innovative ideas and materials, and should also organize and facilitate exchanges of information wiih other countries.

IX. Research and Experimentation

41. Member-States should stimulate and support research on the foundations, guiding principles, means of implementation and effects of international education and on innovations and experimental activities in this field, such as those taking place in the Associated Schools. This action calls for collaboration by universities, research bodies and centres, teacher-training in situations, adult education training centres and appropriate non-governmental organizations.
42. Member-States should take appropriate steps to ensure that teachers and the various authorities concerned build international education on a sound psychological and sociological basis by applying the results of research carried out in each country on the formation and development of favourable or unfavourable attitudes and behaviour, on attitude change, on the interaction of personality development and education and on the positive or negative effects of educational activity. A substantial part of this research should be devoted to the aspirations of young people concerning international problems and relations.

X. International Co-operation

43. Member-States should consider international co-operation a responsibility in developing international education. In the implementation of this recommendation they should refrain from intervening in matters which are essentially within the domestic jurisdiction of any State in accordance with the United Nations Charter. By their own actions, they should demonstrate that implementing this recommendation is itself an exercise in international understanding and co-operation. They should, for example, organize, or help the appropriate authority and non-governmental organizations to organize, an increasing number of international meetings and study sessions on international education; strengthen their programmes for the reception of foreign students, research workers, teachers and educators belonging to workers, teachers' associations and promote reciprocal visits by school children, and student and teacher exchanges; extend and intensify exchanges of information on cultures and ways of life; arrange for the translation or adaptation and dissemination of information and suggestions coming from other countries.
44. Member-States should encourage the co-operation between their Associated Schools and those of other countries with the help of UNESCO in order to promote mutual benefits by expanding their experiences in a wider international perspective.
45. Member-States should encourage wider exchanges of textbooks, especially history and geography textbooks, and should, where appropriate, take measures by concluding, if possible, bilateral and multilateral agreements.

MEETING OF EXPERTS TO CONSIDER IMPLEMENTATION OF UNESCO RECOMMENDATION (1974), 1976

Introduction

A group of 13 experts met at UNESCO House on 15 to 19 March, 1976 to consider ways of implementing the recommendation concerning Education for International Understanding, Co-operation and Peace and Education Relating to Human Rights and Fundamental Freedom, adopted by the general conference at its eighteenth session.

The meeting was convened by the Director-General in pursuance of resolution 1.26 adopted by the General Conference at its eighteenth session in November 1974. The experts came from 13 Member-States and participated in a private capacity. Also attending were four observers, two beneficiaries of UNESCO fellowships awarded in the framework of the Associate Schools Project and an auditor.

Terminology

The phrase "international education" should be considered to embrace the entire range of the Recommendation's concerns and to cover as well the meanings associated with such terms as "development education" and "global education" which have come into use in recent years. It would be advantageous if "international education" or its equivalent in other languages could be used in the sense in all Member-States.

Some factors bearing on implementation. Certain general conditions or circumstances may favour or impede application of the Recommendation. National policy, as represented by, for example, a nation's constitution and educational legislation, obviously will have direct and important effects on implementation of the Recommendation. In some Member-States, national policy reflects principles that are set out in the Recommendation and this will favour its implementation. Of prime importance for the development of international education are equality of educational opportunity for all, regardless of race or national origin, sex, religion, social or marital status; free and compulsory understood and used by students, as a humanistic approach in education.

Implementation of the Recommendation will stand a greater chance of success when policy-making and policy-implementing agencies and institutions have dovetailed their planning strategies, so that government departments, National Commissions for UNESCO, regional or state, educational authorities, teacher-training institutions, teachers' associations, schools and school services, non-governmental organizations, labour unions, the mass media and religious institutions are involved in co-operative interrelated ventures.

Among the obstacles to international understanding and realization of the principles of human rights are such problems as those mentioned in paragraph 6 of the Recommendation: war for purposes of expansion, aggression and domination; colonialism and neo-colonialism, racialism, fascism, apartheid and ideologies which breed national and racial hatred. International education, as is stated in the Recommendation itself, should contribute to the struggle against these evils. The need for international solidarity in solving such problems should be stressed, and due attention should be given to recent and current international action to deal with them, such as, for example, relevant resolutions adopted by the United Nations and other international organizations, including those on peace, human rights, the economic rights and duties of States, the new international economic order, and racialism; progress in peaceful coexistence and *detente*; new proposals on disarmanent; the Helsinki Conference on European Security and Cooperation and other significant events in the domain of international relations.

International education can be developed in different ways. For example, in some countries — perhaps especially newly-independent countries emerging from colonial domination — there is a need to strengthen the sense of national identity and unity. Emphasis must therefore be placed on education concerning national, social and political structures, culture and history. Just the opposite may be true in other countries. One aim may be to foster communication and mutual respect between different cultural groups of the nation. The study of local and national problems can lead on to an examination of the international dimensions of the same or similar questions. It is important in any case that international education should be linked to community issues and national realities.

The weakness of international education in many countries and the difficulties of reinforcing it within the existing structures and the programmes indicate that fully effective application of the Recommendation may in numerous instances depend upon overall educational reforms.

I. Pre-primary, Primary and Secondary Education

General Observations

1. The effectiveness of international education in promoting international understanding, co-operation, peace and human rights derives to a large extent from the climate of life in the school. It should be conducive to the growth of understanding and respect for all peoples; a greater sense of responsibility toward less

privileged groups of people or countries; a conviction that it is necessary to ensure equal rights for all; the acquisition of analytic skills needed for problem solving and rational decision-making; active participation in the affairs of school and society; and a spirit of co-operation.

2. The objectives of international education should permeate the entire curriculum and not merely form part of one or two courses in the field of history and civic education, as has often been the case. All disciplines, including mathematics, science and physics, as well as many combinations of disciplines; can make a significant contribution. The possibilities of such contributions should be assessed with a view to furthering the aims of the Recommendation. It is important to employ appropriate teaching methods and techniques (such as problem-oriented approaches, group dynamics, etc.) which will help students understand the world around them. In addition, if the school is to prepare students to assume their responsibilities at the local, national and international levels, it should provide them with opportunities for active participation through such means as free discussion in the classroom and active involvement in improving the well-being of the school and the community.
3. Many teachers are concerned about the possible conflict between the notion of solidarity, which is an essential factor in cultivating the spirit of international understanding, and that of competition, which is inherent in the examination system on which most school programmes are based. Examinations are still often the only means used to evaluate student's knowledge and progress. Consequently, teachers, students and parents tend to consider any learning activity which is not subject to examination as being irrelevant or of low priority. For this reason many educators feel that international education will be furthered if its subject-matter is included in examination, particularly those leading to certificates, diplomas and degrees.
4. It has been observed that there is sometimes an imbalance in the proportion of men and women teachers at the various levels of education. In many instances most teachers at the primary level are women and at the secondary and higher level are men. This situation may have undesirable effects. For example, it may strengthen among children stereotyped ideas about the respective roles of men and women in society. In addition, psychological

problems may be generated in some children who are almost exclusively in contact with women and their values in the early stages of life and education and with men and their values at later stages. International education and education in general would benefit from a balanced distribution of men and women teachers at all levels.

5. The quality of the home/school relationship is of great significance for international education. Efforts should be made to ensure that it is a positive relationship in which parents might develop an interest in the aims of international education through the experience of their children. Ways should be sought to strengthen parental participation in school programmes of international education.
6. International questions should be dealt with in a spirit of realism. In teaching about the United Nations and its specialized agencies, for example, the limitations as well as the strengths of these international organizations should be examined objectively. Over-idealization often leads to exaggerated expectations and ultimately, when such expectations are inevitably disappointed, to disillusionment with these institutions and their efforts. Particular problems in this respect should be firmly based on factual knowledge and real situations and which should call into play a variety of analytical skills.
7. Another area which deserves special attention is that of education for peace. Although in some countries it is an integral part of school programmes and presents no special problems, in others it has been observed that students are uncertain about the concept of peace. Their images of war, on the other hand, are specific and concrete. In these instances it is necessary to develop teaching methods which will make the meaning of peace clear and vivid. In particular, ways should be found to convey effectively that the goal to be attained is not merely an avoidance of war but rather the achievement of a just and universal peace based on recognition of the equal rights of nations and peoples.
8. The teaching of modern languages can be especially important in international education. In addition to the teaching of the mother-tongue, more schools should provide students with the opportunity to learn one or more languages, particularly languages of wide international communication. Language courses should be designed not only to develop proficiency in linguistic

skills but also to provide a broader knowledge and understanding of the traditions, culture and way of life of the peoples whose language is being studied.

9. Much interesting and effective work is already being done in international education. In a great many countries, however, only a minority of students, teachers, lecturers, inspectors and administrators are involved. There may be a risk that this minority may become a separate "in-group" practising its own form of elitism, with a widening gap between it and an indifferent or even hostile majority. A possible further difficulty is to determine what even such a minority can be expected to accomplish within an educational system which may stress, or even over-stress, the acquisition of knowledge and other skills leading to diplomas or other certification, and which is itself but one part of a society conditioned by the interplay of economic, environmental and political forces. The attitude of students, teachers and parents may be that anything which does not help the student through examinations and improve his employment prospects is a waste of time. In these conditions it is hard for the minority in the vanguard to feel secure, to establish continuity of effort and to make much lasting headway.

Pre-school Education

10. Research indicates that many enduring attitudes are formed in the first five years of the child's existence. Pre-school education within the family as well as in such pre-school educational establishments as the kindergarten can, therefore be of prime importance in furthering the aims of international education. Essentially, what is needed at the pre-school level is a stimulating environment for healthy social and emotional growth in which children can learn to live harmoniously together and can acquire basic attitudes of solidarity and co-operativeness before the educational accent shifts, at the primary level, to the formal acquisition of learning skills.

11. The influence of figures of authority, usually the parents, is decisive at this stage in forming the child's outlook. Thus, as stated in paragraph 24 of the Recommendation, the attitude of parents is an essential factor in the education of children and special attention should be given to the preparation of parents for

their role in pre-school education. In an ever-increasing number of countries the influence of television is also very strong. Figuratively speaking, television may in fact be the only "parent" at home much of the time. While it can have a negative effect — for example, by the constant portrayal of violence or the perpetuation of undesirable national and ethic stereotypes — its potential for good is almost limitless, as the educational television programmes of some countries have demonstrated.

12. In addition to the part it plays in personality development and the inculcation of fundamental values, pre-school education can also help children to gain experience in conflict-resolution and problem-solving. It is self-evident that constructive experience of this kind at an early age is a useful preparation for participation in conflict-resolution and problem-solving at later stages and at other levels.
13. As to specific content, one of the chief centres of interest at the pre-school level can be an introduction to the lives of children in other countries. Learning through stories, picture books, songs and the like can be enhanced by exchange of messages and materials, with schools in other countries and observance of such world events as International Children's Day which will help to develop a sense of solidarity with children of other lands.

Primary Education

1. As pre-school education is institutionalized and generally available only in the developed countries, it is all the more imperative to ensure that the foundations of international understanding and respect for human rights are firmly laid at the primary level. The importance of what is done at this stage is further increased by the fact that many of the world's children receive no other formal education and that many of them do not even complete their primary education.
2. Each school discipline, and many combinations of disciplines, can make an appropriate contribution. Since it is often the case that many and not infrequently all subjects are taught by one teacher, the ability of that person to interpret the curriculum in the light of international education is of crucial importance. Therefore sufficient flexibility of curricula and syllabuses is necessary to permit innovations by the teacher and active participation by

students.

3. The primary stage is particularly suitable for fostering "understanding and respect for all people, their cultures, civilizations, values and ways of life, including domestic ethic cultures and cultures of other nations" [Recommendation, paragraph 4(b)]. It has already been noted that many life-long attitudes are shaped in the early years of childhood. Negative or hostile attitudes towards other cultural or racial groups may already have taken root by the time the child enters the primary school. One task may therefore be to counteract such attitudes through programmes dealing with other peoples and cultures. It is important not to over-emphasize the merely curious, quaint or exotic; instead, stress should be laid on the common realities of life and of the human situation. For this purpose there is a marked need for such suitable reading materials as collections of well-illustrated stories about the life of children in different countries to be more widely available than at present. The production of materials of this kind is a task in which UNESCO's assistance would be useful.
4. The basic concepts with which the Recommendation is concerned — for example, international co-operation, peace, human rights, solidarity — can be presented and interpreted in understandable terms at the primary level. Pupils should also learn of the existence of such international instruments as the United Nations Charter, the Universal Declaration of Human Rights, the Covenants on Human Rights and the International Convention on the Elimination of all Forms of Racial Discrimination. The content of these documents can be woven into teaching in many ways. The basic ideas, however, need to be translated into terms that are within the intellectual and effective grasp of pupils through sound pedagogical approaches.
5. As far as possible concepts should be linked to the children's own situations, experience and environment. For example, with a view to creating awareness of "the increasing global interdependence between nations and peoples" [Recommendation, paragraph 4(c)], teachers can draw attention to familiar raw materials or manufactured products which are of foreign origin. This approach may be used to illustrate global relationships and the workings of world trade and also to serve as the point of departure for the study of other countries and cultures.

Secondary Education

1. Learning is cumulative, and international education at the secondary level should build upon that carried out at the primary level. At this stage the curriculum offers a wider range of possibilities. Cognitive aspects of international education can be treated with greater sophistication. At the same time, effective aspects should not be neglected, as students are usually at a stage of development when they are particularly sensitive to ethical values.
2. In most countries students at the secondary level are made further aware of their national civic responsibilities. As the great majority do not continue their formal education beyond this stage, it is important that they also be prepared for their international civic responsibilities. This cannot be done simply by offering short courses on current events and world problems. As at the primary level, the principles of international education should permeate the entire curriculum, with each discipline making a contribution. As far as possible, the programme should be linked to the life, work and problems of the community — in particular to those problems which have a global dimension and offer opportunities for inter-culture education.
3. As at the primary level, the general climate of the school is an important factor in international education. It is essential to develop participatory modes of education in the classroom, school and community. If students are later to discharge effectively their local, national and international civic responsibilities they need to acquire relevant experience through active participation. In the classroom, for example, less emphasis might be placed on teacher-directed work and more on open discussions and dialogues between the teacher and students. The creation of student councils, with students electing representatives who are entrusted with the responsibility of examining school affairs and organizing student activities, can be effective in providing experience in participation. Community-oriented programmes — for example, to assist minority groups, the elderly or migrant workers — would permit the students to play an active role in improving the well-being of the community. In some countries, students spend a certain amount of time working in the fields or factories, thereby not only contributing to the social and economic development of their communities but also learning by direct ex-

perience the meaning and value of labour.

4. By its very nature, international education involves treatment of political and ideological questions. In many countries teachers are wary of doing this, fearing that it may become a form of indoctrination. Guarantees against such a development should be created. For example, students should learn more about different socio-political systems so that they might, on the one hand, understand better the complexity of international relations and, on the other, be in a better position to make informed political choices and decisions. UNESCO might assist by helping in the preparation of teaching materials on issues with difficult political implications. On such issues, all governments have policies, and students can examine the policies of their government concerning them, as well as the position taken by political parties, labour unions, churches and other institutions of their society. More attention should be given, in particular to the problem of armaments, since it is closely related to the maintenance of peace and to the establishment of a new economic order. Such aspects as the armaments industry and race, disarmament and arms control should be examined. Students should also learn about recent and current international action to the aims of the Recommendation, such as the developments referred to in paragraph 6, examining the various sides of controversial issues and objectively analysing information concerning them as a means of arriving at conclusions.
5. One problem, of course, is to find ways of fitting such teaching into the syllabus. While a certain stability in school programmes and syllabuses is needed and curricula cannot be frequently changed, nevertheless pertinent content can be introduced as and when they are revised. In general, however, secondary school curricula already offer many opportunities for teaching about the contemporary world. The possibilities presented by such courses as history, geography, modern languages, civics and social studies are well known. Other courses can also serve as vehicles for international education, and among these, particular attention might be given to the potentialities of mathematics, physics and chemistry, all of which have a direct relation to technological development in general and the problem of armaments in particular. Home economics and health education provide occasions for dealing with such matters as the world problems of food,

nutrition and population. The expressive arts — music, dance, drama, handicrafts, painting and drawing and physical education — not only present opportunities for students of all abilities to develop and demonstrate their creative skills but also provide a good basis for learning about other cultures, Moreover, by helping to redress the balance in schools where cognitive goals are heavily emphasized, they may also serve to mitigate the frustration and possible aggressivity of the less gifted. Activities in these fields, in addition, can lead to international exchanges and contacts – for example, international arts festivals, contests and sport events of various kinds. Such undertakings, and in particular sport events, should be conducted without excessive emphasis on competitiveness.

6. Again, what is called for is a flexible approach to the organization and interpretation of the curriculum. For several reasons, this may not be easy to achieve. The fact that much specialist teaching takes place in secondary education promotes compartmentalized course and subject-matter. Textbooks are often out of date, and even if other suitable materials are available not all teachers have the necessary skill to select the most appropriate and make the best use of them.
7. Experience shows that these difficulties can be overcome. For example, interdisciplinary teams of teachers can be formed to work out an integrated programme. Through workshops and seminars new materials and methodology can be developed. Full use can be made of the information and materials emanating from the mass media and from the organizations of the United Nations system.
8. Consideration should be given to the possibility of introducing a course on the history of human civilizations. UNESCO might assist in the production of materials for such a course, which would illustrate the principle of unity in diversity and might have as a central theme progress towards realization of the principles of human rights.
9. Special efforts should be made to strengthen international education in prevocational and technical education at the secondary level. Comparatively little has been done in this area, which is increasing in importance as the numbers of vocational and technical institutions grow.

II. Teacher Preparation

1. As the success of international education depends largely on the quality of teaching, priority should be given to teacher education in planning policies to strengthen international education in school systems. Member-States should carry out a thorough assessment of their teacher-training programmes in respect of international education and take appropriate steps to strengthen them in this regard. Teacher education should be a carrier long process, embracing initial training and in-service studies in a process of continually renewed professional and personal development.
2. In many countries, the preparation of teachers is a part of higher education. Both initial training and in-service studies at this level will profit from the point of view of international education if the faculty of education, other faculties of the university and other educational institutions collaborate closely in teacher-preparation programmes. All future and in-service teachers should be made aware of the roles that their disciplines can play in support of international understanding.
3. The importance of teaching at all levels about world problems, international relations and recent international developments which are likely to be the subjects of discussion at international forums for years to come, has already been stressed. Consequently, it is essential that teachers be given opportunities to acquire the knowledge and skills required to deal with this subject-matter in their work.

Pre-service Training

4. Special attention should be given to reinforcing the contribution of teacher-trainers to international education. Much will depend on their ability and willingness to rethink the relevance of international education to their work and to undertake reorientation programmes. If teacher-trainers are to impart the principles of the Recommendation to others they themselves should have respect for people of other countries; be sensitive to the significance of other cultures; have a broad knowledge of child psychology and group dynamics, and be proficient in innovatory learning methods designed to promote active student participation. In most

countries, few teachers have been trained to treat political and ideological questions in the right spirit and there are insufficient members of staff in secondary schools qualified to show the increasingly important contribution of economics.

5. International education will best flourish in those colleges and institutions of higher learning which have established a unified community of staff and students and which are putting into action principles which will bind them together. Among these are respect for the child, and understanding of the needs of the child and a willingness to serve the community. At all levels of education right relationships between staff and students are of paramount importance. Students need to take an active part in learning and in decision-making and to be given genuine freedom to mature.
6. The teaching techniques suggested in the sections on primary and secondary education will not only sharpen the pupils' and students' abilities to analyse and solve problems, make objective value judgements and acquire experience in participation, but will also bring the student and the teacher closer together and provide conditions in which all they learn and evolve together.
7. In multi-ethnic societies teacher-training institutes should draw students from the various ethnic groups. Such a practice will not only enrich the life of the college but will also cultivate a greater understanding, respect and appreciation of other members of society and other cultures. In this connection, it should be recalled that the Recommendation has not only international but also intercultural and inter-group implication.
8. In many countries the curriculum of teacher training institutions is being revised. Where this process is going forward, it may offer a good opportunity to introduce or strengthen the international content of programmes. All students should have possibilities for learning the concepts, content and methods of international education through their regular academic and professional studies. In addition more intensive training should be offered to those who wish to specialize in this field. It would be useful if teacher-certification requirements could include preparation for work in international education.
9. In an effort to help future teachers learn more about other peoples, cultures and systems of education, training institutions should provide, whenever possible, opportunities for students to

take part in study visits to other countries.

In-service Training

1. The objectives of in-service teacher training vary from country to country in accordance with needs. For example, in those countries where there is a dearth of teachers and resources and facilities are insufficient for adequate training, teaching posts, particularly at the primary level, are often filled by people who have had little formal training. In such instances, the aim of in-service training is mainly to raise the general level of professional competence as rapidly as possible. In some other countries a decline in population growth has led to a reduction in the numbers of children, and hence to a decrease in new teaching positions. As a consequence fewer young teachers are coming into the profession with up to date training. In this situation, in-service programmes have a particular value as a means of renovating the methods and content of teaching. Much can be done through them to further the aims of the Recommendation.
2. In-service programmes should be developed which will enable practising teachers to:

- acquire a greater understanding of international education and of major documents pertaining to it;
- know where to obtain materials for use in international education;
- learn how to exercise discrimination in the evaluation, selection and presentation of materials;
- adapt such materials to specific needs and, when necessary, to devise their own materials;
- develop the skills needed to involve school students in active participation in learning experience;
- gain greater insight into the processes of their professional and personal development.

3. In-service training programmes in international education can take a variety of forms. In some countries, teachers are granted sabbatical leaves or a certain number of days or weeks each year to take part in organized programmes of study or carry out personal research. Those who have had such experience in international education can share their ideas and skills with colleagues in

the same institution. Local, national and international workshops and seminars have also proved to be valuable. Correspondence courses represent a possibility which has been little exploited in this field.

4. Some schools are becoming increasingly aware of the value of developing their own in-service studies and of associating specialists from teacher-training institutes and other competent agencies and organizations with their programmes.
5. It would be useful to establish research and advisory centres whose objective would be to assist teachers, upon their request, in the field of international education. These centres could render a number of valuable services. For example, they could:

– help teachers select materials that are already available and guide them in using them;
– produce teaching models which teachers could adapt to their particular needs; devise new teaching techniques and methods;
– help teachers improve their knowledge of specific world events or issues; and
– offer guidance on how to involve the school more actively in the life of the community.

6. Due attention should be given to the in-service training of young teachers so that they can put into practice the aims of international education from the outset of their careers. It would also be useful to arrange courses for school inspectors and head teachers since the introduction of international education generally depends on their co-operation, understanding and leadership.

III. Higher Education

7. As an introduction to this section it is appropriate to recall a statement by the earlier meeting of experts of education for international understanding and peace, with special reference to moral and civic education: "In view of the nature and objectives and missions of higher education in relation to contemporary world problems, the urgency of promoting international understanding at this level is keenly felt. An examination of the development of higher education relating to international understanding is especially important because of the place which it enjoys in the con-

temporary world. It is by its nature, in most countries, the pace-setter for the entire educational process because it is the highest level to which all other levels are preparatory. It is generally the highest level for the education of persons who will carry major responsibilities in government and in other leadership roles. It is here also that special preparation is provided for a wide range of professions, including the mass media, adult education, etc. Higher education provides the preferred setting for research in the natural and social sciences and in the humanities. Especially in the natural sciences great progress has been made in achieving transnational co-operation and thereby, indirectly, in promoting international communication and understanding. It is the principal link for each nation with intellectual leadership throughout the world; but more than this, higher education seems to be the only universally-oriented educational resource found in the nations of the contemporary world community to which mankind can look for leadership in speeding the advancement of international understanding to guide government policy.

8. Institutions of higher education in may countries have more autonomy that institutions at lower levels and more freedom and broader possibilities for innovation. Moreover, in a good many countries they are evolving as a consequence of the restructuring of this part of the educational system, and new relationships between institutions are becoming possible. These circumstances could be propitious for the development of international education.
9. In reinforcing the international components of their programmes at both undergraduate and graduate levels, institutions of higher learning might consider the following suggestions:

- international education should be regarded as an appropriate area for free inquiry and research, with particular emphasis on studies of human rights and of methods of teaching about them;
- interdisciplinary approaches in international education should be further explored and developed;
- programmes of international education which will reach all students regardless of their specialization should be organized;
- teaching methods which encourage the active participation of students (*i.e.*, problem-solving approaches and discussion methods) should be stressed, so that the rigid formality of the traditional

lecture ceases to be the norm;

- the presence of students and staff from a variety of countries should be encouraged; and
- the application of technological studies to the problems of developing countries should be actively pursued.

10. Neglect of teaching about human rights at the higher level has had the effect of inhibiting the development of teaching on this subject at other levels. This makes it all the more urgent that work in this field be intensified and generalized at the higher level. For example, education about human rights should be added to the priorities of the United Nations University, and institutes of higher education specializing in the study of human rights should be established.
11. Teachers who have undertaken projects of education about Human Rights have often had difficulty in maintaining their students' interest in the subject if a too abstract approach has been employed. One way of sustaining interest is to link the theme with the life of the community and the nation as students themselves have experienced it. For example, teachers can help students to determine what their rights mean in practical terms, as this is not always fully apparent in constitutional and legal texts. International instruments on human rights — such as the Universal Declaration of Human Rights, the two International Covenants on human rights adopted by the United Nations General Assembly, and the Convention on the Elimination of all Forms of Racial Discrimination should also be studied and analysed, as these represent the views of the world community on the subject. Attention can be drawn also to violations of human rights and possible remedies.
12. Programmes of international education at technical universities and polytechnical institutes likewise need to be further developed. An example of what can be done is provided by one country where a project has been undertaken to introduce in three technical universities a course on the adaptation of technology to the needs and circumstances of the Third World. Through this course students will be able to deepen their understanding of the developing countries while at the same time advancing in professional knowledge and skills.
13. Institutions of higher learning commonly have faculties or

research centres which specialize in the study of different cultures. It is important that more attention be paid to the way in which other cultures are studied for they are sometimes looked at, perhaps unconsciously, from a paternalistic point of view. It would be helpful if guidelines for such studies could be developed, perhaps with the aid of UNESCO.

14. The possibilities offered by faculties and schools of economics also should receive closer attention. These institutions have an important part to play in furthering the aims of the Recommendation. Their task should be to educate students as to economic relationships in the world today and to develop understanding of the need for sharing the world's resources and for solidarity between the developed and the developing countries.
15. Institutions of higher learning are already international in their orientation and have many contacts abroad. Nevertheless, the establishment of an association of institutions of higher education working in the field of international education, as well as the organization at the higher level of a world-wide programme such as UNESCO's Associated Schools Project, should be considered. Such an association could serve as a forum for the exchange of experience and the development of co-operative ventures. It could also be useful in helping the existing Associated Schools to evaluate the effectiveness of the projects.

IV. Out-of-school Education for Young People and Adults

1. The objectives of out-of-school education necessarily differ from one country to another according to specific needs and circumstances. In many developing countries the majority of young people and adults have had little or no formal education and illiteracy is widespread. Priority is, therefore given to the basic education needed in order to raise standards of living. In many industrially education developed countries, on the other hand, the goals pursued in out-of-school education include career improvement through the acquisition of additional skills and knowledge, development of civic and political consciousness and cultural recreation. As the concept of life-long education finds wider application in practice, the role of out-of-school education will inevitably increase in importance and with it the range of opportunities it offers for international education.

2. For adults as well as young people the point of departure in out-of-school programmes of international education should be the local, regional and national realities. An examination of these can lead to the consideration of relevant aspects of international issues. Young people and adults should be encouraged to take an active part in choosing areas of study, and pedantic approaches and language should be avoided. As far as possible, international education should be built into existing structures, drawing in people and groups who are already involved in conducting out-of-school education programmes, such as non-governmental and labour unions.
3. For young people, "in-depth" experiences should be developed through participation in voluntary service activities, exchanges, community betterment projects, festivals of the arts, work camps, etc., which provide occasions for collaborating with people from other countries or other racial, social or cultural groups within the country. There is little risk of "alienation" among young people who feel they are constructively involved in the development of their own society.
4. In adult education, a promising field which has thus far been little explored is that of international education for "senior citizens". In many countries, the age for retirement is becoming more flexible, the number of retired persons is increasing and preparation for retirement is a growing phenomenon. Many retired persons would have both the time and the motivation to participate in programmes of international education and would welcome the opportunity to refresh their interests and widen their horizons.
5. Experience has shown that UNESCO Clubs and Associations can play an extremely valuable part in international education for young people and adults out of school. It is to be hoped that they will be extended and strengthened in Member-States. Greater efforts should be made to organize them among older people such as the "senior citizens" referred to in the preceding paragraph.
6. However, well developed and effective out-of-school programmes may be, most of the information received by young people and adults about the contemporary world comes through the mass media. These have a crucially important effect on attitudes concerning the issues which form the subject-matter of international education. From the point of view of the aims of the Recommendation this influence is often negative. Every effort

should be made to strengthen the role of mass media in action to attain the Recommendation's objectives. It has been suggested that UNESCO should prepare an international instrument concerning the contribution of the mass media to peace and international understanding.

7. As the Recommendation indicates [paragraph 38(a)], education should include a component designed to help the individual to select and analyse the information transmitted by the mass media. For example, students can be assigned to watch and afterwards discuss a television programme concerning some international matter or to make a comparative study of the treatment of a problem in different media. Such learning experiences can help to develop the individual's ability to judge soundly the information conveyed by the mass media.

V. Equipment and Materials

1. If possible, a wide variety of materials should be used in international education. They should be up to date, of a nature to command the attention of students and written or presented in jargon-free language. For out-of-school education there is a need for more short films, documentaries, television programmes, etc.
2. In each Member-State an analysis should be made of textbooks and teaching materials from the point of view of their contribution to the aims of the Recommendation.
3. There is need to develop strategies which will ensure that the best use is made of materials. These might include: The production of basic scholarly materials — a task to which institutions of higher learning should contribute:

- development of teams of writers, audio-visual specialists, etc., to adapt these materials;
- training of teachers in the use of various kinds of materials;
- establishment of resource centres, perhaps in teacher-training institutions, to assist schools;
- provision of advisory services by experts on the use and evaluation of materials.

4. In many countries the textbook is the main and sometimes the only teaching aid. The co-operation of authors, publishers,

teachers and curriculum developers should be sought in improving textbooks from the point of view of their furtherance of the Recommendation's aims. As revising or replacing textbooks is slow and costly, however, efforts should also be made to prepare up to date, inexpensive supplementary materials for international education. Teachers themselves should be prepared to devise their own equipment and materials, taking into account the aspirations of students.

5. UNESCO might assist by producing prototype materials, facilitating the international exchange of textbooks and other teaching materials and providing consultative services to Member-States in such areas as textbook writing and production and training in the use of audio-visual materials. It would also be useful if UNESCO could aid in developing criteria for the analysis and evaluation of teaching materials.

VI. Further Suggestions on National Action and International Co-operation

1. Member-States should work out a national policy for promotion of international education, using the Recommendation constantly as a working guide. It should be taken into account when educational legislation and programmes are being reassessed and changed. At the same time all existing possibilities for implementation should be utilized.
2. National Commissions for UNESCO should stimulate action for application of the Recommendation and should assist in co-ordinating programmes involving different ministries, government departments and agencies and non-governmental organizations. To these ends National Commissions might consider establishing task forces bringing together officials, educators, administrators, leaders of public opinion, etc., to plan strategies and take the lead in action.
3. The Recommendation should be translated into the national language(s) in each Member-State and should be widely disseminated. If possible it should be distributed together with a document interpreting it and presenting practical suggestions for its implementation.
4. Local groups should have a decisive voice in policy-making and should be given sufficient resources for local initiatives. The ef-

forts of these groups might be co-ordinated at the national level by UNESCO National Commissions in order to strengthen the impact of their work on educational policies and reforms, especially as regards curriculum development, teacher training and educational research.

5. Member-States and UNESCO National Commissions should seek the collaboration of non-governmental organizations in action to disseminate and implement the Recommendation.
6. Research to evaluate the effectiveness of international education should be intensified. It is particularly important to develop evaluative instruments for direct use by teachers. UNESCO should promote parallel comparative research on international education in different countries. Programmes, materials and methods of international education should be modified in the light of research findings.
7. It has been suggested that the aim of international education at all stages should be to develop what might be called "global literacy" — that is, a basic understanding of the contemporary world, its problems and its evolving systems of international relationships. There is need to explore further the concept of "global literacy" and to establish guidelines concerning it for curriculum designers and teachers.
8. In each Member-State existing materials, programmes and educational resources capable of furthering the objectives of the Recommendation should be identified; areas in which such materials, programmes and resources are deficient should be surveyed and appropriate action taken to provide them.
9. Fellowships should be made available to enable students and teachers to study the goals and practical application of the Recommendation in their own and other countries.
10. Exchanges of teachers and students between Member-States, as well as exchanges of information and educational materials, should be encouraged and facilitated.
11. National seminars and workshops should be organized to promote the application of the Recommendation and to consider practical ways of implementing it.
12. Those responsible for the mass media should be encouraged to promote through them the aims of the Recommendation.
13. It is recommended further that UNESCO should:

- convene a committee of specialists to study the reports of Member-States on action to implement the Recommendation submitted to the General Conference at its nineteenth session. It is hoped that the General Conference of UNESCO will decide to invite Member-States to transmit additional reports periodically for study by the Special Committee of the Executive Board. For such reports it would be helpful to seek information on a variety of questions relating to the dissemination and discussion of the Recommendation (e.g., whether it has been translated into a national language, whether it has been published in educational journals, etc.);
- organize international inter-disciplinary seminars and working groups of educators, political scientists, etc., to prepare practical guidelines for implementation of the Recommendation. One task of such groups should be to examine the basic ideology of the Recommendation and transmute it into pedagogical materials;
- draw up for use by Member-States a list of expert consultants qualified to advise on the planning, execution and evaluation of activities to implement the Recommendation;
- send upon request of Member-States mobile teams of experts to assist in action to implement the Recommendation and in the evaluation of such action. The results of assessments should be discussed with the national authorities with a view to strengthening the effectiveness of action;
- accounts of successful activities should be made available by UNESCO to other Member States;
- encourage the collaboration of other international and regional organizations, including the organizations of the United Nations system and especially the United Nations University, in joint programmes to further the aims of the Recommendation. UNESCO should make use of its machinery for relations with international non-governmental organizations to promote action by them and their national branches for the study and implementation of the Recommendation;
- assist in the organization of regional and international seminar and workshops for educators and mass media specialists on implementation of the Recommendation;
- prepare and publish a multilingual bibliography of materials relating to the four main concerns of the Recommendation — international understanding, international co-operation, peace, and human rights;

make use of its existing periodicals and publications to further the implementation of the Recommendation.

INTERNATIONAL MEETING* OF EXPERTS ON EVALUATION AND DEVELOPMENT OF THE ASSOCIATED SCHOOLS PROJECTS ON EDUCATION FOR INTERNATIONAL CO-OPERATION AND PEACE, 1980

I. Suggestions on the Renewal and Further Development of the Associated Schools Project

A.Objectives, Educational Content, Teaching Methods and Materials (at the Primary, Secondary and Teacher-training Levels of Education)

1.*Objectives*: The growing economic, political, cultural and social interdependence of the present day world, the existing international tensions and conflicts, the violations of human rights, the arms race and the persisting inequalities to be observed in many parts of the world, the increasing internationalization of our everyday life show that the need for peace and international understanding and co-operation has never been so pressing as it is now. In the present circumstances education for international understanding, co-operation and peace is a matter of crucial importance for the survival of mankind. The implementation of the UNESCO Recommendation concerning Education for International Understanding, Co-operation and Peace and Education relating to Human Rights and Fundamental Freedoms (to be referred to for the purpose of this report as the Recommendation) which was adopted by the General Conference at its eighteenth session in 1974 therefore, becomes today a predominant task for national educational authorities, international organisations and the whole educational community of the world. Educational authorities in the Member-States should be reminded of the existence of the Recommendations and of the fact that the acceptance of this instrument at the General Conference places responsibility upon them to give the necessary support for its implementation.

---

* Held at UNESCO House, Paris, from 8-12 September, 1980, and attended by 18 Experts from different countries.

While acknowledging that the implementation of the Recommendation is a task which has to be faced by the whole system of education in Member-States it was stated that the UNESCO Associated Schools Project, being at the same time an international and a national pilot programme, has a specific role to play in this respect. For the participating institutions the project is "a window on the world" which opens up possibilities for international exchanges and contacts. On the other hand the Project provides for UNESCO a "window to the school", i.e. it enables the organization to obtain information on classroom activities directly from schools and teachers at the local level. Because of this two-way linkage it was recommended that the Associated Schools Project should be considered both by UNESCO and by Member-States as one of the main vehicles to further the provisions of the Recommendations.

It was recalled that the overriding objective of the Associated Schools Project was until now to conduct, within the framework of the existing curriculum, experimental activities on specific themes in order to further education for international co-operation and peace. These activities were to be designed in a way to develop educational content in a perspective of international education, to elaborate adequate teaching methods and to prepare relevant materials accordingly. Schools and national authorities were to report periodically to the UNESCO Secretariat in order to facilitate the exchange of experience on a world-wide basis. The participants endorsed these overriding objectives of the Project stressing in particular the necessity that any positive results achieved through these activities be widely diffused within and outside the country so that other schools can learn from them and undertake similar action.

In order to enable Associated Schools to play the active and dynamic role that is expected of them, it is necessary that Member-States formulate their own national strategies, operational objectives and, whenever possible, take legislative measures to launch and develop the Project and to ensure its impact on the educational community. Consequently, it is urged that Member-States will make available the necessary moral, human and financial support needed to achieve the objectives of the Project. These strategies should be designed in a flexible way which permit the participating institutions, teachers, students, etc., to take part in their formulation. In this way, the national objectives will be broadly accepted and attainable and will ensure that the work of Associated Schools does not remain in isolation.

One of the main objectives of the Associated Schools Project is to facilitate the communication between teachers and students belonging to different political systems, cultures and regions, and to contribute, by means of educational activities to establishing closer contacts and better understanding. This is particularly true for the communication between industrialized and developing countries. But also within a region the Associated Schools Project provides a most useful framework for exchanges between educators and students of countries that are separated by ideological or other divisions.

In addition some general principles have been formulated for the implementation of the Project:

– Schools, teachers and students involved in the Project have a special commitment to be objective. Objectivity means to avoid a one-sided presentation or interpretation of international events and world issues and to try to understand the positions of all concerned;
– the results of any education for international understanding are very much dependent on the personal commitment of the individual teacher and on the credibility of the message he communicates;
– it is necessary to create within the Associated Schools an atmosphere which encourages initiatives to be taken by teachers or students and which stimulates co-operation among them; and
– the participation in the Project places special responsibility on the director of the school, on the support he gives, and his ability to promote relevant activities.

Suggestions were made as to be type of schools which should take part in the project. In addition to the present primary and secondary schools and teacher-training institutions, it was recommended that the project should include pre-primary and technical and vocational schools. Where appropriate non-formal education centres should also be given the opportunity to join the Project. Being aware that an unlimited expansion of the Project causes problems of financing and coordination, the participants recommended that the schools should represent a cross-section of schools in the country and should be located in rural as well as urban areas. Efforts should be made to encourage all Member-States of UNESCO to join the Project.

On several occasions it was stressed that UNESCO Associated Schools should not be considered as separate and "privileged" schools, but that they have to be seen as an integral part of the education system which could, through their special experience as well as through their linkage with the international community, contribute to the improvement of educational content, methods and material in the perspective of international understanding, co-operation and peace.

2. *Educational Content*: The meeting agrees to the value of having main themes to be studied by participating institutions and endorses the following four main areas:

(a) wrld problems and the role of the United Nations system in solving them;
(b) human rights;
(c) other countries and cultures;
(d) man and his environment.

These themes were considered sufficiently broad to cover a wide range of sub-themes. These themes and sub-themes often interrelate and this can be shown by preparing a matrix. It should, however, be understood that this list is not exhaustive and that Member-States and individual school should select their own themes in accordance with their interest and priorities. Special mention was also made to the study of the major problems of mankind listed in paragraph 18 of the Recommendation.

The meeting felt that emphasis should not only be given to world problems but an equal emphasis should be laid on the many achievements in finding solution to problems. In this connection it was pointed out that the teaching about the United Nations and its specialized Agencies needs to be further developed. Instead of teaching about the complicated structures and procedures of these organizations an issue-oriented approach should be adopted underlining the interdependence of the present-day world which calls for international co-operation.

The importance of the teaching about human rights which were considered as a universally accepted system of values was stressed. Participants recommended that education for international understanding and peace should give more emphasis than in the past to the teaching about human values and about human relations.

The question of human relations is vital for the treatment of the fourth theme "Man and his environment". This topic which found a great interest among participants, should not be restricted to the question of pollution or to the preservation of nature but should cover the whole set of social, cultural, emotional or other relations between man and his milieu. The topic includes not only the local environment of the student but permits teachers to explain to students the specific place their community and country has in the world.

The theme "other countries and other cultures" is one of the most studied subjects of Associated Schools. The appreciation of other cultures was still considered as a valid educational goal. Participants felt, however, that more emphasis should be given to the interrelation of different cultures and their mutual influence than to the teaching about exotic cultures.

In this connection it was pointed out that the study of other cultures does not necessarily relate to other countries. Other cultures are found even in the same country. While some societies continue to be rather homogeneous, other rapidly change through the effect of international mobility into multiethnic, multinational and multicultural societies. The trend of migrant workers presents only one example of this kind. The meeting welcomed therefore the new cross theme proposed by the external evaluators, i.e., "international/cross-cultural education", recommending however that only the term "inter-cultural education" should be introduced.

The second cross-theme proposed by the evaluators, i.e. "Co-operative development education" was accepted in principle. The evaluators defined this term to mean: "education through which children and young people will develop positive attitudes and participate in projects and other activities contributing to such development. The meaning of 'development' should be understood broadly to include social and cultural development as well as the more easily identifiable economic goals which many governments and nations espouse. . . . Co-operative activities within the family, the classroom and the community, where students are most likely to be personally involved, can be related to broader issues of co-operation within nations and between them. This new emphasis should be used as the main integrating concept for activities intended to explicate the role of the United Nations and its related organizations and in dealing with the relationship of man and the environment". It was, however, felt that the title will not be understood in many countries and that a new title should be sought as well as a clearer definition. On the other hand an additional area of study was suggested: "Interdependence between peoples and civilizations" with emphasis on the recognition of the ability of peoples and countries to co-operate in the solving of mutual problems.

Still in connection with the study of other cultures the meeting examined the need to teach about the role of traditions, both social and cultural, in modern society and how we can integrate these traditions into a modern scientific society. It believed that to understand a society or a culture you must also understand its traditions and recognize the conflict which often exists between progress and the preservation of a tradition-based cultural identity. In this context mention was made of the importance of history teaching and the comparative study of arts and literature.

Participants also considered furthermore the possibility of studying the role of science and the effect it has on modern society, the problems it brings and the achievements it has made. It was stated that inventions could not be restricted to the country of origin and the benefits should be world-wide. The need for the transfer of knowledge and technology from industrialized to developing countries has been a question of international debate during the past years, and should be suggested to schools for study.

3. *Methods*: The meeting stressed the importance of seeing education as an integral part of school life, permeating and influencing all facets of the school. An Associated School should in itself, be a reflection in its own community of the lessons which it is aiming to teach. (The school itself must be an understanding society.) It is important that the school accept the responsibility of being considered and accepted within the local community as an institution promoting the ideals of international understanding, co-operation and peace.

While acknowledging that all subjects, especially social studies, have contributions to make to the teaching about international issues, special reference was made to the responsibility of Associated Schools to further interdisciplinary or multidisciplinary teaching methods permitting co-operation among teachers and students and involving the local community. Particular mention was made of problem and action-oriented study programmes and the utilization of active methods, e.g., the *semaine integree* or *project week* (whereby a particular theme or issue is studied through an interdisciplinary approach by students during an entire week) which is now being developed in many countries.

The meeting discussed the relation of cognitive and socio-affective approaches and examined the evaluators views on the role of "socio-affective" methods in teaching. While agreeing that socio-affective methods provide students with skills which foster human relations, interpersonal communications etc., it was felt, however, that these methods constitute only one of the components of the educational methodology to be used. What is needed in teaching international issues is a balanced approach (both cognitive and affective learning) adopted to the specific needs of the age-group concerned.

It was pointed out that the teaching methods used by Associated Schools should be co-ordinated with the methods generally used within the educational system of the country. While agreeing that Associated Schools should explore new methods, mention was made of the desirability of introducing these methods whenever they proved successful, into other schools. In order to facilitate the sharing of experiences such teaching methods should be selected which could easily be adapted by other schools. It was also agreed that educational methods and content should be flexible enough and open in order to help teachers and students to have a readiness to face up to the unexpected and the unforseeable.

It was stated that the educational methods used by Associated Schools must be dynamic and attractive in order to motivate students to participate actively in the prepared activities being promoted. Extra-curricular and community-related activities should also be encouraged. The use of audio-visual materials (films, posters, photographs) was considered as vital to heightening the impact since for many schools it is not possible to send students and teachers to visit other countries or to organize exchange programmes.

4. *Material*: The meeting stressed the importance of having adequate and appropriate teaching material for education for international understanding, co-operation and peace. These materials should not only contain updated and correct information but should also be presented in such a way that it can be understood by the different age-groups. There is a need for constant revision and evaluator of textbooks and teaching materials, which could — where the study of other countries and international relations is concerned — be done in the framework of bilateral or multilateral co-operation between interested countries.

As many of the themes studies by the Associated Schools are comparatively new it is inevitable that Associated Schools will have to prepare their own teaching materials and in doing so they may wish to base them on the information and literature they receive from UNESCO, National Commissions or other sources. The participation of Associated Schools in producing teaching and learning materials adapted to the local needs and often at a low-cost level was considered as one of the strengths of the project. Every initiative to produce self-made teaching materials and modules within the Associated Schools Project should be encouraged. UNESCO and national authorities should, however, review the possibility of contracting some effective schools so as to assist them in the preparation of such materials and to diffuse them both at the national and regional levels. Teacher-training has a specific responsibility to enable teachers to prepare some of their own material and to evaluate it accordingly.

Special reference was made to the importance of audio-visual and graphic material (films, posters, photographs, etc.). UNESCO and the United Nations agencies were requested to provide within their programmes of public information more materials for educational purposes. The Office of Public Information of UNESCO should contact specialized institutions and agencies to produce pedagogical material for use in the classroom and an education officer should be attached to OPI to ensure the production of such material. It was stated that most of the information material produced by the various United Nations agencies is used by educational institutions any way and this justifies the production of more teaching material. National Commissions or other national authorities should be more equipped to translate existing United Nations materials into national languages.

The *UNESCO Courier* was considered to be very valuable to Associated Schools but sometimes teachers have difficulties in using it in the classroom. It was therefore suggested that the circular "International Understanding at School" should include some pedagogical notes relating to past and future issues of the *UNESCO Courier*.

The United Nations agencies should co-operate more closely in the production of educational and information material. Efforts should be made to ensure that material produced by other agencies is in all the official United Nations languages (Arabic, Chinese, English, French, Spanish and Russian) and is distributed systematically to Associated Schools, UNESCO should produce some basic material on learning about the organization and its main fields of action (e.g., struggle against illiteracy, preservation of cultural heritage, earth sciences, man and the biosphere), which would also help schools to develop their own materials. (A basic information brochure replacing "Looking at UNESCO" is needed). Throughout the discussion emphasis was laid on the need for the produced materials to be appropriate and acceptable to both teachers and students. A strong appeal was made to UNESCO that it should encourage and assist Member-States in the translation of the Organization's publications into national languages.

The meeting agreed to the recommendations contained in the evaluators' report, namely:

- material containing a detailed description of teaching practices, together with evaluative information, could be of great utility as a teaching aid by providing teachers with examples and models they could experiment within their classrooms;
- specific attention should be given to the development of teaching aids in the field of human rights education, especially racism. In all countries there is a strong demand for graphic materials, particularly posters and photographs;
- teacher-training institutions in the Associated Schools network should be encouraged when possible to develop teaching materials for use in both primary and secondary schools;
- regional co-operative development of teaching materials should be strongly encouraged, for example, through regional workshops, whereby material would be contributed and exchanged between participating countries;
- efforts should be made to obtain as much UNESCO and United Nations material as possible and whenever necessary, to produce national language versions of them.

Finally it was recommended that UNESCO, National Commissions and other national authorities should encourage the exchange of material and equipment both at the national and international levels, in order to help less well-equipped schools to fulfil their task in the field of education for international understanding and peace.

B. Educational Research, Experiments and Evaluation Techniques

Participants felt that if the Associated Schools Project is to achieve its objectives it must be accompanied by educational research to enhance its content, methods and materials and improve its results. This research should not be purely theoretical but should include teachers and educators who are taking part in the Project. Universities, institutes of pedagogy and other specialized bodies should be encouraged to become more actively involved in the Project for it is obvious that if Associated Schools are to carry out the experimental/experiential activities expected of them, they need to receive assistance from research institutes.

Participants recommend that UNESCO carry out research which will contribute to the design of general guidelines and instruments which could enable teachers to understand better the educational process of infusing education in the light of education for international understanding in the classroom and help them to analyse and self-evaluate the effectiveness of international education. Suggestions should also be provided to teachers on how they can report on their classroom experiences so that their results can be shared with others both nationally and internationally. It was proposed that these general guidelines drawn up by UNESCO should be elaborated further by national authorities in order to take into account local and national situations.

Other areas of research needed were indicated:

- *(i)* The impact of Associated Schools on the school system and how it can be enhanced;
- *(ii)* the planning, conduct and evaluation of interdisciplinary projects such as the "project weeks" indicated earlier;
- *(iii)* the contribution to an effect of in-school and out-of-school activities in international education;
- *(iv)* the relationship of national identity to international understanding;
- *(v)* how the four main themes of the Project can be studied more effectively.

As concerns experimentation it was felt that it was often difficult for Associated Schools to carry out purely scientific experimentation, but they have undertaken considerable experiential activities which have contributed to curriculum development and innovation and they should be encouraged to continue to do so. In the field of education very often new ideas have come from the grassroots level, *i.e.* the schools themselves.

It was suggested that other divisions of the UNESCO Secretariat use the network of Associated Schools for the purpose of experimentation, *i.e.* in the fields of science, culture, etc. Likewise many Associated Schools would probably be interested in such collaboration and which goes beyond the task of promoting international education.

Experimental and experiential activities should not only be carried out at the national level but also at the regional level.

With regard to evaluation, participants expressed their appreciation of the in-depth evaluation on the Associated Schools Project carried out in 1979-80 by the external evaluators and under the auspices of UNESCO. They deemed it to be most useful and the evaluation report should be widely diffused. An evaluation at the international level is required at regular intervals and the results should be submitted to international conferences on the Project.

It was also stressed that evaluations should be regularly carried out at both the national and institutional levels in order to make continuous improvements. The shortcomings of evaluating Associated School activities by only professional evaluators were underlined and it was strongly urged that teachers receive some type of pre-service training to enable them to make self-evaluations of their teaching.

C. Ways and Means to Develop the Project at the National Level

The success of the implementation of the Project depends primarily on how it is implemented at the national level hence, the necessity for national strategies which should include the following:

- The development of a national network of Associated Schools which permits communication and close co-operation among them; a co-ordinating mechanism which could consist of an individual person, a committee, the UNESCO National Commission for UNESCO, etc.;
- financial, human and moral support from the national authorities in order to enable the co-ordinating body to assume its leadership role;
- Associated Schools should be asked to fulfil minimum requirements as a pre-requisite to taking part in the Project which could compromise the obligation to report on an activity at least once a year, and the sharing of experiences with other schools in the community, etc.;
- the periodic conducting of national workshops and seminars of Associated School representatives (including teachers and

principals);

- joint Associated School activities should be carried out on a particular theme, such as was often the case of the International Year of the Child;
- the results achieved by Associated Schools should be broadly diffused by means of workshops, news bulletins, publications, the mass media, etc.;
- whenever possible, the Project should also contribute to the renewal of education in general;
- Member-States should also convene sub-regional, regional and international workshops of Associated School representatives on particular areas of concern.

D. Ways and Means to Develop the Project at the Regional Level

Once the Project has become operational at the national level, measures should be taken to establish regional linkage. Action at this level could be greatly helped by a more active role played by UNESCO Regional Offices for Education. It was noted that suggestions have already been formulated along these lines at the recent regional seminar of Associated School representatives which took place in Buenos Aires, Argentina, in June 1980.

Participants suggested that regional seminars, meetings and training courses be organized in all regions at regular intervals not only for national co-ordinators but for teachers actively engaged in the Project. Member-States should be encouraged to take such regional initiatives. Exchange programmes between schools (both for teachers and students) should also be promoted.

Participants pointed out that co-operation between Associated Schools at the regional level could enable contacts to be made between teachers and students belonging to countries with different ideological and political systems and should therefore be sought whenever possible.

The Regional UNESCO Education Offices could facilitate the preparation of teaching materials to be used in specific regions and it was pointed out that at present there is a particular dearth of such material in Arabic. The co-production of material should be sought whenever possible. Regional Offices should also provide consultant and advisory services to the Project, and regional advisers in international education should be appointed.

Bilateral and multilateral consultations among nations in the region concerning the improvement of content of textbooks (e.g., geography, history and social studies) with regard to international education should be organized and supported by UNESCO.

In order to strengthen contacts between regions, inter-regional co-operation in the Project was advocated e.g., representatives from other regions should be invited to attend regional meetings.

E. Ways and Means to Develop the Project at the International Level

Participants welcomed the convening of an Inter-governmental Conference on the implementation of the Recommendation on Education for International Understanding in 1982 and recommends that the Associated Schools Project be one of the main items on its agenda. They also supported the suggestion to hold the first international congress on the Project in 1983 and hopes that it will receive wide support from Member-States.

International fellowships were considered as a useful means to further co-operation between different regions but it was suggested that the candidates for such fellowships should be carefully selected and be actively involved in the Project. The organization of group study tours of teachers coming from different regions was urged. International seminars for Associated School teachers should also be regularly convened on specific teaching issue for example on the study of the United Nations system and such meetings could most usefully be held at the Headquarters of the United Nations and its Specialized Agencies such as UNESCO, FAO, WHO, UNIDO, etc.

UNESCO should prepare a manual in different languages to help Member-States and teachers implement the Project.

Participants wished to acknowledge the fine work which has been carried out by the UNESCO Secretariat in implementing the Associated Schools Project. However, in view of the magnitude of the task at hand, it was recommended that both the financial and human resources of the Secretariat be increased in order to enable the Organization to further the Project accordingly.

II. Suggestions for Introducing Similar Activities into Certain Establishments of Higher Education

The meeting discussed under item 5 of its agenda the question of how to introduce similar activities into certain establishments of higher education. Participants based their discussion on Part D of the evaluators' report and on the report of the consultation on the extension of the Associated Schools Project to the University level, held in Paris in 1977 (Ref. ED-77/WS/136).

In accordance with the discussion on the previous items participants recalled the need for the further development of the Project to undertake more research on the implementation of the Project, to intensify in-service teacher-training programmes and to prepare adequate teaching material. In order to achieve these objectives co-operation between schools and specialized institutions of the higher education level is essential. Mention was made by several speakers that already university, institutes, educational research centres and teacher-training colleges have contributed effectively. The meeting recognized, therefore, the important role of higher education institutions for the furthering of the Associated Schools Project and for the implementation of the Recommendation concerning Education for International Understanding, Co-operation and Peace and Education relating to Human Rights and Fundamental Freedoms.

On the other hand, it was pointed out that the Associated Schools Project got its vitality on account of the role that it plays in the community and because it was centred on the direct contact between teachers and students at school. The main objective of the project is to improve, by experiential and innovative programmes conducted in the participating schools, the existing curriculum in the field of educational content, methods and materials, and the meeting felt that this goal should remain the central objective of the project. Higher education institutions, however, can help to reach this educational objective and should be invited, wherever possible, to lend their assistance to the project.

Different views were expressed on the question of strategies to be applied for the association of higher education institutions to the project. While some participants felt it necessary to launch a strong appeal among universities and other higher education institutions to join the project others called for a cautious and selective approach. It was said that due to the limited funds available and to the need to strengthen at present the existing network, only those institutions in the field of higher education should be invited which could effectively contribute to the improvement of the project. The meeting recommended that this question should receive further study and the decision should be left to the national level in order to find the most adequate ways of co-operation with the higher education level.

Some participants introduced the idea of changing the name of the project because they felt the existing one was restrictive. "Global education network" or "Associated Institutions Programme in education for international understanding" were two examples of possible changes. Participants felt, however, that the present name of the project was widely known and accepted and that any change needs through deliberation on its positive aspects as well as the negative ones. This question might be raised again at the proposed International Congress of Associated Schools Representatives in 1983.

III. Conclusion

The meeting concluded its work by a strong affirmation of the objectives, achievement and role of the project in contemporary society and its relevance to the great problems of our time. The following statement was unanimously adopted.

The Associated Schools Project and the Education of the Future

As the Associated Schools Project approaches its fourth decade of service to the world's educational community, we reaffirm our commitment to its goals of strengthening international understanding, co-operation and peace. At the same time, we dedicated ourselves to its renewal and further development, as a major educational force for building the defences of peace in the minds and hearts of all peoples and for the evolution of a new world community based on justice, humanity, and harmony with the environment.

In these times, the emerging concept of lifelong education and the new opportunities created by the revolutionary technologies of communication offer the promise of joining education, science and culture together in a new enterprise to liberate the human spirit, to enrich the minds of all persons, and to project human values in the service of international co-operation and peace. The new goals of the education of the future recognize the integrity and diversity of cultures while seeking the universality of thought and embracing the common values and tasks of humanity.

The education of the future providing for a person's entire life span must be directed towards his or her fulfilment as a total person, as a creative worker, and as a member of society at national, regional and global levels. Educational programmes and processes must be related to the needs of the human community in a rapidly changing future and underscore a resurgence of our common human values.

We stand at a critical point in history. We are witnessing for the first time the emergence of a global civilization based on the diversity of cultures and societies. But our technology has far outstripped the capacity of our social institutions to cope with it and both pose a striking challenge to those values which guide all of us in our response to the awesome global problems of conflict, injustice, disease and poverty.

The Associated Schools Project of UNESCO as a voluntary worldwide network of some 1,400 schools in over 70 countries has achieved a remarkable record of helping teachers and students to understand better these awesome problems and the efforts of the international community to deal with them. But its work is only beginning. The challenges to international co-operation and peace which lie ahead are still greater than in the past 30 years and require far more determined efforts to enlist the world's educational community in the cause of peace and justice.

We, therefore, call upon the Member-States of UNESCO, the students, teachers and administrators now participating in the Associated Schools Project, and all who share our desire to build a new education for the future dedicated to justice, humanity and harmony with the environment. Let us embark together on the exciting enterprise of implementing the UNESCO Recommendations concerning Education for International Understanding, Co-operation and Peace and Education relating to Human Rights and Fundamental Freedoms through an expanded and reinvigorated Associated Schools Project.

BIBLIOGRAPHY

UNESCO DOCUMENTS AND PUBLICATIONS*

1. *Apartheid – a teacher's guide* by Godfrey N. Brown. Paris, UNESCO, 1981, 105 p.

* Listing to illustrate the range of UNESCO documents and publications.

2. *Consultative committee on steps to promote the full and comprehensive implementation of the recommendation concerning education for international understanding, co-operation and peace and education relating to human rights and fundamental freedoms.* Paris, 24-28 November 1986. *Final report.* Paris, UNESCO, 1986, 14 p. + annexes. ED-86/CONF. 504/1.
3. *Education for international co-operation and peace at the primary school level.* Paris, UNESCO, 1983, 138 p.
4. *An Experience-centered curriculum – exercises in perception, communication and action* by David Wolsk. Paris, UNESCO, 1975, 52 p. (Educational studies and documents No. 17).
5. *Human rights - questions and answers* by Leah Levin. Paris, UNESCO, 1981, 86 p. [on sale]
6. *Implementation of the plan for the development of education for international understanding, co-operation and peace.* Report of the Director-General. Executive Board document 126 EX/16. Paris, UNESCO, 1987, 11 p. + annexe.
7. *Intergovernmental conference on education for international understanding, co-operation and peace and education relating to human rights and fundamental freedoms, with a view to developing a climate of opinion favourable to the strengthening of security and disarmament.* UNESCO House, 12-20 April 1983. *Final report.* Paris, UNESCO, 1983, 101 p.
8. *International congress on the occasion of the thirtieth anniversary of the associated schools project.* Sofia, Bulgaria, 12-16 September 1983. *Final report.* Paris, UNESCO, 1984, 26 p. + annexes.
9. *International consultation on ways of improving educational action at the level of higher education, to provide students with the necessary knowledge of problems relating to peace and respect for human rights and the rights of peoples.* Athens-Delphi, 20-24 January 1986. *Final report.* Greek National Commission for UNESCO, 1986, 32 p.
10. *International education in twelve countries.* Finnish National Commission for UNESCO, 1986, 497 p. (European joint studies in education No. 9).
11 *International expert meeting on the role of women in the education of young people for peace, mutual understanding and respect for human rights,* New Delhi, India, 7-11 December 1981. *Summary record of discussions.* Paris, UNESCO, 1982, 35 p. +

annexes. ED-82/CONF. 609/4.

12 *International understanding at school.* A bi-annual bulletin published under the Associated Schools Project. Paris, UNESCO

13. *Partners in promoting education for international understanding; for participation in the UNESCO associated schools project. Practical manual.* Paris, UNESCO, 1986, 49 p. + annexes. ED-86/WS/44.

14. *Plan for the development of education for international understanding, co-operation and peace.* Paris, UNESCO, 1986 ED-86/WS/40.

15. *Questionnaire on the application of the recommendation concerning education for international understanding, co-operation and peace and education relating to human rights and fundamental freedoms adopted by the General Conference at its eighteenth session.* Paris, 1974. Executive Board document 126 EX/17, Annex. Paris, UNESCO, 1987, 15 p.

16. *Recommendation on education for international understanding, co-operation and peace and education relating to human rights and fundamental freedoms.* Paris, UNESCO, 1974.

17. *Seeds for peace : the role of pre-school education in international understanding and education for peace.* Paris, UNESCO, 1985, 123 p.

18. *Some suggestions on teaching about human rights.* Paris, UNESCO, 1968, 155 p.

19. *Teaching for international understanding, peace and human rights* by Norman J. Graves et al. Paris, UNESCO, 1984, 244 p.

20. *The Teaching of contemporary world issues* by Robert Harris, Carole Hahn. Paris, UNESCO, 1986, 198 p.

21. *World problems in the classroom.* Paris, UNESCO, 1981, 61 p. (ESD No. 41).

22. *Yes, we can ... together*! UNESCO Clubs and Associations, UNESCO Associated Schools Project. Paris, UNESCO, 1988, 78 p.

See also UNESCO series *International studies in education.*

12

PHYSICAL EDUCATION AND SPORTS

INTERNATIONAL CHARTER FOR PHYSICAL EDUCATION AND SPORTS, 1978*

Preamble

The General Conference of the United Nations Educational, Scientific and Cultural Organization, meeting in Paris at its twentieth session, the twenty-first day of November, 1978,

'Recalling' that in the United Nations Charter the peoples proclaimed their faith in fundamental human rights and in the dignity and worth of the human person, and affirmed their determination to promote social progress and better standards of life,

'Recalling' that by the terms of the Universal Declaration of Human Rights, everyone is entitled to all the rights and freedoms set forth therein without discrimination of social origin, property, birth or other consideration,

'Convinced' that to preserve and develop the physical, intellectual and moral powers of the human being improves the quality of life at the national and the international levels,

'Believing' that physical education and sport should make a more effective contribution to the inculcation of fundamental human values underlying the full development of peoples,

'Stressing' accordingly that physical education and sport should seek to promote closer communion between peoples and between

---

* Resolution 1/5, 4/2 adopted by the General Conference of UNESCO at its Twentieth Session (November 1978).

individuals, together with disinterested emulation, solidarity and fraternity, mutual respect and understanding, and full respect for the integrity and dignity of human beings,

'Considering' that responsibilities and obligations are incumbent upon the industrialized countries and the developing countries alike for reducing the disparity which continues to exist between them in respect of free and universal access to physical education and sport,

'Considering' that to integrate physical education and sport in the natural environment is to enrich them and to inspire respect of the earth's resources and a concern to conserve them and use them for the greater good of humanity as a whole,

'Taking' into account the diversity of the forms of training and education existing in the world, but nothing that, notwithstanding the differences between national sports structures, it is clearly evident that physical education and sport are not confined to physical well-being and health but also contribute to the full and well-balanced development of the human being,

'Taking' into account, furthermore, the enormous efforts that have to be made before the right to physical education and sport can become a reality for all human beings,

'Stressing' the importance for peace and friendship among peoples of co-operation between the international governmental and non-governmental organizations responsible for physical education and sport,

'Proclaims' this International Charter for the purpose of placing the development of physical education and sport at the service of human progress, promoting their development, and urging governments, competent non-governmental organizations, educators, families and individuals themselves to be guided thereby, to disseminate it and to put it into practice.

Article 1. The Practice of Physical Education and Sport is a Fundamental Right for All

1.1. Every human being has a fundamental right of access to physical education and sport, which are essential for the full development of his personality. The freedom to develop physical, intellectual and moral powers through physical education and sport must be guaranteed both within the educational system and in other aspects of social life.

1.2. Everyone must have full opportunities, in accordance with his national tradition of sport, for practising physical education and sport, developing his physical fitness and attaining a level of achievement in sport which corresponds to his gifts.

1.3. Special opportunities must be made available for young people, including children of pre-school age, for the aged and for the handicapped to develop their personalities to the full through physical education and sport programmes suited to their requirements.

Article 2. Physical Education and Sport form an Essential Element of Lifelong Education in the Overall Education System

2.1 Physical education and sport, as an essential dimension of education and culture, must develop the abilities, will-power and self-discipline of every human being as a fully integrated member of society. The continuity of physical activity and the practice of sports must be ensured throughout life by means of a global, lifelong and democratized education.

2.2. At the individual level, physical education and sport contribute to the maintenance and improvement of health, provide a wholesome leisure-time occupation and enable man to overcome the drawbacks of modern living. At the community level, they enrich social relations and develop fair play, which is essential not only to sport itself but also to life in society.

2.3. Every overall education system must assign the requisite place and importance to physical education and sport in order to establish a balance and strengthen links between physical activities and other components of education.

Article 3. Physical Education and Sport Programmes must meet Individual and Social Needs

3.1. Physical education and sport programmes must be designed to suit the requirements and personal characteristics of those practising them, as well as the institutional, cultural, socio-economic and climatic conditions of each country. They must give priority to the requirements of disadvantaged groups in society.

3.2. In the process of education in general, physical education and sport programmes must, by virtue of both their content and their timetables, help to create habits and behaviour patterns conducive to full development of the human person.

3.3. Even when it has spectacular features, competitive sport must always aim, in accordance with the Olympic ideal, to serve the purpose of educational sport, of which it represents the crowning epitome. It must in no way be influenced by profit-seeking commercial interests.

Article 4. Teaching, Coaching and Administration of Physical Education and Sport should be Performed by Qualified Personnel

4.1. All personnel who assume professional responsibility for physical education and sport must have appropriate qualification and training. They must be carefully selected in sufficient numbers and given preliminary as well as further training to ensure that they reach adequate levels of specialization.

4.2. 'Voluntary personnel', given appropriate training and supervision, can make an invaluable contribution to the comprehensive development of sport and encourage the participation of the practice and organization of physical and sport activities.

4.3. Appropriate structures must be established for the training of personnel for physical education and sport. Personnel who have received such training must be given a status in keeping with the duties they perform.

Article 5. Adequate Facilities and Equipment are Essential to Physical Education and Sport

5.1. Adequate and sufficient facilities and equipment must be provided and installed to meet the needs of intensive and safe participation in both in school and out-of-school programmes concerning physical education and sport.

5.2. It is incumbent on governments, public authorities, schools and appropriate private agencies, at all levels, to join forces and plan together so as to provide and make optimum use of installations, facilities, and equipment for physical education and sport.

5.3. It is essential that plans for rural and urban development include provision for long-term needs in the matter of installations, facilities and equipment for physical education and sport, taking into account the opportunities offered by the natural environment.

Article 6. Research and Evaluation are Indispensable Components of the Development of Physical Education and Sport

6.1. Research and evaluation in physical education and sport should make for the progress of all forms of sport and help to bring about an improvement in the health and safety of participants as well as in training methods and organization and management procedures. The education system will thereby benefit from innovations calculated to develop better teaching methods and standards of performance.

6.2. Scientific research, whose social implications in this sphere should not be overlooked, must be oriented in such a way that it does not allow of improper applications to physical education and sport.

Article 7. Information and Documentation help to Promote Physical Education and Sport

7.1. The collection, provision and dissemination of information and documentation on physical education and sport constitute a major necessity. In particular, there is a need to circulate information on the results of research and evaluation studies concerning programmes, experiments and activities.

Article 8. The Mass Media should Exert a Positive Influence on Physical Education and Sport

8.1. Without prejudice to the right of freedom of information, it is essential that everyone involved in the mass media be fully conscious of his responsibilities having regard to the social importance, the humanistic purpose and the moral values embodied in physical education and sport.

8.2. Relations between those involved in the mass media and

specialists in physical education and sport must be close and based on mutual confidence in order to exercise a positive influence on physical education and sport and to ensure objective and well-founded information. Training of personnel for the media may include elements relating to physical education and sport.

Article 9. National Institutions Play Major Role in Physical Education and Sport

9.1. It is essential that public authorities at all levels and specialized non-governmental bodies encourage those physical education and sport activities whose educational value is most evident. Their action shall consist in enforcing legislation and regulations, providing material assistance and adopting all other measures of encouragement, stimulation and control. The public authorities will also ensure that such fiscal measures are adopted as may encourage the activities.

9.2. It is incumbent on all institutions responsible for physical education and sport to promote a consistent, overall and decentralized plan of action in the framework of lifelong education so as to allow for continuity and co-ordination between compulsory physical activities and those practised freely and spontaneously.

Article 10. International Co-operation is a Prerequisite for the Universal and Well-balanced Promotion of Physical Education and Sport

10.1. It is essential that States and those international and regional intergovernmental and non-governmental organizations in which interested countries are represented and which are responsible for physical education and sport give physical education and sport greater prominence in international bilateral and multilateral co-operation.

10.2 International co-operation must be prompted by wholly disinterested motives in order to promote and stimulate endogenous development in this field.

10.3 Through co-operation and the pursuit of mutual interests in the universal language of physical education and sport, all peoples will contribute to the preservation of lasting peace, mutual respect and friendship and will thus create a propitious climate for solving international problems. Close collaboration between all interested national and international governmental and non-governmental agencies, based on respect for the specific competence of each, will necessarily encourage the development of physical education and sport throughout the world.

BIBLIOGRAPHY

UNESCO DOCUMENTS AND PUBLICATIONS*

1. *Ad hoc committee of the intergovernmental committee for physical education and sport.* (First session), Paris, 16-19 December 1981. *Final report.* Paris, UNESCO, 1981, 21 p. ED-81/CONF.20/COL.5.
2. *Development of physical education and sport since 1976.* Second international conference of ministers and senior officials responsible for physical education and sport, Moscow, USSR, 21-25 November 1988. *Reference document.* Paris, UNESCO, 1988, 71 p. ED-88/MINEPS II/4.
3. *Interdisciplinary regional meeting of experts on physical education and sport.* Brisbane, Australia, 19-29 September 1982. *Final report.* University of Queensland/UNESCO, 61 p.
4. *Intergovernmental committee for physical education and sport.* (Second session), Paris, 3-10 March 1981. *Final report.* Paris, UNESCO, 1981, 55 p. ED/MD/64.
5. *Intergovernmental committee for physical education and sport.* (Third session), Paris, 22-29 March 1983. *Final report.* Paris, UNESCO, 1983, 58 p. ED/MD/73.
6. *Intergovernmental committee for physical education and sport.* (Fourth session), Paris, 9-16 October 1984. *Final report.* Paris, UNESCO, 1985, 23 p. + annexes. ED/MD/77.
7. *Intergovernmental committee for physical education and the sport.* (Fifth session), Paris, 7-13 October 1986. *Final report.*

* Listing to illustrate the range of UNESCO documents and publications.

Paris, UNESCO, 1986, 53 p. ED/MD/82.

8. *International charter of physical education and sport/Charte Internationale de l'education physique et du sport/Carta International de la education fisica y el deporte.* Paris, UNESCO, 1980.
9. *International symposium on physical education and sport programs for the physically and mentally handicapped.* Washington, D.C., 22-27 November 1982. *Final report.* Paris, UNESCO, 105 p. ED-84/WS/53.
10. *Physical education and sport in the cause of humanism.* Second international conference of ministers and senior officials responsible for physical education and sport, Moscow, USSR, 21-25 November 1988. Paris, UNESCO, 1988, 18 p. + annexe. ED-88/MINEPS II/3.
11. *Planning inexpensive facilities and equipment for physical education, sports and recreation programs* by Carlos Vera Guardia. Paris, UNESCO/ICHPER, 1985, 139 p. ED-85/WS/5.
12. *The Reduction of current disparities between developed and developing countries in the field of sport and physical education a comparative study* by John F. Coghlan. Paris, UNESCO, 1988, 69 p. ED-88/WS/48.
13. *The Role of girls and women in developing physical education and sport programs* by Carole A. Oglesby and Christine S. Walters. Paris, UNESCO/ICHPER, 1984, 74 p. ED-84/WS/71.
14. *The Role of physical education and sport in the education of youth.* First international conference of ministers and senior officials responsible for physical education and sport organized by UNESCO with the co-operation of the ICSPE. Paris, 5-10 April 1976. *Final report.* Paris, UNESCO, 1976, 26 p. + annexes. ED/MD/43.
15. *Sports facilities for schools in developing countries. An inventory of experiences and proposals for future projects* by F.B. Seriven and Associates. Paris, UNESCO, 1973, 39 p. (Educational studies and documents no. 8).
16 *Sport for all programmes throughout the world.* Report prepared by Peter McIntosh, International Council of Sport and Physical Education. Paris, UNESCO, 63 p. + references. ED-82/WS/65.
17 *Sports for the physically handicapped* by Ludwig Guttman. Paris, UNESCO, 1976, 53 p.
18. *Suggested guidelines for conducting a national status study for*

physical education and sport by Charles L. Heilman and Carl A. Troester, Jr. Paris, UNESCO/ICHPER, 1983, 35 p. ED-85/WS/19.

19. *Ways and means of organizing a system for the standardized collection of documentation in physical education and sport* prepared by Jan Broekhoff. Paris, UNESCO, 1980, 92 p. ED-80/WS/68.

13

MANAGEMENT OF EDUCATION

INTERNATIONAL CONFERENCE OF EDUCATION RECOMMENDATION CONCERNING THE IMPROVEMENT OF THE ORGANIZATION AND MANAGEMENT OF EDUCATION SYSTEMS AS A MEANS OF RAISING EFFICIENCY IN ORDER TO EXTEND THE RIGHT TO EDUCATION, 1978

Preamble

The International Conference of Education convened by the United Nations Educational, Scientific and Cultural Organization in Geneva for its 37th session from 5 to 14 July, 1979.

Considering Article 26 of the Universal Declaration of Human Rights (1948).

Considering the Declaration of the Rights of the Child (1959).

Considering Article 5 of the Declaration on Race and Racial prejudice adopted by the General Conference of UNESCO at its twentieth session (1978).

Considering the provisions of the Declaration on the Promotion among Youth of the Ideals of Peace, Mutual Respect and Understanding between Peoples, adopted by the General Assembly of the United Nations in its resolution 2037 (XX) (1965).

Considering the Convention and Recommendation against Discrimination in Education adopted by the General Conference of UNESCO at its eleventh session (1960).

Considering the UNESCO/ILO Recommendation concerning the Status of Teachers (1966).

Considering the Recommendation on Education for International Understanding, Co-operation and Peace and on Education Concerning Human Rights and Fundamental Freedoms adopted by the General Conference of UNESCO at its eighteenth session (1974).

Considering the recommendations of the International Conference on Education Planning (1968).

Considering the recommendations of the Third Regional Conference of Ministers of Education and Ministers Responsible for Economic Planning in the Arab States (Marrakesh, January 1970); those of the Third Regional Conference of Ministers of Education and those Responsible for Economic Planning in Asia (Singapore, May-June 1971); those of the Conference of Ministers of Education and those Responsible for the Promotion of Science and Technology in Relation to Development in Latin America and the Caribbean (Venezuela, December 1971); those of the Second Conference of Ministers of Education of European Member States (Bucharest, November-December 1973); those of the Final Act of the Conference on Security and Co-operation in Europe (Helsinki, 1975); those of the Meeting of Senior Officials of the Ministries of Education of the 25 Least Developed Countries (Paris, 8-16 September, 1975); those of the Fourth Conference of Ministers of Education of African Member-States (Lagos, January-February 1976); those of the Conference of Ministers of Education and those Responsible for Economic Planning in the Arab States (Abu Dhabi, November 1977); and those of the Fourth Regional Conference of Ministers of Education and those Responsible for Economic Planning in Asia and Oceania (Colombo, July-August 1978).

Noting in particular, that Recommendation No. 23 of the Colombo Conference and Recommendation No. 38 of the Abu Dhabi Conference emphasize the importance of research, exchanges and co-operation, at all levels, in the field of educational planning, management and administration.

Considering the relevant recommendations adopted by the International Conference on Education at its various sessions and, more especially Recommendation No. 66 concerning "the improved effectiveness of education systems particularly through reduction of wastage at all levels of instruction," and Recommendation No. 67 concerning "the social background of students and their chance of success at school".

Considering all the relevant recommendations adopted by the UNESCO General Conference at its various sessions, above all the recommendations on the relation between the full implementation of the right to education and the democratization of education, social progress and the solution of fundamental problems of mankind especially the strengthening of peace, transition to disarmament, and the promotion of human rights.

Considering that, in this International Year of the Child and in the years to come all due attention should be given to the inadequate provision of education at many levels which still exists in various parts of the world.

Considering the resolutions of the UNESCO General Conference and the decisions of its Executive Board concernir.g educational and cultural rights in the occupied Arab territories.

Considering that the right to education is a fundamental human right and that no measure likely to contribute to its wider application should be neglected.

Considering that the problems of educational management and administration are matters of grave concern for the majority of Member States at the present time.

Considering that the improvement and streamlining of educational planning, management and administration methods are likely to contribute to a very great extent to the democratization of education.

Considering that the extensive progress already achieved in the fields of educational planning, management and administration may be further consolidated and promoted through regional and international co-operation.

Considering that not only things but also, basically, human beings should be developed, reappraisal and renewal of education system should necessarily include cultural and educational elements specific to human development, in addition to the effects of rapid technological change and the circumstances of a new world economic order.

Recognizing that greater efficiency is called for in these fields in regard to the mobilization of resources and their administration, in order to achieve that democratization of education on the largest possible scale.

Recognizing the constitutional provisions of each Member-State, and its particular educational needs.

Submits for consideration by the ministers responsible for education and the appropriate authorities and agencies in the various Member-States, the following Recommendation.

A. UNDERLYING PRINCIPLES

1. The improvement of the organization and management of education systems as a means to increase efficiency in order to extend the right to education should be guided by the following principles:

(a) A statement of the aims of policies for the development and strengthening of the right to education and the means required for their application should enable all the administrative authorities to understand the aims pursued and to see what part they play in the application of those policies.

(b) Systems of education must be responsive to the imperatives of such policy direction and, to this end, should be reviewed regularly to ensure that policies relevant to extension of the right to education are optimally implemented and that priorities arising from such policies are being met.

(c) Broad participation of all sectors of the population in appropriate aspects of the educational process is essential to the generalized and effective exercise of the right to education, and educational organization and management should reflect the need to maximize such participation.

(d) The optimum combination of centralization and decentralization in organization and management, taking account of the national systems applied, should be considered as an important means of enlarging participation, provided that such measures maintain or increase the efficiency of education systems.

(e) Resource mobilization and utilization should be a primary concern at each level of educational management in order to make the most effective use of the financial, material and human resources available, to extend the right to education.

(f) The selection and training of administrative personnel at all levels is a key element in the improvement of educational management as the extension of the right to education places new demand on such personnel for specialized knowledge as well as for creative approaches to educational problems.

(g) International co-operation is essential to reinforce the exchange of information among Member-States concerning the improvement of organization and management, and to sustain efforts to provide the necessary training.

B. PRACTICAL MEASURES AT NATIONAL LEVEL

National Goals and Policies

1. Goals and aims embodied in statements of national educational policy should refer explicitly to the objective of extending the right of education to everyone, irrespective of race, nationality, language, sex, religion or any other classification.
2. Legislative provision for free and/or compulsory schooling for certain levels of formal and non-formal types of education, as appropriate, should be expressly mentioned.
3. Due recognition should be given to the special educational needs of the disadvantaged groups in the community wherever they exist. Examples of such groups are ethnic and migrant minorities, adult illiterates, rural children, and others. The same importance should be given to the education of the physically and mentally handicapped. Appropriate legislative action should be taken to guarantee to women and girls the right to equal educational opportunity.
4. Educational policies should, within the overall goal of nation-building, emphasize the aspects of culture, science and technology.
5. The particular needs of the pre-school age child should be expressly recognised.
6. The importance of lifelong education and, consequently, that of non-formal education as a complement to formal education should be given due recognition.
7. The importance of education as a constituent factor in the socio-economic development of the nation, as an overall objective, should be emphasized. At the same time, the relevance of social conditions to the extensive implementation of the right to education should not be overlooked.
8. To facilitate the achievement of national policy which tends to be long-term, it is advisable to identify current priorities for more effective implementation of short- and mid-term goals.
9. A periodical review of priorities is also necessary to redeploy resources to more optimum use, based on an assessment of current needs.
10. To ensure an effective strategy which takes note of the needs, potential and perspective of educational development, due

emphasis should be placed on research and innovative activities contributing to this effort.

11. Provision should therefore be made, as appropriate to the organization of national systems, for the institutional means to pursue effectively the planning and research activities necessary for systematic educational development within the context of overall national development plans.
12. Access to up to date information on contemporary developments in education, in the appropriate cognate fields, not only at the national but also at the international level, is essential for the proper formulation of educational policy.

Improvement of Educational Management

13. While it is evident that a basic aim of better management is to achieve optimum results with a given resource input, this must be qualified by the fact that educational activities cannot be judged wholly in cost-benefit terms, but must also take into account the intangible and unquantifiable aspects of education.
14. It must also be recognized that educational administration and management procedures will necessarily vary between countries depending on the historical, social and cultural background, and on the existing socio-economic structures.
15. Certain broad criteria should be identified for more efficient educational management, including the following:

16. *Educational Planning*

    (a) In establishing targets and strategies for educational plans it is necessary to take into account current and prospective demographic changes and their likely effect on educational growth and the national budget, as well as the results of sociological and economic research relating to the conditions of the development of education.
    (b) An information system should be created which will permit their efficient educational planning through familiarity with past decision-making experiences.
    (c) A review of the education sector, in relation to other sectors in the economy, for the purpose of ascertaining manpower requirements is also needed for an overall planning perspective.

(d) Co-ordination amongst all institutions engaged in providing educational services is essential to avoid duplication of effort and wastage of material resources, and to achieve the best possible learning environment for students, in or out of school, in the education system.

(e) There is a need for more effective liaison and communication between government and non-governmental agencies concerned as regards the fields of both formal and non-formal education.

(f) It must also be recognized that better management of educational resources as a whole may lead to drastic shifts of emphasis on education and training, and educational administrators must be prepared for these changes.

(g) The investment priorities for educational financing should be established within the framework of an overall development programme.

17. *Centralization/Decentralization*

(a) Educational administrators should make the best possible use of the optimum combination of the effects of centralization and decentralization, while respecting national systems, in order to broaden the financial bases of education and foster wider citizen participation in local educational management.

(b) Advisory councils, parent-teacher associations, community assemblies, and similar consultative organs should be considered as a means to encourage closer community involvement.

(c) The mobility of students and personnel should be one of the consequences of the optimum combination of the effects of decentralization in an overall view of the situation.

(d) In any decentralization scheme, adequate provision must also be made to protect the interests of economically deprived communities who may not have sufficient resources to meet their commitments.

(e) It is also necessary to recognize that centralization of certain functions in educational administration, e.g. compatibility of qualifications and service privileges, is necessary in the interests of overall efficiency within the system.

18. *Staff*

(a) Adequate measures, including allocation of the necessary funds, to provide security of tenure, through opportunities for training and appropriate service incentives, are necessary to promote staff morale and improve the quality of education.
(b) This is specially important in relation to the introduction of educational innovations and other reforms, when the full co-operation of all staff concerned is vital for success.
(c) Effective communication at all levels of staff responsibility is indispensable to a proper understanding and appreciation of common objectives, so as to ensure their attainment.
(d) The role of the teachers and heads of educational institutions, as well as of the others directly concerned in the educational process-in-school and out-of-school — is of cardinal importance in this respect.
(e) It is desirable that institutional heads and other supervisors, such as school inspectors, who must provide effective leadership in this regard, should not be overloaded with routine administrative duties.
(f) While the concept of division of labour and task specialization is important, as well as the need for reasonable stability and continuity in post, it is necessary to reconcile this with the need for staff or units to co-operate with each other and with the need for staff reassignments in given circumstances.
(g) In addition, there are other related questions, such as job satisfaction and recycling of hardships posts, which call for a sound empirical approach based on accepted service principles.
(h) It is also recommended that current practice in other countries or regions with similar problems should be taken into consideration.

19. *Evaluation*

(a) A clear definition of objectives being essential for proper evaluation, analysis of expected outcomes for each planned activity or group of activities in programme implementation is necessary both for routine checking and final assessment. In the interest of successful implementation of an overall national plan or the attainment of educational goals, the establishment of common parameters of evaluation is advantageous.

(b) It is desirable that such evaluation should be extended to the educational administrators themselves.

(c) It should be recognized that a system of control of the execution of programmes is indispensable, to enable necessary adjustments and modifications to be made, and thus to improve overall progress and results.

(d) Such control being dependent on data provided by continuous evaluation and feedback, national and regional networks engaged in the collection and dissemination of educational statistics and other information should be capable of performing their functions satisfactorily.

(e) Standardization of administrative practice within any given system or subsystem should be encouraged to promote compatibility of information exchange.

(f) Modern technology should be utilized, to the extent possible, to secure a satisfactory educational administration.

Role and Training of Educational Administrators

20. It is recognized that the growing complexity of administration *per se* as well as the needs of contemporary society, impose new demands on the capacity and therefore the training requirements of educational administrators.
21. Since it is desirable that the training of educational administrators should conform with the principle of lifelong education, i.e. it should be dynamic and continuous such training should, to the extent possible, aim at providing an understanding of broad social, economic, national and international issues, besides covering the administrative and technical aspects of education.
22. In terms of the individual, a job requirement analysis is desirable to enable the competent authorities to develop a professional profile for each type of education administrator, so as to better define his or her role in the educational process and to evaluate performance against assigned responsibilities.
23. Such an analysis is necessary also for a better conceived administrative structure, based on division of labour and task specialization, with clearly defined areas of responsibility without

losing sight of the whole.

24. In recognition of the fact that education is an integral part of community and national development, due allowance must be made in the training content for the supportive roles which educational administrators may be called upon to play in this regard, and especially in relation to the objective of promoting community participation in educational development.
25. Subject to national circumstances and priorities, it is recommended that staff training for educational administrators be institutionalized so as to provide proper support for both pre- and in-service training which will maintain a strong administrative cadre for the service.
26. In conformity with the principle of democratization of educational opportunity, selection of candidates for staff training should be based on clearly defined criteria and proven field experience, in addition to academic or professional status.
27. Based on past experience, a practical scheme of incentives (including non-financial rewards) should be devised to attract candidates for training.

Resource Mobilization and Utilization

28. For effective planning and budgeting in educational development, it is necessary that a regular, broad inventory be made of the financial, human and material resources available for educational programmes.
29. Wider community participation such as parents, civic organizations, commerce and industry should be encouraged, both in the interest of democratization of educational opportunity as well as strengthening the links between education and society.
30. The involvement of the general public, including all social and economic sectors, is also desirable to obtain access to contributions which otherwise would not be available for use in educational development.
31. Volunteer service centres for non-instructional tasks by parents and others offering assistance to educational centres within their individual capacities should be fostered in the same spirit of developing and utilizing latent community resources.
32. New technologies in education, based on distance teaching, external degree programmes, independent study, correspondence

courses, and other such programmes should be further developed for their particular relevance to rural schools, as well as their potential for the "second chance" education of adult students for various types of courses and at all levels.

33. Endogenous approaches, less dependent on technological support, should also be pursued, as appropriate to local conditions.

C. INTERNATIONAL CO-OPERATION

34. Co-operation at the international and regional levels to further the aims of this recommendation should focus on the following suggestions applied by Member-States responding to the pre-Conference questionnaire:

(a) There is a felt need for analytical case studies on current efforts to achieve a better balance between different levels and types of education, within the context of the overall objective of universalization of education.

(b) Such studies should emphasize the concrete and the practical, and should illustrate different types of educational administration and management, paying particular attention to those features which are of common interest for their relevance to other countries or regions, for application or adaptation to their own needs.

(c) A problem-oriented approach is desirable, focusing on such issues as increasing the efficiency of education; raising standards in rural primary schools; the reform of secondary education to respond to contemporary needs; the role immatures and other teacher auxiliaries; and closer involvement of universities in educational development; criteria for the selection and the determination of the content of education; the role of the school in preparing the young generation for life; the requirements to be met if education is to lead to the full development of the personality; and the connection between uniformity and differentiation in the field of education.

(d) In the perspective of recurrent or lifelong education, it is important to assess the future trend of major developments in, for example, the evolving relationship of vocational training to general education.

(e) There is also a need for a pragmatic system of critical indicators to measure the degree to which an education system has been responsive to social requirements, to the extent that such indicators can be established.

(f) The role and function of examinations and related tests of achievement or progress offer another area for fruitful co-operation between countries.

(g) There is a similar demand for comprehensive information on the availability and usefulness of modern techniques in educational administration, including use of the new teaching media with particular reference to the special manpower requirements needed to introduce and maintain such an infrastructure.

(h) Regional centres of educational innovation for development are urged to prepare training modules and other teaching materials for the use of national staff training institutions.

35. UNESCO, particularly through the IBE and in close collaboration with other international agencies and organizations, should be invited to assist Member-States to improve their systems of educational management, with the overall objective of democratization and renewal of education, by intensifying action in the following fields:

(a) Support of action-oriented research in Member States, particularly for innovative projects aimed at widening educational opportunity.

(b) Documentation and dissemination of such research and other relevant information to facilitate the exchange of country experiences between Member-States.

(c) Provision of specialist training facilities in educational planning, research, evaluation, administration, and management for the conditions and needs of Member-States.

(d) Convening regional and international meetings of experts for detailed study of specific problems in educational management related to the universalization of education.

36. The UNESCO Regional Offices for Education should also continue to provide the impetus and support currently given to the regional networks of educational innovation for development, besides offering training and advisory services in cognate fields.

The study of the economics of education should be included in the programmes of the regional centres, particularly those serving the developing countries.

37. The Conference also suggests that:

(a) The International Institute for Educational Planning should continue its programme of training and research activities, oriented particularly with regard to the needs of developing countries.
(b) The International Bureau of Education should further develop its current services for educational documentation and information, and in particular assist in the co-ordination of educational information networks, towards the achievements of a viable global network supplying up to date information for the use of educational administrators and other specialists in Member-States.
(c) Member-States, the United Nations High Commissioner for Refugees, the United Nations Relief and Works Agency for Palestine Refugees and other competent bodies should be requested to step up their efforts to help refugee children and to increase the educational and social services they provide for such children.

38. The Conference emphasizes, in this International Year of the Child, the importance of joint action by UNESCO and other United Nations agencies, notably UNICEF, to ensure that the school, the family and the community may continue to play an important role in the education and welfare of children, especially those in territories under foreign and military occupation, those affected by war, famine or disease, and in regions where the scourges of racism and racial discrimination are still to be found. The priority aim is to give children who are the victims of foreign and military occupation, war, and those who are refugees as a result of natural catastrophes, better opportunities and greater means of fully exercising their right to education and a safe and stable life, and also to help them express their cultural identity through national education programmes based on their own culture and heritage.

BIBLIOGRAPHY

UNESCO DOCUMENTS AND PUBLICATIONS*

1. *The Administrative structures of education. Case studies on sixteen countries* by H.T.B. Harris. Paris, UNESCO, 1983, 110 p.
2. *Annotated bibliography on practice and research in educational administration and management* by Anne Basile. Paris, UNESCO, 1979, 130 p.
3. *Budgeting for education in Alberta (Canada)* by L.P. Gue *et al.* Paris, UNESCO, 1979, 54 p.
4. *Computer applications to educational administration in developed countries : a comparative study* by John Lintott. Paris, UNESCO, 1987, 43 p. ED-87/WS/24.
5. *The Computerized management of educational systems* Vol. 1. Accompanying document (of audiovisual assembly). Paris, UNESCO, 1979, 123p. ED-79/WS/118. Vol. 2. Scenario (of audiovisual assembly). Paris, UNESCO, 1979, 59p. ED-80/WS/157. Vol. 3 : Users' handbook (of audiovisual assembly). Paris, UNESCO, 1979, 50 p. ED-79/WS/155.
6. *The Computerized management of educational systems.* Case studies. Vol. 1 : Accompanying document (of audiovisual assembly). Paris, UNESCO, 1983, 157 p. Vol. 2. : Scenario (of audiovisual assembly). Paris, UNESCO, 1983, 99 p. ED-83/WS/81.
7. *Directory of governmental bodies and institutions dealing with educational planning and administration.* Preliminary version. Paris, UNESCO, 1980, 337 p.
8. *Educational administration and management. Structures and functions at national regional and local levels, dealing with educational administration in Hungary* by Erno Kemenes. Paris, UNESCO, 1983, 50 p.
9. *Educational administration and management. Studies on co-ordinated development of formal and non-formal education* by Trevor Turner and Ganga Persaud. Paris, UNESCO, 1980, 48 p.
10. *Educational administration and management. Studies on co-ordinated development of formal and non-formal education.* The

* Listing to illustrate the range of documents and publications.

U.S. Community College experience in co-ordinating school and out-of-school education by Paul V. Delker. Paris, UNESCO, 1983, 49 p.

11. *Educational Administration terminology* by E. Ortiz and A. Basile. Paris, UNESCO, 1982, 354 p.
12. *Eleven experiences in innovations in decentralization of educational administration and management of local resources* by Z. Yannakopoulos. Paris, UNESCO, 1981, 166 p.
13. *Evaluation of technical co-operation projects in education. Guide for the non-specialist practitioner.* Paris, UNESCO, 1979, 47 p. ED-79/WS/159.
14. *From goal to process concerns in education : a behavioural view of the role of experts in development* by F.L. Higginson and A.S. Hartwall. Paris, UNESCO, 1976, 21 p.
15. *Guide for the preparation of technical co-operation projects in education.* Provisional version. Paris, UNESCO, 1979, 26 p. ED-79/WS/116.
16. *Guide on the organisation and the operation of documentation and information centres and services for technical and vocational education* Paris, UNESCO, 1982 (Info TVE series No. 2).
17. *The management of change in Swedish higher education* by B. Ostergen. Paris, UNESCO, 1979, 58 p.
18. *Monitoring and the management of educational policy implementation – a theoretical approach* by R. Sack. Paris, UNESCO, 1985, 34 p.
19. *An Overview of the administrative situation in education in the Arab countries.* Paper prepared for the symposium on management and administration of educational services and establishments by M. El-Ghannam. Paris, UNESCO, 1976, 16 p.
20. *PMIS – The editing of "project review" printouts. On-going projects. Potential projects – User's guide.* Paris, UNESCO, 1988, 12 p. + annexes. ED/SDI/88/43.
21. *PMIS – guide for the computer-assisted management of operational activities in the field of education.* Provisional version. Paris, UNESCO, 1981, 119 p. ED-81/WS/17.
22. *PMIS – project management information system for the management of operational activities of UNESCO.* Audio-visual presentation. Accompanying document. Paris, UNESCO, 1984, 59 p. ED-84/WS/60.
23. *Planning and management of the integrated development of for-*

mal and non-formal education : a review of the possibilities and difficulties by W. Courtney and G. Kutsh. Paris. UNESCO, 1978, 72 p.

24. *Resource constraints : ways and means to overcome the snortage of qualified educational personnel : experiences from Thailand and Ivory Coast* by K. Vorapipatana *et al*. Paris, UNESCO. 1978, 47 p.

14

POPULATION EDUCATION

UNESCO'S JOINT PROGRAMMES, 1984-1986

Objectives

Taking up research networks in three key areas – internal and international migration; effects of demographic trends and development on the status of women.

Developing a methodology for quantifying the relationship between population, resources and human welfare.

Preparing and publishing technical documents giving an analysis of the pilot experiments integrating human rights factors in population communication programmes.

Recent Activities in the Field of Population

1. Research has been undertaken on the dynamics of internal migration.
2. Four country studies on the dynamics, pattern and consequences of migration in France, India, Mexico and Nigeria have been undertaken.
3. Comparative research projects have been undertaken in India, Pakistan, Sri Lanka and Thailand on the impact of migration in the Middle East (West Asia) on rural communities and families.
4. Studies have been conducted in Africa, Asia and the Pacific, Latin America and the Caribbean, the Middle East (West Asia), Western Europe and North America which aimed at identifying the main trends in international migration.

5. An international symposium was held in October 1983, to investigate migration problems.
6. With the financial assistance of the United Nations Fund for Population Activities (UNFPA) attention has been focused on the development of knowledge about population issues in the overall development context.

Youngest African States Hold Population Training Seminar

For the first time since many of them became independent less than 10 years ago, representatives of five African countries whose official language is Portuguese (Angola, Mozambique, Guinea-Bissau, Cape Verde, Sao Tome and Principe) and Spanish-speaking Equatorian Guinea met to discuss their mutual concerns in matters of population and development, with emphasis on the role of communication. The meeting, organized by UNESCO with financing from the United Nations Fund for Population Activities (UNFPA) from November 12 to December 6, 1984, in Maputo, People's Republic of Mozambique, was attended by high-ranking officials from Ministries of Health, National Planning and Education, and by representatives of women's organizations. UNDP, ILO and UNICEF also sent observers as did the Lisbon-based Commission of Portuguese Women. Work sessions were devoted to the relation of population and natural resources with regard to the satisfaction of basic needs, elimination of hunger, disease, ignorance and unemployment. Particular stress was placed on the development of programmes for maternal and child care, and on the training of specialized personnel responsible for furthering the participation of women in the life of the country.

Co-action Programme Highlights Youth and Women

Youth and women occupied a special place (in 1985) in UNESCO's Co-operative Action (Co-Action) Programme, through which individuals or associations could participate directly in development. In 1984,over $586,000 was made available to about 75 projects which range from "Mothers' Clubs" (UCA/73) in Bolivia, carried out with the Confederation de Clubes de Madres de Bolivia, to "Vocational Courses for Young Blind People" (UCA/614) supported in collaboration with the World Blind Union. In the 1985, Co-Action catalogue, contributors could choose from a long list of projects, corresponding to a wide, but always urgent, variety of needs. "Water for All" (UCA/71), a project in which UNESCO is collaborating with the Associated Country Women of the World (ACWW), is, for instance, improving the provision of drinking water and sanitation in many countries.

Harmonizing Population Growth and Development Goals in Cape Verde

After Independence (in 1975), Cape Verde, an archipelago of nine inhabited islands off the coast of Senegal, is suffering from growing pains. The annual population growth rate of 1.6 per cent is low when compared to that of over 4 per cent in Kenya or over 3 per cent for Africa as a whole. Yet, according to data collected during Phase I of the UNESCO/UNFPA project for "Family and Sex Education", an estimated population increase from 300,000 to over 380,000 by the year 2000, or over 400,000 by 2025, could seriously jeopardize development goals in the small, densely populated country. Massive emigration, once a safety valve, has slowed due to the world recession, and, in any case, planners aim at providing living conditions which would make emigration unnecessary. To take stock of the situation, and formulate an Action Plan in line with Phase II of the UNESCO/UNFPA project, 60 representatives of government bodies, women's, youth and religious organizations. . . met from April 22 to 26, 1985, in Praia, the capital. The plan called for urgent measures, including both in-school and out-of-school courses in family and sex education, counselling centres, and greater participation of women in the development process. Of the 74 projects in population education or communication which UNESCO is currently executing in collaboration with UNFPA on the global, regional, or national – in 43 Member-States level, 23 are in Africa.

UNESCO and WHO Collaboration to Increase Media Involvement in Health Education

Recognizing the mass media as a major determining factor in shaping public attitudes and awareness about health and nutrition, UNESCO and the World Health Organization (WHO) have, since 1984, pooled their expertise in a vast project to increase involvement of the media in this sector. Two initial phases, carried out in 11 Asian countries, resulted in innovative and successful country-level health and nutrition education projects employing a variety of designs and approaches ranging from radio listening groups to promotion campaigns through rural Press to the training of media professionals in health education. A third phase (1986-1988) had been launched with two round-tables for decision-makers in education, health and information services in 17 French-speaking countries – in Yaounde, Cameroon (November 25-28, 1986) for eight Central African countries, end in Dakar, Senegal (December 1-5, 1986) for nine countries in West Africa. At the meetings, financed by the French Foreign Ministry, the Canadian International Development Agency (CIDA) and a $25,000 contribution from UNESCO's International Programme for the Development of Communication (IPDC), participants laid plans for national level mass media/public health pilot projects.

Intensive Seminar on Population Education

An Intensive Seminar on Population Education was held in Dakar (Senegal) from July 7 to August 1, 1986, and was attended by 31 specialists from 10 West African countries, Morocco, Tunisia and Haiti. The Seminar, which preceded a similar meeting for East African Member-States (September 8-30) in Nairobi (Kenya), was largely devoted to the training of teachers, methods and the inclusion in materials used in general education, literacy and post-literacy programmes of subject-matter related to population problems. At both meetings, emphasis was placed on the close interrelationship of these problems with the quality of life, the environment, nutrition and health, ethical and human rights concerns and the role of women in development. While Africa is still sparsely populated when compared to Asia, the continent's population growth rate of 3 per cent (against 1.8 per cent for Asia, 2.3 per cent for Latin America) is the world's highest. About one-third (28) of the 90 national, regional or global projects in population education or communication being executed by UNESCO in collaboration with UNFPA are in Africa. Since close co-operation with the UNFPA began in 1970, UNESCO has assisted in formulation and implementation of $60 million of UNFPA-funded projects. With world population now over the five billion mark, this collaboration is being intensified, both in terms of activities and expenditure – from $11,300,000 in UNFPA-funding for UNESCO's 1984-85 biennium to $14 million for 1986-87 period.

BIBLIOGRAPHY

UNESCO DOCUMENTS AND PUBLICATIONS*

1. *Activities Report, 1984-1985.* Paris, UNESCO, 1985, 29 p. ED-86/WS/4.
2. *Human rights aspects of population programmes with special reference to human right law.* Paris, UNESCO, 1977, 154 p.
3. *Immigrant Workers in Europe: Their legal status* by Eric-Jean Thomas, Study Director, Paris, UNESCO, 1982, 245 p.
4. *Living in two cultures: The socio-cultural situation of migrant workers and their families.* Paris, UNESCO, 1982, 325 p. Co-published with Gower Publishing Co. Ltd.
5. *Managing national population education programmes : issues and actions.* Paris, UNESCO, 1985, 200 p. + annexes. ED-85/WS/56.
6. *Manual on evaluation on population communication programmes*, Paris, UNESCO, 1981, 129 p. (Population Communication Manuals, 2)
7. *Manual on mass media in population and development*, Paris, UNESCO, 1977, 105 p. (Population Communication Manuals, 1).
8. *Population education : a contemporary concern.* Paris, UNESCO, 1978, (Educational studies and documents ESD No. 28).
9. *Preparing teachers for population education : a handbook.* Paris, UNESCO, 1983, 129 p. ED-83/WS/33.
10. *Socio-cultural case studies for population education in Morocco, Peru, Rwanda and the United Republic of Tanzania.* Paris, UNESCO, 1981, 244 p. ED-81/WS/59.
11. *Study of the contribution of population education to educational renewal and innovation in El Salvador, The Republic of Korea, Philippines and Tunisia.* Paris, UNESCO, 1980, 206 p.
12 *Why people move*: comparative perspectives on the dynamics of internal migration, ed. by Jorge Balan, Paris, UNESCO, 1981, 342 p.

* Listing to illustrate the range of UNESCO documents and publications.

15

TECHNOLOGY OF TEACHING

NEW TEACHING METHODS AND APPROACHES, 1964

From the very beginning, UNESCO has been concerned with the new methods and new approaches in the field of education and science. After the Second World War when schools in many countries were destroyed, UNESCO sponsored the production of a small volume which showed how teachers in devastated countries who lacked scientific equipment could build such tools of their classes for a few pennies.

The book was an immediate success. From this was born the famous *Source Book of Science Teaching* which has been UNESCO's biggest single best-seller title. This 'do-it-yourself' since book contains directions for making laboratory equipment and carrying out simple experiments using tin cans, bottles, string, chair springs, knitting needles, clothes pegs, etc.

Another book in the same series, published in 1965, is the *Source Book for Geography Teaching* which shows how the teaching of geography can be improved in the light of our new knowledge of the earth. Other guides deal with secondary-school mathematics, the teaching of biology and chemistry, and planning for health in school.

Of special interest are the regional pilot projects launched by UNESCO to evolve new approaches, methods and techniques in the teaching of physics, chemistry, biology and mathematics. The projects are designed to upgrade science teaching by making possible observation and experimentation by students, followed by interpretation of results, stressing inquiry and discovery over memorization of facts. The participants in the projects have been teacher trainers. They have developed such materials as inexpensive laboratory apparatus, single-concept films and programmed instruction materials.

The first of these research and development projects — on the physics — brought together senior teachers from eight Latin American countries at Sao Paulo (Brazil) in 1964. The second — on chemistry teaching — was at Bangkok (Thailand) with senior teachers from fourteen Asian countries taking part. Similar experimental projects have been carried out in the teaching of biology in Africa and mathematics in the Arab States.

Research into the new techniques making use of films, radio, television and programmed instruction, and efforts to encourage their use, particularly in developing countries, has been another of UNESCO's tasks in recent years. The Organization has sponsored experiments in the application of these techniques, mainly in adult education and in the teaching of science and languages. One experiment was the pilot project launched by UNESCO in Dakar in 1965 to introduce the new methods in Africa. Television programmes produced by a team of young Africans were received in ten 'tele-clubs' in and around Dakar. Literacy broadcasts have been tested and evaluated for groups of factory workers in the Dakar area.

Just as important as new techniques and methods is the spirit in which the subjects are taught. UNESCO's efforts in this field have given impetus to a movement for making school-books more objective and accurate. An important result has been consultations between educational authorities in different countries — the Federal Republic of Germany and France, for example — with a view to removing biased and tendentious references and opinions.

SEMINAR ON EDUCATIONAL TECHNOLOGY, 1984

The seminar was held at the Tokyo Gakugei University, Japan. It was organised jointly by the Japan Council of Educational Technology Centres and UNESCO. Excerpts from a paper '*Impact of Microcomputers on Less Developed Countries*', presented by H.N. Mahabala are given below:

Suggestions for a Plan of Action

(i) Computer professionals and their societies are obsessed with mainframes. Not enough is being done to help the owners of microcomputers. Their activities must become small computer-oriented, and forums must be created to discuss all aspects of a microcomputer installation including the installation itself, the manpower and the selection of packages.

(ii) One can certainly try to monitor the standards of teaching shops. After all, they are only helping (or, as some say, taking advantage of) those who want a computer-oriented career. Assessing objectively the aptitude of a candidate is as important as the subsequent training. Professional societies should provide opportunities for graduates of these programmes to learn about those aspects which they feel are lacking in their training. The emphasis should not be on complete training by the society but on 'make-up' training. One can provide lectures on real-life applications and discussions on meaningful case studies (however micro-oriented).

(iii) Professional societies must recognize the importance of small computers and bring them into the fold through appropriate measures, such as having separate divisions for small computers. It is needless to mention that if it is not done soon, the societies may alienate themselves from the majority of computer users.

(iv) Small computers are best used in a distributed way. As such one must emphasize the parallel growth in computer communications. Vendors must be encouraged to introduce products oriented to Local Area Networks. It is possible to provide logical networks using floppy diskettes for the exchange of data. Experiments show that a distributed approach based on floppies can be quite effective.

(v) Graphics have not been emphasized sufficiently in data processing circles. With school computers going for colour graphics how can professional applications still be text-oriented?

(vi) Whereas it is not necessary to have local language based programming languages one must emphasize the need for data processing using strings in local script, e.g. to print bills. This is one way the computer can be brought closer to the common man in an LDC.

(vii) The future belongs to programmer-less, single-application-oriented, dedicated systems. Obviously, the design of software for such systems which are to be used by lay users needs special attention. Computer education institutions must orient their curricula to train software engineers to develop packages.

(viii) Professional societies must develop extension programmes to advise lay users in the selection of hardware and packages. They should also operate better business bureaux to monitor activities of 'fly-by-night' vendors.

(ix) Countries must view microcomputers as 'mother technology' and take policy decisions to provide hardware at international prices (i.e. the lowest possible) and enforce laws in order to make the development of packages worthwhile for the vendor.

(x) One can expect in the near future, greater impact of microcomputers in the 'information industry' rather than in data processing. One should think in terms of 'electronic publishing', based on diskettes to provide information support to development. A centralized database can be used to produce information tailored to the local context, say of a rural community which is distributed through floppies to be used at local information dissemination centres. At a later date one can replace the transportation of floppies by data communications. Undoubtedly, one cannot reap the full benefits of microcomputers without matching data communication facilities. However, one can do a lot with transportable media.

(xi) Rapid advances in Hardware technology have made standardization difficult. One thought that the 8-inch floppy was going to be the standard only for it to be replaced by 5-inch and now 3-inch diskettes. An imaginative approach is needed to provide a measure of protection to the microcomputer user. Professional societies in LDCs must help in arriving at a plan of action.

(xii) As has been demonstrated in the United Kingdom, radio and television media can be used to distribute software and databases in LDCs along the lines of CEEFAX.

(xiii) The computer profession was obsessed in developed countries up to a few years ago, with the 100 per cent utilization of the processor. One still sees such an approach in LDCs. One must reorient the profession to a user-oriented approach which places only appropriate importance on hardware utilization. Also one cannot directly adapt applications on large systems to small systems. A new approach to system design is needed. The chances are that micro-based networks will provide better decision support to an organization than centralized systems.

(xiv) Because of the economics, microcomputers in LDCs cannot take the place of personal computers in developed countries. Therefore one has to develop strategies for using them as small business computers. One will not find relevant experience in developed countries in such usage is directly transferable to LDCs. In summary, the expectations of a microcomputer in a LDC are different from those in a developed country. They have to serve as workhouses for small businesses. Computer professionals in LDCs have to orient themselves to this challenge, since almost every wisdom about a large system is not applicable in the case of a small system.

CONTENTS OF EDUCATION (A.D. 2000), 1987

The UNESCO commissioned five case studies on the main trends to be seen in the curricula and the results of these studied have been summarised by UNESCO.

The methodological framework for the contents of general education based on these studies is reproduced below:

Subject groupings and/or subjects-formal and non-formal education	Importance of informal education	Goals; remarks	Observations; possible options
1	2	3	4
I. *Education for and through the natural sciences* Mathematics Computer science and/or CAL Physics Chemistry Biology Knowledge of the earth and space: geogra-	link up and informal education	Providing a basic training in the sciences: basic concepts, theories, methodologies and outlooks, mathematical tools to be used Training young people in the use of computers Enabling young people to utilize sour-	Different modes and degrees of subject integration Infusional approach: education relating to the quality of life and environment, the problems of develop-

1	2	3	4
phy, geology, astronomy, etc. Non-formal activities and national and international competitions to identify and encourage talent		ces of information available in society Preparing pupils for continuous and creative self-instruction	ment and underdevelopment
II. *Social and human sciences* National, regional and world history National and world literature Philosophy and philosophy of life Understanding of man, of society and the future	Apply procedures at school for linking formal and informal education	Humanist education Fostering a critical spirit Conclusions on the development of societies, on social in equalities and injustice Knowledge of different societies and acceptance of their diversity Improvement in the quality of school life and the life of the community	Infusional approach: education for democracy and participation Introduction of future-oriented exercises or courses Emphasis on the role of the family Possibility of introducing contents pertaining to education for peace, education relaing to the environment and the quality of life
III. *Education for and through technology and work* In relation to the needs resources and prospects of each national community.		A proper attitude to work; respect for work A technological culture; a critical interest in and attitude to technological progress	Open to boys and girls; option^c Conceived as a component of general culture
In keeping with the computerization of all sectors of social life.		Training of active individuals and inculcation of know-how Preparing pupils to adapt easily to chan-	In keeping with the dynamics of the world of work

	1	2	3	4
	School and or out-of-school activities		ges in the world of work	
IV.	*Mother tongue and foreign languages* Important role of the media and cultural exchanges		Sense of belonging to a given culture; national dignity Means of communication and knowledge of other cultures; open-mindedness Critical analysis of the quality of the messages carried by the media	Systematic teaching and preparation for continuous self-instruction Possibility of fitting in education for peace and co-operation
V.	*Moral and civic education* Courses and exercises or debates or indirect moral education involving the participation of all teachers	Religious education. Greater consultation and/or involvement of the family	Cultivating an interest in the ethical quality of life and in social equality and justice Inculcating moral values likely to further co-operation and participation Defusing aggressiveness, self-interest, racism, etc.	Can include education for democracy and participation and sex education Non-verbal teaching inputs to be taken into account
VI.	*Spiritual and cultural education* Helping young people to steer a course in the world of material and spiritual values and to combat dehumanization. Improving the quality of relations: Pupil-pupil, teacher-pupil, etc.	Important role of the family and youth organizations Importance of traditions and of the cultural training capacities of the local community	Distinction between ends and means Respect for values and talent Giving cultural values priority in life Combating the possible moral disintegration of society	Ensuring balance between the cognitive and affective Educating young people to make rational decisions and choices Possibility of fitting in education for development and international co-operation

1	2	3	4
VII. *Education for and through the arts and manifestations of beauty* Special emphasis on music and the visual arts Multiple and combinable options Importance to be given to artistic events	Very important: hence the need to guide pupils and utilize in the school the aesthetic experience acquired out of school Role of the family	Development of aesthetic taste and acquisition of criteria of judgement Preparing pupils to participate in the artistic life of society Organizing creative artistic exercises Identifying and encouraging talent	Possibility of linking different arts or integrating education in the different arts through common aesthetic concepts; means of expression, styles, etc. Possibility of fitting in education for peace and co-operation
VIII. *Education for and through sport and leisure* Non-formal activities organized by the school (clubs, competitions, excursions, nature classes, etc.) should have an important place	Linkage between formal and informal education is important	Knowledge and know-how with regard to sports and leisure pursuits Developing a sporting outlook Cultivating interest in the various competitions seen as sporting and ethical events Foster enjoyment of life	Possibilities for incorporating new types of education
IX. *Modern domestic science* The home (furnishing, *ikebana*, etc.) Family life Nutritional education Family budget Formal and/or non-formal activities	It is essential to involve parents	Preparing pupils for marriage and family life Indirect preparation for future parenthood Indirect preparation for working life: knowing how to organize one's own life	*cf.* the experience of Japan, the Netherlands, the Federal Republic of Germany, etc. Possibility of introducing population education

1	2	3	4
X. *The new forms of education and contemporary world problem* Environmental education Education for democracy and participation Education for a new international order Education for peace and co-operation Population education, etc.	Informal education is very important here, and not always in accordance with the aims pursued in school	Giving pupils a relevant view of world problems Devising exercises as an approach to specific problems of a global and multidisciplinary nature Improving the quality of school life and relationships Highlighting interdependencies and the responsibilities of each individual Cultivating the idea of the solidarity of modern man	Infusional approach or separate subjects: depending on needs and traditions, the characteristics of the initial and in-service teacher training sub-system, etc. In the case of an infusional approach, one subject should have a co-ordinating role

Source: *The Contents of Education : A World View of Their Development from the Present to the Year* 2000, by S. Rassekh and G. Vaideonu, Paris, UNESCO, 1987

BIBLIOGRAPHY

UNESCO DOCUMENTS AND PUBLICATIONS*

Curriculum Development

1. *Contribution to a study on the evolution of the content of general education (1970-1980)*. Paris, UNESCO, 1980, 39 p. ED-80/CONF.803/4.
2. *Interdisciplinarity in general education*. Paris, UNESCO, 1986, 102 p. ED-86/WS/78.
3. *International investigation into the articulation of the contents of secondary education, of post-secondary education and the world

* Listing to illustrate range of UNESCO documents and publications.

of work by the World Association for Educational Research, Gent, Belgium, July 1982. Paris, UNESCO, 1982, 60 p. ED-82/WS/44.

4. *International consultation concerning the possibility of making the transition between general and technical and vocational education more flexible in both initial and further education.* Paris, 1-4 March 1983. *Final report.* Paris, UNESCO, 1983, 15 p. ED-83/CONF.016/3.
5. *International symposium on the evolution of the content of general education over the next two decades.* Paris, 7-11 July 1980. *Final report.* Paris, UNESCO, 1980, 52 p. ED-80/CONF.803/7.
6. *Lifelong education and school curriculum* by R.H. Dave. UNESCO/UIE, 1973, 92 p.
7. *Lifelong education, schools and curricula in developing countries* by H.W.R. Hawes. UNESCO/UIE, 1975, 110 p. (UIE monograph No. 4).
8. *School curricula and standards of education and training in Madagascar*. Paris, UNESCO, 1978, 79 p.
9. *School curricula and standards of education and training in Portugal*. Paris, UNESCO, 1979, 77 p.
10. *School curriculum in the context of lifelong learning* by Uwe Hameyer. UNESCO/UIE, 1979, 112 p.
11. *Some comments on the socio-economic context of development and its influence on the evolution of content of education during the next two decades.* Paris, UNESCO, 1980, 48 p. ED-80/CONF.803/6.
12. *Standardization of education and curricula for boys and girls in general education, vocational and teacher-training schools in the Mongolian People's Republic*. Paris, UNESCO, 1979, 49 p.
13. *Study on curricula and standards of education and training for boys and girls in secondary schools and teacher-training institutes in Jamaica*. Paris, UNESCO, 1979, 99 p.
14. *Study on curricula and standards of education and training for boys and girls in secondary schools and teacher-training institutes in Jordan*. Paris, UNESCO, 1978, 63 p.
15. *A Study on the differences between the educational programmes of young girls and young boys in Turkey*. Paris, UNESCO, 1979, 44 p.
16. *Study on the differences of curricula for girls and boys in Afghanistan*. Paris, UNESCO, 1978, 87 p.

Exact and Natural Sciences

Biology

1. *Agriculture and biology teaching*. Paris, UNESCO, 1984 (Science and technology education document series (STEDS No. 11) ED-84/WS/81.
2. *Assessment : a practical guide to improving the quality and scope of assessment instruments*. Paris, UNESCO, 1986 (STEDS No. 16) ED-86/WS/17.
3. *Biological system, energy sources and biology teaching*. Paris, UNESCO, 1984, (STEDS No. 9) ED.84/WS/79.
4. *Biology and human welfare. Case studies in teaching applied biology*. Paris, UNESCO, 1988, 64 p. (STEDS No. 25) ED-87/WS/53.
5. *Ecology, ecosystem management and biology teaching*. Paris, UNESCO, 1984 (STEDS No. 10) ED-84/WS/80.
6. *Genetically-based biological technologies*. Paris, UNESCO, 1984, (STEDS No. 8) ED-84/WS/78.
7. *Health education and biology teaching*. Paris, UNESCO, 1984 (STEDS No. 12) Ed-84/WS/82.
8. *Human development and evolution and biology teaching*. Paris, UNESCO, 1985 (STEDS No. 15) ED-85/WS/43.
9. *Leisure, values and biology teaching* by Alan J. Pritchard and Dean J. Buckland. Paris, UNESCO, 1986, 64 p. (STEDS No. 22) ED-86/WS/102.
10. *Methodologies for relevant skill development in biology education*. Paris, UNESCO, 1982, 49 p. (STEDS No. 2) ED-81/WS/139.
11. *Microbiological techniques in school* by Ronald Westphal. Paris, UNESCO, 1988, 118 p. (STEDS No. 28) ED-88/WS/29.
12. *New trends in biology teaching*. Paris, UNESCO 1977.
13. *New trends in biology teaching*. The teaching of basic sciences, Vol. V. Paris, UNESCO, 1987, 222 p.
14. *Teachers' study guide on the biology of human populations, Arab States*. Paris, UNESCO, 1981.
15. *Teachers' study guide on the biology of human populations, Africa*. Paris, UNESCO, 1975.
16. *Teachers' study guide on the biology of human populations, Asia*. Paris, UNESCO, 1975.

17. *UNESCO handbook for biology teachers in Africa.* Paris, UNESCO, 1986, 329 p.
18. *UNESCO handbook for biology teachers in Asia.* UNESCO/ROSTSCA, 1986.
19. *UNESCO handbook for biology teachers in Latin America.* UNESCO/ROSTLAC, 1982, 263 p.
20. *Use of the sea and its organisms.* Paris, UNESCO, 1987, 215 p. (STEDS No. 23) ED-86/WS/111.

Chemistry

1. *Bibliography of chemical education journals* by J.N. Lezomby. Waddington, D.J., University of York, 1981.
2. *Chemistry teaching and the environment.* Paris, UNESCO, 1983 (Science and technology education document series (STEDS No. 6) ED-83/WS/86.
3. *Collection of competition tasks from the international chemical olympiades*, 2nd edition. International Jury of Chemical Olympiades, Czechoslovak Commission for UNESCO. Bratislava, 1985.
4. *Didactics of chemistry.* Selective bibliography for 1984. Central Library, Information and Reference Centre, Pedagogical Faculty of the Charles University in cooperation with UNESCO. Prague, 1985, 177 p.
5. *Didactics of chemistry.* Selective bibliography for 1985. Central Library, Sectional Information Centre, Pedagogical Faculty of the Charles University in cooperation with UNESCO. Prague, 1986, 262 p.
6. *Experiments on chemical equilibrium.* UNESCO/GEEQuim – Group for education and teaching of chemistry, Institute of Chemistry, University of Sao Paulo, Brazil, 1987, 252 p.
7. *International chemistry olympiades (I-XV).* Problems and solutions. University of Moscow, 1986, 191 p.
8. *International chemistry olympiad, 16th.* Frankfurt, Main, 1984. *Report.* Offenbach/Main, 1984 *Out of print.*
9. *International chemistry olympiad, 19th.* Veszprem, Budapest, Hungary, 6-15 July 1987. *Report.* Veszprem, 1987, 52 p.
10. *International conference on chemical education.* Dublin, Ireland, 1979. *Proceedings.* The teaching of chemistry – interaction between secondary and tertiary levels. University College, Dublin,

1980, 176 p.

11. *International newsletter on chemical education*. Published with UNESCO's assistance by the International Union of Pure and Applied Chemistry (IUPAC) and the Committee on the Teaching of Chemistry (CTC).
12. *New trends in chemistry teaching*. Vol. IV. Paris, UNESCO, 1975.
13. *New trends in chemistry teaching*. Vol. V. Paris, UNESCO, 1981.
14. *Report of the 18th international chemistry olympiad*. Leiden, Netherlands, 1986, 59 p.
15. *Teaching school chemistry* by D.J. Waddington. Paris, UNESCO, 1984.
16. *Thirty years of Polish chemistry olympiads*. Translated from Polish by Mrs. Eva Mioduszewska. Warsaw, Ministry of Education and Upbringing, the Main Committee of Chemistry Olympiad, 1986.

Mathematics

1. *All the best from the Australian mathematics competition* by Josephine D. Edwards, Declan J. King, Peter J. O'Halloran. Canberra, Australian Mathematics Competition, 1986, 220 p.
2. *The Caribbean mathematics project : training the teacher as an agent of reform* by Martyn H. Cundy. UNESCO/IBE, 1977 (Experiments and innovations in education No. 32).
3. *The development of science and mathematics concepts in young children in African countries*. Nairobi, 19-27 September 1974. *Final report*. Paris, UNESCO, 1984.
4. *The education of secondary school teachers of mathematics* Vol. IV by R. Morris. Paris, UNESCO, 1984 (studies in mathematics education).
5. *Goals for mathematics education : mathematics teaching and the needs of society*. Paris, UNESCO, 1980. *Final report*.
6. *Innovations in science and mathematics education in schools in the Soviet Union*. Paris, UNESCO, 1987 (STEDS No. 24) ED-87/WS/46.
7. *Interactions between linguistics and mathematics education*. Report of a symposium sponsored by UNESCO/CEDO/ICMI. Nairobi, 1974 ED-74/CONF.808.
8. *Mathematical education of primary school teachers* (The) Vol. III

by R. Morris. Paris, UNESCO, 1984 (studies in mathematics education).

9. *Mathematics for all*. Paris, UNESCO, 1986, 109 p. (Science and technology education document series (STEDS No. 20) ED-86/WS/84.
10. *New trends in mathematics teaching*. Vol. III. Paris, UNESCO, 1972.
11. *New trends in mathematics teaching*. Vol. IV. Paris, UNESCO, 1979.
12. *Out-of-school mathematics education*. Vol., VI by R. Morris. Paris, UNESCO, 1987, 135 p. (Studies in mathematics education).
13. *Science and mathematics education in the general secondary school in the Soviet Union*. Paris, UNESCO, 1986, 211 p. (STEDS No. 21) ED-86/WS/81.
14. *The teaching of basic sciences* by R. Morris. Vol. I Paris, UNESCO, 1980 ISBN 92-3-101779-9 (Studies in mathematics education).
15. *The teaching of basic sciences*. Vol. II by R. Morris. Paris, UNESCO, 1981 ISBN 92-3-101905-8 (Studies in mathematics education).
16. *Teaching of geometry*. Vol. V by R. Morris. Paris, UNESCO, 1986 (Studies in mathematics education).
17. *Teaching school mathematics — a UNESCO sourcebook* by W. Servais and T. Varga. Paris, UNESCO/Penguin, 1971.
18. *Twenty-fifth international mathematical olympiad (IMO)*. Prague, 1984. Compiled by the IMO Organizing Committee. Prague, IMO, 1984.
19. *Twenty-sixth international mathematical olympiad (IMO)*. Joutsa, Heinola, Helsinki, 1985. *Results and problems* by Matti Lehtinen. Helsinki, Organizing Committee of the 26th IMO, 1985.
20. *Twenty-seventh international mathematical olympiad. Results and problems*. Warsaw, Organizing Committee, 1986, 41 p.

Physics

1. *Fifteenth international physics olympiad*. Sigtuna, Sweden, 1984. *Proceedings*.
2. *Collection of competition tasks form the 1st through XV international physics olympiads 1967-1984*. Budapest, Roland Fotvos

Physical Society, 1985.

3. *GIREP conference 1986, COSMOS – an educational challenge.* Proceedings of a conference held in Copenhagen, Denmark, 18-23 August 1986. European Space Agency, 1986, 450 p.
4. *International conference on trends in physics education.* Tokyo, Sophia University, 24-29 August, 1986, *Proceedings.* Tokyo, The Physics Education Society of Japan, 1986, 482 p.
5. *International Physics Olympiad. 16th.* Potroroz, Yugoslavia, 1985. *Proceedings.* Ljubljana, Society of Mathematicians, Physicists and Astronomers of Slovenia, 1985.
6. *International Physics Olympiad. 17th.* London, Harrow, 1986.
7. *International Physics Olympiad. 18th.* Jena, German Democratic Republic, 5-13 July 1987. *Report.* Eggersdorf, GDR, 1987, 73 p.
8. *International pupils physics olympiads* by O.F. Kabardin, V.A. Orlov, Moscow, 1985, 158 p.
9. *The many faces of teaching and learning mechanics in secondary and early tertiary education.* Proceedings of a conference on physics education. Utrecht, The Netherlands, 20-25 August 1984, organized by Groupe international de recherche sur l'enseignement de la physique (GIREP) in co-operation with UNESCO and SVO. Utrecht, 1985.
10. *New trends in physics teaching.* Vol. III. Paris, UNESCO, 1976.
11. *New trends in physics teaching.* Vol. IV. The teaching of basic sciences. Paris, UNESCO, 1984.
12. *Physics olympiads (I-XV). Problems and solutions.* Moscow, 1985, 158 p.
13. *Proceedings of the international conference on physics education.* Nanjing/Jiangsu, The People's Republic of China, August 31-5 September, 1986. Nanjing Institute of Technology, 1986, 352 p.
14. *Teaching school physics — a UNESCO sourcebook* by John L. Lewis. Paris, UNESCO/Penguin, 1972.

Science and Technology

1. *Consultation meeting on pilot project "technology in general education".* Beijing, 3-5 April 1984. *Final report.* Paris, UNESCO, 1986. ED-85/WS/86.
2. *Consultation on the priority needs and activities of the international network for information in science and technology education.* Paris, 27-29 October 1986. *Final report.* Paris, UNESCO,

1986, 16 p.

3. *The Development of science and mathematics concepts in young children in African countries.* Nairobi, 19-27 September 1974. *Final report.* Paris, UNESCO, 1984.
4. *Directory of participating institutions/Repertoire des institutions participantes.* International Network for Information in Science and Technology Education (INISTE). Paris, UNESCO, 1985 ED-85/WS/59.
5. *Elementary school science.* In "*prospects*" quarterly review of education. Paris, UNESCO, 1978.
6. *Encouraging girls into science and technology : some European initiatives.* Paris, UNESCO, 1984 (Science and technology education document series (STEDS No. 7) ED-84/WS/64.
7. *The Experience of GDR in the teaching of science and technology and productive work.* Case study for UNESCO by Dietrich Blandow and Erwin Messner. Erfurt, University College of Education, 1987, 62 p. + annexes.
8. *Five years of Thailand's youth science week, 1982-1986.* Centre for Educational Museums, Department of Non-formal Education, Ministry of Education. Bangkok, 1986, 51 p.
9. *Forty years of science camps.* Bergen, Norway, 1986.
10. *Games and toys in the teaching of science and technology* by Norman K. Lowe. Paris, UNESCO, 1988, 90 p. (STEDS No. 29) ED-88/WS/36.
11. *Glossary of terms used in science and technology education.* Paris, UNESCO, 1981 (STEDS No. 1) ED-84/WS/68.
12. *Information note.* International Network for Information in Science and Technology Education (INISTE). Paris, UNESCO, 1985-1988.
13. *Innovations in science and mathematics education in schools in the Soviet Union.* Paris, UNESCO, 1987 (STEDS No. 24) ED-87/WS/46.
14. *Innovations in science and technology education.* Volume I. ed. by D. Layton. Paris, UNESCO, 1986, 188 p.
15. *Innovation in science education worldwide* by Albert V. Baez. Paris, UNESCO, 1976.
16. *Interest in science and technology education.* 12th IPN symposium by M. Lehrke, L. Hoffmann, P.L. Gardner. University of Kiel, Federal Republic of Germany, 2-6 April 1984. Kiel, Institute for Science Education, 1985, 325 p.

17. *International congress on science and technology education and national development.* Paris, 23 November – 2 December 1981. *Final report.* Paris, UNESCO, 1981 ED-81/CONF.401/COL.10.
18. *International symposium on the teaching of technology within the context of general education.* Paris, 18-22 November 1985. *Final report.* Paris, UNESCO, 1985, 32 p. ED-22 CONF.809/COL.21.
19. *Interregional workshop on methods of production, use and exchange of low-cost science and technology materials at the primary education level.* Pyongyang, Democratic People's Republic of Korea, 13-19 May 1987. *Final report.* Paris, UNESCO, 1988.
20. *Low-cost equipment for science and technology education.* Vol. I. Paris, UNESCO, 1985. ED-85/WS/60.
21. *Manual for the promotion of scientific and technological activities for young people.* UNESCO/OREALC, 1984.
22. *New trends in school science equipment.* Paris, UNESCO, 1983
23. *New trends in the utilization of educational technology for science education.* Paris, UNESCO, 1973.
24. *New UNESCO sourcebook for science teaching.* Paris, UNESCO, 1973.
25. *Out-of-school scientific and technical education.* Journal published with UNESCO's assistance by the International Coordinating Committee for the presentation of science and the development of out-of-school scientific activities (ICC), Brussels.
26. *The place of science and technology in school curricula : a global survey.* Paris, UNESCO, 1986, 77 p.
27. *Practical activities for out-of-school science and technology education.* Paris, UNESCO, 1986, 133 p. (STEDS No. 17) ED-86/WS/16.
28. *Primary science teacher training for process-based learning.* Report of the workshop held in Barbados 31 August – 9 September 1987. Commonwealth Secretariat/UNESCO, 1987, 103 p.
29. *Science and mathematics education in the general secondary school in the Soviet Union.* Paris, UNESCO, 1986, 211 p. (STEDS No. 21) ED-86/WS/81.
30. *Science and technology education and national development.* Paris. UNESCO, 1983
31. *Science and technology education as part of general education.* Paris, UNESCO, 1981 (STEDS No. 4) ED-83/WS/52.
32. *Science and technology in school curricula. Case study 1,*

People's Republic of China. Social needs and the teaching of mathematics, science and technology in primary and secondary schools. Paris, UNESCO, 1987, 39 p. ED-87/WS/36.
33. *Science and technology in school curricula. Case study 2, Uganda.* Paris, UNESCO, 1988, 14 p. ED-88/WS/24.
34. *The social relevance of science and technology education.* Paris, UNESCO, 1986, 172 p. (STEDS No. 18) ED-86/WS/24.
35. *UNESCO handbook for science teachers.* Paris, UNESCO, 1980.
36. *UNESCO sourcebook for out-of-school science and technology education.* Paris, UNESCO, 1986, 145 p.

Integrated Sciences

1. *Children's ideas in science* by R. Driver, E. Guesne, Tiberghien. Milton Keynes (U.K.) and Philadelphia (U.S.A.), Open University Press, 1985.
2. *International workshop on primary science.* Bangalore, conference report. Bangalore, 1985.
3. *New trends in integrated science teaching.* Vol. IV. Paris, UNESCO, 1977.
4. *New trends in integrated science teaching.* Vol. V. Paris, UNESCO, 1982.
5. *New trends in primary school science education.* Vol. I. Paris, UNESCO, 1983.
6. *The training of primary science educators — a workshop approach.* Paris, UNESCO, 1985 (Science and technology education document series (STEDS No. 13) ED-85/WS/8.
7. *The teaching of science and technology in an interdisciplinary context.* Approaches for the primary school. Paris, UNESCO, 1986, 133 p. (STEDS No. 19) ED-86/WS/38.

Media Education

1. *Advanced communication and information technology for education and training : status and prospects* by Henri T. Ingle *et al.* Paris, UNESCO, 1983, 126 p.
2. *Impact of educational television on young children.* Paris, UNESCO, 1981, 60 p. (Educational studies and documents ESD No. 40).
3. *Impact of mass communication media on curriculum development*

and educational methods by Len Masterman. *Final report* of the UNESCO European workshop held at Tutzing, Federal Republic of Germany, 17-20 November 1986. Paris, UNESCO, 1986, 26 p.

4. *International annotated bibliography on media education* by Ingrid Geretschlaeger. Paris, UNESCO, 1987, 194 p. (Communication and Society No. 17) CC/87/WS/9.
5. *Learning about the media. Media education and communication research* by James Halloran and Marcia Jones. Paris, UNESCO, 1986, 183 p. (Communication and society No. 16).
6. *Media education in the United Kingdom : an annotated bibliography* by Dr. L. Masterman. Paris, UNESCO, 1983, 72 p.
7. *Media education materials : an annotated bibliography* by Jung Sook Lee *et al*. Paris, UNESCO, 1982, 40 p.
8. *Regional seminar on the effects of public TV programmes and press on educational process*. Tunis, 10-14 June 1982. *Formation and training of teachers in order to utilize the effects of mass-media messages in school education*. Paper by A.Q. Yousuf. UNESCO/UNEDBAS, 1982, 27 p.
9. *Regional seminar on teacher preparation to utilize mass-media in school education*. Amman, 7-16 May 1983. Towards a minimum strategy of integration between teacher trainers and mass-media personnel (programmers) by A.Q. Yousuf. Paris, UNESCO, 1983, 29 p. ED-83/CONF./713.
10. *School knowledge, media knowledge : media literacy in teacher training and student learning* by Len Masterman. Paris, UNESCO, 1983, 42 p.
11. *Symposium international sur l'education du public aux media de masse : problemes, tendances et perspectives*. Grunwald, 18-22 Janvier 1982. *Rapport final*. Paris, UNESCO, 1982 COM-82/WS/16.
12. *Workshop guide on the use by teachers of the mass-media in the educational process*. Paris, UNESCO, 1983, 98 p.

Language Teaching

1. *Bibliography of major decisions, meetings and documents related to UNESCO's activities in the domain of mother tongue instruction and languages*. Paris, UNESCO, 1981, 72 p. ED-81/CONF.601/4.
2. *Brief description of the spoken and written languages of China's*

minority nationalities and China's educational policy concerning the institutes of nationalities by Lu Bi. Paris, UNESCO, 1980, 25 p. ED-80/WS/151.

3. *A Checklist of pluridisciplinary criteria for the evaluation of materials used in the teaching-learning of the mother tongue in primary and secondary schools in Brazil* by Francisco Gomes de Matos, Universidade Federal de Pernambuco and Associacao Brasileira de Linguistica. Paris, UNESCO, 1983, 23 p. ED-83/WS/21.
4. *Consultation on content and methods that could contribute in the teaching of foreign languages and literature to international understanding and peace.* Kiev, Ukrainian SSR, 26-30 January 1987. *Final report.* Paris, UNESCO, 1987, 22 p. ED-87/CONF/47.
5. *The Educational use of African languages in Sub-Saharan Africa: the state of the art* by David Dalby. Paris, UNESCO, 1985 ED-85/WS/62.
6. *Expert meeting to review the worldwide position as regards to results of activities relating to the use of mother tongue as medium of instruction.* Paris, 30 November – 4 December 1981. *Final report.* Paris, UNESCO, 23 p. + annexes. ED-81/CONF.601/5.
7. *First international symposium on language barriers to science and technology development in the Member-States of the Andres Bello convention.* Trujillo, Peru, 1-5 October 1979. *Analytical report* by Ernesto Zierer, National University at Trujillo, Peru, Paris, UNESCO, 1983, 33 p. ED-83/WS/124.
8. *General survey of aspects of foreign language teacher training* by Reinhold Freduenstein, Philipps University Marburg, FRG. Paris, UNESCO, 1987, 76 p. ED-87/WS/13.
9. *Icelandic as a foreign language* by Jon Friojonsson and Svavar Sigmundsson. Paris, UNESCO, 1987, 55 p. ED-87/WS/17.
10. *The Linguistic situation in Upper Volta : theoretical and applied research on the national languages* by Robert Nikiema. Paris, UNESCO, 1980, 34 p. ED-80/WS/22.
11. *Meeting of experts on language teaching in a bi- or pluri-lingual and multicultural environment.* Paris, UNESCO, 19-23 December 1977. (i) *Academic report.* Paris, UNESCO, 1980 ED-80/WS/112; (ii) *Final report.* Paris, UNESCO, 1978, 14 p. ED-77/CONF.613/7.

12. *National languages and teacher training in Africa. A methodological guide for the use of teacher training institutes* by Joseph Poth. Paris, UNESCO, 1980, 51 p. (ESD No. 32).
13. *National languages and teacher training in Africa.* Report of seminar held in Kaduna, Nigeria, 19-24 January 1976. Paris, UNESCO, 1976, 46 p. ED-76/CONF.817/1.
14. *The Role of teacher training institutions in the promotion of national languages as teaching languages in Africa* by Arame Fal. Dakar, 1979, 73 p.
15. *Seminar on national languages and teacher training in Africa.* Dar-es-Salaam, Tanzania, 12-16 November 1979. *Content and methodology in African language teacher education. Final report.* UNESCO, NEIDA, 1980, 52 p.
16. *The teaching of the mother tongue in Indonesian secondary schools* by P.W.J. Nabahan, Faculty of Languages and Arts, IKIP/Djakarta. Paris, UNESCO, 1983, 41 p. ED-83/WS/5.

Educational Methods, Techniques and Practices

Administrative, Legal and Economic Aspects

1. *Commercial packages. How to use them for educational purposes.* Report elaborated by contract with UNESCO. Lisbon, 1979.
2. *Cost of the new information terminologies in education: characteristics and problems of measurement* by J.C.Eicher. Paris, UNESCO, 1987, 23 p. ED-87/WS/1
3. *The Economics of new educational media.* Vol. 1. *Present status of research and trends.* Paris, UNESCO, 1977, 200 p. (Educational methods and techniques No. 1); Vol. II. *Cost and effectiveness.* Paris, UNESCO, 1980, 316 p. (Educational methods and techniques No. 1); Vol. III. *Cost and effectiveness overview and synthesis.* Paris, UNESCO, 1982, 142 p. (Educational methods and techniques No. 1).
4. *The Educational administrator and instructional materials.* Paris, UNESCO, 1984, 180 p.
5. *Nothing to declare.* A practical guide to using the international convention on the international circulation and importation of visual and/or auditory materials of an educational, scientific or cultural character by Pierre Chesnais. UNESCO, 1982, 20 p.

ED-81/WS/97.
6. *Regulations and legislation regarding correspondence education. A survey of five countries with recommended guidelines for developing countries* by Robert Gunning. London, International Council for Correspondence Education, 1978, 64 p.
7. *Standardization of educational audio-visual equipment.* Yugoslav Commission for Cooperation with UNESCO. Belgrade, Yugoslavia, 1980, 222 p.
8. *Status of staff employing modern educational techniques* by J. Leedham and A. Berruer. Paris, UNESCO, 1979, 122 p. ED-79/WS/49.
9. *Technical and economic criteria for media selection and planning in educational institutions.* Paris, UNESCO, 1984, 81 p. (Educational studies and documents ESD No. 48).

Educational Methods

1. *The child and play.* Theoretical approaches and teaching applications. Paris, UNESCO, 1980, 68 p. (Educational studies and documents (ESD No. 34).
2. *Didactic games in the educational process* Edited by Violeta Mirtcheva, Penka V. Bozarova and Guergana S. Kostadinova. Sofia, Todor Samodoumor Research Institute on General Education. Sofia, 1985, 310 p.
3. *Educational systems regulation : a methodological guide* by Louis D'Hainaut. Paris, UNESCO, 1980, 59 p. (ESD No. 33).
4. *Group techniques in education.* Paris, UNESCO, 1977, 51 p. (ESD No. 24).
5. *Guide for the conversion of school libraries into multi-media centres.* Paris, UNESCO, 1977, 62 p. (ESD No. 22).
6. *The "Macroscope". A methodological approach for a better understanding of educational processes as they relate to social, economic and cultural development.* Paris, UNESCO, 1981, 22 p. ED-82/WS/49.
7. *Programming and complementarity of audio-visual and computer equipment in educational institutions. A methodological guide for administrators.* Report prepared by the International Council for Educational Media (ICEM) under contract with UNESCO. Paris, ICEM, 1987, 38 p. + annexes.
8. *Self-management in educational systems.* Paris, UNESCO, 1981,

48 p. (ESD No. 39).

9. *A Systems approach to teaching and learning procedures.* A guide for educators. Second edition revised and expanded. Paris, The UNESCO Press, 1981, 203 p.
10. *The Use of general TV programmes in school and community. The linkage between in-school and out-of-school education* by Takashi Sakamoto. Tokyo, Institute of Technology. Paris, UNESCO, 1981, 38 p.

Educational Technology, Multimedia Systems and Distance Teaching

1. *Catalogue of non-book materials offered by the member institutions of Avinter–an international exchange mechanism for audio-visual instructional technology resources.* National Centre for Educational Technology, Hungary, 1986, 134 p.
2. *Glossary of educational technology terms.* IBEDATA series, UNESCO/IBE, 1984, 250 p.
3. *Higher level distance education, Perspectives for international co-operation and new developments in technology.* UNESCO international consultation on higher level distance education. Deakin University, Victoria, Australia, 6-11 September 1987. *Proceedings.* UNESCO/Deakin University, 1987, 261 p.
4. *Interactive video in education* by Adolf Melezinek. Programme of joint studies in the field of education carried out by the National Commissions for UNESCO of the European region. Austrian Commission for UNESCO/University of Klagenfurt, Klagenfurt, 1985, 144 p.
5. *Low-cost communication systems for educational and development purposes in third world countries* by R. Postgate, P. Lewis and W. Southwood. Paris, UNESCO, 1979, 225 p. ED-79/WS/70.
6. *Mass media for agricultural extension in Malawi. A case study* by H. Perraton, D. Jamison and F. Orivel. Cambridge, England, International Extension College, 1982, 51 p.
7. *Open learning : systems and problems in post-secondary education* by N. Mackenzie, R. Postgate and J. Scupham. Paris, UNESCO, 1975, 500 p.
8. *Organizing education broadcasting* by D. Hawkridge and J. Robinson. London, Croom Helm/Paris, UNESCO, 1982, 302 p.
9. *Teacher training in educational technology* by Lazar Vlasceanu. UNESCO/CODIESEE, Bucharest, 1986, 192 p.

10. *Techniques for improving educational radio programmes* by James M. Theroux. Paris, UNESCO, 1978, 43 p. (Educational studies and documents (ESD No. 30).
11. *Training farmers by correspondence in Cameroon:A case study* by J. Jenkins and H. Perraton. Cambridge, England, International Extension College, 1982, 42 p.
12. *Use of a newspaper as a distance teaching medium: a case study.* Paris, UNESCO, 1983, 37 p. (Surveys & studies in adult education) ED-83/WS/58.

New Information and Communication Technologies in Education

1. *Applications of computer science to the management and evaluation of the educational process* by Jacques Hebenstreit. Paris, UNESCO, 1984, 15 p. ED-84/WS/10.
2. *Computer applications to educational administration in developed countries : a comparative study* by John Lintott. Paris, UNESCO, 1987, 43 p. ED-87/WS/24.
3. *Computer-assisted school management in the Federal Republic of Germany : the example of microcomputers use in Hessen* by Rudolf Peschke. Paris, UNESCO, 1983. ED-84/WS/104.
4. *Computer-managed learning. A case study : United Kingdom* by W. Broderick. Paris, UNESCO, 1983, 40 p.
5. *Computer-managed instruction in the Japanese secondary school* by Haruo Nishinosono. Paris, UNESCO, 1983.
6. *The Computerized management of educational systems.* Vol. 1 : Accompanying document (of audiovisual assembly). Paris, UNESCO, 1979, 123 p. ED-79/WS/118; Vol. 2 : Scenario (of audiovisual assembly). Paris, UNESCO, 1979, 59 p. ED-80/WS/157; Vol. 3 : Users' handbook (of audiovisual assembly). Paris, UNESCO, 1979, 50 p. ED-79/WS/155.
7. *The Computerized management of educational systems.* Case studies. Vol. 1 : Accompanying document (of audiovisual assembly). Paris, UNESCO, 1983, 157 p.; Vol. 2 : Scenario (of audiovisual assembly). Paris, UNESCO, 1983, 99 p. ED-83/WS/81.
8. *Computers and education. Which role for international research?* by Martin Carnoy and Liza Loop. A report on the Stanford/UNESCO symposium, Stanford University, 10-14 March 1986. Paris, UNESCO, 1986, 17 p. ED-86/WS/86.

9. *Computers in education in developing countries* by Jacques Hebenstreit. Paris, UNESCO, 1984, 28 p. ED-84/WS/10.
10. *Computers in education in developed countries, methods, achievements and problems* by Jacques Hebenstreit. Paris, UNESCO, 1984.
11. *Costs of the new information technologies in education : characteristics and problems of measurement* by J.C. Eicher. Paris, UNESCO, 1987, 23 p. ED-87/WS/1.
12. *Education and computers : vision and reality* by Martin Carnoy, Hugh Daley, Liza Loop, Stanford University, USA. Paris, UNESCO, 1987, 109 p. ED-87/WS/37.
13. *Feasibility study on the use of computer managed learning in secondary schools in the U.S.A.* by Sylvia Charp. Paris, UNESCO, 1984, 27 p.
14. *Informatics and education: a first survey of the state of the art in 43 countries.* Paris, UNESCO, 1986, 308 p. ED-86/WS/9.
15. *New information technologies and education in the USSR : theory and practice* by Valentin M. Kuznetsov. Paris, UNESCO, 1985, 40 p. ED-85/WS/17.
16. *PMIS – guide for the computer-assisted management of operational activities in the field of education.* Provisional version. Paris, UNESCO, 1981, 119 p. ED-81/WS/17.
17. *PMIS – project management information system for the management of operational activities of UNESCO.* Audiovisual presentation. Accompanying document. Paris, UNESCO, 1984, 59 p. ED-84/WS/60.
18. *Study concerning the use of computers in the management and evaluation of instruction in the higher educational establishments of the Union of Soviet Socialist Republics* by V.N. Chetverikov. Paris, UNESCO, 1983.
19. *Study on the use of computers in education in the Soviet Union as well as in other Eastern Socialist countries* by Alexandre I. Saveliev, Director, National Research Institute for Higher Education, Moscow. Paris, UNESCO, 1986.
20. *Training of teacher educators in the use of microcomputers in secondary education on the basis of French and English experiments* by B. Dubreuil. Paris, UNESCO, 1982, 31 p.
21. *The Use of computer-managed learning for media-based informal adult learning* by Ignacy Waniewicz. Paris, UNESCO, 1984, 33 p.

22. *The Use of informatics in education. Present situation, trends and perspectives* by Jacques Hebenstreit. Paris, UNESCO, 1986, 71 p. ED-86/WS/47.
23. *The Use of the microcomputer in teaching and learning* by Jos Beishuizen, Judith Tobin and Peter R. Weston. Swets & Zeitlinger, Amsterdam, 1988, 257 p.

Educational Industries, Teaching Materials

1. *Development of industrial-scale manufacturing of materials and equipment adapted to educational needs in the Third World.* Analysis of the problems and proposals for action. Paris, UNESCO, 1980, 35 p. ED-80/WS/162.
2. *Educational material and media in Japan. A case study.* Paris, UNESCO, 1981, 39 p. ED-81/WS/107.
3. *A Guide to planning and administering government school textbook projects : with special emphasis on cost reduction factors* by Douglas Pearce. Paris, UNESCO, 1988, 95 p. ED-88/WS/33.
4. *The Hungarian experience of OOK : an instrument for the development of educational technology* by Joseph Nagy. Paris, UNESCO, 1980, 102 p. (Experiments and innovations in education No. 43).
5. *The Multilateral exchange of educational audio-visual materials. Existing mechanisms and suggestions for the future.* Paris, UNESCO, 1980, 117 p. (Educational methods and techniques No. 2).
6. *Practical guide for the selection of audio-visual media. General criteria system and evaluation procedure for educational media decisions* by H.J. Klepzig and M. Weiss. Paris, UNESCO, 1979, 50 p. ED-79/WS/26.
7. *The Preparation of minimum performance specifications for audio-visual equipment* by A.H. Crocker. London, UNESCO/International Council for Educational Media (ICEM), 1983, 50 p.
8. *Textbook production in developing countries : some problems of preparation, production and distribution* by Douglas Pearce. Paris, UNESCO, 1982, 66 p. ED-82/WS/60.

See also UNESCO series *Educational methods and techniques*; (ii)

Experiments and innovations in education; *UNESCO source books on curricula* and *methods*. (at the end of Section I)

Common Core Training

1. *The Concept of common core of training applied to complex learning situations* by James Porter. Paris, UNESCO, 1983, 54 p.
2. *The Concept of a common core of training applied to formal and non-formal education* by James Porter. Paris, UNESCO, 46 p.
3. *Conceptual and methodological considerations concerning the notion of a "common core" of training* by L. Vandevelde. Paris, UNESCO, 1983, 28 p.
4. *The Development of core training curricula*. Paris, UNESCO, 1981, 6 p.
5. *A Methodological guide to the application of the notion of common cores in the training of various categories of educational personnel* by Jean-Claude Pauvert. Paris, UNESCO, 1984, 51 p.
6. *Research concerning common cores of training of educational personnel* by Jean-Claude Pauvert. Report of the consultative meeting held at UNESCO, 11-15 April 1983. Paris, UNESCO, 1983, 74 p.

16

ENVIRONMENTAL EDUCATION

INTERNATIONAL ENVIRONMENTAL EDUCATION PROGRAMME, 1975

What is the IEEP ?

The International Environmental Education Programme (IEEP) is a co-operative response at the international level to the pressing concern of nations about their threatened or already damaged environments. Specifically in 1975, UNESCO and United Nations Environmental Programme (UNEP) jointly reacted to Recommendation 96 of the UN Conference on the Human Environment, Stockholm, 1972, after long, consultative preparation, by launching the IEEP.

IEEP, which celebrated its tenth anniversary in 1985, has no closing date: there is no end to efforts to preserve and improve the environment for generations to come.

What Use is Environmental Education?

The last half of the twentieth century witnessed unprecedented economic growth and technological progress. It also witnessed accompanying environmental consequences. In a sense this is not new: interaction between people and their environment has existed since human beings first appeared on earth. But never has the impact been as deep and wide: if now spans the world, affecting flora and fauna, air, soil and the water, thus the quality of human life.

The interaction of humanity and the environment is an intrinsic aspect of human development. Few would wish to stop that development, all would wish it knowledgeable and intelligent, equitable and environmentally sustainable. The technology which brings pollution in its wake can provide the means for the control — indeed the elimination of — the environmental degradation once considered the inevitable price of industrial progress.

The role of education in replying to the challenges of environmental problems and disturbances impressed firmly in our social thinking, the key to their solution is already in our hands – environmental education and training.

Goals, Objectives and Guiding Principles of Environmental Education

The world's first Intergovernmental Conference on Environmental Education, organized in the context of IEEP and convened in Tbilisi (USSR), October 1977, provided, through its recommendations, the framework, principles and guidelines for environmental education at all levels — local, national, regional and international — and for all age groups, inside as well as outside the formal education system.

Accordingly, the goals of environmental education are:

– to foster clear awareness of, and concern about economic, social, political interdependence in urban and rural areas.
– to provide every person with opportunities to acquire, the knowledge, values, attitudes, commitment and skills needed to protect and improve the environment;
– to create new patterns of behaviour of individuals, groups and society as a whole towards the environment.

The objectives of environmental education are:

Awareness – to help social groups and individuals acquire an awareness and sensitivity to the total environment and its allied problems.

Knowledge – to help social groups and individuals gain a variety of experience in, and acquire a basic understanding of the environment and its associated problems.

. *Attitudes* – to help social groups and individuals acquire a set of values and feelings of concern for the environment and the motivation for actively participating in environmental improvement and protection.

Skills – to help social groups and individuals acquire the skills for identifying and solving environmental problems.

Participation – to provide social groups and individuals with an opportunity to be actively and responsibly involved at all levels in working towards resolution of environmental problems.

As for guiding principles, environmental education should:

- consider the environment in its totally — natural and built, technological and social (economic, political, cultural, historical, moral, aesthetic);
- be a continuous lifelong process, beginning at the pre-school level and continuing through all formal and non-formal stages;
- be interdisciplinary in its approach, drawing on the specific content of each discipline in making possible a holistic and balanced perspective;
- examine major environmental issues from local, national, regional and international points of view so that students receive insights into environmental conditions in other geographical areas;
- focus on current and potential environmental situations while taking into account the historical perspectives;
- promote the value and necessity of local, national and international co-operation in the prevention and solution of environmental problems;
- explicitly consider environmental aspects in plans for development and growth;
- enable learners to have a role in planning their learning experiences and provide an opportunity for making decisions and accepting their consequences;
- relate environmental sensitivity, knowledge, problem-solving skills and values clarification to every age, but with special emphasis on environmental sensitivity to the learner's own community in early years;
- help learners discover the symptoms and real causes of environmental problems;
- emphasize the complexity of environmental problems and thus the need to develop critical thinking and problem-solving skills;
- utilize diverse learning environments and a broad array of educational approaches to teaching/learning about and from the environment with due stress on practical activities and first-hand experience.

Target Populations for Environmental Education

As recommended by the Tbilisi Conference, environmental education should be directed to:

- the general public at every age and at all levels of formal education, for pupils, students and teachers, and in the various non-formal education activities for young people and adults;
- specific occupational or social groups with a focus on those whose activity and influence have an important bearing on the environment, for instance, engineers, architects, administrators and planners, industrialists, trade unionists, policy-makers and agriculturists. Various levels in formal and non-formal education should contribute to this training. It is important, moreover, that the training of certain professionals and scientists involved with problems of the environment, such as biologists, hydrologists, sanitary engineers, and others, include an inter-disciplinary environmental component.

How IEEP Works?

From the beginning, the accent of the IEEP has been squarely placed on service to — and participation of — UNESCO's Member-States. The very basis of the Programme was built on a preliminary world survey of the EE needs and priorities of the 136 Member-States at the time, which provided information for determining the most effective strategies for action at the international, regional and national levels.

Seven years after its foundation and five years after the Tbilisi Conference, the IEEP conducted a second worldwide survey with a view to determining new trends and progress of Member-States in relation to environmental education, so as to guide the IEEP in its own planning of future activities. The need and priority of environmental education itself was consistently reported, reflecting the growing concern about a threatened environment.

Actions of IEEP

Successively, actions of IEEP have centred upon:

- development of a general awareness of the need for environmental education;

– development of concepts and methodological approaches in this important field of education;
– efforts for incorporating an environmental dimension into the educational system of Member-States.

Principal Results of IEEP (1975-1985)

Contributing most to the development of global awareness of EE needs was the series of international and regional meetings culminating in the Tbilisi Conference.

A policy of regular, periodical information also contributed to this awareness, notably through the IEEP's international newsletter *Connect*, distributed freely in five languages to 13,000 individuals and institutions throughout the world who are actively involved in environmental concerns as well as environmental education. In parallel, IEEP has been steadily building a computerized information system whose database currently contains information on 900 EE institutions and 300 EE projects, published in regularly updated directories.

IEEP itself has undertaken 31 pilot, experimental and research projects aimed at aiding Member-States to incorporate EE into their national educational processes.

As for EE teacher training, IEEP has organized 13 regional and sub-regional workshops in the five regions of the world as well as 37 national training workshops in the same regions.

Over 130 countries have been directly involved in IEEP's activities – more than 260,000 pupils in primary and secondary schools, about 10,000 teachers, educators and administrators – resulting in the environmental sensitizing of untold thousands worldwide.

Internationalizing Exchange of Information and Experiences

The goal of the IEEP is to provide individuals and institutions, both governmental and non-governmental, with information and opportunities for the exchange of experiences relating to policies, programmes, activities and materials, including publications, in the field of environmental education.

The main activities of the IEEP in this area are:

– computerization of data based on environmental education, resulting in periodical production of three directories – on EE

institutions, on EE projects and activities and on EE periodicals – all three on a worldwide basis;
- publication of the quarterly newsletter *Connect*;
- compilation of a thesaurus of EE terms;
- issuance of an updated bibliography on environmental education;
- organization of multinational meetings and seminars.

Research and Experimentation

Here IEEP's aim is to develop and promote research activities concerning content, methods, mechanisms and strategies for EE, both inside and outside the formal education system.

Principal actions have been:

- surveys on EE needs, priorities, trends and progress internationally;
- studies and research projects on EE contents and methods;
- pilot and experimental projects stimulating EE practices at the national level.

Training of Key Personnel

The pre-service and in-service training of qualified personnel – teachers, educational administrators, planners, curriculum developers and researchers – in environmental education is a priority activity of IEEP.

The main actions concern:

- on international EE training course;
- EE training workshops in all regions of the world;
- subregional EE training workshops;
- EE training workshops at the national level.

Materials and Publications

This area of the IEEP's action involves preparation, adaptation, production and diffusion of EE materials – manuals, guidebooks, modules audio-visuals, etc. – as well as publications concerning various levels and forms of environmental education and training.

Books and brochures of the IEEP, most of which are in several languages, notably include: *Environmental Education in the Light of the Tbilisi Conference; Education and the Challenge of Environmental Problems; EE Needs and Priorities – an International Survey; EE Trends since the Tbilisi Conference, 1977*; two sourcebooks on formal and non-formal environmental education; prototype modules for education and for teacher-training modules; guides on EE methodologies; audiovisual package, etc. – many of them are part of the IEEP's Environmental Education Series of publications.

International Co-operation and IEEP

In the field of international co-operation, the IEEP has significantly aided countries in their efforts to incorporate the environmental dimension into their educational systems. As one result of the various actions of the IEEP in the areas which have been described, and as an outcome of specific technical missions of the IEEP staff, a considerable number of countries have officially introduced EE into their educational plans, policies and reforms.

In most cases, these countries have developed complementary EE legislation or appropriate institutional arrangements. In many cases, they have established ministerial or interinstitutional committees with responsibility for the development of environmental education at all levels of their educational systems.

CONSULTATION MEETING ON THE INCORPORATION OF ENVIRONMENTAL EDUCATION INTO TECHNICAL AND VOCATIONAL EDUCATION, 1986

Background

Within the framework of UNESCO's Approved Programme and Budget for 1984-1985 and as an activity of UNESCO-UNEP IEEP of the Division of Science, Technical and Environmental Education, the Colombo Plan Staff College for Technician Education (CPSC), Singapore organised under UNESCO contract and in co-operation with IEEP the meeting in Singapore from 10-14 March, 1986.

Objectives

1. To study the need and place of environmental education in technical and vocational education.
2. To develop guidelines and strategies for the incorporation of environmental education into technical and vocational education mainly into school curricula and teacher training for industrial and agriculture schools.
3. To recommend activities and documents to be developed by UNESCO-UNEP International Environmental Education Programme for fostering the incorporation of EE into TVE at national, subregional, regional and international levels.
4. To exchange information and experience in the development of environmental education in technical and vocational education.

Participants

Seven participants and one observer from Australia, Egypt, Indonesia, Union of Soviet Socialist Republics, Sri Lanka, Malaysia and Switzerland as well as the Director and two Faculty members of CPSC and the UNESCO Programme Specialist in Environmental Education attended the meeting.

GUIDELINES FOR INCORPORATION OF ENVIRONMENTAL EDUCATION INTO CURRICULA AND TEACHER TRAINING

Although the importance of environmental studies in education and the need for integrating such aspects into the curricula of industrial and agriculture is acknowledged, the extent of integration achieved and the extent of fulfilment of the objectives of Environmental Education depend upon a variety of factors such as:

* Governmental policies on environmental protection and Environmental Education.
* The complexity and size of the industrial/agricultural education system.
* Flexibility and adaptability of the curricula in industrial/agricultural institutions.
* Attitudes and policies of the managements/boards of these institutions.

- Attitudes and commitment of the academic staff and students.
- Responsiveness of the institutions to society's needs.

The purpose of the guidelines presented here is to assist management in achieving a reasonable degree of success.

Policies, Aims and Approaches

The following guidelines reflect important factors in preparing policies and aims for environmental education in curricula:

(a) Environmental Education is a component of education that is essential for the very survival of mankind on the planet earth and is a matter of global concern.
(b) Environmental education objectives can only be attained through clear and explicit policies in general planning.
(c) The policies need to stress that Environmental Education should be integrated into the system so that education becomes a means for bringing about environmental change and awareness.
(d) Components of Environmental Education must be introduced at all levels in education and certain aspects must be compulsory for all students. The compulsory aspects should be drawn up in accordance with the needs of the course and the community.
(e) The aims and objectives of Environmental Education in curricula should be carefully considered and complement those of the technical and vocational education system so that the technological aspects of environmental and ecological problems are fully appreciated.
(f) Environmental Education in Technical and Vocational Education should build on those skills, attitudes, values and knowledge acquired in the high school and relate to technological competencies in a meaningful way.
(g) In Technical and Vocational Education, an exposure to Environmental Education should not be limited to students alone, but should be extended to teachers, workers in industry and the farm, managers and supervisors etc. through appropriate formal and non-formal education programmes.
(h) Components of Environmental Education in Technical and Vocational Education should not be treated as additions to an already crowded curriculum, but as inherent in it and essential for

developing an appreciation for the environment on a scientific and technological basis. A process flow chart for curriculum development in Environmental Education is shown in Fig. 16.1.

Models and Patterns for Incorporating Environmental Education into Curricula

There are several methods of integrating Environmental Education in an educational system. A conceptual model illustrating the integration of curriculum scope through grade levels and across subject areas is shown in Fig. 16.2. In Technical and Vocational Education, the model adopted would depend largely upon the local context and could be decided locally. Whichever model is chosen, it is however, necessary to ensure that:

- the needs of the community at both local and national levels are served;
- the courses are in tune with modern technological developments and the changing needs of the employment market;
- the engineering/agriculture and environmental aspects are integrated;
- Environmental Education should consider the environment in its totality, natural and built, ecological, political, economic, technological, social, legislative, cultural and aesthetic;
- it is a continuous lifelong process: it should link with Environmental Education at other levels and take place through formal and non-formal channels;
- it is transdisciplinary in its approach, drawing on the specific content of each discipline to provide a holistic and balanced perspective;
- it emphasises active participation in preventing environmental problems and working toward the solution of those found;
- it enables learners to play a role in planning their learning experiences and provides an opportunity for making decisions and accepting their consequences;
- it focuses on current and potential environmental situations;
- it explicitly considers environmental aspects in plans for development and growth;
- it examines environmental issues from local, national and international points of view so that learners receive insights into environmental conditions in other geographical contexts;

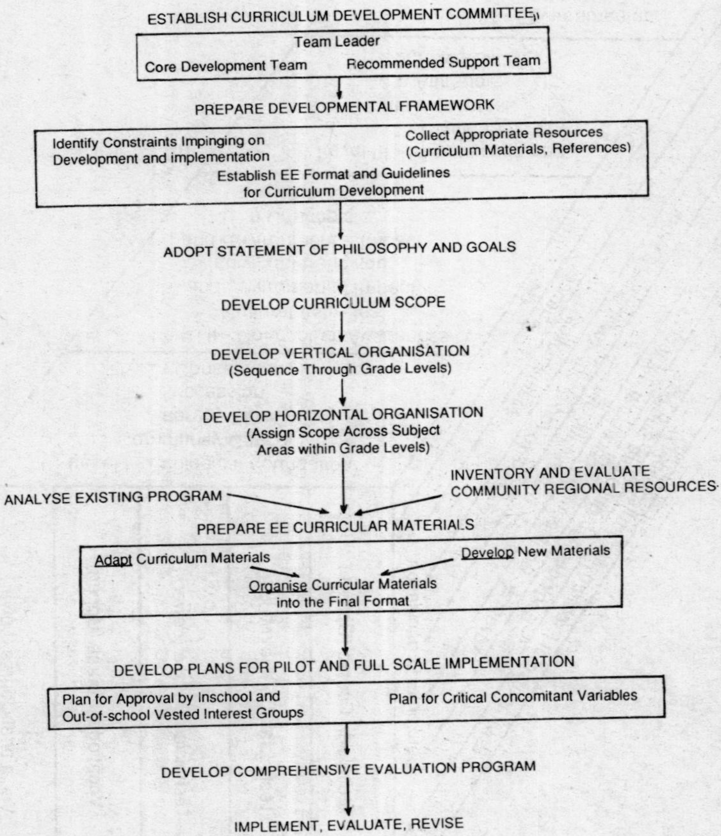

Fig. 16.1: Process Flow Chart for Curriculum Development

Source: UNESCO Document No. ED-80/WS/134 - Harold R. Hungerford.

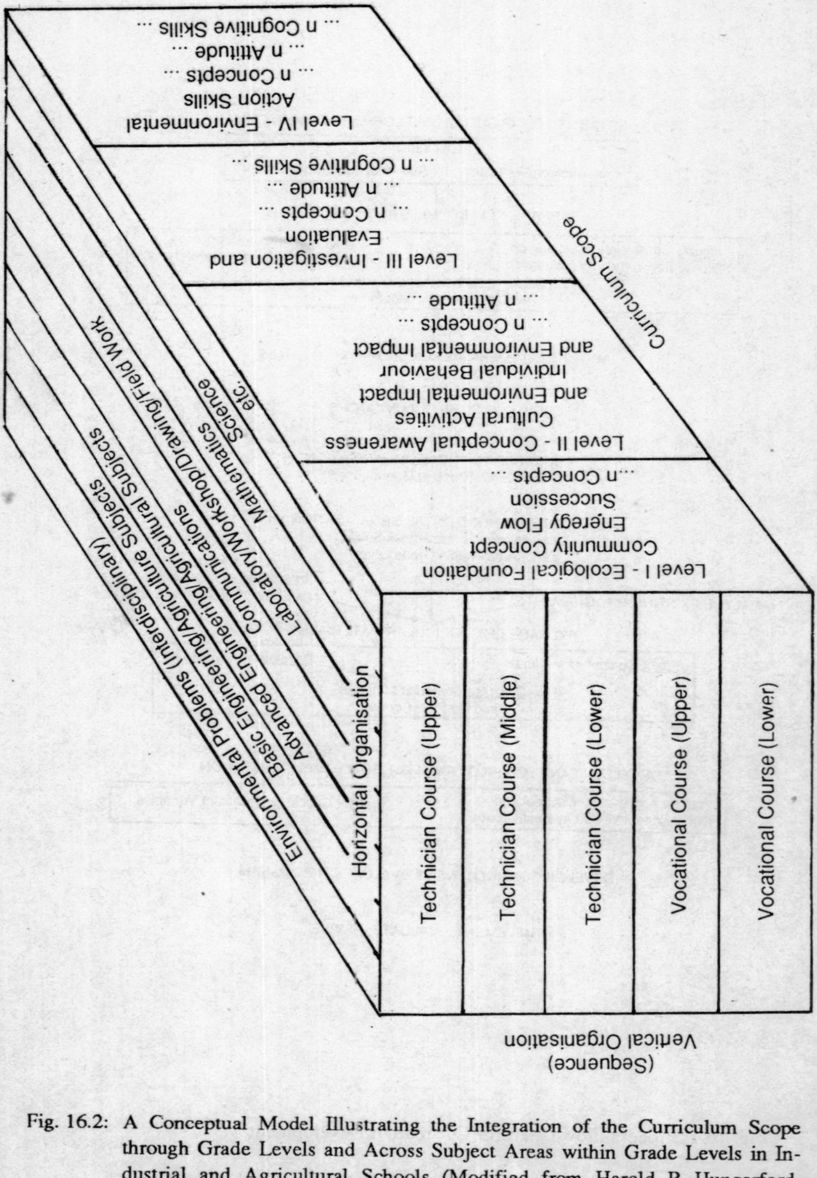

Fig. 16.2: A Conceptual Model Illustrating the Integration of the Curriculum Scope through Grade Levels and Across Subject Areas within Grade Levels in Industrial and Agricultural Schools (Modified from Harold R Hungerford, UNESCO Doc. No. ED-80/Ws/134)

– it focuses on the learner's own community and relates topics being discussed to state, regional, national and international issues and perspectives;
– it relates environmental sensitivity, knowledge, problem-solving and values at every level, but with special emphasis on environmental sensitivity among young people;
– it emphasises the complexity of environmental problems and the need to develop critical thinking and problem-solving skills;
– it utilises diverse learning environments and a broad array of educational approaches to teaching/learning about the environment with due stress on practical activities and first-hand experience.

Curricula

(a) In the case of existing courses, Environmental Education aspects may need to be introduced incrementally with major structural changes taking place in planned stages. This would ensure that present compatibility with career needs is not disturbed and employment prospects not jeopardised. Awareness and sensitivity towards Environmental Education needs to be introduced within current programmes without unduly extending course duration.
(b) The curriculum document is not just a compendium of course/subject syllabii, but includes other components such as:

– topic sequencing
– time allotted for each topic
– instructional objectives (general and specific)
– recommended teaching methods
– instructional resources needed
– assignments/worksheets/exercises
– evaluation scheme
– teacher support materials (teaching schemes, lesson plans)

(c) Curriculum documents may be prepared centrally for all the industrial/agricultural schools and colleges in a country/state and supplied to all institutions. Autonomous institutions might wish to use them as a basis on which to develop detailed curricula from an assessment of their local needs.
(d) Part of curriculum development is the production of instructional

materials for student use – for example notes, textbooks, guides, workbooks, assignment/question banks, audio-visual aids, simulations/games, projects etc. These may be developed by conducting appropriate workshops in which competent teachers and specialists participate.

(e) The curriculum materials so prepared should be adequately pilot tested (evaluated) before they are used in the classroom. Alternatively they may be trial tested on students and subsequently revised.

(f) Curriculum materials in Environmental Education subjects become out-of-date and lose relevance unless periodically reviewed and evaluated. Institutions need to anticipate this need.

Instructional Materials and Media

In most countries, educational systems are often handicapped by a paucity of appropriate print and non-print instructional resources for use by teachers and students. In the case of Environmental Education, the efforts should be made to bridge the gap between the production of this type of material and the demand for them. The potential of the mass media in every country to spread information about environmental matters should be utilised to achieve the goals of Environmental Education. In the light of these recommendations, the following specific guidelines may be helpful:

(a) Environmental experts and teachers in industrial and agricultural schools and colleges could be encouraged to form teams for writing textbooks and other instructional materials for Environmental Education. They could be provided with sufficient financial and other incentives to do so, for example, encouraging them to take up such work during their sabbatical or study leave periods.

(b) Book publishers and media producers in each country should be made aware of their potential role in creating environmental consciousness and be encouraged to produce books, filmstrips, movies. TV programmes, dramas, about environmental awareness for use in Environmental Education.

(c) The management of technical and agricultural schools and colleges could institute national/regional awards annually for the best instructional resource/media software relating to Environmental Education.

(d) Preferably, materials produced should be made with locally available low cost materials relevant to local conditions, and cultural traditions. Media imported from abroad may not always be the most suitable. This should not, however, preclude exchange of resources between countries (e.g. through UNESCO) and their adaptation/modification/translation to meet local needs.

(e) While many countries today have well established systems for radio and TV covering the entire population of the country, the use of these systems for educational purposes is still limited. Since Environmental Education will be a concern of most countries in the years to come, efforts should be made to establish good links between media experts and educationists to develop the effective use of these systems for the dissemination of environmental awareness programmes. In each country, national media systems should be asked to accord priority to Environmental Education, particularly for industrial and agricultural education.

Assessment and Evaluation

The introduction of Environmental Education components into the curricula of industrial and agricultural school could require changes in current student assessment practices. Some important points to consider are:

(a) an assessment scheme closely tied to curriculum objectives, and hence the nature of competencies to be developed, is an essential pre-requisite for success.

(b) the assessment scheme should utilise all the tools and instruments such as objective, short answer and essay type questions, rating scales, case-studies, surveys, interviews, opinionnaires etc. normally used, which are appropriate to the behaviour being tested. In practical and experimental areas a suitable mix of process and product evaluation will need to be used.

(c) cirterion-referenced testing should be used to assess objectives specifying competency and standard performance levels.

(d) specialists in environmental areas both from industry and education will need to design and implement the assessment procedures.

(e) research into assessment methods needs to be undertaken in areas such as the correlation between student performance in environmental subject areas and other subjects.

Teacher Training

One factor effecting the successful implementation of Environmental Education programmes is the training of the personnel responsible for putting the programmes into effect. Both formal and non-formal approaches, pre-service and in-service modes need to be utilised in training programmes for teaching personnel with the objective of developing their ability to incorporate environmental components in their teaching. In addition to the various strategies and methodologies for teacher education and training in environmental areas the following aspects also need to be considered:

(a) while determining the needs of teacher education for Technical and Vocational Education, the special needs of environmental subjects introduced into the curricula of industrial and agricultural schools should be considered.

(b) the approaches and strategies needed for training teachers in Environmental Education may be different from those normally used.

(c) the additional training needs of teachers for Environmental Education can be broadly classified into these areas:

   (i) knowledge of newly introduced environmental subjects.
   (ii) pedagogical skills particularly relevant to the teaching of environmental subjects.
   (iii) exposure to/training in appropriate industries concerned with environmental protection.
   (iv) management of the instructional system to meet the additional demands imposed by the integration of Environmental Education components (e.g. production of instructional materials etc.)

(d) the motivation of teachers to incorporate environmental components in their teaching strategies.

Teacher training colleges may first have to prepare to meet this new challenge by taking measures to orient their teacher-educators to environmental issues.

System Management

Implementation of the kind of changes in the educational system envisaged in this report requires a forward-looking, dynamic and committed senior management. Educational systems are already undergoing changes in several respects, but the changes envisaged pertaining to Environmental Education have far reaching consequences and hence need to be handled with the utmost foresight. Some useful guides to system managers in this regard are:

(a) make special efforts to create an awareness of the need for Environmental Education in industrial and agricultural schools at all levels of the system.
(b) ensure that teachers, students and parents are aware of government and system policies on Environmental Education.
(c) invest time in planning, course design, procurement of resources and curriculum design before venturing to implement Environmental Education.
(d) be flexible in approaches, schedules and targets to ensure adequate co-operation and involvement by all the stakeholders in the project.
(e) take steps to obtain the active co-operation and support of industries (particularly those interacting with the environment).
(f) establish proper links between institutions within the system and the surrounding communities.

The success of the educational approach to solving environmental problems rests heavily on the attitudes exhibited by managements of industrial and agricultural schools.

RECOMMENDED ACTIVITIES AND DOCUMENTS TO BE DEVELOPED BY IEEP

The incorporation of Environmental Education components in the curricula of industrial and agricultural schools needs to be considered as a major "change project" in the educational system. The general guidelines given earlier may be considered as a necessary first step.

This should be followed by a series of activities leading to the development of important policy documents, guidelines, working documents, etc., to be used by various groups of professionals for producing and implementing curricula. In this context the following activities and documents are recommended to be developed:

1. Activities

(i) *Development of prototype curricula, programmes, structures, methodologies as well as teacher-training programmes*

UNESCO has already initiated a number of activities under Environmental Education in a proactive manner and much progress has been made in incorporating Environmental Education into primary and secondary education. Similar initiatives are now to be taken up in the post-secondary sector, particularly in Technical and Vocational Education commencing at the level of the industrial and agricultural schools.

Workshops and training seminars at international, regional and sub-regional levels need to be conducted by IEEP for curriculum developers and teacher trainers in Technical and Vocational Education to identify possible approaches, structures and methodologies, to prepare model curricula in chosen disciplines as well as sample teacher-training programmes. These will provide the required guidance of countries and institutions desirous of incorporating Environmental Education into their Technical and Vocational Education programmes. Experts from organisations such as ILO, CPSC, FAO and WHO should be consulted in the preparation of such programmes.

(ii) *Development of suitable textbooks, workbooks, instructional modules, and teaching aids including film and video programmes*

Lack of suitable instructional resources could emerge as a major handicap in the successful implementation of Environmental Education. This deficiency could be largely overcome by the production of inexpensive local resources and production of standard books and other materials of high quality with support from UNESCO. Organisations with a direct teaching function, such as the Colombo Plan Staff College could be commissioned to extend their services as producers of teaching materials.

(iii) *Exchange of information between countries and supply of resources and media materials*

IEEP should foster the exchange of information on the incorporation of Environmental Education in Technical and Vocational Education as a part of its international network of information exchange.

(iv) *Organisation of periodic conferences, training seminars, and symposia*

The importance of organising training seminars, conferences, and symposia both within a country and at regional and international levels needs no reiteration. At the regional and international levels such meetings bring experts in the field of Environmental Education together and facilitate exchange of successful experiences as well as problems faced and solutions adopted. In this context training seminars should be organised. Furthermore, Environmental Education should be placed on the agenda of Technical and Vocational Education meetings such as the International Congress on Technical and Vocational Education to be organised in 1987.

(v) *Institution of awards and prizes for outstanding achievements in Environmental Education and for the production of innovative media and instructional resources*

Perhaps the surest way to motivate people for greater involvement and effort in Environmental Education is to recognise and reward exceptionally good work done in the field. UNESCO has excellent scope to take up such activities which will eventually lead to the establishment of proper norms and standards at a global level and support such activities at country levels also.

(vi) *Pilot programmes and research projects*

The introduction of Environmental Education into industrial

and agricultural schools might need a cautious approach through the use of pilot studies and impact studies. Such activities quite often require a considerable investment of resources and need to be supported by UNESCO.

(vii) *Establishment of national centres*

Among the several strategies to promote intensified activities in Environmental Education would be the identification of centres of excellence and potential in each country and their designation as national centres for Environmental Education. In Technical and Vocational Education, it would not be difficult to identify such institutions through the respective governments by establishing a set of criteria for selection. If such national centres are provided with adequate funds and expertise through UNESCO, it would be possible to generate replicable models for excellence in Environmental Education in each country.

2. **Documents to be Developed**

A large number of the activities described above would lead to the production of reports, case studies or other publications which would be of use to national organisations working for Environmental Education in Technical and Vocational Education. In particular, international documents of significance would be:

(i) Documents on general guidelines, objectives, concepts, approaches, methodologies etc. for incorporating Environmental Education into the curricula of industrial and technical schools.
(ii) Prototype course structures, syllabii and Environmental Education components for samples of conventional industrial and agriculture courses in Technical and Vocational Education and integrated Environmental Education oriented courses.
(iii) Lists of prototype projects to be undertaken by technician level students in industry/field/farm in the area of environmental protection.
(iv) List of prototype research activities that could be taken up by technician institutions in Environmental Education areas.
(v) National/worldwide directories of institutions in technology and agriculture which offer Environmental Education oriented tech-

nician courses.

(vi) An international directory of eminent educationists/media specialists/teacher trainers in industry and agricultural who have specialised experience in environmental studies.

(vii) An international resource book of industries/farms/organisations taking an active part in imparting Environmental Education.

(viii) An international resource book of teaching aids, educational films, video programmes and gaming/simulation exercises at post-secondary level for students in technician and agriculture education.

(ix) The journal "*Connect*" needs to report on research and innovations in implementing Environmental Education in technician and agriculture subjects.

(x) Simple and concise appreciation documents.

(xi) Environmental Education guides for teacher trainers in Technical and Vocational Education.

See also *Consultative Meeting on the Inforporation of Environmental Education into the Training of Teacher Educators, Planners and Administrators, 1985*. (Chapter 24.XVI)

BIBLIOGRAPHY

UNESCO DOCUMENTS AND PUBLICATIONS*

1. *Activities of the UNESCO/UNEP international environmental education programme (1975-1983)*. Paris, UNESCO, 1983, 35 p. ED-84/WS/36.
2. *Analysis of results of environmental education pilot projects*. (Environmental education series, EES No. 19).
3. *The Balance of "lifekind" : an introduction to the human environment*. Paris, UNESCO, 1986, 26 p. (EES No. 18) ED-86/WS-52.
4. *A comparative survey of the incorporation of environmental education into school curricula*. Paris, UNESCO, 1985 (EES No. 17) ED-84/WS/84.

* Listing to illustrate the range of UNESCO documents and publications

5. *Connect – UNESCO/UNEP international environmental education newsletter* (quarterly), 1976.
6. *Consultation meeting on the incorporation of environmental education into technical and vocational education.* Singapore, 10-14 March 1986. *Final report.* Singapore, 1986, 65 p. + annexes.
7. *Educational module on conservation and management of natural resources.* Paris, UNESCO, 1983, 89 p. (EES No. 3) ED-83/WS/38.
8. *Educational module on environmental problems in cities.* Paris, UNESCO, 1983 (EES No. 4) ED-83/WS/87.
9. *Energy : an interdisciplinary theme for environmental education.* Paris, UNESCO, 1985, 171 p. (EES No. 11) ED-84/WS/76.
10. *Environmental education in Asia and the Pacific.* Bulletin of the UNESCO Regional office for Education in Asia and the Pacific (PROAP) UNESCO/PROAP, June 1981.
11. *Environmental education in the light of Tbilisi conference.* Paris, UNESCO, 1980, 100p.
12. *Environmental education in technical and vocational education.* Paris, UNESCO, 1987, 42 p. (EES No. 24).
13. *Environmental education in vocational agriculture curriculum and agriculture teacher education in Michigan, U.S.A. : a case study.* Paris, UNESCO, 1988, 97 p. + annexes (EES No. 28) ED-88/WS/41.
14. *Environmental education : module for in-service training of social science teachers and supervisors for secondary schools.* Paris, UNESCO, 1985, 125 p. (EES No. 10) ED-84/WS/54.
15. *Environmental education : module for in-service training of teachers and supervisors for primary schools.* Paris, UNESCO, 1985, 172 p. (EES No. 6) ED-85/WS/1.
16. *Environmental education : module for pre-service training of teachers and supervisors for secondary schools.* Paris, UNESCO, 1983, 154 p. (EES No. 8) ED-83/WS/90.
17. *Environmental education: module for pre-service training of social science teachers and supervisors for secondary schools.* Paris, UNESCO, 1985, 133 p. (EES No. 9) ED-85/WS/5.
18. *Environmental education : module for pre-service training of teachers and supervisors for primary schools.* Paris, UNESCO, 1983, 143 p. (EES No. 5) ED-83/WS-912.
19. *Environmental education : module for pre-service training of*

teachers and supervisors for secondary schools. Paris, UNESCO, 1983, 224 p. (EES No. 7) ED-83/WS/89.

20. *Environmental education: module on health, nutrition and the environment*. (EES No. 21).
21. *Environmental education: principles of teaching and learning*. Paris, UNESCO, 1985, 228p. (EEP No. 20).
22. *Environmental education. Training of teacher educators, curriculum developers, educational planners and administrators* by Usha Nayar, Anjana Mangalagiri, New Delhi, National Institute of Educational Planning and Administration, 1988, 327 p.
23. *Evaluating environmental education in schools : a practical guide for teachers*. Paris, UNESCO, 1985, 106 p. (EES No. 12) ED-84/WS/77.
24. *Glossary of environmental education terms*. Hungary, UNESCO, 1983, 67 p.
25. *Guide on environmental values education*. Paris, UNESCO, 1985, 106 p. (EES No. 13) ED-85/WS-94.
26. *Guide on gaming and simulation for environmental education*. Paris, UNESCO, 1983 (EES No. 2) ED-83/WS/64.
27. *Guidelines for developing nonformal environmental education programmes*. A discussion guide for UNESCO training seminars on environmental education. Paris, UNESCO, 1986, 94 p. (EES No. 23).
28. *Interdisciplinary approaches in environmental education*. Paris, UNESCO, 1985, 52 p. (EES No. 14) ED-84/WS/95.
29. *Intergovernmental conference on environmental education*. Tbilisi, USSR, 14-26 October, 1977. *Final report*. Paris, UNESCO, 1977 ED/MD/49.
30. *International directory of individuals active in the field of environmental education*. Paris, UNESCO, 1977, 126 p. ED-77/WS/121.
31. *International directory of institutions active in the field of environmental education*. Revised and enlarged edition. Paris, UNESCO, 1981 ED-81/WS/86 (Fre, Spa) (Eng Out of print available on microfiche) S.A. 02.11.
32. *International strategy for action in the field of environmental education and training for the 1990's*. Paris/Nairobi, UNESCO/UNEP, 1988, 21 p.
33. *Living the environment : a sourcebook in environmental education*. Paris, UNESCO/UNEP, 1985, 230 p.

34. *A Problem-Solving approach to environmental education.* Paris, UNESCO, 1985, 83 p. (EES No. 15) ED-84/WS/96.
35. *Procedure for developing an environmental education curriculum: a discussion guide for UNESCO training seminars on environmental education.* Paris, UNESCO, 1986, 100 p. (EES No. 22).
36. *Strategies for the training of teachers in environmental education.* A discussion guide for UNESCO training seminars on environmental education by Richard J. Wilke, R. Ben Peyton, Harold R. Hungerford. Paris, UNESCO, 1987, 152 p. (EES No. 25) ED-86/WS/117.
37. *Subregional training seminar on the incorporation of environmental education into industrial education for Asia.* New Delhi, India, 20-27 April 1987. *Final report.* New Delhi, National Council of Educational Research and Training, 1987, 116 p.
38. *Subregional training seminar on nonformal environmental education for the Caribbean.* Guyana, 25-31 May 1987. *Final report.* Guyana, 1987, 155 p. + annexes.
39. *Subregional workshop on teacher training in environmental education for the Arab States.* Bahrain, 25-30 January 1986. Bahrain, 1986, 100 p.
40. *Toward interdisciplinary environmental education.* International seminar education and environment. Budapest, Vesprem, Hungary, 10-14 November 1980. *Proceedings.* National Centre for Educational Technology (OOK), 1981, 220 p.
41. *Trends in environmental education.* Paris, UNESCO, 1977, 307 p.
42. *Trends in environmental education since the Tbilisi conference.* Paris, UNESCO, 1983 (EES No. 1) ED-82/WS/125.
43. *UNESCO/UNEP international congress on environmental education and training.* Moscow, USSR, 17-21 August 1987. Paris, UNESCO, 1987, 39 p. ED-87/CONF.402/6.
44. *Universities and environmental education.* UNESCO and the International Association of Universities. Paris, UNESCO, 1986, 127 p.

17

SECONDARY EDUCATION

INTERNATIONAL CONFERENCE ON EDUCATION RECOMMENDATION CONCERNING IMPROVEMENT OF SECONDARY EDUCATION: OBJECTIVES, STRUCTURES, CONTENT AND METHODS, 1986

Preamble

The International Conference on Education, convened by the United Nations Educational, Scientific and Cultural Organization, meeting in Geneva at its 40th session, held from 2 to 11 December, 1986.

Having regard to the relevant conventions, recommendations and declarations adopted at the international level, and more particularly by the UNESCO.

Noting the universal recognition of education as a fundamental right for individuals and a prerequisite for social progress has led over the past two decades to the unprecedented growth of education throughout the world, particularly at the secondary and higher levels.

Recalling that the Convention and Recommendation against Discrimination in Education adopted by the General Conference of UNESCO at its eleventh session stipulate that secondary education, in its different forms, should be made generally available and accessible to all.

Recognizing that each Member-State has its distinctive constitutional features and its particular educational needs and arrangements.

Emphasizing that secondary education should contribute both to the full and all-round development of the individual and to his or her preparation for cultural, social and economic life, and wishing to strengthen, and to seek new forms of, co-operation in education.

Recognizing the importance of relevant secondary education as a contributory factor of foster cultural, socio-economic, scientific and technological development in all contemporary societies.

Recalling that Recommendation No. 68 adopted by the International Conference on Education at its 34th session called on Member-States to reorganize secondary education by transcending its traditional academic emphasis and by associating general, technical and vocational education in one balanced, harmonious and flexibly diversified system.

Noting that the process of bringing together and sometimes of grouping together general education and vocational education has manifested itself in a great number of Member-States.

Noting also that during the last decade, secondary education was subject to profound reform which have affected its structures and curricula, and reaffirming the importance of strengthening the interrelations between the various levels of education.

Recognising that rapid scientific, technological and social developments present new challenges which call for the improvement of secondary education in order to meet the present and future needs of individuals and society.

Believing that the clearly defined goals and objectives of secondary education, derived from the national objectives of education, and their review in the light of changing circumstances and needs constitute significant steps towards the improvement of secondary education.

Recognizing that the essential prerequisites for the improvement of secondary education embrace suitable initial and continuing training of teaching staff, the availability and proper management of physical resources, the updating of curricula and programmes, text-books and teaching aids, and the development of appropriate forms and methods of education.

Adopts on 11th December, 1986 and submits for consideration by the ministries responsible for education and the appropriate authorities and agencies in the various Member-States, institutions within United Nations system having responsibilities in this field, and inter-governmental and non-governmental organizations concerned, the following Recommendation:

A. General Principles and Key Concepts

1. Secondary education is a phase of education during which young people are led to become independent, responsible adults. It is during this period that the young acquire the knowledge and skills needed to prepare them for life in all its aspects.
2. The improvement of secondary education should be seen in the perspective of lifelong education. The organization of secondary education should be flexible enough to provide continuity and complementarity between institutions which are elements of the formal general and vocational secondary school system and institutions and programmes outside this system, as well as providing an opportunity for continuation or re-entry into secondary education for those who left it earlier or who never had a chance to enter secondary education.
3. The choice of objectives, structures, content and methods in secondary education should be guided by the following general principles and key concepts:

(a) promoting the all-round and harmonious development of the individual by providing the conditions needed for his or her intellectual, moral, physical, aesthetic and social education and preparation for life in society, and educating the young generations in the spirit of peace, international understanding, co-operation and mutual respect.

(b) encouraging the participation of the entire population in the development strategy of secondary education, either directly or through the intermidiary of the bodies responsible for educational management, including cultural or scientific institutions.

(c) offering each individual real equality of opportunity and the greatest possible chances of success.

(d) meeting the need of cultural, socio-economic, scientific and technological development and taking account of distinctive national characteristics; respecting, in the case of territories still under the foreign occupation, the right of the population of those territories to an education adapted to their needs. Their national and cultural identities must be preserved and national school curricula should not be modified in such a way as would distort that identity.

(e) ensuring the high quality of instruction and education, which should be regarded as the main task in the circumstances of rapid quantitative growth in secondary education and of its universalisation.

(f) regularly evaluating, reviewing and adjusting curricula, textbooks, methods and teaching-learning processes with a view to improving the quality of education, keeping pace with rapid scientific and technological progress and the resulting development in knowledge and know-how, and producing individual who can, through self-directed learning, orientate themselves in changing industrial, agricultural and social processes and who may themselves promote such changes and progress in society and take an active part in them.

(g) clarifying the objectives, structure, content, forms and methods of secondary education in a continuous process of reflection.

(h) using in the educational and training process approaches and technologies corresponding to those existing in the society, due regard being paid to the need to incorporate modern scientific and technological achievements.

(i) developing and updating science and technology teaching and encouraging an interdisciplinary approach in that type of education, bearing in mind also the need to intensify students' humanistic education with a view to ensuring their harmonious development.

(j) taking into consideration the fundamental role of general education while promoting closer link between general education and technical and vocational education, with a particular view to enhancing the status of the latter.

(k) closely interlinking the education imparted by schools themselves with the many resources offered by the out-of-school environment.

(l) promoting interaction between education and work in accordance with general principles, programmes and measures such as those set forth in Recommendation No. 73 adopted by the International Conference on Education at its 38th session.

(m) putting into practice as far as possible the principles set forth in the other recommendations on secondary education adopted by the International Conference on Education.

B. Practical Measures and Programmes at the National Level

4. National education policies should favour and, whenever necessary, give priority to the improvement of secondary education through:

   (a) continuous reflection on the objective of secondary education with a view to improvement;
   (b) adoption of legislative, administrative, financial, social and educational measures to ensure the further democratization of secondary education and the improvement of its objectives, content, structures and methods;
   (c) re-examination of the share devoted to secondary education within the total expenditure on education;
   (d) reinforcement of educational provisions for disadvantaged groups of the population and regions of the country, and development of special measures at the planning and implementation levels such as a better distribution of schools to reach rural and suburban areas;
   (e) ensuring equal rights to secondary education for migrants and national minorities, while enabling them to maintain links with their culture of origin and their mother tongue, in particular by teaching in those subjects;
   (f) appropriate provision for the education of handicapped young people, including theoretical and practical teacher training;
   (g) development and improvement of secondary technical and vocational education, especially in relation to the changing requirements for qualified manpower brought about by the challenges of science and technology and national development;
   (h) establishment or development of evening courses outside school time and outside the formal education system and of distance-teaching programmes (for example, by correspondence, by radio or by television);
   (i) introduction of measures to motivate and stimulate young people and adults to acquire a secondary education in society, in industrial and agricultural enterprises and in the family;
   (j) to promote greater access for girls and women to scientific studies and to technical and vocational secondary education and encourage them, through appropriate measures, to pursue

their studies particularly in those fields which enable them to participate in all sectors of the national economy.

5. (a) Appropriate mechanisms should be established or further developed to promote an optimal use of available resources, in particular to ensure greater continuity and complementarity between the different types of secondary education.
(b) In addition, training in educational management, for middle-level staff at local and institutional levels in particular, could be promoted.

6. As part of the general improvement of secondary education, in-depth examination of the existing structures is required. Whenever necessary, practical measures should be taken, in order:

(a) to ensure that structures are better adapted to the country's cultural, socio-economic, scientific and technical development;
(b) to develop overall structures, institutions and cycles most conducive to achieving the national goals and objectives for secondary education and in harmony with the current trend of rapprochement between general and technical/vocational education.

7. Educational structures should be developed in a sufficiently flexible manner so as:

(a) to be able to respond to changing societal needs while maintaining continuity and coherence and providing equal opportunity of access and the greatest possible chances of success;
(b) to provide, by appropriate procedures, for the possibility of transfer from one type of course or kind of education to another, thereby making it easier for students to have access to alternatives as they proceed;
(c) to permit the integration of education, science, culture and production and provide for continuous linkage of education and work;
(d) to improve examination and assessment techniques, the latter being considered as an integral part of the teaching-learning process, with a view to continuous monitoring of the progress

and results achieved by students in relation to the objectives of the course;

(e) to design referral and selection procedures in such a way that they are entirely non-discriminatory.

8. The process of improvement of secondary education should lead to a substantial raising of the scientific level of the whole content of secondary education, which should be forward-looking and should be in line with the achievements and requirements of social, scientific and technological progress in order to provide the conditions for new professional qualifications connected with the mastering of integrated technologies.
9. A balanced secondary curriculum is essential for the all-round personal development of students and their personal aptitudes and interests should also be catered for. Continuous curriculum appraisal and renewal are essential to avoid over-loading and imbalance. The subjects taught should include languages, mathematics, natural science, technology and social science studies. Provision should be made for cultural, moral, spiritual, aesthetic and physical education and for education related to new ways of thinking for the nuclear and space age. These components should prepare students for life and work in society in general. The content of secondary education should highlight the cultural and intellectual tradition of each country. It should also be directed to the strengthening of respect for human rights, fundamental freedom and people's rights; it should promote peace, international understanding and friendship among all nations; it should counter racial segregation and discrimination on grounds of race, sex or religion.
10. Curricula should be developed through a broad process of research, evaluation and consultation, involving teachers, teachers' organizations, parents, students and representatives of various sectors of cultural and socio-economic life. Introduction of new curriculum elements should be the subject of prior studies and evaluations.
11. The process of curriculum renewal should make possible the elimination of outdated material to make way for newer elements (for example, environmental and ecological education, informatics, new technology, etc.) called for by scientific and technological challenges. These elements may form part of integrated

or inter-disciplinary course to contribute to coherence in the curriculum and to avoid overloading it.

12. Curricula, especially at the upper secondary level, should provide for creativity, flexibility and diversification. The core of compulsory subjects should be complemented by optional subjects and various extra-curricular activities.
13. Importance should be attached not only to what is taught but also to the way in which it is taught. It follows that the forms and methods of teaching, as well as instructional materials, must be continuously reviewed.
14. Methods should be developed and used which stimulate active participation of pupils in the teaching-learning process and develop their self-learning possibilities, their desire to learn and their taste for the acquisition of knowledge.
15. In the teaching-learning process, emphasis should be laid on 'learning how to learn'. Appropriate methods and forms of the organization of the students' work should be used to this effect, such as, for example, group work, self-directed learning and other forms of individualized learning.
16. The introduction of work experience or familiarization with the world of work in the general education curriculum also calls for a change of emphasis in the methods used: visits, educational excursions and practical work experience outside the classroom should be organized. Outside experts should also be invited into schools more frequently.
17. Science and technology education implies the introduction of more laboratory, experimental and practical activities of all types leading to more active participation on the part of the student in the processes of scientific exploration and technological development. Likewise, arts education should be linked to the use of such sources and means of culture as museums, archives and libraries.
18. Modern technologies, such as, for example, micro-computers, may bring substantial support to the improvement of the teaching-learning process, favour individualized learning and help to develop the pupil's personality. On the basis of analysis of the practical results of the use of computers in schools, appropriate changes should be made to the content of studies utilizing computers. School authorities should assess the usefulness of new equipment before acquiring it.
19. Appropriate steps should be taken to develop national capacities

for the production, at reasonable cost, of instructional materials and equipment, including textbooks, software and other materials for science and technology education.

20. Teachers should be involved in the preparation of the materials needed, as a way of enhancing their professional competence.
21. Guidance and counselling services should be developed and extended to every secondary school and student. Educational and vocational orientation and guidance should, whenever possible, be an integral part of secondary-school life. Girls should be encouraged to pursue further studies leading to scientific and technological careers and more generally to careers in which they are under-represented.
22. It is also essential to develop out-of-school forms of orientation and guidance such as, for example, visits to industrial and agricultural enterprises and other places of work.
23. Due support should be ensured for the development of educational research as an essential tool contributing to the attainment of the established objectives. Educational research and innovative activities should be encouraged at all levels and taken into account in political decisions and educational practice.
24. In order to enhance the contribution that research can make to the improvement of secondary education, appropriate steps should be taken to make the results of educational research and the innovations to which it may lead better known. These results should be taken into account in the pre-service and continuing training of teachers, administrators and other secondary education personnel.
25. The development of national, local and institutional management capacities, especially by training, can enhance the effectiveness of secondary education administration and management methods. The involvement of teachers and parents in this process is also desirable.
26. Performance and efficiency in educational management should benefit from a greater and better use of modern technologies. The development of management resource centres and management information system should be seen as important for the improvement of secondary education.
27. Each country should consider which administrative functions can best be carried out by central services and which by regional or local services with a view to better use of resources, more effective participation of all groups and better information and com-

munication among the different administrative levels.

28. Evaluation of the functioning of the management of secondary education should be an integral part of management. This would require appropriately designed monitoring systems for all aspects of secondary education.
29. It is essential that educational policies encourage, and educational practices secure, wider participation by all sectors of the population in both the democratization and the improvement of secondary education.
30. The improvement of secondary education requires the training of a sufficient number of teachers and other educational personnel and enhancement of the equality of such training.
31. In this connection, long-term and medium-term policies and objectives concerning teacher education should be formulated and practical action foreseen, which may include:

(a) encouraging the most motivated young people to enter the teaching profession;

(b) reorienting teacher education methods and curricula towards an improved balance between subject content and educational psychology components with a view to the harmonious professional preparation of teachers; this preparation should be based on actual teaching practice providing a basis for the analysis and evaluation of educational activity. It should also make possible a reasonable shortening of the period of adaptation of young teachers;

(c) measures to regulate the supply of, and demand for, teachers, particularly in the areas of science and technology, as well as in other areas where a shortage may be perceived;

(d) developing a systematic approach to in-service education aimed at upgrading, updating and generally improving the knowledge and professional qualifications of different categories of secondary educational personnel on a regular and recurrent basis. This approach should be differentiated in accordance with the qualification standards of the various groups of teachers and the concrete needs of pedagogical practice, and should be conducive to exchanges of innovative experience, research and pedagogical reflection thereon;

(e) measures to ensure that educational personnel are promptly provided with scientific and technical information, with the necessary documentation, visual aids and technical equipment for teaching.

32. Other categories of educational personnel, such as administrators, principals, inspectors, guidance and counselling personnel, should receive appropriate pre-service and in-service training for their work in secondary education.

C. International and Regional Co-operation

33. Taking into account the variety and dimensions of problems and issues associated with the development of secondary education, particularly, but not exclusively, in developing countries, a concentrated international and regional approach could help Member-States to find solutions to existing problems and issues at the secondary level.
34. Member-States should strengthen and develop further bilateral regional and international co-operation with a view to the improvement of secondary education and give all necessary support to UNESCO's regional programmes of educational innovation for development. Such co-operation is particularly desirable in the teaching of modern languages as an instrument of education for international understanding.
35. UNESCO, as the leading international organization in the field of education, should endeavour:

    (a) to pay special attention to the development and improvement of secondary education in its programmes for the years to come;
    (b) to promote further international and regional co-operation in the field of secondary education through its various international and regional programmes and projects;
    (c) to foster, particularly through its regional network of educational innovation for development, closer co-operation between Member-States with a view to the improvement of secondary education;
    (d) to encourage international and regional co-operation in the field of training and the raising of the qualification standards of teachers and secondary education managerial staff through various programmes and international and regional projects;

(e) to support efforts aimed at the development of the Associated Schools.

36. UNESCO, and the International Bureau of Education as a specialized body within UNESCO, should also endeavour:

(a) to facilitate the exchange of information and experience in the field of secondary education between different countries, including the exchange of secondary-school curricula, training materials and specialists. International Bureau of Education's (IBE) documentation service should play its role to the full in this connection;
(b) to promote research and studies with a view to the improvement of secondary education;
(c) to carry out follow-up activities to this Conference and to advise Member-States upon request on ways of applying this Recommendation in the light of the real situations prevailing in various countries.

37. UNESCO, in co-operation with other international organizations, should strengthen activities concerning education for international understanding, co-operation and peace and education relating to human rights and fundamental freedom. They should also promote innovative measures in Member-States for the revision of secondary-education curricula in this light and for encouraging the mutual revision of textbooks in order to free them for prejudice, incitement to racial hatred and a hostile attitude to other peoples. International exchanges of information on the results achieved should be encouraged.
38. UNESCO, in co-operation with other international organizations, regional bodies and concerned international non-governmental organizations should further encourage joint activities and contribute efficiently to the systematic exchange of ideas, information and experiences regarding the improvement of secondary education by using various means, such as promoting the organization of regional and international conferences, workshops, seminars and meaning to discuss various aspects of the improvement of secondary education, and supporting the exchange of educational personnel to study other countries' experience.
39. The IBE, in co-operation and co-ordination with other units of UNESCO, should:

(a) within its programme of educational documentation and information, give appropriate attention to secondary education and its improvement by collecting information concerning secondary education curricula and programmes, innovative experiences and reforms in the field of secondary education, analysing this information, disseminating it and making it available to Member-States;
(b) within its study activities, and particularly within its series of studies and surveys in comparative education, study ways and means of improving secondary education in collaboration with national research institutions;
(c) pay special attention to the system for the training of teaching staff and for improving their qualifications and to progress noted in this respect in national programmes, collect information on school documentation and innovatory experience required in teacher and in teachers' professional practice, and transmit such information to Member-States.

RECOMMENDATION ON EDUCATION IN THE FIGHT AGAINST AIDS

The International Conference on Education,

Recognizing that the world is faced with a problem of which the full gravity has become apparent only since the UNESCO Secretariat sent the preliminary draft of Recommendation No. 75 concerning 'the improvement of secondary education: objectives, structures, content and methods' to Member-States, namely the AIDS pandemic, as the Director-General of the World Health Organization (WHO) recently called it,

Noting that many governments and public opinion in general find themselves at present helpless and lacking in the necessary minimum of information to face up to this new disease;

Considering that there is a great deal to be done at the educational level and certainly in schools with a view to implementing emergency programmes of preventive information, and that, in particular, such information should focus upon secondary-school teachers and pupils and on the parents of those pupils;

Considering that UNESCO has an essential role to play in this respect, in close collaboration with WHO and other agencies, organizations and bodies in the United Nations systems;

Recommends the Director-General of UNESCO to examine the

possibility of preparing as a matter of urgency and in co-ordination with other competent bodies in the United Nations system, a draft emergency programme of education and information in schools for AIDS prevention, and to submit such proposals as he deems appropriate to the next session of the General Conference of UNESCO;

Expresses the wish that this programme may become operational in all Member-States as soon as possible and that it may make possible the rapid establishment of co-operation among Member-States that already have experience in this matter;

Appeals urgently to financing agencies and bodies and to foundations to make available to UNESCO the resources needed to important educational aspect of the fight against AIDS.

BIBLIOGRAPHY

UNESCO DOCUMENTS AND PUBLICATIONS*

1. *Comparative study of secondary school building costs* by Hutton and Rostron. Paris, UNESCO, 1971, 77 p. (Educational studies and documents No. 4).
2. *Distance learning for technical and vocational education at pre-university level establishment of open tech type* by D.A. Blackburn and R.C. Smith. Paris, UNESCO, 1987, 47 p. (Studies in technical and vocational education No. 27) ED-87/WS/37.
3. *Measures to provide the access of girls and women to secondary technical and vocational education in New Zealand.* A report on policies and selected activities by Doris MacDonald. Paris, UNESCO, 1987, 47 p. + annexes. ED-87/WS/40.
4. *The Organisation of productive work in secondary, technical and vocational education in the People's Republic of Bulgaria.* Paris, UNESCO, 1984, 17p. (Studies in technical and vocational education No. 3) ED-87/WS/43.
5. *The Organisation of productive work in secondary technical and vocational education in the United Kingdom.* Paris, UNESCO, 1983, 78 p. (Studies in technical and vocational education No. 2) ED-84/WS/49.

* Listing to illustrate the range of UNESCO documents and publications.

18

ADULT EDUCATION AND LITERACY

OVERVIEW/HIGHLIGHTS

Illiteracy: Trends and Prospects

UNESCO's estimates and projections as assessed in 1989 at the world level lead to the following conclusions:

- There were just under 1,000 million adults who could not read nor write in 1985. This number is only marginally projected to decline in 1990 and in the year 2000.
- In 1985, 30 out of 100 adults in the world were illiterate and this proportion should decline to 27 out of 100 in 1990 with a further reduction to 22 out of 100 at the end of this century.
- The overwhelming majority of the illiterate population (921 million in 1990) are and will continue to be found in the developing countries.
- Invariably females constitute the majority of the illiterate population and will continue to do so.
- Worldwide averages disguise important regional disparities.
- Both in absolute and relative terms. Latin America and the Caribbean will have the best literacy situation – a decline from 18 per cent of its adult population illiterate in 1985 to 15 per cent in 1990 and 11 per cent in 2000. Nevertheless, 41 million adults are projected to be illiterate in this region at the end of the century.
- Eastern Asia should reduce the number of illiterates by about 64 million between 1985 and 2000 leading to reduction in the illiteracy rate – from 29 per cent in 1985 to 24 per cent in 1990 and 17 per cent in 2000. Despite this improvement, more than 230

million adults of the region will still be illiterate.

For Sub-Saharan Africa, Arab States and Southern Asia, although the number of illiterates is projected to increase between 1985 and the end of this century, in relative terms the proportion of adult illiterates should decrease. At the end of this century almost 440 million adults will be illiterate in Southern Asia. 147 million in Sub-Saharan Africa and 66 million in the Arab States.

Adult illiterates (age 15 and over) and illiteracy rates

	Adult illiterates (in millions)			Illiteracy rates (%)			Decrease 1985-2000
	1985	1990	2000	1985	1990	2000	% points
World Total	965.1	962.6	942.0	29.9	26.9	22.0	–7.9
Developing countries of which:							
Sub-Saharan Africa	133.6	138.8	146.8	59.1	52.7	40.3	–18.8
Arab States	58.6	61.1	65.8	54.5	48.7	38.1	–16.4
Latin America/ Caribbean	44.2	43.5	40.9	17.6	15.2	11.3	–6.3
Eastern Asia	297.3	281.0	233.7	28.7	24.0	17.0	–11.7
Southern Asia	374.1	397.3	437.0	57.7	53.8	45.9	–11.8
Developed countries	57.0	42.0	23.5	6.2	4.4	2.3	–3.9

THE WORLD CONFERENCE OF MINISTERS OF EDUCATION ON THE ERADICATION OF ILLITERACY, 1965

The World Conference of Ministers of Education on the eradication of illiteracy, convened by the United Nations Educational Scientific and Cultural Organization in Teheran from 8 to 19 September, 1965.

Considering that the Universal Declaration of Human Rights proclaims that everyone has the right to education. Considering that the Constitution of the United Nations Educational Scientific and Cultural Organization proclaims that the whole diffusion of culture and the education of humanity for justice and liberty and peace are indispensable to the dignity of man and constitute a sacred duty which all the nations must fulfil in a spirit of mutual assistance and concern.

Noting that the attainment of literacy by the hundreds of millions of adults who are still illiterate is of fundamental importance for full economic and social development and that without it there can be no complete and active participation of the peoples in national or international civic life.

Noting that illiteracy, which more particularly affects the populations of developing countries and the women of many countries, accentuates the unfavourable position of these people who thus suffer from a form of *de facto* discrimination which must be eliminated.

Convinced, further, that illiteracy affects not only the people directly involved but the whole of mankind, whose progress it impedes, and that all nations must co-operate in the fight against this evil.

Desirous of asserting the principles that should govern the struggle to eradicate illiteracy and of definiting the measures, national and international, that should be taken in this regard.

Adopts the following general conclusions and recommendations.

I. The Place of Literacy Work in National Efforts

The development of the modern world, the accession to independent of a large number of the countries, the emancipation of peoples and for the increasingly active and productive participation, in the economic, social and political life of human society, of the hundreds of millions of illiterate adults still existing in the world, make it essential to change national education policies. Education systems must provide for the educational training needs of both the young generations who have not yet begun working life, and the generation that have already become adult without having had the benefit of the essential minimum of elementary education.

There is no contradiction between the development of the school system, on the one hand, and of literacy work, on the other. Schooling and literacy work, supplement and support each other. National educational plans should include schooling for children and literacy training for adults as parallel elements.

Adult Literacy and Economic Growth

Adult literacy, an essential element in overall development, must be closely linked to economic and social priorities and to present and future manpower needs. All efforts should, therefore, tend towards functional literacy. Rather than an end in itself, literacy should be regarded as a way of preparing man for a social, civic and economic role that goes far beyond the limits of rudimentary literacy training consisting merely in the teaching of reading and writing. The very process of learning to read and write should be made an opportunity for acquiring information that can immediately be used to improve living standards; reading and writing should lead not only to elementary general knowledge but to training for work, increased productivity, a greater participation in civil life and a better understanding of the surrounding world, and should ultimately open the way to basic human culture.

Integration of Literacy Programmes

Literacy teaching should be resolutely oriented towards development, and should be an integral part not only of any national education plans but also of plans and projects for development in all sectors of the national life. In view of mankind's needs today, education can no longer be confined to the school; the necessary promotion of adult literacy makes it essential to integrate all the school and out-of-school resources of each country.

Functional literacy for adults must, moreover, involve the whole of society and not governments only. It demands the co-operation of all the forces in the nation and, in particular, local authorities and communities, educational, scientific and cultural bodies, public and private enterprises, non-governmental organisations, political groups, religious movements, women's organisations, and so on.

Mobilisation of Human and Material Resources. The main responsibility for the struggle against illiteracy rests with the countries which still have illiteracy among their populations. The mobilisation of the human and material resources of these countries is fundamental to the success of the efforts that should be undertaken by all mankind with a view to eradicating this evil.

II. Utilisation of Different Means, Methods, Structures and Techniques

New Techniques

The disproportion between the immensity of the task to be accomplished and the limited material and human resources of the developing countries, and the introduction of new elements in literacy policy, including the transition from rudimentary to functional literacy and the diversification of literacy programmes, call for new solutions to the problems involved in the training of instructors and the selection of techniques and in the educational infrastructure needed to overcome illiteracy.

Personnel Needed

The new concept of functional literacy makes it necessary to reconsider the question of the personnel needed to carry out programmes. To ensure the full mobilisation of resources, the teachers must be supplemented not only by specialised instructors or, if they are not available, by specially trained voluntary workers, but also by the members of all the groups that make up the educated sector of the national community.

Forms of Literacy Programmes

Functional literacy depends for its success upon an appropriate infrastructure, on-the-job educational facilities, out-of-school facilities in the villages and towns, and so on. It also presupposes the use of schools as literacy centres and the creation of a number of services specialised in research and in the preparation of teaching and reading material and publications. The literacy programmes should be considerably enlarged and the duration of teaching extended accordingly.

Programmes Suited to Adult Psychology

To be effective, literacy work demands programmes sufficiently diverse in form and content to take account of differences in age, sex, condition, environment, the field of interest of the adults concerned, their motives and immediate employment openings. This diversity presupposes research into the psychological and social characteristics of the different categories. In addition, the existence of many linguistic groups and the determination of many governments to provide literacy training (and adult education) in the mother tongue of the people concerned will probably involve special linguistic studies and the transcription of non-written languages.

The elaboration of teaching methods adapted to the mental habits of adults, to the psychology and way of life of the different social and occupational groups and to the actual content of this new teaching constitutes one of the major tasks of modern pedagogican science. Literacy and adult education techniques, reading materials and the texts used need greater diversification so that they can be adapted to the differing needs of each society.

Judicious Combination of Traditional and Modern Techniques

The need to carry out an immense task within a short period demands that traditional techniques be judiciously combined with the most modern ones. The lack of qualified teachers, the need to reach millions of illiterates scattered over vast territories, and the power and attraction of sound and image speak in favour of using non-conventional means of communication and modern techniques, e.g., radio, television, films, the press, including pictorial newspapers and certain forms of programmed instruction. Indeed, their utilisation will add a new dimension to adult education. But the massive use of such media to create suitable motivations for learning and provide education, in areas having a high proportion of illiterates, will require experiment and a very careful evaluation of its results.

Systematic Evaluation

The immensity of the task and the degree of social involvement required for its accomplishment make very necessary the judicious use of acquired experience. A series of thorough investigations and a scientific evaluation of programmes and their economic, social and educational aspect should therefore be carried out.

The evaluation should make it possible to compare the results of programmes carried out in different countries, and to estimate the return on investment and the effectiveness of the means used, direct and indirect, long term and short term.

The results of these studies and evaluations should be made available to those who, throughout the world, have a direct or indirect interest in the problem of illiteracy.

III. Role of International Co-operation, Bilateral and Multilateral

(a) Although the chief responsibility for the struggle against illiteracy lies with the countries which still suffer from it, the assistance of the international community as a whole is essential to the success of this great undertaking.

(b) Obviously, every country that is fighting against illiteracy among its people must define its needs and priorities and draw up its plans, and so determine the direction of bilateral and multilateral aid.

(c) An important and early feature of international co-operation should be the exchange of experiences and closer contacts between the countries concerned. The similarity of aims and the variety of solutions chosen make it desirable to strengthen this co-operation between the developing countries.

(d) In determining the priority to be given to literacy work in their bilateral aid programmes, developed countries should take account of the priority fixed by the developing countries which are to receive that aid.

(e) The contribution that literacy can make to the modernisation of agriculture, industrialization, the increased mobility of labour and the strengthening of international trade justifies an increase in international assistance at the preinvestment level. It would be desirable for the United Nations Special Fund to extend its assistance by providing aid for an increasing number of experimental literacy projects carried out in accordance with UNESCO's programme and by including literacy work in various preinvestment projects.

It is highly desirable that UNESCO should be enabled to expand and to extend to a greater number of countries the excellent experimental world literacy programme adopted by the General Conference at its thirteenth session.

(f) To the extent that literacy is essential to the implementation of economic development projects, particularly agricultural and industrial projects, international and regional authorities which have investment funds at their disposal should devote a part of them to literacy work.

(g) The complex nature of literacy work and the many different responsibilities involved in carrying it out call for close co-operation under the aegis of UNESCO, between all the competent international organisations and agencies and in particular the various Specialised Agencies of the United Nations.

(h) It is adjudged desirable that bilateral co-operation programmes and international assistance programmes should be properly fitted into national programmes; here again, UNESCO can play an important part as a catalyst.

(i) In accordance with its mandate and in view of its past and present activities, UNESCO is called upon to play a vital role in the world struggle against illiteracy and in the concerted action which this implies. UNESCO should take action: (1) to promote exchanges of information and a knowledge of the most fruitful experiences; (2) to encourage and organise study of the different aspects of literacy work throughout the world; (3) to carry out a comparative evaluation of the different structures, means, and methods of functional literacy work; (4) to further the training of the personnel required for the implementation of functional literacy programmes; (5) to advise Member-States in the preparation and implementation of literacy programmes; and (6) to encourage and sustain public determination to continue and intensify national efforts and international co-operation until illiteracy is eradicated. For this, UNESCO must be able to devote more substantial means to the struggle against illiteracy, both through the commitment of more of its own resources for the purpose and through the receipt of additional external resources.

The Teheran Conference of 1965, "convinced that the struggle against illiteracy, aimed at the total eradication from our planet of the scourge of ignorance, is a moral imperative for our generation," concluded its recommendations with:

A Solemn and Urgent Appeal

- To the United Nations, its Specialized Agencies and, in the first place to UNESCO;
- To regional bodies concerned with development in general and education in particular;
- To non-governmental organizations which include assistance, direct or indirect, to education in their operational programmes;
- To religious, social and cultural institutions;
- To national and international foundations, both public and private;

To educators, scientists and scholars, to economic and trade union leaders, and to all men of goodwill;

To do everything in their power to arouse public opinion with a view to intensifying and accelerating the world-wide attack on illiteracy; and in particular to exert their influence on all responsible leaders;

- To ensure that literacy work is an integral and essential part of every development plan in countries where illiteracy is rife;
- To increase, so far as may be practicable and appropriate, the national and international resources set aside for the fight against illiteracy;
- To make possible the provision of additional resources for development in general and for literacy work in particular as and when further funds become available through a reduction of military expenditure or for other reasons;
- To harness to the full all available information media for propagating the new concept of adult literacy;
- To ensure that priority in the allocation of available resources is accorded to the fight against the great human afflictions that constitute a major threat to peace, namely, hunger, disease and ignorance, among which illiteracy occupies a place of key importance.

UNESCO GENERAL CONFERENCE RECOMMENDATION, 1976

The General Conference of the United Nationals Educational, Scientific and Cultural Organization, meeting in Nairobi from 26 October to 30 November, 1976, at its nineteenth session,

Recalling the principles set forth in Articles 26 and 27 of the Universal Declaration of Human Rights, guaranteeing and specifying the right of everyone to education and to participate freely in cultural, artistic and scientific life and the principles set forth in Articles 13 and 15 of the International Convenant on Economic, Social and Cultural Rights,

Considering that the education is inseparable from democracy, the abolition of privilege and the promotion within society as a whole of the ideas of autonomy, responsibility and dialogue,

Considering that the access of adults to education, in the context of life-long education, is a fundamental aspect of the right to education and facilitates the exercise of the right to participate in political, cultural, artistic and scientific life,

Considering that for the full development of the human personality, particularly in view of the rapid pace of scientific, technical, economic and social change, education must be considered on a global basis and as a life-long process,

Considering that the development of adult education, in the context of life-long education, is necessary as a means of achieving a more rational and more equitable distribution of educational resources between young people and adults, and between different social groups, and of ensuring better understanding and more effective collaboration between the generations and greater political, social and economic equality between social groups and between the sexes,

Convinced that adult education as an integral part of life-long education can contribute decisively to economic and cultural development, social progress and world peace as well as to the development of educational systems,

Considering that the experience acquired in adult education must constantly contribute to the renewal of educational methods, as well as to the reform of educational systems as a whole,

Considering the universal concern for literacy as being a crucial factor in political and economic development, in technological progress and in social and cultural change, so that its promotion should therefore form an integral part of any plan for adult education,

Reaffirming that the attainment of this objective entails creating situations in which the adults are able to choose, from among a variety of forms of educational activity the objectives and content of which have been defined with their collaboration, those forms which meet their needs most closely and are most directly related to their interests,

Bearing in mind the diversity of modes of training and education throughout the world and the special problems peculiar to the countries whose education systems are as yet underdeveloped or insufficiently adapted to national needs,

In order to give effect to the conclusions, declarations and recommendations formulated by the second and third international conferences on adult education (Montreal, 1960; Tokyo, 1972 and, as far as the relevant paragraphs are concerned, by the World Conference of the International Women's Year (Mexico, 1975),

Desirous of making a further contribution to putting into effect the principles set forth in the recommendations addressed by the International Conference on Public Education to the Ministries of Education concerning the access of women to education (Recommendation No.

34, 1952), facilities for education in rural areas (Recommendation No. 47, 1958), and literacy and adult education (Recommendation No. 58, 1965), in the Declaration adopted at the International Symposium for Literacy in Perspepolis (1975) and in the Recommendation concerning Education for International Understanding, Co-operation and Peace, and Education relating to Human Rights and Fundamental Freedoms adopted by the General Conference at its eighteenth session (1974);

Taking note of the provisions of the Revised Recommendation concerning Technical and Vocational Education adopted by the General Conference at its eighteenth session (1974) and of resolution 3.426 adopted at the same session with a view to the adoption of an international instrument concerning action designed to ensure that the people at large have free democratic access to culture and an opportunity to take an active part in the cultural life of society.

Noting further that the International Labour Conference has adopted a number of instruments concerned with various aspects of adult education, and in particular the recommendation on vocational guidance (1949), the recommendation on vocational training in agriculture (1956), as well as the convention and recommendation concerning paid educational leave (1974), and of human resources development (1975),

Having decided, at its eighteenth session, that adult education would be the subject of a recommendation to Member-States,

Adopts this twenty-sixth day of November 1976, the present Recommendation.

The General Conference recommends that Member-States apply the following provisions by taking whatever legislative or other steps may be required, and in conformity with the constitutional practice of each State, to give effect to the principles set forth in this Recommendation.

The General Conference recommends that Member-States bring this Recommendation to the attention of the authorities, departments or bodies responsible for adult education and also of the various organizations carrying out educational work for the benefit of adults, and of trade union organizations, associations, enterprises, and other interested parties.

The General Conference recommends that Member-States report to it, at such dates and in such form as shall be determined by it, on the action taken by them in pursuance of this Recommendation.

Definition

1. In this Recommendation the term "adult education" denotes the entire body of organized educational processes, whatever the content, level and method, whether formal or otherwise, whether they prolong or replace initial education in schools, colleges and universities as well as in apprenticeship, whereby persons regarded as adult by the society to which they belong develop their abilities, enrich their knowledge, improve their technical or professional qualifications or turn them in a new direction and bring about changes in their attitudes or behaviour in the twofold perspective of full personal development and participation in balanced and independent social, economic and cultural development:

- adult education, however, must not be considered as an entity in itself, it is a sub-division, and an integral part of a global scheme for life-long education and learning;
- the term "life-long education and learning", for its part, denotes an overall scheme aimed both at restructuring the existing education system and at developing the entire educational potential outside the education system;
- education and learning, far from being limited to the period of attendance at school, should extend throughout life, include all skills and branches of knowledge, use all possible means, and give the opportunity to all people for full development of the personality;
- the educational and learning processes in which children, young people and adults of all ages are involved in the course of their lives, in whatever form, should be considered as a whole.

Objectives and Strategy

2. Generally speaking, the aims of adult education should be to contribute to:

(a) promoting work for peace, international understanding and co-operation;
(b) developing a critical understanding of major contemporary

problems and social changes and the ability to play an active part in the progress of society with a view to achieving social justice;

(c) promoting increased awareness of the relationship between people and their physical and cultural environment, and fostering the desire to improve the environment and to respect and protect nature, the common heritage and public property;

(d) creating an understanding of and respect for the diversity of customs and cultures, on both the national and the international planes;

(e) promoting increased awareness of, and giving effect to various forms of communication and solidarity at the family, local, national, regional and international levels;

(f) developing the aptitude for acquiring, either individually, in groups or in the context of organized study in educational establishments specially set up for this purpose, new knowledge, qualifications, attitudes or forms of behaviour conducive to the full maturity of the personality;

(g) ensuring the individuals' conscious and effective incorporation into working life by providing men and women with an advanced technical and vocational education and developing the ability to create, either individually or in groups, new material goods and new spiritual or aesthetic values;

(h) developing the ability to grasp adequately the problems involved in the upbringing of children;

(i) developing the aptitude for making creative use of leisure and for acquiring any necessary or desired knowledge;

(j) developing the necessary discernment in using mass communication media, in particular radio, television, cinema and the press, and interpreting the various messages addressed to modern men and women by society;

(k) developing the aptitude for learning to learn.

3. Adult education should be based on the following principles:

(a) it should be based on the needs of the participants and make use of their different experiences in the development of adult education; the most educationally underprivileged groups should be given the highest priority within a perspective of collective advancement;

(b) it should rely on the ability and determination of all human beings to make progress throughout their lives both at the level of their personal development and in relation to their social activity;
(c) it should awaken an interest in reading and develop cultural aspirations;
(d) it should stimulate and sustain the interest of adult learners, appeal to their experience, strengthen their self-reliance, and enlist their active participation at all stages of the educational process in which they are involved;
(e) it should be adapted to the actual conditions of everyday life and work and take into account the personal characteristics of adult learners, their age, family, social, occupational or residential background and the way in which these interrelate;
(f) it should seek the participation of individual adults, groups and communities in decision-making at all levels of the learning process; including determination of needs, curriculum development programme implementation and evaluation and should plan educational activities with a view to the transformation of the working environment and of the life of adults;
(g) it should be organized and operated flexibly by taking into account social, cultural, economic and institutional factors of each country and society to which adult learners belong;
(h) it should contribute to the economic and social development of the entire community;
(i) it should recognize as an integral part of the educational process the forms of collective organization established by adults with a view to solving their day-to-day problems;
(j) it should recognize that every adult, by virtue of his or her experience of life, is the vehicle of a culture which enables him or her to play the role of both learner and teacher in the educational process which he or she participates.

4. Each Member-State should:

(a) recognize adult education as a necessary and specific component of its education system and as a permanent element in its social, cultural and economic development policy; it should, consequently, promote the creation of structures, the preparation and implementation of programmes and the application of educational methods which meet the needs and aspirations of all categories of adults, without restriction on grounds of sex, race, geographical origin, age, social status, opinion, belief or prior educational standard;

(b) recognize that although, in a given situation or for a specific period, adult education may play a compensatory role, it is not intended as a substitute for adequate youth education which is a prerequisite for the full success of adult education;

(c) in eliminating the isolation of women from adult education work towards ensuring equality of access and full participation in the entire range of adult education activities including those which provide training for qualifications leading to activities or responsibilities which have hitherto been reserved for men;

(d) take measures with a view to promoting participation in adult education and community development programmes by members of the most underprivileged groups, whether rural or urban, settled or nomadic, and in particular illiterates, young people who have been unable to acquire an adequate standard of general education or a qualification, migrant workers and refugees, unemployed workers, members of ethnic minorities, persons suffering from a physical or mental handicap, persons experiencing difficulties of social adjustment and those serving prison sentences. In this context, Member-States should associate themselves in the search for educational strategies designed to foster more equitable relations among social groups.

5. The place of adult education in each education system should be defined with a view to achieving:

(a) a rectification of the main inequalities in access to initial education and training, in particular inequalities based on age, sex, social position or social or geographical origin;

(b) the assurance of a scientific basis for life-long education and learning as well as greater flexibility in the way in which people divide their lives between education and work, and, in particular, providing for the alternation of periods of education and work throughout the life span, and facilitating the integration of continuing education into the activity of work itself;

(c) recognition, and increased exploitation, of the actual or potential educational value of the adult's various experiences;

(d) easy transfer from one type or level of education to another;

(e) greater interaction between the education system and its social, cultural and economic setting;

(f) greater efficiency from the point of view of the contribution of educational expenditure to social, cultural and economic development.

6. Consideration should be given to the need for an adult education component, including literacy, in the framing and execution of any development programme.
7. The objectives and goals of adult education policy should be incorporated in national development plans; they should be defined in relation to the overall objectives of education policy and of social, cultural and economic development policies.

Adult education and other forms of education, particularly school and higher education and initial vocational training, should be conceived and organized as equally essential components in a co-ordinated but differentiated education system according to the tenets of life-long education and learning.

8. Measures should be taken to encourage the public authorities, institutions or bodies engaged in education, voluntary associations, workers' and employers' organizations, and those directly participating in adult education, to collaborate in the task of defining further and giving effect to these objectives.

Content of Adult Education

9. Adult education activities, viewed as forming part of life-long education and learning, have no theoretical boundaries and should meet the particular situations created by the specific needs of development, of participation in community life and of individual self-fulfilment; they cover all aspects of life and all fields of knowledge and are addressed to all people whatever their level of achievement. In defining the content of adult education activities priority should be given to the specific needs of the educationally

most under-privileged groups.

10. Civic, political, trade union and co-operative education activities should be aimed particularly towards developing independent and critical judgment and implanting or enhancing the abilities required by each individual in order to cope with changes affecting living and working conditions, by effective participation in the management of social affairs at every level of the decision-making process.
11. While not excluding approaches intended to achieve a short-term solution in a particular situation, technical and vocational education activities should as a general rule emphasize the acquisition of qualifications which are sufficiently broad to allow of subsequent changes of occupation and a critical understanding of the problems of working life. It is necessary to integrate general and civic education with technical and vocational education.
12. Activities designed to promote cultural development and artistic creation should encourage appreciation of existing cultural and artistic values and works and, at the same time, should aim to promote the creation of new values and new works, by releasing the expressive capabilities inherent in each individual or group.
13. Participation in adult education should not be restricted on grounds of sex, race, geographical origin, culture, age, social status, experience, belief and prior educational standard.
14. With regard to women, adult education activities should be integrated as far as possible with the whole contemporary social movement directed towards achieving self-determination for women and enabling them to contribute to the life of society as a collective force, and should thus focus specifically on certain aspects, in particular:

    (a) the establishment in each society of conditions of equality between men and women;
    (b) the emancipation of men and women from the preconceived models imposed on them by society in every field in which they carry responsibility;
    (c) civic, occupational, psychological, cultural and economic autonomy for women as a necessary condition for their existence as complete individuals;
    (d) knowledge about the status of women, and about women's movements, in various societies, with a view to increased

solidarity across frontiers.

15. With regard to settled or nomadic rural populations, adult education activities should be designed in particular to:

    (a) enable them to use technical procedures and methods of individual or joint organization likely to improve their standard of living without obliging them to forego their own values;
    (b) put an end to the isolation of individuals or groups;
    (c) prepare individuals or groups of individuals who are obliged, despite the efforts made to prevent excessive depopulation of rural areas, to leave agriculture, either to engage in a new occupational activity while remaining in a rural environment, or to leave this environment for a new way of life.

16. With regard to such persons or groups as have remained illiterate or are experiencing difficulty in adjusting to society because of the slenderness of their resources, their limited education or their restricted participation in community life, adult education activities should be designed not only to enable them to acquire basic knowledge (reading, writing, arithmetic, basic understanding of natural and social phenomena), but also to make it easier for them to engage in productive work, to promote their self-awareness and their grasp of the problems of hygiene, health, household management and the upbringing of children, and to enhance their autonomy and increase their participation in community life.
17. With regard to young people who have been unable to acquire an adequate standard of general education or a qualification, adult education activities should, in particular, enable them to acquire additional general education with a view to developing their ability to understand the problems of society and shoulder social responsibilities, and to gaining access to the vocational training and general education which are necessary for the exercise of an occupational activity.
18. If people wish to acquire educational or vocational qualifications which are formally attested by certificates of education or of vocational aptitude and which, for social or economic reasons, they have not been able to obtain earlier, adult education should enable them to obtain the training required for the award of such

certificates.

19. With regard to the physically or mentally handicapped, adult education activities should be designed, in particular, to restore or offset the physical or mental capacities which have been impaired or lost as a result of their handicap, and to enable them to acquire the knowledge and skills and, where necessary, the professional qualifications required for their social life and for the exercise of an occupational activity compatible with their handicap.
20. With regard to migrant workers, refugees, and ethnic minorities, adult education activities should in particular:

    (a) enable them to acquire the linguistic and general knowledge as well as the technical or professional qualifications necessary for their temporary or permanent assimilation in the society of the host country and, where appropriate, their reassimilation in the society of their country of origin;
    (b) keep them in touch with culture, current developments and social changes in their country of origin.

21. With regard to unemployed persons, including the educated unemployed, adult education activities should be designed, in particular, to adapt or modify their technical or professional qualification with a view to enabling them to find or return to employment and to promote a critical understanding of their socio-economic situation.
22. With regard to ethnic minorities, adult education activities should be designed in particular:

    (a) to give all a better understanding of contemporary problems and of the younger generation;
    (b) to help acquire leisure skills, promote health and find increased meaning in life;
    (c) to provide a grounding in the problems facing retired people and in ways of dealing with such problems, for the benefit of those who are on the point of leaving working life;
    (d) to enable those who have left working life to retain their physical and intellectual faculties and to continue to participate in community life and also to give them access to fields of knowledge or type of activity which have not been opened to them during their working life.

Methods, Means, Research and Evaluation

24. Adult education methods should take account of :

(a) incentives and obstacles to participation and learning specially affecting adults;
(b) the experience gained by adults in the exercise of their family, social and occupational responsibilities;
(c) the family, social or occupational obligations borne by adults and the fatigue and impaired alertness which may result from them;
(d) the ability of adults to assume responsibility for their own learning;
(e) the cultural and pedagogical level of the teaching personnel available;
(f) the psychological characteristics of the learning process;
(g) the existence and characteristics of cognitive interests;
(h) use of leisure time.

25. Adult education activities should normally be planned and executed on the basis of identified needs, problems, wants and resources, as well as defined objectives. Their impact should be evaluated, and reinforced by whatever follow-up activities may be most appropriate to given conditions.
26. Particular emphasis should be placed on adult education activities intended for an entire social or geographical entity, mobilizing all its inherent energies with a view to the advancement of the group and social progress in a community setting.
27. In order to encourage the broadest possible participation, it may be appropriate in some situations to add, to locally based adult education, methods such as:

(a) remote teaching programmes such as correspondence courses and radio or television broadcasts, the intended recipients of such programmes being invited to form groups with a view to listening or working together (such groups should receive appropriate pedagogical support);
(b) programmes launched by mobile units;
(c) self-teaching programmes;
(d) study circles;

(e) use of voluntary work by teachers, students and other community members.

The various services which public cultural institutions (libraries, museums, record libraries, video-cassette libraries) are able to put at the disposal of adult learners should be developed on a systematic basis, together with new types of institutions specialising in adult education.

28. Participation in an adult education programme should be a voluntary matter. The State and other bodies should strive to promote the desire of individuals and groups for education in the spirit of life-long education and learning.
29. Relations between the adult learner and the adult educator should be established on a basis of mutual respect and co-operation.
30. Participation in an adult education programme should be subject only to the ability to follow the course of training provided and not to any (upper) age limit or any condition concerning the possession of a diploma or qualification; any aptitude tests on the basis of which a selection might be made if necessary should be adapted to the various categories of candidates taking such tests.
31. It should be possible to acquire and accumulate learning, experiences and qualifications through intermittent participation. Rights and qualifications obtained in this way should be equivalent to those granted by the systems of formalized education or of such character as to allow for continued education within this.
32. The methods used in adult education should not appeal to a competitive spirit but should develop in the adult learners a shared sense of purpose and habits of participation, mutual help, collaboration and team work.
33. Adult education programmes for the improvement of technical or professional qualifications should, as far as possible, be organized during working time and, in the case of seasonal work, during the slack season. This should, as a general rule, be applied also to other forms of education, in particular literacy programmes and trade union education.
34. The premises necessary for the development of adult education activities should be provided, depending on the case, these may be premises used exclusively for adult education, with or without residential accommodation, or multi-purpose or integrated

facilities or premises generally used or capable of being used for other purposes in particular, clubs, workshops, school, university and scientific establishments, social, cultural or socio-cultural centres or open air sites.

35. Member-States should actively encourage co-operative research in all aspects of adult education and its objectives. Research programmes should have a practical basis. They should be carried out by universities, adult education bodies and research bodies, adopting an interdisciplinary approach. Measures should be taken with a view to disseminating the experience and the results of the research programmes to those concerned at the national and international levels.
36. Systematic evaluation of adult activities is necessary to secure optimum results from the resources put into them. For evaluation to be effective it should be built into the programmes of adult education at all levels and stages.

The Structures of Adult Education

37. Member-States should endeavour to ensure the establishment and development of a network of bodies meeting the needs of adult education; this network should be sufficiently flexible to meet the various personal and social situations and their evolution.
38. Measures should be taken in order to:

(a) identify and anticipate educational needs capable of being satisfied through adult education programmes;

(b) make full use of existing educational facilities and create such facilities as may be lacking to meet all defined objectives;

(c) make the necessary long-term investments for the development of adult education in particular for the professional education of planners, administrators, those who train educators, organizational and training personnel, the preparation of educational strategies and methods suitable for adults, the provision of capital facilities, the production and provision of the necessary basic equipment such as visual aids, apparatus and technical media;

(d) encourage exchanges of experience and compile and disseminate statistical and other information on the strategies, structures, content, methods and results, both quantitative and qualitative, of adult education;

(e) abolish economic and social obstacles to participation in education, and to systematically bring the nature and form of adult education programmes to the attention of all potential beneficiaries, but especially to the most disadvantaged, by using such means as active canvassing by adult education institutions and voluntary organizations, to inform counsel and encourage possible and often hesitant participants in adult education.

39. In order to achieve these objectives it will be necessary to mobilize organizations and institutions specifically concerned with adult education, and the full range, both public and private of schools, universities, cultural and scientific establishments, libraries and museums, and, in addition, other institutions not primarily concerned with adult education, such as:

(a) mass information bodies: the press, radio and television;
(b) voluntary associations and consortia;
(c) professional, trade union, family and co-operate organisations;
(d) families;
(e) industrial and commercial firms which may contribute to the training of their employees;
(f) educators, technicians or qualified experts working on an individual basis;
(g) any persons or groups who are in a position to make a contribution by virtue of their education, training, experience of professional or social activities and are both willing and able to apply the principles set forth in the preamble and the objectives and strategy outlined in the Recommendation;
(h) the adult learners themselves.

40. Member-States should encourage schools, vocational education establishments, colleges and institutions of higher education to regard adult education programmes as an integral part of their own activities and to participate in action designed to promote the development of such programmes provided by other institutions, in particular by making available their own teaching staff, conducting research and training the necessary personnel.

Training and Status of Persons engaged in Adult Education Work

41. It should be recognized that adult education calls for special skills, knowledge, understanding and attitudes on the part of those who are involved in providing it, in whatever capacity and for any purpose. It is desirable therefore that they should be recruited with care according to their particular functions and receive initial and in-service training for them according to their needs and those of the work in which they are engaged.
42. Measures should be taken to ensure that the various specialists who have a useful contribution to make to the work of adult education take part in those activities, whatever their nature or purpose.
43. In addition to the employment of full time professional workers, measures should be taken to enlist the support of anyone capable of making a contribution, regular or occasional, paid or voluntary, to adult education activities, of any kind. Voluntary involvement and participation in all aspects of organizing and teaching are of crucial importance, and people with all kinds of skills are able to contribute to them.
44. Training for adult education should, as far as practicable, include all those aspects of skill, knowledge, understanding and personal attitude which are relevant to the various functions undertaken, taking into account the general background against which adult education takes place. By integrating these aspects with each other, training should itself be a demonstration of sound adult education practice.
45. Conditions of work and remuneration for full-time staff in adult education should be comparable to those of workers in similar posts elsewhere, and those for paid part-time staff should be appropriately regulated, without detriment to their main occupation.

Relations between Adult Education and Youth Education

46. The education of young people should progressively be oriented towards life-long education and learning, taking into account the experience gained in regard to adult education, with a view to preparing young people, whatever their social origins, to take part in adult education or to contribute to providing it.

To this end, measures should be taken with a view to:

(a) making access to all levels of education and training more widely available;
(b) removing the barriers between disciplines and also between types and levels of education;
(c) modifying school and training syllabuses with the aim of maintaining and stimulating intellectual curiosity, and also placing greater emphasis, alongside the acquisition of knowledge, on the development of self-teaching patterns of behaviour, a critical outlook, a reflective attitude and creative abilities;
(d) rendering school institutions of higher education and training establishments increasingly open to their economic and social environment and linking education and work more firmly together;
(e) informing young people at school and young people leaving full-time education or initial training of the opportunities offered by adult education;
(f) bringing together, where desirable, adults and adolescents in the same training programme;
(g) associating youth movements with adult education ventures.

47. In cases where a training course organized as part of adult education leads to the acquisition of a qualification in respect of which a diploma or certificate is awarded when the qualification is acquired through study in school or university, such training should be recognized by the award of a diploma or certificate having equal status. Adult education programmes which do not lead to the acquisition of a qualification similar to those is respect of which a diploma or certificate is awarded should, in appropriate cases, be recognized by an award.

48. Adult education programmes for youth need to be given the highest priority because in most parts of the world the youth form an extremely large segment of society and their education is of the greatest importance for political, economic, social and cultural development of the society in which they live. The programmes of adult education for youth should take account not only of their learning needs, but should enable them to orient themselves for the society of the future.

The Relations between Adult Education and Work

49. Having regard to the close connecion between guaranteeing the right to education and the right to work and to the need to promote the participation of all, whether wage-earners or not, in adult education programmes, not only by reducing the constraint to which they are subject but also by providing them with the opportunity of using in their work the knowledge, qualifications or aptitudes which adult education programmes are designed to make available to them, and of finding in work a source of personal fulfilment and advancement, and a stimulus to creative activity in both work and social life, measures should be taken:

(a) to ensure that, in the formulation of the curriculum of adult education programmes and activities, the working experience of adults should be taken into account;
(b) to improve the organization and conditions of work and, in particular, to alleviate the arduous character of work and reduce and adjust working hours;
(c) to promote the granting of educational leave during time, without loss of remuneration or subject to the payment of compensatory remuneration and payments for the purpose of offsetting the cost of the education received and to use any other appropriate aid to facilitate education or updating during working life;
(d) to protect the employment of persons thus assisted;
(e) to offer comparable facilities to housewives and other home-makers and to non-wage-earners, particularly those of limited means.

50. Member-States should encourage or facilitate the inclusion in collective labour agreements of clauses bearing on adult education, and in particular clauses stipulating:

(a) the nature of the material possibilities and financial benefits extended to employees, and in particular those employed in sectors where rapid technological change is taking place of those threatened with being laid off, with a view to their participation in adult education programmes;
(b) the manner in which technical or professional qualifications

acquired through adult education are taken into account in determining the employment category and in establishing the level of remuneration.

51. Member-States should also invite employers:

(a) to anticipate and publicize, by level and type of qualification, their skilled manpower requirements and the methods of recruitment which are envisaged to meet such needs;
(b) to organize or develop a recruitment system such as will encourage their employees to seek to improve their occupational qualifications.

52. In connecion with adult training programmes organized by employers for their staff, Member-States should encourage them to ensure that:

(a) employees participate in the preparation of the programmes;
(b) those taking part in such programmes are chosen in consultation with the workers' representative bodies;
(c) participants receive a certificate of training or paper qualification on completion of the programme enabling them to satisfy third parties that they have completed a given course or received a given qualification.

53. Measures should be taken with a view to promoting the participation of adults belonging to labouring, agricultural or craft communities in the implementation of adult education programmes intended for such communities; to this end they should be granted special facilities with the aim of enabling the workers to take those decisions which primarily concern them.

Management, Administration, Co-ordination and Financing of Adult Education

54. There should be set up, at all levels, international, regional, national and local:

(a) structures or procedures for consultation, co-ordination between public authorities which are competent in the field of adult education;

(b) structures or procedures for consultation, co-ordination and harmonization between the said public authorities, the representatives of adult learners and the entire range of bodies carrying out adult education programmes or activities designed to promote the development of such programmes.

It should be among the principal functions of these structures, for which resources should be made available, to identify the objectives, to study the obstacles encountered, to propose and, where appropriate, carry out the measures necessary for implementation of the adult education policy and to evaluate the progress made.

55. There should be set up at national level, and, where appropriate, at sub-national level, structures for joint action and co-operation between the public authorities and bodies responsible for adult education on the one hand and the public or private bodies responsible for radio and television on the other.
It should be among the principal functions of these structures to study, propose and, where appropriate, carry out measures designed to:

(a) ensure that the mass media make a substantial contribution to leisure-time occupations and to the education of the people;
(b) guarantee freedom of expression, through the mass media, for as opinions and trends in the field of adult education;
(c) promote the cultural or scientific value and the educational qualities of programmes as a whole;
(d) establish a two-way flow of exchanges between those responsible for or those professionally engaged in educational programmes broadcast by radio or television and the persons for whom the programmes are intended.

56. Member-States should ensure that the public authorities, while assuming their own specific responsibilities for the development of adult education:

(a) encourage, by laying down an appropriate legal and financial framework, the creation and development of adult education associations and consortia on a voluntary and administratively independent basis;

(b) provide competent non-governmental bodies participating in adult education programmes, or in action designed to promote such programmes, with technical or financial resources enabling them to carry out their task;

(c) see that such non-governmental bodies enjoy the freedom of opinion and the technical and educational autonomy which are necessary in order to give effect to the principles set forth in paragraph 2 above;

(d) take appropriate measures to ensure the educational and technical efficiency and quality of programmes or action conducted by bodies in receipt of contributions from public funds.

57. The proportion of public funds, and particularly of public funds earmarked for education, allocated to adult education, should match the importance of such education for social, cultural and economic development, as recognized by each Member-State within the framework of this Recommendation. The total allocation of funds to adult education should cover at least:

(a) provision of suitable facilities or adaptation of existing facilities;
(b) production of all kinds of learning materials;
(c) remuneration and further training of educators;
(d) research and information expenses;
(e) compensation for loss of earnings;
(f) tuition, and, where necessary and if possible, accommodation and travel costs of trainees.

58. Arrangements should be made to ensure, on a regular basis, the necessary funds for adult education programmes and action designed to promote the development of such programmes; it should be recognized that the public authorities, including local authorities, credit organizations, provident societies and national insurance agencies where they exist, and employers should contribute to these funds to an extent commensurate with their respective responsibilities and resources.

59. The necessary measures should be taken to obtain optimum use of resources made available for adult education. All available resources, both material and human, should be mobilized to this

end.

60. For the individual, lack of funds should not be an obstacle to participation in adult education programmes. Member-States should ensure that financial assistance for study purpose is available for those who need it to undertake adult education. The participation of members of underprivileged social groups should, as a general rule, be free of charge.

International Co-operation

61. Member-States should strengthen their co-operation, whether on a bilateral or multilateral basis, with a view to promoting the development of adult education, the improvement of its content and methods, and efforts to find new educational strategies.
To this end, they should endeavour to incorporate specific clauses bearing on adult education in international agreements concerned with co-operation in the fields of education, science and culture, and to promote the development and strengthening of adult education work in UNESCO.

62. Member-States should put their experience with regard to adult education at the disposal of other Member-States by providing them with technical assistance and, in appropriate cases, with material or financial assistance.
They should systematically support adult education activities conducted in countries so wishing, through UNESCO and through other international organizations, including non-governmental organizations, with a view to social, cultural and economic development in the countries concerned.
Care should be taken to ensure that international co-operation does not take the form of a mere transfer of structures, curricula, methods and techniques which have originated elsewhere, but consist rather in promoting and stimulating development within the countries concerned, through the establishment of appropriate institutions and well co-ordinated structures adapted to the particular circumstances of these countries.

63. Measures should be taken at national, regional and international level:

(a) with a view to making regular exchanges of information and documentation on the strategies, structures, content, methods and results of adult education and on relevant research;

(b) with a view to training educators capable of working away from their home country, particularly under bilateral or multilateral technical assistance programmes.

These exchanges should be made on a systematic basis, particularly between countries facing the same problems and so placed as to be capable of applying the same solutions; to this end, meetings should be organized, more especially on a regional or sub-regional basis, with a view to publicising relevant experiments and studying to what extent they are reproducible; similarly joint machinery should be set up in order to ensure a better return on the research which is undertaken.

Member-States should foster agreements on the preparation and adoption of international standards in important fields, such as the teaching of foreign languages and basic studies, with a view to helping create a universally accepted unit-credit system.

64. Measures should be taken with a view to the optimum dissemination and utilization of audio-visual equipment and materials, as well as educational programmes and the material objects in which they are embodied. In particular, it would be appropriate:

(a) to adapt such dissemination and utilization to the various countries; social needs and conditions, bearing in mind their specific cultural characteristics and level of development;

(b) to remove, as far as possible, the obstacles to such dissemination and utilization resulting from the regulations governing commercial or intellectual property.

65. In order to facilitate international co-operation, Member-States should apply to adult education the standards recommended at international level, in particular with regard to the presentation of statistical data.

66. Member-States should support the action undertaken by UNESCO, as the United Nations Specialized Agency competent in this field, in its efforts to develop adult education, particularly in the fields of training, research and evaluation.

INTERNATIONAL LITERACY YEAR, 1990

Illiteracy Situation and Trends

Awareness of the problem of illiteracy is at present becoming increasingly acute in the international community, and the importance of literacy training is now universally recognized. Many countries have already taken important measures in this area. The organization of mass literacy campaigns, some of which have had remarkable results – sometimes in a relatively short space of time, at the cost of considerable sacrifice – the implementation of selective literacy programmes of varying scope and the efforts made to enrol in schools all children of school age illustrate the determination of Member-States to wipe out the scourge of illiteracy.

If we take stock of what has been achieved over the past two decades, even without wishing to minimize the progress made, it becomes apparent that the record of the struggle against illiteracy is on the whole far from satisfactory given the means at our disposal and all that remains to be done to ensure effective access to education for everyone.

Illiteracy statistics, however, afford no grounds either for pessimism or for discouragement. Enrolment ratios, which had improved considerably in the 1960s, began to climb faster, mainly in the developing countries during the 1970s and early 1980s.

This rapid expansion of primary school enrolments was accompanied by a perceptible increase in the world total of adults (15 years and over) who had received literacy training, which rose from 1,708 million in 1975 to 2,314 million in 1985, an increase of some 35 per cent in ten years.

Despite these efforts illiteracy persists, often going hand in hand with poverty, and there continue to be disturbing trends. In spite of the decrease in the global illiteracy rate the absolute number of adult illiterates is steadily increasing at the same time as the world adult population, which is 1985 had increased by nearly 40 per cent since 1970.

According to estimates and projections made by UNESCO's Office of Statistics, in 1985 there were throughout the world some 889 million illiterates aged 15 and over, or 27.7 per cent of the population in that age-group. The worst affected regions were Asia, with an illiteracy rate (36.3 per cent) higher than the average, but above all with an extremely high absolute number of illiterates (666 million), and Africa, with a lower absolute number (162 million) but a higher illiteracy rate (54 per cent). It is also to be noted that in 1985 three quarters of the world's illiterates, i.e. 669 million, were to be found in nine countries, six of which are in Asia.

While illiteracy affects primarily the developing countries (869 million persons or some 98 per cent of the total number of illiterates in the world) and, furthermore, absolute illiteracy is rather rare in the industrialized countries (20 million persons) it should be mentioned that a new phenomenon is being taken into consideration: in recent years certain industrialized countries which thought they had solved the problem of illiteracy 50 years back, or more, have discovered, and officially, admitted the existence of a non insignificant percentage of '*functional illiterates*' among their nationals. Unlike illiterates, as the term is usually understood, functional illiterates may know the alphabet or figures, but their rudimentary knowledge is too scant to enable them to participate effectively in social life or to find employment in a modern economy. Surveys have shown that in some countries the proportion of the population faced with difficulties of this kind may attain from 5 to 10 per cent, in some cases even more.

Overall, considerably more women than men suffer from illiteracy, 34.9 per cent of women being illiterate at the present time as against 20.5 per cent of men. Illiteracy is also to be found among young people: 84,300,000 illiterates are aged between 15 and 19. Furthermore, in 1985, more than 100 million children aged between 6 and 11 in the developing countries were not attending school.

Background to UN Proclamation

It should be recalled that the proposal concerning an international literacy year was put forward at the 121st session (May-June 1985) of the Executive Board, which recommended to the General Conference that it 'address to the United Nations General Assembly an appeal to proclaim an international Literacy year'.

The General Conference of UNESCO, at its twenty-third session, held in Sofia in 1985, considered that the eradication of illiteracy by the year 2000 was of special urgency and should be a priority objective of the international community as a whole and of UNESCO. It launched an appeal to proclaim an International Year, the observance of which would contribute to greater understanding by world public opinion of the various aspects of the problem of illiteracy and to intensified efforts to spread literacy and education.

In response to this appeal, the United Nations General Assembly, in December 1987, adopted resolution 42/104 proclaiming 1990 as International Literacy Year (ILY) and inviting UNESCO to assume the role of lead organization for its preparation and observance.

Why ILY

Firstly, because illiteracy is one of the major global problems of our era. Secondly, because illiteracy is closely related to underdevelopment and poverty and, moreover, because the elimination of illiteracy represents an essential condition for the development and the well-being of peoples and nations. Thirdly, because illiteracy is not a fatality but a condition – often a deep-rooted and refractory one – which, if combated with commitment, persistence and imagination, can be, and in numerous countries is being, overcome.

Illiteracy is a deep-rooted social phenomenon and many years of dedicated, persevering and imaginative effort in several related fields are normally required to eliminate it. To begin with, the eradication of illiteracy is inseparable from the objective of primary education for all. It is only through the universalization of primary education that illiteracy can be checked at its source. But if the problem of illiteracy is to be solved in a decade, not a generation, large-scale literacy programmes for out-of-school youth and adults will also be required. Indeed, such programmes are necessary, in any case, to create a supportive environment for the promotion of primary education. But it does not suffice to concentrate on literacy instruction, be it for children or adults; literacy skills cannot be maintained in an illiterate environment. Hence, literacy work must be accompanied and supported by post-literacy measures which make reading and writing useful, rewarding and increasingly necessary skills to possess.

It must also be borne in mind that the struggle against illiteracy is bound up with the quest for development. Illiteracy and poverty go not only hand in hand, but shoulder to shoulder, each supporting the other. Those who live in want today, in fear of tomorrow, who have neither a stake in society nor a hope in the future, are unlikely to be strongly motivated to become literate. What would prompt them to allot several hundred hours, needed in a harsh struggle for survival, to the arduous task of mastering in alphabet? To become literate, people must be motivated to learn and this will occur only when they perceive the possibility of improving their living conditions. Thus, the struggle for literacy is also, and at the same time, a struggle for development, justice, greater equality, respect of cultures and recognition of the human dignity of all and the claims of each to an economic, social and political role in society and the fruits which derive therefrom. It is this which makes the struggle against illiteracy difficult; it is also this which makes it essential and worthwhile.

What will ILY Achieve and What Activities should be Carried Out?

This will depend entirely upon what the international community and, more especially, national communities around the world make of this occasion. It could be a unique opportunity to renew commitments and reinvigorate actions to combat illiteracy throughout the Year and all through the ensuing decade. The Year should not be a celebration but a summons to action.

Then again, there is common agreement that the year should be planned as a means, and a step in the process, of launching a global attack on illiteracy with the ambitious goal of eliminating it by the end of the century. Also, 1990 is the first year in which UNESCO's third Medium-Term Plan will be applied, and International Literacy Year will help create a climate favourable to the launching of the plan of action to eradicate illiteracy by the year 2000, which is being prepared and will be submitted to the General Conference for consideration at its forthcoming session (autumn 1989).

In a preliminary document examining the possibilities and the problems involved in carrying out such a plan, UNESCO stressed the fact that the task could not be accomplished unless Member-States evinced a *political will and commitment*, unless a wide movement of *international solidarity* was established and unless the intergovernmental and non-governmental organizations, the community groups working in the field in particular, played an active part.

Consulted in 1987 on the objectives for International Literacy Year and the procedures for its preparation and implementation, some 82 Member-States and 40 international non-governmental organizations put forward pertinent comments and suggestions, which were to serve in the elaboration of *A Practical Guide* for the organization of the activities of the Year, which is in the course of preparation. The themes which emerged from Member-States' replies were:

- need to alert and mobilize world public opinion in favour of action to promote literacy, particularly through the mass media;
- need for international co-operation and solidarity;
- leadership expected of UNESCO in planning and implementing the programme of the Year;
- identification of priority, 'target populations': rural residents, women and girls, as well as such groups as out-of-school youth, migrants and the handicapped;
- need to make literacy instruction functional by relating it to the needs of learners and to ensure follow-up in the form of post-literacy activities;
- importance of NGO participation in the year.

Two conclusions can be drawn regarding the role Member-States expect UNESCO to play: firstly, the Organization is expected to promote public awareness of the problem of illiteracy and support for combating it; secondly, it is desired that UNESCO continue and, to the extent possible, increase its services to Member-States in the formulation and implementation of national and regional strategies for literacy, especially through facilitating regional co-operation and providing training and advisory services. Many Member-States stress the need for UNESCO to concentrate on 'practical' activities in planning the programme for ILY. The view of NGOs do not differ essentially from those expressed by Member-States, the importance of 'concrete' activities being stressed even more strongly. In general, they replied in the manner which would be expected given their objectives and their memberships. Thus, students' organizations propose to direct their activities towards mobilizing students to participate in literacy work; women's organizations have a particular interest in schooling for girls and literacy instruction for women; labour organizations see literacy in its relation to the world of work. Still, certain general tendencies are evident concerning the activities NGOs propose to organize or consider should be organized during ILY:

- incorporation of literacy components into small-scale development projects or activities;

- preparation of projects designed for particular populations; e.g. women, the urban poor or unskilled workers;
- production of teaching and learning materials;
- training of extension workers;
- promotion of participation in literacy campaigns, especially that of students;
- stepping up of exchanges of information and experience in the field of literacy work.

Objectives for ILY

The objectives of International Literacy Year as approved by the UNESCO General Conference at its twenty-fourth session, in the autumn of 1987, are:

(i) increasing action by the governments of Member-States affected by illiteracy or functional illiteracy to eliminate these problems, particularly through education in rural areas and urban slums, in favour of women and girls and among populations and groups having special educational problems and needs;

(ii) increasing public awareness of the scope, nature and implications of illiteracy as well as of the means and conditions of combating it. In particular, an effort should be made to alert public opinion to the rate of illiteracy among women and its implication for the well-being of their children, the lower rate of school attendance among girls than among boys and connection between illiteracy, on the one hand, and poverty, underdevelopment and economic, social and cultural exclusion on the other;

(iii) increasing popular participation, within and among countries, in efforts to combat illiteracy, particularly through activities of governmental and non-governmental organizations, voluntary associations and community groups;

(iv) increasing co-operation and solidarity among Member-States in the struggle against illiteracy;

(v) increasing co-operation within the United Nations system and, more generally, among all intergovernmental and non-governmental organizations in the struggle against illiteracy;

(vi) using International Literacy Year for launching the plan of action for the eradication of illiteracy by the year 2000 and for addressing issues of critical importance for the progress of literacy, such as reducing the number of primary school drop-outs and establishing post-literacy programmes to prevent relapse into illiteracy.

One of the main goals of International Literacy year is therefore to lay the foundations for long-term action, to create conditions favourable to the launching of a plan of action for the decade, from 1990 to the end of the century, by mobilizing international public opinion in support of the literacy teaching efforts of the governments and organizations.

Goals for the Year 2000

As part of ILY, the *42nd Session of the International Conference on Education*, to be held in Geneva on 8th September, 1990, will focus on literacy as its main theme.

The heads of World Bank, UNDP, UNESCO and UNICEF met in Washington D.C. (U.S.A.) to discuss the launching of a worldwide education initiative to be implemented throughout 1990. At the meeting, William H. Draper (Administrator of UNDP), Federico Mayor (Director-General of UNESCO), James P. Grant (Executive Director of UNICEF) and Barber B. Conable laid the groundwork for a conference to forge a global commitment to providing (i) high quality primary schooling for children around the world, and (ii) access to essential knowledge enabling adults to cope with the demands of the modern world.

The heads of the four agencies agreed that the conference should consider fixing the following educational goals for the year 2000:

- a common basic level of primary educational achievement for at least 80 per cent of all 14 year-old boys and girls;
- access to basic knowledge and skills training for all adults so as to allow them to improve their quality of life;
- massive reductions in the rate of illiteracy, each country setting specific targets and priorities in terms of age or sex.

Source: *Adult Education Information notes.*

BIBLIOGRAPHY

UNESCO DOCUMENTS AND PUBLICATIONS*

Adult Education

1. *Adult education information notes* (quarterly). Paris, UNESCO.
2. *Adult education series – co-operative educational abstracting service (CEAS).* UNESCO/IBE.
3. *Adult education since the third international conference on adult education (Tokyo, 1972).* Round-up of replies to the survey carried out by UNESCO among National Commissions with a view to gathering information on the development of adult education. Paris, UNESCO, 1985, 71 p.+annexes ED-85/CONF.210/4.
4. *Co-operation between the media and adult education bodies* by Henry R. Cassirer. Paris, UNESCO, 1985, 77 p. (Surveys & Studies in Adult Education) ED-85/WS/29.
5. *Current status of vocational education and training in the Republic of Korea* by Jeoung-Keun Lee *et al.* Paris, UNESCO, 1980, 31 p. (Surveys & Studies in Adult Education) ED-80/WS/7.
6. *The Development of adult education : aspects and trends.* Paris, UNESCO, 1985, 83 p. ED-85/CONF.210/3.
7. *Directory of adult education periodicals.* Paris, UNESCO, 1985, 151 p. ED-85/WS/55.
8. *Directory of adult education and research institutions 3rd ed.* Paris, UNESCO, 1984 (IBEDATA series).
9. *Directory of national adult education co-ordinating bodies.* Paris, UNESCO, 1984, 167 p. ED-84/WS/34.
10. *Education and training of adults in the context of scientific and technological development. A summary* by Marit Ohayon-Kaczmarek. Paris, UNESCO, 1988, 62 p. ED-88/WS/7.
11. *Education for liberation and development. The Tanzanian experience* edited by H. Hinzen and V.H. Hundsdorfer. UNESCO/UIE, 1982, 266 p.

* Listing to illustrate the range of UNESCO documents and publications.

12. *Fourth international conference on adult education.* Paris, 19-29 March 1985. *Final report.* Paris, UNESCO, 1985, 68 p. + annexes ED/MD/81.
13. *Functional illiteracy and literacy provision in developed countries : the case of the Federal Republic of Germany* by E. Fuchs-Bruninghoff, W. Kreft, and U. Kropp. UNESCO/UIE, 1986, 90 p.
14. *General educational requirements for access to manual skills training in Botswana.* Paris, UNESCO, 1979, 116 p. (Surveys & Studies in Adult Education) ED-79/WS/160.
15. *Guidelines for the establishment of adult education mechanisms for employment-oriented training* by Sushila Singhal. Paris, UNESCO, 1986 ED/PLA/AD.
16. *Interaction between adult education and universalization of primary education in the context of integrated rural development* (A research study conducted in Sri Lanka) published by UNESCO in co-operation with Faculty of Education, University of Colombo, Sri Lanka. Paris, UNESCO, 1984, 131 p. ED-84/WS/69.
17. *Making higher education accessible to young workers and peasants : the soviet historical experience* by V. Onushkin and V. Zubkov. Paris, UNESCO, 1982, 42 p. (Surveys & Studies in Adult Education)ED-82/WS/26.
18. *Meeting of experts to consider ways and means of taking the workers' interests into consideration when formulating and implementing adult education policies.* Paris, UNESCO, 1983, 12 p. + annexes ED-83/CONF.614/COL.3.
19. *The potential contribution of adult education to the reduction of economic and social inequalities in developing countries* by P.H. Bertelsen. Madras, UNESCO-University of Madras, 1980, 19 p. ED-80/WS/62.
20. *A Primer of adult education.* Paris, UNESCO, 1987 ED-87/WS/10
21. *Recommendation on the development of adult education* adopted by the general conference at its nineteenth session, Nairobi, 26 November 1976. Paris, UNESCO, 1977, 18 P.
22. *Seminar for Nordic countries on adult education and education concerning the problems associated with the use of drugs* by Christian Gunther. E Skilstune, Sweden, 18-22 April, 1977, 21p. EPDAN/1.

23. *A Study on the general educational requirements for access to vocational education.* Progress report by Le Thanh Khol. Paris, UNESCO, 1980, 33 p. (Surveys & Studies in Adult Education) ED-79/WS/161.
24. *Study on the general educational requirements for access to vocational education in the Arab Republic of Egypt.* Paris, UNESCO, 1980, 39 p. (Surveys & Studies in Adult Education) ED-80/WS/6.
25. *Study on the general educational requirements for access to vocational education in the Republic of Argentina.* Paris, UNESCO, 1980, 55 p. ED-80/WS/8.
26. *Survey of adult education legislation.* Report published by the European Bureau of Adult Education with the support of UNESCO, 1985, 207 p.
27. *Terminology of adult education.* UNESCO/IBE, 1985 (IBEDATA series).
28. *Transition from education to working life ; the role of part-time education* by Wim H.M.L. Hoppers. Paris, UNESCO, 1986 ED/PLA/AD.
29. *Use of a newspaper as a distance teaching medium : a case study.* Paris, UNESCO, 1983, 37 p. (Surveys & Studies in Adult Education) ED-83/WS/58.

Literacy

1. *Adult literacy in the third world. A review of objectives and strategies* by Agneta Lind and Anton Johnston. Stockholm, Swedish International Development Authority, 1986, 101 p.
2. *Backgrounder : literacy education.* Paris, UNESCO, 1983, 19 p.
3. *Campaigning for literacy. Eight national experiences of the twentieth century, with a memorandum to decision-makers* by H.S. Bhola. Paris, UNESCO, 1984.
4. *Compendium of statistics on illiteracy* (Statistical reports and studies, 30) Paris, UNESCO, 1988, 122 p.
5. *Declaration of Persepolis.* International symposium for literacy. Persepolis, 3-8 September 1975. Paris, International Coordination Secretariat for Literacy, 1975, 3 p.
6. *Education for liberation and development. The Tanzanian experience* edited by H. Hinzen and V.H. Hundsdorfer. UNESCO/UIE, 1982, 266 p.

7. *Employment-oriented educational programmes for disadvantaged youth : a memo to municipal decision-makers*. Paris. UNESCO, 1986, 61 p. ED-86/WS/22.
8. *Functional illiteracy and literacy provision in developed countries : the case of the Federal Republic of Germany* by E. Fuchs-Bruninghoffs, W. Kreft and U. Kropp. UNESCO/UIE, 1986, 90 p.
9. *A Guide to UNESCO sources on literacy*. Morges, Switzerland, World Confederation of Organizations of the Teaching Profession/UNESCO, 1986, 15 p.
10. *Learning strategies for post-literacy and continuing education : a cross-national perspective* by R.H. Dave, D.A. Perera and A. Ouana with contributions from A. Bordia and H.S. Bhola. UNESCO/UIE, 1985, 269 p.
11. *Learning strategies for post-literacy and continuing education in Algeria, Egypt and Kuwait* edited by R.H. Dave, A Ouane and A.M. Ranaweera, Hamburg, UNESCO Institute for Education, 1988, xviii+210 pp., tables. (UIE studies on Post-literacy and continuing education, 6).
12. *Learning strategies for post-literacy and continuing education in Brazil, Colombia, Jamaica and Venezuela* by R.H. Dave, A. Ouane and A.M. Ranaweera with contributions from A.M. Coutinho, L.M. Carmo Chaves and V. Galvao, L. Hurtado, M. Moulton-Campbell and A. Valbuena Paz. UNESCO/UIE, 1986, 282 p.
13 *Learning strategies for post-literacy and continuing education in China, India, Indonesia, Nepal, Thailand and Vietnam* with contributions from Li Jiyuan, D.V. Sharma, A. Iskandar, U. Sihombing *et al*. UNESCO/UIE, 1986, 284 p.
14. *Learning strategies for post-literacy and continuing education in Kenya, Nigeria, Tanzania and United Kingdom* with contributions from D. Macharia, C.O. Akinde, Z.J. Mpogolo and A. Stock. UNESCO/UIE, 1985, 284 p.
15. *Learning strategies for post-literacy and continuing education in Mali, Niger, Senegal and Upper Volta* with contributions from A. Ouane, O. Kane, F. Badiane and P.T. Ilboudo. UNESCO/UIE, 1984, 206 p.
16. *Literacy campaigns*. In "Prospects" quarterly review of education. Paris, UNESCO, 1982, 256 p.

17. *Literacy education for young people, by young people*. Paris, UNESCO.
18. *Literacy for women : a development priority*. Paris, UNESCO.
19. *Literacy : gateway to fulfilment*. UNESCO Courier, June 1980. Paris, UNESCO, 1980, 34 p.
20. *Literacy : the ladder of achievement. UNESCO Courier*, February 1984. Paris, UNESCO, 1984, 34 p.
21. *Literacy : the right of every human being*. Paris, UNESCO.
22. *Nicaragua : for the eradication of illiteracy*. Published by "Gloverio Castaneda de Leon" International Union of Students Literacy Brigade with UNESCO financial assistance, 1980.
23. *Objective : literacy*. Report on literacy. Paris, UNESCO, available as from 1983.
24. *An Orientation seminar for the Arab States on the development of learning strategies for post-literacy and continuing education in the perspective of lifelong education*. Hamburg, 28 October-8 November 1985. *Final report*. UNESCO/UIE, 1986, 91 p.
25. *Theory and practice of literacy work : policies, strategies and examples* by A. Hamadache and D. Martin. Paris/Ottawa, UNESCO/CODE, 1986.
26. *Towards international literacy year. Illiteracy in industrialized countries : situation and action*. In "Prospects" quarterly review of education. Paris, UNESCO, 1987, 109 p.

19

INFORMATICS AND LIBRARIANSHIP

SYMPOSIUM OF EDITORS OF DOCUMENTATION, LIBRARY AND ARCHIVES JOURNALS, 1972

This symposium was held at UNESCO House from 16 to 18 May, 1972. It was attended by 55 editors of documentation, library or archives journals from 29 countries.

The aim of the symposium was to seek ways and means of improving the periodical literature of the profession and its bibliographical control and to obtain closer co-operation and co-ordination between documentation, library and archives journals, with a view to increasing the exchange of information, achieving more unified methods of presentation and encouraging greater use of authors abstracts.

During the general discussion various topics such as content of journals, standardization, abstracting and indexing services, international co-operation, etc. were discussed. At the close of the meeting the following recommendations were adopted:

1. Editors should quote always the original source of any article republished or translated, noting title changes, within copyright requirements.
2. Editors be urged to accept the abbreviations of titles and the International Standard Serials Number (ISSN) to be formulated by the International Serials Data System (ISDS) in collaboration with ISO and with the competent national bodies.
3. National meetings of editors should be organized.
4. A booklet based upon the essential content of the various relevant ISO standards should be published.

5. UNESCO should undertake a study of the presentation of periodicals in the field; a statistical study of the major abstracting and indexing services; a feasibility study of an indexing or abstracting network based upon a survey of the world's primary literature in the field.
6. Countries without an indexing or abstracting service should be encouraged by UNESCO to set up such services to cover their national literature in the field; at least an indexing service should be set up. Such services could be either national or regional.

INTERNATIONAL CONGRESS ON EDUCATION AND INFORMATICS FOR STRENGTHENING INTERNATIONAL CO-OPERATION, 1989

Nearly 500 participants from 96 countries, 5 United Nations Agencies, 6 intergovernmental organizations and 15 NGOs attended the Congress, held at UNESCO House in April 1989, in order to take stock of experience acquired in introducing informatics at different levels of formal and non-formal education and to draw up recommendations on how computers can best be used to develop and improve both the educational process and on the form international co-operation should take.

The general conclusions emphasized that:

- information technology has come to stay as an effective instrument for the improvement of the internal and external efficiency of the system of education;
- with the introduction of new information technologies, educational disparities may further grow within and between countries unless immediate and determined steps are taken to avoid such a development;
- the implementation of new information technologies and the pace of implementation should be based on a need analysis of any particular country, balanced against social, economic and cultural perspectives;
- higher education should be developed before consideration is given to the introduction of new information technologies

programmes in other sectors of education;

- a commitment to new technology requires continuous financial investment to respond to the ever-changing world of new technologies.

In its Recommendations, the Congress underlined the following priorities:

- exchange of information and data on experience acquired;
- exchange and joint production of software and selection of standards;
- training of specialists and teachers;
- research;
- education and industry co-operation;
- financial and technical assistance

BIBLIOGRAPHY

UNESCO DOCUMENTS AND PUBLICATIONS*

Periodical

PGI-UNISIST Newsletter. Quarterly.

Documents and Publications

1. *ASCOBIC manual on bibliographic control in Africa/* by Saliou M'Baye. Paris: UNESCO; Dakar: African Standing Conference on Bibliographic Control, 1981, 61 p. (PGI-81/WS/29).
2. *The Applicability of UNISIST guidelines and ISO international standards to archives administration and records management: a RAMP study* by James B. Rhoads, Paris, UNESCO 1982, 95 p. (PGI-82/WS/4).
3. *CCF: The Common Communication Format* by Peter Simmons and Alan Hopkinson. Paris, UNESCO, 1984, 185 p.

* Listing to illustrate the range of UNESCO documents and publications.

4. *Guide to the production and use of audio-visual aids in library and information science teaching*, by Anthony H. Thompson, Paris, UNESCO, 1983, 127 p. (PGI-83/WS/17).
5. *Guidelines for curriculum development in information studies*, by W.L. Saunders, Paris, UNESCO, 1978, 38 p. (PGI-78/WS/27).
6. *UNISIST guide to statistical information handling*, Paris, UNESCO.
7. *UNSIST reference manual for mechine-readable bibliographic descriptions*, 2nd ed., Paris, UNESCO, 1982.

DOCUMENTATION ENCYCLOPAEDIA
OF
UNESCO AND EDUCATION

Concepts in Communication
Informatics & Librarianship - 16

General Editor: S.P. AGRAWAL

DOCUMENTATION ENCYCLOPAEDIA OF UNESCO AND EDUCATION

PART TWO

J. C. AGGARWAL
S. P. AGRAWAL

CONCEPT PUBLISHING COMPANY, NEW DELHI 110059

ISBN 81-7022-329-6

First Published 1991

J.C. **AGGARWAL** (*b.* 1928)
S.P. **AGRAWAL** (*b.* 1929)

Published and Printed by
Ashok Kumar Mittal
Concept Publishing Company
A/15-16, Commercial Block, Mohan Garden
NEW DELHI 110059 (India)

Lasertypeset by
Microtech Advance Printing Systems (Pvt.) Ltd.
H-13, Bali Nagar
NEW DELHI-110015

Contents

SECTION IV
EDUCATIONAL PROGRAMMES ROUND THE WORLD

SECTION IV

EDUCATION PROGRAMMES ROUND THE WORLD

20

EDUCATION PROGRAMMES IN AFRICA

OVERVIEW/HIGHLIGHTS

Priority: Education for Economic Recovery and Development

Strengthening education at all levels is a major task of UNESCO for regional co-operation in the framework of the United Nations Programme of Action for African Recovery and Development.

Eradication of Illiteracy in Africa

Launched in 1984, this regional programme provides Member-States in the region with support and a framework for action for the eradication of illiteracy through a twofold approach involving expansion of primary education and literacy training for young people and adults. A Consultative Committee and a Technical Secretariat (based at BREDA) provide support, at regional level, for the implementation of the programme and National Committee for the programme have been set up in each participating State.

Renewal of Science and Technology Teaching

A Regional Consultative Committee responsible for establishing a programme of renovation of science and technology teaching was set up in 1984. Its activities are concerned mainly with the methodology of science and technology teaching, the training of personnel, and the production of teaching materials.

Strengthening the Role of Higher Education in Society

Another Regional Consultative Committee has been set up in this field and has prepared a special programme to improve higher education in Africa. Its objectives concern the training of personnel, the pooling of resources, and the promotion of scientific and technical research in the service of development.

The Network of Educational Innovation for Development in Africa (NEIDA)

The purpose of this network is to promote co-operation in educational research and innovation through exchanges, publications and meetings.

Technical Co-operation for Training and Research in Educational Planning and Administration (COFORPA)

This regional project — which also encompasses subregional projects – is designed to develop technical co-operation for national training and research in the field of educational planning and administration through the organization of training programmes, the production of teaching materials, and the development of research.

TABLE 20.1: UNESCO, 1984-1989: Technical co-operation in education

	Number of countries concerned	Resources utilized (MS)	Number of projects		
			Completed	On-going	In preparation
Total	46	79.0	117	144	49
Of which least Dev. Countries	26	39.6	67	78	32

Regional Conferences

From its inception UNESCO has acknowledged the need for educational planning. It has organized a series of regional conferences bringing together, in most cases, both ministers of education and ministers in-charge of economic development. At these conferences the participating Member-States have taken decisions of considerable bearing on educational progress.

Addis Ababa Plan (1961)

Realising its responsibilities to this part of the world UNESCO, jointly with U.N. Economic Commission for Africa convened a Conference of African States on the Development of Education in Africa, at Addis Ababa (5-12 May, 1961) to establish an inventory of educational needs in Africa and a programme to meet these needs. The conference was attended by the representatives from 34 African States and Territories as well as four European countries (Belgium, France, Spain, United Kingdom) and it lasted for ten days. (Two delegates from the 35th, the Republic of Chad, were tragically killed in air crash on their way to Conference). Experts from UNESCO, International Bank, the ILO, the FAO, the WHO and UNICEF also attended the conference. In addition, observers from twenty-four other States (including Austria, Brazil, Bulgaria, Canada, Formosa, Cuba, Czechoslovakia, Federal Republic of Germany, Greece, Hungary, India, Israel, Lebanon, Netherlands, Poland, Sweden, Switzerland, Turkey, USSR, USA, Vietnam, Yugoslavia). The African countries were represented by the Ministers or Directors of Education.

The conference adopted an 'Outline Plan for the Development of Education in Africa' which stipulated *inter alia* an annual increase of 5 per cent in school development of children having reached the age of compulsory schooling, a rise of enrolments into secondary schooling from 3 per cent in 1961 to 9 per cent in 1966, an increase in the proportion of GNP earmarked for education from 3 per cent in 1961 to 4 per cent in 1965, 5 per cent in 1970 and 6 per cent in 1980.

The Plan (1961) was revised at Paris (March 1962) and at Tananarive later in the same year.

Paris Conference (March 1962)

The situation was reviewed at the Paris Conference which recommended the creation or improvement of educational planning bodies. The Paris Conference suggested urgent measures to reduce the cost of secondary schooling.

The Tananarive Conference (1962)

The Tananarive Conference on the Development of Higher Education in Africa made recommendations on higher education estimating that during the next fifteen years, the growth of university students would require recruitment of 7,000 non-African and 14,000 African professors assuming an average student-teacher ratio of 15 : 1.

Abidjan Conference (March 1964)

The year 1964 witnessed conference of African Ministers of Education under the UNESCO's auspices at Abidjan, the capital of the Ivory Coast. Abidjan also became, for eight days, the intellectual capital of Africa.

All the African States, Members and Associate Members of UNESCO were represented by persons responsible for education at all levels; there were also observers from eleven non-African States and nine International Organizations, bringing the total number of participants more than 200, including 30 ministers.

(a) *Short Term Plan*: The short-term Five Year Plan (1961-66) called for raising primary school enrolment from the overall average in Africa of 40 per cent of the school-age population to 51 per cent during this period i.e. from a little over 11 million pupils to about 15 million, and for increasing secondary school enrolment from the present figure of about 3 per 100 of the age group to 9 per 100, i.e. from some 800,000 pupils to about 2,500,000.

(b) *Long Term Plan*: This plan called for:

(i) Establishment by 1980 of universal primary education throughout Africa.

(ii) Enrolment at secondary school level for 30 per cent of children leaving primary schools.

(iii) Enrolment at higher institutions for 20 per cent or one out of every five young pupils completing secondary education.

Both Plans also provided for a great increase in the training of teachers at all levels and for stepped-up courses in specialized, vocational and technical training as well as for greater efforts in carrying out programmes of adult education, including the task of reducing Africa's percentage of adult illiterates.

Finances: The bulk of the costs for the plans was to be borne by the African States themselves. The African States at the conference approved the recommendation that they make every effort to raise the percentage of their respective national incomes devoted to education, from 3 to 4 per cent during the next five years, and up to 6 per cent by 1980.

INFRASTRUCTURE INSTITUTIONS

Secondary Teacher Training Colleges

To help meet the shortage of teachers twenty secondary teacher training colleges were set up between 1962 and 1966 by seventeen States in Africa, with substantial financial assistance from the Special Field sector of the United Nations Development Programme administered by UNESCO. In 1965, 1,500 fully qualified teachers graduated from these colleges.

At the request of Member-States in Africa and in other regions UNESCO has provided experts, fellowships and equipment for the development of pre-service and in-service training both for primary and secondary school teachers. Moreover, in 1966 fifty-eight Member States were receiving financial assistance from the United Nations Children's Fund for teacher-training projects under a UNICEF-UNESCO agreement.

Regional School Building Centres

To meet the urgent need for schools adapted to local conditions, UNESCO has supported a Regional School Building Centre for Africa in Khartoum where studies, research and training courses are carried on. A similar centre exists in Bangkok for Asia, and another in Mexico City for Latin America.

Curriculum Reform Centre

Another UNESCO Regional Centre for Africa, the Accra Centre for Educational Information and Research has assisted ministries of education in reforming curricula in the light of new trends in education and in ensuring that they are properly related to African cultures instead of reflecting European conditions and attitudes. UNESCO has also provided expert services for two regional textbook production centres at Yaounde and Addis Ababa, and recently helped in the establishment of a unified alphabet for six major West African languages.

Experts for Educational Planning

Planning sections have been set up in most of the ministries of education, and UNESCO has sent expert missions to twenty African countries, at their request, to help in planning the development of their educational systems. At Dakar, the UNESCO Regional Group for Educational Planning and Administration organizes courses and seminars for senior civil servants and workshops for specialists in educational planning.

In these and many other ways UNESCO is helping its African Member-States to achieve the educational targets they have set themselves and on which some are spending as much as 25 per cent of the national budget and 5 per cent of their gross national product.

EDUCATIONAL PLANNING AND ADMINISTRATION

On their accession to independence in the early 1960s, African countries were convinced that the development of education constituted the main instrument of their progress. They were aware of the need to call into question the educational systems inherited from the colonial period which no longer responded to the fundamental aspirations and needs of their peoples. African States were persuaded of the necessity to accelerate the training of the officials they greatly needed, to initiate reforms for the purpose of adapting their school curricula to the demands of their development and to eradicate illiteracy. UNESCO immediately set itself the task of contributing to the achievement of these objectives. On the question of educational planning and administration, the African countries did not have any operating units in the proper sense of the world.

The Addis Ababa Conference (5-12 May, 1961) which was the first Conference of African States on educational development in Africa organized by UNESCO, thus marked the beginning of actions to promote educational planning and administration in Africa. In discussions during this conference, as a rule, only the clauses of the long term plan (1961-1980) setting 1980 as the target date for the achievement of universal primary education are recalled.

Beside the creation of services, the main objectives of educational planning could be summarized as follows:

- assist in formulating educational policies by providing the necessary basic data, analysing the possible strategies and estimating the costs of implementing the various plans, projects and programmes:
- assist in evaluating educational systems;
- assist in preparing the implementation of reforms.

Concerning educational administration, the African countries had more or less services which were not in a position, however, to cope with the implementation of reforms. The question, therefore, was not so much to create such services but to improve, strengthen, transform and modernize them.

These objectives were pursued from 1961 to date as it was necessary to proceed by stages. In the first phase, it was particularly necessary to act at the central levels, that is to say, for educational planning, set up central units within the Ministries of Education and, for educational administration, strengthen national departments. The objective of the second phase, in which we presently find ourselves, was to set up regional, provincial and district branches of planning services and also to strengthen the administrative services in the same areas.

On the field, UNESCO developed three main activities:

- technical co-operation;
- training in educational planning and administration;
- development, of national training capabilities (training of trainers and researchers).

Technical Co-operation

As a follow-up of this recommendation between 1962 and 1965, a number of Member-States requested consultancy services from UNESCO which contributed to the creation and establishment of the first educational planning structure. The majority of structures thus set up were educational statistics bureaux which subsequently obtained project help for launching planning units. The funding agencies mainly include:

- UNDP (United Nations Development Programme);
- ADB (African Development Bank);

– Bilateral sources, especially the SIDA (Swedish International Development Association).

Training

Starting in 1965, UNESCO set up a Regional Group for Educational Planning and Administration, soon to be renamed the Regional Centre for Educational Planning and Administration. The Regional Centre was integrated into the Regional Office for Education in Africa (BREDA) in 1970.

BREDA has been implementing since the beginning of 1984 a project of 'Regional Technical Co-operation for Training and Research in Educational Planning and Administration.' Popularly known under the name of COFORPA, this project has already received the support of twenty-six countries of the Region (Angola, Benin, Burkina Faso, Burundi, Cape Verde, Central African Republic, Chad, Comoros, Ethiopia, Gabon, Gambia, Guinea, Guinea-Bissau, Kenya, Malawi, Mali, Mauritania, Niger, Rwanda, Senegal, Seychelles, Sierra Leone, Swaziland, United Republic of Tanzania, Zaire and Zambia) and has obtained financing for a period of two and a half years within the framework of the UNDP Regional Programme for Africa (project RAF/81/047).

With regard to its main objective of developing national capabilities in the field of educational planning and administration, the project has contributed in its first phase in:

– Sensitizing the Government and national authorities to the necessity of organizing permanent training in educational planning and administration;
– Setting up the national mechanisms (National COFORPA teams and co-ordinators) for participation in the execution of the project;
– Strengthening educational planning and administration:

  . training and research needs determined and national training programmes developed in all the countries visited by an identification mission;
  . initiation to planning techniques applicable to the duties of planning officials and technicians in the ten countries that organized seminars, workshops, or developed national training

programmes;
. setting up of new educational planning structures at central level and in the regions;
. preparation of small number of national specialists to supervise the curricula and methods applied in national training programmes in educational planning and administration;

– raise funds from other sources to finance additional projects.

The essential condition for developing national training programmes, whether in educational planning or in educational administration, is to ensure the training of trainers as the most urgent need. According to the project document, this is one of the functions of the COFORPA project.
(*Source*: *UNESCO and Asia: Some Regional Activities*.)

UNESCO PROGRAMME IN HIGHER EDUCATION

Studies and Research

1. Study on the human, scientific and technological potential of higher education and research centres in East Africa: Ethiopia, Kenya, Somalia, Tanzania, Uganda, Zambia and Zimbabwe, by Professor Keto E. Mahigeni, Ph.D., University of Dar-e-Salaam, 1984.
2. Study on the human, scientific and technological potential of higher education and research centres in Central Africa: Burundi, Rwanda, Zaire, by Professor Gerard T.K.M. Buakasa, University of Kinshasa, 1984.
3. Study on the brain drain in African countries by Dr Thiedel Camara, Ministry of Planning and Co-operation, Dakar, Senegal, 1984.
4. Study on the human. scientific and technological potential of higher education and research centres in Benin and Togo by Professor Lucien G.A. Chede, National University of Benin, Cotonou, 1985.
5. Study on the ways and means of making the most economical use of the human and material resources of universities in Africa by Professor Lucien G.A. Chede, 1986.
6. Study of the conditions of the personnel of higher education: for

generalizing the 1966 recommendation on (improving) the conditions of the teaching staff, by Professor Kalemba Vita Kanga, University of Kinshasa, Zaire, 1986.

7. Study on the brain-drain in African countries by Dr. T.O. Fadayomi, Senior Research Fellow, University of Ibadan, Nigeria, 1986.
8. Study on the ways and means of making the most economical use of the human and material resources of universities, by Professor Nnoli Okwudiba, Nsukka University, Nigeria, 1987.

Documentation and Information

'Case studies on higher education in Africa', — a special edition of *Educafrica*, December 1986, devoted to the higher educational institutions of the following countries: Benin, Burkina Faso, Burundi, Central Africa, Cameroon, Cote d'Ivoire, Ethiopia, Gabon, Lesotho, Madagascar, Malawi, Mali, Niger, Senegal, Sierra Leone, Zaire.

Personnel Training

1. Workshop on project evaluation (University of Lusaka, Zambia, December 1984).
2. Seminar on the use of the computer in scientific and technical information (Conakry, 28 May-8 June, 1985).
3. Introduction of the computer in management methods (Bangui, 12-21 October, 1985).
4. National workshop on instructional technology and communication in higher education, Makerere University, (Uganda, December 1985).
5. Subregional workshop on teacher training for the personnel of higher education (Abidjan, 9-18 December 1985).

Consultative Services

Benin: Joint activities between higher educational institutions in the sub-region, December 1986.

Chad: Identification of problems connected with the reorganization of the University of Ndjamena.

Guinea: National conference on education in Guinea, 19 May - 4 June, 1984. Several missions on higher education.

Mauritania: Studies on the modalities of extending the scope of the Nouakchott University Project.

Mali: In-depth study on higher education in Africa, 11-27 May, 1983.

Mauritius: Problems of acceptance of degrees, 11-28 July, 1984.

Mozambique: Evaluation of the activities of the Eduardo Mondlane University, 5-14 October, 1984.

Guinea-Bissau: Establishment of a co-operative training network, a joint project of Guinea-Bissau, Cape Verde, Sao Tome and Principe.

Support to Operating Programmes

Evaluation of the BEPUZA (Post-Graduate Consulting Firm of Zaire) project.

Network of higher educational training institutions (Cape Verde, Guinea-Bissau, Principe and Sao Tome).

UNESCO PROGRAMMES IN SCIENCE AND TECHNOLOGY EDUCATION

Improvement of the Curricula and Teaching Methods

UNESCO/BREDA provided technical and financial assistance: for the following activities among others:

Guinea 1981: A national workshop on the revision and design of a biology syllabus for secondary and higher educational institutions;
Guinea 1981: A national workshop on the revision and design of a syllabus for teaching mathematics;
Central African Republic then Mauritius 1983: A sub-regional workshop on pedagogical renovation and innovation in the field of mathematics;
Sierra Leone 1981 and 1983: A workshop on the production of methodological modules for teaching physics at the secondary school level;
Zaire, then Malawi 1984: A national workshop on the revision and development of agricultural education at the middle school level.

Out of School Education in Science and Technology

Science and technology constitute today not only the main factors of economic development but also the fundamental components of modern civilization. It was deemed necessary to develop extra-mural knowledge by using such varied means as:

- scientific days for science fairs;
- training workshops for key-personnel;
- scientific competitions and olympiads;
- activities for popularizing science and technology through the radio, television and the press.

Training of Teachers and Trainers

UNESCO's assistance in the field of scientific training is pursued through training courses, seminars and workshops, financing consultancy missions and exchanges of information and experiences. The following activities may be cited as examples:

- *Senegal*, 1981 : a sub-regional seminar on the training of the supervisory staff of education in nutrition.
- *Nigeria*, 1981 : a chemistry training course organized at the University of Ibadan.
- *Burkina Faso*, 1982 : a national training workshop for ecology teachers.
- *Zaire*, 1982 : a sub-regional training workshop for lecturers and assistant lecturers in ecology.
- *Rwanda*, 1982 : a national training workshop for the administrative staff and teachers responsible for teaching ecology.
- *Senegal*, 1983: a sub-regional training workshop for supervisory staff in the field of home economics.
- *Cote d'Ivoire*, 1984 : a sub-regional workshop on the modular approach to technical and vocational education.

Design and Development of Teaching Materials and Infrastructure

UNESCO's aim in this field is to develop local production of easily made and low-cost teaching materials. It ensures, through the organization of regional, sub-regional and national workshops, the training of officials who may initiate or develop in their respective countries the local production of low-cost teaching materials.

A few examples of the activities organized by UNESCO/BREDA in this field are given below:

– *Zimbabwe*, 1982, and Botswana, 1984

A sub-regional workshop on the study and production of teaching materials for integrated science teaching using new low cost material:

– *Senegal*, 1983 : BREDA's preparation of a guide on innovation for key-staff of out-of-school scientific and technological education.
– *Madagascar*, 1984 : Sub-regional workshop on the study and production of low-cost teaching materials for science and technology education.

UNESCO's ASSOCIATED SCHOOLS PROJECT

Since the 1960s, the Associated Schools Project (ASP) has expanded considerably throughout Africa. The first country from the African continent to take part in the Project was Egypt in 1960 and several others followed in that decade. 24 African countries are taking part in it with a total of 336 institutions (145 primary schools, 152 secondary schools and 39 teacher-training institutions).

Two African regional ASP seminars, which were held respectively in Nairobi, Kenya, in January 1979 and in Dakar, Senegal, in June 1981, contributed to the extension of the Project in the continent. These seminars were conducted in close co-operation with the National Commission for UNESCO in the two host countries and resulted in a number of recommendations for the development of the Project at both the national and regional levels.

World ASP Congress

Delegates from 21 African nations and observers from South West African People's Organization (SWAPO) and the Pan African Congress of Azania (the nationalist name for South Africa) attended the first International Congress on the occasion of the 30th anniversary of the Associated Schools Project took place in Sofia, Bulgaria, from 12-16 September, 1983.

Some of the proposals made by the African/Arab group included:

- close co-operation with the Ministries of Education with a view to ensuring that ASP innovations are incorporated into the educational policies and programmes of a given country; and
- increased co-operation between Associated Schools and UNESCO Clubs in order to reinforce out-of-school activities in the spirit of international understanding.

Implementation at National Level

In all countries taking part in the Project in the African region, the national co-ordination is ensured by the National Commission for UNESCO.

A national conference took place in Kinshasa, Zaire, on 14 June, 1986 with a view to launching the Project in the country. The Conference was organized by the Regional Council of UNESCO Clubs and Associations in co-operation with the Zaire National Commission for UNESCO.

In Taza (Morocco) some 70 educators and UNESCO Club representatives as well as specialists from Belgium and Switzerland, from the World Federation of UNESCO Clubs Associations and from the UNESCO Secretariat met from 24 to 27 March, 1986 in order to examine ways and means to develop and Project further in the country and to establish a closer link between Associated Schools and UNESCO Clubs.

A national seminar took place in Nairobi, Kenya, from 21 to 24 April, 1986 under the auspices of the Kenya National Commission for UNESCO and under contact with BREDA. The participants formulated a series of recommendations for strengthening the Project in Kenya, which included:

- More workshops and seminars at the national, provincial and district levels in order to create greater awareness of the Project and to provide information for participation in it;
- The preparation and publication of an ASP teachers' guide to help teachers incorporate more easily the aims and objectives of the Project into the school curriculum;
- The diffusion of the results of the Project to the general public through the mass media, film shows, lectures by officials, etc.

The preparation of appropriate teaching material pertaining to international education is another important facet of the Project. In Chad, several workshops were conducted in 1985-86 to prepare material, on teaching about human rig' 's for use by schools in the country. In Zambia, the National Commission for UNESCO, in collaboration with ASP teachers, prepared teaching guidelines for the observance of World Environment Day (5 June).

Realising that, if the Project its to attain its objectives at the national level, it is important that information about positive results be widely diffused so that other schools can learn about them and undertake similar action. Some countries (Tunisia is one example) diffuse information through national ASP news bulletins or circular letters. The media can also be an effective way to inform others about contributions made by Associated Schools to furthering peace and international understanding and national co-ordinators are encouraged to invite the press, educational journals, etc., to report on significant activities carried out by Associated Schools.

Burendwa Primary School, Kakamega, Kenya

This school conducted a number of activities to enhance the role of youth in community development. Some of the students visited a centre for adults in the village and witnessed the problems faced by both teachers and learners. As a result of the visit, they decided to become actively involved in the adult literacy campaign in the village and to work closely with an individual in teaching her/him how to read and write. Other students visited the elderly in the village and helped them with some household chores. The students also examined how crop production could be increased and they took part in an Irish potato-growing project.

'Germaine le Goff' Teacher Training Institution for Girls, Thies, Senegal

This school celebrated the 40th anniversary of the end of the Second World War and the creation of the United Nations and UNESCO. Contacts were made with the "Association des anciens combattants" (war veterans' association) in order to learn more about their memories of war days and the strategy of their association in finding solutions for the maintenance and reinforcement of peace.

Several other activities were conducted to heighten awareness of the importance of peace as opposed to war. In art classes, the students did paintings on peace themes and in music class they composed a peace hymn. In psychology, discussions were held on a programme for peace education on one of five main themes: co-operation at school, solidarity, hospitality, comprehension and tolerance.

Further Developments

On the occasion of the International Year of Peace (1986) and the 40th anniversary of the coming into effect of the UNESCO Constitution (4 November, 1986), two regional African seminars for ASP national co-ordinators took place : in Benin (for French-speaking national co-ordinators) and in Zambia (for English-speaking national co-ordinators) before the end of 1986. The objectives of the seminars were : to enable co-ordinators to exchange information on experience acquired within the framework of the Project, results achieved and problems encountered: and to make plans for the future, including the preparation of teaching material on UNESCO — its objectives, history and achievements — for use in upper primary and junior secondary schools.
(*Source*: Based on a report by Elizabeth Khawajkie, UNESCO, Paris.)

NETWORK OF EDUCATIONAL INNOVATION FOR DEVELOPMENT IN AFRICA

Network of Educational Innovation for Development in Africa (NEIDA) was established in 1978, at the request of the Ministers of Education of African Member-States, meeting in Lagos, Nigeria, in January-/February 1976. Its seven fields of action, which were endorsed at the Conference of Ministers of Education and those responsible for Economic Planning in African Member-States, are:

- Education and productive work
- Education for development in rural areas
- Administration and supervision of educational systems
- training and retraining of educational personnel
- Production and distribution of educational materials
- Use of national languages in education
- Science and technology education.

Modes of Action

NEIDA promotes exchanges among Member-States:

a. by bringing specialists from different countries together at various meetings, seminars and workshops:

   (i) to inform one another of the educational innovations that are taking place in their respective countries;
   (ii) to exchange views on ways and means of developing, organizing, improving, generalizing and evaluating the innovations;
   (iii) to seek solutions to common problems;
   (iv) to produce materials that can be used in various countries; and
   (v) to undergo training in specific areas of innovation;

b. by giving specialists from various countries an opportunity to visit projects in countries other than their own, with a view:

   (i) to examining an innovation *in situ*; and
   (ii) to learning from one another's experience;

c. by providing consultants, in preference from African countries, to assist other countries launch, develop, evaluate an innovation, at the latter's request;
d. by disseminating written information/materials throughout the Africa regions through:

   (i) a direct exchange of printed materials and correspondence between countries/projects/programmes; and
   (ii) the publications of the NEIDA Co-ordinating Unit:

Periodical and serial publications:

– NEIDA Information
– NEIDA Digest
– Innovations and Change
– Inventory of Innovations
– Annual Calendar of NEIDA Activities
– Directory of NEIDA Institutions.

Non-periodical publications:

- Reports on meetings, seminars and workshops
- Guides of NEIDA personnel and of specific activities at national level
- Regional and case studies
- Miscellaneous.

NEIDA has conducted seminars and/or workshops in all seven of its programme areas; it has enabled over 200 specialists from 36 countries to visit innovative projects in other African countries; it has completed or is in the process of conducting regional studies or surveys in the areas of Education and Productive work. Education for Development in Rural Areas, Teacher Education, the Use of Appropriate Technologies for Educational Purposes and the Use of National Languages in Education. Numerous case studies have been undertaken, mostly in preparation for regional and sub-regional activities. A directory of innovative educational institutions, an annotated bibliography on appropriate educational technologies and guidelines for running national in-service training exercises for middle and lower level educational planning and administration personnel, have been published and circulated throughout the region. This is in addition to the periodical and serial publications of the NEIDA Co-ordinating Unit. NEIDA has also launched a Regional Programme for the publications of works in African Languages in the African countries. The programme is aimed at the popularization of high quality writing in the African Languages, as well as the development of African language publishing in the countries.
(*Source*: UNESCO.)

BIBLIOGRAPHY

UNESCO DOCUMENTATION AND PUBLICATIONS*

1. *Buildings for school and community use : five case studies* (University groups in : Australia, Federal Republic of Germany,

* Listing to illustrate the range of UNESCO documents and publications.

Greece, Kenya and USA). Paris, UNESCO, 1977, 122 p. (Educational studies and documents No. 26).

2. *Course for English-speaking African educators on the methodology of education concerning the problems associated with the use of drugs.* Reports of the working groups by Edmee Moutandon. Eimu, Kenya, 1983, 135 p. EPDAF/COURS II.
3. *Educating handicapped young people in Eastern and Southern Africa*, by D.H. Ross. Paris, UNESCO, 1988, 153 p.
4. *Eduafrica.* As from December 1981 : Bulletin of the UNESCO Regional Office for Education in Africa.
5. *Forms of pre-primary education appropriate to the socio-demographic conditions and cultural tradition — Kenya* by E.M. Mugiri. Paris, UNESCO, 1980, 34 p. ED-80/WS/98.
6. *Handicapped children : early detection, intervention and education.* Selected case studies from Argentina, Canada, Denmark, Jamaica, Jordan, Nigeria, Sri Lanka, Thailand and the United Kingdom. Paris, UNESCO, 1981, 142 p. ED/MD/63.
7. *Higher education in Trinidad and Tobago : a focus on organisational development and change*, by Gwendoline Williams and Claudia Harvey. UNESCO/CRESALC, 1985, 145 p. (Monograph series)
8. *National languages and teacher training in Africa : A methodological guide for the use of teacher training institutions*, by Joseph Poth. Paris, UNESCO, 1988, 49 p.
9. *Regional conferences and educational development in Africa, Arab States, Asia and Latin America : Bombay 1952 — Mexico City 1979* by F.L. Bartels. Paris, UNESCO, 1983, 187 p.
10. *Regional conferences and educational development in Africa from the Addis Ababa conference 1961 to the Lagos conference 1976*. by F.L. Bartels. Paris, UNESCO, 1983, 93 p.
11. *Regional convention in the recognition of studies, certificates, diplomas, degrees and other academic qualifications in higher education in the African States*. Paris, UNESCO, 1981.
12. *Regional meeting on education concerning problems connected with the use of drugs in six African countries*, Lome, Togo, 13-17 September 1976. *Final report.* Paris, UNESCO, 1977, 12 p. ED/MD/44.
13. *Regional seminar in Africa on the recognition and reorganisation of studies and research in higher education having regard to the requirements of endogenous development*, Yaounde, 30 May-5

June 1983. *Results of the work.* Paris, UNESCO, 1983, 20 p. ED-83/CONF.710/3.

14. *The Role of parents in the education of children of pre-school age in Tropical Africa, India, and the Maghreb countries* prepared by the International Federation for Parent Education. Paris, UNESCO, 1980, 48 p. ED-80/WS/97.
15. *Special education in Africa : research abstracts.* Nairobi, Kenya, 1986. ED-86/6.
16. *Stocktaking of needs and resources relative to training and research,* Vol. 1 : *Australia, Hungary, Kenya, Syrian Arab Republic.* Paris, UNESCO, 1987, o.p. (Papers on higher education No. 10).
17. *A Survey on dangerous drugs and narcotics in Togo.* Regional meeting on education concerning problems connected with the use of drugs in six African countries. Lome, Togo, 13-17 September 1976. *Working Document* by Tevi Sedalo, YaoTossou and Dovi Feli. Lome, 1976, 28 p. EPDAF/3c.
18. *Technical co-operation in education in Africa — review and prospects.* Paris, UNESCO, 1984, 56 p. ED-84/WS/47.
19. *The use and abuse of drugs in Kenya. A survey of the need for drug education* by C.A. Mwakwers, G. Muito, A. Ananda and G.P. Oluoch. Regional meeting on education concerning problems connected with the use of drugs in six African countries. Lome, Togo, 13-17 September 1976, 29 p. EPDAF/3d.

See also UNESCO series *African research monographs* (UNESCO/IIEP), and *Educational studies and documents* (New series).

21

EDUCATION PROGRAMMES IN ARAB STATES

OVERVIEW/HIGHLIGHTS

Priority: Human Resource Development

Regional co-operation lays special emphasis on the renewal of education in order to strengthen its ability to contribute to social and economic development.

The Universalization and Renewal of Primary Education and the Eradication of Illiteracy by the Year 2000: ARABUPEAL

This regional programme was launched in 1989 following a meeting of senior officials of Ministries of Education in the Arab States, held in Amman, Jordan, in 1987. This meeting had recommenced that UNESCO should establish in the Arab Region a co-operative programme for the provision of universal literacy similar to those already established in Latin America, Africa and Asia.

The main objectives of this programme are:

- to ensure primary education for all;
- to eradicate illiteracy;
- to enhance socio-economic development and release creative social energies.

Educational Innovation for Development: EIPDAS

Co-operation and the exchange of information, experience and exper-

tise among Member-States is the keynote of EIPDAS, the Educational Innovation Programme for Development in the Arab States.
EIPDAS is located in Kuwait and is supported by UNESCO and UNDP. It operates through a Co-ordinating Unit — which in turn, has the backing of specialists from UNESCO Regional Office for Education in the Arab States (UNEDBA) — to achieve the following objectives:

* to help Member-States introduce fundamental changes in their educational systems so as to make education more relevant to community needs;
* to make teachers and education officials more aware of the need for educational innovation;
* to promote understanding of the process of educational innovation, how this process is related to social and economic development and the constraints to which it is subject in developing countries;
* to promote co-operation among Arab Member-States in establishing the infrastructures necessitated by educational innovation.

Strengthening National Capacities in Educational Planning and Management

UNESCO assists Member-States in the region, especially through UNEDBAS, in the formulation and application of educational policies and in the improvement of educational planning, management, administration and facilities. National capacities in educational planning, administration and management are strengthened by the provision of advisory services and the organization of training courses, workshops and seminars.

TABLE : 21.1: UNESCO, 1984-1989: Technical co-operation in education

	Number of countries concerned	Resources utilized (M$)	Number of projects		
			Completed	On-going	In preparation
Total	17	22.2	39	43	17
Of which Least Dev. Countries	4	6.3	15	9	5

Since the early days, UNESCO has been providing assistance and guidance to the Arab States in organising many educational programmes.

The programme of education for Arab refugees from Palestine was begun in 1950 in co-operation with the United Nations Relief and Works Agency (UNRWA). At present it is offering education to about 351,000 children in more than 600 elementary and junior secondary schools.

Since 1952, UNESCO, has helped the operation of the Arab States Training Centre for Education for Community Development, established in the United Arab Republic.

UNESCO contributed to the cost of operating the Arab States Regional Centre for the Advanced Training of Educational Personnel established in 1961.

In April 1964, a meeting of experts on the access of education to girls was organised in Algiers. A regional conference on the planning and organization of literacy campaigns was convened in Alexandria in October 1964. An Institute of Education was created in Beirut in 1964 by UNESCO and UNRWA.

Since the Tripoli Conference in April 1966, the Ministers of Education and those responsible for Economic Planning have been meeting regularly. The Tripoli Conference stressed the need to organize educational planning, provide functionally training for adults, develop scientific and technical education and promote the access of women to education. In most of these UNESCO initiated action and provided assistance.

To extend and improve teacher training UNESCO, with aid from United Nations Development, has set up many teacher training colleges.

UNESCO has sent many expert missions to various Arab States to advise governments on such questions as educational planning, teacher training, the improvement of teaching methods, and techniques and the production of materials and audio-visual aids for education.

Algeria was one of the first three countries to receive aid from the United Nations Development Programme for implementing a pilot project in functional literacy, whose execution was entrusted to UNESCO. Nearly one lakh industrial and agricultural workers were affected by this project. UNESCO has provided expert services, fellowships and equipment for the development of audio-visual aids for schools and out of school education to Algeria, Iraq, Lebanon, Syria,

Tunisia and United Arab Republic.

UNESCO has given assistance to Jordan, Lebanon and Yemen for the development of their library services and to Algeria, Iraq, Kuwait and Syria for the organization and development of their museums.

In the field of service, as early as 1947, UNESCO set up in Cairo an International Science Co-operation Office. As a part of the Major Project on Arid Zone Research, UNESCO has helped to create scientific research institutes in Iraq, Saudi Arabia and Sudan and has given financial help to the United Arab Republic's Desert Research Institute. Under the same programme UNESCO has given assistance to a number of institutions for scientific and technological research and training in the Arab States, UNESCO has organised important regional meetings to discuss science policy : Cairo (1960), Beirut (1963) and Algeria (1966).

Very valuable work has been done as a result of the Major Project on Mutual Appreciation of Eastern and Western Values.

The Arab States have played a major role in international campaigns initiated by UNESCO for the development of museums and the protection of monuments. The laying of the foundation stone of the Great Temple of Abu Simbel at its new site on December 1965 marked a high point in the international campaign to save the monuments of Nubia. UNESCO has given financial aid to the centre for Documentation and Research on the History and Art of Ancient Egyptian Civilization in Cairo.

Fruitful collaboration has been established between UNESCO and the National Commissions in the Arab States.

Present Policies and Programmes

The Amman Conference (22-26 June, 1987) convened by UNESCO Regional Office for Education in the Arab States (UNEDBAS) in collaboration with the Ministry of Education of the Hashemite Kingdom of Jordan provides an overview of the state of education in the Arab States.

In pursuance of the programme and Budget for 1986-87, approved by the General Conference of UNESCO at its twenty-third session, a meeting of senior education officials of the Arab States organised by UNESCO was attended by 25 participants from 16 Arab States and 18 observers representing regional and international organizations. Specialists from the UNEDBAS and the UNESCO Secretariat also participated in the meeting.

The meeting was assigned the following tasks:

(a) to review educational achievements, trends and problems in the Arab States region since the Conference of Ministers of Education and those responsible for Economic Planning held in Abu Dhabi in 1977;
(b) to study possible strategies for the development, renewal and democratization of education and for literacy teaching in the context of cultural, social and economic development;
(c) to establish guidelines for Member-States in the Arab States region and specialized regional and international organizations to assist them in the development and renewal of education at the national level and in the context of regional and international co-operation.

EXCERPTS FROM PROCEEDINGS

Regional and International Co-operation for the Development of Education in the Arab States

The participants expressed their satisfaction at the establishment, since the Abu Dhabi Conference, of a number of regional and sub-regional governmental and non-governmental educational institutions and at the activities that UNESCO had organized during that period or in which it had played an active role in co-operation with Arab organizations and regional and international funds.

The meeting emphasized the need for continued co-operation and co-ordination between UNESCO, the Arab Educational, Cultural and Scientific Organization and other Arab governmental and non-governmental organizations working in UNESCO's fields of competence in the execution of activities in the Arab region. It also stressed the necessity for co-ordination with the Arab Literacy and Adult Education Organization in organizing regional activities within the framework of International Literacy Year.

Educational Innovation Network

A document on the Educational Innovation Programme for Development in the Arab States was presented to the meeting. The document dealt with the Programme's objectives, structure, types and fields of activity, its achievements hitherto and the difficulties it had encountered.

The meeting stressed the Programme's important role in developing and strengthening basic structures aimed at educational innovation in the Arab States, in encouraging those States to introduce fundamental changes in their education systems in order to make them more effective and more relevant to social and economic development, and in promoting co-operation between the existing structures, enabling them to exchange knowledge, experience, information and advice in the field of educational innovation and undertake innovative projects of common interest, thereby increasing their awareness of innovation and increasing their determination and capacity to direct their action towards that objective.

The meeting emphasized the need for the Arab States to promote this Programme and to provide moral and financial support for its activities. It was also essential for UNESCO to provide the Regional Co-ordinating Unit for the Programme with human and material support. The participants also considered that the United Nations Development Programme should contribute to the financing of the Programme, as it had done in the case of other comparable programmes. They hoped that the impact of the Programme would be felt at the school and classroom level and urged Arab organizations to continue co-operating with the Programme's Regional Co-ordinating Unit in the implementation of its activities.

RECOMMENDATIONS

I. Co-ordinated Strategies to Universalize Primary Education and Eradicate Illiteracy

Recommendation No. 1

The Meeting,

Realizing that widespread illiteracy constitutes a major constraint on the development of individuals and societies,

Noting that despite the significant progress in the universalization of primary education and in literacy education achieved by the Arab States since the Abu Dhabi Conference in 1977, with enrolment rates in primary education exceeding 90 per cent in several countries, these rates, among women in particular, are still below the desired level in other countries of the region, where the illiteracy rates are among the highest in the world,

Conscious that illiteracy can only be eradicated by providing all children with a suitable quality of primary education over an adequate period accompanied by intensive out-of-school education for young people and adults,

Emphasizing that the principle of equal opportunity and the democratization of education can only be put into practice by improving the quality of the content of education and increasing its quantity,

Convinced that the best way to execute co-ordinated strategies for the universalization of primary education and the improvement of its quality and to eradicate illiteracy among young people and adults in the Arab regions is to co-ordinate educational efforts at the national level and to consolidate co-operation and solidarity among the Member-States in all fields,

Appreciating the positive co-operation in these fields between ALECSO and its specialized agencies and UNESCO and its Regional Office,

Recommends to the Arab States that they:

1. renew their commitment to joint action to achieve full literacy in the region by the year 2000 by taking all the necessary measures to provide primary education for all school-age children and to establish flexible, co-ordinated structures for both formal and non-formal education;
2. provide more human, technical and material resources in order to achieve universal primary education in the 1990s;
3. consolidate the links between primary and literacy education programmes so as to achieve the objectives of the co-ordinated strategies, through planning and research, curriculum development, teacher training and making good use of educational facilities;
4. prepare effective training programmes for primary school teachers so that they can teach both children and adult learners, thereby making up for the great shortage of trained adult education teachers;
5. step up current efforts on behalf of girls and women, especially in

rural areas, in both the formal and the non-formal sectors of education;

6. stimulate and support all traditional educational and cultural institutions (mosque, shrine and brotherhood schools - *kuttab, zawaya, khalawi* — and single classroom schools) so as to enlist them in the service of the universalization of primary education and literacy education;
7. make effective use of the communication media and modern technology to achieve the goals of primary and literacy education;
8. reinforce pre-school education as an important aid to success in primary school;
9. continue to support the Arab Fund for Literacy and Adult Education;

Recommends to the Director-General of UNESCO that he:

10. strengthen co-operation and consultation between UNESCO and ALECSO regarding primary, literacy and adult education so as to support Arab efforts in these fields;
11. propose to the General Conference at its twenty-fifth session that it provides in the Programme and Budget for 1988-1989 for assistance to the Arab States in setting up a regional co-operation programme based on the principle of co-ordinated strategies in primary and literacy education that would back up the efforts of the Arab Literacy and Adult Education Organization to eradicate illiteracy by the year 2000, that assistance taking the form of the Organization's support for regional projects and programmes in Latin America, Asia and Africa;

Recommends to UNESCO that it:

12. provide the Member-States of the region with technical and other forms of assistance so as to enable them to universalize primary education and improve its quality and to eradicate illiteracy among young people and adults;
13. assist the Member-States of the region, especially those in greatest need of international support (technical and financial), to achieve their national objectives in primary and literacy education;
14. provide special support to educational programmes for girls and

women, particularly in rural areas and poor urban areas;

15. provide special support to national and regional programmes for the education of disabled children and adults;
16. provide assistance to Member-States suffering from drought, famine, war and other forms of natural disaster so that they can reconstruct and improve their education systems and promote equality by linking these systems to their development plans.

International Literacy Year - 1990

Recommendation No. 2

The Meeting,

Welcoming the resolution of the United Nations General Assembly adopted in response to the appeal of the General Conference of UNESCO that it proclaim an international literacy year as a way of drawing world attention to the problem of illiteracy and giving momentum to the struggle against it,

Considering that the proclamation of an international literacy year is of particular importance to the peoples and States of the Arab region and that that year should be used as an opportunity to launch regional and national actions and to strengthen current programmes and activities that stress the right of education for all,

Concurring with the proposal of the Director-General of UNESCO that 1990 be proclaimed International Literacy Year and that that Year should mark the beginning of a decade of intensive efforts lasting to the end of the century for the universalization and reform of primary education,

1. *Recommends* to the Director-General of UNESCO that he takes steps to ensure that the international programmes for the year are designed to support and strengthen national efforts to teach reading and writing, particularly in countries suffering from high rates of illiteracy;
2. *Calls on* the Arab States to take immediate steps to set up national co-ordination committees and to provide the opportunity for all qualified members of society to participate in improving the standards of reading and writing; to prepare and implement permanent and effective national programmes for that year and to

facilitate regional and international co-operation to follow up the purposes and aims of International Literacy Year;

3. *Invites* ALECSO and other regional governmental and non-governmental organizations to participate actively in the regional and national activities of International Literacy Year.

II. General and Technical Secondary Education in Relation to the Needs of Development and the Employment Market

Recommendation No. 3

The Meeting,

Noting the importance of secondary education in the preparation and training of students for higher education or for enrolment in technical and training institutions,

Stressing the role of secondary education in providing trained human resources for comprehensive development plans, programmes and projects,

Recognizing that its general aims and purposes are to prepare individuals for life in the advanced Arab societies of the future.

Recommends the following measures:

1. establishment of a centralized national body to plan, guide and supervise vocational schools and centres with a view to formulating and executing policies serving the objectives of development and its labour requirements;
2. development of counselling and guidance programmes for technical and vocational education, encouraging private institutions to become involved in this endeavour in co-operation with public institutions;
3. introduction of agricultural and environmental activities and handicrafts at all educational levels in order to develop an attraction for manual work among young people and to endeavour to change the negative social attitude to manual labour and handicrafts;
4. establishment at the national and regional levels, of specialized institutes for the technical and pedagogical training of teachers and for improving their performance;
5. diversification of technical and vocational disciplines in order to

meet the requirements of development projects;

6. stressing the role and importance of agricultural education in rural development and the need to support and improve its programmes by relating education and training in agricultural institutions to the conditions and problems of rural areas;
7. organization of more seminars on technical education in general and agricultural education in particular, so as to make good use of and exchange experience and innovations in various fields at the regional and the international levels;
8. integration of the programmes of general education and those of technical and vocational education; relating education to work so as to provide school leavers with the basic skills and qualifications they need to meet the personal, social and occupational challenges of life, provided that this does not occur at the expense of academic excellence and creativity;
9. strengthening the science, technology and mathematics curricula in general secondary education in order to provide learners with the scientific and technical knowledge and skills they need later in life;
10. introduction of population and family planning programmes in curricula at all educational levels, in teacher training institutions and in literacy and adult education programmes and using the mass media to disseminate population information in order to increase public awareness of population phenomena and their effects on individuals, families and society.

III. The Contribution of Science and Technology to Development

Recommendation No. 4

The Meeting,

Convinced of the importance of teaching science and technology so as to provide Arab individuals with the basic knowledge and skills they need for full personality development,

Conscious of the role of science and technology in enabling the members of modern society to deal with the conditions and achievements of human civilization and to keep pace with the knowledge explosion and modern technological progress,

Recommends to the Arab States that they:

1. adopt an integrated approach to science and technology curricula instead of confining their attention to the individual courses of a syllabus;
2. stress the training of academically and pedagogically qualified personnel, endeavouring to dissuade them from leaving the Arab region;
3. Arabize the terminology of science and technology in order to overcome the linguistic barriers to educational success;
4. promote the introduction into curricula of the principles and concepts of environmental education;
5. link science and technology education to productive work, moving beyond its theoretical dimensions and applying methods of independent and creative scientific thinking in the educational process;
6. spread scientific knowledge and attitudes through out-of-school activities, using the written and the audio-visual media and concentrating on young people and women;
7. introduce the principles of biotechnology and informatics into the educational process so as to modernize its methods and improve its results;
8. establish scientific and professional associations, which could organize meetings and competitions in their respective fields for secondary school students at the national and regional levels;
9. develop Arabic reference works in various branches of knowledge and standardize Arabic terminologies in order to overcome linguistic barriers to scientific expression and promote the translation of great scientific works from and into Arabic;
10. use the services of ARABSAT for the more effective dissemination of scientific knowledge and attitudes among Arabic language speakers and other peoples.

IV. The Contribution of Higher Education to Development, the Strengthening of Cultural Identity and the Improvement of the Education System

Recommendation No. 5

The Meeting,

Recognizing the importance of using national languages in all systems and at all levels of education as an important way of strengthening cultural identity and stemming the brain drain,

Considering that despite the major achievements of Arab education systems since the Abu Dhabi Conference the efforts made to meet the increasing social demand on education through the expansion of existing educational institutions have remained incommensurate with that demand,

Emphasizing the fact that development needs require greater use of advanced technology as well as participation in its production,

Conscious of the shortcomings of concentrating higher education institutions in urban areas and neglecting productive rural areas,

Appreciating the efforts made to promote scientific research in higher education institutions through the establishment of specialized research centres,

Recognizing the need to develop infrastructures for technologically based information systems, which are an essential tool for the effective planning of higher education and for interlinking it closely with overall development planning,

Calls upon the Arab States:

1. to step up their campaigns to Arabize higher education by implementing past recommendations in this regard;
2. to step up national efforts to diversify the structures of higher education systems so as to make them more responsive to labour needs and more democratic, and to invite them to experiment with alternative and innovative methods such as open universities, distance teaching and practical learning, while introducing the necessary safeguards;
3. take steps to ensure the optimum distribution of students between the humanities and social science on the one hand and science and technology on the other;
4. take measures to ensure equitable geographical distribution of higher education institutions between urban and rural areas;
5. assign more human and material resources to scientific research and training activities within and outside higher education establishments;
6. take all necessary measures and mobilize available resources for the development of modern information systems for higher education; make greater use of advanced technology in this field and participate in its production;

Invites UNESCO to :

7. help the Arab States to develop their research and training activities and provide them with the technical assistance they need to develop information infrastructures for higher education.

V. Regional and International Co-operation for Educational Development in the Arab States

Recommendation No. 6

The Meeting,

Believing in the importance of co-operation for providing the Arab States with useful information concerning the experiences of other regions, associating them fully with the progress achieved by the international community in education, science and technology, and establishing an international order based on justice and equality.

Conscious of the importance of Recommendation No. 28 adopted by the Fourth Conference of Ministers of Education and those responsible for Economic Planning in the Arab States, pursuant to which the Educational Innovation Programme for Development in the Arab States (EIPDAS) was established.

Emphasizing the importance of EIPDAS and its role in introducing educational innovations in the Arab region through co-ordination with Arab organizations, particularly the Arab Educational, Cultural and Scientific Organization, the Arab Bureau of Education for the Gulf States and other Arab organizations involved in educational innovation,

Recommends:

1. that UNESCO be invited to continue its support for the regional co-ordinating unit of EIPDAS and to provide this unit with the human and material resources it needs to strengthen the ability of EIPDAS to co-ordinate educational innovation efforts in the Arab region so that new methods corresponding to the needs of the region can be devised;
2. that the United Nations Development Programme be invited to contribute to the financing of EIPDAS activities just as it

contributes to other regional programmes;

3. that the Arab States be invited to make financial or material contributions to the EIPDAS work plan and to encourage their experts to participate in its activities, thereby giving Arab experts an opportunity to work together and become familiar with the background and needs of innovation, supporting the national institutions that participate in EIPDAS and helping them to play an active role in educational innovation at the national level;
4. that the Educational Innovation Programme be invited to:

   (a) set up an information system to facilitate the exchange of information on science and technology education and the findings of educational research among national institutions and regional and international educational organizations;
   (b) design and produce tools for educational evaluation;
   (c) publicize new experiments in reducing the cost of educational facilities and equipment;
   (d) follow up and publish the experiences of Arab and non-Arab Member-States in all areas of EIPDAS activity, particularly in basic education, science and technology education at primary school and all levels of teacher training, so that they can be consulted on educational innovation and improvement and on efforts to develop new teaching methods in the Arab States;
5. that UNESCO be invited to intensify its efforts to follow up the execution of regional projects, in particular the following:

   (a) the introduction of computers into Arab education systems;
   (b) distance higher education in the Arab region;
   (c) educational and cultural industries;
   (d) low-cost educational premises, facilities and materials.

VI. Education of the Arab People of Palestine

Recommendation No. 7

The Meeting,

Expressing its support for the Palestinian cause in its Arab and national dimension and for the Arab people of Palestine, inside and outside the occupied territories, so that they can prepare future generations to continue their legitimate struggle for self-determination, and seeking to implement the resolutions and recommendations of UNESCO regarding the education of the Arab people of Palestine,

Recommends:

1. that UNESCO intensify its efforts to ensure the protection of educational institutions at all levels inside and outside the occupied territories, to enable them to absorb the growing number of young Palestinian Arabs and to provide them with the educational resources they need to ensure the preservation of the Palestinian Arab identity in the educational process;
2. that the competent authorities in the Arab world be encouraged through support for their efforts, to find new ways of providing Palestinian Arabs with continuing education opportunities at all levels, such as the Open University of Jerusalem.

VII. **General Recommendations**

In the light of both the general and the detailed discussions that took place at the opening meetings, the Meeting adopted the following recommendations:

Recommendation No. 8

The Meeting recommends to UNESCO that it call for the establishment, in co-ordination with competent Arab organizations, of an inter-Arab body that would place the potential of ARABSAT (the Arab satellite) at the service of culture, education and science, so as to strengthen Arab cultural identity and the sense of belonging to the Arab nation all over the Arab world.

Recommendation No. 9

The Meeting recommends to UNESCO that it endeavour, with the help of Arab funds in particular and international funds in general, to finance and rationalize the execution of joint educational projects such as the project for introducing informatics, educational industries and low-cost school facilities and equipment into the educational process in the Arab region so as to keep in touch with the spirit of the times and to meet the urgent needs of an age of exponential growth in knowledge; and that it co-operate to this end with regional organizations such as ALECSO, the Arab Bureau of Education for the Gulf States, the Association of Arab Universities and similar Arab and international organizations.

Recommendation No. 10

The Meeting calls on UNESCO to strengthen the role and the resources of its Regional Office for Education in the Arab States as part of its commendable decentralization policy and in view of the impact that the Regional Office has had in the area, and to support it technically and materially by providing it with adequate funds and qualified human resources so that it can continue to carry out its responsibilities to the full in the service of education in the Arab world.

Recommendation No. 11

The Meeting invites the Arab States to search for new sources of funds with which to finance educational projects, programmes and plans, such as special taxes, voluntary contributions, contributions by local communities and external loans and grants, as a number of Arab States have reached the upper limits of what they can allocate to education under their regular budgets.

Recommendation No. 12

The Meeting invites UNESCO to consider the possibility of establishing a board of advisers from Arab Member-States, who would meet in a personal capacity to follow up and co-ordinate the Organization's efforts in literacy teaching and other educational development projects, while respecting UNESCO's rules and regulations in this regard.

Recommendation No. 13

The Meeting invites the Arab States to execute the recommendations of the International Conference on Education (Geneva) on secondary education and calls on UNESCO's Regional Office for Education in the Arab States to follow up such efforts through contacts and consultations with the Arab States and through its own plans, programmes and activities.

BIBLIOGRAPHY

UNESCO DOCUMENTS AND PUBLICATIONS*

1. *Convention on the recognition of studies, diplomas and degrees in higher education in the Arab States.* Paris, UNESCO 1978.
2. *Directory of teacher training institutions in the Arab States* (first elements). Paris, UNESCO, 1979, 63 p.
3. *Identification and elimination of sex stereotypes in and from school textbooks.* Some suggestion for action in the Arab World. Paris, UNESCO, 1983, 59 p. ED-84/WS/31.
4. *International convention on the recognition of studies, diplomas and degrees in higher education in the Arab and European States bordering on the Mediterranean.* Paris, UNESCO, 1976.
5. *Learning strategies for post-literary and continuing education in Algeria, Egypt and Kuwait.* Paris, UNESCO, 1988.
6. *Meeting of senior officials responsible for education in the Arab States.* Amman, Jordan, 22-26 June 1987. *Final report.* UNESCO/Mineduc, Jordan. Paris, UNESCO, 1987, 41 p. ED-87/WS/39.
7. *Orientation seminar for the Arabs States on the development of learning strategies for post-literacy and continuing education in the perspective of life long education.* Hamburg, 28 October — 8 November 1985. *Final report* 1986.
8. *Overview of the administrative situation in education in the Arab countries.* Paris, UNESCO, 1976.
9. *Perspectives of the development of the university in the Arab region from the present to year 2000* by Omer M. Osman. Paris, UNESCO, 1983, 44 p. (Papers on higher education No. 4) ED-83/WS/78.
10. *Regional conferences and educational development in Africa, Arab States, Asia and Latin America, Bombay, 1952 — Mexico City 1979* by F.L. Bartels. Paris, UNESCO, 1983, 187 p.

* Listing to illustrate the range of UNESCO documents and publications.

11. *The role of working mothers in early childhood education in Arab Republic of Egypt*. Paris, UNESCO, 1978, 31 p.
12. *Stocktaking of needs and resources relative to training and research*, Vol. I : *Australia, Hungary, Kenya, Syrian Arab Republic*. Paris, UNESCO, 1987, v p. (Papers on higher education No. 16).
13. *Status of teachers in the Arab region*. UNESCO/UNEDBAS, 1983, 120 p.
14. *Study of problems relating to drug abuse in Arab countries and the role of information and education in the prevention* by C. Ougouag. Paris, UNESCO, 1979, 36 p. EPDAR/1.
15. *Study on the general educational requirements for access to vocational education in the Arab Republic of Egypt*. Paris, UNESCO, 1980, 39 p. (Surveys and studies in adult education) ED-80/WS/6.
16. *Sub-regional workshop on teacher training in environmental education for the Arab States*., Bahrain, 25-30 January 1986. Bahrain, 1986, 100 p.
17. *Technical and vocational education in the Arab Gulf countries*. Paris, UNESCO, 1986, 89 p. (Studies in technical and vocational education No. 20) ED-86/WS/66.
18. *Technical education and vocational training in Egypt*. Paris, UNESCO, 1987.
19. *UNRWA 1989: Summary of the report of the Commissioner-General of UNRWA to the United Nations General Assembly for the period 1 July 1988 — 30 June 1989*. UNRWA.

See also UNESCO series *Educational studies and documents* (new series).

22

EDUCATION PROGRAMMES IN EUROPE, USA AND CANADA

OVERVIEW/HIGHLIGHTS

Priority: Humanistic and Cultural Dimensions within Modernized Educational Systems

The priorities set out for European region co-operation aim at developing:

* international education within the context of common European cultural traditions;
* educational programmes, teacher training and research in response to the new information and communication technologies.

Co-operation in Research and Development for Educational Innovation (CODIESEE)

Twenty-four research institutions in ten countries — Bulgaria, Greece, Hungary, Italy, Malta, Portugal, Romania, Spain, Turkey and Yugoslavia — are members of UNESCO's CODIESEE co-operative network.

Co-operation in Research and Development for Educational Innovation in South and South-East Europe (CODIESEE) promotes co-operation in educational research and development in three priority areas:

* primary education in the perspective of life-long education;

- education, technology and the world of work;
- the application of information technologies in education.

Higher Education

The European Centre for Higher Education (CEPES) was established in 1972, in Bucharest, Romania. Its goal is to promote co-operation, the exchange of information, research and development and regional and international mobility in higher education in the European region.

The main activities of the Centre include:

- *Publications*: the quarterly review *Higher Education in Europe*; monographs on national higher education systems; studies on key issues and statistical surveys.
- *Networks*: national information centres on academic mobility and mutual recognition of academic qualifications.
- *Meetings*: symposia, seminars, training workshops.

TABLE 22.1 UNESCO, 1984-1989: Technical co-operation in education

	Number of countries concerned	Resources utilized (M$)	Number of projects		
			Completed	On-going	In preparation
Total	5	0.6	8	1	—
Of which Least Dev. Countries	—	—	—	—	—

EDUCATIONAL PLANNING[1]

When we talk of education and national development, our thoughts turn away from Europe to Asia, Africa and Latin America, the areas where education is battling the dire enemies of development–poverty, hunger, ignorance and disease, where the comparatively poor three-quarters of humanity, despite their struggle for advancement are growing comparatively poorer. Why this neglect of Europe, of

1. Extracts from the opening address by the Deputy Director-General of UNESCO on 12 June 1967 at Finish Educational Planning Seminar organized by the Finnish National Commission for UNESCO and Seinajoki Summer University.

industrialized societies?

Dimension of the Problem

Perhaps because of the terminology we use in referring to so-called "developed" countries, perhaps because that terminology expresses a kind of deep-rooted belief that these societies have solved all their really serious problems in becoming comparatively rich and in growing steadily comparatively richer, we tend to discuss the role of their educational systems almost exclusively in terms of past achievements and historical models for others to follow. We sometimes forget that the process of development poses for the industrialized, highly-advanced quarter of our globe a whole new series of problems, no less urgent because they are more complex, no less dramatic because the goals are more difficult to define, and no historical models exist to help in defining them.

These problems are often different from those faced at earlier stages of development; they call no less imperatively for decision and choice. They pose questions more of purpose and direction than of competing priorities, yet they demand immediate attention. And the development problems of the industrialized countries, like those of all countries, involve fundamentally and centrally the education system through which the accumulated experience of the human race is not only preserved and transmitted, but also renewed and restored, and education is no less fundamental to their solution. . . .

The contribution which education is making to development in industrialized countries can and should be radically increased — by a deliberate effort to respond more adequately to three sets of growth problems: the economic problems of stagnation and under-development, technological unemployment and under-employment and skill shortages; the social problems of community wastes, use of leisure, youth and special education; and the international problems of economic equity and peace.

Such an increased contribution imposes a number of constraints on educational systems. It is these constraints and the adequacy of response to them that will determine, for industrialized countries and indeed for the entire world, the perspective of the future.

The first imperative that the industrialized country faces is the planning of education. Too long, in these countries, has planning been dismissed as a socialist fantasy or something smacking of under-development. It has been held that unplanned chaos is a mark of advancement, that the *laissez-faire* ostrich is the lamp post of development. These short-sighted ideas and misleading slogans now belong entirely to the past in the industrialized countries. One should take seriously the ominous paraphrase of Clemenceau's memorable words heard repeatedly in these countries : "Education has become too important to be left to the educator." Education is going to be planned for a variety of reasons. If educators do not plan education, it will be planned by the technocrat and the amateur.

Planning: A Tool, not a Master

This does not mean that planning is a substitute for innovation — the outpouring of the free human spirit. Nor does it mean that from somewhere up atop, decisions on education will be handed down. Educational planning is a tool, not a master. It simply enables the alternative educational paths, which are consistent with national objectives to be set forth clearly, and so provides a rational basis for decision by the appropriate authorities. Its necessity follows the recognition that in the complex demand and supply relationships that comprise education, the market mechanism is incapable of functioning adequately and can provide no assurance that anything like optimum investment will be reached. What are these demand and supply relationships? They include technological unemployment, disguised unemployment, skill shortages, bulging defence and service-producing sector demands and reconciliation of all these production constraints with the all important demands of consumption education. But this is not all.

In terms of policy, educational planning must also assist in reconciling such contradictions as the objective of economic growth with the principle of equalization of opportunity, international understanding and co-operation with the need for national defence and integration, the increased payoffs to educational investment in the developed regions of an industrialized country with the need to develop the backward areas and the nation's poverty pockets. . . .

In all educational planning there is one risk. In the absence of planning, this risk becomes a certainty. The risk is that a given strategy with its priorities for action might sacrifice what is most fundamental to all education — its content and quality. In the last resort, what justifies the high investments in education prevalent in industrialized countries and what makes education a dynamic factor of growth and development is quality as well as quantity, the standards of education as well as the output in numbers.

Referring to the serious migration of talent and skill — the "braindrain" — from Britain to the United States (it is estimated that 20 per cent of the annual output of 2,000 Ph.D. scientists so emigrate), Quintin Hogg, Minister of Science in the then Government, declared in the debate in the British House of Commons : "Our only prospect (to counter this outflow) is excellence in everything, politically, socially, economically and technologically. Three broad conditions are necessary for that. A first-class system of primary education is the first." And that is where educational planning begins.

The price of quality is eternal vigilance. The continuing breakthroughs in content and methods in many subjects make it vital to up-date teaching programmes in schools and colleges. The methods of learning and the techniques of instruction are also undergoing rapid change and need similar evaluation and up-dating. Referring to the use of new media by industrialized countries. Wilbur Schramm describes the development in graphic terms. Italy uses them to make up for a shortage of secondary schools; Japan to provide further education for young people who have full-time jobs; and Washington County (Maryland) in the United States is using six channels of closed-circuit television throughout the school day to make expert teachers available in the classrooms, where otherwise their specialities would not be taught as well.

A number of courses have always been considered necessary to general education courses — namely mathematics, history and science — not merely because of their practical value but also and primarily because of their contribution to the individual student's culture and mental discipline. This means that in contrast to earlier school days, when language and literature were compulsory and a choice had to be made between science and mathematics or history and arts, there is need today for the educationist to re-examine the content of general education. In view of the diversity of life and complexity of problems confronting contemporary man, why should not courses which have greater practical value and increasing social meaning be evolved to deal with these problems and likewise be considered compulsory. These matters have been under discussion long enough, now for over a century and a quarter. Grundtvig started the debate in 1840 in Denmark. Is it not time that they should pass from the desirable to the necessary and from there on to being considered compulsory, just as elementary education itself has passed from being considered desirable, to necessary and now to being compulsory?

Machinery for Innovation

More generally, curriculum reform and development require the urgent attention of industrialized countries as part of their educational policy and planning. The curriculum must be continuously adjusted to meet the new and different interests represented by their expanding school population. It must provide for the incorporation of new knowledge and for reinterpretation and reorientation of the existing corpus. It must enable the identification and nurturing of individual and unusual talent. It must mobilize the wealth of knowledge and experience of the teaching profession in the planning and execution of these tasks.

Indeed it is time for the very machinery for continuous reform, revision and updating of the content, the teaching techniques and the learning methods of education to be provided in every industrialized country. Such machinery must rely for its substance and technical guidance on the research work and potential of the universities. The university tradition of being in the vanguard of human knowledge, probing into the unknown and providing stimulation for young inquiring minds, as well as an association and interaction between different disciplines, places the university and its research resources for educational and scientific content and methods in a key position. And as the portals of the university open out to the community on the one hand, and industry and governmental research establishments on the other, the resulting cross fertilization can only enhance the service of the universities to the reform movement in education.

This contribution of universities is part of a larger contribution that they must make to growth in the industrialized countries. And that contribution is to humanize technology, to ensure that growth serves its objective, which is man.[2]

FUNCTIONAL ILLITERACY

In 1980, the UNESCO Institute for Education (UIE) in Hamburg

2. *Source*: *Unesco Features*, July (II) 1967.

(Federal Republic of Germany) launched an international research, training, documentation, publication and distribution project on the post-literacy and continuing education of newly-literate adults and children outside the school system in the developing countries, in the wider context of lifelong education. Between 1980 and 1987, as work proceeded with the publication of many studies, the training of some 300 key persons in over 90 developing countries and the compilation of a great variety of documents from those countries, the scope of the project was gradually extended to include the study of the problems of functional illiteracy in the industrialized countries. Two case-studies on functional illiteracy (in the Federal Republic of Germany and the United Kingdom) were published between 1982 and 1986, and samples of teaching materials and books on this subject were collected from 15 industrialized countries.

In December 1986, on the basis of these activities at UNESCO's request, the Institute organized the first working meeting on the problems of functional illiteracy for the Europe region (Technical Meeting of European Specialists on the Prevention of Functional Illiteracy and the Integration of Young People into Working Life). Published in 1987, the report of this meeting was followed by an analytical bibliography on the subject (*Functional illiteracy in industrialized countries: an analytical bibliography*, by Ursula Giere).

In November 1987, the General Conference of UNESCO at its twenty-fourth session approved of the recommendations of the Hamburg meeting, which called for the establishment of a network for the exchange of information and documentation on functional illiteracy in the industrialized countries concerned. Since then, a work plan and timetable of activities for this network have been prepared by UIE with UNESCO co-operation and assistance.

With an address list and a continuously updated documentary collection, UIE, in co-operation with UNESCO and within the limits of its resources, acts as a clearing-house for documents and other information and carried out promotional activities in the field of functional illiteracy. More specifically, it would serve as:

- a central contact point between sources and seekers of information;
- a resource centre, providing bibliographical and documentary reference services, besides publications and extracts in limited numbers;

— a study centre for visitors who may wish to consult its holdings for purposes of information and research;
— a contact agent between well-developed and embryonic or informal networks;
— an agent for promoting personal contacts between field workers (trainers), researchers and decision-makers throughout the region;
— a distributor, as far as possible, of appropriate experiments, methods and materials that are suitable for transfer to and from developing countries.

In the effort to promote a multidimensional exchange between network members and institutions, UIE would act, with UNESCO's support, both as principal agent and as intermediary, and its role should contract as exchanges between members become more intensive.[3]

On 4 June, 1984, one of the topics discussed by the Council of Europe and the Ministers of Education was, for the first time, the problem of functional illiteracy in the Member-States of the European Community. They reached a number of conclusions. Some concerned action which Member-States should take at the national level (mainly preventive measures at primary school; but also, for example, action in the field of adult education, when this problem fell within the province of ministries of education: literacy campaigns and distance education, for example). Other conclusions concerned the implementation of a community policy to combat illiteracy and to support national policies in this domain.

The Commission of the European Communities was assigned the main task of organizing the exchanges of information among national experts. Such exchanges should help to determine the causes and scope of the phenomenon, to analyse experiments undertaken in school systems and to define specific measures to combat illiteracy, particularly at primary school.

One of the first contributions of the Commission was the publication of a report on progress made in implementing literacy education policies in the European Community. This report was prepared in close co-operation with national officials in this field. Moreover, in addition to the first symposium organized in Athens,

---

3. *Source*: UNESCO Institute for Education (UIE), Feldrunnestrasse 58, D-2000 Hamburg 13, Federal Republic of Germany.

Greece, in September 1987, the Commission drew up a programme of action for *1988* which provided, *inter alia*, for the continuation of a working group which meets twice a year in Brussels, Belgium; study visits; the launching of a research project in a number of pilot schools in several Member-States; two specific studies (one on NGOs involved in the field of literacy education, the other on tests to gauge numbers of illiterates); the launching of an information campaign for decision-makers and support for, or organization of, meetings.

For example, following the 'Seminaire europeen sur la formation des formateurs d'adultes dans leur langue maternelle', held at the 'Centre universitaire de formation continue de l'universite d'Angers', France, in May 1987, a small number of European specialists and field workers met between 1 and 3 July, 1988 on the premises of FUNOC ('Formation pour l'universite ouverte de Charleroi') in Charleori, Belgium, to study syllabuses for the training of literacy teachers. Similarly, between 7 and 12 July, 1988 a Summer University was organized by the University of Toulouse-Le-Mirail, France, on the subject of 'Writing and first contact with the written word'. The purpose of that meeting, which was attended by European experts and observer-participants, was to collate the experience acquired in this field in Europe and to pass it on to teacher and trainers working in the field of literacy education for children and for adults in Europe.[4]

At a press conference in Washington DC (U.S.A.) in March 1988, Education Secretary William J. Bennet along with Labour Secretary Ann McLaughlin and Commerce Secretary C. William Verity announced the publication of '*The Bottom Line: Basic Skills in the Workplace*'. This booklet contains guidelines to help businesses, education and local governments identify workplace literacy problems and establish sound programmes to upgrade labour force literacy. Mr. Bennett said, 'It's not that business has a problem and they don't know it. . . , [but] education and training does not stop with the schools, and industry must take an active role in training workers today for the future'. Ann McLaughlin noted that '75 per cent of the United States work force for the year 2000 is already out of school' and added that 'Many of these workers are ill-prepared to deal with rapidly changing

4. *Source*: Commission of the European Communities, Directorate-General V, Employment Social Affairs and Education, run de la Loi 200, B-1049, Brussels, Belgium.

technology because they lack adequate basic skills'. Mr. Verity said: 'Basic workplace literacy is an absolute necessity if we are to increase our productivity, remain competitive in the global economy and continue to be a world leader'.[5]

On 25 May, 1988 a symposium was held in Washington D.C. (U.S.A.) on the Image of Print Media and the Problem of Functional Illiteracy in the United States. It was organized jointly by the Academic Advisory Council of the U.S. Government Printing Office and the Adult Literacy Initiative of the U.S. Department of Education. The administrative functions were handled by the Research and Engineering Council of the Graphic Arts Industry, Inc. Several prominent officials participated in the Symposium, at which many subjects were considered. Most dealt with the print media and reading and their relationship to functional illiteracy, — (The role of the graphic arts industry in the war on illiteracy; The economic impact of illiteracy on the graphic art industry; Print media image; Growing apathy towards print media and reading; Getting the youth of Nation to understand the importance of print media; Dealing with educators; primary, secondary, higher education; Programmes for business; programmes for the community; Dealing with functional illiteracy of employees; How to motivate employees to seek help).[6]

On 17 and 18 May, 1988 an international meeting of experts was held at the Adolf Grimme Institute in Marl, Federal Republic of Germany, (Expertinnen-Tagung Analphabetismus/Alphabetisierung). Its purpose was to consider the relations between the written word and the audio-visual media and to try to take stock to a decade in which these media have been used in action to combat illiteracy. The Adolf Grimme Institute is the media arm of the German Adult Education Association — (Deutscher Volkshochhul-Verband, DVV).[7]

'Learn to Read' is an adult literacy programme in the U.S.A. which

---

5. *Source*: Division of Adult Education, U.S. Department of Education, 400 Maryland Avenue, SW, Room 522, Reporters Building, Washington, D.C. 200202, United States of America.

6. *Source*: Research and Engineering Council of the Graphic Arts Industry, Inc., P.O. Box 639, Chadds Ford, PA 19317, United States of America.

7. *Source*: Adolf-Grimme Institute, Eduard-Weitsch-Weg 25, 4370 Marl, Federal Republic of Germany.

involves television, newspapers and telephone and is intended for illiterates who feel too embarrassed to tell anyone about their handicap. The rights of this series of 30 one-hour broadcasts initially produced by WXYZ, a subsidiary of the ABC station in Detroit, were bought by KET, the Kentucky Network, which has since increased the number of broadcasts and produced a telephone back-up service and two 32-page magazines of printed news. In this way an illiterate adult can watch a television programme without troubling anyone else, can telephone for help, and do exercises on the newspaper pages.[8]

EUROPE

Social Europe, report on the fight against illiteracy, Supplement 2/88.

This report[9] by the Commission of the European Communities reviews policy on combating illiteracy within the Community. In addition to sections on 'Background', 'Introduction', 'Conclusions' and 'Work programme 1987-88', there are two main sections as follows: 'Summary of the activities carried out by the Member-States to combat illiteracy, by (A) adapting teaching to overcome the learning difficulties of disadvantaged pupils; (B) reconsidering and developing the objectives of language skills at primary level; (C) preventing loss of skills; (D) initial and in-service teacher training; (E) literacy campaigns; (F) distance learning'; and 'Review of community action: (i) measures taken by the Commission to organize exchanges of information; (ii) taking account of the literacy problem in other community action'.

The report also contains a number of annexes: the 12 national reports submitted by the Member-States; the list of responsible national officials; the list of official authorities active in the fight against illiteracy; a bibliography on the measures taken by the Member-States of the European Community to combat illiteracy (January 1985 to January 1988); an account of the research co-ordinated in 1985 on behalf of EEC by the Belgian Association Lire at Ecrire, entitled *The*

8. *Source*: *Press to Read*, Vol. 3, No. 2, May 1988: American Newspaper Publishers Association Foundation. The Newspaper Center, Box 17407 Dulls Airport, Washington, D.C. 20041, U.S.A.

9. *Source*: Commission of the European Committees, Directorate-General for Employment, Social Affairs and Education, Rue de la loi 200, B-1049, Brussels, Belgium.

Paths of Illiteracy: and the conclusions of the Council of Ministers of Education.

CANADA

Adult Illiteracy in Canada: Identifying and Addressing the Problem. Statement by the Council of Ministers of Education (Canada), March 1988.

During the past decade it has become evident that approximately one-quarter of Canadians over the age of 18 are inadequately educated in terms of the requirements of an industrialized, high-technology society. Although precise figures are not available, it is estimated that some 1.5 million people in this group, many of whom have less than Grade 5 education, lack basic literacy skills. A further 3 million are considered functionally illiterate or under-educated because their levels of language and computational skills are judged inadequate for the demands of present day Canadian society.' In addition to an Executive Summary and a Preface, this document consists of sections on: the problem of adult illiteracy; addressing the problem (administrative and educational arrangements; curricula, methodology and training; institutions and agencies involved; adult participants: their requirements and aspirations); future directions.

Source: *UNESCO Adult education Information Notes*, No. 2-3/1988, Adult Education Section, UNESCO, Paris.

BIBLIOGRAPHY

UNESCO DOCUMENTS AND PUBLICATIONS*

1. *Building for school and community use five case studies.* (University groups in: Australia, Federal Republic of Germany, Greece, Kenya and USA). Paris, UNESCO, 1977, 122 p. (Educational studies and documents No. 26).
2. *Computers in technical teacher education in the United Kingdom.* Paris, UNESCO, 1984, 61 p. (Studies in technical and vocational education No. 9).

---

* Listing to illustrate the range of UNESCO documents and publications.

3. *The connection between formal and non-formal education at university level: the experience of the German Democratic Republic* by G. Roger, K. Jackstel and H. Mohle. Paris, UNESCO, 1982, 53 p.
4. *Content of general education in technical and vocational schools — USSR*. Paris, UNESCO, 1986, 19 p. (Studies in technical and vocational education No. 14).
5. *Convention on the recognition of studies, diplomas and degrees concerning higher education in the State belonging to the Europe region*. Paris, UNESCO, 1979.
6. *Determinants and options in the development of higher education in Poland*, by A. Josefowicz and J. Klucznski. Paris, UNESCO, 1980, 43 p.
7. *The Diversification of the educational field in Hungary*, by Peter Inkei with G'âbor Konez and G'âbor Poeze. Paris, UNESCO, 1988, 61 p.
8. *Economic aspects of special education : Czechoslovakia, New Zealand, United States of America*. (Special education). Paris, UNESCO, 1978, 152 p.
9. *Education of deaf children and young people* by the Centre for Total Communication, Denmark. Paris, UNESCO, 1987, 84 p. (Studies for special education No. 4).
10. *The Education of migrant workers and their families: Case studies undertaken for the National Commissions of Finland, France, Sweden, Yugoslavia*. Paris, UNESCO, 1978, 44 p.
11. *European regional workshop on the implications of the educational integration of disabled children and adolescents into normal structures of general education for teacher training*. Bologna, Italy, 30 September — 4 October, 1985. *Final report*. Paris, UNESCO, 1985, 11 p. + annexes ED-86/WS/31.
12. *Fourth Conference of Ministers of Education of Member-States of the Europe region* organised by UNESCO with the co-operation of United Nations Economic Commission for Europe. Paris, 21-27 September, 1988. *Final report*. Paris, UNESCO, 1989, 41 p. + annexes ED/MD/86.
13. *Handicapped children : early detection, intervention and education*. Selected case studies from: Argentina, Canada, Denmark, Jamaica, Jordan, Nigeria, Sri Lanka, Thailand and the United Kingdom. Paris, UNESCO, 1981, 142 p.
14. *Higher education and economic development in Europe,*

1975-1980 : a statistical and economic study, Vols. I + II. UNESCO/CEPES, 1983, 160 + 200 p.

15. *Higher education in Albania.* UNESCO/CEPES, 1986, 51 p. (Monographs series No 10).
16. *Higher education in Bulgaria* by Vladimir Topencharov. UNESCO/CEPES, 1983, 114 p. (Monographs series No. 4).
17. *Higher education in the Byelorussian SSR* by E.G. Bondarenko, V.T. Vodnev, A.P. Kandybo. UNESCO/CEPES, 1983, 72 p. (Monographs series No. 6).
18. *Higher education in the German Democratic Republic* by H.J. Scherlz. UNESCO/CEPES, 1983, 77 p. (monographs series No. 5).
19. *Higher education in Hungary*. UNESCO/CEPES, 1985, 107 p. (Monographs series No. 9).
20. *Higher education in the Ukrainian SSR* prepared by the Ministry of Higher and Specialized Secondary Education of the Ukrainian SSR. UNESCO/CEPES, 1985, 80 p. (Monographs series No. 8).
21. *Netherlands commissioned by the Ministry of Education and Science of the Netherlands.* UNESCO/CEPES, 1985, 72 p. (Monographs series No. 7).
22. *Higher education Norway*. UNESCO/CEPES, 1983, 72 p. (Monographs series No. 3).
23. *Higher education in Switzerland.* UNESCO/CEPES, 1984, 83 p. (Monographs series No. 1).
24. *Higher education in the United States* by Donald S. Doucette, UNESCO/CEPES, 1982, 83 p. (Monographs series No. 2).
25. *Innovations in teacher training in the field of agriculture — Federal Republic of Germany*. Paris, UNESCO, 1986, 118 p. (Studies in technical and vocational education No. 24) ED-86/WS/118.
26. *International convention on the recognition of studies, diplomas and degrees in higher education in the Arab and European States bordering Mediterranean.* Paris, UNESCO, 1976.
27. *Interuniversity co-operation in the Europe region* UNESCO/CEPES, 1981, 75 p.
28. *Media education in the United Kingdom : an annotated bibliography*, by L. Masterman. Paris, UNESCO, 1983, 72 p.
29. *Meeting of experts on co-operation in research and development of education in Europe.* Schloss Ottenstein, Austria, 11-13 May 1987. *Final report.* Austrian Commission for UNESCO, 1987,

26 p. + annexes. *Information document* by Hans-Wolf Rissom. Paris, UNESCO, 1987, 8 p. + annexes.

30. *Mobile units for vocational education — USSR*. Paris, UNESCO, 1986, 52 p. (Studies in technical and vocational education No. 18) ED-86/WS/45.
31. *National inventory on the status of women in the USSR*. Paris, UNESCO, 1977, 25 p.
32. *Study on portrayal of men and women in school textbooks and children's literature in the Ukrainian Soviet Socialist Republic*. Paris, UNESCO, 1982, 56 p., ED-82/WS/109.
33. *National Inventory on the studies of women in the USA*. Paris, UNESCO, 1976, 78 p.
34. *National inventory on the studies of women in the United Kingdom*. Paris, UNESCO, 1976, 51 p.
35. *Organisation of centralised workshops — USSR*. Paris, UNESCO, 1986, 51 p. (Studies in technical and vocational education No. 16) ED-86/WS/39.
36. *The Organisation of productive work in secondary technical and vocational education in the United Kingdom*. Paris, UNESCO, 1983, 78 p. (Studies in technical and vocational education No. 2).
37. *Policy, planning and administration of technical and vocational education in the Netherlands*. Paris, UNESCO, 1984. (Studies in technical and vocational education No.7).
38. *Progress report on graphic communication course experiments conducted in Belgium, China, Cyprus, Finland, Hungary, India, Korea (Republic), Philippines, Sweden*. Paris, UNESCO, 1984, ED-84/WS/61.
39. *The Role of working mothers in the early childhood education in Hungarian People's Republic*. Paris, UNESCO, 1977, 77 p.
40. *Stocktaking of needs and resources relative to training and research*, Vol. 1: *Australia, Hungary, Kenya, Syrian Arab Republic*. Paris, UNESCO, 1987, up (Papers on higher education No. 16).
41. *A Study of the portrayal of women and men in school textbooks and children's literature in France*. Paris, UNESCO, 1983, 66 p.

23

EDUCATION PROGRAMMES IN LATIN AMERICA AND CARIBBEAN

OVERVIEW/HIGHLIGHTS

Priority: Improving the Quality of Education

Initiated in 1979, the Major Project in the Field of Education in Latin America and the Caribbean provides an overall framework for the improvement of education in each country of the region.

The Major Project in the Field of Education: Ten Years of Co-operation

The objectives of the Major Project are as follows:

- To provide schooling for all children and young people of school age and to provide them with a general education lasting for at least eight to ten years, by combating grade repetition, drop-out and scholastic failure, and developing pre-school education.
- To eradicate illiteracy and extend adult education. The greatest advances have been made in the fields of basic education for adults, the further training of educational personnel and the education of women.
- To improve the quality and efficacity of education. Emphasis is placed on the modernization of school curricula through the introduction of subjects relating to peace and understanding among peoples and the inclusion of bilingual an intercultural educational projects.

The Major Project is implemented mainly through a system of regional co-operation networks comprising national projects and institutions:

- The Regional Network for Training, Innovation and Research in the Fields of Planning and Administration of Basic Education and Literacy Training Programmes (REPLAD). Activities launched by REPLAD, which covers nineteen Member-States and is active in the field of training, particularly training in educational planning and administration, include:

  — research and studies designed to facilitate decision-making;
  — production of training materials;
  — exchange of experience and information.

- The Regional Network of Innovation and Change in Preparation of Educators with a view to the improvement of Education (PICPEMCE), which groups twenty-two countries and is active in producing teacher training material and promoting the exchange of experience and information on new curricular dimensions.
- The Regional Network for the Training of Personnel and for the Back-up of Literacy Training and Adult Education Programmes (REDALF), which groups institutions in fifteen countries, as well as three regional or sub-regional bodies, the Latin American Council for Adult Education (CEAAL), CREFAL and CARCAE linking adult education centres in the Caribbean countries. Major activities include a thirteen-country regional research project on post-literacy training linked with productive work and the writing of instructional manuals for indigenous populations.
- A Regional Information System (SIRI) linking national information units in twenty-five countries of the region.

TABLE 23.1: UNESCO, 1984-1989: Technical co-operation in education

	Number of countries concerned	Resources utilized (M$)	Number of projects		
			Completed	On-going	In preparation
Total	25	23.7	55	60	22
Of which, Least Dev. Countries	1	4.4	5	3	—

SECOND MEETING OF THE INTERGOVERNMENTAL REGIONAL COMMITTEE, 1987

Background

Following a recommendation of the Second Inter-American Conference of Ministers of Education held at Lima in April-May 1956, an Inter-American Seminar on Overall Planning of Education (Washington, June 1958) was organized jointly by UNESCO and the Organization of American States. This seminar marked the inception of planning within the framework of the Major Project on the Extension and Improvement of Primary Education in Latin America. Its recommendations deal primarily with the problems relating to the organization and methods in the field of educational planning, administration and finance.

The Washington Seminar (1958) was followed by the Santiago de Chile Conference (March 1962) convened by UNESCO, the Economic Commission for Latin America and the Organization of American States. This conference studied the relationship between education and the economic, social and demographic situation in Latin America and defined the objectives of a ten-year plan of educational development in the region. Among the recommendations it adopted appeared the 'Santiago Declaration' which envisaged an increase in the proportion of national income earmarked for educational investment to 4 per cent by 1965.

The Conference of Buenos Aires (June 1966) concentrated its attention on the qualitative aspects of education such as contents, methods and evaluation.

The Second meeting of the Intergovernmental Regional Committee for the Major Project in the Field of Education in Latin America and the Caribbean organized by UNESCO, was held in Bogota from 24 to 28 March, 1987 at the generous invitation of the Government of Colombia. It was convened by the Director-General of UNESCO pursuant to resolution 2.1 adopted by the General Conference at its twenty-third session.

The Regional Conference of Ministers of Education and those responsible for Economic Planning of Member-States of Latin America and the Caribbean held in Mexico City in December 1979 unanimously adopted the Mexico City Declaration, which urges the use of all available resources and means to ensure the general introduction of complete primary or basic education for all children of school age to eliminate illiteracy and to intensify programmes designed to make provision for children of pre-school age who live in conditions of social deprivation. On that occasion the Member-States appealed to UNESCO to take the initiative of putting forward a major project designed to overcome the fundamental problems of education identified in the Mexico City Declaration.

Pursuant to resolution 1/07 adopted by the General Conference at its twenty-first session (1980), the Director-General convened an Intergovernmental Regional Meeting on the Objectives. Strategies and methods of Action for a Major Project in the Field of Education in Latin America and the Caribbean, which took place in Quito in April 1981. At that meeting, besides defining the objectives of the Major Project a: designing the initial planning phase for the implementation of the Major Project at the national level, the Member-States undertook to prepare national plans of action within the framework of the Project.

. The Executive Board of UNESCO at its 113th session (September 1981) approved the establishment of an interim Intergovernmental Regional Committee for the Major Project, which met in Castries (Saint Lucia) in July 1982, to examine the formulation and application of the national plans of action, establish priorities and lay down guidelines for the development of the Project at the regional level. The Saint Lucia meeting also drew up the draft statutes of the Intergovernmental Regional Committee, which were subsequently adopted in resolution 11.2 by the General Conference at its twenty-second session (1983).

The first meeting of the Intergovernmental Regional Committee for the Major Project in the Field of Education in Latin America and the Caribbean was held in Mexico City from 5 to 9 November 1984. It elected the Bureau of the Intergovernmental Regional Committee and defined the basic components of a Regional Plan of Action. It also reviewed the activities carried out by Member-States in implementation of their national plans of action and studied the current situation and new trends and prospects regarding subregional, regional and international co-operation in the framework of the Major Project.

This second meeting of the Intergovernmental Regional Committee had at its disposal a main working document entitled *Major Project in the Field of Education in Latin America and the Caribbean: Progress Made, Obstacles Encountered and Priorities for the Future* (ED-87/PROMEDLAC/3).

RECOMMENDATIONS

1. *Considering* the need for a general frame of reference for the development of the Major Project that, as well as ensuring continuity with the work carried out to date, specifies priorities for action in the near future,
2. *Bearing in mind* the content of the national documents submitted by Member-States, the documentation prepared by the Secretariat of UNESCO and, in particular, the discussions of this meeting on the progress made and the limitations and obstacles encountered in the course of past efforts, at both the national and regional levels, to attain the objectives of the Major Project,
3. *Reaffirming* the support of Member-States for the Major Project in the Field of Education in Latin America and the Caribbean and their commitment to its objectives.

The Intergovernmental Regional Committee for the Major Project in the Field of Education in Latin America and the Caribbean, at its second meeting held in the city of Bogota from 24 to 28 March, 1987, unanimously adopts the following guidelines:

General Considerations

1. The Committee was unanimous in recognizing that the efforts deployed and the progress made in the next four or five years will determine the degree to which Member-States of the region are able to achieve the objectives of the Project before the end of the century. To succeed in this will require a renewal of the commitment and the political decision necessary for the structuring and adoption of national plans of action and the mobilization of the human and material resources essential to the task.
2. The Committee, though not unaware of the constraints imposed by the economic difficulties facing the countries of the region, considers that the objectives of the Major Project are priorities that should not be affected by present financial restrictions. The chances of making progress in the building of societies that are juster, better integrated and more capable of a concerted effort to inject the necessary dynamism into the process of socio-economic, socio-political and socio-cultural development

depend in large measure on the ability to overcome deficiencies and cater to the basic educational needs of the population that the Major Project seeks to satisfy.

3. At the same time, this situation calls for efforts to increase the internal efficiency of education systems themselves and to introduce innovations to overcome the dichotomy between growing educational needs and increasingly limited resources.
4. The basic character of these needs and socio-educational deficiencies and the inescapable necessity of attending to them can and should constitute a meeting point for — and a factor making for consensus among — the different political and social sectors of the countries of the region, in view of education's fundamental role, in the context of development policies and strategies, in overcoming poverty and deprivation.
5. While all sectors should contribute to the task of tackling systematically and as a matter of priority the educational shortcomings and needs affecting children, young people and adults belonging to disadvantaged population groups in urban and rural areas, it is clear that it is for the public sector to play the leading role of stimulating the initiatives and efforts of society as a whole. In this connection, the Committee is convinced that pertinent and effective educational action for the disadvantaged presupposes the need for educational action proper to be systematically and explicitly linked with action at the national, regional and local levels in such fields as nutrition, health care, housing and employment, backed up by, among other things, systematic programmes of family and community education. In this task the private sector is called upon to make a greater and more systematic contribution.
6. With the aim of stepping up and ensuring the effectiveness of measures related to the objectives of the Major Project the Committee assigns considerable importance to the updating and effective implementation of the national plans of action or equivalent documents, to the expansion and strengthening of the co-operation networks already established under the Regional Plan of Action for the Major Project, and to increased and better co-ordinated international co-operation.

National Plan of Action for the Major Project

15. More meticulous planning, organization, administration,

monitoring and evaluation of literacy campaigns and programmes will also be necessary. Within them, but without abandoning the objective of the total eradication of illiteracy, attention should be focused on literacy education for adolescents and adults in the lower age-brackets and illiterate mothers. Programmes for mothers should include components of health, nutrition and early stimulation and incitement to families to encourage their children to stay on at school. It is also important to design, and extend the scope of special literacy programmes for ethnic groups, taking account of their linguistic differences and safeguarding their cultural identity. Another sector that merits special attention in literacy and adult-education programmes is that of handicapped persons or those with learning difficulties. Where low rates of illiteracy are achieved it will be necessary to develop appropriate policies to deal with residual illiteracy.

There is likewise a need for a close linkage between literacy work, specific job-training or work-skill schemes and socio-economic programmes or projects for community development. Such a linkage would provide an effective application of acquired knowledge and skills to everyday working, civic and family life. It would also serve as an incentive to adults to participate in and remain in literacy schemes, thereby preventing the substantial drop-out rates frequently noted.

16. The Committee is highly appreciative of the growing importance accorded to the problem of illiteracy in recent years by the governments of the region and the increase in the number of measures directly carried out or financed by ministries of education or bodies dependent on them. But it noted with serious concern that in many cases the efforts of the education authorities are not matched by those of all the economic and cultural sectors of the nation. This could reflect, in some instances, an inadequate collective awareness of the seriousness of the consequence of illiteracy for the individual and for society or else the fact that campaigns and programmes do not succeed in motivating and generating a concerted national effort linking ministries of education with other ministries and public bodies and involving the various social, economic, political and cultural sectors of national life. The Committee is convinced that the Major Project objective of eradicating illiteracy by the end of the century can be achieved by many countries if such a concerted national effort is

organized and takes practical shape in the short-term

17. In connection with this objective, the Committee feels that each Member-State, in accordance with its political organizations and specific characteristics, should pay special attention in its national plan of action to the following:

    (i) Strengthening national capabilities to enable countries to take on the responsibility of providing their own training in the formulation of comprehensive literacy, post-literacy and adult education strategies for cadres, especially central managerial and technical personnel, regional technical teams (at the State, departmental or provincial level) to put the policies and strategies adopted into effect; local personnel, co-ordinators, supervisors, activity organizers or community action workers; literacy workers and adult educators; and personnel in grassroots and community institutions and organizations for support work.

    (ii) Incorporating post-literacy programmes dealing with civic and social rights and responsibilities and the occupational or employment needs of the newly literate, school drop-outs and functionally illiterate adults. The design, adoption and implementation of these post-literacy programmes, and of their content and methodology, calls for the joint involvement of — among others — ministries or secretaries of education and labour, bodies responsible for economic planning, employers' associations and naturally those for whom they are intended.

    (iii) strengthening formal and informal basic-education activities for adults — a measure that should play a key role in meeting the educational needs of poverty-stricken adults. Such a measure could be achieved with the assistance of other government agencies concerned with such matters as health, housing and rural development and of an increasingly influential body of grassroots organizations and non-governmental institutions promoting education.

    (iv) Action concerning the objective relating to the effectiveness and quality of education.

18. It was basically with a view to ensuring the right to education and equal educational opportunities of children, young people and

adults in Latin America and the Caribbean that the Major Project was launched. For that reason it was considered necessary, in both the strategies and the programme of action, to link the objectives concerning school enrolments and literacy teaching and adult education closely with those concerning the relevance, quality and effectiveness of the educational services provided.

19. The Major Project should be shaped to overcome the dichotomy between quantity and quality in two basic ways. On the one hand, the extension of coverage and the reduction of the high failure and drop-out rates necessarily implies a set of qualitative changes in educational provision that promote and ensure more relevant and better adapted pedagogical practices. On the other hand, improvements in quality presuppose a policy with regard to the allocation of resources that gives priority to those sectors of the education system catering for the broad masses of the population, offsetting the frequently observable differentiation between an elitist education and an education marked by deficiencies that make any guarantee of quality impossible.
20. The Committee has taken the opportunity to note some of the efforts undertaken in the majority of the countries of the region to improve quality, efforts promoted in some cases by official educational bodies themselves and in others by private institutions or groups. Outstanding among these efforts are those aimed at adapting curricula to regional and local conditions and to the special characteristics of children and adults belong to rural and deprived urban populations, without losing sight of national goals and objectives, such as the establishment of links between general education and the world of work. The Committee also appreciates the initiatives taken to increase the functionality of teaching and its effect on personal development through education relating to population issues, environment, health, nutrition, human rights and international understanding.
21. Bilingual intercultural education for indigenous peoples has made strides as a strategy for highlighting an important element of national cultures and at the same time catering for the needs and special characteristics of these groups. Mention should also be made of the experiments being undertaken in the design, production and utilization of low-cost teaching materials employing craft techniques and locally available resources and of the growing interest in participatory approaches and the use of

modern information technologies, especially those employed in distance-education experiments, which have yielded encouraging results in a number of countries in the context of teacher upgrading. More emphasis on the teaching of science and scientific methods in the education of children is another important strand in educational innovation.

22. However, these and many other initiatives are still no more than microexperiments, innovative exercises by individual institutions or groups, in some cases finding barriers or restrictions impeding their gradual extension and seemingly failing as yet to constitute a marked trend towards change or improvement. The Committee therefore recommends that Member-States give special attention, in drawing up and executing national plans of action, to the gradual spread of innovations designed to enhance the relevance, quality and efficiency of pre-school and primary or basic education for children and literacy and post-literacy programmes for adolescents and adults.

(i) Of crucial importance in this task of improving quality are establishments for the pre-and in-service training of teachers, headmasters, supervisors, administrators and planners, educational research and experimentation centres and programmes, child and adult educators, parents and the public and private agents within local communities.

(ii) Generally speaking, the Committee deems it desirable to encourage education personnel to become more closely and actively involved in all the processes concerned with the formulation and implementation of the national plans of action and the evaluation of their achievements. This calls for greater and more accurate knowledge on the part of such personnel and of student teachers of the socio-educational needs catered to by the Major Project, of its objectives and of the measures that must be taken in order to attain them. Establishments responsible for the initial, further and in-service training of education personnel, professional associations and the mass media all have a key responsibility in this field.

(iii) However effective teacher participation is dependent largely on improvement of the teachers' technical skills to match up to their job requirements. It will therefore be necessary to encourage close co-ordination between educational-research institutions and teacher-training establishments and schemes.

(iv) Strategic devised to improve teachers' professional and social status by finding ways of attracting the society's most talented members to the teaching profession and incentives to teachers to work in disadvantaged areas are a *sine qua non* if the quality of education is to be improved.

23. The achievement of this objective is closely linked to the introduction of reforms in educational organization and administration that would ensure their adequate functioning and permanent incentives for improvement in the quality of education. In this regard the Committee notes with satisfaction the great strides that have been made in recent years in some countries in decentralization, educational regionalization, microplanning and the introduction of new and modern management techniques designed to increase the efficiency and relevance and widen the participation of local agents in the education process while bearing in mind the need to maintain quality on the national level.
24. The difficulties most commonly found in these processes stem from the need to train local staff to undertake the new tasks efficiently and also from the need to define adequate countervailing strategies to avoid intensifying inequalities between regions.
25. The need to design reliable systems for evaluation of the quality of teaching is also becoming more and more important for equipping education authorities with firm diagnoses on which to base their decisions.
26. Pursuant to the above, the Committee invites Member-States to make a more systematic and intense effort to meet the objective of the Major Project relating to quality of education by including in their national plans of action specific strategies and programmes encompassing and dovetailing all the factors, both internal and external, that determine quality, paying particular attention to the relevance and content of the educational services supplied, innovations in teaching methods, teacher training, greater recognition for education professionals and improvement of their working conditions, the design and comprehensive use of

school buildings, and financial assistance for pupils, whether children, young people or adults. belonging to disadvantaged sectors of the society.

Regional Plan of Action for the Major Project

27. The formulation and unanimous adoption of a Regional Plan of Action for the Major Project by the Intergovernmental Regional Committee at its first meeting (Mexico City, November 1984) was a decisive step towards promoting, systematizing and boosting, through horizontal co-operation, a joint and mutually supportive effort by the Member-States of the region to achieve the objectives of the Project. At this second meeting the Committee notes with the greatest satisfaction the progress that has been made in implementing and developing the first phase of the Regional Plan, with the participation of numerous national bodies and with UNESCO's co-operation.
28. At its first meeting, as well as specifying the objectives, fields of application and practical priorities of the Regional Plan, the Committee made provision, among the basic operational mechanisms, for a system of regional networks for horizontal co-operation, made up of national institutions and projects engaged in activities in the priority areas of the Plan and a Regional Information System for the Major Project. The Committee considers that the effectiveness and relevance of the networks' activities will depend on the extent to which they constitute a means of achieving the objectives of the Major Project rather than an end in themselves.
29. In their first phase, both the system of networks and the Information System have begun to be organized and to operate with promising results.
30. The system of networks is composed of the Regional Network for Training, Innovation and Research in the Planning and Administration of Basic Education and Literacy Programme (REPLAD), the Regional Network of the Programme on Innovation and Change in the Training of Educators for the Improvement of the Quality of Education (PICPEMCE) and the Regional Network for the Training of Personnel and Specific Support for Literacy and Adult Education Programme (REDALF).

31. The Regional Information System (SIRI) set up to facilitate follow-up of the implementation of the Regional Plan and of the national plans of action provides information that is useful for the evaluation of activities developed in order to attain the objectives of the Major Project and comprises a Regional Co-ordinating Centre, Subregional Operational Units and National Co-ordinating Units for information, all of which are interconnected. The information submitted to this meeting regarding the progress of the Major Project at regional, subregional and national levels was largely made possible by this system.
32. Reaffirming the vitally important role to be played by both the system of co-operation networks and the Regional Information System in the development of the Major Project and for achieving systematic co-operative action by Member-States for the attainment of its objectives, the Committee deems it appropriate to formulate a number of recommendations, which it hopes may help to strengthen those systems and improve their functioning and activities.

    (i) The longevity, scope and effectiveness of the activities and results of these systems depend in large measure on the integration of the institutions, programmes and activities composing the networks and the Information System into the Major Project's national plans of action and into such machinery as may be set up for their implementation. It is also necessary to set up national networks that are sufficiently flexible for the design and execution of innovative activities, that co-ordinate their activities within the regional networks and whose results are used to the greatest extent possible by national education systems.

    (ii) The Committee considers four aspects of the development of the regional co-operation networks to be partially noteworthy. The first is the progressive increase in the number of Member-States whose institutions form part of the networks. The second is the need to ensure that the bodies responsible for co-ordination have sufficient convening authority. The third concerns the need to guarantee the greatest possible compatibility of objectives and co-ordination of activities among institutions and programmes in order to avoid overlapping and guarantee complementarity and pooling of results. The aim is to achieve a critical mass of innovative experiences at the national, subregional and regional levels that will have a decisive impact on the attainment of the objectives of the Major Project. The fourth is the desirability of further progress in the appropriate distribution of the networks' responsibilities, tasks and resources for the development of projects promoted by their member institutions, in accordance with the needs identified by the participating countries.

(iii) In this connection, basic practical issues such as repitition and drop-out, the development of low-cost teaching aids, adapting the supply of education to the needs and characteristics of underprivileged or disadvantaged groups, interlinking formal with non-formal education and education with work, and community participation could constitute areas of common interest for co-operative action on the part of the networks.

(iv) Some higher-education establishments have become involved in the networks. In view of the role they have to play, essentially in the training of human resources and in educational research, the Committee recommends that their participation in those networks should be gradually increased. The Regional Centre for Higher Education in Latin America and the Caribbean (CRESALC) will be responsible for compiling and disseminating information and documentation relating to the activities of the higher-education institution under the Major Project. In addition, CARNEID will be responsible for ensuring that the Caribbean countries have greater access to the regional networks.

(v) The Committee notes that, among the Regional Plan's priority fields of action and programmes, topics relating to 'physical infrastructures and school buildings' and to 'socio-educational research' have so far not been accorded attention by the system of networks. It considers that they should be taken up as quickly as possible, drawing on the potential of the countries of the region in terms of experience and human resources.

(vi) With regard to the Regional Information System (SIRI), mention has already been made of the speed with which its structure, machinery and instruments were devised and with which it was set in motion. However, the real effectiveness of the system will depend essentially on improvements in the national education information systems. National information systesm need to be strengthened for two reasons: firstly, to ensure that countries possess full, objective and accurate information on the quantitative and qualitative development of education, to serve as a surer and more relevant basis for the formulator of educational policies and plans and for decision-making; and secondly, to provide information on the way the Major Project is progressing in the region, the subregions and among groups of countries.

International Co-operation for Development of the Major Project

33. The Intergovernmental Regional Committee has studied with satisfaction and assessed very highly the continuity, growing scale and efficiency of the support UNESCO, at the request of Member-States, has provided for regional, subregional and national action carried out under the Major Project in Latin America and the Caribbean, especially the comprehensive way in which it has responded to the requests submitted to it by the first meeting of the Committee with regard to the application of the Regional Plan of Action for the Project. With regard to this co-operation, mention should be made of the efficient part played by the Regional Office of Education in Latin America and the Caribbean (OREALC), the Major Project Support Unit in Quito, the Subregional Office for Central America, the Office of the UNESCO Representative in the Caribbean, and the Caribbean Network of Educational Innovation for Development (CARNEID). As well as giving continual support to national action under the Project, UNESCO has co-operated in an outstanding way in the establishment of the Regional System of Networks and the Regional Information System and in supporting their operations, in compliance with the request made by the Committee at its first meeting.
34. The Committee likewise expresses its gratitude to other United Nations bodies such as ECLAC, FAO, UNFPA, UNDP, UNEP, UNICEF, WFP and the World Bank for the actions they undertook, individually or jointly with UNESCO, in areas related to the Major Project. It also wishes to express its appreciation to

regional co-operation bodies such as OAS, IDB and OEI, to subregional co-operation bodies such as CARICOM, CECC, and SECAB, and to regional non-governmental bodies such as CARCAE, ALER, CEAAL and others.

35. The Committee wishes to make special mention of the generous co-operation of the Spanish Government, which has provided large-scale financial support for regional, subregional and national activities under the Major Project and for the co-operation and information-network systems; the Committee hopes that other countries outside the region will join in this co-operative effort in the near future.

36. The Committee also wishes to express its gratitude to the Governments of Italy and the Federal Republic of Germany for their assistance with the Major Project activities and the Arab countries, which are providing substantial support through AGFUND for specific projects in various countries of the region.

37. The Committee formulates the following guidelines and recommendations regarding co-operation:

(i) While hoping that the above-mentioned bodies will maintain and step up their assistance and that their ranks will be swelled by many more, the Committee feels that one general point should be made about assistance, namely the frequently emphasized need for greater consultation and co-ordination with regard to the action to be taken by the bodies concerned, both regionally and nationally. Given the financial conditions prevailing both in organizations engaged in international, regional and subregional assistance work and in the countries of Latin America and the Caribbean themselves, this is not only desirable but imperative.

(ii) The Committee wishes to stress the importance it attaches to horizontal co-operation as a means of furthering achievement of the objectives of the Major Project. During the next two years the Committee wishes to encourage measures for the exchange of specialists within the region for the exchange of publications and translations of material of relevance to the problems facing certain countries and for the undertaking of joint studies on the problems impeding attainment of the objectives of the Major Project. The activities planned can be carried out effectively through the regional networks, which already have a good many achievements to their credit in that area, and through subregional structures.

(iii) The Committee also agrees that, alongside the activities to be carried out through the regional networks, regional and subregional projects should be developed for submission to international co-operation bodies with the aim of supporting and speeding up Member-States' own efforts. In this connection, the needs already identified in respect of literacy teaching, pre-school education, the training of education personnel, the production of textbooks and teaching materials, basic educational facilities, and research on the problems impeding attainment of the objectives of the Major Project are concrete examples of areas in which groups of projects could be developed at the regional and subregional levels with a view to obtaining international co-operation.

(iv) The Committee recognizes that, under the financial conditions prevailing both in organizations engaged in international, regional and subregional assistance work and in the countries of Latin America and the Caribbean, there is a need for greater consultation and co-ordination of efforts among the organizations involved with a view to their maintaining and stepping up their activities at the regional, subregional and national levels. To that end, the Committee intends to contribute to this process of consultation and co-ordination by promoting in the coming biennium among other initiatives — a regional meeting of representatives of the Member-States of the region, of other Member-States form outside the region and of organizations engaged in assistance work, in order to pursue further the dialogue on their possible contributions to the attainment of the objectives of the Major Project. The Committee calls on UNESCO and UNDP to support the holding of this meeting, to which the Member-States of Latin America and the Caribbean attach the highest importance.

(v) In view of the obstacles resulting from the economic crisis that are impeding execution of the national plans of action in the countries of the region, the Committee renews its appeal to UNESCO to continue extending vigorous assistance for the preparation and development of strategies, programmes and projects designed to ensure optimum utilization of the basic facilities, means and resources available for education in

Member-States and for the preparation of specific projects likely to secure support from funding agencies.

(vi) Finally, the Committee requests the Director-General of UNESCO, in the preparation of the Draft Programme and Budget for 1988-1989 (document 24C/5), to provide for activities conducive to the continuation and strengthening of the Organization's technical support for both national and regional activities under the Major Project in the Field of Education in Latin America and the Caribbean, having regard to the priorities set out in this recommendation.

BIBLIOGRAPHY

UNESCO DOCUMENTS AND PUBLICATIONS*

1. *Aspects of training and research in higher education with case studies on India and Venezuela.* Paris, UNESCO, 1987, 308 p. (Paper on higher education No. 19).
2. *Bulletin.* The major project in the field of education in the Latin America and the Caribbean UNESCO/OREALC, No. 1, April 1986.
3. *Handicapped children: early detection, intervention and educative.* Selected case studies from : Argentina, Canada, Denmark, Jamaica, Jordon, Nigeria, Sri Lanka, Thailand and the United Kingdom. Paris, UNESCO, 1981, 142 p. ED/MD/63.
4. *National inventory on the studies of women in Brazil.* Paris, UNESCO, 1977, 52 p.
5. *Outflow of professionals with higher education from and among states parties to the regional convention on the recognition of studies, diplomas and degrees in higher education in Latin America and the Caribbean.* Paris, UNESCO, 1984, 54 p. (Educational studies and documents No. 45).
6. *Regional conferences and educational development in Africa, Arabs States, Asia and Latin America : Bombay 1952 — Mexico City 1979* by F.L. Bartels. Paris, UNESCO, 1983, 187 p.

* Listing to illustrate the range of UNESCO documents and publications.

7. *Regional convention on the recognition of studies, diplomas and degrees in higher education on Latin America and the Caribbean.* Paris, UNESCO, 1974.
8. *Regional expert meeting in Latin America and the Caribbean on the role of teachers of educational science in the improvement of teacher training at all levels and the improvement of the education system as a whole*, Caracas, CRESALC, 1-5 November, 1982. *Final report.* Paris, UNESCO, 1983, 28 p. ED-82/CONF.627.
9. *Regional meeting on education concerning the problems associated with the use of drugs in Latin America and the Caribbean.* Buenos Aires, Argentina, 1-7 July 1982. *Final report.* Paris, UNESCO, 1982, 16 p. ED/MD/70.
10. *Second meeting of the intergovernmental regional committee for the major project in the field of education in Latin America and the Caribbean*, Bogota, 24-28 March 1987. Paris, UNESCO, 1987.
11. *Study on the general educational requirements for access to vocational education in the Republic of Argentina.* Paris, UNESCO, 1980, 55 p. ED-80/WS/8.
12. *Trends and prospects in the development of higher education in Latin America and the Caribbean* by Juan Carlos Tedesco. Paris, UNESCO, 1983, 47 p. (Papers on higher education No. 3) ED-83/WS/75.

24

EDUCATION PROGRAMMES IN ASIA AND THE PACIFIC

OVERVIEW/HIGHLIGHTS

Within the regional co-operation programmes such as APEID and APPEAL new partnerships are stimulating educational development.

Educational Innovation for Development: APEID

Twenty-eight Member-States of the region participate in the Asia and the Pacific Programme of Educational Innovation for Development (APEID). Established in 1973, APEID aims to:

* strengthen capabilities and self-reliance in educational matters;
* find innovative solutions to educational problems and achieve development goals.

At the heart of APEID are its 186 Associated Centres — specialized educational institutions nominated by participating governments — which form a network for the exchange of experience and ideas. UNESCO's principal function is to ensure the programme's smooth operation.

To focus its activity on critical issues, APEID selects special themes, or 'Joint Innovation Projects' (JIPs) in which a number of Associated Centres are interested.

A recent JIP dealt with ways of improving the quality of primary education. Work has begun on the preparation of an inventory of common problems and possible solutions to them. When this phase of the work has been completed, experts from the Associated Centres will meet to assess results and agree upon follow-up measures.

TABLE 24.1: UNESCO, 1984-1989: Technical co-operation in education

	Number of countries concerned	Resources utilized (M$)	Number of projects		
			Completed	On-going	In preparation
Total	31	62.7	101	127	43
Of which, least Dev. Countries	11	30.3	27	44	17

MAJOR EDUCATION PROGRAMMES

Karachi Plan (1960)

Around the beginning of the 1950s, the development of education appeared as an essential pre-requisite for the raising of living standards and primary education became top priority. In 1952, UNESCO organized in Bombay a regional conference on free and compulsory education in South Asia to determine the region's main needs and problems in setting up compulsory primary education. Studies and thorough surveys of the situation in the various countries of the region were undertaken and their results transmitted to the representatives of seventeen Asian Member-States at a meeting convened by UNESCO in the capital of Pakistan during the last days of 1959 and the early days of 1960. It was this conference that adopted the plan commonly known as the "Karachi Plan" which set out to establish at least seven years of free and compulsory education for all Asian children by 1980. This Plan foresaw a total enrolment of 156 million children and adolescents, implying the hiring of more than five million teachers and the building of some five million classrooms, the total cost being estimated at 56,000 million dollars.

The Karachi Plan was a landmark in the evolution of education in Asia and as a reference document, it was also destined to facilitate concerted international action.

Tokyo Conference (1962)

In 1962, it was extended and complemented by the Tokyo Conference of ministers and high officials of education and economic planning in 18 Asian Member States. It was extended so as to cover all levels of education — primary, secondary, higher, technical, etc. — without overlooking adult education; and complemented so that it could be integrated into the national development plan of each country which would have to devote about 5 per cent of its gross national product to education in 1980.

Participants in the Tokyo conference asked UNESCO to help them establish long-term educational plans and to derive from these plans a "draft Asian model" to be submitted to a second conference of ministers.*

Bangkok Conference (1965)

Like the one at Tokyo, this conference was convened jointly by UNESCO and the United Nations Economic Commission for Asia and the Far East (ECAFE). It met at Bangkok in November 1965 to elaborate principles and criteria to help Member-States plan the development of education on a national level. It examined the "draft model" which indicated requirements for development expressed in quantitative terms, proposed criteria, objectives and an evaluation of foreseeable expenses and recommended that it serve as a guide to the goals of each country and a way of verifying them. The conference also took up such questions, diverse but indissolubly linked in the context of an overall educational policy, as literacy, the access of girls and women to education, school drop-outs, agricultural education, higher education, the teaching of science, long-term planning, educational administration, and the training or status of teachers.

Regional Offices and Institutions

A regional office, destined to help all Asian Member-States applying the Karachi Plan, was created in Bangkok in 1961. An integral part of the UNESCO Secretariat, it performs functions in research and educational documentation and information and maintains liaison with ECAFE. It also co-ordinates the activities of the three specialized centres founded in 1962, upon the request of States participating in the

Plan and with UNESCO's aid, by India, Indonesia (later transferred to Ceylon) and the Philippines.

The Asian Institute for Educational Planning and Administration (now National Institute of Educational Planning and Administration – NIEPA) was established in New Delhi for organizing training and study courses and meetings of experts.

The Institute for School Building Research, which operated at Bandung before moving to Colombo, has carried out many remarkable studies of specific problems faced by countries in the dry and wet zones or by countries vulnerable to storms, typhoons or cyclones. Many national development groups have been set up by Member-States.

As for the Institute for Training Teacher Educators at Quezon City, it developed a system bringing together about twenty associated institutions. This enables the big national teacher training schools to keep abreast of the most recent educational concepts and techniques. It also organizes training courses.

Collaboration between UNESCO and Other United Nations Bodies

This collaboration has been developed to further education. The Organization was given charge of the project concerning the creation of a higher teacher training school in Kabul — a project receiving financial assistance from the United Nations Development Programme (UNDP, Special Fund sector). Under an agreement reached in 1964 with the International Bank for Reconstruction and Development in which the latter agreed to grant loans to develop education, UNESCO sent technical assistance missions to the governments of Afghanistan, Pakistan and the Philippines. It assisted in the supplying of aid by the United Nations Children's Fund (UNICEF) to several Asian States. Various such other projects have been started.

Science Teaching

To facilitate and improve teaching, the Organization has published a Source Book for Science Teaching, brought out in many Asian languages, which contains information needed for a broad range of experiments that can be done with local materials and, consequently, are of particular interest to developing countries. It also started on a regional level a pilot project for the teaching of chemistry in secondary schools. Destined to increase the number of qualified teachers through intensive use of audio-visual aids, this experiment began in 1965 at Bangkok.

While necessary for economic progress, a mere increase in the number and quality of science teachers is not enough. To achieve true independence, a country must have its own researchers, engineers and technicians and it must be able to undertake in its own laboratories and factories the research and the applications that it chooses. This is why UNESCO endeavours to help its Member-States in establishing their policy of scientific and technological planning. Since 1959, it has organized regional meetings of specialists for this purpose and it has sent advisory missions to several countries requesting them.

Social Sciences

In the social sciences, as in the natural sciences, problems of development took on utmost importance at a certain point. At the start, UNESCO limited its activities to countries where study of the social sciences was already well-advanced. But beginning in 1950, it sent survey missions to Indonesia and Pakistan while it undertook studies on such subjects as social tensions in India or on the consequences of technical progress, industrialization and urbanization on populations. In 1953, a social scientist was attached to the science co-operation office in New Delhi and, in 1956, a regional centre was established in Calcutta to encourage research on problems of economic and social development in thirteen Asian Member-States. Transferred to New Delhi in 1961, this centre carries out various studies on evolution of social structures, social aspects of education or of small industries, new patterns of leadership in rural areas, etc.

INTERGOVERNMENTAL MEETING OF EXPERTS ON THE MEANS OF IMPROVING THE QUALITY OF EDUCATION IN ASIA, 1964

Introduction

The Meeting organized by UNESCO in collaboration with the

Government of the Philippines, was held in the WHO Building (Manila) from 21 to 28 April, 1964, with the participation of experts from seven Member-States from Asia. (1. Afghanistan, 2. Ceylon, 3. India; 4. Iran, 5. Japan, 6. Pakistan, and 7. Philippines) and four experts from other regions (France, Union of Soviet Socialist Republics, United Kingdom and United States of America).

Recommendations

I. *Meaning of quality in education and the relationship to the aims and objectives of education in the present technological age.*

The following conclusions were arrived at:

(a) Quality in education depends on the basic principle that all educational institutions should be conducted solely to ensure the spiritual, moral, mental and physical development of their pupils and to promote the advancement of knowledge.
(b) When a senior educational institution assumes university status, that is to say, engages in specialist teaching at the highest level and in research, the degree which it awards should be reasonably equivalent in standard to the best degree offered elsewhere.
(c) The pressure of admissions of existing Asian universities should not be allowed to become so great that they inevitably bring about a lowering of academic standards.
(d) In each country there should be an agency working on behalf of the government which would be empowered to ensure that university standards are maintained and withhold recognition from any institution which laid claim to university status but failed to achieve those standards.
(e) There should be sound and effective alternative routes in education so that those who can pursue their studies in an institution other than a university may do so in other appropriate institutions and so avoid the overcrowding of universities.
(f) Standards should be raised to the highest level in the training of those who in the next generation will teach in universities and institutions of higher education, including teacher training colleges.
(g) The secondary schools supply the universities and provide the model management of industry and commerce. In this field,

therefore, quality must also be maintained at all costs.

(h) A proper balance must always be kept between development in higher education and development at the primary stages, and to ensure this every major educational advance should be preceded by a detailed study of such vital matters as the money available, building facilities, teacher supply, salary structure and the manpower demands of the several branches of the nation's economy.

II. *Teachers as focal figures in improving standards. Recruitment, selection, training, status, conditions, etc.*

(a) Teachers' salaries in both public and private schools be comparable to those with men and women which their length and quality of training could command in other branches of the public service.

(b) Teachers should be employed full time in their respective institutions and their conditions of service, such as pensions, holidays, working hours and conditions of tenure, should be made sufficiently attractive to encourage recruitment to the profession, and the burden of their duties should in many instances be reduced.

(c) There should be a basic salary scale for all teachers, differentiated according to the length and quality of experience.

(d) The training of secondary school teachers who will have to teach at the pre-university level should be a matter for the universities, and colleges for the training of primary school teachers should also fall within the ultimate academic jurisdiction of the universities, which should be responsible for the trainees' final certifications as teachers.

(e) In all public systems of education there should be lively and stimulating activities for service training of a kind that will continually revitalize the teaching in the area.

(f) The quality of teaching is related to the number of hours of instruction given daily by the teacher and the number of pupils in each class. Research should be carried out to determine optimum teaching loads and class sizes.

(g) Secondary school teachers should have a minimum of four years of education beyond the secondary stage, but in a period of rapid expansion this period may have to be considerably reduced.

(h) In the teacher education course, academic and professional studies should be appropriately balanced. Each potential teacher should undergo a course in research methodology with special emphasis on action research, and should have undertaken the preparation of a comprehensive research paper.

(i) To recruit teachers of high quality, training scholarships should be awarded on a competitive basis. Such scholarships should be equal in value to those offered for research and for other forms of professional training.

(j) Appointment and placement of graduate teachers should be made on the basis of their qualifications and the recommendations of the training authority.

III. *Organizing schools for improving quality, selection, grouping, streaming, identification of talent, catering for able early leavers, further education etc.*

(a) Benefits and dangers attend almost all methods of segregating children according to ability. If segregation does take place it is important to ensure that the selection of the more able does not automatically imply rejection of the less able.

(b) There may be an advantage in putting clever children through an accelerated course of study, but there is a danger of mistaking intellectual precocity for maturity of growth; a pupil may lose something by doing under pressure at 15 what he would do normally at 16.

(c) When children have to be selected according to their ability, no single criterion of selection should be relied upon. Rather, it is advised that a variety of criteria such as well-kept records, standardized tests, the teacher's views and other recognized guidance procedures should be taken into account.

(d) The educational facilities of a community can be greatly enriched by using the schools in the evening to provide instruction in a great range of adult activities which may vary from specific vocational training to purely recreational crafts and sports or to classes designed to reduce adult illiteracy. The development of a full range of further educational activities is of particular importance in rural areas.

(e) The problem of early school leaving and ill health might well be reduced if free mid-day meals were provided in schools. Asian countries are urged to experiment with this step, which has been so conspicuously successful in other countries where it has been taken.

(f) Scholarships should be provided for pupils of outstanding ability who would otherwise be unable to attend a secondary school.

(g) As long as the number of places available in secondary schools is less than the number of applicants, selection is necessary, and selective places should not be available only to those whose main qualification is the ability to pay for them.

IV. *General discussion of the role of the school (in its many forms) in socio-economic development. Orientation- relationship with community, industry, agriculture, other agencies, etc., curriculum emphasis — local needs*

(a) The meeting endorses the present UNESCO approach to planning and emphasizes that the most detailed and thorough economic planning should precede such major educational advance so that the needs of society for professional men, technicians, skilled craftsmen and workers can be accurately assessed.

(b) The meeting urges the importance, in implementing the Tokyo Resolutions, of relating education to the life of the community and to the environmental needs and activities as a means of developing the faculties of the student.

(c) If at a given moment of expansion a country cannot produce the trained manpower that it needs, it should not hesitate to draw experts from abroad and to send its own young men and women abroad for training.

(d) In a period of rapid technological change it is important that the secondary schools should be sufficiently flexible to provide adequately for the academic, vocational and technical needs of their pupils and society. Advisory committees should be established at each level of education to integrate the schools with industry and commerce.

(e) Vocational interests of young people uninterested in, or, for many reasons unable to give the time for, the longer, basic studies of university can be effectively served by post-secondary institutions. Such schools can also make significant contribution to the economy by supplying technicians, nurses, agricultural extension workers, school teachers, clerical supervisors, and professional assistants as needed by society. Such schools should be set up in such a way that individual enrolled can with appropriate supplementary study transfer to or subsequently proceed to degree awarding institutions.

V. *Curriculum and methods of teaching, length and range of courses, kinds of teaching methods, textbooks — teaching aids (television)*

(a) At the primary stage the child's environment and his first hand experiences should be used to the full in his education and less reliance should be placed on memorizing 'book knowledge'.
(b) At this stage, however, the child be offered as rich a variety of reading material as circumstances permit in order that he may, in his early years, acquire and enjoy the habit of reading.
(c) UNESCO should call together a team to produce a textbook on a suitable science subject for use in secondary schools in Asian countries.
(d) As an antidote to the present demand for technical and scientific education, each country should promote a special study which would attempt to answer the question, "what, in our day, is meant by the spiritual and cultural traditions of our country and what part should they play in the education of our children?"
(e) In the near future, countries may be able to afford the expensive apparatus implied by the newer and more inexpensive teaching aids, and they should therefore conduct experiments so that they will be experienced in their use when they can be made available.
(f) The secondary stage of education should develop a power of objective and critical thought, a desire for further comparative study and knowledge, efficient habits of study and the ability to analyse and synthesize.
(g) At the university stage it is important that the staff-student ratio should be such as to permit the effective use of seminars, tutorials and discussion groups.
(h) No student of science or technology should completely severe his connection with humanistic studies and no student of the humanities should leave the university ignorant of the main processes of science and of the scientific methods.

VI. *Objectives and methods of science teaching, importance of science, relationship with other subjects, curricular essential guidelines for selection of content-teaching approaches*

(a) Considering the importance of science in the economic

development of the Asian countries, it is desirable that scientific studies and even a scientific study of the humanities should be made compulsory in the schools.

(b) In the teaching of science, the emphasis should at all time be on enquiry and discovery by the pupil himself.

(c) In order to ensure that the content of the courses in science at the various levels of education is both up-to-date and suitable for students at their respective stages of development, it is desirable that specialists in the various branches of science be employed to assist classroom teachers in the construction of curricula and the preparation of syllabuses. The help of such experts should also be sought in the preparation of textbooks in science.

(d) It is recommended that the Asian countries take the necessary steps to establish national workshops for the production of low-cost science apparatus. UNESCO is requested to provide the Asian Member-States with necessary technical help for the production of such apparatus.

(e) There is considerable scope for research in the methods of teaching science at the different levels of education. Universities and teachers colleges should be committed to undertake research projects in science methodology with a view to discovering the most effective techniques of science teaching.

(f) UNESCO is requested to set up a committee to study what ways and means may be adopted to use such media of instruction as television and radio in order to offset the difficulty of finding an adequate number of well-trained teachers of science.

(g) In the interest of good science teaching there should be close connection between the schools and industry.

VII. *Evaluation and research. Kind of evaluation procedures, examinations, assessing the intangibles, etc. Research in teaching and teacher education-research as an attitude of mind*

(a) It is important that information concerning methods of selecting pupils of ability for secondary education without exposing them to examinations should be collected and made available; and there should be experiments in Asian countries into the use of a variety of ways of selection in order to find out which is the best in the Asian context. In some of these experiments the oral test should play a considerable part.

(b) In any country there should be opportunities for educational investigation and research, and this should preferably be undertaken or sponsored by a university department.

(c) It is of fundamental importance, both for the universities and for the advancement of the countries which they serve, that adequate founds be provided to enable universities to carry out programmes of research and publication.

VIII *Administration and Supervision*

(a) In order to achieve stability in education and continuity of policy, Minister of Education should be served by an advisory committee consisting mainly of teachers, which they should consult before any major steps are taken affecting the service.

(b) Educational administrators should be recruited from among those thoroughly experienced in the problems of teaching and preferably from the teaching profession itself.

(c) A corps of enlightened supervisory teachers should be available to help and advise the schools, to conduct in-service courses of all kinds and to carry out "follow-up" studies.

(d) There should always be some effective way of associating every school with the adult members of the community which it serves.

(e) For the proper functioning of universities and for ensuring quality and standards in university education, it is fundamental to protect and preserve the autonomy of universities in internal administration and freedom of teaching.

(f) The main emphasis in supervision (inspection) should be on the guidance of teachers for the improvement of teaching and the promotion of their personal and professional growth.

MEETING OF EXPERTS ON EDUCATIONAL PLANNING IN ASIA, 1966

A meeting of Experts on Educational Planning in Asia was organized at Simla (India) from 16 to 28 May, 1966, by the Asian Institute of Educational Planning and Administration, New Delhi, under the auspices of UNESCO. The meeting was attended by 21 participants including delegates from 10 countries (Philippines, Afghanistan,

Thailand, Ceylon, Malaysia, Iraq, Japan, Iran, India and France).

IMPORTANT RECOMMENDATIONS

The Concept of Educational Planning with Particular Reference to Training and Research

The meeting felt that educational planning was not a science but an operation, drawing upon various disciplines (Statistics, Economics, Pedagogy, Sociology, etc.) Planning was, therefore, essentially teamwork and involved collaboration at various stages between several specialists of the administrative and educational services.

Task of Educational Planners

According to the Seminar, in general terms, persons engaged in educational planning may be said to constitute all those in any nation or in international organizations, who carry significant responsibility for the formulation, implementation and revision of educational policy of a forward looking character.

There tasks include:

(a) Diagnosis and appraisal of the existing educational system in relation to the population of school-going age, its performance and its relation to the economic and social situation. (Planning of adult education is normally administratively separate but should be linked to the planning of formal education.)

(b) Setting special basic objectives, priorities and directions for change in the broad magnitude of resource-allocation to education over the long-term. This would involve the establishment of relevant quantitative projections in the light of economic, demographic and social factors and also the reform of contents, methods and structure of education.

(c) Practical elaboration and programming in conjunction with other national plans and in terms of specific educational goals, i.e., pupils by sex, by level and by type of education training and recruitment of teachers, location and construction of school buildings, production of books and equipment, programming of external assistance requirements, costing and financing of programmes.

(d) Implementation of plans and initiating appropriate action for the same (e.g., budget contracts, school-mapping, educational and vocational guidance, etc.).

(e) Evaluation and revision of plans in the light of implementation and taking into account new educational, political, technological, economic and demographic developments.

(f) Administrative reforms and inter-ministerial co-operation at the central and local levels.

(g) Maintenance of the necessary contacts with national research groups of educators, economists, demographers and sociologists, with a view to ensure the effective use of resources in education through research findings.

In brief, within the overall national planning body, the Ministry of Education and other public and private agencies, there should be people who understand how to look at the educational system in relation to the contribution which, at various levels and according to different types, it can make an economic and social development, and how in practical terms resources should be organized, quantitatively and qualitatively, it can contribute to this end.

Categories of Personnel Needed

The meeting identified the following categories and personnel needed:

(i) Junior officers of central and local educational planning units, without specialization;

(ii) Senior educational planners responsible for the overall co-ordination of the educational plan;

(iii) Specialists of various disciplines, such as economics, statistics, demography, manpower etc.;

(iv) Highest level officials responsible for policy-making at the ministerial or under-secretary level;

(v) Administrators of the Ministry of Education at the central and local levels;

(vi) Officials outside the Ministry of Education concerned with educational planning.

Concerning the above classification, a number of comments were made. First, a distinction between training and information was emphasized; for some categories, orientation programmes and dissemination of information were considered to be sufficient. It was also suggested that the specialists included under category (iii) would not be necessarily located in the planning unit of the Ministry of Education, and that the contribution of specialists from other departments could be suitably drawn upon.

Organization and Training Courses

The general problems of organizing a course on educational planning was summarized as follows:

(a) A successful course requires: a competent staff, an able and appropriately qualified body of students and good curriculum material;
(b) A satisfactory balance between (i) Lectures, (ii) informal discussions and seminars, (iii) practical work and case-studies, and (iv) individual reading.

The meeting recommended the desirability of organizing training courses around the process of educational planning. In this respect, the meeting suggested that statistics should be directly related to the different problems and not taught as separate academic subject.

The participants felt that before making recommendations on training at the national, regional and international levels, there should be an evaluation of the efficiency of existing training facilities.

Training at the National Level

The meeting felt that undoubtedly, training in educational planning will ultimately be given in national institutions, such as teacher-training colleges or universities.

The meeting felt that when national courses are organized an attempt should be made to harmonize their contents, so that they provide a common background for the participants who proceed to join international training courses. The Regional Institute might assist in the preparation of curricula for such courses.

Aid offered at the International Level

The meeting suggested that until a network of national training insututions was established, the Member-States of the region would have to continue utilizing the facilities offered by UNESCO.

The participants examined the possibilities offered by long-term UNDP fellowships. It was felt that in selecting prospective fellowship holders, the variations between different levels of training should be borne in mind, and continuity of training should be evolved in the field of educational planning.

Such continued training should normally start with elementary national or regional course, and then proceed to longer and more comprehensive training either at the regional institutes or in a national university, ultimately ending at the International Institute for Educational Planning.

In between such periods of training, the meeting felt that the selected official would naturally work for a sufficiently long time in his own administration. The pattern will, however, have to be applied with flexibility, taking into account the particular circumstances of each country.

The members were of the opinion that it would help the regional and international institutions concerned if a plan could be drawn in each country indicating its future need of planners and administrators at various levels.

Training Programmes

Composition and Basic Tasks of an Educational Planning Office

In most countries of the region where educational planning offices exist, the staffing pattern is as follows:

(a) A number of junior officers engaged in detailed operations of educational planning;
(b) A departmental head assisted by one or more senior officers;
(c) A number of specialists in the field of statistics, school buildings, budgeting, etc.

The meeting suggested that following basic operations are required in the analysis of the actual educational situation in formulating the educational plans and in the process of evaluating them: collection of statistics, tabulation and elementary analysis, projections; costing; assessment of the efficiency of the school system and school mapping.

Course for Junior Planning Officers

The meeting considered the syllabus for a training course for junior planning officers in the Ministry of Education and for provincial educational officers dealing with educational planning. The objective of this course was to acquaint them with the necessary practical techniques so that they could carry out their jobs efficiently.

In performing the basic tasks described above, the junior planning officer will also have to:

(a) analyse a provincial educational report, summarize reports, write official letters, etc.;
(b) maintain liaison with other ministries (defence, culture, health, labour, etc.) as well as the press;
(c) possess a knowledge of foreign assistance programmes of the relevant agencies and their operations.

In the light of these observations, the following majer-headings were suggested for the syllabus:

(i) General issues in educational planning;
(ii) Basic training in statistics, school mapping and demography;
(iii) Costing, financing and budgeting;
(iv) Evaluation;
(v) Office practices, reporting and data compilation; and
(vi) Practical planning exercises.

It was strongly recommended that instruction should not be carried out mainly along the various disciplines which go to make up the course, but that it should have a strong emphasis on operational practices. Practical exercises, for example, in the form of preparing a provincial plan in alternative contexts, should get a high priority in the training course. In short, the training should be plan-oriented.

It was suggested that the course should cover a minimum of 160 and a maximum of 230 class hours, the suggested division of time over the various subjects being as follows:

Practical exercise	25%
General issues in educational planning	20%
Statistics	20%

Costing and financing	20%
Evaluation	10%
Offices practices	5%

These percentages as well as the duration of the course could be adjusted in the light of the outcome of the first experimental programmes.

Comprehensive Long-term Course

The meeting considered the syllabus for a comprehensive long-term course for the preparation of senior officers in the field of educational planning.

It was recognized that for a course of this nature the "problem-oriented" approach was the most appropriate method of instruction.

As the participants would normally have widely varying backgrounds and capacities, it was felt that in the initial stage of the course their specific remedial needs should be met.

The core of the programme could be organized around six key areas:

(i) Analysis and diagnosis of the existing situation;
(ii) Preparation of long-term perspectives;
(iii) Detailed consideration of short-term plans;
(iv) Evaluation and revision of plans and programmes;
(v) Action-oriented research.

The course should comprise a variety of selected practical exercises and case-studies which would be continuously and appropriately interwoven with the programme of studies. The intention is not merely to enable the participants to deal with the total process of educational planning but also to give them improved understanding of the operational techniques. This would enable them to face in realistic and flexible ways the situations as they present themselves.

Orientation Seminars for Specialists

The meeting agreed that specialists, whether in or outside the Ministry of Education, should have some basic knowledge of educational planning so that they may adapt their specialized competence to the interdisciplinary operation of planning in education.

Two kinds of specialists were considered:

(i) Specialists in one phase or level or education. It was felt that basic orientation in educational planning could be given to these specialists through meeting of experts in specific types of education.

(ii) Specialists who are more or less directly involved in educational planning, such as:

(a) Economists (including cost accountants, development economists, etc.),
(b) Social scientists,
(c) Statisticians,
(d) Demographers,
(e) School building specialists, and
(f) Educational and vocational guidance counsellors.

The main elements in the orientation seminars for these specialists would be:

(i) General consideration on educational planning and administration;
(ii) General consideration on socio-economic development;
(iii) Application of specialised knowledge and techniques in educational planning and development.

It was suggested that orientation seminars should be held for a period of 10 to 15 days and, if possible, simultaneously for the various types of specialists. However, they could also be held separately according to the needs of the situation.

Information Programmes

The meeting also discussed various means of providing information on educational planning to a variety of persons who were concerned with it. It was suggested that, apart from the categories considered below, it was necessary to involve a wide variety of people in the planning process by information through appropriate documentation and the extensive use of mass media.

Four major categories and the ways of providing information to them were examined:

(i) The first, and also the most important, category is of the highest level officials, either in the Ministry of Education or in other ministries (e.g. planning) and also key personalities concerned with education. Those responsible for policy-making at the ministry level, get opportunities for information on educational planning through conferences organized by UNESCO. For other high officials, meeting may be convened, and by the Regional Institutes if only one region is concerned, and by the IIEP if officials from various regions are invited for examining problems of a common nature. The main purpose of such meetings would be to assist the participants in developing and improving the quality and effectiveness of policy-making and administration through educational planning. In view of the limited time available, no attempt would be made to deal with the whole problem during one single meeting. The topics for discussion would neither be too general nor too academic but rather oriented towards concrete problems. The discussion would remain at the level of policy and technique and would indicate how planning may help to solve these problems.

(ii) The second category would comprise mainly officials of ministry other than the Ministry of Education, who are concerned with educational problems, at the administrator level and for whom information seminars would be organized. These seminars would not normally include specialists, as specialists are expected to undergo the courses indicated above. In cases, however, where they could not be released, they might also participate in such seminars. It is expected that, in the majority of cases, much seminars would take place at the national level but that the Regional Institute might participate in their preparation and organization. Such seminars would provide opportunities for these officials to meet their counterparts in the Ministry of Education. The seminars might last for one to two weeks. Having convinced the participants of the necessity of co-ordination between the various departments, these seminars would attempt to arrive at concrete solutions. Emphasis would be laid on the fact that planning is necessary before action at all levels and that it is an integrated process. The topics to be discussed might be somewhat similar to those for category (i), but should be examined on practical considerations.

(iii) A third category would comprise officials of the Ministry of Education, provincial administrators, supervisors, directors of schools and professors of teacher-training colleges. Associations of lectures and workshops organized at the national or provincial levels, for a few days but not exceeding two weeks and preferably during the vacation period. While broadening the views of the participants on the changing role of education, such workshops would focus on immediate problems of planning in their respective areas of responsibility within the over-all system of social and economic planning.

(iv) Although the above categories comprised essentially Government officials, it was agreed that information should also be disseminated to persons outside the ministerial organization but concerned with specific or general aspects of education. In some cases, they might be included in the first two categories, but it was felt that they would not be much concerned with the problems of integration and co-ordination which would be the main topics of discussion in the above seminars. For this type of person, one kind of seminar would not be sufficient but a number of them would be required, each focusing but a different aspect of educational planning. The following topics were suggested as suitable for discussion: (a) educational research in relation to educational planning (involving universities, research institutions, etc.); (b) enlisting public co-operation (with mass media specialists); and (c) manpower aspects (involving industrial managers, economists, specialists of vocational training and technical education).

In each seminar of two to five days' duration, outsiders could also participate along with the administrators of the educational system.

Such seminars should be supplemented by the distribution of appropriate material on problems of educational planning.

Research Requirements for Educational Planning in Asia

As far as research was concerned, it was agreed that a clear distinction should be made between:

(a) The work necessary for the improvement of the training programme of the Institute, which would be in the nature of "studies" in whose conduct the Institute would play a direct and essential role.
(b) Fundamental research concerning problems of educational planning which are not directly connected with the training programme of the Institute. The Institute could promote this type of research and co-ordinate it at the regional level.
(c) The participation of the Asian Institute in International studies undertaken by UNESCO's Office of Educational Planning.

Training Programme of the Asian Institute

Three main principles were accepted with regard to studies of this type:

(a) They should be problem-oriented and should contribute to the solution of the problems they study;
(b) They should generally comprise collection or analysis of data;
(c) They should be undertaken in close co-operation with other existing institutions, either in UNESCO (OEP, IIEP, the Bangkok Regional Office) or outside the organization.

The large number of suggestions made by the participants which are illustrative of the kinds of studies needed are grouped under three main headings: (a) Methodology, (b) Case-studies and data collection, and (c) Evaluation.

(a) *Methodology*. The following suggestions were made:

(i) Studies concerning educational planning are often hampered by problems of vocabulary and of definitions. Further work could be undertaken in this field, including the preparation of uniform definitions, where feasible, for comparative purposes.
(ii) It was also suggested that studies could be undertaken to establish some basic standards, such as pupil-teacher ratios, area per pupil, etc.
(iii) Considerable attention was also to be given to the planning process, particularly as it prevailed in Asia. From the practical point of view, it was recognized that basic data required for

planning are often missing and that a methodology should be developed, which would make some kind of planning possible without them.

(b) *Case-studies and Data Collection.* The following fields of study were mentioned:

(i) School wastage;
(ii) Statistics: the collection of satisfactory statistics being essential for planning, the problem of their reliability and of their significance should receive more attention;
(iii) Cost of education and the problem of 'productivity' (a preliminary study of this subject is being undertaken jointly by the Asian Institute and the Bangkok Office);
(iv) Manpower information, such, for example, as would be recorded by a study of the follow-up of graduates at different levels;
(v) Assessment of the quantitative need for personnel specialized in educational planning;
(vi) Educational policies of the countries of the region;
(vii) Social and pedagogic data on changes and innovations in the educational system;
(viii) Improvement of the curriculum.

(c) *Evaluation.* The need for evaluation at different levels was considered by the meeting:

(i) It was felt that it would be useful to devise methods or tests which would apply to and educational system as a whole and which would provide a basis for a preliminary assessment of its performance.
(ii) It was also felt that, generally speaking, the trainees should be familiar with the techniques of evaluation, which are directly relevant to programmes or projects in their own country.
(iii) It was suggested that one of the responsibilities of the Institute should be to evaluate its own training programme, by following up the work of the trainees after they had completed the course.

A significant contribution to the Institute's programmes of studies could be expected from the trainees themselves. Information could be obtained from them on the planning situation in their respective countries.

It was agreed that the suggestions made by the participants were of an indicative character and that the Director of the Institute should feel fresh to adapt them in the light of available staff and financial resources.

Co-ordination of Research at the Regional Level

In this connection, reference was made to the recommendations of the Bangkok Conference of Ministers of Education, which invited further research in the field of manpower planning, drop-outs and wastage, scientific testing and evaluation procedures, adult education as well as literacy programmes.

Studies undertaken by UNESCC's Office of Educational Planning

Two international studies are actually being carried out by the Office of Educational Planning:

(a) A survey of the situation of educational planning in the world for the preparation of which information sheets are being circulated to Regional Centres, experts in the field, etc.
(b) Practice of educational planning in developing countries.

REGIONAL SYMPOSIUM ON IN-SERVICE TRAINING OF PRIMARY SCHOOL TEACHERS IN ASIA, 1967

Organisation

A Regional Symposium on the In-Service Training of Primary School Teachers in Asia, sponsored by UNESCO, was convened by the Asian Institute for Teacher Educators in the University of the Philippines, Quezon City, Philippines, from 5 to 19 July, 1967. This was the first meeting of its kind in the programme of the Institute. The organization of the Symposium was authorized by the 1966 General Conference of UNESCO and received assistance from UNESCO.

In recognition of the importance of in-service training for teachers, the Conference of Ministers of Education and Ministers responsible for Economic Planning of Member-States in Asia, convened by UNESCO with the co-operation of ECAFE in 1965, in Bangkok, made a special recommendation about this problem, urging that Member-States "organize in-service training of teachers in order to keep the teacher abreast with modern advances in educational theory and practice and in his own subject field and to enable those who do not possess adequate qualifications or are untrained, to acquire needed qualifications."

In pursuance of the above decision and recommendation, the Asian Institute invited experts, in their individual capacity, from the Member-States in Asia as well as observers from UNICEF, WCOTP, the Asia Foundation and UNESCO sponsored regional institutes. Experts from sixteen Member-States submitted reports on their respective countries and fifteen participated in the Symposium.

Objectives of the Symposium

These were defined as follows:

(i) To review the in-service training programmes in the countries of the region;
(ii) In the light of the above review, to prepare a basic statement of principles for the organization and conduct of in-service training programmes; and
(iii) To identify the areas where further research is needed and to develop research designs for such studies.

Principal Findings and Recommendations

Need for In-service Training Aims and Objectives

In-service training of primary school teachers in Asia is vital to the progress and qualitative improvement of education in the region, particularly at the primary level, and should be considered as both complementary and supplementary to the normal pre-service programmes.

In view of the rapid expansion of education in all Member-States, particularly at the primary level, many countries have had to recruit teachers with qualifications which are lower than either the minimum prescribed qualifications at the time of admission to training or the present prescribed minimum requirements. In addition; these countries have had to resort to emergency of "crash" training programmes to prepare as quickly as possible new teachers for the fast expanding school programme. As a consequence, there is a rather high proportion of unqualified or inadequately trained teachers in primary schools in many Member-States, who must be given regular in-service training to ensure that the quantitative expansion in education is accompanied by qualitative improvement.

The tendency in most countries today, especially among the advanced nations, is to lengthen the period for pre-service training and to raise the present minimum qualifications with a view to improving the quality of teachers and teacher training. Most developing countries, however, cannot yet afford to think in terms of lengthening the period of pre-service training because of the urgent need of producing new teachers for immediate service in schools. In any case, pre-service training, however long, does not and cannot fully prepare a person to function efficiently as a teacher throughout his professional life. Pre-service training must be followed by career-long in-service training and education if the quality of teachers and of education in primary schools is to be maintained and improved. It is, therefore, essential that the pre-service training of student teachers should be closely integrated and co-ordinated with the in-service training programme for trained teachers in order to provide a programme of continuous teacher education and to foster their professional growth.

There is a great deal of wastage in primary schools in some countries resulting from uninteresting and ineffective teaching by the large number of underqualified or inadequately trained teachers particularly from the emergency training courses. A programme of teacher education for these inadequately trained teachers will help to reduce the high percentage of dropouts from primary schools and ensure equality of opportunity for children in primary schools and better returns on educational investment.

In the rural areas, the teacher is likely to suffer from intellectual and professional isolation and from low morale. In view of the fact that in some countries teachers have to serve not only as teachers in the classroom but also as leaders and guides in the social, cultural and economic life of the community, it is essential that these teachers be given in-service training to refresh their minds and keep abreast of cultural and educational developments.

There has been a great deal of research and experimentation in the behavioural sciences in respect of the social, psychological and emotional development and growth of children and the learning process, which have revolutionized educational theory and practice and have contributed to the establishment of a sound, scientific basis for education. In addition, rapid changes are taking place in science and technology, resulting in an ever increasing use of new instructional materials and equipment including audio-visual aids and mass media. All these developments have led educators to review and revise curricula on the basis of the new concepts of education. It is vital for teachers in primary schools to understand these developments and their far-reaching implications for teaching, administration and supervision in the total educational system and be prepared adequately for giving effect to curricular changes.

In-Service training should also be designed to help teachers to become well-adjusted members of a society in the process of change. For this, they have to keep themselves constantly abreast of the rapid changes that take place in society and in the world around them. Negative attitudes to change have to be broken down and positive attitudes built to broaden their cultural backgrounds, cultivate their personalities and improve their professional techniques. Since the content of education draws its vitality from the personality of the teacher, it is essential that teachers be given in-service training to enable them to find the resources to grow from within by refreshing their minds, strengthening their convictions, awakening their interests and curiosity and instilling professional pride and respect for high standards of performance.

In-service training provides an excellent opportunity to Ministries of Education to offer further and specialized training to promising teachers for promotion to positions of greater responsibility in education. The concepts of administration and supervision have changed materially during the past few decades and in-service programmes have become necessary to bring practice up to date. The new concept changes the role of the administrator from the autocratic to the democratic approach. Likewise, the supervisor in the new situation becomes a valuable resource to teachers who collaborate in the planning of curricula and the improvement of instruction.

In-service training promotes professional growth and thus enhances self-confidence and security of tenure. The promise of a career resting on the firm foundation of social and economic security is a very important aspect of in-service training.

Planning and Administration of In-service Training

Planning

In many of the Asian countries today, the national plan for education does not make a distinguishable provision for in-service training, thus making it difficult to obtain adequate financial support for such training. It is necessary that the needs for in-service training should be carefully assessed in every country and a definite plan to meet these needs formulated, which would form part of the plan for education within the overall national plan of economic and social development.

Planning as an in-service training programme has certain special features which call for a considerable measure of flexibility. In planning for the development of schools and colleges, the number of students to be catered for and the qualifications to which the curricula lead can be clearly and simply stated. In the case of in-service training, numbers will fluctuate according to the length of courses, that is, the shorter the courses the greater the number of teachers who can be accommodated in any one year. Again, the objectives of the courses must be allowed to vary according to current needs. Nevertheless, in spite of these difficulties, a plan or in-service training expressed in terms of the numbers and costs involved and the objectives is necessary if it is to be accepted as a normal and permanent part of an educational plan. Within this general framework, details of specific courses should be left to local decision.

An important aspect of planning as it relates to the in-service training of teachers is to provide for ample and adequate consultation not only among teacher educators, supervisors, administrators and others involved in the organization of training programmes but also with teachers for whom these programmes are intended.

Administrative Machinery

Even a carefully conceived plan for in-service training with an adequate financial provision may prove ineffective if there is no proper machinery for its implementation. It is, therefore, desirable that there should be a special administrative machinery at all levels of administration to take care of in-service training.

At the national level, this could take the form of a department (or division or unit) of teacher education which takes care of both pre-service and in-service training. It is important, however, that this unit functions as a part and parcel of the total administration of the Ministry or Department of Education. Corresponding units should also be set up at the regional and local levels.

For an effective functioning of this machinery, it is imperative that it be headed by an officer of sufficient seniority and status and be staffed at all levels by properly qualified and competent personnel. If such personnel is not readily available, it will be necessary either to provide the facilities needed for their appropriate training or to utilise similar facilities available elsewhere either in the region or outside it.

The machinery set up by the government for the administration of in-service training should include arrangements for utilising the services of other agencies or organizations that can contribute effectively to this programme, such as universities, professional associations of teachers, other government departments, local authorities, cultural and civic groups, local communities and international organizations.

Effective co-operation and co-ordination among these agencies is of prime importance. A suitable way of ensuring co-ordination is to establish a co-ordinating body composed of the representative of all the agencies concerned at the different levels.

Co-operation should be particularly strong between teacher educators and supervisors in view of the fact that these two groups share the main task of organizing and carrying out the in-service training programmes. The administrative personnel occupy a pivotal position in the total scheme of co-operation and co-ordination since it is they who not only determine the general policies on which the in-service training programmes will be based and provide the necessary financial and material support but also license teachers and enforce service regulations.

There should be a gradual movement in the direction of a decentralized system of organization and administration for in-service training. While overall planning and determination of policy are inseparable from the functions of the Central authority, it is highly desirable that agencies of in-service training at the regional and local levels should be encouraged to assume increasing responsibility for the organization and implementation of in-service training programmes. One of the main advantages of decentralization lies in the fact that local educators, provided they are qualified are in the best position to know the local conditions in which in-service training operates as well as the needs of children and the problems of teachers in their areas.

Supervisors have a very important role to play in the in-service training of teachers. In the past they have been concerned more with the inspection of school facilities and with the assessment of teachers' competencies than with assisting teachers in their professional growth. In future, every encouragement and help should be given to them to enable them to assume a leadership role, in collaboration with other educators, in the development of effective programmes of in-service training.

In their own particular role as supervisors, they can also help teachers to grow professionally by making use of such diverse means as providing individual guidance, holding group conferences, giving demonstrations of teaching, distributing professional literature, and organizing study groups of teachers.

There are at least two restrictive factors that prevent many supervisors in the Asian countries from making an effective contribution to the in-service growth of teachers. These are (i) the unduly large number of schools and teachers that they are required to supervise, and (ii) the enormous amount of clerical work that they have to do for lack of adequate clerical assistance. If these two inhibiting conditions are improved, supervisors could be expected to play a more useful role in the in-service training of teachers provided, of course, they are properly qualified and competent to take on this special assignment.

Finance

Investment in an in-service training programme aims primarily, through upgrading of factor skills, at increasing the returns on existing investments by reducing dropouts and improving output. As such, it contributes directly to social and economic development and should be conceived as an essential component in resources allocation policies.

To enable programmes to be efficiently planned ahead, budgetary provision over a period of years is necessary and efficient evaluation procedures must be devised to ensure economical functioning.

Supplementary funds may be available from other sources such as foreign and international organizations and national non-governmental agencies such as banks, local foundations, business groups, teachers' organizations, civic and cultural groups, parent-teacher organizations, and local communities; but these will be insufficient for a systematic and full programme without the main support from public funds.

Evaluation

Evaluation of in-service training programmes is needed both to measure the economic returns on the investment and, to assess in educational terms, their impact on schools and teachers.

Such evaluation may take the following forms:

(i) Evaluation of a particular in-service training activity in the total programme in terms of the extent of involvement of the participants in the activity, the quality of thinking that took place, and the usefulness of the activity to the participants.

(ii) Assessment of the impact made on the schools by a particular activity in the programme, which may be done through such means as follow-up visits by staff, a study of reports made by participants, and the reactions of principals and supervisors.

(iii) Periodical evaluation of the total programme for the benefit — firstly, of the organizers, who could then effect improvements in it, and secondly, of the government, who could decide to expand, curtail or modify it.

Role of Various Agencies

Primary Teacher Training Institutions

In most of the Asian countries, the primary teacher training institutions have been concerned mainly, if not exclusively, with providing pre-service training. In future, they should be expected to be equally concerned with providing in-service training. In order, however, to facilitate their participation in this aspect of teacher training, there should be appropriate adjustments in their organization and staffing, including the addition of necessary personnel and facilities not only for the actual in-service training but also for follow-up.

Among the functions that such institutions may be expected to undertake, the most important are:

(i) Participating in the development of a comprehensive programme of in-service training at all levels;

(ii) Providing courses for both trained and untrained teachers;

(iii) Organizing seminars and workshops to deal with specific problems faced by teachers;

(iv) Helping teachers to adapt the curriculum to local requirements; and

(v) Undertaking the evaluation and follow-up of the training that has been given.

Special Centres or Institutes

In some countries, special centres or institutes have been set up for the express purpose of providing in-service training to primary school teachers, thus complementing the efforts of the regular primary teacher training institutions and other agencies engaged in this work. Such centres, wherever they exist, could also undertake to organize correspondence courses, long-term courses for untrained teachers and refresher courses for trained teachers. However, in view of the sound principle that pre-service training should not be divorced from in-service training, it might not be desirable to delegate the responsibility for fresher courses entirely, or even largely, to such special centres or institutes.

There are other useful functions that such special institutes could perform:

(i) Provide in-service training for teacher educators, supervisors and administrators who are concerned with the training of primary school teachers:

(ii) Take part in or undertake research and experimentation in primary education and primary teacher training; and

(iii) Produce and distribute educational literature such as educational abstracts, teachers guides, etc.

There are also some institutes in this region which are primarily engaged in educational research but which also conduct in-service training. This is a useful service which all educational research institutions should be encouraged to render.

Universities

In very few countries in Asia are the universities directly involved in the pre-service training of primary school teachers, and it will, perhaps, be a long time before they assume this responsibility. They can nevertheless play an important role in the in-service training of primary school teachers, provided the personnel involved are given the necessary facilities. In particular, they should have opportunities for familiarising themselves with primary schools.

Some of the ways in which they can participate in such training are:

(i) Assisting in the planning of in-service training programmes;
(ii) Organizing training courses, or providing resource persons for courses in such areas as the primary school subjects, or the social sciences which have a bearing on education, such as philosophy, psychology and sociology, or such specialised fields as art, music or agriculture, if and where these subjects are taught in the university;
(iii) Providing special courses for teacher educators, educational administrators and supervisors; and
(iv) Assisting in evaluation and research relating to in-service training.

Other Governmental Departments and Agencies

Other governmental departments such as the Ministries or Departments of Health, Agriculture, and Community Development and governmental agencies such as museums, public libraries and government broadcasting systems can assist the Ministry or Department of Education in implementing in-service training programmes by providing the needed resource persons, useful data and information, pertinent publications and literature, and other facilities needed for in-service training programmes.

Teachers' Organizations

Teachers' organization can make a useful contribution to the in-service training of teachers in a number of ways. They can assist in the formulation of plans and programmes; stimulate teachers to attend in-service training activities through such means as educational broadcasts and financial assistance to teachers for attending such activities; publish professional literature for use in in-service training activities; organize professional meetings to discuss new trends and development in education; and finally, lend support to training programmes organized by other agencies.

Associations of teacher educators, where they exist, should also engage themselves actively in the in-service training of teachers. In countries where such associations have not yet been formed, it is desirable that teacher educators should take the initiative in organizing them. At a later stage, a federation of all such associations in the Asian region could be formed to promote an exchange of views and experiences among teacher educators in the region and to develop programmes of mutual professional assistance.

Other Non-Governmental Agencies

Depending upon their interests and resources, other national non-governmental agencies can render the same kind of support to programmes of in-service training as teachers' organizations can.

Foreign and international agencies can assist in this direction by co-sponsoring with national governmental agencies special programmes of in-service training. Such joint sponsorship can take the form of (i) joint effort in planning, financing and implementation of programmes; (ii) technical and/or material assistance; (iii) scholarships for the training of personnel, especially for teacher educators, administrators and supervisors; and (iv) exchange of personnel and intercountry visits of educators.

Regional Co-operation

It is highly desirable that regional and bilateral co-operation should be developed among the Asian Member-States for the purpose of implementing programmes for the in-service training of primary school teachers. Such co-operation may take the form of exchange of personnel—students, educators, specialists, etc.; co-operative research; exchange of professional literature; and inter-country visits.

In developing co-operative activities among the countries of the region, the facilities provided by several regional institutes, such as the Asian Institute for Teacher Educators and the Asian Institute of Educational Planning and Administration, should be availed of. There are also other regional programmes such as those relating to educational research, science teaching, reading materials and school buildings which could assist in promoting the in-service training of primary school teachers in the region.

Programmes for In-service Training

This section reviews first the in-service programmes for untrained and trained teachers and then certain requirements common to all programmes; finally, it deals with the special needs of rural and remote areas. The problems that in-service training is attempting to solve are common to both men and women teachers.

Untrained Teacher

The number of untrained teachers in over half of the Member-States is staggering. The problem is often a double problem of how to give these untrained teachers enough general education for their task as well as how to train them in the necessary professional skills. The matter is of such urgency that exceptional measures need to be taken and comprehensive plans to cover a period of years (including continuing budgetary commitment) are essential.

To reduce the size of the problem two suggestions are made:

(a) That untrained teachers of long teaching experience should not be required to take a full course of training but should be given trained teacher status after an appropriate short course;

(b) That so far as general education is concerned, teachers who are much below the required standard should not be required to follow the same course of study as that for secondary school children but should take a special course more suited to their needs and shorter in length.

To reduce the time needed to catch up with this backlog of untrained teachers, part of the training should be given through media which large numbers can use simultaneously, such as correspondence courses, programmed instruction, teachers' guides, radio and possibly television. Provided the numbers involved are large (which in most countries they are), the costs per untrained teacher are definitely lower than those incurred by using only traditional methods.

Some use of traditional methods is nevertheless essential. The media to which reference has just been made are sometimes called 'indirect' media because teacher and pupil cannot directly discuss problems. For this reason any programme of in-service training for the untrained teacher which uses these media must be accompanied by more traditional means, such as vacation courses, weekly seminars, and visits by training staff to observe the teacher in school. In particular, four ingredients should find a place in every complete programme:

(a) Group discussions of problems,
(b) Individual counselling,
(c) Supervised classroom teaching, and
(d) Library facilities.

To encourage the teacher the whole course should be broken down into units, each of which earns credit.

On the subject of indirect media, the possibilities in the use of correspondence courses with or without programmed instruction are distinctly encouraging and should be considered. Specialist staff would be required as in the case of all the other indirect media. The Asian Institute for Teacher Educators might be prepared to assist by a preliminary survey of the experiences so far acquired of correspondence courses and techniques, and making this information available to Member-States in the region.

In concluding this section on the untrained teacher, it is necessary to emphasise speed not only because the problem hangs like a millstone round the neck of educational progress but also because the lack of professional status amongst a large number of teachers is bad for the morale of the teaching service and the welfare of the schools. Most untrained teachers should be able to qualify within three or four years.

Trained Teacher

It is evident that in a number of Member-States the in-service training of trained primary teachers takes a very low priority. Many reasons could be produced in support of a much higher priority, but perhaps these can best be summarised by two statements:

(a) It is difficult to introduce improvements and changes throughout the primary schools by any other means as speedily as by in-service training, and for many changes there are no other means.

(b) Even in conditions where improvements must be postponed for a time, in-service training can help to prevent a lowering of standards and loss of morale.

It may be useful to distinguish certain broad categories of in-service programmes according to the type of teacher catered for and the objectives of the course. First, there are *courses for the sub-standard trained teacher*. As standards rise many teachers find themselves below the latest requirements for a qualified teacher either on the general education side or professional side. These courses are designed specifically to upgrade them and their value is clear.

Then there are *courses for the fully qualified teacher*. These can have a large variety of objectives and perhaps, because of this, they often suffer from two weaknesses: (a) a lack of continuity and sequence, and so their effect is weakened and dispersed; and (b) a failure to recognise that when the objective of the course is to introduce something radically new in the schools, the co-operation of heads and supervisors must first be sought and follow-up arrangements must be intensified. The remedy lies in sequence planning of courses where necessary (this is not desirable in all cases), proper attention to preparing opinion for the acceptance of change, and follow-up visits to schools to encourage and advise the teachers who have taken courses.

The detailed content of the courses for fully qualified teachers must depend on local circumstances, but three considerations should be borne in mind when devising the programmes:

(a) If the felt needs of teachers are given prominence, those attending the courses are more likely to become genuinely interested and actively involved.

(b) If in-service programmes can be seen to be contributing to the solution of widely recognised problems — such as wastage from the primary school or weaknesses in the basic subjects — they will gain more support from the authorities.

(c) If due attention is paid in the courses to the teacher's social needs, his effectiveness as a person will be increased and his morale raised.

The length of courses and the methods used can cover a wide variety. The only point to be made here is concerning method. There should be an increasing use of methods which require active participation by the teacher — such as discussion groups, seminars, workshops and action research. In contrast, lectures should only be used when there is no other way. These "participating" methods are more suitable for experienced adults, especially when dealing with the practical problems of education.

Requirements Common to All Programmes

These requirements include the provision of incentives to teachers to attend courses, the involvement of teacher's interests in the programmes, the support of school principals, supervisors, and pre-service training staff, the follow-up of teachers who have been on courses, and provision for training of teacher educators engaged in in-service training.

Incentives may be used to persuade teachers to take part in in-service training programmes and can be positive or negative. They can be positive by offering rewards, such as credit points towards promotion and/or increases in salary, travel allowances, "release time", etc., or they can be negative by providing penalties for non-attendance, such as "efficiency bars" and limited certification. Or attendance may be made compulsory and become part of the accepted life of a teacher.

Though incentives are valuable, and in most circumstances necessary, they are not by themselves sufficient. A teacher's attendance can be ensured, but more than lip service is not certain unless he becomes genuinely convinced that what he is learning will benefit his pupils and his school. It above refers to the desirability of giving prominence during courses to those needs which are felt by teachers to be important. The point to be made here is that for teachers to feel that they are being consulted and involved in the courses, it is not enough for supervisors, who are in a position of authority, to report their views. Those who are engaged in planning and running the courses must also have the opportunity of informal consultations with teachers. Involvement is largely an emotional problem and therefore the promotion of a climate of harmony, goodwill and close personal relations must always be a main consideration both in the preparation for, and the day-to-day conduct of, in-service courses.

Where radical changes, such as a new approach to the teaching of arithmetic, are to be introduced into the school through in-service courses, it is more than ever necessary to secure the understanding and sympathy of supervisors, heads of schools and pre-service teacher educators before any in-service courses are held. Otherwise, opposition arising out of lack of understanding may easily nullify the influences of the teacher who has attended a course. Short conferences, demonstrations and personal explanations can be used to secure this co-operation.

Courses introducing radical changes also need more follow-up support than do courses which improve on already accepted practices. It is very desirable that follow-up visits to schools should be made by the staff who were involved in the in-service course and every effort should be made to release them to undertake at least part of the follow-up programme.

On the subject of quality of in-service courses, there have been complaints of a shortage of suitable staff in some countries. So it may be helpful to suggest what are the minimum qualifications needed by in-service staff. These are three:

(a) Practical experience of some continuous teaching at the primary level, without which it is not easy to win the real respect of experienced teachers. That the experience should be continuous is important because teaching isolated lessons does not allow one to acquire practical experience of child development at this level.
(b) A knowledge of, and some skill in, the methods of teaching experienced adults (as is distinct from pre-service training college students). These methods are referred to above.
(c) Specialised knowledge in his subject fields, usually of a higher level than that required for pre-service training.

Training schemes to meet these special requirements of in-service teacher educators could most economically be arranged in conjunction with any national schemes for training pre-service teacher educators (who in many cases will be the same people). Such training could be given in special institutions or in universities but perhaps the most suitable setting would be in primary teacher training institutions already engaged in some in-service training.

Special Problems of Rural and Remote Areas

Rural primary schools constitute the vast majority of primary schools in this region and the rural primary teacher carries the extra responsibility of contributing to rural leadership. In-service courses could play an important part in keeping the rural primary teacher informed of economic and social development policies and the part he could play in them as well as in maintaining the isolated teacher's interest and enthusiasm.

Research for In-service Training

The emergence of most Asian countries into independent status during the last two decades has brought about unprecedented social and economic changes all of which, in various ways and degrees, require corresponding changes in education. Educational leaders are becoming increasingly aware of the need for educational reforms. Since action must keep pace with rapid changes, and resources in experts and money are limited, educational research must perforce be largely functional and action-oriented. Moreover, research in in-service training will have to take related problems into account. Although basic or fundamental research is not precluded, it is strongly felt that in the present stage of educational development in Asian countries, primary emphasis should be on practical problems and needs. These practical problems about which great concern was expressed and which require urgent investigation relate to the following four major areas:

(i) Primarily administrative and supervisory in nature;
(ii) Primarily concerned with curriculum and methods;
(iii) Primarily dealing with school personnel; and
(iv) Primarily related to the social context matters.

In developing a programme of research, priority should be given to surveys and reviews, action research, comparative and evaluative studies, opinion and attitude surveys, pilot studies and experimentation, and analytical and descriptive studies. The approach and method to be used in the research will be determined by the specific nature of the problem.

The following criteria might be found helpful in determining priorities in educational research:

(i) Educational research must have a direct bearing on contemporary educational problems.

(ii) Research should develop and utilize common standards of comparison.
(iii) The terms used must be precisely defined.
(iv) Research should be useful and functional.
(v) Research should lead to action for improvement.
(vi) Research should relate to local situations and conditions.
(vii) Research should be designed to have value and importance for the needs of the country.

In the present stage of development of educational research in Asian countries, it will be particularly useful to undertake co-operative research, within each country as well as regionally, because it develops co-ordinated effort among participating entities, helps by mutual exchange of information, avoids unnecessary duplication and makes it possible to share the limited resources of expertise. The areas of the teacher training curriculum, student teaching, and evaluation of training are especially suitable for co-operative research.

For the systematic organization and encouragement of research in elementary education and teacher education in the Member-States an appropriate central organization or unit in each country is desirable. Wherever such a central organization does not exist, it should be established to discharge the following functions:

(i) Development of co-operative research;
(ii) Co-ordination of research carried out at various levels in the country;
(iii) Promotion of training of research workers;
(iv) Dissemination of available information;
(v) Organization of training programmes for encouraging teachers to design simple studies and conduct practical research in classroom problems; and
(vi) Involvement of post-graduate university students in educational research related to urgent practical problems.

If some such central body is organized to fulfil the above functions, it would serve as a professional arm of the Ministry of Education for collaboration with national and international organizations for educational research.

It is vitally important that teachers themselves should be helped to analyze the problems felt by them in reasonably objective and informed manner. They should be given the necessary training through in-service programmes to collect relevant facts and evidence, assess them and arrive at working decisions with a view to carrying them out. Such "action studies" are considered more valuable and meaningful to the teacher than sophisticated fundamental or theoretical research because they help teachers to identify problems and to weigh the pros and cons of evidence in arriving at decisions and carrying them out.

Almost all the country reports presented to the Symposium draw attention to the lack of professional literature available to the teacher and the paucity of library facilities. In any programme of book development, the need for educational literature should be given high priority. International assistance could be particularly useful in promoting the production of modern educational literature for teachers. In addition, educational research organizations and teacher training institutions in Member-States should undertake the preparation and production of instructional materials for the use of teachers this activity being considered as an essential part of their "extension" function.

The Asian Institute for Teacher Educators should play an important role in the promotion and development of research in this region, and therefore it should be suitably strengthened. Its programme should include:

(i) The publication of abstracts of research done in the Member-States;
(ii) Regular dissemination of research findings for the use of teachers;
(iii) Training in research methodology of selected research fellows;
(iv) Planning and execution of co-operative research projects.

It is noted with satisfaction that a small provision has been made in the Institute budget for developing co-operative research. It is recommended that the programme in this regard should be expanded urgently and additional resources provided to the Institute which may be used to finance research projects in teacher education in the Member-States on a matching basis.

In the Institute's programme of co-operative research, high priority should be given by it to conducting a comprehensive survey of teacher training in the Asian region, at all levels (primary as well as secondary) and forms (general, vocational, special etc.). A status study of this kinds is essential if further research is to be directed to assessing the assumptions on which present practices and methods are based.

One important direction for the development of Asian Institute for Teacher Educators would be to provide for teacher educators from Asian Member-States to come to the Institute for a specific period to participate in its training and research programmes.

UNESCO may appoint a panel of consultants from among the Asian Member-States to advise the Institute on its programme of research and to act as a liaison with research organizations and institutions in the region.

UNESCO may be requested to establish research fellowships in each Asian Member-State to carry out specific research projects within the framework of the co-operative research projects. The selected research fellows should be provided opportunities to meet periodically at the Institute.

ASIAN REGIONAL WORKSHOP ON THE PROGRESS OF INTEGRATED SCIENCE TEACHING, 1970

Organisation

"The Asian Regional Workshop on the Progress of Integrated Science Teaching" was held in Manila, by invitation of the Government of the Philippines, from 3-17 August, 1970. It was convened by UNESCO, with financial assistance from UNICEF, following Programme Resolution 2.211 of the UNESCO General Conference at its 15th session. National participants from 12 Asian countries attended the workshop as well as UNESCO experts in science education associated with UNESCO/UNICEF projects in Asian countries, observers from regional organizations concerned with science education, invited consultants, and UNESCO and UNICEF staff members.

Objectives

The objectives of the Workshop were:

1. To review progress in the teaching of integrated science in countries in the Asian Region.
2. To review developments in integrated science teaching made

outside the Region, and to consider their relevance and applicability to Asian countries.

3. To suggest guidelines for future developments in the teaching of integrated science.
4. To draw up a plan of action to foster collaboration in this field among countries participating in the workshop.

The level of work discussed at the workshop covered the teaching of science as an integrated subject during the first eight or nine years of schooling. The workshop, made suggestions for the approaches to the needs of the participating countries. It also suggested ways in which suitable programmes of integrated science could be devised, tested and implemented. As the teacher is the key to effective science teaching both pre- and in-service training was considered. The workshop also reviewed the physical requirements for integrated science teaching including space, facilities and equipment.

Concept of Integrated Science Teaching

The place of science as an essential ingredient in the education of all children is widely recognized. Furthermore, it is also recognized that the role of science teaching is not limited to that of being one subject among many in the curriculum. By sharpening the sense or curiosity of children in a manner that leads to their independent thinking and to their intelligent awareness of the world in which they live, science teaching has become one of the best vehicles we have for educating the child. In order to be effective in their role, the teaching of science should begin when the child's attitudes to the primary and pre-primary level.

In most Asian countries, the vast majority of children do not continue their schooling beyond primary or junior secondary school level. Thus, the courses in science which they receive at these levels are not only foundation courses but terminal courses as well, and their only formal scientific preparation for adulthood. Furthermore, many of these children are brought up, in their homes, with little opportunity to appreciate scientific ideas in a concrete way and to develop manipulative skills through, for example, playing with toys or taking machinery apart and putting it together again. They may also not be encouraged to be curious about their environment or to ask questions about it. It is thus through science teaching in schools that the experiences must be provided which, to a much greater extent, would have been automatically supplied by the environment in more technologically advanced countries.

To cater for these needs, attempts are being made to devise science courses in which concepts of science are developed, so as to reflect the fundamental unity of scientific thought. Such, integrated science courses aim to present science in a coherent way, and to avoid pre-mature or undue stress on the distinctions between the various scientific fields. They emphasize the underlying methodology and processess which characterize the scientific outlook. By a judicious choice of experience and activities, children learn how to think productively about the natural world and man's interaction with it by calling upon knowledge and skills from the various parts of science as needed.

Plan for Future Action

It is recognized that plans for future action must encompass both national and regional activities. Such activities are complementary. While national activities can be greatly strengthened and improved through regional inputs, regional activities can only be successful when they draw on soundly-based national experience.

While it is unlikely that a scheme of work developed in one country would be suitable for another, there are a large number of common problems which would be nearer solution if experiences in science curriculum development were shared. In particular, it is felt that experience gained in individual countries of Asia with similar climate, cultural and sociological backgrounds should be shared. These countries are at present too dependent on schemes originating in countries of high per capita income with a warm temperate climate.

1. An exchange of information is needed. This will involve the establishment of a clearing house for information, and a further development of the bulletins from the UNESCO Regional Office for Education in Asia would be most welcome. Consideration should also be given to the publication of newsletter "Science Education in the Asian Region". The newsletter might give information about forthcoming conferences, visits of consultants and news about curriculum trials in the countries of Asia.
2. The sharing of the evaluation of trials would save much time and

expense. This kind of information may not be suitable for wide publicity and may best be done by correspondence, or better still be regular meetings of curriculum developers. Any expenditure on such dissemination of research findings is likely to be very rewarding, and the help of the aid-giving agencies should be made available for such a purpose.

3. The cost of bringing a consultant to the region is high and a more effective use of his services would result from a careful programme of visits to a number of countries, rather than to just one. In many fields it would be desirable to request the international and other agencies to deploy advisers to cover a number of countries. The service of regional officers from the UNESCO Regional Offices has already established the value of such posts.
4. Full use of existing regional organizations should be made. The contribution to Asian educational development of such organizations as the Asian Association for Biology Education, the Asian Institute for Teacher Educators, the Asian Regional Institute for School Building Research, and the Regional Centre for Education in Science and Mathematics should be recognized and exploited to the full.
5. There is a need for more regional and sub-regional workshops. These could well be on specific topics of curriculum development. Workshops are needed on science equipment design and production. There is a strong case for a closer liaison between groups of countries with a similar economic and cultural history than now exists. Two obvious groups, for instance, would be Korea, Taiwan, and Japan and the countries and territories of the Western Pacific.
6. Many international and bilateral agencies are working in the field of educational development in Asia. Where co-operation between them is established, progress will be more rapid. For co-operation to be effective, a national body such as a science education co-ordinating committee is needed.
7. The evaluation of pupil achievement in modern science courses is not easy. If we are to teach for understanding we must test for understanding, not recall. Suitable examination and not test questions are very difficult to devise. The building up of a book of such questions, suitably graded, would be most valuable.
8. An advisory panel on integrated science teaching should be

established by UNESCO which should meet regularly to review current developments in integrated science teaching in the region and to plan future collaborative activities.

9. UNESCO should facilitate the exchange of information among science teachers associated in the Asian region and, as a first step, should organize a meeting of secretaries of these associations.

International Activities

International follow-up can be carried through UNESCO's programme of integrated science teaching which comprises the following elements:

— A series of publications on integrated science teaching.
— Technical services to Member-States through UNESCO field experts concerned with integrated science teaching.
— Experimental projects for the development of new methods and materials for integrated science teaching at the primary and lower secondary stages.
— A series of regional, sub-regional and national integrated science teaching workshops.

These activities should be carried out in such a way as to provide maximum assistance to Asian Member-States and to provide maximum input to the Asian collaborative programme in integrated science teaching.

REGIONAL SEMINAR ON SCHOOL SCIENCE EQUIPMENT IN ASIA, 1972

Organization

The Regional Seminar on School Science Equipment in Asia was held at the invitation of UNESCO at the Indian National Science Academy (INSA), New Delhi, from 11 December to 20 December, 1972, with the Government of India generously acting as host. It was convened in co-operation with UNICEF, following Programme Resolution 2.21 adopted by the General Conference of UNESCO at its sixteenth session in 1970. The Seminar was attended by participants from 14 countries in the Asian region, who were science curriculum developers, equipment design specialists or specialists in the manufacturing of science education equipment at the primary and lower secondary levels. It was also attended by invited consultants and UNESCO experts in science education/science equipment production associated with UNESCO/UNICEF Projects in Asian countries, and observers from Hong Kong and India as well as representatives from the UNICEF Regional Office for South Central Asia, New Delhi, the UNESCO Field Science Office for Asia, New Delhi, and the UNESCO Regional Office for Education in Asia, Bangkok, were also present.

The Seminar was the first of its kind held in the Asian region and provided a forum for an exchange of knowledge and experience of the work that has been carried out in the field of school science equipment. It focused attention on the problems of design, prototype manufacturing, mass production, marketing and distribution of science equipment. The training of teachers and laboratory technicians in the use of modern equipment was another major concern of the Seminar.

The activities during the Seminar included the presentation of country reports which outlined the present situation of school science equipment in participating countries; discussions in plenary sessions; visits to science equipment exhibitions, school science equipment manufacturers and training institutions for instrument technicians.

Recommendations

1. That the local design and production of school science equipment be initiated and encouraged in Asian countries;
2. that the regional exchange of ideas on science curriculum development and the design and production of school science equipment be encouraged;
3. that Asian countries promote the use of regional and national science newsletters and other media for the exchange of ideas and use of equipment;
4. that Asian countries promote standardization of school science equipment to encourage its wider use within the region;
5. that national science fairs encourage the development and use of innovative school science equipment;
6. that the training of teachers on the use, maintenance and repair of equipment be included in pre-service and in-service programmes;
7. that a regional fellowship programme be made available through

UNESCO/UNICEF or other sources for giving experience in the design and production of science teaching equipment and curriculum matters;

8. that the UNESCO Regional Office for Education in Asia publish a science education newsletter for the dissemination of information about science curriculum development teaching materials and equipment from within as well as outside the region;
9. that UNESCO and UNICEF assist in the translation of educational materials into English and French;
10. that Member-States which manufacture school science equipment make available for regional use catalogues of their equipment and thereby encourage the export and exchange of materials within the region;
11. that seminars be arranged on specific subjects related to science curriculum development and school science equipment production;
12. that the development and use of school science kits be encouraged by the inclusion of some selected kits in the UNICEF EVE List;
13. that the UNESCO Regional Office, Bangkok assist in preparing evaluation programmes and guides for manufacturing quality control and standardization of school science equipment.

REGIONAL SEMINAR ON LIFE-LONG EDUCATION, 1976

Organization

Following the report of the International Commission on the Development of Education ("Learning To Be") which *inter alia* proposed, "lifelong education as the master concept for educational policies in the years to come for both developed and developing countries", UNESCO organized a seminar in June 1976 at Chiangmai, Thailand to promote reflection on the theme of lifelong education.

Objectives

The Seminar considered the concept of lifelong education and its implications for curriculum with particular reference to the basic cycle of education. This was intended to be done in the context of some of the major concerns which are reflected in national policies for educational development in Asian Member States. As the Seminar examined the concepts of lifelong education and of the "basic" cycle, it found it necessary to drop the term "basic" cycle and to use "basic learning needs".

Participation

At the invitation of UNESCO, 16 Member-States in Asia designated participants to attend the Seminar in their individual capacities. Organizations of the U.N. system, inter-governmental organizations and other organizations also sent their representatives and observers.

Conclusions and Recommendations

1. Lifelong education is viewed as a strategy for educational action directed to the development of societies and of individuals. The concept of lifelong education should, therefore, act as an energizing force for the reform of education systems, and as an organizing principle by which the various components and types of education are brought together in a coherent strategy for educational action.
2. Meeting the basic learning needs of various categories of learners is fundamental to lifelong education as a strategy of educational action.
3. While basic learning needs pertain to all sections and age groups of population, their application in terms of programmes of action has necessarily to be directed first to priority areas. In the circumstances of many countries in Asia, priority emphasis should be on meeting the basic learning needs of the deprived and the disadvantaged sections of the society.
4. Curriculum development for lifelong education would call for a fundamental reconsideration of principles currently used in curriculum construction. To this end, it is necessary to identify the organizing principles for curriculum development in the perspectives of lifelong learning and education.
5. In order to meet the requirements of lifelong education conceived in terms of basic learning needs of the deprived and the

disadvantaged groups of population, each country would need to develop a comprehensive statement of objectives and content of the curriculum, using real-life and problem-solving methodologies.

6. Curriculum development centred round basic learning needs would call for new methods for preparing relevant learning materials and of evaluation.
7. For implementing an integrating strategy of educational action based on lifelong education it is necessary that various agencies, both government and non-government, should be associated in this task. Furthermore, optimum use of resources should be made by rational utilization and reallocation.
8. It was agreed that the present Regional Seminar on Lifelong Education and the Curriculum should be followed by seminars at the national level. It was further suggested that UNESCO and other international agencies be asked to assist in conducting these national seminars. The report of the present Seminar would provide one starting point. A clear and practical framework for discussion would be useful. Participants should be drawn from various government ministries, appropriate non-governmental agencies and local communities.
9. An exchange of information and materials should be actively promoted through in-country workshops and a forum for a continuous regional sharing of experiences. Possibly APEID might collaborate in this by providing a channel for regional dialogue and by monitoring initiatives taken by Asian countries in the field of lifelong education. More specifically, APEID might offer resource assistance to experimental projects. Among the projects proposed to follow up the seminar are the following:
   (i) Inventories and case studies should be prepared of programmes and projects of lifelong education initiated in the Member-States;
   (ii) Collaboration of a curriculum development centre and the people of a given community in the design and pretesting of a curriculum for a particular public;
   (iii) preparation of comprehensive planning exercises (preferably at district or provincial level) for integrated development of educational opportunities and facilities (for formal, non-formal and informal learning), taking into account national educational requirements and the totality of learners'

needs;

(iv) Experiments in compressing the duration of existing school curricula in order to gain greater flexibility and also wider spread of benefits;

(v) Experiments with new non-formal programmes;

(vi) A public awareness programme using all available media to familiarize people with the concept of an opportunities for lifelong education;

(vii) Inventories of existing underutilized resources for lifelong education, e.g., school, hospitals, museums, etc., and available personnel, e.g., government employees, village leaders etc.;

(viii) The establishment of resource centres at different levels (district/provincial/national) to rationalize and co-ordinate resources and services;

(ix) Teacher re-education and re-orientation to play an appropriate role in the lifelong education system;

(x) The development of low-cost self-learning materials.

The representative of International Labour Organisation (ILO) brought to the attention of the Seminar for commendation to the Member-States, the convention and recommendation adopted by the ILO in 1974 with respect to "paid educational leave" for education and training at any time, in order to realize the idea of lifelong education.

REGIONAL SEMINAR ON ALTERNATIVE APPROACHES TO SCHOOL EDUCATION, 1976

Organisation

The Regional Seminar was held at Manila from 6-14 December, 1976. It was one of the series of activities undertaken by UNESCO towards promoting reflection on the needs for evolving "complete flexible and diversified structures" notably aimed at the realization of equality in education. Meetings of this series included the Meeting of Experts on Services to Out-of-School Youth in the Asian Region (Bangkok, 9-13 October, 1972), the Regional Seminar on Rural Youth and Out-of-School Education in Asia (Tagaytay, Philippines, 30 September–1 October, 1974), and the Regional Seminar on Lifelong

Education, the Curriculum and Basic Learning Needs (Chiangmai, Thailand, June 1976). The theme of "Alternative Approaches to School Education at the Primary Level" was also examined in a Meeting of Experts in Africa (Addis Ababa, October 1975).

Participation

The eleven Member-States (1. Bangladesh, 2. India, 3. Indonesia, 4. Japan, 5. Korea, 6. Malaysia, 7. Nepal, 8. Philippines, 9. Singapore, 10. Sri Lanka, 11. Thailand) responded and participated in the Seminar.

Representatives or observers from ILO, UNICEF, WHO and South East Asian Ministers of Education Organization (SEAMEO) also attended the Seminar.

Agenda

1. Review of national experiences in developing alternative approaches to school education at primary level (for various learner groups: non-school-enrolled children and young people; enrolled children and young people; children and youth without adequate schooling).
2. In the light of Item 1 above , consideration of the main principles and concepts underlying the search for alternatives:

   (a) Development of strategies to meet learning needs of various groups in the young population.
   (b) Organization and adaptation of content and methods.
   (c) Organization and adaptation of teaching/learning resources.
   (d) Problems of management and administration in designing alternative approaches.

3. Suggestions for future action at country, regional and international levels: research, planning, implementation, evaluation, intercountry collaboration.

Suggestions for Future Action

The Seminar is convinced that alternative approaches to meeting the learning needs of young people, in school or out of school, cannot be developed by making marginal changes in the existing structures and content of primary education programmes. This is particularly so where the learning needs of deprived populations are concerned. The development of viable alternatives and a simultaneous reorientation of the existing systems call for systematic experimentation, with new techniques, methodologies and materials. Inter-country and regional co-operation in this area would be a particularly productive ground for international action.

With the above considerations in mind and recognizing the co-operative interest of international agencies, notably UNICEF, and UNESCO, the Seminar recommends the following areas for action and assistance at the national and regional levels:

National Level

1. Action-research, studies and projects on the development and adaptation of *learning content* in the delivery of education to deprived populations including:

— Identification and analysis of learning content for mass education (national basics and local variants), and supportive parental instruction;
— Utilization of learner experiences as formative learning content and development of consistent, relevant post-formative learning content;
— Making learning content implicit in socio-economic development programmes and specific programmes for the removal of poverty.

2. Action-research, studies and projects on the development and adaptation of *methodologies* in the delivery of education to deprived populations, including:

— *Pedagogical methodologies* in particular those incorporating the attributes of the various and diverse learners, such as socio-economic-cultural aspects, learning styles, motivations, availability of time, educational deprivation;
— *Delivery and infrastructure methodologies* in particular, training methodologies for various implementors and changes in methodologies for formal school teachers to provide them with competencies to meet new social-action-based educational needs; methods for using under-utilized and unutilized indigenous

learning techniques, institutions (especially the school in its new roles), and people, for the delivery of education to deprived populations; decentralized resource and learning centres;

— *Planning and management methodologies* including those for decentralized planning and management, communication, feedback and plan reformulation and, in particular, incentive systems for facilitators of learning; inter-sectoral co-ordination; community participation in decision making; removal of barriers;
— to poverty strategies;
— *Knowledge and information dissemination methodologies* including national coverage (and regional and international transmission of information on projects) for the delivery of education to deprived populations, through networks of national change-agent groups at various levels, which would also take on advocacy roles in the country.

Regional and International Level

1. Financial and technical assistance support, at the request of Member-States, for country actions for the delivery of education to deprived population, without producing distorting effects on indigenous development;
2. Support for providing access to significant educational experiences in the delivery of education to deprived populations in other countries through documentation flow and clearing house services; case study analyses; and study/exchange visits by country project personnel for on-the-job training at on-going projects;
3. Support (in co-operation with Member-States) for the utilization of selected national centres and projects for the periodic training of personnel from other countries.
4. Support to Member-States, as required for translation into English, of representative samples of learning/teaching materials (originally in national languages) successfully developed and used by the Member-States, which may be shared with other countries; the development and dissemination of multi-media packages (films, charts, slides, tapes, VTR and printed matter) depicting country experiences, which may be shared with other countries;
5. Support for regional field-operational seminars and experts'

meetings to analyze and synthesize experiences in the delivery of education to deprived populations;

6. Support for regional and international surveys and analyses, with the co-operation of Member-States, of the follow-up of the recommendations for the delivery of education to deprived populations;
7. Support for preiodic meetings of high-level decision makers, to provide a forum for discussions on policy matters related to the delivery of education to deprived populations, and monitor progress in the Asian region.

SUB-REGIONAL CURRICULUM WORKSHOP, 1976

Organisation

The workshop, organized by the Asian Centre of Educational Innovation for Development, Curriculum Development Centre, Ministry of Education, Sri Lanka and Sri Lanka Foundation Institute, met in Colombo from 1-30 October, 1976. The purpose of the Workshop was, broadly, to provide experiences in the analysis of curriculum materials with a view to fostering awareness of alternative approaches to the attainment of educational goals, and to provide experiences in developing instructional materials for grades VI through IX or X relating to the areas of health and nutrition, the development of skills and rural transformation.

Objectives

1. To familiarize the participants with curriculum projects relating to the three areas of (a) health and nutrition, (b) skills training and (c) rural transformation in grades VI through IX or VI through X (whichever range is applicable to their countries);
2. To develop in the participants the skills in preparing criteria for curriculum analysis and to enable them to learn the techniques of curriculum analysis and development;
3. To develop in the participants the skills in the application for curriculum analysis in revising their own curricula for the respective grades; and

4. To provide experiences for the participants in developing instructional materials in the above three areas for the respective grades.

Broad Guidelines for Development and use of Criteria

A. *Development of criteria*

Owing to the variety of conditions which obtain in the different countries participating in the Workshop, it was felt that the development of a single set of criteria applicable to all the countries may neither be possible nor desirable. The Workshop was of the view that each country should evolve its own set of criteria for curriculum analysis and therefore favoured the preparation of broad guidelines which each country may use in the development of its own criteria. The following guidelines were discussed:

1. *The assumptions implicit in the criteria should be acceptable to the country:* In the development of criteria it is essential to recognize explicitly the assumptions implied by the criteria one accepts.
2. *The criteria should be feasible*: The resources available for using the criteria for curriculum analysis should be kept in mind in developing the set of criteria. The time of professionally competent people is at a premium in most countries. Criteria which demand an excessive use of highly trained professional time may actually not be feasible. Applying the criteria should not involve the use of procedures which may be too expensive either in terms of time or money.
3. *Criteria should be relevant to curriculum development*: The curriculum analysis should lead to the improvement of the curriculum materials. Hence, the criteria should cover the aspects directly relevant to curriculum development and not so much other matters such as school supervision or teacher education.
4. *Criteria should be comprehensive*: Various factors should receive adequate consideration in developing criteria. One needs to study the curriculum development process and the structure of the curriculum materials which are to be produced to ensure that all aspects directly relevant to curriculum development are taken note of by the criteria.

5. *Analysis of curricula should elicit to what extent the existing curriculum is workable and suits the changing needs of the community*: In developing a set of criteria for analysis of curricula, it is essential to keep in mind the major purpose for which the criteria were evolved, namely, the improvement of the curriculum development process resulting in improved curriculum materials. Curriculum analysis is not a barren academic exercise. It should result in some corrective measures being taken. Hence in designing criteria one should be careful to ensure that remedial action is possible.
6. *Criteria should be reviewed periodically*: Innovative practices are likely to arise. Current practices may no longer be adequate. In other words, the assumptions implicit in the criteria may no longer be valid. Hence criteria should be reviewed and renewed periodically.

B. *Use of criteria*

1. *A variety of people should be involved in the analysis of the curriculum materials*: It is desirable that people who were not directly involved in the development of the curriculum materials be involved in their analysis. Depending on the particular way in which the criteria are structured, different groups of people may take part in the analysis. For example, in the criteria relating to strategies or methods of teaching, it would be very desirable to involve teachers in the analysis. At least some of these teachers should be outside the curriculum development groups.
2. *An appropriate sample of curriculum materials should be subjected to analysis*: As it may not be possible to analyse all of the curriculum materials relevant to the areas of concern, a sample may be selected. Each country should determine what is an appropriate sample considering the resources which it can command and its own national priorities.
3. *The analysis should be done quickly*: If the analysis of the curriculum materials takes as long a time or more than the time required to develop the materials themselves, then the analysis may not be useful. In the context of many Asian countries, action needs to be taken quickly to remedy existing defects. A quick analysis resulting in some remedial action being taken quickly may permit innovative curriculum development procedures.

REGIONAL WORKSHOP ON EDUCATIONAL TECHNOLOGY WITH SPECIAL REFERENCE TO DEVELOPMENT OF LOW-COST EDUCATIONAL MATERIAL, 1977

Organization

In accordance with the Work Plan of the Asian Programme of Educational Innovation for Development (APEID), the Regional Workshop in Educational Technology with Special Reference to Development of Low-cost Educational Materials was held at Kuala Lumpur, Malaysia from 5-15 December, 1977. The Workshop was jointly organized by the Curriculum Development Centre, Ministry of Education, Malaysia, an Associated Centre of APEID and the Asian Centre of Educational Innovation for Development (ACEID), UNESCO Regional Office for Education in Asia and Oceania.

Objectives

The objectives of the Workshop were (i) to exchange experiences in the development of educational materials with special emphasis on prints, games, toys and other low-cost/simple materials and (ii) to consider the use of the environment and locally available materials and other appropriate or adapted methods and techniques being used and developed in the Asian countries.

Participation

There were 23 participants: three from Thailand; two each from Japan and the Philippines; one each from Afghanistan, Bangladesh, India, Indonesia, Iran, Republic of Korea, Nepal, Singapore and Sri Lanka; and seven from Malaysia.

A representative of the United Nations Development Programme (UNDP) Kuala Lumpur, one from UNESCO, Paris, and seven from the Ministry of Education, Malaysia attended as observers.

ACEID was represented by the Chief of ACEID, the Specialist in Curriculum Development and the Associate Expert in Educational Technology.

Guidelines for Designing, Developing and Evaluation of Low Cost Educational Materials

The development of low-cost educational materials is one of the most crucial areas in the development of education in a sense that this process would contribute in overcoming many of the problems which Asian countries are now facing. The development efforts in this respect should therefore be further strengthened in a number of ways.

Low-cost educational materials have an advantage of offering a "do-it-yourself" approach to the teaching-learning situations, and they bring into the classrooms more humanized and personalized teaching strategies especially in the underprivileged schools. When teachers and pupils plan, produce or create their own educational materials, they invariably manifest pride and pleasure in utilizing them to the maximum, because such materials are almost certain to be related directly to the objectives of their class activities. Pupil participation in the preparation of educational materials stimulate learning and develop skills in manipulation and production of worthwhile and useful articles. Co-operative endeavours among school administrators, supervisors, teachers, pupils, parents and the community in the production of low-cost educational materials could provide breakthroughs with the attempt to solve problems of how to provide the children in the available budgetary allotment and with the maximum use of local resources.

An effective design for a realistic programme of the developing low-cost educational materials should consider foremost the improvement of instruction for quality education of the children. It should employ the best that can be done with the available materials and human resources to solve present problems in instruction and to meet the desired objectives and needs of the children. It should provide for practical production activities as well as maximum utilization of the finished materials by teachers and pupils. The programme should also include the evaluation and revision of the educational materials on a continuous basis for the improvement and validation of such materials.

A. *Toward Designing, Development/Production and Evaluation of Low-cost Educational Materials*

During the workshop, it was observed that the processes of actual design and development of low-cost educational materials have some fundamental features in common. These features could broadly be classified under four important aspects for considerations, namely: psychological, instructional, materials, and production.

Psychological Aspect. As regards the psychological consideration needed for designing low-cost educational materials, one has to pay due attention to the following factors:

(i) the "target-group" that is, for whom it is designed;
(ii) the types of experience that would best stimulate the group in terms of their age, intellectual level, socio-cultural background, aptitudes and interests; and
(iii) a clear identification of the actual needs for low-cost materials before settling down to the actual designing.

Instructional Aspect. It was the unanimous agreement of the participants that designing of low-cost educational materials without due consideration of the real instructional factors related to the product, is of little use. The most important instructional factors that are to be considered in the design process are the educational objectives that the educational materials may help to achieve. These objectives may include, among others, knowledge, skills and attitudes. One has to consider the points such as:

(i) How best could these objectives be met?
(ii) What would be the best process to transfer the expected experiences to the pupils?
(iii) What is the best process that would stimulate the pupils?
(iv) Which process would help the pupils to relate the learning experience with their social and cultural environment?

In addition to the above, it was noted that the designer should consider the possibilities of broadening the utilization of the product to the maximum. For example, low-cost educational materials could be utilized in various learning situations, and could make a number of concepts more comprehensible for teaching different disciplines. During the Workshop, the participants recognized the importance of designing multi-purpose low-cost educational materials.

Materials Aspect. On being sufficiently enlightened on the psychological and instructional factors that are related to the anticipated product, one may proceed to the actual designing. At this juncture, it is of prime importance for a designer to consider the nature of the final product rather than be influenced by an existing piece of equipment or aid.

A designer, however, may have the freedom to be guided by an existing piece of educational material while considering the possibilities of improving its quality, widening its usability and reducing the complexity of its production process and manipulations. A good designer therefore has to be a "dreamer" who thinks from varióus angles.

Production Aspect. Finally, this is the phase of actual production of the design. Assuming that the psychological and instructional factors are duly recognized, the next step would be to consider the following three factors:

(i) material factors;
(ii) production factors; and
(iii) quality factors.

Material factors to be considered are the availability, cost, and flexibility of use. The last one is essential to broaden the utility value of a material for many or multi-purposes.

At the next stage, the production factors to be considered are:

(i) the persons who are involved in actual production work;
(ii) skills needed by such persons;
(iii) contributions that may be received from concerned persons/agencies (*e.g.*, for collecting waste and scrap materials from domestic, commercial or industrial sectors);
(iv) the machines and the number of operational-phases involved in the production process;
(v) the sources of energy that may be needed for completing the product; and
(vi) the time needed for producing a unit item.

The quality factors play an important role in the performance and durability of the products. However, throw-away types of materials may also be designed from freely available materials provided that they need the least efforts in reproduction.

When the above sequences are undertaken at an institutional level such as audio-visual materials centre, an educational technology centre or a curriculum development centre, a prototype has to be produced and tested in actual classrooms. This try-out process should be carefully observed and analyzed not only by the people who are involved in designing and in the production process but also other educators in the field to find out problems and possible solutions for improving the original prototype. This process may be repeated until and appropriate material is developed and finalised. The final product will be reproduced on a large scale and distributed to schools.

It is expected that all the personnel involved in the design, development and production process would meet regularly to exchange ideas and to conduct evaluations so that the quality of the materials may be improved continuously throughout the process.

The total process mentioned above is simplified and illustrated as follows:

a. Identifying the need	—nature of need —sources of need —cultural background
b. Specifying target audience	—cultural background —level of education —age —urban or rural
c. Defining objectives	—knowledge —skills —attitudes
d. Identifying skills, procedures and techniques for realizing the objectives	—feasibility —suitability/appropriateness —types of materials, *e.g.* charts, games, etc.
e. Specifying approaches to design	—creating new materials —modifying/improvising exemplar materials
f. Considering raw materials and tools needed	—availability in local environment —cost
g. Identifying the involvement of different people	—skills required —teachers, parents, pupils —community, curriculum specialists

h. Producing prototype	—relevance to curriculum needs
i. Testing try-out model	—cost —time for production —feedback
j. Modifying of the try-out model	—objectives achieved —effectiveness
k. Finalization of the materials	

(*Note*. The above process is not necessarily to be linear, and a certain portion of the process may be repeated.)

B. *Teachers as Agents of Development of Low-cost Educational materials*

The above process is also applicable in a situation when a school teacher himself develops low-cost educational materials using locally available materials. In this case, a teacher may carry out all the processes either by himself or as a co-operative effort among teachers, pupils, parents and the community. In order to facilitate the development efforts and the use of low-cost educational materials in Asia for improving the teaching-learning activities in the classroom, teachers have to take active part in the development of the low-cost educational materials.

Basic to the design for effective low-cost educational materials is the teachers' thorough knowledge of the objectives and contents of education which contribute to the appropriate changes in the pupils' behaviour. Adequate knowledge of the patterns for learning experiences is another concern whereby the teachers and pupils have specific roles to perform and for each learning situation, there are materials, equipment and environmental conditions that can most effectively facilitate learning.

Teachers who are keen to improve the education of their children prepare their own teaching aids and devices. However, the quality and effectiveness of these teacher-made materials have been limited by the kinds of raw materials available, their limited knowledge of effective visual designs and construction techniques, and the insufficient encouragement from their superiors, parents, and the community. With financial and administrative support, professional help from educational media supervisors and technicians, and the co-operative thinking and efforts of parents and the community, it is possible to produce various types of educational materials.

C. *Basic Principles for Developing Low-cost/Simple Materials*

(i) A practical step to be taken in production is to identify or isolate the critically needed instructional materials which teachers alone or the teachers and pupils together can produce out of the available local resources. The production of inexpensive educational materials frees the schools and teachers from over-dependent on commercial and profit-oriented suppliers or producers.

(ii) A survey and an inventory of the local raw materials and resources will spark in the teachers and pupils stock of ideas and thinking on forms and types of materials which they can create to solve their instructional problems.

(iii) A great deal of research, reading, observation, listening, and purposeful exposures to new ideas, information and types of teaching materials will generate much needed motivation and creative ideas for the production of novel or new educational materials. Improvisation of old devices and the utilization of discarded materials are usually the result of imaginative thinking and resourcefulness.

(iv) Start with the simple and easy production techniques or procedures such as learning to draw letters; doing simple sketching; designing simple layouts of posters, diagrams and graphs; and making effective use of the chalkboard, and flannelboard. Such simple skills are fundamental for the production of more difficult materials like displays, charts, puppets, models, etc.

(v) Individual as well as group judgement, common sense, resourcefulness and hard work are important factors in the production programme. "Openness" of one's mind to a variety of ideas and principles in the creation of different forms of educational materials is essential for maximum use of indigenous raw materials.

(vi) Minimize the production of "one-time" or "one-shot" educational materials as this will prove to be a very expensive venture. Multi-purpose materials, cross media kits and packages will surely induce greater participation and several exposures of the children to the development of meaningful learning experiences.

(vii) All low-cost materials must be pupils-oriented to provide for expanding the learning opportunities of children. Maximum participation of pupils and parents in the production of such materials develops better motivation for learning, improves the school and community relations, and ensures economy in the school budget.

D. *Principles for Effective Design of Educational Materials*

The qualities of arrangement, spacing, colour, and overall attractiveness are elements to be achieved in every good educational material. Together they build the design of the visual materials and are usually found in graphic presentations, diagrams, charts, posters, bulletin boards, and other display materials. Good design must be functional.

The following basic principle may summarize the elements of good design for any educational materials:

(i) Clarity is the key. The central idea must be simple, direct and accurate. It must be legible in terms of layout, size, contrast and colour.

(ii) It is compelling. It must attract attention, spark the learners' reaction and promote sharp thinking. Its message must stick; its colour, symbolism, phraseology, and overall form contribute to the lasting impression on the learners.

(iii) It is easy to use. It must be simple and easy to be handled, manipulated and understood by the learners.

(iv) It is appropriate. The material must reflect its purpose and form is closely tied to its content. Its form reflects the experience and age level of the users.

(v) It is worth what it costs. It must be produced as economically as possible in terms of time, efforts and money. It must produce desired results. Careful planning and familiarity with the various types and purposes of inexpensive visual materials contribute economy in production.

E. *Principles for the Utilization of Educational Materials*

The key to the effectiveness of educational materials is the wise use of the available materials in the improvement of the learning process. A teacher may use educational materials in the initiation, presentation, development, application and follow-up phase and time of the lesson, and use them in the right way for effective teaching-learning experiences. The effectiveness of educational materials depends upon the skill and imagination of the teacher using them. There is no magic about them. A teacher may follow this pattern of good teaching.

(i) *Careful selection.* The teacher should examine the materials to find out their suitability or appropriateness to the learning task, ages and abilities of her pupils. The materials should be selected in relation to the learning objectives.

(ii) *Teacher preparation.* The teacher should preview the materials, read the study guides if available, plan the class preparation and follow-up so as to achieve the purposes for using such materials.

(iii) *Class preparation.* The teacher and pupils should discuss the reasons for using the materials, the questions or problems the materials might help solve, the new concepts that might be gained, and the points to look for. The teacher should make sure that the pupils are properly motivated to use the materials.

(iv) *Presentation of materials.* The teacher should have the right materials at the right time. They should be checked and ready for use. The teacher should know how to handle the presentation of such materials before her class.

(v) *Follow-up and application.* The teacher and pupils should discuss the questions or problems suggested in the preparation period; check on the information gained; discuss the parts not clear; and review any part of the media which needs further clarification. Other materials may be used in the follow-up Tests may be given when needed.

(vi) *Evaluation of the lesson and methods used.* The teacher and pupils should discuss whether the materials helped to achieve the purposes set up during the preparation period. The entire learning experience and the outcomes should be appraised as basis for continuous improvement of the learning processes.

F. *Criteria for Evaluating Low-cost Educational Materials*

For realistic judgement about simple, low-cost educational materials the following questions may help:

(i) Will the material be usable in direct relation to a teaching unit? To a specific experience or a problem solving activity?

(ii) Is the content of the material useful and relevant to the learning experiences of the children? Will it increase the depth and richness of their learning?

(iii) Does the material stimulate thinking, reacting, discussing, deciding or further study on the content portrayed?

(iv) Is the content of the material free of conflicts, distractions or bias? Is it in good taste?

(v) Will the material help in the development of wholesome attitudes, values, ideas and concepts?

(vi) Does the material facilitate the process of inference, action or sound conclusion?

(vii) Is the material accurate, typical, and up-to-date?

(viii) Does the workmanship in the construction of the material show careful planning and satisfactory quality? Is it visually strong in verbal, pictorial or graphic design?

(ix) Is the material constructed to withstand hard usage and several handling? Can it be used again and again, and in a number of teaching-learning situations?

(x) Are the physical size, formal and artistic quality satisfactory?

(xi) Are the letterings, label of caption on the material legible and comprehensible? Is there no misleading statement or label or caption on the material?

(xii) Is the material worth the time, effort and money spent in constructing or preparing it?

G. *Production of Low-cost Educational Materials*

Only a few of the commonly used educational materials are considered here:

(i) *Flat pictures.* Flat or still pictures are among the most accessible and least expensive of all educational materials. Usable illustrations can be found in most periodicals and magazines.

The following are the guidelines for the selection and preparation of such materials:

(a) A picture should present a single, clear centre of interest related to the teacher's purpose. The main idea visualized should be apparent and relevant to the unit under study.

(b) The picture should be truthful and present scenes which are typical, rather than unique or starting.

(c) High technical and artistic quality should characterize each picture. Photography, composition, and colour should be attractive.

(d) In most cases the picture should stimulate the imagination, through suggestion of new experiences or re-creation of previous ones.

(e) A picture should be suitable to the age and background of the pupils.

For neatness and effectiveness in presentation, pictures should be mounted. Mounting is also a means of protection and will ensure longer life of the pictures.

(ii) *Other flat visual materials.* These refer to diagrams, charts, graphs, maps, posters, and cartoons, all of which are symbolic representations or explanations, rather than pictorial reproductions.

(a) *Diagrams and charts* are condensed visual summaries of facts and ideas, clarifying relationships. Charts are orderly arrangements of words and figures, but diagrams feature lines and symbols. Charts and diagrams are more useful in summary and review than in introduction of materials.

(b) *Turnover charts or flip charts* often include not only charts and diagrams but also pictures, graphs, and whatever symbols may be helpful for the presentation. These are mounted or printed on large sheets which are shown in sequence by flipping them over the top.

In making a chart or a diagram (1) concentrate on key ideas and dispense with non-essentials; (2) use symbols large enough to be seen easily; (3) make it attractive through use of contrast, space and appropriate colours.

(c) *Graphs* are forms of diagrams but they represent numerical data. They include (1) line graphs, probably the most accurate of all graphs and useful in plotting trends, growth, or frequency; (2) bar graphs, useful for teaching the relationship of individual items to a whole; (3) pictorial graphs, using figures of varying sizes to represent large numbers.

(d) *Maps* are another form of diagrams visualizing geographical relationships. If a small map must be enlarged, use the opaque projector technique or the method.

(e) *Cartoon* is another graphic form of representing ideas, situations, and relationships; and its effectiveness depends upon unity and clarity of the visual presentation. Distinctively, however, a cartoon features exaggeration and humour.

(f) *The feltboard* or adhesive board takes advantage of the facts that wool and cotton felt will adhere to like surfaces. On a board covered with felt or napped material various pictures of wood symbols are placed. A presentation can be built-up piece by piece, dismantled, and reassembled for review. Children especially enjoy placing the pieces on the board as a story is told.

(g) *Posters* are visual materials that put across an idea in one fleeting glance. They exert great visual power through their qualities of boldness, directness, simplicity and dynamism to drive home their the message two components of a good poster are:

(1) Pictorial elements which consist of the major illustrations, secondary or supplementary illustrations (optional), logo—a sign for rapid identification (optional), white or "silence" space, and colour.

(2) Word elements which consist of the *headline* or statement of the theme or idea, secondary or amplifying statements, and command or the "call to action".

(iii) *Three-dimensional materials.* Some materials add a third dimension to visual images. Their realism offers a supplementary appeal to the sense of touch.

(a) *Objects and specimens* are simply the real things, usually taken from their natural setting to be used by a group of pupils. Objects of art from other civilizations may contribute to inter-cultural understanding.

(b) The terms, *model* and *mock-up* are frequently interchangeably used. Models of various animals are useful in animal study; a mock-up of a clock helps in developing skills in telling time among the children. Both model and mock-up may increase understanding by enlarging small items or reducing the size of unwieldy one.

(c) *Globes* and *relief* or *terrain maps* are forms of models. They visualize geographical relationships and may be used for such varying purposes as explaining principles of soil conservation, studying highway problems, or planning a trip.

(d) *Puppets and marionettes* make strong appeal to the imagination especially of children. Featuring whimsy and fancy rather than realism, they can be used to tell stories at little risk of stereotyping characters. Some types of drama not easily presented with human actors, adaptations of classic plays, visual interpretation of music and development of fantasy are ideally suited to the use of puppets or marionettes.

(iv) *Use of colours.* Educational materials in black and white are usually cheaper and more available than those produced in colour. However, in local production discreet use of colours add to the effectiveness of the materials for the following reasons: legibility and visibility, truthfulness, psychological effect, dramatic impact, interest created, colour contrasts, colour coding, and active reaction. Visibility and contrast are two most important points in the use of colour for visual materials. High contrast range is often desirable and good visibility is always a must for all visual materials. Red and orange are colours which have good eye catching qualities for they activate the nerve endings of the eyes much more than any other colours.

Teachers who have to plan and make-up educational materials must consider the theories of colour which are based on lights and pigments as well as the viewing location and the effects upon the users of the materials.

(v) *Lettering educational materials.* Lettering on visual materials can make or break the visual presentation. Teachers should develop skills in lettering techniques. Lettering brushes, speedball pens, ink, crayons, coloured pencils, and lettering manuals/instructions will prove helpful. Tracing or cutting out suitable letters from newspapers, magazines and advertisements give good effects.

The titling of any visual material is of primary importance. Titles should always be:

Brief — usually two lines, but only one is preferable.
Accurate — saying no more and no less than intended; make them telegraphic.
Arresting — the emotional impact of a visual material can be heightened by the use of appealing work symbols to reinforce the message.
Legible — the spacing between letters, their thickness, or thinness, spacing between lines or words and the arrangement of the parts give the total effect of attractiveness and clean-cutness of the whole message. Legibility also depends on colour and larger letters.

All graphic materials must be properly titled; objects, specimens, models, and other 3-dimensional materials must be labelled to add meaning to their visual impact.

(vi) *Designing layout format.* In planning effective graphic educational materials a good layout is essential. It should have the following elements:

(i) *Balance.* Are both sides of the layout equal? Does one side appear to be heavier than the other?
(ii) *Emphasis.* Decide which parts are the most important and emphasize them.
(iii) *Contrast.* If something is important enough to be included in the layout, it is important enough to be seen. Contrast light with dark and dark with light so that the parts are clearly visible.
(iv) *Harmony.* Do all the parts go together? Does the lettering fit

the subject of the visual presentation?

(vii) *Reference files for layouts and sketches.* In the preparation of a variety of educational materials, it is necessary to develop some reference files for layouts and sketches. These serve as basic resource for hand-made graphic materials. Tear sheet files can be assembled from the following:

(a) Pictorial, diagrammatic and allied graphic contents and cuttings from newspapers, magazines, comics, and other discarded booklets. Some of the most common pictorial magazines for this purpose are magazines, supplements of the daily newspapers, and many other local and foreign periodicals and publications.

(b) Pamphlets and pictorial display materials from embassies, tourist information centres and offices as well as dealers of audiovisual materials and equipment.

(c) Advertisement materials from government and private industrial agencies.

(d) Sets of picture postcards and pictorial cut-outs produced commercially.

(e) Tracings of sketches and other pictures from encyclopaedias, pictorial books, etc.

The collection of pictorial materials will serve as a rich source of ideas to develop educational materials. Some of them can even be mounted for use on bulletin boards, feltboards, and magnetic boards. The tear sheets may be arranged under different sub-headings according to the different categories of the pictures and illustrations.

FOURTH REGIONAL CONFERENCE OF MINISTERS OF EDUCATION AND THOSE RESPONSIBLE FOR ECONOMIC PLANNING IN ASIA AND OCEANIA, 1978

Organization

The Fourth Regional Conference of Ministers of Education and those responsible for Economic Planning in Asia and Oceania was held in Colombo, Sri Lanka, from 24 July to 1 August, 1978 with the

Government of the Republic of Sri Lanka acting as the generous host. It was organized by the United Nations Educational, Scientific and Cultural Organization with the co-operation of the United Nations Economic and Social Commission for Asia and the Pacific.

The Governments of 25 Member-States of UNESCO in Asia and Oceania were invited, in accordance with the decision of the Executive Board, to take part in the Conference. Twenty-two Member-States sent their delegations to participate and 20 of them were led by Ministers or Vice-Ministers. Observers from other Member-States (the Holy See, Fiji and the Maldives) as well as representatives of the organizations of the United Nations system and observers from intergovernmental and non-governmental organizations attended the Conference. In all, 177 delegates from 22 Member-States in the region, representing both national Ministries concerned with education and Ministries/agencies concerned with national planning, and 37 observers and representatives took part in the Conference.

Background

This Conference was the fourth in a series of Regional Conferences of Ministers of Education and Those Responsible for Economic Planning. The first was held in 1962 in Tokyo, Japan, and was attended by the Member-States participating in the Karachi Plan which was evolved at a regional meeting held in Karachi in 1959-60, for the development of primary education in Asia. The second conference, held in Bangkok, Thailand in 1965, adopted the Asian Model of Educational Development which presented a set of suggested targets for national action and regional co-operation. The third conference in Singapore in 1971 marked a further step in the progressive development of initiatives for regional and international co-operation in education, and, among other things, initiated the Asian Programme of Educational Innovation for Development.

Declaration of the Conference

1. The Fourth Regional Conference of Ministers of Education and Those Responsible for Economic Planning in Asia and Oceania, organized by UNESCO with the help of the United Nations Economic and Social Commission for Asia and the Pacific, and meeting in Colombo from 24 July to 1 August, 1978, at the

generous invitation of the Government of Sri Lanka, solemnly adopts the following Declaration.

2. Considerable progress has been made since the Conference held at Singapore in 1971: the increase in enrolments has been accompanied by a substantial increase in educational personnel and facilities and by numerous improvements and innovations carried out in the education system of the different Member-States of the region. There has been a marked trend to move away from elitist education towards broadly-based education. This progress, however, should not disguise the magnitude of the task which remains to be achieved. The higher percentages which young people and the population of rural areas represent in relation to the population as a whole, and the ever growing number of children, young people and adults who have to be educated, provide the measures of what has still to be done. Tens of millions of children do not have access to education; in absolute terms the number of illiterates is increasing; and in many cases educational disparities are widening.
3. On the eve of the Third United Nations Development Decade and in the context of a new international economic order, it is clear that education, whose ultimate goal is to promote the full development of the human personality, will be faced with increased responsibilities for contributing to the economic, social and cultural progress of societies, for consolidating national independence and for strengthening peace and international co-operation and understanding.
4. Despite the wide diversity of situations and cultures of the countries of the region, the Member-States of Asia and Oceania share the following particular concerns and convictions:

(a) The Conference considers that implementation of the right to education is essential for the exercise of, and for strengthening respect for, all other human rights and fundamental freedoms without distinction of any kind.

(b) The Conference declares itself unequivocally in favour of education which is open wide to all. It reaffirms its commitment to the principle of universal schooling of children, and considers it essential to take vigorous steps to eliminate illiteracy and provide out-of-school and non-formal education for adults as well as children and young people, particularly those who have had no schooling or only inadequate schooling. Special attention should be given to those groups which often remain educationally disadvantaged, in particular in rural areas, and appropriate measures should also be taken in favour of those who suffer from economic or social disadvantages, notably the rural and urban poor, and in favour of the handicapped.

(c) The Conference is convinced that high priority should be given to the education of girls and women on a basis of equality with men, in order to enable them to achieve self-fulfilment as well as to make them fully aware of, and prepare them for, their role in social life and national development.

(d) The Conference wishes to stress that in order to achieve genuine democratization, equality of prospects of success in education must go on a par with equality of access. Equality of access and of prospects of success entail the qualitative improvement and renewal of education in the framework of policies based on national choices, conducive to social justice and designed to provide education geared to the conditions, needs and culture of each country.

(e) The Conference considers that the improvement of the pre and in-service training of teachers and of other educational personnel, the improvement of the status of teachers and also their participation in the reform of education, are indispensable for the success of any education system.

(f) The Conference considers it essential that education should be closely linked to life and to the world of work and should impart to children and young people the attitudes and skills which will prepare them for their role as producers, citizens and participants in the development of the community. Education should accord a prominent place to science and technological education and make experience of productive work an integral part of general education. By drawing their inspiration from the thriving cultural traditions of many countries of the region, educational institutions will be more closely associated with the economic, social and cultural life of the communities they serve and will contribute to strengthening national unity. It is also incumbent on education to ensure the harmonious development of the personality in its intellectual, physical, aesthetic and ethical aspects and in particular to encourage behaviour conductive to the strengthening of, and respect for, basic human rights and fundamental freedoms.

(g) The Conference is convinced that higher educational establishments should shoulder a greater share of responsibility in order to contribute to indigenous development and the progress of local and national communities, both by their teaching and research activities in the field of science and technology and by the part they can play in preservation of the national heritage and in cultural development.

(h) The Conference is fully aware that the tasks mentioned above require the mobilization and effective utilization of all available financial, physical and human resources. If the efforts made to develop and improve education are to bear fruit it seems to it essential that the population as a whole — teachers, pupils and students, parents, various community groups — should participate actively and on a large scale in them.

In adopting the present Declaration the Conference, *convinced* of the particular gravity attaching in the Asia and Oceania region to the problems referred to above and the urgency of taking energetic steps to find rapid solutions to them, by effective regional and international co-operation, *Deems it essential* that the Member-States of the region:

(i) Take the necessary steps, and mobilize the necessary financial and human resources, to provide education for the broad mass of the people, by achieving as rapidly as possible, where this is still necessary, universal primary education, the elimination of illiteracy and the intensification of efforts directed to providing non-formal education for the benefit of adults and children or young people, particularly those who have had no schooling or only inadequate schooling, removing any impediment to equality of access and of prospects of success for women and paying special attention to the most disadvantaged groups;

(ii) endeavour to improve the quality of education and make it more relevant, not only by modernizing it and gearing it to development objectives but also by rooting it in national, cultural and human values;

Appeals to the international community to have recourse to new forms of co-operation based on the concept of a new and more equitable international economic order for the purpose of giving wide-ranging assistance to the Member-States of Asia and Oceania in their efforts to develop their education system;

Invites UNESCO, in collaboration with other international or regional organizations concerned, to continue and intensify its regional action with a view to fostering technical co-operation between the countries of the region, in particular developing countries, and in this connection to strengthen the regional co-operation machinery operating within the framework of the Organization and arrange for it to be extended to the field of higher education.

REGIONAL MEETING OF EXPERTS ON NEW APPROACHES TO EDUCATION OF CHILDREN OF PRE-SCHOOL AGE, 1978

Organization

In pursuance of Resolution 1.151 of the General Conference at its Nineteenth Session, UNESCO convened a Regional Meeting of Experts on "New Approaches to Education of Children of Pre-School Age". The Meeting was held at the UNESCO Regional Office for Education in Asia and Oceania, Bangkok, Thailand, from 4 to 12 September, 1978. This Report is a contribution by UNESCO to the International Year of the Child (1979).

Objectives

The main purpose of the Meeting was to exchange and study experiences among the Member-States in the Asia and Oceania region, in regard to new approaches which may have been adopted for early childhood education, with particular reference to disadvantaged rural and urban populations, and to provide suggestions for future practical programmes of action.

Participation

In preparation for the Meeting, each Member-State was requested to send in a report on the status of early childhood education, and a case study on a project for the delivery of early childhood education to learners in disadvantaged areas. Sixteen Member-States responded by sending in their country reports. Twenty participants from sixteen Member-States and ten observers from interested agencies, including those from the UN System, attended the Meeting. Two resource persons, Mrs. Mina Swaminathan (India) and Dean (Dr.) Aurora G. Corpuz (Philippines) assisted the Meeting.

Recommendations

National Level

1. It is recommended that Member-States consider including specifically the concerns for young children in their socio-economic *policies*, and incorporating in these policies the following:

— the emphasis on children of disadvantaged populations;
— the inclusion of the whole age-range 0 to 6+ years;
— the need to provide integrated services for the development of the whole child, including health, education and nutrition;
— the focus on the child in the family, and where possible, the child and the family;
— the role of early childhood services as vehicles for social change;
— the place of early childhood education as a component of lifelong education.

2. It is recommended that Member-States, in developing *strategies* and plans to carry out these policies, consider that:

— a range and diversity of programmes be developed in recognition of differences that exist among various sections of the population in a country, seeking to complement these differences in order to enable each child to attain his or her full potential, and all groups to participate in the mainstream of development;
— emphasis be placed on a decentralized approach to programme design, and on the pivotal role of the local worker, including the

parent;

— a consistent methodology be built around the principle of 'participation' which would pervade all the programmes;
— continuity be established with informal education in the home, with other stages of education, and other social services, so that early childhood education could make a significant contribution to social change;
— public awareness of the importance of early childhood be created, and support for the policies and programmes be generated.

3. It is recommended that Member-States, in the *implementation* on policies, plans and strategies, consider the following:

— the development and strengthening of *institutions*, specially for: research in early childhood; production of literature materials and equipment for children; production of teaching/learning material for the preparation of personnel;
— the development and strengthening of *infrastructures*, especially for: mass communication for support of programmes; decentralization of programme and curriculum planning; the delivery of integrated services; the delivery of mass training, continuous supervision, monitoring and evaluation;
— the development and strengthening of *competencies* required for the above institutional and infrastructure operations;
— the development and strengthening of *field experimental projects*.

International Level

1. *It is recommended that*, at the request of Member-States, *UNESCO and other interested organisations*:

— provide assistance to the above actions at the national level;

2. *It is recommended that UNESCO:*

— establish a net-working of national centres, programmes, and projects for early childhood education in Member-States, with the UNESCO Regional Office for Education in Asia and Oceania acting as a facilitating agent;
— arrange for inter-country exchange of experiences through

regional and sub-regional meetings and seminars, study visits and placement programmes;

— develop comparative studies in co-operation with Member-States;
— set up a data bank and a Clearing House Service in the area of early childhood development;
— convene, at regular intervals, a regional panel of early childhood educators and researchers to monitor progress in the region and suggest future directions for action.

3. *It is also recommended that UNESCO:*

— circulate the Final Report of this Meeting widely to national agencies dealing with early childhood programmes both within and outside the education departments;
— present the Final Report of this Meeting to the UNESCO Programme of the International Year of the Child.

REGIONAL SEMINAR ON TECHNICAL AND VOCATIONAL EDUCATION IN ASIA AND OCEANIA, 1979

In addition to the suggestions made at the plenary and group discussions, the Seminar held at Singapore from 20-27 November, 1979, considered the Revised Recommendation concerning Technical and Vocational Education adopted by the General Conference of UNESCO at its 18th Session (1974), and the relevant recommendations of the Fourth Regional Conference of Ministers of Education and those responsible for Economic Planning in Asia and Oceania.

The Seminar discussed the issues related to productive work as part of the learning process, and technical and vocational education in relation to rural development. It decided to make a series of recommendations for consideration by governments or education agencies, and urged that priority be given to this approach to technical and vocational education.

The Seminar also discussed continuing education, and the appropriateness of formal and non-formal methods of learning. These points were taken into account when the following suggestions were being prepared, with the intention that many of these apply to relevant aspects of continuing education.

SUGGESTIONS FOR FUTURE ACTION

National Level

I. Productive Work

A. *Curriculum design, development and evaluation related to productive work.* In these processes, the Seminar recommends that consideration be given to:

(a) the proportion of time to be spent on productive work throughout each course;
(b) the proportion of time given at each level of technical and vocational education;
(c) the ways in which productive work is most appropriately undertaken:

(i) in the sandwich mode;
(ii) after the theoretical studies have been completed;
(iii) concurrently with theoretical stuies , such as part-time study and part-time work;

(d) which aspects of the several objectives should be given priority at each stage of technical and vocational education;
(e) whether simulated work places or actual, real-life work places are more appropriate, specifically the placement of the productive work and whether it is best undertaken in:

(i) the educational institution's own training facility or workshop;
(ii) a special production unit or centre attached to the school;
(iii) an on-the-job site, in industry;
(iv) in a training centre attached to industry.

2. The appointment of officials to co-operate with, and to co-ordinate the activities of the teaching institutions and the industries and services, in order to;

(a) work out with industries or services the nature of the productive work experience required by the learners;
(b) explain to the teaching institutions the nature of the curriculum most required by the learners to fit them for work in the industries or services;
(c) assess the effectiveness of the productive work experience;
(d) provide vocational guidance to learners.

3. Providing equal access in all areas of technical and vocational education to boys and girls, men and women.
4. Providing special opportunities for those who are disadvantaged, such as those handicapped by poverty or physical problems.
5. The need to give priority to the educational objectives of technical and vocational education programmes (that is, to contribute effectively to the learning process) rather than to allow the production outcome to be of greater importance.
6. The desirability, within the process of curriculum design and implementation, of including:

(a) surveys of manpower needs to determine necessary priorities in implementing courses and associated productive work programmes;
(b) task analyses of jobs in industries so that courses may be designed in terms of appropriate behavioural objectives and the correct productive work experience be provided;
(c) analyses of the learners' productive work experience to assist further reinforcement of learning in the institution.

7. The incorporation of productive work as an integral and essential component of the curriculum by involving the following design actions:

(a) task analyses of productive work jobs for matching with the competencies developed in institutional training, and specification of behavioural objectives for systematic curriculum development for the institutional programme;
(b) surveys of the community for location of service needs and subsequent task analyses of these;
(c) placement of the productive work experience in the total learning sequence planned for the learner to ensure the most

effective reinforcement and new learning;

(d) analyses of the experiences of the learner in productive work for further reinforcement of learning in the institution.

8. The incorporation of productive work experiences early in school education and its continuation, with greater emphasis and sophistication, into technical and vocational education.
9. Flexible design of the curriculum in order to allow for productive work to be completed either on the job or in a school situation.
10. Decentralizing, to the local level, decision-making about the curriculum in order to facilitate the implementation of both productive work and course work.
11. The use of local resources and materials in curriculum development.
12. The inclusion in the curriculum documents of:

    (a) the relationship of productive work objectives to the course objectives;
    (b) recommended teaching sequences necessary to link productive work to theory;
    (c) methods of assessment of the productive work for in-course and terminal purposes;
    (d) the proportion of overall assessment to be awarded to productive work.
13. The degree of importance to be given to such factors as cost effectiveness, entrepreneurial skills and marketing.
14. Methods of evaluating productive work in the curriculum, including the:

    (a) relevance of productive work to the overall curriculum;
    (b) problems of implementation of productive work;
    (c) problems of procurement of resources, and problems concerned with finished products.

B. *Staff development for productive work.* In this connection, the Seminar recommends that consideration should be given to:

1. The policy decisions that should be made and carried out about the recruitment and development of staff.
2. The importance of recruiting staff who are experienced and able

in productive work.

3. Policy decisions about the proper and necessary status of teachers, (*Note:* Policy statements should acknowledge that a skilled educational staff is as important a resource as are facilities and finance in the provision of technical and vocational education staff the status which matches the importance of their contribution to social and economic development. Specifically they should be paid salaries and employed under terms of service which are at least as attractive and those they would obtain in industry.)
4. Given present difficulties in recruiting people, the design of staff development programmes and their high priority to support the successful introduction and maintenance of productive work in technical and vocational education programmes.
5. Preparing staff development programmes for all personnel engaged in productive work programmes — including policy-makers, teachers, instructors, administrators and clerical staff, industry liaison officers and personnel in industries.
6. The inclusion within pre- and in-service staff training programmes, of courses and activities which foster positive attitudes toward productive work and which enhance skills in planning and managing productive work programmes. The trained staff, may thereby become agents of curriculum reform capable of integrating productive work with technical and vocational education programmes and administrating such programmes, particularly with regard to facilitating the liaison and interface with industry.
7. Staff development programmes which include the requirement that personnel undertake and the given appropriate recognition for such activities as:

   (a) pre-training industrial experience, or
   (b) periods of 'return to industry' after the pre-training course so that the teacher may both bring existing skills up to date and learn new ones.

8. Allocating priority to staff development programmes for skills necessary to carry out productive work.
9. Designing staff development programmes which produce teachers competent in the skills required for productive work,

together with the necessary theory and attitudes.

10. The design and implementation of staff development programmes which can be carried out by staff at the local level (including enhancing the competence of local staff to allow this to be done).

C. *Development of learning resources for productive work.* In this context, the Seminar recommends that consideration be given to:

1. The development of materials directed to a variety of groups (teachers, instructors, administrators and clerical peoples, students, and personnel engaged in industry — employers, union members, and the self-employed).
2. Materials which would explain—

   (a) the aims and objectives of productive work;
   (b) the importance of productive work in technical and vocational education courses;
   (c) the complementary roles of each group—their rights and responsibilities;
   (d) the types of productive work which are more suitable.

3. The development of guidelines for both the learners and the industries, which:

   (a) indicate the details of the curriculum which the learners are undertaking;
   (b) indicate the types of productive work they should have;
   (c) record what productive work each learner has undertaken.

4. The development of worksheets for productive work which may consist of:

   (a) the objectives of the productive work experience;
   (b) the necessary pre-requisite theory;
   (c) the materials required;
   (d) the methods of production.

D. *Planning and organization for productive work.* The Seminar recommends that consideration be given to:

1. The determination of policies which should be made at each appropriate level affirming the importance of productive work programmes as a necessary component of technical and vocational education.
2. The establishment of effective national support structures to co-ordinate activities among a number of agencies.
3. The establishment of productive work committees, comprising members from industries and the community, at appropriate levels — particularly the local level — to:

   (a) advise the technical and vocational education authorities on the needs for, the provision of, and the effectiveness of such programmes;
   (b) assist with the liaison and interface between the educational institution and industries;
   (c) provide assurance of relevance of the programmes to changing demands.

4. Appropriate legislation and legal offices for such arrangements as learner stipends, insurance and agreements with employers.
5. Official inspection systems which might be applied to the implementation plan to ensure that there is co-operation between the institutions and the industries.
6. The adjustment of class scheduling in technical and vocational education programmes to facilitate the inclusion of productive work.

E. *Research and development for productive work.* In regard to this area, the Seminar recommends that consideration be given to:

1. Action-oriented research and development programmes which might be initiated to investigate the effectiveness of curriculum development programmes, specifically:

   (a) the existing research literature to be analysed, synthesized and disseminated;
   (b) case studies and longitudinal studies of curriculum development programmes and their effectiveness within the geographical area.

2. Action-oriented curriculum research and development programmes which might be initiated in co-operation with staff development programmes, specifically:

   (a) the existing research literature might be searched, synthesized and disseminated;
   (b) case studies and longitudinal studies of staff development programmes within the geographical area.

3. The establishment, by each country, of a National Technical and Vocational Education Clearing House, which will co-operate with a Regional Clearing House. The clearing house service is an urgent need in all countries in the region, to prevent wasteful duplication of efforts, and to facilitate immediate supply of resources.
4. Determining the functions and operations of such clearing houses, which could have as their primary mission the collection and dissemination of all available information about productive work programmes within the Member-States, specifically:

   (a) research and development activities;
   (b) course design and implementation activities;
   (c) staff development activities;
   (d) learning resources development and production;
   (e) planning and organization of programmes;
   (f) provision of and utilization of resources;
   (g) statistics including cost data and other information.

5. The range of items to be included, such as descriptions of research studies; descriptions of successful programmes (lists of objectives, descriptions of learning resource materials, examples of learner record cards), accounts of effective procedures (liaison between institutions and industries); and location of people with particular expertise who may be consulted. (Selection of items should be governed by their validity and usability to the potential users.)
6. How the retrieval system could be kept simple and readily available to practitioners and administrators in the field.
7. The method of operation of such clearing houses, specifically:

(a) a regular contribution of items to the clearing house headquarters;
(b) a standard format for listing items, such as:

— title of the item;
— classification and code;
— grade level;
— brief description of the information, materials and activities;
— location—name and address of the source.

(c) a printed booklet or loose-leaf sheets which list the existing items and are regularly added to, on a quarterly basis;
(d) the likelihood that the clearing house would cover topics other than 'productive work'; for example, rural technical and vocational education, teacher education and the like. (It would be necessary to use a coding system which could be expanded as required.)

8. The allocation of funds for the purpose of establishing the clearing houses.

II. Technical and Vocational Education in Rural Areas

The Seminar recognized that the issues raised concerning productive work as part of the learning process had a special relevance to the expansion of technical and vocational education in rural areas. For this reason, a separate section was set aside for some recommendations.

The Seminar had an opportunity to discuss only a few of the major issues relating to technical and vocational education in rural areas, and has been able to make only a few recommendations. Participants felt that discussion at much greater depth is necessary. It is declared, therefore, that more seminars are needed specifically to discuss and make recommendations on this matter.

A. *Curriculum.* In this connection the Seminar recommends that consideration be given to:

1. The value of relating the curriculum to the needs of the community.

2. The flexibility of curriculum design, to allow for regional differences in rural areas to suit local needs (possibly leading to a modular approach).
3. Basing the curriculum upon a survey of the area where it is to be taught, learned and used.
4. Emphasis upon entrepreneurial skills.
5. Basing the design of the curriculum on current and emerging patterns of development, and providing for new skills which will diversify employment, including self-employment opportunities.

B. *Development of staff*. For this area, the Seminar recommends that consideration be given to:

1. Staff development programmes which emphasize entrepreneurial skills.
2. Programmes which aim to improve the skills and attitudes necessary for rural development.
3. Programmes which aim to provide teachers with the necessary skills and attitudes to develop curriculum and learning resources for rural areas.
4. Programmes designed to allow staff to become involved in community activities.
5. Including in teacher training programmes, optional components which develop skills and attitudes appropriate for technical and vocational education in rural areas.
6. The use of local expertise and resources, wherever practicable, in the conduct of staff development programmes.

C. *Learning resources development*. In relation to these the Seminar recommends that consideration be given to:

1. The establishment of central workshops for the development of resource materials related to rural areas.
2. The involvement of the local community in the production of resources.
3. The development of resources which facilitate distance learning (e.g., radio, TV, self-instructional materials).
4. The development of resources at the appropriate level of sophistication and cost-effectiveness.

D. *Planning and organization.* In this context the Seminar recommends that consideration be given to:

1. Policy decisions being made at each appropriate level which affirm the importance of special technical and education programmes for rural areas.
2. Rural area committees comprising of educational and local members being established to:

   (a) advise the technical and vocational education authorities on the needs for the provision, and the effectiveness, of such programmes;
   (b) assist with the liaison and interface between the educational institution and industry;
   (c) ensure recognition and acceptance.

E. *Research and development for rural areas.* In this connection the Seminar recommends that consideration be given to:

1. The development of techniques to evaluate the needs of rural areas in order that relevant curriculum be designed.
2. The development of special modules for teacher training for rural areas.

Regional Level

The primary objective of inter-country co-operation at the regional level will be to contribute to the enhancement of the capacity of each Member-States to develop an appropriate technical and vocational education system suited to its needs and conditions, in particular with respect to integrating productive work in the system and contributing to rural development.

UNESCO, the Colombo Plan Staff College, and other organizations and institutions that have regional coverage, have important work to do in enhancing these national capacities. In addition to direct support to national level actions, activities such as the following may be taken account of when UNESCO and other organizations plan their regional programmes related to technical and vocational education:

1. Action-oriented studies, such as those which investigate — the

existing role of productive work, such as income-generating activities, work experience and socially useful activities in relation to educational content, paying attention to different socio-cultural milleux, and to needs in human resources development at different stages of development

— alternative strategies aimed at making educational content, structures and teaching methods at the different levels relevant to social, cultural and economic development needs;
— the occupational preferences and employability of secondary school leavers.

2. Policy-oriented studies such as those which investigate:

necessary changes in curricula, methods and other relevant aspects of the educational system in order to develop attitudes, skill and knowledge in their graduates that are conductive to their employment;

— ways and means of assisting graduates in their efforts to obtain employment for themselves.

3. Exchange of experiences and personnel among the countries in regard to innovative developments in technical and vocational education — and in particular integration of productive work in technical and vocational education – and contributions to rural development, such as through:
— regional and sub-regional meetings;
— study tours.

4. Inter-country transfer of expertise through means such as:

— regional and sub-regional training programmes including those specifically for curriculum development and staff training;
— mobile teams for in-country training courses;
— placement and attachment programmes in which staff from one country are attached as fellow workers to relevant projects in another country for on-the-job training.

5. Co-operative research on problems of common concern among two or more countries, particularly those related to costs, curriculum design and development, and human resources development aspects.
6. At the request of Member-States, assist in carrying out joint appraisal studies of the problems in the country relating to the development of technical and vocational education.
7. Establishing a Regional Technical and Vocational Education Clearing House in Asia and Oceania (RETVECH/AO) for the exchange of information and documentation, at the most appropriate place for the effective functioning of the Clearing House; *i.e.* in close association with curriculum design and development programmes and staff development programmes at a regional level. Further, in the manner that UNESCO has assisted Member-States in establishing a national system for scientific information, similar assistance should be provided for a national information, system for technical and vocational education. Considering the urgency for interchange of information, documentation services may be initiated immediately through existing regional agencies. The National Technical and Vocational Education Clearing Houses should be 'networked' into the Regional Clearing Houses Service. Member-States will retrieve information from the Regional Service, and will have responsibility to contribute to the Regional Service on a regular basis.
8. In support of the above activities, establishing a Panel of Experts from the Member-States in the Region, to monitor and review periodically the progress of technical and vocational education in the Region, and advise on emerging aspects of regional co-operation and regional action.

TECHNICAL WORKING GROUP ON LEARNING NEEDS AND PROBLEMS IN PRIMARY EDUCATION, 1983

Participants

The Working Group held at Bangkok from 6 to 12 September, 1983 included participants from Afghanistan, Australia, Bangladesh, India,

Malaysia, Nepal, Pakistan, Philippines, Representatives. of Korea and Thailand. One representative of SEAMES (Southeast Asian Ministers of Education Secretariat and nine staff members of the Regional Office for Education in Asia and the Pacific also attended the meetings.

Overview of Research Studies in the Region

The investigation of children's learning needs and problems in the Region has consisted of a variety of approaches adopted in different countries by various agencies, such as University, College, and Ministry/departments. In addition, research institutes have been established in several countries in the Region—for example, the Australian Council for Educational Research; the Institute of Education and Research in Bangladesh; the National Council of Educational Research and Training in India; the Curriculum Textbook and supervision Centre in Nepal; the National Institute of Psychology in Pakistan; the Centre for the study of Children and Youth in the Philippines; the Korean Institute for Research in the Behavioural Sciences in the Republic of Korea; and the Institute of Behavioural Sciences Research in Thailand.

In studies of the learning problems of children, the plight of children from disadvantaged groups has received considerable emphasis.

With respect to language in education, it has been observed that children who are required to learn to read, and receive educational instruction in, a language with which they have not been previously familiar; frequently encounter learning problems. Language problems are also prevalent in children from low socio-economic backgrounds, a finding reported by the great majority of countries in the Region. It has also been found in Pakistan that children of parents whose educational level is low often do not exhibit high-level verbal and abstraction skills, a contributory factor to low school achievement. The attainment of good verbal and communication skills in primary schooling has also been observed to be relatively poor in disadvantaged groups in studies completed in the Philippines and Thailand. With respect to the oral language of children and the language of the school, several studies in India have drawn attention to the adverse effects that can arise when there is "dissonance between the language spoken by disadvantaged groups and the (middle class) language used in books and instruction".

Studies of relationships between the learning problems of children and levels of parental education have also received attention.

Children's low achievement in school is often associated with parental illiteracy. India has also found that "first generation learners", i.e., children whose parents have not been educated, often perform poorly on abstract reasoning tasks. In Nepal, it has been found in some parts of far western regions that girls of parents who are illiterate are often prevented from attending school and are married at an early age. The Republic of Korea has introduced parent education programmes designed to provide basic information on child development, improved child rearing techniques, and advice on improving the family environment. In Australia, research on parent involvement in primary education has found that parents from low socio-economic backgrounds are willing to be involved in their children's education, provided that schools and teachers can communicate the aims of such involvement in a way that parents can understand, and provided that schools and teachers provide appropriate advice and resources which parents can utilize.

With regard to cognitive development, and amount of research has been completed in the Region, often within a Piagetian framework, which assumes that children proceed through stages of cognitive development. (Here it should be noted that the results of recent research, completed mainly in Europe and the United-States of America, indicate that children can exhibit certain intellectual and social skills at a considerably earlier age then is predicted in Piagetian theory. These recent findings have considerable implications for practice in early childhood development and education, particularly in relation to the pre-school and early primary school years.)

Research in the Philippines has found that middle class children complete conservation tasks about one year ahead of their completion by children from low socio-economic groups. However, in Pakistan, studies of primary school children's completion of Piagetian cognitive tasks found no difference between the performances of children from urban and rural areas. Rather than, cognitive level underlying learning difficulties in such children, unsuitable educational activities were more important factors. Research in the Philippines has attributed poor performance in classification, attention and perception to impediments to cognitive development, such as children's low socio-economic background.

With regard to the development of "cognitive competence", the importance of good nutrition, and the importance of adequate early stimulation, have been reported. Research in India has drawn attention to the need for adequate nutrition if the child is to develop adequate mental capacities, and has also noted that inadequate nutrition is more prevalent in lower socio-economic groups. Research in India has also found that children who perform significantly better on cognitive tests tend to have mothers who are rated high on the cognitive stimulation of then infants and children.

Research has also been conducted on the learning styles of children. For example in the Philippines, the preferred method of learning of children who have had no kindergarten experience at the pre-school level has been investigated. Lack of pre-school experience was found to affect children's attention skills, and the way in which they attempted to learn. In India, a study of children's attention to relevant and irrelevant learning cues has found this to be associated with performance or cognitive tests in the age range 6-9 years, although after several years of schooling (ages 11-12 years), this is no longer the case.

Attitudes towards learning have also been studied in the Region. In Nepal, it has been found that in some parts of far western regions negative attitudes towards the education of females are prevalent. To encourage the enrolment of females in literacy programmes, special reading materials for females have been prepared in Pakistan, instruments for measuring the attitudes of rural populations towards the education of boys and girls have been developed.

School achievement and drop-out from schools have also been widely studied. Assessment of scholastic achievement in the "basic subject" in Nepal has found that children of upper primary stages find it easier to use numerical systems which employ Hindu Arabic symbols rather than alternatives such as Devnagiri numerals. Studies in Thailand have found that scholastic achievement is closely related to parental vocation and socio-economic status, geographical region, dialects spoken at home, and school size. To increase scholastic achievement, Malaysia has laid considerable stress on the acquisition of the 3Rs in early primary education, seeing this as the essential stepping stone to subsequent education. In Australia, scholastic achievement was surveyed nationally in 1975 and 1980. However it has recently been decided to abandon further national surveys of achievement for a variety of reasons, one of which is that the findings of national surveys were found to have little impact on the educational system, which is a State, not a National, responsibility. In future, achievement is to be monitored at State level.

With regard to drop-out rates from primary education, studies in Bangladesh have found that high drop-out is associated with a number of factors, including poor economic conditions at home, pressure to leave school to help support the family, parental indifference, negative parental attitudes which consider education to be "ungainful", and unfair treatment in school and negligence by teachers. In Pakistan, high drop-out rates have been found to be related to school curricula which are inappropriate to children's cognitive levels. India also has high drop-out rates, and particular problems with children from scheduled castes and tribes.

In conclusion, while it should be noted that no attempt has been made here to provide an exhaustive survey of the research conducted in the Region, the studies mentioned here nevertheless illustrate the types of research being conducted in several of the countries of the Region, and provide some indication of what problems are being identified and how they are being tackled.

CONSULTATIVE MEETING ON THE INCORPORATION OF ENVIRONMENTAL EDUCATION INTO THE TRAINING OF TEACHER EDUCATORS, CURRICULUM DEVELOPERS AND EDUCATIONAL PLANNERS AND ADMINISTRATORS, 1985

The meeting was organised from 11-15 February, 1985 by the National Institute of Education Planning and Administration (NIEPA), New Delhi in Co-operation with UNESCO-UNEP International Environmental Education Programme (IEEP). Reports on environmental education were presented by the representatives of Afghanistan, Nepal, Sri Lanka, Bangladesh, Malaysia and India.

A. Environmental Education in the Region — Major Trends

The participating countries belonged to the South Asian Region that has varied geographical locations, climatic conditions, population density and cultural background. Though diverse in several aspects, they have a common concern in fighting the grim battle of environmental pollution by struggling against the related and immediate socio-economic and political problems and issues, on the one hand, and those of poverty and over-population on the other. Each country feels the need for raising the environmental awareness of the people at large. The vital need to develop an awareness of environmental problems to initiate concerted action for environmental protection, is also realised.

The major environmental problems common to the participant countries were noted as follows:

(i) Devastation brought about by natural calamities such as heavy rains and cyclones, which are, an annual feature in Bangladesh.
(ii) Problem of impure drinking water and ensuing epidemics of water borne diseases prevalent throughout the year.
(iii) Excessive land-use for feeding multitude of population.
(iv) Depletion of natural forest cover, clearing of forest land for developmental purpose and shifting cultivation practised since ancient times, causing denudation of large forest areas. These practices lead to inland water imbalance, severe flooding and soil erosion.
(v) Severe sea erosion resulting from removal of sand and coral reef from coastal sea beds, for example, in Sri Lanka.
(vi) Pollution of air and water due to indiscriminate disposal of garbage, affluents from factories and other industrial wastes.
(vii) Unplanned urban development.
(viii) Preponderance of environmentally illiterate citizens.

B. **Conclusion and Recommendations**

The meeting discussed various issues in the training of Curriculum Developers, Teacher Educators and Educational Planners in the framework given below:

Environmental Education in the Region

Conceptual Frame

Training

Curriculum Developers	Teacher Educators	Educational Planners

Recommendations
and
Follow-up Action

It was recommended that, for a proper impact of EE programme it was necessary to develop courses on the basis of teaching ecological objectives. The curricular and instructional processes needed to be interlinked and resources had to be augmented and chiselled to provide functional support to the process of implementation. Some of the important, general recommendations and observations of the Group were as follows:

1. Educational Planners, Curriculum Developers and Teacher Educators have to take cognizance of the needs for inclusion of the component into the total system of education. They must incorporate these ideas into the teaching-learning situation with a view to developing awareness and committed action.
2. Educational administrators and planners, curriculum developers, and teacher educators should have commitment and orientation for environment education.
3. For its conceptual framework the group proposed the systems model for Environmental Education. It was recommended that under the systems model all activities pertaining to environmental education could be classified under policy, planning and management.
4. Appropriate policy formulation was essential to understand the environment and the problems of its maintenance in the context of local situations and circumstances. This would imply ecological analysis, forecasting and prioritization of objectives for developing a policy on environment education.
5. Planning would have to start firstly with developing curriculum with objectives of awareness, knowledge, attitudes and skills to significantly interlink with other subjects for designing integrated instructional approaches. Secondly, it involved evaluating the overall development of concern for skills concerning environmental protection and lastly planning for EE would have to relate to resource utilization — human and material resources for development.
6. It was necessary that the planners and administrators in education developed sensitivity, awareness and relevant skills in environmental education. The systems model would indicate that planning and management activities are spread over all levels.
7. Self-learning modules in environmental education may be

developed for various functionaries.

8. Orientation programmes on environmental education may be provided through the mass media. Radio and television programmes may be used for in-service training in this area.
9. Environmental education should be considered in a holistic manner in the context of the realities of the cultural and socio-economic milieu.
10. Environmental education programme should be planned with multi-agency participation, including both experts and grassroot level workers.
11. Collaborative research into problems of environmental education may be undertaken by the member-countries and the findings may be exchanged among themselves.
12. Specialised university departments and research organisations and other agencies like the Department of Environment should disseminate the latest research findings and data to the education sector for incorporation in the teacher training curriculum.
13. Teacher Educators and Educational Planners should utilise the opportunities coming through national policy statements and programmes concerning environment, e.g., the movement for reforestation, social forestry, land-use, water management, community development programmes, for promoting EE in the training of teachers.
14. They should be familiarised with and prepared for utilisation of all possible resources within their institutions and also those available with governmental agencies and voluntary groups.
15. Area-specific case studies be conducted in the field of EE which should become an input into the training of various categories of educational personnel in EE.

(*Source* : *Environmental Education*, NIEPA, New Delhi, 1988).

ASIA-PACIFIC PROGRAMMES OF EDUCATION FOR ALL (APPEAL), 1986

Background

The Fifth Regional Conference of Ministers of Education and those responsible for Economic Planning in Asia and the Pacific (Bangkok, 4-11 March, 1985) had recommended (Recommendation No. 10) to the Director General of UNESCO to study the possibility of launching a regional programme, to eradicate illiteracy and to universalize primary education in Asia and the Pacific before the end of the century.

The Twenty-third Session of the UNESCO General Conference (Sofia, 1985) by its Resolution 2.3 had authorized the Director, General to launch a regional programme for universal provision and renewal of primary education and eradication of illiteracy in Asia and the Pacific. To develop the programme, a technical meeting of experts was convened by the UNESCO Regional Office for Education in Asia and the Pacific in January 1986.

Guided by its deliberation, the programme was prepared and submitted to the Regional Experts Meeting on the Regional Programme for Universalization and Renewal of Primary Education and the Eradication of Illiteracy in Asia and the Pacific (Bangkok, 20-27 May, 1986).

The Meeting unanimously endorsed the programme under the title "Asia-Pacific Programme of Education for All", acronym APPEAL, and recommended to the Director General to launch it on 4 November, 1986, on the occasion of the 40th Anniversary of UNESCO.

APPEAL is built on the premises that education is a fundamental human right, and that it is a critical means for development. In the context of the problems of illiteracy and the need for universalization of primary education, it is realized that education cannot be treated as a closed system. It should be regarded as a sub-system of the wider society, having interfaces with the economic, political, social and cultural domains; actions should be planned taking into account all these domains.

The programme acknowledges the rich cultural and civilizational heritage of the region. The existence of indigenous languages and the long literary tradition of many of them is another unique feature. There is also a renewed assertion of cultural identity by the Nation States. Furthermore, there is an increase in the tempo of development and strong emphasis on enhancing the absorptive capacities of their economies.

Education is expected to support these trends and contribute to national development. Rather than being a goal by itself, education is to be treated at a means for development. This newer role requires not only to enlarge the existing structures to impart conventional education, but to create new ones — both within and outside the education system and to fashion new curricula with contents relevant to the nationally defined goals for development. The technological breakthroughs made in recent years provide newer tools and techniques which could be fruitfully and imaginatively utilized for the Programme.

The Programme is a response to the resolution of Member-States to eradicate illiteracy and to universalize primary education. It is intended to backstop national efforts and promote intra-regional co-operation so that inequalities in literacy profiles are wiped out, and prophylactic action be taken against the possibility of lapse into illiteracy.

Its focus will primarily be on the children and the younger age groups of the adult population who have somehow remained outside the catchment area of the existing educational system. The Programme would initiate research to investigate the factors that were responsible for their neglect, and encourage Member-States to evolve suitable strategies to ensure their involvement and participation.

Aim, Objectives and Tasks

The aim of APPEAL is to facilitate, through regional co-operation, the national efforts of the Member-States in Asia and the Pacific with a view to:

(a) Achieving universal primary education;
(b) eradicating illiteracy; and
(c) providing continuing education in support of (a) and (b) above.

Objectives of APPEAL would be to promote and strengthen mutual co-operation among the Member-States in the Region to fulfil their resolve to:

(i) continue and intensify their effort to eradicate illiteracy by the year 2000 by adopting effective policies and strategies;
(ii) consider literacy programmes as an integral part of socio-economic development plans of the countries, especially of local development efforts;
(iii) link universal primary education (UPE) to literacy programmes by facilitating and strengthening their potential complementarity;

(iv) create appropriate infrastructures for effective planning, management, and research and development supports for attaining the goals of eradication of illiteracy and UPE;

(v) strengthen training programmes for all types of literacy workers from central to field levels;

(vi) mobilize on the widest possible basis the human, material and financial resources;

(vii) encourage community participation and utilization of local resources involving all sectors of society including local leaders, industries, religious and social organizations in the planning and implementation of literacy programmes;

(viii) develop special programmes for women and disadvantaged population groups to ensure that they derive full benefit from them;

(ix) promote and strengthen post-literacy and adult education programmes to check lapsing into illiteracy and to upgrade general and vocational skills of youth and adults to make them more employable and productive;

(x) take appropriate measures for achieving universal enrolment and retention at the primary level to meet the target of universal primary education well before the year 2000; and

(xi) give special attention to the problem of quality, the renewal of educational content and raising the levels of learning achievement.

In support of achieving the above objectives, the Fifth Regional Conference of Ministers of Education and Those Responsible for Economic Planning in Asia and the Pacific (MINEDAP) also indicated the following as among the tasks to be undertaken by APPEAL:

(i) provide increased technical and other necessary assistance to the Member-States to strengthen their national capabilities or the eradication of illiteracy and the achievement of UPE within the century, and to promote exchange of experiences, expertise and information;

(ii) undertake comparative studies on the effective strategy for linking education and the world of work in literacy and UPE programmes;

(iii) focus, to an increasing extent, on programmes of education, innovation in science and technology within the programme of

UPE in view of the changing environment; and

(iv) mobilize international resources from international organizations and IBRD to promote programmes for universal access to, and retention and quality in, primary education in the Member-States, and to eradicate illiteracy, especially to assist the least developed countries and disadvantaged sectors of the people in the region.

Principles, Strategies and Guiding Actions

To achieve the above objectives and undertake the stated tasks APPEAL has identified specific principles and strategies for action.

The overriding principle governing APPEAL is its actions for in-puts into, and in support of, national activities for UPE and the eradication of illiteracy.

APPEAL would attempt to enhance national capabilities, leading to self-sufficient growth and independent development.

This enhancement of national capabilities is to take place using the strategy of mobilizing regional co-operation, including technical co-operation among developing and developed countries in the region.

This would involve:

1. The maximum mobilization of existing national and regional structures, within the education sector and outside it, and their appropriate co-ordination to encompass innovation, and implementation on a mass scale against quantitative and time targets;
2. The conjoining of quantitative expansion and quality improvement and renewal, including the redefinition of curricular specifications and incorporation of technological breakthroughs in support of both quantitative expansion and quality improvement; and
3. The special attention on population groups such as women, the primary school child populations in poverty environments, out-of-school early drop-out youth populations, minority groups displaced and nomadic groups, and groups living in remote areas.

The regional attributes of high programme, thus, are:

(a) the sharing of common objectives for universalizing primary education and eradicating illiteracy; and

(b) the shared determination of Member-States to achieve these objectives.

Action Areas

Education of Illiteracy (EOI) through:

— development of appropriate and viable literacy strategies;
— development of programmes designed to serve the needs of women, out-of-school children and youth and/or other defined disadvantaged groups;
— development of post-literacy activities;
— mobilization of community support and resources;
— strengthening of programmes in critical areas such as production of learning materials and, resources training of instructors, research and evaluation;
— linking literacy with development.

Universalization of Primary Education (UPE) through:

— enrolment and retention of girls;
— enrolment and retention of defined disadvantaged groups;
— improvement of the quality and/or relevance of primary education;
— provision of preparatory, complementary or supplementary education to primary school age children;
— planning and management of UPE at the micro level.

Continuing Education for Development (CE) through:

— parental education;
— improved linkages between formal and non-formal education;
— continuing education and its applications to work.

Modalities and Regional Co-operation

— mobilization of public and resources through dialogue and discussion;
— exchange information, experiences and expertise;
— conduct joint consultation, research evaluation and other actions;

— train personnel at national, regional and sub-regional levels.

WORKSHOP ON LEARNING ENVIRONMENTS OF EARLY CHILDHOOD, 1986

Organization

With a view to promoting research which would bring to light the resources related to learning which are already available in the immediate environments of the very poor — research which would also suggest ways in which those resources could be built upon to ease the transition from home to school, thus rescuing disadvantaged children from early failure and drop-out, IDRC, UNICEF and UNESCO, jointly sponsored a workshop, held on December 1-5, 1986 in Bangkok, entitled 'The Learning Environment of Early Childhood: Research Perspective and Prospects". Researchers and early childhood educators from seven countries, India, Indonesia, Malaysia, Nepal, Philippines, Sri Lanka and Thailand plus resource persons from four continents were involved. They were charged with 'exploring the features of the home and community environment of pre-school children in disadvantaged areas, which are conducive to cognitive and social development' and considering implications of this for 'the design of home and institution-based programmes in pre- and early primary school education in order to enhance a successful transition from home to school.'

Objectives

The Workshop on Learning Environments sought to draw upon and to strengthen the knowledge and research base within the region, with the explicit objective of facilitating the contribution of local indigenous research and knowledge to policy and programming for ECCE. More specifically, the objectives of the workshop were:

- to explore features of the home and community environments of pre-school children conducive to cognitive and social development, in so-called 'disadvantaged' rural, urban or minority group areas;

— to consider implications of these environmental features for the design of home or institution-based child care and education programmes and for early primary schooling, in order to enhance a successful transition from home to school;
— to consider research strategies, methods and designs which have been, and/or can be, used to assess and characterize home and community environments in disadvantaged areas, and their effects on cognitive and social development; and
— to develop agenda for research on priority issues in ECCE in the Asia and Pacific region.

Conclusions

Guidelines for Research

1. Given the criticality of early childhood, high priority should be assigned to research on early childhood education. Such research must be consciously drawn upon, both as input to policy and as feedback to programmes.
2. Research themes and topics may be suggested not only by researchers, but also by community members, programme designers, teachers, parents, and caregivers. Whenever possible, research should be participatory, drawing local groups into the research process itself.
3. Research in early childhood must be holistic and synthesizing in approach, and multi-disciplinary in character. It will need to use both qualitative and quantitative research designs, sometimes in combination.
4. Assessment instruments and processes which have been shown to be culturally biased must be adapted to local circumstances and norms. Local assessment tools should be developed drawing on indigenous psychological concepts and traditions.

Suggested Research Outlines

As an exercise, rough outlines for research programmes are prepared, in an attempt to answer the question:

'What are the strengths in disadvantaged environments that can be utilized in the design of programmes for child development in homes, in early childhood education centres, and in primary school?'

Implications for Programme Design and Action Research

Designers of ECCE programmes are urged to promote and use research more effectively, as well as to integrate research into their activities. The following points require attention.

Promoting concern for the development of the whole child. Most early childhood education programmes in the countries of the region appear to be downward extensions of the primary school, catering to the demands of parents and educators that the child be ready to perform well in school tasks. Such pressures often force children into tasks for which they are not ready (reading and mathematics at age 3 or 4), or into situations which neglect or devalue already well established competencies (the capacity to handle farm animals or different kinds of plants). Yet research indicates that the most effective pre-school programmes seemed to be those which focus on proper nutrition, socio-emotional development, self-concept and self-esteem, motor skills development and language production skills (often in a second language). *Programmes should build upon the competencies developed in the natural environments of early childhood*, and avoid the trap of accepting narrowly defined goals.

Handling divergence of programmes goals between parents and programme designers. Parents who wish to give their children a good foundation for school generally believe that programmes should concentrate on the 3R's, not on other areas of development. They may also expect pre-school or early primary school programmes to teach moral values, discipline and good (docile) behaviour. Such expectations are clearly at odds with programmes which stimulate children to be active, inquisitive, expressive and exacting. Such behaviours may be especially irritating to parents who themselves are suffering from lethargy resulting from malnutrition and drudgery. Another possible area of conflict is between parental emphasis on collective group achievement and social harmony, and the school's emphasis on individualistic and competitive goals. Although parental goals must be taken into account, programmers will also need to develop acceptable ways of communicating the value of other goals. Community involvement at every stage will help to settle differences.

Avoiding unwarranted assumptions about impact. Programme

planners often make some unwarranted assumptions, which may lead to a failure to demonstrate programme efficacy. An example is the following:

1. The assumption is often made that pre-school programmes will have a homogeneous effect; that most children will benefit equally and that all undergo the same experience. Both assumptions have been shown to be untrue.

   The rate of progress is largely dependent on the child's level of functioning on entry into the programme and the type of disadvantages suffered during the early years. The intensity of exposure is related to the parents' motivation, the difficulty of getting to and from the family's home, competing demands on family time, the service providers' skill and interest, and family income. Programmes must begin to operate under the assumption that they will affect children differently. They will then be able to determine who benefit most positively.
2. The duration of the programme is often decided based on funding or political considerations, and may result in an intervention of limited duration which cannot produce results of sufficient magnitude to be measurable. Programme design must provide for variations in intensity and length of contact. The results may then be used to determine the best combination for the population under consideration.

Modifying and integrating existing systems. ECCE programmes should be designed not only to promote children's all-round development, but also to ease the transition from home to school, building on the strengths of the former. In addition, educational designers should re-examine the structure and demands of early primary education, with a view to making it more consistent with local conditions, needs and cultural patterns; as well as with the needs, abilities and learning styles of young children, focusing on what children bring with them from home.

Utilizing available strategies. Toys, objects, activities, and materials from the local environment should be introduced into programmes immediately, since their role in concept learning is already known. The appropriate sequencing of materials and activities, based on research feedback, can be introduced later. Similarly, wider use should be made of the dramatic mode in teaching, with its rich

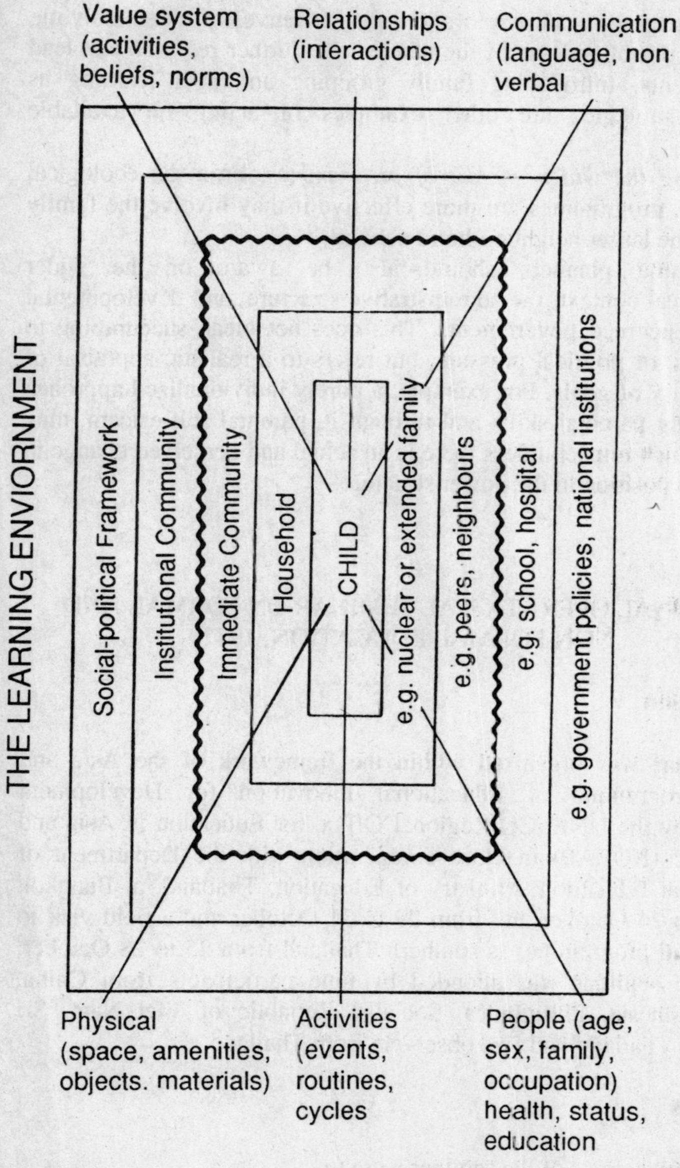

Fig. 24.1

Source APEID - UNESCO regional Office Bangok

possibilities for the safe exploration of alternatives, problem-solving, repetition, control and use of the whole self. Further research can lead to refinements. Introducing family grouping and peer learning as classroom strategies are other examples of acting on available knowledge.

Assessing the wider context of programmes. From an ecological perspective, programmes are more effective if they involve the family as well as the larger neighbourhood network.

Programme planners should also be aware of the wider socio-political context, the administrative structure, and developmental goals of concerned governments. This does not mean succumbing to bureaucratic or political pressure, but refers to a realistic appraisal of the feasibility of goals. For example, a purely individualized approach to improving parental skills and through it, parental self-esteem, may not have much impact unless there is an actual and perceived change in the group's position in the power structure.

REGIONAL OPERATIONAL SEMINAR ON FORMAL AND NON-FORMAL EDUCATION, 1987

Organization

The seminar was organised within the framework of the Asia and Pacific Programme of Educational Innovation for Development (APEID) by the UNESCO Regional Office for Education in Asia and the Pacific (ROEAP) in close co-operation with the Department of Non-Formal Education, Ministry of Education, Thailand, at Bangkok from 22 to 24 October and from 29 to 31 October and a field visit to projects and programmes is southern Thailand from 25 to 28 October, 1987. The seminar was attended by nine participants from China, India, Indonesia, Philippines, Socialist Republic of Viet Nam, Sri Lanka and Thailand and five observers from Thailand.

Objectives

The main objectives of the seminar were to:

1. review the current situation on the region on the subject in the

context of life long education;
2. visit field projects in Thailand and discuss the experiences gained; and
3. suggest ways and means to solve identified problems and possible actions to strengthen co-ordinated planning and complementarity between formal and non-formal education at the national and regional levels.

Recommendations

A. *Recommendations for Member-States*

It is recommended that the Member-States:

1. have a well defined policy statement requiring the establishment of complementarity between formal and non-formal education programmes;
2. establish a mechanism at various levels, with participation of the representatives of different agencies involved in the co-ordinated planning and implementation of universalization of primary education, science education, and basic skills training in the context of lifelong education, which should form a part of the national planning and development set-up;
3. take steps to develop awareness, interest and positive attitude for the establishment of co-ordinated planning and complementarity between formal and non-formal education among planners, decision makers, administrators, and other key personnel at all levels;
4. adopt an operational strategy which could help enhance the degree of participation of all concerned in the planning and implementation of formal and non-formal education programmes aiming at establishing complementarity;
5. make provision for developing training facilities and appropriate curricula which could aim at training teachers to be used both in the formal and non-formal education programmes;
6. ensure the provision of adequate funds and assignments of qualified staff for planning and implementation of formal and non-formal education programmes aiming to achieve universal primary education, science education and basic skills training objectives;

7. establish institutional linkages for identifying, mobilizing and sharing resources such as personnel, buildings, equipment and other materials to ensure maximum utilization of existing and new resources for the promotion of complementarity between formal and non-formal education programmes;
8. take appropriate steps to involve inter-agency/inter-disciplinary teams of experts including representatives of programme beneficiaries for developing, producing and disseminating low-cost and appropriate teaching-learning materials for use in the formal and non-formal education programmes to achieve complementarity;
9. strengthen the management information system as a part of the planning process;
10. make special efforts to promote activities aiming at action research and evaluation studies to determine alternative modes of complementarity between formal and non-formal education programmes; and
11. promote activities for developing criteria and procedures to establish equivalence of certificates awarded to participants in formal and non-formal education programmes.

B. *Recommendations to UNESCO*

It is recommended that UNESCO:

1. organize regional/sub-regional workshops for designing training courses and developing prototype training materials for educational planners, administrators and other key personnel on co-ordinated planning and complementarity between formal and non-formal education;
2. assist the Member-States in organizing follow-up national workshops for designing training courses and developing training materials for educational planners, administrators and other key personnel from related development agencies in co-ordinated planning and complementarity between formal and non-formal education;
3. organize attachment programmes for the operational staff of Member-States to successful and innovative programmes/ projects in a host country on co-ordinated planning and complementarity between formal and non-formal education;

4. provide financial assistance to document innovative experiences generated in different projects/programmes within the region; and
5. assist in undertaking studies to develop different modes of complementarity between formal and non-formal education programmes.

MULTIPLE CLASS TEACHING IN PRIMARY SCHOOLS, 1988

Genesis

The UNESCO Regional Office for Asia and the Pacific, Bangkok has brought out a publication entitled *Multiple Class Teaching in Primary Schools : A Methodological Guide* (1988) which points out strategies and approaches of teaching on multiple class teaching in single teacher primary schools. Also included in the book are a few specimen lesson plans and examples of useful educational material for better classroom teaching in a multiple class situation. This methodological guide is a synthesized version of similar guides prepared on the same subject by four Asian countries namely Japan, Malaysia, India and Nepal. Significant material is summerised below from chapters of the guide.

What is Multiple Class Teaching?

Multiple class teaching is a form of teaching in which a single teacher teaches in one classroom children of two or more grades. It also connotes teaching by a teacher in one classroom more than one age-cohort group of children with varying levels of ability.

Why Multiple Class Teaching?

Multiple class teaching is a device undertaken to meet a situation in which there is a need for teaching children in a combined group. To quote from the methodological guide prepared by India, some 77 per cent of the total number of primary schools in that country have adopted the multiple class teaching system in varying degrees. A compelling situation which requires the adoption of multiple class teaching can arise from various causes, e.g.

— *Geographical*: — The difficult terrain, the lack of easy means of transportation, straggling settlement areas, small islands, fishing and forestry areas, etc. can make multiple class teaching necessary.
— *Demographic*: — To teach the few children living in thinly populated pockets, and small-sized settlements of educationally backward communities, the use of multiple class teaching device may be practical.
— *Teacher Shortage*: — Adequate number of teachers may not be available for various reasons like scarcity of funds, teacher's unwillingness to work in remote rural areas, general shortage of trained and competent teachers, etc.
— *Absence of Teachers*: — Sometimes even in large schools some teachers may be absent or the vacancies for some teachers may remain unfilled for a long time. In this situation some classes may require to be combined and placed under one teacher.
— *Shortage of Classrooms*: — In some schools, there may not be enough number of classrooms so that two or three grades may need to be put together in one classroom under one teacher.
— *Migration and Displacement*: — Multiple class teaching is a practical device for imparting education to children of displaced people, nomadic tribes, and temporary migrants.
— *Disadvantaged People*: — To provide education for those people, especially girls, who cannot be brought to the formal school, multiple class teaching can perhaps be applied with advantage.

Advantages of Multiple Class Teaching

The multi-grade teaching methodology has its own advantages, e.g.

— The same teacher teaches the same group of children each year. Hence, he/she will know the child as an individual better and will thus be able to give him/her the right kind of help and guidance.
— The senior pupils can help the junior ones in learning and this in turn helps the senior ones to reinforce what they have-learnt.
— Pupils are assessed also on the basis of the teacher's judgement more than on the basis of one-shot examination.
— There is greater chance for mutual understanding and

co-operation to grow among the children of various ages and grades while staying, together in the same classroom and participating together in various, activities.

— Every child can get a chance to learn at his/her own pace.
— It is less expensive than the grade or subject teaching system.

Limitations of Multiple Class Teaching

Multiple class teaching has also its limitations, e.g.

— Multiple class teaching can be handled only by an experienced and competent teacher because of the diversity of the pupils in their achievement levels.
— Individualized instruction is not an easy job for a motley group of pupils.
— A teacher in a single classroom school has a heavy work-load and so he is apt to neglect the need for paying individual attention.
— Usually the classroom is not spacious enough for all groups of pupils to carry out their activities under the guidance of the teacher. And a large collection of instructional materials will be required to keep the class busy.

Hindrances to Effective Multiple Class Teaching

— In most countries, because the same primary school curricular and methodologies are prescribed for both urban and rural areas, the multiple class teacher finds it difficult to make the content of his teaching meaningful to the rural children.
— Besides, classroom teaching is apt to be artificial because of the lack of relationship between what is taught and what is accepted as needed.
— There are learning differences between fast and slow learners. The right materials may not be available for both these groups in a usually ill-equipped multiple class.
— The system of multiple class teaching expects the teacher to play a more-than-average role. Lack of slackness in the work efficiency of the teacher will give very poor results.
— The classroom may often be too small and inconvenient.
— The local people's support may be at a low ebb. There may be

even problems of getting the people to realize the need of education itself.

— Divergence of values held at home and propagated at school may antagonize the local people.
— Lack of educational atmosphere at home may retard the progress a child can make.
— There are difficulties in planning lessons for every child due to the limitation of time available for teaching two or more classes within the same duration. As children wait for their turns when the teacher is engaged with another class, they will be either killing time or disturbing others.
— The remote location of a single classroom school generally places the teacher outside the receiving end of support. Resource inputs such as reference materials, supervision, in-service education, participation in teacher centre are not usually available to him/her.
— The general atmosphere of socio-economic depression and neglect of prevailing in the community lowers the self-concept of the teacher which in turn results in his/her inefficient performance.
— When the teacher is on leave, the class cannot run.
— Lack of accommodation locally may require the teacher to travel a long distance every day. This may enervate him/her everyday and he/she will have little time to make lesson plans and to upgrade himself/herself professionally.

General Background of Pupils in Multiple Class Schools

The general background of children who come to study in multiple class schools can be described as follows:

Living in Rural Isolated Areas: Many of the children live in remote areas, distant islands or new settlement areas. So most of these pupils have little or no exposure to modernity. As they are not reached by mass media of communication, their experience is much limited.

Economically Poor: Most children come from comparatively poor families. In some places, especially in India and Nepal, facilities of electricity, piped water, medical services, etc. are lacking. Parents in general cannot afford to pay even small expenses required for their children's schooling.

Higher Rate of Diseases and Malnutrition: Lack of awareness and of means result in poor living conditions and neglect of the rules of hygiene and sanitation. So the incidence of diseases is high especially among the young children who are also mostly under-nourished.

Need to Work at Home: Children are often required to work at home. They take care of their younger siblings or take the animals out to graze or help their parents during the busy agricultural seasons. In some places, parents tell their children to carry their baby brothers and sisters to school to save themselves from the need to look after the young ones.

Lack of Parental Support: Because of ignorance and illiteracy in general, parents cannot or do not care to give necessary support for their children's education.

Discriminatory Treatment: In a number of rural societies, girls and women are discriminated against. People belonging to disadvantaged communities, hill tribes, and scheduled castes are often not treated on an equitable basis by the other privileged class in the society. This makes some pupils feel inferior to others.

Superstitions and Stereotypes: Most rural people are victims of superstitions and have several fixtures and prejudices. Because of their limited human relations, the pupils lack the feeling of competitiveness, independence and positiveness. Some of their attitudes and habits are deep-rooted and not amenable to change easily.

General Classroom Conditions in Multiple Class Schools

Because the people living in one settlement cluster are normally few in number and again because some of them may be on the move most of the time, the community interest to run a school will be minimal. For lack of wider community support classroom conditions in multiple class type of schools are, in most cases, poor and inconvenient. A survey made in Nepal indicated that more than 71 per cent of primary school houses are no better than temporary sheds. In Japan, however, as a result of the ever-increasing urbanization of the life-style and improved transportation system, there has been a marked improvement in the conditions of even small schools.

The teacher's role in arranging one room available in his school both for the classroom purpose and for other curricular activities is therefore paramount. He/she has to organize the room wisely and imaginatively so that he/she is able to not only seat his/her pupils properly but also utilize the room for the library, science study, music lessons and workshop corners for various activities like woodwork, drawing, painting and claywork.

Role of a Multiple Class Teacher

Given the limited facilities and other constraints, a multiple class teacher plays a very important but almost a solitary role in making his/her classroom instruction effective. In fact, the teacher's job is not confined to classroom teaching only. He/she has to play the role of an educator, a school administrator, a researcher in quality teaching and a community adviser all rolled in one. Some of the important aspects related to the role that a multiple class teacher is expected to play are as mentioned below:

As a curriculum planner. The teacher selects the items in the curriculum that need to be emphasized, decides upon the grading and sequencing of these concepts of teaching items and finds out areas in other subjects where he/she can integrate them.

As an administrative worker. The teacher has to plan and arrange the classroom as well as the teaching schedule with aims to maximize the results. This task also requires the teacher to use the services of his pupils effectively and mobilize the local people to the best possible extent to help him/her in his/her work.

As a successful teacher. With the minimal facilities available to him/her, the teacher has to be creative and resourceful. He/she uses his/her discretion in such a way that he/she can give maximum attention to each pupil, minimize wastage of time and energy and get every child engaged as much as possible in some kind of learning activities. The teacher relates the subject matter taught to the daily activities of the children and their local environment.

As a professional. The teacher must always be effortful to enhance his own competency and to improve his teaching style.

As a change agent. The teacher plays a pastoral role towards the pupils under his care. He/She represents the community's morals and values and passes them on to his/her pupils and at the same time he/she tries to bring about a positive change in the attitude and behaviour of the people in the community by means of his/her own teaching at school and by interacting with the local people.

School Management

In a single teacher school the task of school management falls entirely on the teacher. The teacher has to follow a system of school management which, by and large, bears a congenial atmosphere for learning and yet has a local colour which makes the local people look upon the institution as part of their life and the community. Explaining the nature of the task of school administration, the methodological guide prepared by Japan expects the teacher to consider four important aspects — people, things, budget and method. The people-related factor in this connection consists in getting uninterrupted support and service from concerned people, from the related education authority and the school management board to the pupils and workers at school. When there are no other staff to do part of the school work, the teacher himself/herself has to take care of the official work like enrolling, testing and certificating students, getting necessary furniture and equipment and making budgetary expenses and book-keeping. It is also important for the teacher to see that the present plan to action he/she prepares has a good linkage with the previous academic year's work. He/she must, in this respect, bear in mind how the last academic year's plans were set, what achievements were made and what problems occurred and then determine what should be stressed in the current academic year.

Classroom Organization

Classroom organization is one of the important factors to help improve effectiveness of teaching. No matter how well the lesson plan has been prepared, if the classroom arrangement is made in a poor and cumbersome manner, the effectiveness of the lesson will be considerably reduced.

An ill-managed classroom means a disorganized crowd of pupils which hardly lead itself to effective learning. A multiple class teacher has to organize both the classroom and the seating of children by himself/herself which is a very important task in which students of all grades have to be placed and taught in just one class room. Again, because it takes time to organize the class for the day's lessons, it is better if these things are planned and done earlier, so that full time can be devoted entirely to teaching during the actual lesson period. About the need for arranging the classroom wisely and the important role the teacher plays in this connection, the methodological guides of all the concerned four countries have similar views.

However, the methodological guide from Japan makes one good suggestion to the effect that in the regular task of arranging the classroom, if things are placed everyday in a variety of ways it will enliven the atmosphere in the classroom. And this in itself is a nice way of getting the children to warm up for the day's lessons. An element of change together with a fresh look heightens the interest of pupils to be attentive to the teacher.

Physical Organization of the Classroom

Some of the practical suggestions made in the context of Malaysia are mentioned below.

(a) Deciding which parts (usually the walls) of the classroom are appropriate for the display of the children's work, charts, etc.
(b) Selecting strategic corners for various subjects.
(c) Finding a corner for some simple activities so that learning by other groups of children is not hampered. (Partitions made with local materials are useful in minimizing the noise and other disturbing factors).
(d) The teacher's table should be placed in a strategic position which gives the teacher an unobstructed view of the whole classroom.
(e) In the arrangement of desks and chairs the teacher should bear in mind the need to provide for traffic in the room and for group work, individual instruction, etc.

In order to arrange for learning corners, the Malaysian guide-book goes on to describe how odd and empty corners can be converted into interesting, exciting and fun-filled learning corners or cubicles. Some of the ideas suggested are as follows:

1. *The Home Corner*
The home corner consists of a 3/4 size bed which also serves as a sofa for any child who needs a rest. It can also be used for quiet study, for some kind of play or for story-telling. (Japan has also suggested one corner like this).
2. *The Science/Nature Corner*
Insects/Animals/Fish are kept in special transparent containers

for scientific observation — their feeding habits, physical characteristics, movements, etc. (Japan's guide-book stressed the need of such a corner).

3. *Place for Boxes and Cubes*
Boxes and cubes are for building complex structures. The use of boxes helps to make mathematical concepts more concrete and less abstract. These objects can be used for making models of houses, etc. This area can also be used for some kinds of exercise like jumping, balancing, and climbing.
4. *The Book Corner*
There must be a book corner where carefully selected books, magazines and other reading materials are placed for children to browse through. A dynamic teacher can find some means to make a good collection of useful reading materials.
5. *Place for Woodwork*
This corner will have things like hammers, saws, nails, screws, screwdrivers, etc. Children can try their hands at making various objects from wood.
6. *Place for Clay-modelling*
A corner for this unit includes spaces for wet and dry clay in plastic bins, for aprons, and for tools and clay boards and a working table locally made to seat six children.
7. *Corner for making models from scrap materials*
Children can learn the skill of making various objects like fan, clock, boat, house, etc. from various cheap materials. Things needed for this purpose are: (a) a corner big enough to accommodate six children (if a table cannot be procured, squatting on a mat will equally serve the purpose); and (b) materials like cardboard containers, string, wire, adhesive tape, postcards, paper, plastics, hammers, scissors, paints, brushes and so on. (After work, these things must be kept away so that there is no mess all around).
8. *Place for Art and Craft*
Materials required for this purpose are mostly brushes, paints, papers, scissors, adhesive paper, etc.
9. *Sand and Water*
This learning corner should have trays for dry/wet sand and for water, materials of various shapes and sizes that float and sink, spoons, small rakes, spades, plastic and rubber containers, funnels and knives.

10. *The Shop*
 This corner is valuable for children's social development and for language practice. Bills are written for every purchase made and simulated money used as coins and bank notes.
11. *Discovery Table*
 Teachers and sometimes the children bring objects of interest like pets, curios, etc. to the class room. This practice has a great impact on the imagination of the children.
12. *The Reading Area*
 The children come to this area for reading where the teacher can give them individual attention. Each child's reading record should be kept there. The teacher can discuss large pictures, use flash cards and reading assignment sheets and so on and so forth.
13. *The Music Area*
 Musical instruments such as cymbals, drums, and other local musical instruments are kept in a specially designed trolley. The music area can be used individually or in a small group (of about 4).
14. *Displays and Exhibits*
 The aims of exhibits are to sharpen the child's perception and interpretation of the common place and to show objects of good design. Display can be made on walls, partition walls, etc.

Note: Besides sheets for the above-mentioned activities, the guide-book from Japan has reference to the need for storing short materials and for a more organized music class.

As pointed out in the beginning, classroom organization can be made for functional purposes in various ways according to the shape and size of the room, the user and groups of pupils and the different purposes envisaged. One of the possible ways of classroom organization as suggested by Malaysia is given on next page (Fig. 24.2).

A more simple way of arranging the classroom, according to the suggestion made in the Malaysian guide-book is suitable for the teacher to teach two groups simultaneously and to let others go on with some kind of individual work like self-study, etc.

Besides the organization of the classroom, the guide-book from Malaysia deals also with the organization of the playground where there is one. The playground, if there is one, must be seen and organized as part of the learning environment. The playground should not be a facility limited only to physical education or games associated with physical education. Measurement in mathematics, compass direction in geography are examples of topics which can make use of the facilities provided in the playground. In this respect, local materials should be fully utilized. Some examples of their use are:

(a) sawn logs — for measurement of circumference; radius, diameter, in mathematics lessons.
(b) used oil drums — for measurement of volume.
(c) marked direction of sunrise – for compass, direction, in geography lesson.
(d) ropes — for climbing skills in physical education.

ASIA-PACIFIC PROGRAMME OF EDUCATIONAL INNOVATIONS FOR DEVELOPMENT (Taget Date: year 2000)

The Asia-Pacific Programme of Educational Innovation for Development (APEID) of UNESCO has been in operation since 1974. Twenty- four countries of Asia and the Pacific jointly design, execute, supervise and evaluate APEID and the relationship among them is based on reciprocity for mutual learning and self-reliance. The primary focus of Regional co-operation in APEID is educational innovation for social and economic development.

The member-countries of APEID are: Afghanistan, Australia, Bangladesh, China, Fiji, India, Indonesia, Iran, Japan, Lao People's Democratic Republic, Maldives, Nepal, New Zealand, Pakistan, Papua, New Guinea, Philippines, Republic of Korea, Samoa, Socialist Republic of Vietnam, Sri Lanka, Thailand, Tonga and Turkey.

The following priority areas of work were identified during the first three programming cycles of APEID:

First Cycle (1974-1977)

1. New orientations and structures in education.
2. Management of educational innovations.

3. Curriculum development.
4. Educational technology.
5. New structures and methods in teacher training.
6. Science education.

Second Cycle (1978-1981)

1. Non-formal and alternative structures in education.
2. Administration and management of educational innovation.
3. Curriculum development.
4. Educational technology.
5. Training of teachers, teacher-educators and other educational personnel.
6. Science (including mathematics) and technology education.
7. Vocational and technical education.

Third Cycle (1982-1986)

1. Universalisation of education: access to education at the first level by both formal and non-formal means.
2. Education for promotion of scientific and technological competence and creativity.
3. Education and work.
4. Education and rural development.
5. Educational technology.
6. Professional support services and training of educational personnel.
7. Co-operative studies and innovative projects of research and research-based experiments related to educational development.

As a result of evaluation of APEID, the following recommendations about programme areas for concentration of efforts and modalities of operation were made.

Programme Areas

1. The seven programme areas of the third cycle should be maintained in essence for the fourth cycle, with modifications in content and emphasis emerging from the points below:

Multiple Class Teaching

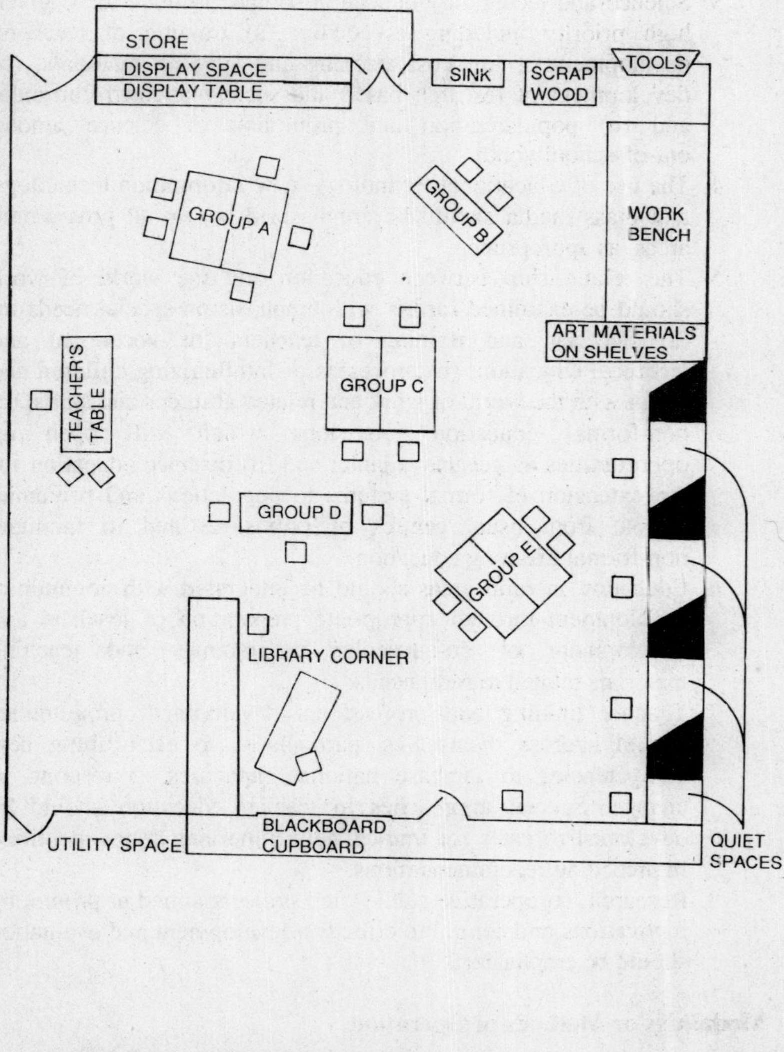

Fig. 24.2: Physical organisation of the classroom

2. Universalisation of primary education remains the major priority and should be continued with attention being directed, as appropriate, to extension of literacy and improved quality of basic education.
3. Science and technology education should continue to be given high priority including especially: (a) training of teachers, development of low-cost teaching and learning materials; (b) development of research based and society-oriented curricula; and (c) popularization and promotion of science among out-of-school youth.
4. The use of educational technology, new information technology and mass media should be emphasized across all programme areas, as appropriate.
5. The relationship between education and the world of work should be examined further with emphasis on special needs in: (a) selection and training of teachers for vocational and technical education; (b) processes of familiarizing children and youth with the world of work and related attitudes and skills; (c) non-formal education provisions which will open up opportunities as yet unavailable; and (d) distance education for the extension of formal systems to populations and personnel remote from usual centres of provisions and to facilitate non-formal life-long education.
6. Education in rural areas should be integrated with community development through appropriate preparation of teachers and development of co-curricular programmes and teaching materials related to rural needs.
7. Teacher training and professional development programmes should address themselves, particularly, to establishing new competencies to increase national capacities to respond to change. Special approaches in teacher education should be developed to cater for immediately important issues identified in preceding recommendations.
8. Research, co-operative studies and projects aimed at promoting innovations and central to effective development and evaluation should be emphasized.

Modalities or Methods of Operation

9. With regard to modalities or methods of operation, the

overriding recommendation is concerned with the need for good communication and dissemination. APEID should make a major effort to strengthen the dissemination process considering the following possible means:

- The development of a news digest which gives brief statements on developments in various centres and which could be of value to others;
- Where the original material is not in English, if felt to be of value, a translation service into English might be provided centrally. Translation from English into the language of a member-country would be responsibility of that country;
- The feasibility of a computer-based information service;
- Procedures for the dissemination of material listed in the news digest and judged to be of value to other countries;
- The development of a staff member to take particular responsibility for the identification and transmission of information on valuable materials, activities to increase national capacities to assess innovations.

10. Whilst acknowledging that all existing modalities satisfy the range of objectives Member-States wish to meet, those which should be further strengthened in the fourth cycle are:

- Joint innovative projects, study group meetings, technical working groups;
- Inter-country/inter-project study and exchange visits;
- Mobile teams, attachments/internships.

11. The selection, briefing and follow-up utilization of participants in APEID activities should be considered one of the most important and pivotal issues in ensuring the success of activities and their effective dissemination and follow-up at the national level.
12. The continuing relevance of Associated Centres and their quality of participation in APEID activities should be monitored to ensure that appropriate expertise is represented for current and potential programmes, and that cost effectiveness and efficiency are maintained.

Fourth Cycle (1987 to 1991)

A combined meeting of the Regional Consultation Meeting (RCM) on APEID and the Regional Expert Meeting on the Regional Programme for Universalisation and Renewal of Primary Education and the Eradication of Illiteracy in Asia and the Pacific was held in Bangkok on 20-27 May, 1986. As a result of discussions in this meeting, following major programme areas of interest were identified for the Fourth Cycle:

1. Education for all,
2. Making education relevant to the societal requirements, and
3. Supporting activities and infrastructures common to all educational levels and systems.

1. *Education For All (Target Date—Year 2000)*

Rationale—Education is a fundamental human right and is a critical means for development.

Current status—Education for all includes the eradication of illiteracy, the universalization of primary education and continuing education. A few countries have achieved universalization of primary education though none claims to have yet achieved complete literacy. All are engaged in varying degrees of continuing education.

General issues—(i) ensuring all children of primary school age have access to education; (ii) retaining all children who enrol in primary school for the full courses; (iii) providing appropriate education for all out-of-school youth; (iv) achieving universal adult literacy; (v) providing continuing education facilities for all; (vi) improving the quality of education and enhancing the achievement levels of education; (vii) creating supportive learning environments; and (viii) improving the capability of the entire education system to provide education for all.

Overall aim—To stimulate through regional co-operation, national efforts of the member-states to: (i) achieve universal primary education; (ii) eradicate illiteracy; and (iii) provide continuing education for all.

Objectives—The objectives are to promote and strengthen mutual cooperation among member-states to: (i) Continue and intensify their efforts to eradicate illiteracy and to achieve universal primary education before the year 2000; (ii) Create appropriate infrastructures for integrated and effective planning, management, research and development for literacy, primary education and continuing education, with special emphasis on women and disadvantaged population groups; (iii) Mobilize human, material and financial resources, as well as encourage community participation and utilization of local resources; (iv) Give special attention to raising the level of learning achievements of pupils through curriculum renewal, training of personnel, and research, etc.; (v) Promote and strengthen continuing education, especially for out-of-school children and youth.

Outcomes—Achievement of education for all by the year 2000. The following should also be expected: (i) Effective policies and strategies for the eradication of illiteracy and the achievement of primary education and continuing education; (ii) The development of appropriate infrastructures for those; (iii) Community participation and utilization of local resources; (iv) A raised level of learning achievement of pupils; (v) Strengthened continuing education programmes.

2. *Making Education Relevant to Social Requirements*

Rationale—The participants to the Regional Consultation Meeting agreed that effort should be concentrated on three major programmes areas. Programme area II carried the title *Making education relevant to societal requirements*. Seven sub-programme areas were arranged under this major heading. The gathering chose "requirements" rather than the "needs" to indicate that it was time to focus on priorities for action and not merely to assess needs.

During the time that UNESCO has been in existence, considerable effort has been expanded to make education relevant to societal conditions, and yet this goal still remains to be achieved. The changes that have occurred within society itself coupled with the conservatism of education systems has meant that social relevance as a goal has proved to be elusive. In addition, there has been a growing demand from parents, students and the general public for education to be related to conditions in the modern world. Therefore, the consultation meeting adopted the concept of social relevance as a criterion for the evaluation of educational systems, curriculum, and teaching methods in seven areas of educational innovation.

Although social relevance will differ from one country to another, and from one cultural setting to another within a country, nevertheless, there will be a set of societal factors which will need to be taken into account in all settings. These factors include the status of science and technology, the demographic pattern, the population size, the degree of isolation, the moral and religious values, the prevailing political ideas, the economic condition, and the physical resources. When the goal adopted for education is social relevance, then it is necessary to forecast these factors and to determine their configuration. For the purposes of the 1987-1991 APEID work plan, the time frame of this forecast will cover five years.

In addition, however, there is a need to develop scenarios for long-term futures with the aim of understanding, controlling and shaping the future.

Education for Rural Development: The products of rural peoples are still the economic mainstay of the majority of countries throughout the region, and there is a disaproportionate incidence of problems of illiteracy and failure to complete schooling. The educational problems of rural areas include difficulty of access, inequality of service in comparison with urban areas, low levels of literacy within communities as a whole and poverty.

Education and Work: There are common problems in many countries of the region in relating education to the world of work. The supply of skilled manpower for the developmental needs of the countries and the problem of unemployment demand that education and work should remain a major area of concern during the fourth programming cycle of APEID.

The major problems include the difficulty of access to appropriate technology, inadequate arrangements for preparation and continued retraining of personnel and teachers of technical subjects, lack of proper equipment and facilities, and lack of effective linkages between educational systems and agricultural and industrial enterprises.

In recent years, the definition of work has been broadened to include productive labour carried out inside or outside the home, whether or not for cash returns. The effect of this definition is that women's work can be viewed as having economic value. More research is required in this field in order to provide more and better information on the vocationalization of general education, relationship between education and the world of work, in particular the implications of science and technological development towards educational policy and *vice versa*.

Science and Technology Education: The past two decades have seen a remarkable change in the perception of developing countries of science and of education. There is a greater awareness and realization that applied science and technology are key factors in the modernization and industrialization process. It is therefore, important that education in science (including technology and mathematics) begins as early as possible and is directed to all sections of the population. The preparation for improving science education and extending scientific literacy to all sections of the population is, therefore, an urgent need to enable the applications of science and effective use of technologies in national development.

Considerable efforts have already been directed towards the improvement of science education in almost all APEID countries during the past two decades and many advances can be identified in the area of curriculum development, development of instructional materials, training of teachers, and other aspects of education. However, the majority of these efforts have mainly been confined to the formal school system with the result that a sizeable population of out-of-school children and a large population of adults have had little chance of developing a minimum level of scientific literacy and appreciation of the potentialities of science and technology for improving their living conditions.

Education for the Future and Future Studies: The rate of change has produced a worldwide interest in the future not just to predict future change but to understand and influence those factors over which we have some control. Futurology or the study of the future has implications for the future of education itself and for the relationships between educational goals and other social parameters.

Restructuring Secondary Education: Countries in the region have changing profiles in their school populations. There is universal primary education in many countries and approaching universalization of primary education in many others. An increasing number of countries have achieved universal secondary education. This has brought young people with a wider spread of ability into the schools of the region. A more diversified occupational structure and a greater scarcity of jobs has placed new demands on the schools including the unjustified charge that unemployment is a consequence of the educational level of the youthful population.

The increasing democratization of secondary education has contributed to, and responded to, the aspirations of families and communities for their children to have the same access as other children both to school itself and to leave the same opportunity to be taught those subjects with the greatest prestige. At the same time if there were no difference in the prestige accorded to white collar jobs and manual activities, it might be better for national development.

The principal of equity is being extended to the education of girls and to the rights of minority ethnic groups. The issue of the rights of minority groups has in turn led to the requirement that schooling and school texts should be available in vernacular and in national languages.

Rising standards of education amongst populations have frequently resulted in the desire of parents to have closer contact with the schools their children attend; to know what goes on within them and to have some part in decisions made that will affect their children. This phenomenon has been accompanied by a recognition that families are, on their own account, sources of learning and that, in addition, they have the capacity to be powerful reinforcing agents for the work of the school.

These changes in education have focused attention on secondary education and several countries of the region are introducing reforms in the structure, the curriculum and the assessment procedures used in secondary schools.

Morals and Values Education: The pace of change, the influence of the mass media and the different life experiences of the older and younger population groups have all produced dislocations in traditional values and in many cases in the patterns of family life.

For achieving national development goals, strengthening national identity and maintaining desirable traditional values in an age of rapid changes in social as well as technological development, moral/religious values, eaucation, whatever the course title may be at school, is given special attention in every society of the region. Increasing concern over the problems and issues of formal education have emerged as a consequence of national efforts to strengthen moral education.

Special Education: While some advances in medical technology have reduced the incidence of disabling conditions, others have contributed to the survival of children who in earlier times would have died at a young age. Therefore, the incidence of young people who need some kind of special education has remained much the same over the year.

The recognition of the rights of the disabled population to equal educational opportunities has led to a worldwide movement to integrate or *mainstream* children with disabilities into normal primary and secondary schools.

APEID, therefore, will carry out innovative studies and projects in the following areas for which the rationale has been briefly set out above:

1. Education for rural development (EDRUDEV).
2. Education for the world of work (EDV).
3. Science and technology education including science for all (STE).
4. Education for the future (EDFUT).
5. Restructuring secondary education (RESEC).
6. Morals and values education (MORED).
7. Special education (SPED).

3. *Supporting Activities and Infrastructures Common to All Educational Levels and Systems*

Innovatives, studies and projects in the following areas have been envisaged:

(a) Research and Development Including Measurement and Testing.
(b) Curriculum Development.
(c) Training of Personnel Including Professional Services.
(d) Distance Education.

(*Source*: *Educational Innovations*, Newsletter of the National Development Group, NCERT, Vol. III, No. 1, January-June 1986.)

BIBLIOGRAPHY

UNESCO DOCUMENTS AND PUBLICATIONS*

1. *Asian regional seminar on access of girls to primary education*, Kathmandu, Nepal, 2-6 October, 1978. *Final report*. Paris, UNESCO, 1978, 37 p.

* Listing to illustrate the range of UNESCO documents and publications.

2. *Educational facilities in the city: the challenge in Asia and the Pacific.* Bangkok, 14-17 February 1983. *Proceedings.* Published with the assistance of UNESCO/Scretariat of the Working Group. Athens, The Technical Chamber of Greece, 1984, 134 p.
3. *Handicapped children: early detection, intervention and education.* Selected case studies from Argentina, Canada, Denmark, Jamaica, Jordan, Sri Lanka, Thailand and the United Kingdom. Paris, UNESCO, 1981, 142 p. ED/MD/63.
4. *Higher education in Asia and the Pacific: a perspectives study* by S.C. Siel. Paris, UNESCO, 1983, 74 p. (Papers on higher education No. 5) ED-83/WS/99.
5. *Interaction between adult education and universalization of primary education in the context of integrated rural development* (A research study conducted in Sri Lanka),published in co-operation with Faculty of Education, University of Colombo, Sri Lanka. Paris, UNESCO, 1984, 131 p., ED-84/WS/69.
6. *International co-operation in education: the Burmese experience* by Dr. Nyi Nyi. Paris, UNESCO, 1979, 52 p.
7. *International co-operation in education in countries of Asia and the Pacific: objectives, statistical trends and prospects* by Peter Herold *et al.* Paris, UNESCO, 1983, 53 p.
8. *International co-operation in education in Sri Lanka/The Marga Institute.* Paris, UNESCO, 1979, 40 p.
9. *Integrated rural development and the role of education.* Report of the Bangladesh—UNESCO field operational seminar held in Bangladesh, 4-19 March 1979. Paris, UNESCO, 1980, 97 p.
10. *Inventory of the results of experience of Japan in developing successful approaches to improving the status of women.* Paris, UNESCO, 1976, 87 p.
11. *Meeting on education concerning problems connected with the use of drugs in ten Asian Countries.* Penang, Malaysia, 5-12 December, 1977. *Final report.* Paris, UNESCO, 1978, 16 p. ED/MD/51.
12. *A Profile of 20 villages in Islamabad federal area* (Experimental pilot project integrating education in rural development). Islamabad, Ministry of Education/UNESCO, 1980, 93 p.
13. *Regional conferences and educational development in Africa, Arab States, Asia and Latin America: Bombay 1952 — Mexico City 1979* by F.L. Bartels. Paris, UNESCO, 1983, 187 p.

14. *Regional convention on the recognition of studies, diplomas and degrees in higher education in Asia and the Pacific*. Paris, UNESCO, 1983.
15. *Studies of girls in primary education in some Asian countries and prospects*/Working documents of Asia regional seminar on access of girls to primary education. Paris, UNESCO, 1978, 37 p.
16. *Study on access of women to science education and training and associated careers in Malaysia*. Paris, UNESCO, 1983, 77 p.
17. *A Study on educational opportunities and employment opportunities open to women in Sri Lanka*. Paris, UNESCO, 1974, 73 p.
18. *Teaching agriculture economics and management in Asia*, ed. by Owen McCarthy, published with financial assistance from UNESCO. New Zealand, Lincoln College, 1977, 124 p.
19. *Women's education in rural Thailand*. (A survey of facilities, needs and opportunities for basic scientific knowledge). Paris, UNESCO, in co-operation with Faculty of Education, Chulalongkorn University, Bangkok, 1980, 39 p. ED-80/WS/165.

Publications of UNESCO Principal Regional Office For Asia and the Pacific, Bangkok, Thailand

Regional Education Programmes in Asia and the Pacific (REPAP)

Education in Asia and the Pacific: Reviews, Reports and Notes.

Bibliographical Documents

Accessions List.

Periodicals of Asia and the Pacific; a selected list of titles received and their contents.

Directories

Directory of national institutions of educational planning and administration in Asia and the Pacific. Bangkok, 1984, 69 p.

Education for Peace

UNESCO Regional Meeting to Formulate Strategies of Action for National Co-ordinators of UNESCO Associated Schools Project, Bangkok, 16-22 December 1986. *Strategies of action for strengthening the Associated Schools Project in the Asia-Pacific region.* Bangkok. UNESCO, 1987, 128 p.

Higher Education

Higher agricultural education and rural development in developing countries in Asia and the Pacific, by Gil C. Saguiguit Jr. Bangkok, 1987.

Pedagogical staff development in higher education, by R.S. Adams and D. Battersby. Bangkok, 1987, 107 p.

Special Education

UNESCO Regional Planning Seminar and Workshop on Special Education, Coimbatore, India, 12-24 August, 1985. *Educating the disabled.* Bangkok, 1987, 79 p.

Asia-Pacific Programme of Education for All (APPEAL)

General

APPEAL Newsletter for the Asia Pacific Programme of Education for All. Vol. 1, No. 1, 1987.

Literacy

Developing personnel training plans for literacy and continuing education. Bangkok, 1987, 38 p.

Posters and leaflet

Illiterates in Asia and the Pacific, 8 September 1987 — International Literacy Day.

International Literacy Day Calendar, 8 September 1987 — 8 September 1988.

Educational Planning and Management Service (EPMS)

Educational Planning

Micro-level educational planning and management; case studies from India, by Satya Bhushan, Brahm Prakash, V.A. Kalpande, Yash Aggarwal, Pramila Menon; ed. by Warren Mellor. Bangkok, UNESCO, 1987, 104 p.

Educational Statistics

Education in Asia and the Pacific: 1987 statistical indicators (leaflet).

Occasional Papers

Education and employment; the case of Thailand, by Vichai Tunsiri. Bangkok, 1987, 48 p.

Asia and the Pacific Programme of Educational Innovation for Development (APEID)

General

APEID Newsletter.

Distance Education

Study Group Meeting on Evaluation of Distance Learning Projects, in Co-operation with the Jiangsu Department of Education, Nanjing, China, 16-25 August, 1986. *Evaluation of distance education projects under APEID, a report*. Bangkok, UNESCO, 1987, 47 p.

Educational Development

Interface of education with employment and leisure in the context of alternative futures: Malaysia, by Rahimah Haji Ahmad, T. Marimuthu and Norjamah Ismail. Bangkok, PROAP/APEID, 1987, 65 p. (Education and Polity No. 5),

Education of Teachers

UNESCO Regional Workshop on Teacher Education in collaboration with the Centre of Education, University of Tasmania, Hobart, 4-10 December, 1986. *Teacher education; issues, needs and plans for action*. Bangkok, PROAP/APEID, 1987.

Science and Technology Education

Technical Working Group Meeting on Training of Primary Education Personnel, Chiangmai, 26 August—4 September, 1986. *Education in difficult contexts; a report*. Bangkok, UNESCO, 1986, 38 p.

Educational Facilities Development Service (EFDS)

Design ideas for play spaces for three to six year olds. (Educational Building Digest series No. 79.)

Population Education Programme Service

Abstracts, Bibliographies

Management, planning and monitoring population education programmes. Bangkok, 1987, 55 p. (Abstract—bibliography series No. 8).

Selected entries on demography and its bearing on population education in seven Asian countries (Abstract—bibliography series No. 7).

Social and Human Sciences in Asia and the Pacific

Regional Research Seminar on Perspectives on Asia's Futures. Bangkok, 20-24 July, 1987. *Perspectives on Asia's futures: report of the seminar*, Bangkok, UNESCO, 1987, 83 p.

RUSHAP Series of Occasional Monographs and Papers

Youth profile: India, prepared by RUSHAP with inputs from Kaushal K. Siddh and Surendra K. Gupta. Bangkok. 1987, 79 p.

Migration of talent: causes and consequences of brain drain; three studies from Asia, edited by Yogesh Atal and Luca Dall Ogho. Bangkok, UNESCO, 1987, 241 p.

Food deficiency: studies and perspectives; papers presented at an International Seminar of Anthropologists, organized by the Division for Social and Economic Sciences, Sector for Social and Human Sciences, 6-9 August 1985. Mexico City. Bangkok, UNESCO, 1987, 234 p.

Bulletin of the UNESCO Principal Regional Office for Asia and the Pacific, Bangkok, Thailand

The Bulletin was established in 1966 then published twice annually from 1967 to 1972. It is now an annual publication. Special issues were published in January and December 1982. Each issue contains a bibliographical supplement.

Topics of various Issues

Review of educational progress in the Asian region. Vol. 1, No. 1, September 1966.

The Problem of educational wastage at the first level. Vol. 1, No. 2, March 1967.

Widening horizons of education in the Asian region. Vol. II, No. 1, September 1967.

Educational research in the Asian region. Vol. II, No. 2, March, 1968.

Organization of educational planning in the Asian region. Vol. III, No. 1, September 1968.

General secondary school curriculum in the Asian region. Vol. III, No. 2, March 1969.

Science education in the Asian region. Vol. No. 1, September, 1969.

Reform and reorganization in education in the Asian region. Vol. IV, No. 2, March 1970.

Education in rural areas in the Asian region. Vol. V, No. 1, September 1970.

Literacy and adult education in the Asian region. Vol. V, No. 2, March 1971.

Exploring new approaches and methods in education in Asia. Vol. VI, No. 1, September 1971.

Education in Asia. Vol. VI. No. 2, March 1972.

Higher education in the Asian region. Vol. VIII, No. 1, September 1972.

First level of education in the Asian region. No. 14, June 1973.

Administration of education in the Asian region. No. 15, June 1974.

Educational planning in the Asian region. No. 16, June 1975.

Educational building and facilities in the Asian region. No. 17, June, 1976.

Science education in the Asian region. No. 18, June 1977.

Open education: experiments and experiences in Asia and Oceania. No. 19, June 1978.

Education in Asia and Oceania. No. 20, June 1979.

Technical and vocational education in Asia and Oceania. No. 21, June 1980.

Environmental education in Asia and the Pacific. No. 22, June 1981.

Adult education in Asia and the Pacific. January 1982.

Population education in Asia and the Pacific. No. 23, June 1982.

Out-of-school science education in Asia and the Pacific. December 1982.

Higher education in Asia and the Pacific. No. 24, April 1983.

Science education in Asia and the Pacific. No. 25, June 1984.

Distance education in Asia and the Pacific. No. 26, December 1985.

Unesco in Asia and the Pacific, 40 years on. No. 27, November 1986.

Continuing Education in Asia and the Pacific. No. 28, September 1987.

25

UNESCO AND INDIA

India is a founder member of UNESCO and it has played an active role in its activities. In addition to paying its share of UNESCO's operating budget India has made available many of its leading educators, scientists and specialists in various fields to serve as members of the UNESCO Secretariat, as UNESCO experts and consultants to other Member-States, and as members of various international panels, conferences, advisory committees, and the UNESCO Executive Board. Distinguished Indians including two former Presidents and one Prime Minister have served on the UNESCO Executive Board.

India is also the first developing country to host UNESCO's General Conference (9th Session, 1956). The Vigyan Bhawan at New Delhi was built specially for that Session. Because of the leading role played by India in the conference, UNESCO's major project for the mutual appreciation of Eastern and Western cultural values was launched. Subsequently, India has hosted many other UNESCO conferences, meetings, seminars, symposia, workshops and training courses. The first UNESCO Conference on the Application of Science and Technology to the Development of Asia (CASTASIA I) was held in New Delhi in 1968, followed by CASTASIA II at Manila (Philippines) in 1982.

UNESCO has collaborated with the Government of India in numerous development projects under its Regular programme as well as with the financial assistance of the United Nations Development Programme (UNDP). UNESCO provides required expertise, administers fellowships for selected Indian personnel for study abroad, and purchases imported equipment according to the agreed plan of action; the Government, which bears the main responsibility for the projects, appoints Indian staff, including a project directory; makes necessary institutional and administrative arrangements; and provides equipment and material manufactured in India. Apart from national development projects, India also participates in and benefits from many of international activities sponsored by UNESCO, such as International Educational Year, International Book Year, International Literacy Day, International Year of the Child, International Year of the Disabled, International Communication Year, International Youth Year, and has been an outstanding contributor to other specialized programmes which include International Hydrological Programme (IGP), Man and the Biosphere (MAB) Programme, International Geological Correlation Programme (IGCP), U.N. Science Information System (UNISIST) and Intergovernmental Oceanographic Commission (IOC), as well as regional activities, such as conferences, meetings, symposia, seminars, workshops and training courses, organized by UNESCO's Regional Offices in Asia.

EDUCATION

In the field of education UNESCO has assisted India in establishing a number of central institutions to strengthen and develop its educational system. The present National Institute of Educational Planning and Administration, New Delhi, was first established in 1962 as the Asian Institute of Educational Planning and Administration and was jointly run by UNESCO and the Government of India for 10 years. In 1973 it was turned over to India as a national institute. During this period the Institute trained some 300 fellows from the Asian Region, promoted research in educational planning, administration and supervision and organized educational services including adult literacy, university teaching, life-long integrated education, educational statistics and modern management techniques.

Many specialists were provided by UNESCO to assist the Indian Education Commission, 1964-66. India's example of including foreign specialists in a national commission has been followed by others.

In India, UNESCO, under the "Secondary School Science Teaching Project", has assisted the National Council of Educational Research and Training (NCERT), New Delhi, with a team of science teaching experts in the improvement of curricula, production of science textbooks and teacher guides, developing new syllabi and samples of model school science equipment. Science equipment has been provided for almost all the teacher training institutions and science kits to nearly 30,000 schools.

UNESCO has helped various programmes of book development. The Delhi Public Library was established as a joint UNESCO India project. India Classics have been translated and works of art reproduced in the UNESCO series.

In the field of literacy UNESCO has assisted India, in collaboration with FAO and UNDP, in establishing the Farmers' Training and Functional Literacy Programme. During 1970-74, more than 300,000 farmers benefited from the Government's high-yielding seeds programme. Also, in collaboration with FAO, UNDP and the Indian Council of Agricultural Research (ICAR), centres of excellence for post-graduate agricultural education research were established at 23 agricultural universities. Along with 34 central research institutes and 54 nationally co-ordinated research projects, these helped to bring together the functions of research, teaching and extension.

Under the National Council of Educational Research and Training, the Centre for Educational Technology was set up with technical assistance from UNESCO and UNDP during 1972-80. The nomenclature of this Centre has since been changed to "Central Institute for Educational Technology". UNESCO was the executing agency for this project for a period of five years (1984-88). This centre is engaged in raising the quality of Educational media utilization at the Central and State levels in India. A notable aspect of this collaboration was the pilot project SITE (Satellite Instructional Television Experiment) for large-scale use of satellite television as an educational medium.

India is a member of the Asian Programme of Educational Innovation for Development (APEID) located at the UNESCO Regional Office for Education in Asia and the Pacific, Bangkok, since its very inception in 1974. The Programme is financially supported by UNESCO, UNDP and voluntary contributions from participating Member-States. In addition, there are contributions in kind by all the participating Member-States. The main objective of the Programme is to assist the participating countries to build up their national capacities for design and introduction of educational innovations for development through relationship of equality, reciprocity and mutual learning among the leading research and development institutions of the

Asia-Pacific region. In India, through this network, five Associated Centres of APEID have been established.

Among the other fields of co-operation in education are educational planning and management, low-cost school buildings, vocational and technical education, environmental education, services, and the UNESCO-UNICEF co-operative programme for reforming primary level curricula. UNESCO also participated in other UNICEF-assisted projects in India like the Applied Nutrition Project, Children's Media Laboratory and the Community Education Project. In association with UNFPA (United Nations Population Fund Activities), UNESCO has supported the National Population Education Project through advisory missions to 18 States and Union Territories in India.

India is very active in UNESCO's Associated Schools Project for promoting international understanding. Presently there are 37 educational institutions all over India participating in this programme.

SOCIAL SCIENCES

In the field of social sciences in India, UNESCO assisted the Government of India in establishing in 1956 a Research Centre in Calcutta on Social Implications of Industrialization in South Asia. The work evolved into research in social and economic development. The Centre was shifted to Delhi and later transferred to the Institute of Economic Growth in 1967, with UNESCO assistance continuing for some years.

In promoting social science development in India, UNESCO has collaborated with the Indian Council of Social Science Research (ICSSR). UNESCO has laid emphasis on co-operation between the social and natural sciences and mutual answers to problems arising from scientific and technological advance. Among specific problems recently addressed are the situation of women and the impact of science and technology on cultural values and the quality of life.

SCIENCE AND TECHNOLOGY

In science and technology, India has close relationships with UNESCO as the host of the organization's Regional Office of Science and Technology for South and Central Asia (ROSTSCA) at New Delhi which serves 11 Member-States in the region including Afghanistan, Bangladesh, Bhutan, Burma, India, Iran, Maldives, Mongolia, Nepal, Pakistan and Sri Lanka.

Many of the meetings, seminars, symposia, workshops and courses organized by the New Delhi Regional Office are hosted by the Government of India at various scientific institutions in the country. Recent examples include: UNESCO Regional Working Group Meeting on Metrology for South and Central Asia, New Delhi, 9-11 August, 1982; Sub-Regional Workshop on Low-cost Locally Produced Equipment for Chemistry Teaching, Chandigarh, 7-9 January, 1983; Second Meeting of the Asia Regional Co-ordinating Committee on Hydrology, New Delhi, 10-12 January, 1983; Inter-Regional meeting on Research and Human Needs, Madras, 14-19 February, 1983; UNESCO Regional Seminar on the Application of Informations in South and Central Asia, New Delhi, 13-16 April, 1983; International Course on Analysis and Design of Machine Foundations, University of Roorkee, 23 February to 15 March, 1983; International Post-graduate Diploma Course in Hydrology and Water Resources Engineering, Anna University, Madras, August 1983 to July 1984; Workshop on Choice of Technology for Endogenous Development, New Delhi, 24-27 October, 1983; Regional Training Programme on Appropriate Technology for South and Central Asian Countries, Allahabad, 12-23 December, 1983; Regional Workshop on Biogas Energy Management in Rural Areas for South Asia, Hyderabad, 27-29 December, 1983; and International Conference on the Rôle of Laboratory in Physics Education, Jaipur, 29 December, 1983 to 2 January, 1984; Regional Seminar on Power System Reliability: Planning, Operation and Management, Indian Institute of Science, Bangalore, 19-23 March, 1984; International ICRO UNESCO/Training Course on Immunogenetics, Cancer Research Institute, Bombay, 19 to 6 April, 1984; Regional Seminar on Use of Information Systems and Services on Research in Progress, Hyderabad (India), 26-30 March, 1984; Regional Seminar on Management of Engineering and Technical Institutions, Indian Institute of Technology, Kanpur, 2-5 April, 1984; Regional Seminar-cum-Workshop on Small Scale Energy Systems in Rural Areas, Madras, 19-28 April, 1984; UNESCO Regional Course on Computer Network Design and Management, New Delhi, 28 May to 16 June, 1984; Regional Training Seminar on Higher Technicians

Education, Madras, 17-21 December, 1984; Regional Training Course on application of Computers to Hydrological Studies, Pune, 7-25 January, 1985; UGC-India/UNESCO/ASPEN Workshop on TV Programmes for Science and Technology Education, Pune, 15-31 January, 1985; Second Regional Training Course in Structural Geology, Dehra Dun, 6 March to 3 April, 1985; Regional Meeting of Man and the Biosphere (MAB) National Committees of South and Central Asia, New Delhi, 18-20 March, 1985; International Seminar on Research in Science and Technology Education (University Level), Himachal Pradesh University, Simla Hills, 21-28 June, 1985; 14th International Postgraduate Diploma and Master's Course in Hydrology, Roorkee, July 1985 to June 1986; International Conference on Science and Technology Education and Human Needs, Bangalore, 8-14 August, 1985; Third International Postgraduate Diploma Course in Hydrology and Water Resources Engineering, Anna University, Madras, September 1985 to August 1986; Regional Symposium on Creation of Awareness about Earthquake Hazards and Mitigation of Seismic Risks, Gauhati, 4-5 October, 1985; UNESCO-INSDOC Asian Regional Seminar/Workshop on Thesaurus Construction, New Delhi, 18-29 November, 1985; Training Course/Workshop on Modern Aspects of Monoclonal Antibody Production by Hybridoma Techniques, National Institute of Immunology, New Delhi, 2-14 December, 1985; International Workshop on Amelioration of Soil by Trees, National Botanical Research Institute, Lucknow, 2-9 March, 1986; Third UNESCO Regional Training Course in Structural Geology, Dehra Dun, 1-16 March, 1986; Third Regional Training Seminar on Ice and Snow Hydrology, Manali, 14 March to 1 April, 1986, IOC/UNESCO Regional Training Workshop on Ocean Engineering and its interface with Ocean Science, Madras, 17 March to 5 April, 1986; Workshop on Technology Policies Comparative Perspectives, Hyderabad (India), 13-14 August 1986; National Symposium on Geomicrobiological Techniques in Biohydrometallurgical Practices, Pune, 25-27 November, 1986; Fifth International Postgraduate Course of Physics on Materials, Indian Institute of Technology, Madras, 10-24 December, 1986, Regional Workshop on Ground Water Models, Water Resources Development Training Centre, Roorkee, 12-17 December, 1986; International Workshop and School on Modern Optics, Laser and Laser Spectroscopy, Indian Institute of Technology, Kanpur, 19-29 January, 1987; Regional Training Workshop on Some Contemporary Areas in applicable Mathematics, Calcutta, 29 January to 1 February, 1987;

International Symposium "Towards Fifth Generation Computer Systems", Madras, 25-27 February, 1987; Regional Workshop on National Issues on Computers in Education, Indian Institute of Technology, Bombay, 16-19 March, 1987; Workshop on Economic and Technological Aspects of Chemical Processes (ECO-TECH-V), M.S. University of Baroda, Baroda, 30 March to 11 April, 1987; Sixteenth International Post-graduate Course in Hydrology, University of Roorkee, Roorkee, 16 July, 1987 to 15 July, 1988; Regional Workshop on Surface and Interface of Metals and Semiconductor Devices, Pune, 3-14 August, 1987; Fifth International Post-graduate Diploma Course in Hydrology and Water Resources Engineering, Anna University, Madras, commencing 17 August, 1987 for a period of one year; Regional Workshop on Solar Energy Utilization, Global Energy Centre, New Delhi, 8-14 September, 1987; Regional Workshop on Science Writers, Calcutta, 11-13 September, 1987; AFRO-ASIAN Conference on Integrated Water Management in Urban Areas, Nehru Centre, Bombay, 3-6 December, 1987.

UNESCO has also assisted the Governments of India in its efforts to expand and improve the body of technical teachers and specialists, with the establishment of several engineering colleges and institutions in India which include : Regional Engineering Colleges at Allahabad, Bhopal, Durgapur, Jamshedpur, Mangalore, Nagpur, Rourkela and Tiruchirapalli. Some other Institutions established with the assistance of UNESCO are : Teacher Training for Engineering Colleges, Warangal; Indian National Scientific Documentation Centre (INSDOC), New Delhi; Central Scientific Instruments Organizations (CSIO), Chandigarh; Central Arid Zone Research Institute, Jodhpur; Power Engineering Research Organizations at Bhopal and Bangalore; National Institute of Foundry and Forge Technology, Ranchi; Central Mechanical Engineering Research Institute, Durgapur; Mechanical Engineering Research and Development Organizations at Ludhiana, Madras and Durgapur; Indian Ocean Biological Centre, Cochin; School of Planning and Architecture, New Delhi; Indian Institute of Petroleum, Dehra Dun; and Turbo-Machinery and Combustion Laboratory, Bangalore. UNESCO has also extended financial assistance to various institutions.

UNESCO Project in the Field of Science and Technology Education

Some significant projects executed by the UNESCO Regional Office, for Science and Technology for South and Central Asia, New Delhi, are given below:

- National Institute of Hydrology, Roorkee (India), 1979-1984.
- Post-graduate Hydrological Education and Research, Roorkee, 1981-1985.
- Special Assistance to Selected University Departments (Phase 11), University Grants Commission, New Delhi, 1979-1984.
- Post-graduate Engineering Education and Research, Coimbatore, 1982-1984.
- Compressibility, Viscosity and Solidification Behaviour of Liquids at Ultra-High Pressures, Department of Astrophysics, Delhi University, Delhi, 1983-1985.
- Water and Power Information Systems, Central Water and Power Research Station, Pune, 1982-1986.
- Study of Environmental Effect on Cultural Properties, Lucknow, 1983-1986.
- Establishment of Central Institute of Educational Technology (INSAT for Education), National Council of Educational Research and Training, New Delhi, 1984-1988.
- Curriculum Development for Technician Education (Phase 11), Technical Teachers Training Institutes in Chandigarh, Calcutta, Bhopal and Madras, 1985-1987.

The Organization has provided assistance by way of (i) offering the services of UNESCO experts of international repute and consultants, (ii) making available the services of UNESCO Advisory Missions from headquarters, (iii) supplying latest equipment for laboratories, and (iv) providing fellowships for advanced studies abroad.

In the present phase, the focus of UNESCO activities is on the application of science and technology to development in fields like rural development, mineral and energy resources, biotechnology, and the biosphere, water resources, ocean and coastal marine systems and information systems and services.

CULTURE

UNESCO's contribution in the field of culture is quite significant.

Through its various programmes of international cultural co-operation carried out by government agencies and autonomous bodies, there has been an increasing awareness of the culture of different countries of the world. India has participated in numerous cultural activities such as the 10-year (1957-66) "Major Project on the Mutual Appreciation of Eastern and Western Cultural Values" through which many works of Indian literature have now been translated into different foreign languages and published by UNESCO. UNESCO has assisted in the renovation and conservation of the Ranganathaswami Temple in Tamil Nadu and in the restoration of the Ajanta Cave frescoes. The Bureau of the World Heritage Committee, at its 1985 session, recommended the inclusion of Ajanta Caves, Elora Caves, Agra Fort, Taj Mahal, the Sun Temple at Konarak, and the group of monuments at Mahabalipuram in the World Heritage List. UNESCO has also extended its co-operation in the building of "Auroville-international city of the future" at Pondicherry.

India on its part has contributed to UNESCO's campaign to save the Nubian monuments in Egypt from the rising waters of the Nile as well as several other international campaigns to save precious-monuments.

Under the five year, (1978-1983) UNDP/UNESCO Project entitled "National Research Laboratory for Conservation of Cultural Property, Lucknow", support was provided to the Government of India in the development of a National Laboratory for Conservation in the fields of museum objects made of wood, paper, metal, miniatures, textiles as well as monuments, archaeological sites and related materials and to make the laboratory a training centre for conservation in India and in the countries of the South and South East Asian Region. The Laboratory has organized many training courses on conservation of cultural property with the financial assistance of UNESCO. The Organization has also been offering fellowships for each course. The conservative trainees have been drawn from several museum, art and cultural institutions in India as well as abroad.

The UNESCO Literature Translation Programme, out of which has grown the "UNESCO Collection of Representative Work's", has been a continuing activity of the Organization since 1948. Under UNESCO's programme of "Collection of Representative Works: India Series", the Organization has so far translated and published 101 titles of different Indian languages into foreign languages including 24 (French), 62 (English), 7 (German), 2 (Spanish), 2 (Hungarian) and 4 (other languages).

MASS COMMUNICATION

In the field of mass communication, UNESCO promotes the free flow of idea by word and image. The Organization develops and improves the means and techniques of mass communication and their use for educational, scientific and cultural purposes. UNESCO helps to stimulate communication as a means of democratic development. It is promoted with assistance, for example, expansion of the television network, television training and satellite instructional television through the Film and Television Institute of India, Pune, established with the assistance of UNESCO and Ford Foundation.

The National Book Trust, India, at New Delhi, which produces and encourages the publication of good literature and makes such literature available at moderate prices to the public, has been assisted by UNESCO. The other institutions in this field which have been assisted by UNESCO include : the Southern Languages Book Trust at Madras, International Institute of Tamil Studies, Madras, and Indian Institute of Mass Communication, New Delhi.

India is a member of the Inter-governmental Council of the International Programme for the Development of Communication (IPDC) which came into existence on the recommendation adopted by the Inter-Governmental Conference for Co-operation on Activities, Needs and Programmes for Communication Development, Paris, in April 1980. UNESCO, under the International Programme for the Development of Communication, has recently supplied important equipment of a substantial amount to the Indian Institute of Mass Communication, New Delhi, in order to help and develop the Institute's programme.

The Delhi Public Library was established in 1951 in association with UNESCO, as a model for public library development in South Asia. This Library was the first UNESCO Public Library Pilot Project.

UNESCO's public information activities are designed to promote international understanding and co-operation by making known to people what UNESCO is doing for the betterment of mankind. Such activities include distribution of informative literature and publications to several institutions and individuals in India. This distribution includes *UNESCO Features, UNESCO News, UNESCO Courier*, and booklets and leaflets, giving an account of UNESCO's programmes and activities. UNESCO films and tapes are also supplied to interested institutions and societies in the country. *UNESCO Courier* is also published in Hindi and Tamil Languages with the financial assistance of UNESCO.

UNESCO films are also supplied to interested institutions in the country.

At the closing meeting of the 6th Session of the Council of IPDC, held in Paris (France) from 4 to 11 March, 1985, the first IPDC/UNESCO prize worth 20,000 dollars for Rural Communication was awarded to the Indian Kheda Communication Project which consists of a low-power television transmitter linked to a study and earth station complex that relays local programmes or central programmes received by Satellite. Community television sets enable the population to view these programmes, which are essentially development and educational oriented.

The office of the UNESCO Representative to India and the Regional Office of Science and Technology for South and Central Asia is responsible for liaison with the Government of India; Indian National Commission for Co-operation with UNESCO, Ministry of Education and Culture; and the United Nations Development Programme in regard to Regular Programmes and UNDP activities. The UNESCO Representative provides technical support for the planning and implementation of UNESCO's programme of aid for development in India. Since its inception in 1949, the Indian National Commission has been closely associated with this office and all the projects are executed and implemented in consultation with the National Commission.

ASSISTANCE TO INSTITUTIONS

A number of educational and scientific institutions in India have received assistance from UNESCO, in the form of technical know-how, equipment, etc. A brief account of each such institution with special reference to the help from UNESCO is given below:

1. *Delhi Public Library, Delhi* It was established as a Public Library Pilot Project in 1951 by UNESCO in collaboration with the Government of India, Ministry of Education. It was intended that the Library would provide a Public Library Service for the people of Delhi

and that it would be a model for all Public Library development in India and in all countries where similar development of public libraries can be undertaken. Under the financial arrangement agreed upon, UNESCO initially contributed a total of about $60,000 during the years 1951-54 and the Government of India 1,20,000 (in rupees) during the same period.

2. *UNESCO Research Centre on Social and Economic Development in Southern Asia, Delhi*: A Social Science Research Centre was established by UNESCO at Calcutta in 1956. It was devoted to research on the impact of urbanization and industrialization in South and South-East Asia. The Centre was shifted to Delhi in 1961 and located there in the premises of the Institute of Economic Growth. After its transfer to Delhi, the centre expanded its aims and activities.

In accordance with the recommendations made by a UNESCO Evaluation Commission, and with the agreement of the Government of India, the UNESCO Research Centre was closed on 31 December, 1966. Its Library and some other assets were transferred to the Institute of Economic Growth which organized its own Asian Research Centre during 1967 with the assistance of the Government of India and UNESCO. UNESCO assistance was available for four years only, ending in 1970, but the Centre continues to be run on finances made available by the Ministry of Human Resource Development, Government of India.

3. *Asian Institute of Educational Planners and Administrators*, now *National Institute of Educational Planning and Administration, New Delhi*: The Institute was set up in 1962 by the Government of India in collaboration with UNESCO under a 10-year agreement for the training of educational planers and administrators to meet the growing educational needs of the different Asian countries.

On the expiry of this agreement in 1972, the Government of India decided to merge the Asian Institute into the National Staff College for Educational Planners and Administrators.

On the recommendation of the Government of India, the NSC has been identified as an Associate Centre of the Asian Centre for Educational Innovation for Development (ACEID), which has been established in Bangkok as an integral part of the UNESCO Regional Office for Education in Asia. As an Associate Centre of ACEID, the main function of the National Staff College is to co-operate with ACEID in promoting reform and innovation in India and other Member-States of the Region in the field of educational management.

The primary modalities of such programmes are surveys, case studies, pilot experiments, field operational and training seminars, workshops, production of instructional materials, etc.

4. *Centre for Educational Technology, NCERT, New Delhi*: Realizing the possibilities which educational technology can offer to education both in respect of improving its quality and extending its reach, the Centre for Educational Technology was set up as a separate institute under the National Council of Educational Research and Training in May 1973 with a special grant from the Government of India. With this, the Centre became one of the 10 constituent units of NCERT.

The UNDP/UNESCO also agreed to assist the Government of India in the initiation, growth and development of the Centre. A project known as IND/711/612-Project was accordingly formulated. The project document was signed by the Government of India and UNDP/UNESCO in May 1974. On account of the initial delay, the project was extended further.

The UNDP/UNESCO assistance in IND/711/612 is being given in the form of experts, equipment and fellowships for training abroad. The assistance indicated in the project document is of the order of $762,903. But as the prices of the equipment soared the figure was revised to $855,137 for the first phase from 1973 to 1976. With a view to giving a boost to the promotion of educational technology for the improvement and spread of education in the country, the Central Institute of Educational Technology (CIET) was set up in May 1984 by the merger of the erstwhile Centre for Educational Technology and the Departments of Teaching Aids of the NCERT. Earlier three-year UNDP Project INSAT for Education was signed by the Government of India in February, 1984.

5. *Indian National Scientific Documentation Centre (INSDOC), New Delhi*: The Centre was set up in 1952 by the Government of India with the technical assistance from UNESCO to provide a full range of documentation services in the field of science and technology. The Centre is functioning under the Council of Scientific and Industrial Research. The assistance of UNESCO covered the provision of experts, fellowship, equipment, etc., during the period 1952-1955. Again in 1964, INSDOC received assistance from UNESCO for setting up its Regional Centre in Bangalore.

It is also actively collaborating with UNESCO in its various projects and programmes. Under scientific and cultural exchange programmes, INSDOC has established exchange relationships with a number of countries in the field of scientific information.

6. *Central Scientific Instruments Organization (CSIO), Chandigarh*: It is a National Laboratory engaged essentially in research, design and development of instruments of scientific and industrial importance. The Organization was set up in 1959 under the Council of Scientific and Industrial Research (CSIR), New Delhi.

During its infancy, the Organization was nurtured by UNESCO/UNDP which provided considerable aid in the form of equipment, UNESCO experts and fellowships.

7. *Central Arid Zone Research Institute, Jodhpur*: The Institute, with its strength of about 500 scientific and supporting staff, library and laboratory facilities, 15 research sub-stations in the desert regions, aerial photo-interpretation centre, solar and wind power harvesting yard and up to date instrumentation facilities stands today on the fringe of the great Indian desert as an evidence of the service rendered by UNESCO to the International community and as its accomplishment in the field of regional development programme through aid and intellectual co-operation.

The Desert Afforestation Research Station at Jodhpur, which had been functioning since October 1952 was redesignated and reorganized as the Central Arid Zone Research Institute in October 1959 on the basis of the recommendations of a UNESCO adviser. At the time of the inception of the institute, UNESCO rendered aid for diverse purposes, such as (a) training of staff, (b) Providing experts, and (c) for equipping the laboratories of the different divisions under the "Major Project of Scientific Researches on Arid Lands".

8. *Films and TV Institute of India (Television Wing), Pune*: The expansion of the television network in the country was a long-felt need. A formal request by the Government of India to UNDP/ UNESCO in 1968 which evoked a favourable response resulted in the establishment of a Television Training Centre on 10 August, 1971. This Centre which was functioning at new Delhi on a temporary basis was shifted to its permanent complex within the campus of the Film Institute, Pune, on 6 July, 1974. The collaboration with UNDP which was for a period of three years ended on 10 August, 1974. The UNDP assistance to this Institute was of the order of US $1.44 million in the form of equipments, experts and fellowships.

9. *National Institute of Foundry and Forge Technology, Ranchi (Bihar)*: The Government of India in 1961 formulated a scheme to

provide improved academic and practical education and training for engineers of the foundry and forge industries by creating a National Institute of Foundry and Forge Technology. In July 1965, the Government of India submitted a request to the United Nations Special Fund for assistance for the above scheme in the form of services of specialists from other countries, equipments not manufactured in India and the fellowships for training Indian counterpart staff outside the country. The NIFFT project was approved by the governing council of the United Nations Special Fund in January 1965. UNESCO was designated as Executing Agency and the Ministry of Education as Government co-operating agency. The plan was signed on 14 December, 1966, and UNESCO was authorized to begin operation on 16 February, 1967. The institute, in consultation with UNESCO experts, took action to procure the equipments on a priority basis both from indigenous sources and from abroad. The equipments received through UNESCO funds were worth $280,790, in addition one induction furnace was received at an approximate cost of $50,000 from UNESCO.

10. *Centres of Advanced Study*: On the basis of the discussions and the report made by the UNESCO Advisory Mission of Science Education which visited India and Moscow in 1962, the programme of assistance to Centres of Advanced Study Project in Indian Universities under UNESCO's Technical Assistance Programme was initiated from 1963-64 with the inclusion of seven Centres/Departments. The assistance made available was in the form of (i) Services of Experts/Consultants, (ii) Training Fellowships and (iii) Supply of Scientific Equipments. The Programme was again reviewed in 1967 and three additional Centres were included under this programme. The list of Centres is as follows:

1. Centre of Advanced Study in Physics, Delhi University.
2. Centre of Advanced Study in Chemistry, Bombay University.
3. Centre of Advanced Study in Chemistry, Delhi University.
4. Centre of Advanced Study in Botany, Delhi University.
5. Centre of Advanced Study in Botany, Madras University.
6. Centre of Advanced Study in Zoology, Delhi University.
7. Centre of Advanced Study in Geology, Panjab University.
8. Centre of Advanced Study in Mathematics, Panjab University.
9. Centre of Advanced Study in Mathematics, Madras University.
10. Centre of Advanced Study in Biochemistry, Indian Institute of

Science, Bangalore.

This programme was completed in 1974. The new project under which the following 10 selected departments were provided UNDP assistance of $771,900 was started from October 1975: Department of Chemistry (Rajasthan University); Department of Pure Chemistry (Calcutta University); Department of Physical Chemistry (Madras University); Department of Inorganic and Physical Chemistry (Indian Institute of Science, Bangalore); Department of Geology (Jadavpur University); Department of Biochemistry (Lucknow University); Department of Physics (Andhra University); Department of Physics (Allahabad University).

11. *Indian Institute of Technology, Bombay*: Established with the co-operation and participation of UNESCO, utilizing the contribution of the Government of the USSR towards building up one of the centres of higher technological education by the Government of India, the Project is a unique adventure with international co-operation in the post-independence era.

The UNESCO Project at the Indian Institute of Technology, Bombay, was nomenclatured as UNESCO Technical Assistance Project No. 12. Under this Project the Institute received 59 Experts, 12 Technicians and 9 Translators.

The most significant contribution made by the UNESCO experts was in the preparation of course material. Lecture notes, monographs and books published by the Experts individually and jointly with the faculty staff ran to 103.

Twenty-seven faculty members of the Institute received higher training in the USSR under the UNESCO Fellowship programme.

The total value of the equipments received by the Institute through UNESCO stood at Rs. 170,60,071.

12. *Motilal Nehru Regional Engineering College, Allahabad*: The Laboratories of all the Departments have been equipped with the latest machines and instruments. The College received assistance from the UNESCO Special Fund, besides funds from the Government of India for equipment.

Four faculty members were sent abroad — three to the UK and one to the USA — for training and advanced studies by the College under the UNESCO Programme for Higher Studies/Research and three for observing the educational pattern in the Western countries.

Eight UNESCO experts and one guest Professor served the College for varying periods. Their contribution in the successful organization of the Industry Oriented Postgraduate courses, and the Under-graduate courses has been appreciable. They have trained some of the staff members of the college in their respective fields of specialization apart from participating in the lecture work and project and thesis guidance. Thirteen lecture notes were prepared on specialized topics.

13. *Maulana Azad College of Technology, Bhopal*: UNESCO, after examining the potentialities of the College and the industrial environment in imparting post-graduate education and training in engineering, selected the College for assistance in (i) equipping its laboratories with necessary sophisticated and precision equipment especially for post graduate and research work, (ii) providing international experts to provide guidance, and train junior faculty and (iii) to train faculty members in advanced countries as summed up below:

> Cost of equipment provided was $300,000. Nine members of the faculty were provided fellowship for research, training and study in the advanced countries of the world. Six experts in the various subjects of post-graduate specialization were provided for a total of about seven years.

14. *Regional Engineering College, Durgápur*: UNESCO assistance has gone a long way in consolidating the existing undergraduate courses by better equipping the laboratories and improving standard of teaching by providing better training facilities to the teachers. It has also been instrumental in developing the industry-oriented M.Tech. courses and initiating industrial research. The assistance consisted of providing the services of eight international experts, offering 10 fellowships for the training of teachers abroad and providing funds worth $0.44 million for the purchase of selected equipment.

15. *Visvesvaraya Regional College of Engineering, Nagpur*: This college, one of the first six Regional Colleges established under the scheme sponsored by the Government of India and the State Government, has been allotted three industrially-oriented post-graduate courses under the UNESCO Project, and these have become popular.

Under the UNESCO Scheme, the College had the advantage of the services of six Experts — four from the USSR and one each from Poland and the UAR — for the various post-graduate courses. Nine staff members of the college also got an opportunity to go abroad with a UNESCO fellowship either for study tour/practical training or post-graduate studies. The College has also received substantial equipment under the UNESCO Scheme.

16. *Regional Engineering College, Rourkela*: The College has received substantial help from UNDP.

17. *Karnataka Regional Engineering College, Surathkal (Karnataka)*: M.Tech. Courses were started in the College as part of the UNESCO Special Fund Project for development of Regional Engineering Colleges.

The College came under the "Six Regional Engineering Colleges Project" (IND-50 and IND-104) of the UNESCO Special Fund Programme. Under this Project the College:

(a) received equipment for undergraduate and post-graduate courses started under this Project;

(b) received fellowships for its staff members for higher studies;

(c) started industrially-oriented post-graduate courses in the following fields:

1. Industrial Structures
2. Marine Structures
3. Industrial Electronics

(d) received services of UNESCO Experts to develop the post-graduate courses.

The College received equipment valued at $310,677. Nine staff members availed themselves of UNESCO fellowships and went abroad — three to the USA, three to the UK and Italy and one each to the USSR, Japan and the UK — either for training/study tour or for post-graduate studies.

18. *Regional Engineering College, Tiruchirapalli (Tamil Nadu)*: The programme of UNDP aid to this college commenced from October 1970, with the starting of an industry-oriented post-graduate degree course in Design and Production of Thermal Power Equipment.

Essential equipment for the conduct of research work and post-graduate and undergraduate laboratory work was envisaged and UNDP funds to the tune of $145,000 were made available.

Items of equipment purchased out of these funds are not only used in the laboratory of the departments but are also utilized by the collaborating industry (such as Bharat Heavy Electrical Limited).

Three fellowships were also made available to the college and the selected candidates obtained training experience in Germany and Czechoslovakia.

19. *Regional Engineering College, Warangal (Andhra Pradesh)*: The UNESCO Programme was originally a Five-Year project extending from 1964 to 1969 which overflowed up to 1972. This was mainly intended to introduce the new concept of industry-oriented courses at the post-graduate level and to strengthen the existing post-graduate programmes in the College. Subsequently, in 1972, a Fellowship Project was started to strengthen the U.G.C. Programme on the one side and to initiate research of a high order in the form of (1) Doctoral Programmes, (2) Joint Research and Developmental Activity between the College and Industries and (3) to develop this College as a Research Centre in certain selected fields of specialization, on the other.

It has also received equipment worth Rs. 1 lakh from abroad under UNDP.

INDIAN NATIONAL COMMISSION FOR CO-OPERATION WITH UNESCO

India has been a member of the United Nations Educational, Scientific and Cultural Organization since its inception in 1946. Article VII of the Constitution of UNESCO requires that "each Member-State shall make arrangements as suit its particular conditions for purposes of associating its principal bodies interested in educational, scientific and cultural matters with the work of the Organization preferably by the formation of a National Commission or any representative of the Government and such bodies" and further provides that "National Commissions or national co-operating bodies, where they exist, act in an advisory capacity to their respective delegations to the Central Conference and to their Governments in matters relating to the Organization and shall function as agencies of liaison in all matters of interest to it". Accordingly, an interim Indian National Commission for Co-operation with UNESCO was set up in 1949, and a permanent Commission was established in 1951.

As a member of UNESCO, the Government of India, in compliance with Article VII of the Constitution of the Organization, established, in 1949, the National Commission for Co-operation with UNESCO to involve in UNESCO's activities, various departments, agencies, institutions, organization — both governmental and non-governmental — and individuals working for the advancement of education, science, culture and communication; to collaborate with each other and UNESCO's Regional Offices and Centres fostering regional, sub-regional and bilateral co-operation in education, science, culture and information, particularly through the joint formulation and execution of programmes. The Commission performs as role not only as a co-ordinating body at the national level but also collaborated with the National Commissions of Asia and the Pacific and with UNESCO's regional offices and centres for bringing about a better understanding of UNESCO's projects and activities. Besides, the Commission identifies and recommends Indian candidates for various posts under UNESCO, arrange placement of UNESCO fellows from Member-States in various universities, institutions, laboratories, etc., in India and helps in handling contracts offered by UNESCO to experts and institutions in India for undertaking specific studies of specialized nature as well as administration of funds allocated under the Participation Programme of UNESCO.

Recent Activities of the Commission

India hosted an International Seminar on UNESCO — In Retrospect and Prospect at the India International Centre, New Delhi, from 1 to 3 January, 1986, with financial assistance from UNESCO under the Participation Programme. Thee Seminar was attended by four members of the Executive Board of UNESCO and delegates from Algeria, Bangladesh, India, Nepal, Sri Lanka and the USSR. Eminent Indian personalities in the fields of education, science, culture, communications and social sciences also participated in the Seminar. The Seminar reviewed UNESCO's work over the past 40 years, examined the nature and ramifications of its present situation and made several recommendations for the future orientation of its programmes.

The Centre for Cultural Resources and Training, New Delhi, in collaboration with the Indian National Commission, organized a Training Workshop in Documentation and Dissemination of Performing Arts at New Delhi from 31 March to 5 April, 1986. The objectives of the Workshop were to evolve a methodology for research and documentation, suitable for the region; to formulate a framework of a scheme for documentation of the Performing Arts of the region; to provide guidelines on production of programmes for dissemination of information about the artistic and cultural heritage using the materials collected during documentation; and to evolve a methodology for cataloguing and indexing the documented materials collected.

Delegates from Bangladesh, Bhutan, Burma, India, Indonesia, Japan, Malaysia, Maldives, Nepal, Pakistan, Sri Lanka and Thailand participated in the Workshop. The Assistant Director General for Co-ordination of UNESCO Activities in Asia and the Pacific, Bangkok, and the Regional Adviser for Culture in Asia and the Pacific, Bangkok, also participated in the Workshop.

In response to a fresh appeal launched by the Director General of UNESCO, a sum of US $25,000 was contributed by the Indian Government for the campaign to safeguard the monumental site of Mohonjodare in Pakistan. With this the total contribution made by India towards the campaign amounts to US $100,000 approximately.

Another sum of US $25,000 has been contributed to UNESCO's International Institute for Educational Planning, a premier institute in the field of Educational Planning located in Paris.

Associated Schools Project

India joined the Associated Schools Project in 1953 with six institutions. The number has now risen to 37 which comprise 10 teacher training institutions and 27 composite schools having both primary and secondary departments. These schools work on three main themes: teaching about the United Nations and its specialized agencies; teaching about human rights and fundamental freedoms; and teaching about other countries. The Indian National Commission for UNESCO has always held the view that the Associated Schools Project is of vital importance for India and the world and that more schools and teacher training institutions should be established to increase the number of Indian Schools linked directly with UNESCO Secretariat in Paris under the Associated Schools Project. The National Commission, therefore, prepared an expanded programme in India to cover a large number of schools and teacher training institutions in the country. There are about 330 institutions which have been covered under the expanded programme.

UNESCO Clubs

The Indian National Commission has been promoting the establishment of UNESCO clubs in various centres including universities, libraries and educational and cultural institutions. So far 133 such clubs have been established throughout the country. These clubs undertake activities such as disseminating information about the aims and policies of UNESCO, the UN and similar bodies and arrange various programmes in education, science, culture, etc., to promote international understanding, co-operation and world peace. The Commission has been sending publications, periodicals and other materials received from UNESCO or brought out by the Commission itself to all the clubs regularly. Special kits of material are sent to the clubs to enable them to celebrate UN Day and Human Rights Day in a befiting manner.

The UNESCO Courier

The Indian National Commission for UNESCO gets the Hindi and Tamil editions of *The UNESCO Courier* published by the Central Hindi Directorate, a subordinate office under the Department of Education and the Southern Languages Book Trust, Madras, respectively.

UNESCO Coupons

The Commission operates the UNESCO International Coupons Scheme designed to assist institutions and individuals working in the fields of education, science, culture and communication to import educational and scientific material from foreign countries on payment in Indian rupees.

Newsletter and UNESCO Publications

The Commission brings out the quarterly *Newsletter* in English to publicize information about the activities of the Commission and UNESCO in India. The Library and Documentation Unit of the Commission makes available copies of the UNESCO publications/periodicals including the *Newsletter* to educational and research institutions/ organizations all over India and abroad. The Unit brings out a monthly annotated list (*Current Awareness*) of publications/periodicals/reports, received from UNESCO Headquarters/regional offices and UNESCO's other research and planning institutions in Member-States.

BIBLIOGRAPHY

UNESCO DOCUMENTS AND PUBLICATIONS*

1. *Aspects of training and research in higher education with case studies on India and Venezuela.* Paris, UNESCO, 1987, 308 p. (Paper in higher education No. 16).
2. *Formal and non-formal education in rural development* (A sample survey in the State of Karnataka, India). Paris, UNESCO, in co-operation with the Asian Institute of Rural Development, Bangalore, 1980, 77 p. ED-80/WS/158.
3. *Policy, planning and administration of technical and vocational education in India.* Paris, UNESCO, 1985, 172 p. (Studies in technical and vocational education No. 8).
4. *Progress report on graphic communication course experiments conducted in Belgium, China, Cyprus, Finland, Hungary, India, Korea (Republic), Philippines, Sweden.* Paris, UNESCO, 1984. ED-84/WS/61.
5. *The Role of parents in the education of children of pre-school age in tropical Africa, India, the Maghreb countries.* Prepared by the International Federation for Parent Education. Paris, UNESCO, 1980, 48 p. ED-80/WS/92.
6. *The role of working mothers in early childhood education in India.* Paris, UNESCO, 1977, 200 p.

* Listing to illustrate the range of UNESCO documents and publications.

APPENDICES

APPENDIX A

UNESCO CONSTITUTION

"Since wars begin in the minds of men, it is in the minds of men that the defences of peace must be constructed".

The Governments of the States parties to this Constitution on behalf of their peoples declare:

- That since wars begin in the minds of men, it is in the minds of men that the defences of peace must be constructed;
- That ignorance of each other's ways and lives has been a common cause, throughout the history of mankind, of that suspicion and mistrust between the peoples of the world through which their differences have all too often broken into war;
- That the great and terrible war which has now ended was a war made possible by the denial of the democratic principles of the dignity, equality and mutual respect of men, and by the propagation, in their place, through ignorance and prejudice, of the doctrine of the inequality of men and races;
- That the wide diffusion of culture, and the education of humanity for justice and liberty and peace are indispensable to the dignity of man and constitute a sacred duty which all the nations must fulfil in a spirit of mutual assistance and concern;
- That a peace based exclusively upon the political and economic arrangements of governments would not be a peace which could secure the unanimous, lasting and sincere support of the peoples of the world, and that the peace must therefore be founded, if it is not to fail, upon the intellectual and moral solidarity of mankind.

For these reasons, the States parties to this Constitution, believing in full and equal opportunities for education for all, in the unrestricted pursuit of the objective truth, and in the free exchange of ideas and knowledge, are agreed and determined to develop and to increase the means of communication between their peoples and to employ these means for the purposes of mutual understanding and a truer and more perfect knowledge of each other's lives;

In consequence whereof they do hereby create the United Nations Educational, Scientific and Cultural Organization for the purpose of advancing, through the educational and scientific and cultural relations of the peoples of the world, the objectives of international peace and of the common welfare of mankind for which the United Nations Organization was established and which its Charter proclaims.

ARTICLE I. Purposes and Functions

1. The purpose of the Organization is to contribute to peace and security by promoting collaboration among the nations through education, science and culture in order to further universal respect for justice, for the rule of law and for the human rights and fundamental freedoms which are affirmed for the peoples of the world, without distinction of race, sex, language or religion, by the Charter of the United Nations.
2. To realize this purpose the Organization will:

(a) Collaborate in the work of advancing the mutual knowledge and understanding of peoples, through all means of mass communication and to that end recommend such international agreements as may be necessary to promote the free flow of ideas by word and image;

(b) Give fresh impulse to popular education and to the spread of culture:

- By collaborating with Members, at their request, in the development of educational activities;
- By instituting collaboration among the nations to advance the ideal of equality of educational opportunity without regard to race sex or any distinctions, economic or social;
- By suggesting educational methods best suited to prepare the children of the world for the responsibilities of freedom;

(c) Maintain, increase and diffuse knowledge:

- By assuring the conservation and protection of the world's inheritance of books, works of art and monuments of history and science, and recommending to the nations concerned the necessary international conventions;

– By encouraging co-operation among the nations in all branches of intellectual activity, including the international exchange of persons active in the fields of education, science and culture and the exchange of publications, objects of artistic and scientific interest and other materials of information;
– By initiating methods of international co-operation calculated to give the people of all countries access to the printed and published materials produced by any of them.

3. With a view to preserving the integrity and fruitful diversity of the cultures and educational systems of the State-Members of the Organization, the Organization is prohibited from intervening in matters which are essentially within their domestic jurisdiction.

ARTICLE II. Membership

1. Membership of the United Nations Organization shall carry with it the right to membership of the United Nations Educational, Scientific and Cultural Organization.
2. Subject to the conditions of the Agreement between this Organization and the United Nations Organization, approved pursuant to Article X of this Constitution, States not Members of the United Nations Organization may be admitted to membership of the organization, upon recommendation of the Executive Board, by a two-thirds majority vote of the General Conference.
3. Territories or groups of territories which are not responsible for the conduct of their international relations may be admitted as Associate Members by the General Conference by a two-thirds majority of Members present and voting, upon application made on behalf of such territory or groups of territories by the Member or other authority having responsibility for their international relations. The nature and extent of the rights and obligations of Associate Members shall be determined by the General Conference.
4. Members of the Organization which are suspended from the exercise of the rights and privileges of membership of the United Nations Organization shall, upon the request of the latter, be suspended from the rights and privileges of the organization.

5. Members of the Organization which are expelled from the United Nations Organization shall automatically cease to be Members of this Organization.
6. Any Member-State or Associate Member of the Organization may withdraw from the Organization by notice addressed to the Director General, such notice shall take effect on 31 December of the year following that during which the notice was given, no such withdrawal shall affect the financial obligations owed to the Organization on the date the withdrawal takes effect. Notice of withdrawal by an Associate Member shall be given on its behalf by the Member-State or other authority having responsibility for its international relations.

ARTICLE III. Organs

The Organization shall include a General Conference, an Executive Board and a Secretariat.

ARTICLE IV. The General Conference

A. Composition

1. The General Conference shall consist of the representatives of the State Members of the Organization. The Government of each Member-State shall appoint not more than five delegates, who shall be selected after consultation with the National Commission, if established, or with educational scientific and cultural bodies.

B. Functions

2. The General Conference shall determine the policies and the main lines of work of the Organization. It shall take decisions on programmes submitted to it by the Executive Board.
3. The General Conference shall, when it deems desirable and in accordance with the regulations to be made by it, summon international conferences of States on education, the sciences and humanities or the dissemination of knowledge; non-governmental conferences on the same subjects may be summoned by the General Conferences or by the Executive Board in

accordance with such regulations.

4. The General Conference shall, in adopting proposals for submission to the Member-States, distinguish between recommendations and international conventions submitted for their approval. In the former case a majority vote shall suffice; in the latter case a two-thirds majority shall be required. Each of the Member-State shall submit recommendations or conventions to its competent authorities within a period of one year from the close of the session of the General Conference at which they were adopted.
5. Subject to the provisions of Article V, paragraph 5(c), the General Conference shall advise the United Nations Organization on the educational, scientific and cultural aspects of matters of concern to the latter; in accordance with the terms and procedure agreed upon between the appropriate authorities of the two Organizations.
6. The General Conference shall receive and consider the reports sent to the Organization by Member-States on the action taken upon the recommendations and conventions referred to in paragraph 4 above or, if it so decides, analytical summaries of these reports.
7. The General Conference shall elect the members of the Executive Board and, on the recommendation of the Board, shall appoint the Director-General.

C. Voting

8. (a) Each Member-State shall have one vote in the General Conference. Decisions shall be made by a simple majority except in cases in which a two-thirds majority is required by the provisions of this Constitution, or the Rules of Procedure of the General Conference. A majority shall be a majority of the members present and voting.
   (b) A Member-State shall have no vote in the General Conference if the total amount of contributions due from it exceeds the total amount of contributions payable by it for the current year and the immediately preceding calendar year.
   (c) The General Conference may nevertheless permit such a Member-State to vote, if it is satisfied that failure to pay is due to conditions beyond the control of the Member-Nations.

D. Procedure

9. (a) The General Conference shall meet in ordinary session every two years. It may meet in extraordinary session if it decides to do so itself or if summoned by the Executive Board, or on the demand of at least one-third of the Member-States.
   (b) At each session the location of its next ordinary session shall be designated by the General Conference. The location of an extraordinary session shall be decided by the General Conference if the session is summoned by it, or otherwise by the Executive Board.
10. The General Conference shall adopt its own rules of procedure. It shall at each session elect a President and other officers.
11. The General Conference shall set up special and technical committees and such other subordinate bodies as may be necessary for its purposes.
12. The General Conference shall cause arrangements to be made for public access to meetings, subject to such regulations as it shall prescribe.

E. Observers

13. The General Conference, on the recommendation of the Executive Board and by a two-thirds majority, may, subject to its rules of procedure, invite as observers at specified sessions of the Conference or of its Commissions representatives of international organizations, such as those referred to in Article XI, Paragraph 4.
14. When consultative arrangements have been approved by the Executive Board for such international non-governmental or semi-governmental organization in the manner provided in Article XI, Paragraph 4, those organizations shall be invited to send observers to sessions of the General Conference and its Commissions.

F. Transitional Provision

15. Notwithstanding the provisions of Paragraph 9(a) of this Article, the General Conference shall hold its twenty-second session in the third year following its twenty-first session.

ARTICLE V. Executive Board

A. Composition

1. The Executive Board shall be elected by the General Conference from among the delegates appointed by the Member-States and consist of fifty-one members each of whom shall represent the Government of the State of which he is a national. The President of the General Conference shall sit ex-officio in an advisory capacity on the Executive Board.
2. In electing the members of the Executive Board the General Conference shall endeavour to include persons competent in the arts, the humanities, the sciences, the education and the diffusion of ideas, and qualified by their experience and capacity to fulfil the administrative and executive duties of the Board. It shall also have regard to the diversity of cultures and a balanced geographical distribution. Not more than one national of any Member-State shall serve on the Board at any one time, the President of the Conference excepted.
3. Members of the Board shall serve from the close of the session of the General Conference which elected them until the close of the second ordinary session of the General Conference following that election. They shall not be immediately eligible for a second term. The General Conference shall, at each of its ordinary sessions, elect the number of members required to fill vacancies occurring at the end of the session.
4. (a) In the event of the death or resignation of a member of the Executive Board, his replacement for the remainder of his term shall be appointed by the Executive Board on the nomination of the Government of the State the former member represented.

   (b) The Government making the nomination and the Executive Board shall have regard to the factors set forth in Paragraph 2 of this Article.

   (c) When exceptional circumstances arise, which, in the considered opinion of the represented State, make it indispensable for its representative to be replaced, even if he does not tender his resignation, measures shall be taken in accordance with the provisions of sub-paragraph (a) above.

B. Functions

5. (a) The Executive Board shall prepare the agenda for the General Conference. It shall examine the programme of work for the Organization and corresponding budget estimates submitted to it by the Director-General in accordance with Paragraph 3 of Article VI and shall submit them with such recommendations as it considers desirable to the General Conference.
   (b) The Executive Board, acting under the authority of the General Conference, shall be responsible for the execution of the programme adopted by the Conference. In accordance with the decisions of the General Conference and having regard to circumstances arising between two ordinary sessions, the Executive Board shall take all necessary measures to ensure the effective and rational execution of the programme by the Director-General.
   (c) Between ordinary sessions of the General Conference, the Board may discharge the functions of adviser to the United Nations, set forth in Article IV, Paragraph 5, whenever the problem upon which advice is sought has already been dealt with in principle by the Conference, or when the solution is implicit in decisions of the Conference.
6. The Executive Board shall recommend to the General Conference the admission of new Members to the Organization.
7. Subject to decisions of the General Conference, the Executive Board shall adopt its own rules of procedure. It shall elect its officers from among its members.
8. The Executive Board shall meet in regular session at least twice a year and may meet in special session if convoked by the Chairman on his own initiative or upon the request of six members of the Board.
9. The Chairman of the Executive Board shall present, on behalf of the Board, to each ordinary session of the General Conference, with or without comments, the reports on the activities of the Organization which the Director-General is required to prepare in accordance with the provisions of Article VI 3(b).
10. The Executive Board shall make all necessary arrangements to consult the representatives of international organizations or qualified persons concerned with questions within its competence.

11. Between sessions of the General Conference, the Executive Board may request advisory opinions from the International Court of Justice on legal questions arising within the field of the organization's activities.
12. Although the members of the Executive Board are representatives of their respective Governments they shall exercise the powers delegated to them by the General Conference on behalf of the Conference as a whole.

C. Transitional Provisions

13. Notwithstanding the provisions of Paragraph 3 of this Article,

  (a) Members of the Executive Board elected prior to the seventeenth session of the General Conference shall serve until the end of the term for which they were elected.
  (b) Members of the Executive Board appointed, prior to the seventeenth session of the General Conference, by the Board in accordance with the provisions of Paragraph 4 of this Article to replace members with a four-year term, shall be eligible for a second term of four years.

ARTICLE VI. Secretariat

1. The Secretariat shall consist of a Director-General and such staff as may be required.
2. The Director-General shall be nominated by the Executive Board and appointed by the General Conference for a period of six years, under such conditions as the Conference may approve, and shall be eligible for reappointment. He shall be the chief administrative officer of the Organization.
3. (a) The Director-General, or a deputy designated by him, shall participate, without the right to vote, in all meetings of the General Conference, of the Executive Board, and/or the committees of the Organization. He shall formulate proposals for appropriate action by the Conference and the Board, and shall prepare for submission to the Board a draft programme of work for the Organization with corresponding budget estimates.
   (b) The Director-General shall prepare and communicate to

Member States and to the Executive Board periodical reports on the activities of the Organization. The General Conference shall determine the periods to be covered by these reports.

4. The Director General shall appoint the staff of the Secretariat in accordance with staff regulations to be approved by the General Conference. Subject to the paramount consideration of securing the highest standards of integrity, efficiency and technical competence, appointment to the staff shall be on as wide a geographical basis as possible.
5. The responsibilities of the Director-General and of the staff shall be exclusively international in character. In the discharge of their duties they shall not seek or receive instructions from any Government or from any authority external to the Organization. They shall refrain from any action which might prejudice their positions as international officials. Each State Member of the Organization undertakes to respect the international character of the responsibilities of the Director-General and the staff, and not to seek to influence them in the discharge of their duties.
6. Nothing in this Article shall preclude the Organization from entering into special arrangements within the United Nations Organization for common services and staff and for the interchange of personnel.

Transitional Provision

7. Notwithstanding the provisions of Paragraph 2 of this Article, the Director General nominated by the Executive Board and appointed by the General Conference in 1980 shall serve for a term of seven years.

ARTICLE VII. National Co-operating Bodies

1. Each Member-State shall make such arrangements as suit its particular conditions for the purpose of associating its principal bodies interested in educational, scientific and cultural matters with the work of the Organization, preferably by the formation of a National Commission broadly representative of the Government and such bodies.
2. National Commissions or National Co-operating Bodies, where they exist, shall act in an advisory capacity to their respective

delegations to the General Conference and to their Governments in matters relating to the Organization and shall function as agencies of liaison in all matters of interest to it.

3. The Organization may, on the request of a Member-State, delegate, either temporarily or permanently, a member of its Secretariat to serve on the National Commission of thAT State, in order to assist in the development of its work.

ARTICLE VIII. Reports by Member-States

Each Member-State shall submit to the Organization, at such times and in such manner as shall be determined by the General Conference, reports on the laws, regulations and statistics relating to its educational, scientific and cultural institutions and activities, and on the action taken upon the recommendations and conventions referred to in Article IV, Paragraph 4.

ARTICLE IX. Budget

1. The Budget shall be administered by the Organization.
2. The General Conference shall approve and give final effect to the budget and to the apportionment of financial responsibility among the State-Members of the Organization subject to such arrangement with the United Nations as may be provided in the agreement to be entered into pursuant to Article X.
3. The Director-General, with the approval of the Executive Board, may receive gifts, bequests, and subventions directly from Governments, public and private institutions, associations and private persons.

ARTICLE X. Relations with the United Nations Organization

This Organization shall be brought into relation with the United Nations Organization, as soon as practicable, as one of the Specialized Agencies referred to in Article 57 of the Charter of the United Nations. This relationship shall be effected through an agreement with the United Nations Organization under Article 63 of the Charter, which agreement shall be subject to the approval of the General Conference of this Organization. The agreement shall provide for effective co-operation between the two Organizations in the pursuit of their common purposes, and at the same time shall recognize the autonomy of this Organization, within the fields of its competence as defined in this Constitution. Such agreement may, among other matters, provide for the approval and financing of the budget of the Organization by the General Assembly of the United Nations.

ARTICLE XI. Relations with other Specialized International Organizations and Agencies

1. This Organization may co-operate with other specialized inter-governmental organizations and agencies whose interests and activities are related to its purposes. To this end the Director-General, acting under the general authority of the Executive Board, may establish effective working relationships with such organizations and agencies and establish such joint committees as may be necessary to assure effective co-operation. Any formal arrangements entered into with such organizations or agencies shall be subject to the approval of the Executive Board.
2. Whenever the General Conference of this Organization and the competent authorities of any other specialized inter-governmental organizations or agencies whose purpose and functions lie within the competence of this Organization deem it desirable to effect a transfer of their resources and activities to this Organization, the Director General, subject to the approval of the Conference, may enter into mutually acceptable arrangements for this purpose.
3. This Organization may make appropriate arrangements with other inter-governmental organizations for reciprocal representation at meetings.
4. The United Nations Educational, Scientific and Cultural Organization may make suitable arrangements for consultation and co-operation with non-governmental international organizations concerned with matters within its competence, and may invite them to undertake specific tasks. Such co-operation may also include appropriate participation by representatives of such organizations on advisory committees set up by the General Conference.

ARTICLE XII. Legal Status of the Organization

The provisions of Articles 104 and 105 of the Charter of the United

Nations Organization concerning the legal status of that Organization, its privileges and immunities, shall apply in the same way to this Organization.

ARTICLE XIII. Amendments

1. Proposals for amendments to this Constitution shall become effective upon receiving the approval of the General Conference by a two-thirds majority; provided, however, that those amendments which involve fundamental alterations in aims of the Organization or new obligations for the Member-States shall require subsequent acceptance on the part of two-thirds of the Member-States before they come into force. The draft texts of proposed amendments shall be communicated by the Director-General to the Member-States at least six months in advance of their consideration by the General Conference.

ARTICLE XIV. Interpretation

1. The English and French texts of this Constitution shall be regarded as equally authoritative.
2. Any question or dispute concerning the interpretation of this Constitution shall be referred for determination to the International Court of Justice or to an arbitral tribunal, as the General Conference may determine under its rules of procedure.

ARTICLE XV. Entry into Force

1. This Constitution shall be subject to acceptance. The instrument of acceptance shall be deposited with the Government of the United Kingdom.
2. This Constitution shall remain open for signature in the archives of the Government of the United Kingdom. Signature may take place either before or after the deposit of the instrument of acceptance.
3. This Constitution shall come into force when it has been accepted by twenty of its signatories. Subsequent acceptances shall take effect immediately.
4. The Government of the United Kingdom will inform all Members of the United Nations of the receipt of all instruments of accept-

ance and of the date on which the Constitution comes into force in accordance with the preceding paragraph.

In faith whereof, the undersigned, duly authorized to that effect, have signed this Constitution in the English and French Languages, both texts being equally authentic.

Done in London the sixteenth day of November, one thousand nine hundred and forty-five, in a single copy, in the English and French languages, of which certified copies will be communicated by the Government of the United Kingdom to the Governments of all the Members of the United Nations.

•

UNESCO MEMBER-STATES*

Afghanistan	4 May 1948
Albania	16 October 1958
Algeria	15 October 1962
Angola	11 March 1977
Antigua and Barbuda	15 July 1982
Argentina	15 September 1948
Australia	11 June 1946
Austria	13 August 1948
Bahamas	23 April 1981
Bahrain	18 January 1972
Bangladesh	27 October 1972
Barbados	24 October 1968
Belgium	29 November 1946
Belize	10 May 1982
Benin	18 October 1960
Bhutan	13 April 1982
Bolivia	13 November 1946
Botswana	16 January 1980
Brazil	4 November 1946
Bulgaria	17 May 1956
Burkina Faso	14 November 1960
Burma	27 June 1949
Burundi	16 November 1962
Byelorussian Soviet Socialist Republic	12 May 1954
Cameroon	11 November 1960
Canada	4 November 1946
Cape Verde	15 February 1978
Central African Republic	11 November 1960
Chad	19 December 1960
Chile	7 July 1953

* As in January 1986.

China	4	November 1946
Colombia	31	October 1947
Comoros	22	March 1977
Congo	24	October 1960
Costa Rica	19	May 1950
Cote D'Ivoire	27	October 1960
Cuba	29	August 1947
Cyprus	6	February 1961
Czechoslovakia	4	November 1946
Democratic Kampuchea	3	July 1951
Democratic People's Republic of Korea	18	October 1974
Democratic Yemen	15	October 1968
Denmark	4	November 1946
Dominica	9	January 1979
Dominican Republic	4	November 1946
Ecuador	22	January 1947
Egypt	16	July 1946
El Salvador	28	April 1948
Equatorial Guinea	29	November 1979
Ethiopia	1	July 1955
Fiji	14	July 1983
Finland	10	October 1956
France	4	November 1946
Gabon	16	November 1960
Gambia	1	August 1973
German Democratic Republic	24	November 1972
Germany, Federal Republic of	11	July 1951
Ghana	11	April 1958
Greece	4	November 1946
Grenada	17	February 1975
Guatemala	2	January 1950
Guinea	2	February 1960
Guinea-Bissau	1	November 1974
Guyana	21	March 1967
Haiti	18	November 1946
Honduras	16	December 1947
Hungary	14	September 1948
Iceland	8	June 1964
India	4	November 1946
Indonesia	27	May 1950

Iran, Islamic Republic of	6 September 1948
Iraq	21 October 1948
Ireland	3 October 1961
Israel	16 September 1949
Italy	27 January 1948
Jamaica	7 November 1962
Japan	2 July 1951
Jordan	14 June 1950
Kenya	7 April 1964
Kuwait	18 November 1960
Lao People's Democratic Republic	9 July 1951
Lebanon	4 November 1946
Lesotho	29 September 1967
Liberia	6 March 1947
Libyan Arab Jamahiriya	27 June 1953
Luxembourg	27 October 1947
Madagascar	10 November 1960
Malawi	27 October 1964
Malaysia	16 June 1958
Maldives	18 July 1980
Mali	7 November 1960
Malta	10 February 1965
Mauritania	10 January 1962
Mauritius	25 October 1968
Mexico	4 November 1946
Monaco	6 July 1949
Mongolia	1 November 1962
Morocco	7 November 1956
Mozambique	11 October 1976
Namibia	2 November 1978
Nepal	1 May 1953
Netherlands	1 January 1947
New Zealand	4 November 1946
Nicaragua	22 February 1952
Niger	10 November 1960
Nigeria	14 November 1960
Norway	4 November 1946
Oman	10 February 1972
Pakistan	14 September 1949
Panama	10 January 1950

Papua New Guinea	4 October 1976
Paraguay	20 June 1955
Peru	21 November 1946
Philippines	21 November 1946
Poland	6 November 1946
Portugal	12 March 1965
Qatar	27 January 1972
Republic of Korea	14 June 1950
Romania	27 July 1956
Rwanda	7 November 1962
Saint Christopher and Nevis	26 October 1983
Saint Lucia	6 March 1980
Saint Vincent and the Grenadines	15 February 1983
Samoa	3 April 1981
San Marino	12 November 1974
Sao Tome and Principe	22 January 1980
Saudi Arabia	4 November 1946
Senegal	10 November 1960
Seychelles	18 October 1976
Sierra Leone	28 March 1962
Somalia	15 November 1960
Spain	30 January 1953
Sri Lanka	14 November 1949
Sudan	26 November 1956
Suriname	16 July 1976
Swaziland	25 January 1978
Sweden	23 January 1950
Switzerland	28 January 1949
Syrian Arab Republic	16 November 1946
Thailand	1 January 1949
Togo	17 November 1960
Tonga	29 September 1980
Trinidad and Tobago	2 November 1962
Tunisia	8 November 1956
Turkey	4 November 1946
Uganda	9 November 1962
Ukrainian Soviet Socialist Republic	12 May 1954
Union of Soviet Socialist Republics	21 April 1954
United Arab Emirates	20 April 1972
United Republic of Tanzania	6 March 1962

Uruguay	8 November 1947
Venezuela	25 November 1946
Viet Nam	6 July 1951
Yemen	2 April 1962
Yugoslavia	31 March 1950
Zaire	25 November 1960
Zambia	9 November 1964
Zimbabwe	22 September 1980

Associate Members

British Virgin Islands	26 October 1983
Netherlands Antilles	24 November 1983

APPENDIX C

UNESCO DIRECTORS GENERAL

1. *Julian Huxley* (1946 to 1948)

A British biologist, who had earlier headed the preparatory Commission which had launched UNESCO, became the first Director General of UNESCO in 1946 and served till 1948 when the Organization set up its headquarters in Paris using the temporary premises in the Hotel Majestic on the Avenue Kleher. Stated that UNESCO activities can best be expressed in five words, "The Advance of World Civilization".

2. *Jamine Torres Bodet* (1949 to 1952)

A Mexcian who knew well what development and underdevelopment meant. His major development programme was the creation of two fundamental education centres—one for Latin America and the other for Arab States. Torres Bodet instinctively and wholeheartedly backed the early efforts on UNESCO's participation in the United Nations Technical Assistance Programme.

3. *Luther H. Evans* (1953 to 1958)

Laid the firm foundation for the spectacular growth of the Organization in the development field. UNESCO, he wrote, "is a living presence in the sense that it is a voice heard by many, a guide followed in a good few places, more and more a searchlight thrown on dark places, to point the road to advance in all the countless cases where advance is sought. But all this stimulus is preparatory to action—action in the schools and laboratories, action in the libraries and museums, in the fields and villages, in a word, action in the Member-States".

4. *Vittorino Veronese* (1958 to 1961)

Became the Director General at the moment of Africans liberation. He often referred to the golden rule, "primum vivere deinde philosophare" which means "live first then philosophize about".

5. *Rane Maheu* (1962 to 1974)

Observed, "education, science, culture and communication are not ends in themselves for UNESCO, but simply ways and means of a spiritual undertaking and moral effort that constitutes its true mission".

On his election to the position of Director General of UNESCO, in a message to Prospects, he observed, "It is education which enables the concept of justice, fraternity and progress to take root in the minds of men by linking them closely to the acquisition of knowledge and the expansion of the intellectual, creative and moral faculties in the children and young people who will be the adults of tomorrow. The first task which its constitution calls on UNESCO to perform is to "contribute to peace and security by promoting collaboration among the nations through education, science and culture in order to further universal respect of justice, and I believe that, for more than a quarter of a century, the organization has shown itself worthy of this noble and difficult mission".

6. *Amadow-Mahtar M'Bow* (1974 to 1987)

On his election to the position of Director General of UNESCO, in a message to Prospects, he observed, "It is education which enables the concept of justice, fraternity and progress to take root in the minds of men by linking them closely to the acquisition of knowledge and the expansion of the intellectual, creative and moral faculties in the children and young people who will be the adults of tomorrow. The first task – which its constitution calls on UNESCO to perform is to "contribute to peace and security by promoting collaboration among the nations through education, science and culture in order to further universal respect of justice, and I believe that, for more than a quarter of a century, the organization has shown itself worthy of this noble and difficult mission".

7. *Federico Mayor Zaragoza* (1987 -)

The Twenty-third Session of the UNESCO's General Conference (Oct.-Nov. 1987) elected through secret ballot Professor Federico Mayor Zaragoza as the new Director-General of the Organization. He assumed his office on 6 November, 1987 for a six-year period.

Professor Mayor (*b.* 27 January, 1934), Spanish by nationality, is a well-known Biochemist with wide-ranging academic interests. Besides being Professor of Biochemistry at the University of Madrid, Professor Mayor has been a member of the Spanish Parliament and later Minister of Education and Science (1981-82) in his country. During 1978-81, Professor Mayor served as UNESCO's Deputy Director-General, and later as Special Adviser to the Director-General. In 1987, he became a member of the European Parliament.

A scholar of distinction, author of several books and scientific articles, poet and politician, Professor Mayor is a member of several academies and scientific societies, including the Club of Rome. He is recipient of several awards and decorations.

Besides his original contributions on cerebral metabolism and molecular pathology of the new born, Professor Mayor has extensively written and spoken on issues such as: science policy, role of the university, science and development, role of science and technology in the society of the future, regional cultures, scientific community and peace, and implications of development on the environment.

Professor Mayor continues to be an ardent supporter of the Human Rights and of International Intellectual Co-operation.

APPENDIX D

LIST OF UNESCO REPRESENTATIVES AND LIAISON OFFICES

I. *Full-time UNESCO Representatives*

1. *BRAZIL*

UNESCO Representative in Brazil
Sector Commercial Norte
Quadra CN2, Lote B
Caixa Postal 04 0063, D.F.
70710 BRASILIA

2. *CAMEROON* (covers also the Central African Empire, Chad, People's Republic of the Congo, Gabon and OCAM)

Bureau due Representant de l'UNESCO en Afrique centrale et aupres de l'OCAM
B.P. 1168
YAOUNDE

3. *CARIBBEAN* (covers Bahamas, Barbados, Belize, British Eastern Caribbean Group, British Virgin Islands, Dominica, Grenada, Guyana, Jamaica, Surinam, St. Lucia, St. Vincent and the Grenatdines, St. Christopher/Nevis, Netherlands, Antilles, Trinidad and Tobago)

UNESCO Representative to the Caribbean
First Floor
30 Grenada Crescent
Post Office Box 8203 C.S.O.
KINGSTON 5

4. *EGYPT* (covers also Sudan)

UNESCO Representative in the Arab Republic of Egypt
8 Abdel Rahman Fahmy Street
Garden City
CAIRO
Arab Republic of Egypt

5. *ETHIOPIA*

UNESCO Representative to Ethiopia and
Liaison Officer with ECA and OAU
Rooms 427, 429 and 433
4th Floor – Old Building UN – ECA
Menelik Avenue
P.O. Box 1177
ADDIS ABABA

6. *MEXICO*

Representante de la UNESCO
Brasil, 31, 2 piso,
Despacho 329
Apartado 45-611
MEXICO, D.F.

7. *NIGERIA* (covers also People's Republic of Benin, Ghana and Togo)

UNESCO Representative a.i. in Nigeria
C/o Federal Ministry of Education
P.O. Box 2823
LAGOS

via Lagos Pouch

8. *QATAR* (covers also Saudi Arabia, Bahrain, United Arab Emirates, Iraq, Kuwait and Oman)

UNESCO Regional Representative Office
P.O. Box 3945
DOHA

Via Doha Pouch

9. *TUNISIA* (covers also Algeria, Libya, Morocco, Arab League and Agencies)

Representant de l'UNESCO aupres des pays
du Maghreb et de la Ligue arabe
C/o UNDP
B.P. 863
TUNIS

10. *UPPER VOLTA* (covers also Mali, Niger, CEAO and CILSS)

Representant de l'UNESCO pour les Affaires saheliennes
s/c Representant resident PNUD
B.P. 575
OUAGADOUGOU

11. *ZAIRE* (covers also Burundi and Rwanda)

UNESCO Representative Office
C/o Resident Representative of the UNDP
P.O. Box 7248
KINSHASA

12. *ZAMBIA* (covers also Botswana, Lesotho, Namibia and Swaziland)

UNESCO Representative to Southern African Countries
P.O. Box 50591
LUSAKA

II. *Part-time UNESCO Representatives*

1. *CHILE* (covers also Bolivia and Peru)

Director de la Oficina Regional de
Education para America Latina Yel Caribe
Representante de la UNESCO en Chile
Calle Enrique Delpiano 2058
Casilla Postal 3187
SANTIAGO DE CHILE

via Santiago Pouch

2. *COSTA RICA* (covers also El Salvador, Guatemala, Honduras, Nicaragua and Panama)

Representante de la UNESCO en Costa Rica
C/o Resident Representative UNDP
Apartado postal 4540
SAN JOSE

3. *CUBA* (covers also Dominican Republic)

Jefe de la Oficina Regional de Cultura
para America Latina yel Caribe,
Representante de la UNESCO en Cuba
Calzada n 551 Esq. a D. Vedado
LA HABANA, 4

via Havana Pouch

4. *ECUADOR* (covers also Colombia)

Representante de UNESCO

C/o Resident Representative UNDP
P.O. Box 4731
QUITO

5. *HAITI*

Conseiller sous-regional d'education
Representant de l'UNESCO en Haiti
C/o PNUD
B.P. 557
PORT-AU-PRINCE

6. *INDIA*

Director, Regional Office for Science
and Technology for South & Central Asia
UNESCO Representative a.i.
UNESCO House
17 Jor Bagh
NEW DELHI 110003

7. *INDONESIA* (covers also Malaysia, Philippines and Singapore)

Director, Regional Office for Science and
Technology for Southeast Asia
UNESCO Representative
United Nations Building (2nd Floor)
Jalan Thamrin 14
273/JKT Tromolpos
JAKARTA

via Jakarta Pouch

8. *KENYA* (covers also Mauritius, Somalia, Tanzania and Uganda)

Director of the UNESCO Regional Office
for Science and Technology for Africa
UNESCO Representative

P.O. Box 30592
NAIROBI

via Nairobi Pouch

9. *LEBANON* (covers also Jordan and the Syrian Arab Republic)

Representant de l'UNESCO
transferee temporairement et jusqu'a nouvel
ordre a Paris 7 Place de Fontenoy
75700 PARIS

10. *PAKISTAN*

Director, Regional Office for Culture and
Book Development in Asia,
UNESCO Representative in Pakistan
39 Delhi Housing Society
P.O. Box 8950
Bahadur Shah Zafar Road
KARACHI 29

11. *SENEGAL* (covers also the Gambia, Guinea, Liberia, Mauritania and Sierra Leone and Cap Verd)

Directeur, Bureau Regional de l'UNESCO
Pour l'Education en Afrique
Representant de l'UNESCO
B.P. 3311
DAKAR

via Dakar Pouch

12. *THAILAND* (covers also Burma, Democratic Kampuchea, Laos People's Democratic Republic and Socialist Republic of Viet Nam)

Assistant Director-General, Regional Office
for Education in Asia and Oceania
UNESCO Representative
P.O. Box 1425
BANGKOK 10500

via Bangkok Pouch

13. *URUGUAY* (covers also Argentine and Paraguay)

Director de la Oficina de Ciencia
Technologia Para America Latina y el Caribe
Representative de la UNESCO en Uruguay
1320-24 Blv. Artigas
P.O. Box 859
MONTEVIDEO

via Montevideo Pouch

14. *VENEZUELA*

Representat de l'UNESCO au Venezuela
Apartado de Correos 68394
Altamira
CARACAS 1062 A

15. *ZIMBABWE* (covers also Angola, Malawi, Mozambique, Sao Tome and Principe)

UNESCO Representative
C/o Resident Representative of the UNDP
P.O. Box 4775
HARARE

III. *LIAISON OFFICES*

1. GENEVA

Charge de Liaison Pincipal

UNESCO Liaison Office
Villa des Feuillantines
Palais des Nations
CH-1211 GENEVE 10

2. *NEW YORK*

Director
United Nations
9th Floor, DC-II Building
2 UN Plaza, Office No. 900
NEW YORK, N.Y. 10017

3. *WASHINGTON*

Director, Liaison Office
918 16th Street N.W.
Suite 301
WASHINGTON D.C.
D.C. 20006

APPENDIX E

UNESCO NATIONAL COMMISSIONS

Genesis

The United Nations Educational, Scientific and Cultural Organisation (UNESCO) came into being in 1946 but its Constitution had been adopted earlier at a meeting of representatives of 43 nations who met in London in November 1945. The world had gone through nearly six years of horror and futility of the Second World War which had caused immense destruction and loss of innumerable human lives unprecedented in history. It was but natural that the thoughts of the peoples of the world should turn to peace and security. Another war, which would threaten the very existence of the human species, was unthinkable. It was, therefore, in this context that the UN system was established as part of the new international order in the hope that peace could be strengthened through fostering human welfare, preventing conflict and promoting respect and understanding among nations.

UNESCO, as one of the Specialized Agencies of the United Nations Organization has the mission of building the bulwarks of peace and global co-operation by transforming the minds and hearts of men through the media of Education, Science, Culture and Communication.

Concept of Co-operation

According to Article I of the Constitution of UNESCO :

> The purpose of the Organisation is to contribute to peace and security by promoting collaboration among the nations through education, science and culture in order to further universal respect for justice, for the rule of law and for the human rights and fundamental freedoms which are affirmed for the peoples of the world, without distinction of race, sex, language of religion by the Charter of the United Nations.

The preamble to the Constitution says that "since wars begin in the minds of men, it is in the minds of men that the defences of peace must be constructed". All activities of UNESCO are, therefore, directed to the task of influencing the minds of men in the interest of security and peace and promotion of co-operation.

UNESCO's Constitution, in order to achieve this end, provides for the establishment of National Commissions in each country. Article VII States :

1. Each Member-State shall make such arrangements as suit its particular conditions for the purpose of associating its principal bodies interested in educational, scientific and cultural matters with the work of the Organisation, preferably by the formation of a National Commission broadly representative of the government and such bodies.
2. National Commissions or National Co-operating Bodies, where they exist, shall act in an advisory capacity to their respective delegations to the General Conference and to their governments in matters relating to the Organisation and shall function as agencies of liaison in all matters of interest to it.
3. The Organisation may, on the request of a Member-State, delegate, either temporarily or permanently, a member of its Secretariat to serve on the National Commission of that State, in order to assist in the development of its work.

The aim of UNESCO is to secure, in every Member-State the collaboration of all elements of the community including intellectuals, teachers, scientists, technicians, artists, writers and journalists in the pursuit of international understanding and co-operation. The framers of the Constitution intended that a National Commission in each Member-State be set up which would provide the best forum for enlisting the support and assistance of institutions/persons in each country most capable of creating international harmony, good-will and co-operation. The National Commissions, one of the original features of the UNESCO system, are the vital agencies for achieving the aims of UNESCO, and which could most effectively come to grips with the future direction and programme priorities of UNESCO.

National Commissions exist in almost every Member-State but not all the Commissions are able to function or exercise their responsibilities as effectively as they should. UNESCO's programmes are implemented through the Governments of Member-States but it is the National Commissions which mobilise active moral support from the intellectuals for these programmes.

Development of National Commissions

The Constitutional provisions envisage two strands of action. *Firstly*, Member-States are expected to set up National Commissions, to serve the aims of UNESCO. *Secondly*, the Director-General of UNESCO is expected to provide training facilities, equipment and other assistance to National Commissions, to make them effective instruments of UNESCO's programme. At each session of the General Conference, ever since the inception of UNESCO, resolutions have been adopted to give effect to this constitutional provision.

As UNESCO's programmes developed over the years, greater emphasis came to be placed on the role and functions of the National Commissions. Originally, they were expected to act in *an advisory capacity* and *as agencies of liaison*. In course of time, the Commissions assumed more and more functions and responsibilities including *executive functions*.

Resolutions 7.11 and 7.12 adopted at the 9th Session (1956) of the General Conference of UNESCO state :

> 7.11 Member-States are invited to give full effect to Article VII of the Constitution by establishing National Commissions comprising representatives of their respective governments and of national groups concerned with the problems of education, science, culture and mass communication, and by providing existing National Commissions with sufficient staff and financial resources to enable them to discharge their duties successfully as advisory, liaison and executive bodies.
>
> 7.12 The Director-General is authorized to give National Commissions any assistance needed in order to facilitate and improve their functioning as bodies for co-operation between Member-States and the Organization :
>
> (a) By affording the secretaries of National Commissions an opportunity of visiting the Headquarters of the Organization;
> (b) By sending members of the Headquarters staff on mission to National Commissions;

(c) By furnishing technical and financial help to regional conferences of National Commissions;

(d) By furnishing technical and financial help to National Commissions which are in process of development;

(e) By promoting the translation, adaptation and publication of UNESCO publications and documents, by means of contracts, on the responsibility of National Commissions;

(f) By continuing the preparation of an up to date Guide and Directory of National Commissions.

Present Functions

Although the responsibilities assigned to National Commissions, as far back as 1945, remain valid even today after the lapse of 30 years, they are not in themselves sufficient to meet contemporary needs. Indeed, in addition to advice and liaison, National Commissions many years ago accepted responsibility for information activities and many have also mounted programmes in the general area of intellectual co-operation and reflection. Further, many National Commissions have assumed executive functions as well by signing contracts with UNESCO for specific programmes. There seems every prospect that this trend will continue in the next few years and will imply changes in the network of relations established by each National Commission, in the substance of their work and in the way they proceed to discharge their responsibilities. This trend will necessarily call for the updating of provisions relating to role and functions of the National Commissions, and may usefully call for an amendment of Article VII of the UNESCO's Constitution in order to conform its provisions to actual needs and requirements of the present times.

UNESCO had, of course, always envisaged the strengthening of the National Commissions by Member-States by way of enlisting support from intellectuals and providing the financial resources. On its own UNESCO has provided technical and financial assistance to the Commissions in various ways.

It was at the 14th Session (1966) that the General Conference mentioned the National Commissions as *advisory, liaison, information and executive bodies*, having accepted the role of National Commissions in activities concerned with information as well. Resolutions 5.21 and 5.22 adopted at this Session are relevant :

Resolution (5.21) of this Session, while recalling Resolution 7.11

adopted by the General Conference at its ninth session, *inter alia* invited Member-States:

(a) to give full effect to Article VII of the Constitution by establishing National Commissions comprising representatives of their governments and of national groups concerned with problems of education, science, culture and communication and by providing these National Commissions with staff and financial resources to enable them to discharge their duties successfully and to become increasingly active;

(b) to pay due attention to the fact that the effectiveness and moral authority of a National Commission depends upon the support of all the governmental and administrative authorities concerned, the interest and work of individuals, the active participation of specialists, and the vitality of the agencies and non-governmental organizations represented in it;

(c) to make increasing use, within the framework of their national legislation, of the National Commissions as advisory, liaison, information and executive bodies at the national level :

(i) as planning and advisory organs in the preparation and execution of UNESCO's programmes;

(ii) where appropriate, as executive organs participating in the execution of UNESCO's programmes requiring the co-operation of National Commissions;

(iii) in the evaluation of UNESCO's activities and of UNESCO's programmes;

(iv) as advisers to governments, particularly to the national authorities concerned with planning and economic and social development, with a view to promoting integration of national and external resources for programmes in the fields of UNESCO's activities;

(v) as organs for information on and diffusion of UNESCO's aims, principles and activities in order to reach ever-widening national audiences;

(vi) in co-operating with national organizations and with national branches of international non-governmental organizations whose activities contribute to the objectives of UNESCO;

(d) to further and facilitate co-operation and exchange of persons, information and materials between the National Commissions on a regional and universal basis and to include, where appropriate, in cultural agreements a specific clause facilitating such exchanges.

By another Resolution (5.22) adopted at the 1966 General Conference, the Director-General was asked to assist in the development of National Commissions by various ways.

This resolution reads :

5.22 The Director-General is authorized to assist the continued development of the National Commissions of Member-States, within the framework of their national legislation, so that they may increase their efficiency and become better able to exercise their growing responsibilities for consultation, liaison, information and executive action :

(a) by affording the secretaries of National Commissions periodic opportunity of studying the work of the Organization at its Headquarters;
(b) by furnishing technical and financial support to regional conferences of National Commissions;
(c) by furnishing technical and financial support and equipment for the activities of National Commissions, particularly those of the developing countries;
(d) by encouraging the translation, adaptation and publication by National Commissions of UNESCO publications and documents in languages other than English, French and Spanish;
(e) by collecting and distributing information on the forms of organization and means of action of the National Commission; and
(f) by inviting the National Commissions and Member-States to initiate and maintain a reciprocal exchange of information, to develop the exchange of exhibitions, documentation and persons, and to undertake joint activities, broadly in line with the Organization's programme, to strengthen the principles of international co-operation.

Similar Resolutions were adopted by the General Conference at its 15th (1968), 16th (1970), 17th (1972), and 18th (1974) and in other sessions also.

The General Conference of UNESCO, for example, at its 18th Session held in Paris in October-November 1974, passed the following Resolution (6.21) inviting Member-States, *inter alia*, to make increasing use at all levels within the framework of their national legislation of the National Commissions, as liaison, information, advisory and executive bodies :

6.21 *The General Conference*,

Bearing in mind the varied organisations and functioning patterns of National Commissions and the right of each country to make such arrangements as suit its particular conditions,
Recalling resolution 5.21 adopted at its seventeenth session (1972),

Invites Member States :

(a) to give full effect to Article VII of the Constitution regarding the establishment of National Commissions by ensuring wide representation within those Commissions of government authorities, national professional organisations, university institutions, organized workers groups, trade unions and non-governmental organisations active in the fields of education, science and communication and concerned with social and economic development and the promotion of human rights;
(b) to provide their National Commissions with adequate permanent staff, financial resources and authority to enable them to perform their functions efficiently and increase their participation in the activities of the Organization;
(c) to make increasing use at all levels, within the framework of the national legislation, of the National Commission as liaison, information, advisory and executive bodies :

(i) in the formulation, implementation and evaluation of UNESCO's programme and, where appropriate, of the Country Programmes assisted by the United Nations Development Programme;
(ii) in associating national intellectual communities actively in

UNESCO's international work;

(iii) in co-operating with national professional organisations and with national branches of international non-governmental organisations whose activities contribute to the attainment of the objectives of UNESCO;

(iv) in collaborating more closely with national trade unions and co-operatives, as well as with youth organizations;

(v) in disseminating information on UNESCO's principles, aims and activities so as to reach a wide national audience, and particularly the younger generation which can be attracted to the ideal of UNESCO through the Associated Schools system, the UNESCO Clubs and sporting activities;

(vi) in helping to circulate UNESCO publications in libraries, schools, universities and cultural centres, as appropriate;

(vii) in acquainting establishments of higher education, research institutes and universities with UNESCO's research projects;

(viii) in collaborating more actively with national planning bodies as well as other administrative channels of government involved in development;

(d) to avail themselves of the potential of National Commissions for effective action in areas of UNESCO's special moral responsibility, such as peace and human rights, the combating of racism and the promotion of international understanding among young people;

(e) to further the exchange of persons, information and materials between National Commissions, on a regional as well as international basis, and to include, where appropriate in cultural agreements, a specific clause facilitating such exchanges.

The General Conference also adopted a resolution (6.22) authorizing the Director-General :

to assist in the development of the National Commissions of Member-States with the aim of increasing the efficiency with which they exercise their responsibilities as liaison, information, advisory and executive bodies, as well as of increasing their participation, in the preparation, implementation and evaluation of

UNESCO's programme;

(a) by furnishing adequate financial support for regional conferences of National Commissions;

(b) by affording the secretaries of National Commissions opportunities to study the work of the Organization and fostering co-operation between the National Commissions and the Secretariat through exchange of information and mutual consultation, in particular by means of :

(i) collective consultations of secretaries of National Commissions;

(ii) training courses for new secretaries and officials of National Commissions, particularly those in the developing countries;

(iii) study visits of officials of National Commissions to UNESCO's Regional Offices;

(iv) meetings between senior staff members, when visiting a Member-State, and responsible officers of the National Commission as well as government authorities on the role and functions of the National Commissions;

(v) missions, upon request, to National Commissions for the purpose of strengthening their organization and improving their functioning;

(vi) collection and dissemination of information on the organization, working methods and activities of National Commissions;

(c) by making use of the National Commissions in the implementation of projects so as to contribute to the decentralization of the Organization's activities;

(d) by furnishing under the Participation Programme, upon request, technical and financial support in accordance with the main priorities of UNESCO in order to :

(i) foster bilateral, sub-regional, regional and inter regional co-operation between National Commissions, particularly with a view to strengthening international understanding, human rights and peace;

(ii) assist States which have recently become members of

UNESCO in constituting their National Commissions, as well as recently established National Commissions and other National Commissions which may require assistance in developing an effective and adequate structure and equipment;

(iii) help National Commissions in promoting UNESCO's principles, aims and activities;

(iv) support National Commissions in having UNESCO publications and documents translated, adapted and disseminated in languages other than English and French, and assist them in the production of their own publications;

(v) encourage and support the exchange of visits between members of National Commissions with a view to studying problems of common interest and developing mutual aid among National Commissions;

(vi) improve communication and co-operation between National Commissions and the Secretariat;

(vii) provide financial and technical support for the existing regional liaison centres and for the new ones which may be established by National Commissions;

(viii) assist the sub-regional meetings of National Commissions.

New Phases in the Activities

Every National Commission of UNESCO functions in a dual capacity; it is constituted by the National Government and it is a part of the apparatus of that Government. But at the same time, it is, in a sense, a projection of UNESCO. The functions of a National Commission can broadly be classified as advisory, liaison, information, execution and evaluation; but none of these functions are carried out in isolation and depend largely on the relations with (a) the National Government itself, (b) other Non-Governmental Organizations or groups within the country, (c) UNESCO, (d) other National Commissions, and (e) Non-Governmental Organizations in other Member-States and International Non-Governmental Organizations. The network of these relationships has to be strengthened and promoted in order to give meaning to the work of the National Commissions and to ensure that they are able to contribute effectively to the preparation and implementation of UNESCO's programmes.

With a few exceptions, almost all Member-States of UNESCO

have set up National Commissions to co-operate with UNESCO. There is no uniform pattern for National Commissions. They differ in structure, powers and the *modus operandi* they adopt to achieve their ends. It has been pointed out that the uniqueness of UNESCO's contribution to the maintenance of peace and security lies in the methods used; it is through essentially non-political means e.g., Education, Science and Culture, that UNESCO seeks to achieve its aims. At the non-governmental level, UNESCO has to work through two primary agencies : (i) International Non-Governmental Organizations, and (ii) the National Commissions in Member-States. While UNESCO has taken considerable trouble in strengthening the International Non-Governmental Organizations and has found them an excellent instrument to serve its ideals, it has not so far been able to make equally strong efforts to strengthen and vitalise the National Commissions in the Member-States.

Financial Provisions

Since the National Commissions have been increasingly entrusted with additional functions and responsibilities, the question of providing adequate financial provision had been engaging the attention of UNESCO. It has now been recognised that at least 1 per cent of the Regular Budget (Part II) of UNESCO should be allocated to programmes of co-operation with National Commissions.

Future Potentialities

The pattern of UNESCO's relations with National Commissions has now been well-established and the lines of communications are clearly defined. The National Commissions should now be able to establish lines of direct Communication and co-operation with other National Commissions and prepare plans for projects reflecting the aspirations of the people of the countries since the next phase of advance depends almost entirely on the role and effectiveness of the National Commissions in achieving the noble objectives set fourth in the preamble of UNESCO's Constitution. There is need not only for bilateral and multilateral co-operation/collaboration between National Commissions of UNESCO within the same region but between National Commissions on intra-regional basis as well.

UNESCO NATIONAL COMMISSIONS

AFGHANISTAN
P.O.B. 717 - KABUL - Tel. : 717

ALBANIE
Ministere des affaires etrangeres
Service de l'UNESCO -
TIRANA
Telegramme : NINJATM
TIRANA
Telex : 2164 MPJ AB

ALGERIE
Ministere de l'enseignement superieur
et de la recherche scientifique
23, avenue de la Robertsau - bd Salah Bouakouir
ALGER - Tel. : 64.47.54 - Telex : 61460-66512

ANGOLA
Ministere de l'education
C.P. 1451 - LUANDA
Tel. : 37.010 - Telex : 4186 MIREX AN
(attention COMNAT UNESCO)

ANTIGUA AND BARBUDA
Ministry of Education and Culture
Church Street St. Johns
ANTIGUA - Tel. : 46-20192

ARGENTINE
Cordoba 831 - 3er piso
1054 BUENOS AIRES
Tel. : 311-0333 - Telex : 25753 MEYJCI AR

AUSTRALIA
Department of Education
P.O.B. 826 - WODEN A.C.T. 2606
Tel. : CANBERRA 83 76 58

AUSTRIA
Mentergasse 11
1070 VIENNA - Tel. : (0222) 93.64.21

BAHRAIN
Ministry of Education
P.O.B. 43
MANAMA - Tel. : 25.84.00 -
Telex :9094 TARBIA BN

BANGLADESH
Ministry of Education
1, Asian Highway, Palassy, Nilkhet
DHAKA 5
Tel. : 50.84.32

BARBADOS
Ministry of Education
Jemmott's Lane
ST. MICHAEL -
BRIDGETOWN
Tel. : 426.5416 or 427.3272

BELGIQUE
Ministere des affaires etrangeres
2, rue Quatre Bras
B-1000 BRUXELLES -Tel. : 516.84.58

BELIZE
Ministry of Education, Youth, Sports & Culture
Belmopan BELIZE - Tel. : 08-2329/2324

BENIN
B. P. 520 PORTO-NOVO - Tel. : 21.25.30

BHUTAN
Ministry of Social Services
THIMPHU - Tel. 2912 - Telex : 203 BT (203 MSS)

BOLIVIA
Ministerio de Educacion y cultura
Av. Arce n.º 2405 - LA PAZ
Tel. : 37.32.69 - Telex : 3373 INSINT BV

BOTSWANA
Ministry of Education - Private Bag 005 - GABORONE
Tel. : 37.56.05 -Telex : 'THUTO' 2944 THUTO BD

BRESIL
Institut bresilien pour l'education,
la science et la culture
196, Avenida Marechal Floriano - Palacio Itamaraly
20080 RIO DE JANEIRO R.J.
Tel. : 263-9919 ou 291-4411
Telex : 2122563 IBECC RIO DE JANEIRO

BULGARIE
96 b, rue Rakovsky
B. P. nº 386 - SOFIA 1000 -
Tel. : 87.54.49

BURKINA FASO
Ministere des enseignements secondaire,
supeieur et la recherche scientifique
B. P. 7046 - OUAGADOUGOU - 03
Tel. : 30.72.15 - Telex : 5555 SECGOUV

BURUNDI
Ministere de l'enseignement superieur
et de la recherche scientifique
B.P. 1990- BOJUMBURA
Tel. 24517 : 22 162 - Telex 5166
MINEDUC BDI

CAMEROUN
Ministere de l'education nationale
B.P. 1600 - YAOUNDE
Tel. 23.40.50 - Telex :
MINEDUC 8551 KN Yaounde

CANADA
99 Metcalfe
Box/C.P. 1047 - OTTAWA K1P 5 V8
Tel. : (613) 237-34000
Telex: 053-4573
CANCONARTS OTT

CAP-VERT
Parque 5 de Julho - C.P. 51-A - PRAIA
Tel. : 611.079 - Telex : 6057 ME CV

CHILE
Ministerio de Educacion Publica
Avenida Libertador Bernado O'Higgins 1371
SANTIAGO DE CHILE
Tel. : 6983351 - Telex : 240.567 MEDUC CL

CHINA
35, Damucanghutong - Xidan - BEIJING
Tel. : 66.27.30 - Telex : 22014 SEDC CN

COLOMBIA
Ministerio de Educacion Nacional
Avenida El Dorado - Oficina 510
Apartado Aereo 077983 - CAN BOGOTA
Tel. : 222.46.91 - Telex : 42456 SGMEN

COMORES
Ministere de l'education nationale,
de la culture, de la jeunesse et des sports
B. P. 73 - MORONI
Tel. : 73.04.32 - Telex : 229 MIEDUC

CONGO
B.P. 493 - BRAZZAVILLE -
Tel. : 81.19.86

COSTA RICA
Ministerio de Educacion Publica
Apartado postal 393.2050 SAN JOSE
San Pedro de Montes de Oca - SAN JOSE
Tel. : 24.43.20 - Telex : 2107

COTE D'IVOIRE
Ministere de l'education nationale
15, avenue Nogues (Immeuble Nogues, 2e e age)
B. P. 297 - ABIDJAN 01
Tel. : 32.48.25 - Telex : 22151 UNESCO CI

CUBA
Ave. Kohly No. 151, esq. 32
Nuevo Vedado - LA HABANA -
Tel. : 3-6161

CYPRUS
Ministry of Foreign Affairs
NICOSIA - Tel. : 40-2493 - Telex : 3001/3002

CZECHOSLOVAKIA
Toskansky, palac
Hradcanske nam. 5
125 10 PRAGUE 1 - Tel. : 2193 3163

DEMOCRATIC YEMEN
Ministry of Education
Madinat Asha-Ab
P.O.B. 7042 - ADEN - Tel. : 82-111

DENMARK
Vester Voldgade, 117, st.
1552 COPENHAGEN V
Tel. : 92.52.16 - Telex : 11.21.12 Copenhagen

DOMINICA
Ministry of Education
ROSEAU - Tel. : 2401

ECUADOR
Calle Buenos Aires 136, 5.º piso
Direccion postal: Casilla 561
QUITO - Tel. : 540.701

EGYPT
17 Shareh Ismail Abu El Fotooh
Dokki
P.O.B. 12311 - CAIRO - Tel. : 716.659

EL SALVADOR
Ministerio de Educacion
Apartado postal 1175
NUEVA SAN SALVADOR - Tel. : 28.34.93

ESPANA
Escuela Diplomatica
Paseo de Juan XXIII
28023 MADRID - Tel. : 233.96.39 - Telex : 49924

ETHIOPIA
P.O.B. 2996 - ADDIS ABABA
Tel. : 11.82.19 - Telex : 21435 MOE

FINLAND
Ministry of Education
Meritullinkatu 10 - PL 293
00170 HELSINKI
Tel. : 134.171 - Telex : 1220-79
mined sf

FRANCE
42, avenue Raymond-Poincare
75116 PARIS - Tel. : (1)
40.66.66.21

GABON
Ministere de l'education
nationale
B. P. 264 - LIBREVILLE - Tel. :
72.20.49 - Telex : 5501

GAMBIA
Ministry of Education
Bedford Place Building
BANJUL
Tel. : (228) 69.20.91 - Telex :
2204 PRESOF GV

GERMAN DEM. REPUBLIC
Ministry of Foreign Affairs
Marx-Eingels-Platz 2
Postfach 101 - 1020 BERLIN
Tel. : 582.4307 - Telex : 11.46.21
AUMI DD

GERMANY (FED. REPUBLIC OF)
15, Colmantstrasse
5300 BONN 1
Tel. : (0228) 69.20.91 - Telex :
886326 duk d.

GHANA
Ministry of Education
P.O.B. 2739 - ACCRA - Tel. :
665-421

GREECE
8, Acadimias
106.71 ATHENS
Tel. : 36.10.581 - Telex : 218213 - 216593 YPEX GR

GRENADA
Ministry of Education
Young Street - ST GEORGE'S - Tel. : 440-2791

GUATEMALA
Ba., avenida 13-30, Zona 1,
Apartado postal 244
GUATEMALA, C.A. - Tel. : 86.171

GUINEE
Ministere de l'information et de la culture
B. P. 964 - CONAKRY - Tel. : 44.49.57 - Telex : 22331

GUINEE-BESSAU
Secretariat d'Etat a l'information
B. P. 248 - BISSAU - Telex : 246 ANG BI

GUINEA ECUATORIAL
Ministerio de Education y Deportes
MALABO - Tel. : 2653 - Telex : CBNOM 913107 EG

GUYANA
Dargan House
0, Robb & Oronoque Streets
P.O.B. 1014 - GEORGETOWN - Tel. : 54.306

HAITI
Ministere de l'education nationale
5, avenue Marie Jeanne
B. P. 1347 - PORT-AU-PRINCE - Tel. : 20.747

HONDURAS
Ministerio de Educacion Publica
Edificio Lazo, 3[er] piso. n°, 14, 2da calle,
entre 2da y 3ra Ave.
Comayaguela
TEGUCIGALPA - Tel. : 22.74.97

HONGRIE
Magyar UNESCO Bizottsag
Muvelodesi Ministerium
(Ministere de la culture)
Szalay u. 10-14
1884 BUDAPEST Pf, 1
Tel. : 313.526 - Telex : 225.935

ICELAND
Ministry of Education and Culture
Menntamalaraduneytud
150 REYKJAVIK - Tel. : 250.00 - Telex : 2111

INDIA
Ministry of Human Resource Development
Department of Education
Room 203, 'C' Wing,
Shastri Bhavan
NEW DELHI 110 001
Tel. : 38.45.89/38.44.42 - Telex : 3161336

INDONESIA
Ministry of Education and Culture
Jalan Jenderal Sudirman - Senayan
JAKARTA - Tel. : 58.16.65 - Telex : 44471

IRAN, ISLAMIC REPUBLIC OF
1188 Enghelab Avenue (Rostam Building)
P.O.B. 11365-4498 Zip code: 13158
TEHERAN - Tel. : 66.83.65 to 67

IRAQ
Ministry of Education
BAGHDAD
Tel. : 887.29.47 - Telex : 2259 EDUCATE IK

IRELAND
Department of Education
Marlborough Street
DUBLIN 1 - Tel. : 734.700 - Telex : 31136 EDUC

ISRAEL
Ministry of Education and Culture
34, Shivtey Yisrael Street
JERUSALEM 91911
Tel. : (02) 89.15.66 - Telefax : (972-2) 891518

ITALIE
Piazza Firenze 27 (3e etage)
00186 ROME - Tel. : 68.73.684

JAMAICA
25, Dominica Drive
P.O.B. 202 - KINGSTON 5 - Tel. : 926.54.80
Telex : 2422 UNESCO JA (for NATCOM)

JAPAN
Ministry of Education, Science and Culture
3-2-2 Kasumigaseki, Chiyoda-ku, TOKYO
Tel. : (03) 581.4211 (ext. 2551)

JORDAN
Ministry of Education
P.O.B. 1646 - AMMAN
Tel. : 669181-91 - Telex - 21396 EDUCATE JO

KAMPUCHEA DEMOCRATIQUE
c/o Permanent mission of Democratic Kampuchea
to E.S.C.A.P Lard Yao, Bangkhen
BANGKOK 9 - (Thailand) - Tel. : 588.17.46

KENYA
Ministry of Education
Commerce House (4th Floor)
Moi Avenue
P.O.B. 72107 - NAIROBI
Tel. : 33.89.80
(Secretary-General)

KUWAIT
Post Box 3266
13033 SAFAT - KUWAIT-
Tel. : 24.444.01/3
Telex : 23656 UNESCO KT -
Telefax: (965) 2469512

LESOTHO
Ministry of Education, Sports and Culture
Constitution Road - P.O.B. 47
MASERU - Tel. : 32.59.32

LIBAN
Palais de l'UNESCO
BEYROUTH - Tel. : 300.962

LIBERIA
Ministry of Education
Broad Street - MONROVIA
Tel. 22.26.54 - Telex : 44449 MINEDU

LIBYAN ARAB JAMAHIRIYA
P.O.B. 1091 - TRIPOLI
Tel. : 41.572 - Telex : 20367 AMANTA LY

LUXEMBOURG
Ministere de l'education nationale
et de la jeunesse
29, rue Aldringen - 2926 LUXEMBOURG
Tel. : (352) 478-11 - Telex : 2111

MADAGASCAR
11, Naka Rabemanantsoa - Behoririka
B. P. 331 - TANANARIVE
ANTANANARIVO (101) -
Tel. : 217.61

MALAWI
Taurus House
P.O.B. 30278
Capital City - LILONGWE 3
Tel. : 73.30.77 - Telex : 4769
UNESCO MI

MALAYSIA
Ministry of Education
5th Floor, Block F (North)
Damansara Town Centre
50604 KUALA LUMPUR
Tel. : 292.77.67 - Telex : MA
33547

MALDIVES
Ministry of Education
MALE 20.05
Tel. : 3524; 3148 - Telex : 66032
FINANCE

MALI
Ministere de l'education
nationale
B. P. 119 - BAMAKO - Tel. :
22.25.15 - Telex : 2602

MALTA
Ministry of Education
Beltissebh - FLORIANA
Tel. : 231.385 - Telex : 1100
MOD MLT MT

MAROC
24, rue du Senegal -Ocean
B. P. 420 - RABAT -
Tel. : 712.21 - Telex : 31016/61

MAURITANIE
B. P. 5115
NOUAKCHOTT - Tel. : (222.2) 528.02

MAURITIUS
Ministry of Education, Arts and Culture
Rainbow House, Edith Cavell Street (2nd Floor)
PORT LOUIS - Tel. : 24915, 080410, 25974

MEXICO
Secretaria de Educacion Publica
Brasil nº 31 (2º piso)
MEXICO 1, D.F. - Tel. : 521.65.42
Telex : 1773860 PSEPME + 1772067

MONACO
4, rue des Iris - 98000 MONACO
Tel. : 93.30.19.21 - Telex : 469942

MONGOLIE
Ministere des Affaires etrangeres
OULAN BATOR
Adresse telegraphique
MOUNESCO OULAN BATOR

MOZAMBIQUE
Ministry of Education and Culture
45, rua Dr. Egas Monis
P.O.B. 3674 - MAPUTO
Tel. : 744.090 - Telex : 6148 M.E.C.

MYANMAR (Union of)
Department of Higher Education
Ministry of Education
Office of the Ministers - Theinbyu Street
RANGOON - Tel. : Secretary 86.704

NEPAL
Ministry of Education
Kaiser Mahal, Kantipath
KATHMANDU - Tel. : 14.064

NETHERLANDS
Oranjestraat 10
2514 JB THE HAGUE
Tel. : 070 - 644.655 - Telex : 32636 MINO NL

NEW ZEALAND
c/o Department of Education
Government Building, Lambton Quay
P.O.B. 1379 - WELLINGTON 1
Tel. : 735.499 - Telex : NZ 31586

NICARAGUA
Ministerio de Education
Complejo Civico "Camilo Ortega Saavedra"
Apartado postal 108 - MANAGUA NIC A.C.
Tel. : 50.342 - Telefax : (505-2) 51595
Telex : 2427 MED

NIGER
Ministere de l'education nationale
B. P. 557 - NIAMEY
Tel. : 72.23.65 - Telex : 5512 NI

NIGERIA
Federal Ministry of Education
14, Broad Street (3rd. Floor)
PMB 2823 LAGOS
Tel. : Secretary-General 615.795 (residence)
Tel. : 276.111 - Telex : NE 22193

NORWAY
P.O.B. 1507, Vika
Klingenberggaten 5 (7th Floor)
OSLO 1 - Tel. : (472) 83.30.56
Telefax : (472) 83.16.89 - Telex : 71004

OMAN
Ministry of Education
P.O.B. 3 - MUSCAT - Tel. : 704.852 - Telex : 3369

PAKISTAN
Ministry of Education
Plot n.° 30, Sector H-8,
UNESCO House - ISLAMABAD
Tel. : 8527.31 - Telex : 5591 UGC PK

PANAMA
Ministerio de Education
Apartado 2440
PANAMA 3 - Tel. : 62.41.77 (ext. 138)

PAPUA NEW GUINEA
Ministry of Education
Private Mail Bag PSA Haus Post Office
BOROKO Port Moresby

PARAGUAY
Ministerio de Education y
Culto/Chile 864
Casilla de Correos n.° 1080
ASUNCION - Tel. : 43.919

PERU
Ministerio de Education
Piso 16 - Oficina n.° 1608
Apartado postal n.° 4681 - Correo Central
LIMA - Tel. : 28.12.09
Telex : MINISTERIO EDUCACION 25803

PHILIPPINES
Department of Foreign Affairs
PICC Building, CCP Complex,
Roxas Bvld
MANILA - Tel. : 831.88.73 -
Telex : 40.257

POLOGNE
Palac Kultury i Nauki (17 pietro)
00-901 VARSOVIE
Tel. : 20.33.55 - Telex : 816025 PKPL

PORTUGAL
Ministere des Affaires etrangeres
Avenida Infante Santo n.° 42 - 5°
1300 LISBONNE
Tel. : 60.49.42
Telex : 18332 ETRAN P (ref. CUNESCO c/CLT)

QATAR
Ministry of Education (opp. Government House)
22nd. February Street - P.O. Box 9865
DOHA - Tel. : 86.14.12
Telex : 4316 Mined DH -
Telefax : 820911

REPUBLICA DOMINICANA
Secretaria de Estado de Education
Bellas Artes y Cultos
Avenida Maximo Gomez
SANTO DOMINGO -
Tel. : 689-9410

REPUBLIC OF KOREA
UNESCO House 50-16 2 Ka
Myung-Dong. Choong-Gu
Postal address: C.P.O. Box 64
SEOUL
Tel. : Secretary-General 776.3950
Telex : MOCNDM K23231-2 (ext. 6364)

REPUBLIQUE ARABE SYRIENNE
Ministere de l'education
DAMAS - Tel. : 444.702/703/705/706

REPUBLIQUE CENTRAFRICAINE
ministere de l'education nationale
et de l'enseignement superieur
B. P. 1583 - BANGUI - Tel. : 61.43.00
Telex : MINEDUC 5333 RC
BANGUI

REP. DEMOCRAT. POPULAIRE LAO
Ministere de l'education
B. P. 67 - VIENTIANE
Tel. : 2213 (postes 132-133) -
Telex : 4317; 4320

REP. POP. DEMOCRAT. DE COREE
Ministere des Affaires etrangeres
PYONGYANG - Telex : 5350

RSS DE BIELORUSSIE
8, avenue Lenine
MINSK - Tel. : 22.29.22

ROUMANIE
Soseau Kiseleff n° 47
B. P. 71268 - BUCAREST -
Tel. : 17.42.49

RWANDA
Ministere de l'enseignement superieur
et de la recherche scientifique
B. P. 624 - KIGALI -
Tel. : 72.747 - Telex : 502
MINAFFET RW

SAINT LUCIA
Ministry of Education and Culture
CASTRIES
Tel. : 809.45.27286
(Secretary-General)
Telex : 6394 FORAFF LC

SAINT MARIN
Ministere de l'education nationale
Palazzo Maggio - SAN MARINO 47031
Tel. : 0541/99.28.13 - Telex : 330 ESTER SM

ST. VINCENT & THE GRENADINES
Ministry of Education
ST. VINCENT & THE GRENADINES
Tel. : Secretary-General 711.04
Telex : 7531 FOREIGN VQ

SAO TOME-ET-PRINCIPE
Ministere de l'education et de la culture
SAO TOME

SAUDI ARABIA
Ministry of Education
RIYADH - Tel. : 404.28.88 (ext. 1485)
Telex : 40.1673 SJ SAUDINESCO

SENEGAL
Ministere de l'education nationale
87, rue Carnot x Bayeux (1er etage)
PAKAR - Tel. : 22.57.30

SEYCHELLES
Ministry of Education, Information and Youth
P.O.B. 48 - Mont Fleuri - VICTORIA MAHE
Tel. : 247.77 - Telex : SZ 2305 MINED

SIERRA LEONE
Ministry of Education, Cultural Affairs and Sports
New England - FREETOWN - Tel. : 40.560

SOMALIA
Ministry of Education and Culture
P.O.B. 1182 - MOGADISCIO
Tel. : 80.204 (ext. 57)

SRI LANKA
Office of the Minister of State for Information
Transworks House
Lower Chatham Street - COLOMBO 1 - Tel. : 33.301

SUDAN
Ministry of Education
13, 17th Street - P.O.B. 2324
KHARTOUM EAST
Tel. : 79.888 - Telex : 220051 SD ESCOM

SUISSE
Department federal des Affairs etrangres
71, Eigerstrasse - 3003 BERNE
Tel. : (031) 61.35.50 - Telex : 911440; 911450

SURINAME
Ministry of Education, Science and Culture
P.O.B. 3017
Cattleyastraat 14, Zorg & Hoop
PARAMARIBO - Tel. : 61.865 - Telex : 376

SWAZILAND
Ministry of Education
P.O.B. 39 - MBABANE
Tel. : 42.491 - Telex : 2293

SWEDEN
Ministry of Education and Cultural Affairs
Street address: Mynttorget 1, STOCKHOLM
Postal address: S-103.33 STOCKHOLM
Tel. : 763.1952 - Telex : 13284 Mineduc S

TCHAD
Ministere de l'education nationale B. P. 731
Rond Point Fontaine de l'Union,
Avenue Mobutu Sesse Seko
N'DJAMENA - Tel. : 51.46.71

THAILAND
External Relations Division
Ministry of Education
Rajdamnern Avenue
BANGKOK 10300 - Tel. : 281.63.70

TOGO
Ministere de l'education nationale
et de la recherche scientifique
B. P. 3226 - LOME
Tel. : 21.61.54 - Telex : 5322

TONGA
Ministry of Education
P.O.B. 61 - NUKU'ALOFA
Tel. : 21-511

TRINIDAD AND TOBAGO
Ministry of Education
8, Elizabeth Street - St. Clair
TRINIDAD. W 1 - Tel. : 622.0939

TUNISIE
Ministere de l'education, de l'enseignement
et de la recherche scientifique
22, rue d'Angleterre
B. P. 1280 R.P. - 1000 R.P. TUNIS
Tel. : 258.290 - Telex : MEDNAT 13004 TUNIS

TURQUIE
7, Goreme Sokak
Kavaklidere - ANKARA
Tel. : 126.58.94 - Telex : 46585 UNES TR

UGANDA
Crested Towers
Hannington Road
P.O.B. 4962 - KAMPALA - Te. : 25.97.13

UKRAINIAN SSR
Ministry of Foreign Affairs
15, Karl Liebknecht. Str.
KIEV - Tel. : 293.42.33

USSR
Ministry of Foreign Affairs
9, Kalinine Avenue
MOSCOW G-19 - Tel. : 290.08.53 - Telex : 41.15.87

UNITED ARAB EMIRATES
Ministry of Education and Youth
P.O.B. 295 - ABU DHABI
Tel. : 34.39.33 - Telex : 22581 TARBI EM

UNITED REPUBLIC OF TANZANIA
Jengo la Umoja wa Vijana
Morogoro Road
P.O.B. 20384 - DAR ES SALAAM - Tel. : 27211

URUGUAY
Ministerio de Educacion y Cultura
Reconquista 535, 8.° piso
MONTEVIDEO
Tel. : 95.92.92 - Telex : 6682 (MEC UY 23133)

VENEZUELA
Ministerio de Relaciones Exteriores
Casa Amarilla - CARACAS 1010
Tel. : 81.81.74 - Telex : 22721

VIET NAM
10, Le Phung Hieu
HANOI - Tel. : 55.441

YEMEN
Ministry of Education
Gamal Abdul Nasser Street
SANA'A
Tel. : 274.550-274.551 - Telex : 2759 EDU YE

YUGOSLAVIA
Mose Pijade 8 (6th Floor)
BELGRAD - Tel. : 335.814

ZAIRE
Commissariat d'Etat charge de l'enseignement primaire et secondaire
B. P. 3163
KINSHASA/Gombe - Tel. : 30.617

ZAMBIA
Ministry of Higher Education
P.O.B. 50619 - LUSAKA - Tel. : 25.00.95
Telex : 42621 (or 43930 UNESCO attention NATCOM)

ZIMBABWE
Ministry of Higher Education
Union Avenue
P.O.B. U.A. 275 - HARARE
Tel. : 72.54.30 - Telex : 4235 ZIMGOV ZW

Note: Names of countries are given in the UNESCO working language utilized in official correspondence.

APPENDIX F

UNESCO-UNDP SUPPORTED TEACHER TRAINING INSTITUTIONS

Primary Teacher Training

1. *Bangladesh*	Primary Teacher Training (1975-77)
2. *Bhutan*	Teacher Development Centre (1974-77)
3. *Cameroon*	Rurally-Oriented Primary Teacher Training Institute Yaounde (1967-72).
4. *Chad*	Further Training of Primary School Teachers (1969-77).
5. *Ivory Coast*	Programme of Training for Primary Schools Teachers, Bouake (1969-72).
6. *Zaire*	National Institute for the Training of Primary School Staff (1972-77).

Secondary School and Higher Teacher Training

7. *Afghanistan*	Higher Teachers College, Kabul (1964-71).
8. *Australia*	Secondary Teacher's College, Goroka, New Guinea (1968-72).
9. *Burundi*	Secondary School Teacher's Institute, Bujumbura (1967-77).
10. *Cape Verde Islands*	Training Staff for Education (1975-77).
11. *Colombia*	The Training of School Teachers and Educational Specialists, University of Antioquia and the National Pedagogical University (1970-74).
12. *Congo (B)*	Secondary Teacher Training Institute, Brazzaville (1968-72).
13. *Congo (K)*	National Pedagogical Institute, Kinshasa (1964-71).
14. *Domican Republic*	Secondary Teacher Training (1971-73).

15. *Ethiopia*	Training of Secondary School Teachers at Faculty of Education, Haile Selassie University, Addis Ababa (1965-79).
16. *Ghana*	Secondary School Teachers Training Institute, Cape Coast (1964-77).
17. *Guatemala*	Secondary Teacher Training School, Guatemala City (1969-74).
18. *Honduras*	Secondary Teachers Training (1975-78).
19. *India*	National Staff College for Educational Planners and Administrators, New Delhi (1974-79).
20. *Iran*	Higher Teacher Training College (1974-78).
21. *Kenya*	Training of Secondary School Teachers, Department of Education, University College, Nairobi (1968-73).
22. *Lesotho*	National Teacher Training College (1974-79).
23. *Liberia*	Rural Primary Teacher Training Institute, Kakata (1974-77).
24. *Libya*	Teachers College, University of Libya, Tripoli (1965-71).
25. *Mali*	Secondary School Teachers Training Institute (1962-71).
26. *Morocco*	Secondary School Teacher Training Institute, Rabat (1963-71).
27. *Mauritius*	Institute of Education (1972-77).
28. *Niger*	Teacher Training College, Zinder (1968-72).
29. *Nigeria*	Abrake College of Education (1970-75).
30. *Nigeria*	Advance Teacher Training College, Zaria (1973-78).
31. *Saudi-Arabia*	Secondary School Teacher Training College, Riyadh (1966-71).
32. *Sierra Leone*	Training of Secondary School Teachers at Milton Margai Training College, Freetown (1966-71).
33. *Sudan*	Training Institute for Secondary Teachers (1968-71).
34. *Tanzania*	Training of Secondary School Teacher at Faculty of Science, University College,

	Dar-es-Salaam (1965-71).
35. *Togo*	Teacher Training College, Atakpame (1969-72).
36. *Tunisia*	Secondary School Teacher Training Institute, Tunis (1965-71).
37. *Zambia*	Training of Secondary School Teachers at the University of Zambia, Lusaka (1967-71).
38. *Africa Regional*	Regional Science Teacher Training Programme of the University of Botswana, Lesotho and Swaziland (1970-73).

Technical Teacher Training

39. *Algeria*	Higher Teacher Training College for Polytechnic Education (1970-77).
40. *Greece*	Training of Technical Teachers for Vocational-Industrial Schools (1966-71).
41. *Nigeria*	National Technical Teacher Training College, Lagos (1967-71).
42. *Singapore*	Technical Teacher Education and Vocational Training.
43. *Thailand*	Technical Teacher Training College, Thonburi (1967-71).
44. *Upper Volta*	Training and Reinforcement of Technical Teachers (1974-77).

MAJOR INTERNATIONAL ASSOCIATIONS/ORGANISATIONS IN THE FIELD OF EDUCATION

1. African and Malagasy Council on Higher Education (1968)(Conseil africain et malgache de l'enselgnement superieur – CAMES): B.P. 134, Ouagadougou, Upper Volta.
2. Association des Universities Parliament ou Entirement d-e Langue Francaise (AUPELF) (1961); Universite de Montreal, B.P. 6128, Montreal (H3C 3J7) Canada.
3. Association for the European University Community (1965) (Association pour la Communaute Europeenne Universitaire): 2 rue Merimee, Paris 16, France.
4. Association of African Universities (1967) (Association des Universities Africaines): P.O.B. 5744, Accra-North, Ghana.
5. Association of Arab Universities (1964): Scientific Computation Centre, Tharwar St., Orman P.O., Giza, Egypt.
6. Association of Caribbean Universities and Research Institutes (1968): P.O.B. 417, Kingston 6, Jamaica, W.I.
7. Association of Commonwealth Universities (1913): 36 Gordon Square, London WCIH oPE, England.
8. Association of Institutes for European Studies (1951): (Association des institutes d'etudes europeennes), Centre Europees de la Culture, 122 rue de Lausanne, Geneva, Switzerland.
9. Association of International Colleges and Universities (1971): 27 place de l'Universitie, 13625 Aix-en-Provence, France.
10. Association of Southeast Asian Institutions of Higher Learning: C/o Exec. Sec. Prof. Prachoom Chom Choi, Ratasastra Building, Chulalong Korn University, Bangkok 5, Thailand.
11. Centre for Educational Research and Innovation (1968): C/o OECD, 2 rue Andre-Pascal, 75016 Paris, France.

12. Comparative Education Society in Europe (L'Association d'education comparee en Europe) (1961): University of London Institute of Education, Malet St., London WCIB 7HS, England.
13. Confederation of the universities of Central America (1948) (Confederacio'n Universitaria Centroamericana): Apdo, 37, Ciudad Universitaria, San Jose, Cose, Costa Rica, C.A.
14. Council for Cultural Co-operation (1962): Council of Europe, ave. de l'Europe, 67006 Strasbourg-Cedex, France.
15. European Association of Teachers (1956) (Association europeenne des enseignants – AEDE): 122 rue de Lausanne, Geneva. Switzerland.
16. European Bureau of Adult Education (1953) (Bureau eurọpe'en de l'education populaire): Nieuweweg 4, P.O.B. 367, 3800 AJ Amersfoort, Netherlands.
17. European Foundation for Management Development (EFMD) (1971): Place Stephanie, 1050 Brussels, Belgium.
18. Federation Internationale des Professurs de Francais (1969) (International Federation of Teachers of French): I ave. L'eon Journault, 92310 Sevres, France.
19. Ibero-American Bureau of Education (1949) (Officina de Education Ibero-American): Ciudad Universitaria, Madrid 3, Spain.
20. Institute of Education (1975): Foundation Europeenne de la Culture Universite Dauphine, I place de Marechal de Latre de Tassigny, 73116 Paris, France.
21. Inter-American Council for Education, Science and Culture (1970): General Secretariat of the Organization of American States, Washington, D.C. 20006, USA.
22. Inter-American Education Association (1962) (Association Inter-americana de Education): Room 401, ii50 Ave. of the Americas, New York (N.Y.), 36, USA and Rio Bamba 1059, Buenos Aires, Argentina.
23. International Association for Educational and Vocational Guidance (1951) (Association Internationale d'Orientation Scolaire et Professionnelle – AIOSP): 257 route d'Arlon, Strassen, Luxembourg.
24. International Association for Educational and Vocational Information (1956) (Association internationale d'information scolaire universitaire et professionnelle): 20 rue de l'Estrapade, 75005 Paris, France.

25. International Association for the Exchange of Students for Technical Experience (IAESTE) (1948): Odos Patission 42, Athens, Greece.
26. International Association of Dental Students (1951): C/o Dr. John E. Seear, the Medical Protection Society Led., 50 Hallam St., London W/N 6DE, UK.
27. International Association of Students in Economics and Commercial Sciences (1950) (Association Internationale des Etudiants en Sciences Economiques of Commerciales – AIESEC): Ave. A. Bayl 123, 1949 Brussels, Belgium.
28. International Association of University Professors and Lectures (1944): 6 rue de la Re'publique, 94160 Saint Mande, France.
29. International Baccalaureate Office (IBO) (1964): Palais Wilson, 1211 Geneva 14, Switzerland.
30. International Bureau of Education (Bureau internationales d'education): 15, route des Morillons, Boite postale 199, 1211 Geneva 20, Switzerland.
31. International Centre for Agricultural Education (CIEA) (1958) (Internationales Studienzentrum fur landwirlschaftliches Bildungswesen): Federal Office for Agriculture, CH-3003 Berne, Switzerland.
32. International Coordinating Committee for the Presentation of Science and the Development of Out-of-School Scientific Activities (ICC) (1962): 125 rue de Veeweyde, 1070 Brussels, Belgium.
33. International Council for Adult Education (1973): 29 Prince Arthur Ave., Toronto, Canada M5R 1B2.
34. International Council on Higher Education (ICHE) (1958): C/o Pres. Wallace B. Edgerton, Institution of International Education, 809 United Nations Plaza, New York, N.Y., 10017, USA.
35. International Federation of Catholic Universities (1949) (Federation Internationale des Universities Catholiques – FIUC): Secretariat, 77 bis rue de Grenelle, Paris 7e, France.
36. International Federation of "Ecote Moderne" Movements (1957) (Federation internationale des mouvements d'ecole modern): 42 Grande Rue, 92310 Sevres, France.
37. International Federation of Organizations for School Correspondence and Exchange (1929) (Federation Internationale des organisation de correspondance de'changes scolaires – FLOCES): 29 rue d'ULM, 75230 Paris, Cedex 95, France.

38. International Federation of University Woman (1919) (Federation internationale des femmes diplomees des universites): 37 Quai Wilson, 1201 Geneva, Switzerland.
39. International Federation of Workers' Educational Associations (1947): OGB, Postrach 155, Vienna, Austria.
40. International Institute for Adult Literacy Methods (1968): P.O.B. 1555, Teheran, Iran.
41. International Institute for Educational Planning, 7 rue Eugene-Delacroix, 75016 Paris, France.
42. International Institute for Educational Studies (1969) (Institut International d'Etudes sur l'Education–IIES): P.O.B. 34, 1000 Brussels 23, Belgium.
43. International League for Child and Adult Education (1947) (Ligue Internationale de l'Enseignement, de l'Education et de la Culture Populaire): 3 rue Recamier, 75341 Paris Cedex 07, France.
44. International Phonetic Association (IPA) (1886): University College, Gower St., London, WCIE 6BT, UK.
45. International Schools Association (ISA) (1951): Palais Wilson 35, 1211 Geneva 14, Switzerland.
46. International Society for Business Education (1901) (Societe internationale pour l'enseignement commercial): 1952 Le Mont sur Lausanne, Switzerland.
47. International Society for Education through Art (INSEA) (1951) (Societe Internationale pour l'Education Artistique): C/o 106 rue du Point du jour, 92100 Boulogue, France.
48. International Union of Students (1946) (Union internationale des etudiants): P.O.B. 58, 17th November St., 11001 Prague Ol, Czechoslovakia.
49. International University Exchange Fund (1961): P.O.B. 108, 1211 Geneva 24, Switzerland; Regional Offices: P.O.B. R.W. 334, Ridgeway, Lusaka, Zambia, Apdo, 381, San Pedro Montes de Oca, San Jose, Costa Rica; London Office: International Development Centre, Parnell House, 25 Wilton Rd., London, SWIV IJS.
50. International Young Christian Workers (1925): (Jeunesse ouvriere chretienne internationale): 26 rue Juste Lipse, 1040 Brussels, Belgium.
51. International Youth and Student Movement for the United Nations (ISMUN) (1949) (mouvement international des jeunes et

des etudiants pour les Nations Unies): 5 chemin des Iris, 1216 Cointrin, Geneva, Switzerland.

52. Latin American Institute for Educational Communication (1956) (Instituto Latinoamericano de la communication educativa): Apdo, Postal 18-1862, Mexico 18, D.F., Mexico.
53. Montessori International Association (1929) (Association Montessori Internationale): Koninginneweg 161, 1075 Amsterdam, Holland.
54. Organization of the Catholic Universities of Latin America: (1953) (Organization de Universidades Catolicas de America Latina – ODUCAL); Pax Romana, (1921) B.P. 1062, 1701 Fribourg, Switzerland.
55. Regional Centre for Adult Education and Functional Literacy for Latin America (1951) (Centro Regional de Alfabetizacion Funcional en las Zonas Rurales de America Latina): Patzcuaro Michoacan, Mexico.
56. Southeast Asian Ministers of Education Organization (SEAMEO) (1965): C/o SEAMES, Darakarn Bldg., 920 Sukbumvit Rd, Bangkok Thailand.
57. Standing Conference of Rectors and Vice-Chancellors of the European Universities (CRE) (1959) (Conference permanente des recteurs et vice-chancellers des universities europeennes – CRE): 10 rue du Conseil General, 1211 Geneva 4, Switzerland.
58. Standing Conference on University Problems (1960): C/o Council of Europe, F-67006 Strasbourg-Cedex, France.
59. UNESCO European Centre for Higher Education (1972) (Centre europeen pour l'enseignement superieur–CEPES): 39 str. Stirbei Voda, 70732 Bucharest, Romania.
60. UNESCO Institute for Education: (1952) (Institut de l' UNESCO pour l'Education/UNESCO Institut for Padagogik): 58 Feldbrunnenstrasse, D-2000 Hamburg 13, Federal Republic of Germany.
61. Union of the Universities of Latin America (1949) (Union de Universidades de Admerica Latin): Secretariat, Apdo. 70232, Ciudad Universitaria, Mexico 20, D.F. Mexico.
62. World Association for Educational Research (1953) (Association Mondiale des Sciences de l'Education): Pres. Prof. M.L. Van Herreweghe (Belgium); Secretariat, Henri Dunantlaan I, B-9000 Ghent, Belgium.
63. World Confederation of Organisations of the Teaching Profes-

sion: (WCOTP) (1952) 5 Avenue du Moulin, 1110 Morges (Vaud), Switzerland.

64. International Council on Health, Physical Education and Recreation (1958): 1201 Sixteenth St. N.W., Washington, D.C. 20036, USA.
65. World Education Fellowship (1921): 33 Kinnaird Ave, London, W 4 3SH, UK.
66. World Student Christian Federation (WSCF) (1895) (Federation Universelle des Associations Chetiennes d'Etudiants–FUACE): 37 quai Wilson, 1201 Geneva, Switzerland.
67. World Union of Jewish Students (1924): 247 Gray's Inn Rd., London, WCIX 80Z, England.
68. World University Service (1920): 5 chemin des Iris, 1216 Cointrin, Geneva, Switzerland.

INTERNATIONAL BANK OF RECONSTRUCTION AND DEVELOPMENT (IBRD), INTERNATIONAL DEVELOPMENT ASSOCIATION (IDA) AND AFRICAN FACILITY ASSISTANCE (AFA) PROJECTS ON EDUCATION, 1988

Algeria. Dollars 54 million. The Ministry of Education and Training will be assisted in upgrading its network of training institutions by the provision of training equipment, technical books consumable materials, and civil works for fifty-seven vocational training centres, four instructor training institutes, and the Maintenance Training Institute. Technical assistance is included. Total cost: Dollars 101.3 million.

Bhutan. Dollars 4.2 million. The government's plan for primary education – designed to accommodate an enrolment growth rate of about 6 per cent a year, raise educational quality and student achievement and lower unit costs of primary schooling – will be supported. Co-financing from Switzerland (Dollars 5.9 million) and UNICEF (Dollars 1.5 million). Total cost: Dollars 13.6 million.

Burundi. Dollars 31.5 million. An education-sector development project seeks to increase access to basic education and to improve the quality of primary and general secondary education while maintaining the share of the sector within the government's recurrent budget at a level of about 20 per cent. Co-financing is anticipated from UNICEF (Dollars 1 million) and the UNDP (Dollars 500,000). Total cost: Dollars 37.5 million.

Cape Verde. Dollars 4.2 million. So as to help improve the quality and efficiency of basic education, a policy and institutional framework will be put into place and necessary education inputs provided for the phased countrywide establishment of a six-year basic education system and for the improvement of education-sector management. Total cost: Dollars 5.3 million.

Central African Republic. Dollars 18 million. The government's education strategy, within its structural-adjustment framework, will be supported by reviewing annually an action plan containing sector budgetary targets, the scholarship programme and budget, and staffing and pedagogical targets. Co-financing (Dollar 100,000) is anticipated from the UNDP. Total cost: Dollars 20.7 million.

China. Dollars 50 million. The government will be assisted in addressing urgent needs for an expanded and improved national lower secondary teacher-training system so as to meet the mandate for a nine-year universal basic-education programme by the year 2000. Total cost: Dollars 104.8 million.

Ethiopia. Dollars 70 million. A seventh education project seeks to improve the quality and volume of manpower training, continue or reinforce educational quality and equity, and strengthen institutional development in the education sector. Total cost: Dollars 95.2 million.

Guinea-Bissau. Dollars 4.3 million. The quality, efficiency, and relevance of, as well as access to, primary education will be improved, and the institutional capacity of the Ministry of Education, Culture, and Sports to plan and manage the development of the education system will be strengthened. The cost: Dollars 4.7 million.

Indonesia. Dollars 140.3 million. Selected activities in the government's higher-education programme, which is based on a medium-term subsectoral strategy and action plan that gives priority to improvements in quality and efficiency, instead of relying on capital expansion, will be supported. Total cost: Dollars 257.3 million.

Indonesia. Dollars 113 million. Accounting practices will be improved through support for the first-phase implementation of a programme to modernize government accounting practices and related efforts to strengthen the professional association of accountants, to develop accounting and auditing standards, and to strengthen the capital market. In addition, the government's programme to raise the quality of accounting staff and to prepare for future expansion of accountancy training will be supported. Total cost: Dollars 164.5 million.

Jamaica. Dollars 8.3 million. The government will be assisted to prepare and evaluate options for a rehabilitation-and-development programme aimed primarily at the first nine grades, mainly grades seven through nine. In addition, the student-loan programme for higher education will be strengthened by improving its collection performance and overall administration. Total cost: Dollars. 11.1 million.

Jordan. Dollars 40 million. A seventh education project has been designed to improve the quality of teaching and learning, provide a better learning environment at reduced costs per student place, improve physical facilities, reinforce planning and management of education, and strengthen the linkage between education/vocational training and skilled manpower demand. Co-financing is anticipated from the EEC (Dollars 2.5 million). Total cost: Dollars 108.3 million.

Malaysia. Dollars 48.2 million. This first Bank-assisted project for universities in the country will support limited new investment to expand university enrolment capacity to meet priority manpower needs, strengthen university management and improve the planning of university development and operations. Total cost: Dollars 81.4 million.

Mexico. Dollars 80 million. Human-resource constraints on growth should be reduced, labour productivity increased, and the social costs of adjustment lessened through a project that seeks to strengthen employment services (in particular expansion and increased effectiveness of retraining programmes), assist enterprises (especially small and medium-sized ones) to provide in-service training, and upgrade training institutions. Total cost: Dollars 156 million.

Mozambique. Dollars 15.9 million. A first IDA operation in the country's education sector seeks to raise the quality and efficiency of primary education, strengthen the training system in order to fill critical manpower gaps, and strengthen the capacity for education-sector policy analysis, with a focus on financial management and planning. Total cost: Dollars 17.9 million.

Nigeria. Dollars 23.3 million. This first Bank involvement in Nigeria's education sector in over a decade aims at upgrading the quality, efficiency; and throughout of selected federal technical training institutions and at strengthening the institutional capability for planning and co-ordinating technical education. Total cost: Dollars 27.9.

Portugal. Dollars 32 million. Portugal will be assisted to adapt its education and training system to the requirements of a modern economy through a project that focuses on rationalizing and strengthening university applied research to meet the needs of industry and agriculture, expanding polytechnic agricultural education and introducing computers in primary and secondary schools. Total cost: Dollars 77.1 million.

Turkey. Dollars 115.8 million. The Council for Higher Education will receive assistance in strengthening its capacity to plan and co-ordinate technician and technical/vocational teacher-training programsme; in alleviating scarcities of technicians in industry through the development of preservice technician-training programmes; and in expanding and improving training programmes at three faculties of technical education and one faculty of vocational education. In addition, the Ministry of Culture and Tourism will be helped to develop and implement a national training plan for tourism occupations. Total cost: Dollars 165.8 million.

Zaire. Dollars 11 million. Through a process of developing a strategy for the higher education subsector, coupled with programmes to improve administration and management, upgrade teaching and learning and provide priority teaching materials, the subsector will be brought within the Bank-supported adjustment framework, which emphasizes improved management and expenditure rationalization. Total cost: Dollars 12.2 million

Source: World Bank, ***Annual Report, 1988***.

UNIVERSAL COPYRIGHT CONVENTION, 1955

Genesis

This convention, signed in Geneva in 1952 at a UNESCO-sponsored inter-governmental conference, besides ensuring compliance with national and international formalities on the one hand, and the legitimate interests of the public, the authors and the various industries for the diffusion of artistic and literary works and of culture generally facilitates the dissemination of works and contributes to better inter-national understanding. The Universal Convention came into force on 16 September, 1955, and is binding in 56 States in Africa, America, Asia and Europe.

Main Features

The following are the main features of the convention:

1. The universal recognition of the principle that a foreign author enjoys the same protection as an author who is a national of a State (Article II).
2. The simplification of formalities which are replaced by the requirement that, when a work is first published, all copies bear the symbol, followed by the name of the copyright owner and the year of the first publication (Article III).
   This provision presents great advantages for the protection of the author's rights because it obviates numerous, costly formalities required by many American legislations.
3. The introduction of special provision governing translation rights. In this connection, the experts who drew up the Universal Convention have attempted to ensure a balance between the protection of the rights of authors in the producing countries, and the undisputed interests of the diffusion of culture in other countries. To this end, Article V includes the following essential provisions:

For the first seven years after publication of a work, the permission of the author in person must be obtained for translation of the Work;
After expiration of this period, a licence to translate may be granted by the State desiring the translation, provided it ensures compensation conforming to international standards for such work.

4. The fixing of a minimum period of protection covering the life of the author and 25 years after his death.
However, States providing protection for a period calculated from the date of publication of the work may retain this system as long as it covers a minimum of 25 years after publication of the work (Article IV).

INTERNATIONAL CONVENTION FOR THE PROTECTION OF PERFORMERS, PRODUCERS OF PHONOGRAMS AND BROADCASTING ORGANIZATIONS, 1961

This convention was adopted in 1961 by a diplomatic conference convened jointly by the Director-General of UNESCO, the Director-General of the International Labour Organization (ILO) and the Director of the United International Bureaux for the Protection of International Property (BIRPI). The convention entered into force on 18 May, 1964 and is at present binding in ten States.

The convention is based on the principle of national treatment, subject to the protection specifically guaranteed, and the limitations specifically provided for, in the text, national treatment means the treatment accorded by the contracting State in which protection is claimed to performers who are its own nationals, and to producers of phonograms and broadcasting organizations on its territory.

However, since national legislations in this field vary–where they exist–provision is made for a "specified" protection which covers:

1. For performers, the possibility of preventing the broadcasting, communication to the public, fixation and reproduction of a fixation of their performances, or some of their performances (Article 7).
2. For producers of phonograms, the right to authorize or prohibit their reproduction (Article 10).
3. For broadcasting organizations, the right to authorize or prohibit the rebroadcasting of their broadcasts, the fixation of their broadcasts, the reproduction of a fixation of their broadcasts made without their consent, and the communication to the public of their television broadcasts if such communication is made in places accessible to the public against payment of an entrance fee (Article 13).

Another important provision concerns what are known as "secondary" uses. According to Article 12, "if a phonogram published for commercial purposes, or a reproduction of such phonogram is used directly for broadcasting or for any communication to the public, a single equitable remuneration shall be paid by the user to the performers, or to the producers of the phonograms, or to both".

To ensure the universal application of the principles of legal and its protection defined in existing multilateral copyright conventions, UNESCO assists its Member-States in drawing up national legislation, or in harmonizing existing laws with international standards.

Two regional seminars have been organized with this aim in view.

Firstly, in application of resolution 4.32 adopted by the General Conference at its twelfth session (Paris, 1962), an African Study meeting on copyright was convened in Brazzaville in August 1963 by UNESCO and the United International Bureaux for the Protection of Intellectual Property. The purpose of the meeting was to help UNESCO Member-States and Associate Members in Africa define the general principles applicable in their territories to the protection of authors, and particularly writers, composers and artists, in respect of their literary, musical and dramatic works and works of the plastic arts.

To give effect to recommendations adopted at this meeting, draft model laws were drawn up by a committee of Africans.

With a view to encouraging the practical application of national copyright laws, another committee of African experts was convened in 1969, in collaboration with the United International Bureaux for the Protection of Intellectual Property, to draw up a model constitution for societies of authors, for the use of African States.

Similarly, in application of resolution 3.336, Section II, paragraph (b), adopted by the General Conference at its thirteenth session, UNESCO in co-operation with the International Confederation of Societies of Authors and Composers (CISAC) convened an inter-American meeting of copyright experts in Rio de Janeiro in July 1966. The aim of this meeting was to study national legislations on copyright in UNESCO Member-States and Associate Members in America and adopt recommendations which would contribute to the development of this legislation.

UNESCO also gives assistance of an intellectual and technical nature to Member-States which request it, either by sending experts to assist national authorities in the preparation of projects for drafting or revising copyright legislation, to create local offices or local societies of authors, and to advise on the improvement of methods of collection and distribution of royalties; or by awarding fellowship to officials responsible for copyright problems to enable them to study legislation on copyright and the organization of societies of authors.

RIGHTS OF THE CHILD

DECLARATION OF THE RIGHTS OF THE CHILD, 1959

Background

The United Nations General Assembly, on November 20, 1959 unanimously adopted and proclaimed a Declaration of the Rights of the Child on 20 November, 1959, setting forth those rights and freedoms which, the international community has agreed, every child, without any exception whatsoever, should enjoy.

Many of the rights and freedoms proclaimed were already mentioned in the Universal Declaration of Human Rights adopted by the General Assembly in 1948. It was, however, thought that the special need of the child justified a separate declaration. In the preamble to the new Declaration it is specifically stated that the child, by reason of his physical and mental immaturity, needs special safeguards and care before as well as after birth. The preamble also affirms that mankind owes to the child the best it has to give.

Like the Universal Declaration, the Declaration of the Rights of the child sets a standard which all should seek to achieve. Parents, individuals, voluntary organisations, local authorities and governments are also called upon to recognize the rights and freedoms set forth and to strive for their observance.

The United Nations first indicated its interest in such a declaration as long ago as 1946, inspired by the Declaration of Geneva adopted, on September 26, 1924, by the Assembly of the League of Nations. A recommendation was made to the Economic and Social Council of the United Nations in 1946 that the Geneva Declaration "should bind the people of the world today as firmly as it did in 1924". Two of the Council's functional commissions – the Social Commission and the Commission on Human Rights – were responsible for the preliminary drafting of the new Declaration. The Social, Humanitarian and Cultural Committee of the General Assembly gave it its final form. Representatives of seventy-eight countries were present when the unanimous vote was taken in the General Assembly.

The full text of the United Nations Declaration of November 20, 1959, is reproduced below. In ten carefully worded principles the Declaration affirms the rights of the child to enjoy special protection and to be given opportunities and facilities to enable him to develop in a healthy and normal manner and in conditions of freedom and dignity; to have a name and a nationality from his birth; to enjoy the benefits of social security, including adequate nutrition, housing, recreation and medical services; to receive special treatment, education and care if he is handicapped, to grow up in an atmosphere of affection and security and, wherever possible, in the care and under the responsibility of his parents; to receive education; to be among the first to receive protection and relief in times of disaster; to be protected against all forms of neglect, cruelty and exploitation; and to be protected from practices which may foster any form of discrimination. Finally, the Declaration emphasizes that the child shall be brought up "in a spirit of understanding, tolerance, friendship among peoples, peace and universal brotherhood".

Preamble

Whereas the peoples of the United Nations have, in the Charter, reaffirmed their faith in fundamental human rights, and in the dignity and worth of the human person, and have determined to promote social progress and better standards of life in larger freedom,

Whereas the United Nations has, in the Universal Declaration of Human Rights, proclaimed that everyone is entitled to all the rights and freedoms set forth therein, without distinction of any kind, such as race, colour, sex, language, religion, political or other opinion, national or social origin, property, birth or other status,

Whereas the child, by reason of his physical and mental immaturity, needs special safeguards and care, including appropriate legal protection, before as well as after birth.

Whereas the need for such special safeguards has been stated in the Geneva Declaration of the Rights of the Child of 1924, and recognized in the Universal Declaration of Human Rights and in the statutes of specialized agencies and international organizations concerned with the welfare of children.

Whereas mankind owes to the child the best it has to give. Now therefore, the General Assembly proclaims this Declaration of the Rights of the Child to the end that he may have a happy childhood and enjoy for his own good and for the good of society the rights and freedoms herein set forth, and calls upon parents, upon men and women as individuals and upon voluntary organizations, local authorities and national governments to recognize these rights and strive for their observance by legislative and other measures progressively taken in accordance with the following principles:

Principle 1

The child shall enjoy all the rights set forth in this Declaration. All children, without any exception whatsoever, shall be entitled to these rights, without distinction or discrimination on account of race, colour, sex, language, religion, political or other opinion, national or social origin, property, birth or other status, whether of himself or of his family.

Principle 2

The child shall enjoy special protection, and shall be given opportunities and facilities, by law and by other means, to enable him to develop physically, mentally, morally, spiritually and socially in a healthy and normal manner and in conditions of freedom and dignity. In the enactment of laws for this purpose the best interest of the child shall be the paramount consideration.

Principle 3

The child shall be entitled from his birth to a name and nationality.

Principle 4

The child shall enjoy the benefits of social security. He shall be entitled to grow and develop in health; to this end special care and protection shall be provided both to him and to his mother, including adequate pre-natal and post-natal care. The child shall have the right to adequate nutrition, housing, recreation and medical services.

Principle 5

The child who is physically, mentally or socially handicapped shall be given the special treatment, education and care required by his particular condition.

Principle 6

The child, for the full and harmonious development of his personality, needs love and understanding. He shall, wherever possible, grow up in the care and under the responsibility of his parents, and in any case in an atmosphere of affection and of moral and material security; a child of tender years shall not save in exceptional circumstances, be separated from his mother. Society and the public authorities shall have the duty to extend particular care to children without a family and to those without adequate means of support. Payment of state and other assistance towards the maintenance of children of large families is desirable.

Principle 7

The child is entitled to receive education, which shall be free and compulsory, at least in the elementary stages. He shall be given an education which will promote his general culture, and enable him on a basis of equal opportunity to develop his abilities, his individual judgement, and his sense of moral and social responsibility, and to become a useful member of society.

The best interests of the child shall be the guiding principle of those responsible for his education and guidance; that responsibility lies in the first place with his parents.

The child shall have full opportunity for play and recreation, which should be directed to the same purposes as education; society and the public authorities shall endeavour to promote the enjoyment of this right.

Principle 8

The child shall in all circumstances be among the first to receive protection and relief.

Principle 9

The child shall be protected against all forms of neglect, cruelty and exploitation. He shall not be the subject of traffic, in any form.

The child shall not be admitted to employment before an appropriate minimum age; he shall in no case be caused or permitted to engage in any occupation or employment which would prejudice his health or education, or interfere with his physical, mental or moral development.

Principle 10

The child shall be protected from practices which may foster racial; religious and any other form of discrimination. He shall be brought up in a spirit of understanding, tolerance, friendship among peoples, peace and universal brotherhood and in full consciousness that his energy and talents should be devoted to the service of his follow men.

CONVENTION ON THE RIGHTS OF THE CHILD, 1989

On Monday, the 20th November, 1989, on the 30th Anniversary of the Declaration of the Rights of the Child, the United Nations 159-member General Assembly adopted a global Convention on the Rights of the Child.

The Secretary-General, Mr. Javier Perez de Cuellar, said: it was "the most important step towards realising our common purpose of promoting and encouraging respect for human rights and fundamental freedom for all."

The convention is "as visionary as it is timely", noting that it "addresses the needs of humanity's most vulnerable and most cherished resource".

"It calls for the development of children through access to information, education, play, leisure and cultural activities and the right to freedom of thought, conscience and religion."

The convention sets the end of childhood at age 18, but does not say whether childhood begins at birth or earlier, a key controversy dividing anti-abortion and pro-choice advocates.

The General Assembly's President, Maj. Gen. Joseph Garban, said:

"Today, with the adoption of the convention on the rights of the child, our Assembly has taken a new and decisive step along the road towards assuring respect for dignity and the rights of the child.

"For the rights of the child have now gone from a declaratory statement of purpose into what will become a binding piece of international legislation."

It wraps together all international laws on rights of minors, which were scattered among more than '80 treaties and declarations' drafted over the past 60 years.

When at least 20 nations ratify the convention, it will become binding on ratifying nations.

Many more countries are expected to sign quickly, but ratification requires a country to bring all its laws into line with the convention.

BIBLIOGRAPHY OF UNESCO DOCUMENTS AND PUBLICATIONS ON TOPICS NOT ADEQUATELY COVERED ELSEWHERE IN THE PUBLICATION*

AESTHETIC EDUCATION

1. *Aesthetic education*. Bulletin of the IBE. Educational documentation and information. UNESCO/IBE, 1978, 84 p.
2. *Aesthetic education in Japan* by Shigeyasu Nakamura. Reprinted from *Research Bulletin of the National Institute for Educational Research*, No, 19, 1980
3. *Case study on significant realizations in the field of aesthetic education in Sri Lanka*. Paris, UNESCO 1982, 44 p.
4. *Classroom use of artistic and cultural heritage*. Report of a regional meeting. UNESCO/PROAP, 1983, 36 p.
5. *Culture as the methodological guarantor of relevance in the education system* by A. Yerodia. Paris, UNESCO, 1981, 15 p. ED-81/WS/126
6. *For an interdisciplinary aesthetic education : objectives orientation - methodology* by H. Gratiot Alphandery. Paris, UNESCO, 1983, 97 p. ED-83/WS/79
7. *Museums and children* by Ulla Keding Olofsson, general editor. Paris, UNESCO, 1979, 179 p. (Monographs on education)
8. *Portugal : une politique de l'enseignement musical* par Marcel Landowski. Paris, UNESCO, 1981, 8 p. FMR/ED/SC/81/307
9. *Study on the development of museums for improved integration of the cultural heritage into the education system in French speaking countries* by J.M. Essomba. Subregional seminar on the use of cultural heritage in education. Freetown, 29 September - 3 October 1980. Paris, UNESCO, 1980, 51 p.

* Listing to illustrate range of UNESCO documents and publication.

ED/CC/BREDA/80/SCM/CRE/9

10. *Subregional seminar on the use of the cultural heritage in education.* Freetown, 29 September - 3 October 1980. *Final report.* UNESCO/BREDA, 1981, 31 p. ED/CC/BREDA/80/SCM/CRE/8
11. *Using the African oral heritage for educational purposes* by J.B. Dongala. Paris, UNESCO, 1981, 24 p. ED-81/WS/125

EDUCATION CONCERNING USE AND ABUSE OF DRUGS

1. *The Aetiology of psychoactive substance use* by C. Fazey. A report and critically annotated bibliography on research into the aetiology of alcohol, nicotine, opiate and other psychoactive substance use. Paris, UNESCO/UNFDAC. 1977, 226 p.
2. *Course for english-speaking African educators on the methodology of education concerning the problems associated with the use of drugs.* Report of the working groups by Edmee Montandon. Embu, Kenya, 1983, 135 p. EPDAF/COURS II
3. *The Drug dilemma. UNESCO Courier*, January 1982. Paris, UNESCO, 1982, 34 p.
4. *Drug problems and drug education in Nigeria* by M.O. Olatawura. Ibadan, 1978, 38 p. EPDAF/3f
5. *Drug problems and education on the use of drugs in Senegal.* Regional meeting on education concerning problems connected with the use of drugs in six African countries. Lome, Togo, 13-17 September 1976. *Working paper* by Paul Ndiaye. Dakar, 1976, 21 p. EPDAF/3a
6. *Drugs demystified* by Helen Nowlis. paris, UNESCO, 1975, 92 p.
7. *Educating against drug abuse.* Paris, UNESCO, 1987, 86 p.
8. *Education and drugs. UNESCO Courier*, July 1987. Paris, UNESCO, 1987, 34 p.
9. *Educational approaches to problems associated with the use of drugs in Denmark* by Peter Schieler. Copenhagen, 1982, 21 p.
10. *Impact of science on society : man's addictions and how to deal with them.* UNESCO, 1984, 176 p.
11. *The Magnitude of the drug problem in the Sudan "A survey of the need for drug education"* by Hakim Abd El Rehman, Ali Mohamed Yousif, Hamid Mohamed El Hussan and Salah Merghami, 1980m 15 p. EPDAF/3h

12. *Meeting of experts on the coordination of school and out-of-school education concerning the problems associated with the use of drugs.* Lisboa, Portugal, 8-12 September 1980. *Final report.* Paris, UNESCO, 1981 , 15 p. ED/MD/62
13. *Meeting on education concerning problems connected with the use of drugs in ten Asian countries.* Penang, Malaysia, 5-12 December 1977. *Final report.* Paris, UNESCO, 1978, 16 p. ED/MD/51
14. *Meeting on the role of education in the social reintegration of former drug users.* Hong Kong, 9-14 April 1980. *Final report.* Paris, UNESCO, 1980, 17 p. ED/MD/60. *Working paper* by G. Krishna Iyer, 41 p. EPDAS/SR/2.
15. *Problems and rewards of evaluation of European drug education* by Nicholas Dorn. Report of a meeting of the study group for evaluation of European drug education and policy. London, 8-11 September 1975, 31 p. EPDAY/5 ED-76/WS/53
16. *Regional meeting on education concerning problems connected with the use of drugs in six African countries.* Lome, Togo, 13-17 September 1976. *Final report.* Paris, UNESCO, 1977, 12 p. ED/MD/44
17. *Regional meeting on education concerning the problems associated with the use of drugs in Latin America and the Caribbean.* Buenos Aires, Argentine, 1-7 July 1982. *Final report.* Paris, UNESCO, 1982, 16 p. ED/MD/70
18. *Report on the problem of drugs in Sierra Leone* by the Department of Extra-mural Studies, Fourah Bay College, in collaboration with the National Association for Drug Abuse Control. Regional meeting on education concerning problems connected with the use of drugs in six African countries. Lome, Togo. 13-17 September 1976, 49 p. EPDAF/3b
19. *A Report on Some studies and trials in Finland concerning health education on smoking, alcohol and drugs* by Anna-Ester Limatainen-Lamberg. Helsinki, 1981, 30 p.
20. *Seminar for Nordic countries on adult education and education concerning the problems associated with the use of drugs* by Christian Gunther. Eskilstuna, Sweden, 18-22 April 1977, 21 p. EPDAN/1
21 *Studies and surveys of the use and abuse of drugs in Zambia, 1966-1981* by A. Haworth. 1983, 63 p. EPDAF/3i
22. *Study of problems relating to drug use in Arab countries and-*

the role of information and education in prevention by C. Ougouag. Paris, UNESCO, 1979, 36p. EPDAR/1

23. *Study on drug problems and drug education in African schools from the point of view of teachers and the teaching profession* prepared by the World Confederation of Organizations of the Teaching Profession, for Regional meeting on education concerning problems connected with the use of drugs in six African countries. Lome, Togo, 13-17 September 1976. Paris, UNESCO, 1977, 42 p. EPDAF/3e
24. *A Study on problems associated with the use of drugs and drug education in Ghana* by Kodjo A. Senah. Accra, Ghana, 1980, 24 p. EPDAF/3e
25. *Sub-regional workshop on educational and information material concerning the problems associated with the use of drugs*. Presentation of the workshop and documents by Edmee Montandon. Freetown, 1980, 87 p. EPDAF/MAT/2/Prov.
26. *Survey of some educational experiments of particular interest in the search for solutions to the problems associated with the use of drugs in the Federal Republic of Germany* by Margareta Nilson-Giebel. Cologne, 1982, 38 p.
27. *Survey of some educational experiments of particular interest in the search for solutions to the problems associated with the use of drugs in the United Kingdom* by Mary Holmes. 1982, 36 p.
28. *A Survey on dangerous drugs and narcotics in Togo*. Regional meeting on education concerning problems connected with the use of drugs in six African countries. Lome, Togo, 13-17 September 1976. *Working document* by Tevi Sedalo, Yao Tossou and Dovi Feli. Lome, 1976, 28 p. EPDAF/3c
29. *Survey on some educational experiments of particular interest in the search for solutions to the problems associated with the use of drugs in Australia* by Hans Hovorka. Wien, 1985, 27 p.
30. *Three alternative approaches to alcohol and drug education in the secondary schools in the country of Akershus, Norway* by Mons Georg Rud. Oslo, 1981, 34 p.
31. *Trends in drug use and preventive education in industrialized countries* by D. Irvine. Meeting of experts on the coordination of school and out-of-school education concerning the problems associated with the use of drugs. Lisboa, Portugal, 8-12 September 1980. *Working paper*, 30 p. EPDA/2
32. *The use and abuse of drugs in Kenya.* A survey of the need for

drug education by C.A. Mwakwers, G. Muito, A. Ananda and G.P. Oluoch. Regional meeting on education concerning problems connected with the use of drugs in six African countries. Lome. Togo, 13-17 September 1976, 29 p. EPDAF/3d

33. *What's being done? - school activities for preventing drug abuse - interchange of strategies for the teacher.* (DINEMS/UNESCO/UNFDAC Project), 1983, 112 p. ED-83/WS/24

EDUCATION, EMPLOYMENT AND PRODUCTIVE WORK

1. *Analytical study of the interrelations between demographic, technological and socio-cultural factors in the process of educational and employment planning in the Kazakh SSR* by Evgeny Zhiltsov et al. Paris, UNESCO, 1986, 75 p.
2. *Annotated bibliography of recent literature on "employment and education in the informal urban sector".* Paris, UNESCO, 1977, 28 p.
3. *Cooperative school-industry education in Turkey.* Case study prepared by Prof. Hifzi Dogan. Paris, UNESCO, 1986, 29 p. (CODIESEE Doc. 3/86
4. *The Coordination of educational policy and planning and employment policy and planning.* (Vol. I: A state of the art review by Angela Little. Paris, UNESCO, 1984, 48 p. Vol. II: An annotated bibliography by Angela Little and Audrey Nunn. Paris, Unesco, 1984, 126 p.
5. *A Cross-cultural analysis of transition from school to work* by William C. Bingham for the International Association for Educational and Vocational Guidance. Paris, UNESCO, 1986, 94 p.
6. *Determinants and options in the development of higher education in Poland* by A. Josefowicz and J. Klucznski. Paris, UNESCO, 1980, 43 p.
7. *Education and the changing world of work in southern Africa* ed by Patrick Van Rensburg. Paris, UNESCO, 1987, 70 p.
8. *Education and employment: a methodology for local policy research* by M. Carnoy. Paris, UNESCO, 1979, 31 p.
9. *Education and work: the case of Bangladesh.* Paris, UNESCO, 1986, 72 p. ED-86/WS/23.

10. *Education and work: links between higher education and employment* by A. Jozefowicz, T. Obrebski and H. Jabalonska-Skinder. Paris, UNESCO, 1981, 31 p. ED-81/WS/83.
11. *Education and work: a review of major issues and experiences* by J. Casassus. Paris, UNESCO, 1976, 41 p.
12. *Education and work in the Spanish educational reform* by R.D. Hochleitner, J. Tena Artigas and M. Garcia Cuerpo. Paris, UNESCO, 1981, 64 p. (Experiments and innovations in education, No. 42, IBE/UIE).
13. *Examples of work components in non-formal education in Africa* by M. Muro. Paris, UNESCO, 1976, 28 p.
14. *Educational and vocational guidance as means of increasing mobility in the educational system* by Donald E. Super for the International Association for Educational and Vocational Guidance. Paris, UNESCO, 1985, 73 p.
15. *The forms, methods and techniques of vocational and educational guidance International case studies.* Paris, UNESCO, 1983, 134 p. ED-83/WS/102
16. *Guide to the workshop on the introduction of productive work in African schools.* Volume A, B, C. Paris, UNESCO, 1983, 3 fascicules
17. *The Interaction between education and productive work.* Bulletin of the IBE. Educational documentation and information. UNESCO/IBE, 1982 112 p.
18. *Interaction between education and work in CODIESEE countries* ed. by Andras Timar. Budapest, Hungarian National Institute of Education (OPI), 1986, 122 p.
19. *The preparation of teachers for their tasks in polytechnic education and the productive and socially useful work of pupils in the ten-class general and polytechnic secondary education in the German Democratic Republic* by H. Frankiewicz, 37 p.
20. *The Problems and forms of interaction between school and out-of-school education in the USSR* by V.G. Onuchtine. Paris, UNESCO, 1985, 30 p.
21. *Problems in the relationship between education and employment in Sweden* by K. Eliasson. Paris, UNESCO, 1980, 28 p.
22. *Productive work and the partial self-funding of schools.* (Part I) by Roselyn R. Gillespie et al. *The fete and the flea market : the many faces of productive labour in schools* (Part II) by Roselyn R. Gillespie and Colin B. Collins. Paris, UNESCO, 1987.

23. *Recent experiences in the coordination of education, employment and technology in Latin America and the Caribbean. A state of the art review and annotated bibliography* by Noel McGinn, Nancy Barra, Christopher Harris. Paris, UNESCO, 1985, 105 p.
24. *Regional seminar for directors and specialists from national training institutions on the training of teachers, inspectors and teacher educators for the introduction of productive work into education.* Baghdad, Iraq, 24-28 November 1979.

    1. *A case study on India* by M.B. Buch and Piloo Buch. Working paper No. 1. Paris, UNESCO, 1979, 25 p. ED-79/CONF.704/COL.1
    2. *A case study on the introduction of practical productive work in the teacher training curriculum in Tanzania.* Working document by A.G.M. Ishumi. Paris, UNESCO, 1979, 17 p. ED-79/CONF.704/COL.3
    3. *Major working document* by Keith Jackson. Paris, UNESCO, 1979, 33 p. ED-79/CONF.704/COL.4
    4. *Report and general trends.* Paris, UNESCO, 1980, 21 p. ED-79/CONF.704/COL.5

25. *Regional seminar on the introduction of productive work into education and its implications for the training of educational personnel.* Porto Novo/Come, Benin, 8-12 December 1980. *Discussion guide* by I. Beraho-Beri. Paris, UNESCO, 1980, 14 p. ED-80/WS/159 *Final report.* Paris, UNESCO, 1981, 18 p. ED-81/WS/16.
26. *The Relationship between education and employment in Spain* by J.T. artigas. Paris, UNESCO, 1981, 34 p.
27. *Relationship of education to employment in the United States* by B.E. Stern. Paris, UNESCO, 1981, 56 p.
28. *Report on the relationship between educational opportunities and employment opportunities for women.* Paris, UNESCO, 1975, 144 p. ED-74/WS/56.
29. *A Study on the relevance of education to work in Bangladesh.* UNESCO in cooperation with the Institute of Education and Research, University of Dacca, Bangladesh. Paris, UNESCO, 1982, 110 p. ED-82/WS/93.
30. *Suggestions for policy regarding the integration of young*

people into working life by William C. Bingham. Paris, UNESCO, 1987, 22 p.

31. *Teacher education and the production workshop* by J.A. Hendry. Paris, UNESCO, 1979, 38 p.
32. *Technological occupational challenge, social transformation and educational response* by Edmund King. (International yearbook of education), Vol. XXXVII, 1985, 366 p.
33. *Training of youth for working life in the Soviet Union* by N.P. Semykin. Paris, UNESCO, 1981, 31 p.
34. *The transition from technical and vocational schools to work.* Paris, UNESCO, 1983 (Trends and issues in technical and vocational education No. 2).
35. *Vocational guidance within the context of the democratization of education* by Anselm Siebel. Paris, UNESCO, 1986, 22 p.
36. *Workshop on productive work and teacher education.* New Delhi, 5-14 April 1982. Sets I-IV. Paris, UNESCO, 1982 ED-82/CONF.704/COL.4.

EDUCATION FOR SPECIAL GROUPS

Education for the Disabled

1. *Access by young handicapped persons to communication and language* by Aime Labregere. Paris, UNESCO, 1987, 130 p. (Guides for special education No. 5) ED-87/WS/2.
2. *Bibliography of books for handicapped children,* Part I and II. Compiled by the International Youth Library, Munich, Paris, UNESCO, 1982, 103 p. (Studies on books and reading No. 11) S.A. 01.6.
3. *Books for language-retarded children : an annotated bibliography* compiled by the International Board on Books for Young Children. Paris, UNESCO, 1985.
4. *Constructive education for special groups : handicapped and deviant children* by W.D. Wall. Paris, UNESCO/Harrap, 1979, 144 p. (IBE Studies and surveys in comparative education) UNESCO/Harrap.
5. *Consultation on alternative approaches for the education of the deaf.* UNESCO, Paris, 18-22 June 1984. *Final report.* Paris, UNESCO, 1984 ED-84/WS/102.
6. *Directory of special education.* Second edition, Paris,

UNESCO, 1986, 106 p. (IBE DATA series).

7. *Early intervention with young visually handicapped children.* A 1-slide/script presentation. Paris, UNESCO, 1985.
8. *Economic aspects of special education : Czechoslovakia, New Zealand, United States of America.* (Special education). Paris, UNESCO, 1978, 152 p.
9. *Educafrica.* As from December 1981. Bulletin of the UNESCO Regional Office for Education in africa.
10. *Educating handicapped children and youth.* In *"Prospects"* quarterly review of education. Abstracts from Vol. XI, No. 4. Paris, UNESCO, 1981, 65 p.
11. *Educating handicapped young people in Eastern and Southern Africa* by David Ross. Paris, UNESCO, 1988, 153 p.
12. *Education and training of children and young people with cerebral palsy.* Paris, UNESCO, 1988 (Guides for special education No. 7).
13. *The education of children and young people who are mentally handicapped* by Dorothy M. Jeffree. Paris, UNESCO, 1986, 79 p. (Guides for special education No. 1) ED-86/WS/25.
14. *Education of deaf children and young people* by the Centre for Total Communication, Denmark. Paris, UNESCO, 1987, 84 p. (Guides for special education No. 4) ED-87/WS/6.
15. *European regional workshop on the implications of the educational integration of disabled children and adolescents into the normal structures of general education for teacher training.* Bologna, Italy, 30 September-4 October 1985. *Final report.* Paris, UNESCO, 1985, 11 p. + annexes ED-86/WS/31.
16. *Handicapped children : early detection, intervention and education.* Selected case studies from : Argentina, Canada, Denmark, Jamaica, Jordan, Nigeria, Sri Lanka, Thailand and the United Kingdom. Paris, UNESCO, 1981, 142 p. ED/MD/63.
17. *Helping handicapped pupils in ordinary schools : strategies for teacher training.* Report on a survey of fourteen countries. Paris, UNESCO, 1985, ED-86/WS/88.
18. *Information on UNESCO projects and activities in the field of special education during 1984/85.* Paris, UNESCO, 1985.
19. *Innovations and practical applications in special education.* Paris, UNESCO, 1981.

    1. *The living classroom* (Ethiopia)

2. *Education of spastic children* (India)
3. *Towards total education* (India)
4. *Education of handicapped pupils in ordinary classes* (Italy)
5. *Early intervention with deaf children* (World Federation of the Deaf)
6. *Early childhood stimulation* (Jamaica)
7. *Early intervention with families of handicapped infants* (Uruguay)
8. *Adult education for the deaf* (World Federation of the Deaf).

20. *Integration of technical and vocational education into special education.* Four studies : Austria, Colombia, Iran and Tunisia. Paris, UNESCO 1977, 220 p.
21. *International round table on the theme : "how the handicapped are presented to the general public".* UNESCO, Paris, 1 June 1977. *Final report* by P. Saint-Martin. Paris, UNESCO, 1977, 18 p. OPI-77/WS/10.
22. *International symposium on services for young disabled children, their parents and families.* Washington, D.C., 6-11 December 1981. *Final report.* Paris, UNESCO, 29 p. ED-82/WS/79.
23. *International year of disabled persons. World conference on actions and strategies for education, prevention and integration.* Torremolinos, Malaga, Spain, 2-7 November 1981. *Final report.* Paris, UNESCO, 1982, 72 p. ED/MD/68.
24. *Language curriculum planning for deaf children.* A training manual for developing a curriculum, with a commented slide presentation. Paris, UNESCO, 1988, 37 p.
25. *Meeting of experts on integration of severely and multiply handicapped persons into general and vocational education.* Heidelberg, FRG, 26-30 October 1981. *Final report.* Paris, UNESCO, 1982, 6 p. ED-82/WS/80.
26. *Museum and disabled persons. Museum* Vol. XXXIII, No. 3, 1981. Paris, UNESCO, 1981, 196 p.
27. *New information and communication technologies : their impact upon educational opportunities for disabled people.* Paris, UNESCO, 1988.
28. *New information technology applied to special education.* Bibliography. Paris, UNESCO, 1985.
29. *New ways to learning.* International year of disabled, special

issue of *UNESCO Courier*, June 1981. Paris, UNESCO, 1981, 36 p.

30. *The protection of the rights of disabled persons afforded under various international instruments* by Maurice Torrelli, University of Nice, 1980. Paris, UNESCO, 1981, 21 p. SS-81/WS/43.
31. *Review of the present situation of special education.* Paris, UNESCO, 1988, 134 p.
32. *The role of children's books in integrating handicapped children into everyday life* by Tordis Orjasaeter. Paris, UNESCO, 1981, 46 p. (Studies on books and reading No. 1).
33. *Selected case studies on special education.* Paris, UNESCO, 1988.
34. *Sociocultural aspects of disability a commented bibliography.* Paris, UNESCO, 1988, 50 p.
35. *Special education.* Bulletin of the IBE. Educational documentation and information. UNESCO/IBE 1983
36. *Special education in Africa : research abstracts.* Nairobi, Kenya, 1986 ED-86/6.
37. *Sport for the physically handicapped* by Ludwig Guttman. Paris, UNESCO, 1976, 53 p.
38. *Sub-regional seminar for administrators and teacher trainers of special education.* Limuru, Kenya, 10-21 September 1984. *Report of the seminar.*
39. *Sub-regional seminar on planning of special education.* Nairobi, 20-31 July 1981. *Report.* Kenyatta International Conference Centre. Paris, UNESCO, 1981, 6 p.
40. *Sub-regional training seminar for teachers of visually handicapped children.* Malawi, 2-20 November 1981. *Final report.* Paris, UNESCO, 1981, 16 p. ED-82/WS/51.
41. *Sub-regional training seminar on the education of hearing handicapped children.* Lusaka, Zambia, 1-19 March 1982. *Final report.* Paris, UNESCO, 1982. 9 p. ED-82/WS/110.
42. *Sub-regional training seminar on the education of mentally retarded children.* Harare, Zimbabwe, 24 May-11 June 1982. *Report of the seminar.* Paris, UNESCO, 1982 ED-83/WS/19.
43. *Teaching visually impaired pupils in the ordinary class-room* by Kirk Horton. Paris, UNESCO, 1988 (Guides for special education No. 6).
44. *Testing and teaching handicapped children in developing countries* by David Baine. Paris, UNESCO,1986, 63 p. (Guides

for special education No. 3) ED-86/WS/59.

45. *Terminology of special education.* 2nd ed. UNESCO/IBE, 1983, 167 p. (IBEDATA series).
46. *UNESCO consultation on special education.* UNESCO, 2-6 May 1988. *Final report.* Paris, UNESCO, 1988, 17 p.
47. *UNESCO expert meeting on special education.* UNESCO, Paris, 15-20 October 1979. *Final report.* Paris, UNESCO, 1979 ED-79/CONF.606/COL.28.
48. *UNESCO statistics on special education 1972/1973 to 1976/1977.* Paris, UNESCO, 1981, 42 p. ST-81/WS/10.
49. *Working together:Guidelines for partnership between professionals and parents of children and young people with disabilities* by P. Mittler, H. Mittler and H. McConachie. Paris, UNESCO, 1986, 63 p. (Guides for special education No. 2) ED-86/WS/47.
50. *Working with Braille : a study of Braille as a medium of communication.* Paris, UNESCO, 1981.

Education for Prevention of Aids

1. *Consultative meeting of national specialists on AIDS prevention.* Organized jointly by WHO and UNESCO. Paris, 29 June-1 July 1987. *Final report.* UNESCO, Paris, 1987, 24 p. + annexes.
2. *Global strategy for the prevention and control of AIDS.* Economic and Social Council 2nd regular session. Statement of the UNESCO representative. Geneva, 6-29 July 1988, 2 p.
3. *Global strategy for the prevention and control of AIDS.* Resolution of the fortieth World Health Assembly. Geneva, WHO, 1987, 3 p. WHA40.26.
4. *Report by the Director-General on the implementation of the recommendation on education in the fight against acquired immunodeficiency syndrome (AIDS), adopted by the International Conference on Education at its fortieth session.* General Conference document 24 C/33. Paris, UNESCO, 1987, 8 p. + annexes.
5. *Strategies and structure, projected needs. Special programme on AIDS.* Geneva, World Health Organization, 1987, 20 p. + annexes WHO/SPA/GEN/87.1.
6. *UNESCO's action concerning AIDS prevention in schools.*

World summit of Ministers of Health on programme for AIDS prevention. London, 26-28 January,1988. Paris, UNESCO, 1988, 2 p.

7. *UNESCO'S role in AIDS prevention and control.* Inter-Agency Advisory Group on AIDS. Geneva, 1-2 September 1988, 2 p.

Education for Rural Areas

1. *Decentralised planning and people's participation in the general provision of education in rural areas.* Report of an inter-regional meeting of experts in Nazareth, Ethiopia, 9-16 December 1985. UNESCO/The Ethiopian National Agency for UNESCO, Addis Ababa, 1986, 113 p.
2. *Education and essential needs of the rural population of Central America.* Paris, UNESCO/Unicef, 1980, 155 p.
3. *Formal and non-formal education in rural development* (A sample survey in the State of Karnataka, India). Paris, UNESCO in co-operation with the Asian Institute for Rural Development, Bangalore, 1980, 77 p. ED-80/WS/158.
4. *Integrated rural development and the role of education.* Report of the Bangladesh-UNESCO field operational seminar held in Bangladesh, 4-19 March 1979. Paris, UNESCO, 1980, 97 p. ED-81/WS/7.
5. *Integrated rural development and the role of education.* Report of the Sudan-UNESCO field operational seminar held at Bakht-er-Ruda, 6-13 February 1981 Paris, UNESCO, 1982, 65 p. ED-82/WS/55.
6. *Interaction between adult education and universalization of primary education in the context of integrated rural development* (A research study conducted in Sri Lanka) published by UNESCO in co-operation with Faculty of Education, University of Colombo, Sri Lanka. Paris, UNESCO, 1984, 131 p. ED-84/WS/69.
7. *A Profile of 20 villages in the Islamabad federal area* (Experimental pilot project integrating education in rural development). Islamabad, Ministry of Education, 1980, 93 p.
8. *Role of education in rural development.* Report of the Malawi-UNESCO operational seminar held in Salima, Malawi, 4-11 December 1983. Paris, UNESCO, 1984, 72 p. ED-84/WS/67.
9. *Teaching agricultural economics and management in Asia,* ed.

by Owen McCarthy, published with financial assistance from UNESCO. New Zealand, Lincoln College, 1977, 124 p.

10. *Training for agriculture and rural development.* A joint authorship publication of FAO, UNESCO and ILO. (Annual review of current opinions and experience in agricultural extension and their contribution to rural development). Roma, FAO, available as from 1984.
11. *Universal primary education and its significance for rural development in China* published by UNESCO in co-operation with the Central Institute of Educational Research, Peking, People's Republic of China. Paris, UNESCO, 1984, 136 p. + appendix ED-84/WS/68.
12. *Women's education in rural Thailand* (A survey of facilities, needs and opportunities for basic scientific knowledge). Paris, UNESCO in co-operation with the Faculty of Education, Chulalongkorn University, Bangkok, 1980, 39 p. ED-80/WS/165.

EDUCATIONAL FACILITIES (INCLUDING SCHOOL CONSTRUCTION)

1. *Building community schools. An analysis of experiences* by M.I. Kennedy. Paris, UNESCO, 1979, 155 p.
2. *Building for school and community use : five case studies.* (University groups in : Australia, Federal Republic of Germany, Greece, kenya and U.S.A.). Paris, UNESCO, 1977, 122 p. (Education studies and documents [ESD]), (ESD No. 26).
3. *Building schools as a learning resource for science and technology education* by Margrit kennedy. Paris, UNESCO, 1985, 47 p.
4. *The Challenge of providing educational facilities in marginal urban areas – the case of Mexico city* by R. Almeida and C. Rodriguez. Paris, UNESCO, 1982, 111 p. + appendices.
5. *Community participation in comprehensive social facilities.* U.I.A. (International Union of Architects) seminar. Washington D.C., 23-27 September 1979. Paris, UNESCO, 1979.
6. *Community participation in the construction of educational facilities* by Y. Friedman. Paris, UNESCO, 1984, 62 p.
7. *Comparative study of the design and management of educational buildings and furniture in Europe and North America* by

Roger and Edith Aujame. Paris, UNESCO, 1986, 138 p.

8. *Comparative study of secondary school building costs* by Hutton and Rostron. Paris, UNESCO, 1971, 77 p. (ESD No. 4).
9. *The Development of the educational environment in favour of the child's development – a case study on the city of Helsinki* by T. Koivula. Paris, UNESCO, 1983, 114 p.
10. *Digest on earthquake protection of educational building* by A.S. Arya and B. Chandra. Extracted from the comprehensive reports prepared by the authors under UNESCO contract. Paris, UNESCO, 1982, 33 p.
11. *Educational facilities in the city : the challenge in Asia and the Pacific.* Bangkok, 14-17 February,1983. *Proceedings.* Published with the assistance of UNESCO/Secretariat of the Working Group. The Technical Chamber of Greece, Athens, 1984, 134 p.
12. *Educational facilities planning spatial inter-relations* by Jaya Appalraju. Paris, UNESCO, 1978, 67 p. ED-78/WS/89.
13. *Educational facilities thesaurus. Descriptor list.* Paris, UNESCO, 1981, 80 p.
14. *Elements for a dossier : architecture and educational space.* Articles reprinted from "*Prospects*", quarterly review of education. Paris, UNESCO, 1972, 99 p.
15. *Facilities for formal and non-formal education* by Thija Geursen. Paris, UNESCO, 1985, 59 p.
16. *First world directory of services in the field of educational buildings and furniture (provisions).* Paris, UNESCO, 1988, 53 p.
17. *Flexibility of building for education.* U.I.A. Seminar. berlin, 10-14 June 1974. *Proceedings.* 148 p. *Final report.* Paris, UNESCO, 1974, 6 p.
18. *Housing, cultural and educational facilities in rural areas in China.* UNESCO/PROAP, 1988, 68 p. (Educational buildings occasional paper No. 5).
19. *Implementation and management of educational building programmes* by R. Almeida and K. El Jack. Paris, UNESCO, 1981, 18 p.
20. *Improvement of the design, planning and management of educational buildings and furniture* by Lajos Jeney. Paris, UNESCO, 1985, 57 p.
21. *Innovation in primary school construction. Maldives community*

schools. UNESCO/PROAP, 1987, 35 p. (Educational building report No. 12).

22. *The Integration of educational and community facilities.* U.I.A. Seminar. Athens, 2-6 October,1976. *Proceedings.* Paris, UNESCO, 1976
23. *Iran : a case study on research and development of the indigenous buildings methods, materials, local skills and resources in Selselen, Luristan in the Caspian region – training workshop for local builders* by J. Norton. Paris, UNESCO, 1980, 63 p.
24. *Iran : a case study on stimulation and improvement or establishment of locally-based materials or elements production, in the Luristan and Caspian region* by J. Norton. Paris, UNESCO, 1980, 53 p.
25. *Mexico: Proposal for a rural community education centre* by R. Almeida and Beatriz Gutierrez. Paris, UNESCO, 1985, 29 p.
26. *Mexico: School construction* by R. Almeida and G. Reyes. UNESCO/CAPFCE, 1980, 95 p.
27. *Oman : a case study on research and development of the indigenous building methods, materials, local skills and resources* by J. Norton. Paris, UNESCO, 1980, 37 p.
28. *Peruvian rural school construction system* by M. Cangiano. Paris, UNESCO, 1979, 21 p.
29. *Planning educational building : basic concepts* by K. El Jack and R. Almeida. Paris, UNESCO, 1981, 22 p.
30. *Planning standards for higher education facilities. Examples from national practice* by Y. Chahrouzi et al. Paris, UNESCO, 1979, 328 p.
31. *Playing and learning opportunities for children in urban areas. Play, spaces and equipment* by J. Knight. Paris, UNESCO, 1983, 62 p.
32. *Primary school building : Standards, norms and design.* UNESCO/PROAP, 1986.
33. *Protection of educational buildings against earthquakes* by Prof. A.S. Arya. UNESCO/PROAP, 1987, 67 p. (Educational, building report No. 13).
34. *School buildings.* Bulletin of the IBE. Educational documentation and information. UNESCO/IBE, 1978, 71 p.
35. *School buildings and natural disasters* by D.J. Vickery. Paris, UNESCO, 1982, 95 p.

36. *School furniture development : an evaluation* by F.B. Scriven and Associates. Paris, UNESCO, 1975, 54 p.
37. *School furniture handbook* by F.B. Scriven and Associates, B. Fritzell. Vol. I : *General and specific aspects*, 259 p. Vol. II : *Practical examples and illustrations*, 246 p. Paris, UNESCO, 1979.
38. *Self-reliance in educational facilities.* U.I.A. seminar. Dakar, 7-10 March 1978. *Proceedings.* Paris, UNESCO, 1971, 163 p.
39. *Sports facilities for schools in developing countries. An inventory of experiences and proposals for future projects* by F.B. Scriven and Associates. Paris, UNESCO, 1973, 39 p. (ESD No. 8).
40. *The story of a prototype in Senegal.* Paper presented at the 4th seminar on the I.U.A. : "Self-reliance in educational facilities", Dakar, 7-10 March 1978, EFS/BREDA. Paris, UNESCO, 1978, 55 p. [C.68].
41. *The wider use of educational spaces.* International seminar, Paris, 2-6 December,1985. *Proceedings.* UIA working group on educational and cultural spaces, published with the assistance of UNESCO. U.I.A., Athens, 1986.

EDUCATIONAL RESEARCH

1. *Activities related to research and development of education in Europe.* Paris, UNESCO, 1988, 13 p. ED-88/WS/32.
2. *Consultation with non-governmental organization on research priorities and action in education that UNESCO could undertake during the Third Medium-Term Plan (1990-1995).* UNESCO Institute for Education, Hamburg, 6-7 May 1988. *Information document.* Paris, UNESCO, 1988, 13 p. + annexes ED-88/WS/37.
3. *Directory of educational research institutions.* Paris, UNESCO, 1980, 208 p. IBEDATA.
4. *Ergonomics in school and within the educational system.* Annotated bibliography by G. Lambert and R. Pascal. Paris, UNESCO, 1983.
5. *Evaluation of nonformal education programs : the applicability and utility of the criterion-sampling approach* by Richard J. Shavelson with contributions by Michael Brophy, Jiyono and Joseph O. Obemeata. UNESCO/UIE, 1985, 160 p.

6. *European expert meeting on joint studies in the field of education reunion d'experts europeenne sur des etudes en commun dans le domaine de l'education.* Vienna, 31 March-2 April 1982. *Final report.* Austrian Commission for UNESCO, 1982, 70 p.
7. *Forecasting methodologies with special reference to education. The experience of the USSR and socialist countries* by G.M. Dobrov. Paris, UNESCO, 1980, 15 p. ED-80/WS/42.
8. *International French-language seminar on the dissemination of educational research findings.* Paris, UNESCO, 1985, 133 p. ED-85/WS/17.
9. *Meeting of experts on cooperation in research and development of education in Europe.* Schloss Ottenstein, Austria, 11-13 May, 1987. *Information document* by Hans-Wolf Rissom. Paris, UNESCO, 1987, 8 p. + annexes. *Final report.* Austrian Commission for UNESCO, 1987, 26 p. + appendices.
10. *Priority research topics in education sources : UNESCO documents 1976-1981.* Paris, UNESCO, 1983, 73 p.
11. *Promoting the publication of research in order to link research more closely with practice : a survey of the question* by Tania Catz. Paris, UNESCO, 1988, 52 p. ED-88/WS/9
12. *Research and practice in education : how to strengthen links between research and practice in order to improve general education.* Final report (of) international colloquium. European Centre for Higher Education, Bucharest, Romania, 10-15 November 1980. Paris, UNESCO, 1981, 146 p. ED-80/CONF.816/12.
13. *Structures and organization of national research institutions* (a synthesis of eleven case studies) by Wolfgang Mitter. Paris, UNESCO, 1987, 98 p. ED-87/WS/26.
14. *Structures and organization of national education institutions and their role in the development of applied research* by W. Mitter. Paris, UNESCO, 1986.

FINANCING OF EDUCATION

1. *Budgeting for education in Alberta (Canada)* by L.R. Gue et al. Paris, UNESCO, 1979, 54 p.
2. *Inventory of international and regional sources of funding for education* by Nayereh Pourdanay and Jean Masini. Paris,

UNESCO, 1985, 43 p.

3. *Public expenditure on education in countries of Asia and the Pacific : goals, trends (1970-1980) and future prospects* by Peter Herold et al. Paris, UNESCO, 1983, 69 p.
4. *Resource constraints : ways and means to overcome the shortage of qualified educational personnel : experiences from Thailand and Ivory Coast* by K. Vorapipatana et al. Paris, UNESCO, 1978, 47 p.

HIGHER EDUCATION

1. *Adult higher education : a case study on the workers' colleges in the People's Republic of China* by Yu Bo and Xu Hong Yan. UNESCO:IIEP, 1988, viii + 110 p.
2. *Annotated bibliography of selected UNESCO publications and documents relative to training and research.* Paris, UNESCO, 1986, 44 p. (Papers on higher education No. 15).
3. *Aspects of training and research in higher education with case studies on India and Venezuela.* Paris, UNESCO, 1987, 308 p. (Papers on higher education No. 19).
4. *Combination of education, research and production in higher education.* A report on the seminar to study formulae combining education, research and production in higher education. Sofia, 1-5 December 1980. Paris, UNESCO, 1981, 123 p.
5. *The connection between formal and non-formal education at university level : the experience of the German Democratic Republic* by G. Roger, K. Jackstel and H. Mohle. Paris UNESCO, 1982, 53 p. ED-82/WS/19.
6. *Convention on the recognition of studies, diplomas and degrees concerning higher education in the states belonging to the Europe region.* Paris, UNESCO, 1979.
7. *Convention on the recognition of studies, diplomas and degrees in higher education in the Arab States.* Paris, UNESCO, 1978.
8. *Democratization of higher education through new admissions strategies : a comparative study of theory and practice* by S. Spaulding and A. Kargodorian. Paris, UNESCO, 1981, 117 p. ED-31/WS/4.
9. *Determinants and options in the development of higher education in Poland* by A. Josefowicz and J. Kluczynski. Paris, UNESCO, 1980, 43 p.

10. *A digest of UNESCO studies and documents on the democratization of higher education* by R. Geodridge and A. Layne. Paris, UNESCO, 1984, 95 p. (Papers on higher education No. 7) ED-84/WS/52.
11. *Distance education for the up-dating of knowledge at post-graduate level.* Report on a symposium organized by CEPES. Madrid, 25-28 November 1980. UNESCO/CEPES, 1982, 115 p.
12. *Education and work links between higher education and employment* by A. Jozefowicz, T. Obrebski and H. Jablonska-Skinder. Paris, UNESCO, 1981, 31 p. ED-81/WS/83.
13. *Efficiency in higher education.* Results of a workshop on the evaluation of UNESCO-sponsored postgraduate training courses in the basic sciences. Suzdal, U.S.S.R., 12-15 December 1983. UNESCO/CEPES, 1985, 149 p.
14. *Evaluation of innovative experiments in the democratization of higher education* by G. Berger, T.K. Thevenin and A. Coulon. Paris, UNESCO, 1985, 72 p. (Papers on higher education No. 10) ED-85/WS/1
15. *Graduate employment and higher education in West Bengal.* UNESCO/IIEP, 1988.
16. *Higher education and economic development in Europe, 1975-1980 : a statistical and economic study.* 2 Vols. UNESCO/CEPES, 1983, 160, 200 p.
17. *Higher education and manpower planning — a comparative study of planned and market economies* by O. Fulton, A. Gordon and G. Williams. Geneva, UNESCO/CEPES/ILO, 1982, 127 p. (WEP study).
18. *Higher education in Albania.* UNESCO/CEPES, 1985, 107 p. (Monographs series No. 9).
19. *Higher education in Asia and the Pacific : a perspective study* by S.C. Goel. Paris, UNESCO, 1983, 74 p. (Papers on higher education No. 5) ED-83/WS/99.
20. *Higher education in Bulgaria* by Vladimir Topencharov. UNESCO/CEPES, 1983, 114 p. (Monographs series No. 4).
21. *Higher education in the Byelorussian SSR* by E.G. Bondarenko, V.T. Vodnev, A.P. Kandybo. UNESCO/CEPES, 1983, 72 p. (Monographs series No. 6).
22. *Higher education in the German Democratic Republic* by H.J. Schulz. UNESCO/CEPES, 1983, 77 p. (Monographs series No. 5).

23. *Higher education in Hungary*. UNESCO/CEPES, 1986, 51 p. (Monographs series No. 10).
24. *Higher education in the The Netherlands commissioned by the Ministry of Education and Science of The Netherlands*. UNESCO/CEPES, 1985, 72 p. (Monographs series No. 7).
25. *Higher education in Norway*. UNESCO/CEPES, 1983, 72 p. (Monographs series No. 3).
26. *Higher education in Switzerland*. UNESCO/CEPES, 1984, 83 p. (Monographs series No. 1).
27. *Higher education in Trinidad and Tobago : a focus on organizational development and change* by Gwendoline Williams and Claudia Harvey. UNESCO/CRESALC, 1985, 145 p. (Monographs series).
28. *Higher education in the Ukrainian SSR* prepared by the Ministry of Higher and Specialized Secondary Education of the Ukrainian SSR. UNESCO/CEPES, 1985, 80 p. (Monographs series No. 8).
29. *Higher education in the United States* by Donald S. Doucette. UNESCO/CEPES, 1982, 83 p. (Monographs series No. 2).
30. *Higher level distance education. Perspectives for international cooperation and new developments in technology*. UNESCO international consultation on higher level distance education. Deakin University, Victoria, Australia, 6-11 September 1987. *Proceedings*. UNESCO/Deakin University, 1987, 261 p.
31. *The Impact of satellite technology on university teaching and research* by Jose L. Braga, Martin Meyerson, Shoichi Noguchi et al. Paris, UNESCO, 1988, 189 p. (Papers on higher education No. 27) ED-88/WS/44.
32. *Interdisciplinarity in higher education*. A study established by Thor Einar Hanisch. UNESCO/CEPES, 1983, 107 p.
33. *International convention on the recognition of studies, diplomas and degrees in higher education in the Arab and European States*. Paris, UNESCO, 1976.
34. *International directory of research institutions on higher education, 2nd rev. ed.*. Paris, UNESCO/CEPES, 1988 134 p. (IBEDATA series)
35. *International symposium on the probable developments in the goals and social roles of higher education during the coming decades*. Sofia, 5-9 December 1983. (Results of the work.) Paris, UNESCO, 1984, 19 p. ED-83/CONF.806/3 ED-

84/WS/20 *Working document.* Paris, UNESCO, 1983, 30 p. ED-83/CONF.806/2.

36. *Interuniversity co-operation in the Europe region.* UNESCO/CEPES, 1981, 75 p.
37. *Inventory of educational research on higher education problems undertaken by higher education institutions* (Preliminary version). Paris, UNESCO, 1987, 310 p. (Papers on higher education No. 18).
38. *Outflow of professionals with higher education from and among states parties to the regional convention on the recognition of studies, diplomas and degrees in higher education in Latin America and the Caribbean.* Paris, UNESCO, 1984, 54 p. (Educational studies and documents).
39. *Perspectives of the development of the university in the Arab region from the present to year 2000* by Omer M. Osman. Paris, UNESCO, 1983, 44 p. (Papers on Higher education No. 4) ED-83/WS/78.
40. *Planning standards for higher education facilities. Examples from national practice.* Y. Chahrouzi et al. Paris, UNESCO, 1979, 328 p.
41. *Recognition of studies and competence. Implementation of conventions drawn up under the aegis of UNESCO. Nature and role of national bodies.* Paris, UNESCO, 63 p. (ESD No. 44).
42. *The recognition of studies and diplomas of higher education : the contribution of UNESCO* by Rene Ochs. Paris, UNESCO (Papers on higher education, No. 23) (bilingual).
43. *Regional convention on the recognition of studies, certificates, diplomas, degrees and other academic qualification in higher education in the African States.* Paris, UNESCO, 1981.
44. *Regional convention on the recognition of studies, diplomas and degrees in higher education in Asia and the Pacific.* Paris, UNESCO, 1983.
45. *Regional convention on the recognition of studies, diplomas and degrees in higher education in Latin America and the Caribbean.* Paris, UNESCO, 1974.
46. *Regional expert meeting in Latin America and the Caribbean on the role of teachers of educational science in the improvement of teacher training at all levels and in the improvement of the education system as a whole.* Caracas, CRESALC, 1-5 November, 1982. *Final report.* Paris, UNESCO, 1983, 28 p.

ED-82/CONF.627.

47. *Regional seminar in Africa on the recognition and reorganization of studies and research in higher education having regard to the requirements of endogenous development.* Yaounde, 30 May-5 June 1983. *Results of the work.* Paris, UNESCO, 1983, 20 p. ED-83/CONF.710/3.
48. *Stocktaking of needs and resources relative to training and research, Vol. 1 : Australia, Hungary, Kenya, Syrian Arab Republic.* Paris, UNESCO, 1987 (Papers on higher education No. 16).
49. *Study service : problems and opportunities* by A. Dickson. Paris, UNESCO, 1980, 41 p. ED-80/WS/130.
50. *Study service : a tool of innovation in higher education.* Paris, UNESCO, 1984, 97 p. (Papers on higher education No. 6) ED-83/WS/101.
51. *Towards lifelong education : a new role for higher education institutions* by Gareth Williams. Paris, UNESCO, 1977, 188 p. (The development of higher education).
52. *Trends and prospects in the development of higher education in Latin America and the Caribbean* by Juan Carlos Tedesco. Paris, UNESCO, 1983, 47 p. (Papers on higher education No. 3) ED-83/WS/75.
53. *World-wide inventory of non traditional post-secondary institutions.* Paris, UNESCO, 1984.

MIGRANT'S EDUCATION

1. *Consultative meeting to formulate suggestions for educational action in favour of migrant workers and their families.* Paris, 13-16 June 1988. *Final report.* Paris, UNESCO, 1988, 15 p. ED-88/CONF.604/COL.1.
2. *The Education of migrant workers and their families : case studies undertaken for the National Commissions of Finland, France, Sweden, Yugoslavia.* Paris, UNESCO, 1978, 44 p.
3. *Meeting of experts to discuss the factors to be taken into account in extending the programme of the education of migrant workers and their families to other Member States concerned.* Paris, 10-13 September 1979. *Final report.* UNESCO, Paris, 1979, 10 p. + annexes ED-79/CONF.605/COL.7.
4. *Programme of exchanges between educators of migrant*

workers in the host countries and educators in the countries of origin by Mrs. S. Lundgren-Turiaf. Paris, UNESCO, 1986, 42 p. ED-86/WS/87.

5. *Rural-urban migration and the Jamaican child* by Erna Brodber. UNESCO/OREALC, 1986, 40 p. (PICPEMCE, technical documents No. 5).

NON-FORMAL EDUCATION

1. *Connection between formal and non-formal education at university level (The) : the experience of the German Democratic Republic* by G. Roger, K. Jackstel and H. Mohle. Paris, UNESCO, 1982, 53 p. ED-82/WS/19.
2. *Educational administration and management. Studies on co-ordinated development of formal and non-formal education* by Trevor Turner and Ganga Persaud. Paris, UNESCO, 1980, 48 p.
3. *Educational administration and management. Studies on co-ordinated development for formal and non-formal education.* The U.S. Community College experience in co-ordinating school and out-of-school education by Paul V. Delker. Paris, UNESCO, 1983, 49 p.
4. *Five years of Thailand's youth science week, 1982-1986.* Centre for Educational Museums, Department of Non-formal Education, Ministry of Education. Bangkok, 1986, 51 p.
5. *Manual for the promotion of scientific and technological activities for young people*. UNESCO/OREALC, 1984.
6. *Non-formal education and teacher participation in French-speaking Africa south of the Sahara* by T. Trevisini. Paris, UNESCO, 1975, 75 p. ED-75/WS/20.
7. *Non-formal education and teacher participation in the People's Republic of Benin* by Michael Gomez. Paris, UNESCO, 1977, 29 p. ED-77/WS/149.
8. *Out-of-school activities and influences and the extent to which they are taken into account in the training of teachers* by Jean-Marie Moeckli. Paris, UNESCO, 1980, 51 p.
9. *Out-of-school scientific and technical education.* Journal published with UNESCO's assistance by the International Coordinating Committee for the presentation of science and the development of out-of-school scientific activities (ICC), Brussels.

10. *Planning and management of the integrated development of formal and non-formal education : a review of the possibilities and difficulties* by W. Courtney and G. Kutsh. Paris, UNESCO, 1978, 72 p.
11. *The problems and forms of interaction between school and out-of-school education in the USSR* by V.G. Onuchkine. Paris, UNESCO, 1985, 30 p.
12. *Regional seminar on the effects of public TV programmes and press on educational process.* Tunis, 10-14 June 1982. *Formation and training of teachers in order to utilize the effects of mass-media messages in school education.* Paper by A.Q. Yousuf. UNESCO/UNEDBAS, 1982, 27 p.
13. *Regional seminar on teacher preparation to utilize mass-media in school education.* Amman, 7-16 May 1983. *Towards a minimum strategy of integration between teacher trainers and mass-media personnel (programmers)* by A.Q. Yousuf. Paris, UNESCO, 1983, 29 p. ED-83/CONF/713.
14. *Resource constraints : ways and means to overcome the shortage of qualified educational personnel : experiences from Thailand and Ivory Coast* by K. Vorapipatana et al. Paris, UNESCO, 1978, 47 p.
15. *School knowledge, media knowledge : media literacy in teacher training and student learning* by Len Masterman. Paris, UNESCO, 1983, 42 p.
16. *Symposium on conditions for effective participation by teachers in non-formal education in Africa.* Dakar, 3-7 May 1976. (i) *Report.* Paris, UNESCO, 1977, 56 p. ED-76/WS/90 (ii) *Working document* by Richard Quetel. Paris, UNESCO, 1976, 34 p. ED-76/WS/10.
17. *Teachers and out-of-school education.* Paris, UNESCO, 1980, 22 p.
18. *The use of general TV programmes in school and community. The linkage between in-school and out-of-school education* by Takashi Sakamoto. Tokyo, Institute of Technology. Paris, UNESCO, 1981, 38 p.
19. *Workshop guide on the use by teachers of the mass-media in the educational process.* Paris, UNESCO, 1983, 98 p.

POLICIES FOR FUTURE DEVELOPMENT OF EDUCATION

1. *An assessment of educational reform in India and lessons for*

the future by J.P. Naik. Paris, UNESCO, 1980, 75 p.

2. *Co-ordinating the forecasts and policies of technological, employment and educational development experiences in Poland. (A synthesis of research and practical experiences and a selected annotated bibliography)* by Karol I. Pelc. Paris, UNESCO, 1986, 39 p.
3. *Educational employment : speculations for the future.* Paris, UNESCO, 1978 (Info TVE series No. 4).
4. *The future of education.* Bulletin of the IBE. Educational documentation and information. UNESCO/IBE, 1981, 69 p.
5. *Reflections on the future development of education.* Paris, UNESCO, 1985, 291 p. + annexes.
6. *Reflection on the future development of education : educational development and forecasting in socialist societies* by L. Rybalkov and E. Soloviev. Paris, UNESCO, 1980, 31 p.
7. *Reflection on the future development of education : prospects of educational development in the OECD countries* by W. Van Vliet. Paris, UNESCO, 1980, 58 p.
8. *Reflection on the future development of education : a selective and annotated bibliography.* Part I by U. Von Haumeder. Paris, UNESCO, 1979, 35 p. Part II by R. Di Carlo. Paris, UNESCO, 1980, 70 p.
9. *Reflections on the future development of education.* Summaries of the discussions of the regional symposia, working documents and final reports of the 1st and 2nd meetings of the International Panel on the Future Development of Education. Paris, UNESCO, 1984, 123 p. + annexes (Educational studies and documents No. 49).
10. *Reflection on the future development of education Trends and projections of enrolment by level of education and by age. World and regional aggregates 1960-2000.* 1981 assessment (Provisional). Paris, UNESCO, 1981, 45 p. + annexes.

PRE-SCHOOL EDUCATION

1. *The child and his development from birth to six years old.* Better understanding for better child-rearing. Paris, UNESCO, 1976, 56 p. ED-78/WS/9.
2. *The child's right to education* ed. by Gaston Mialaret. Paris, UNESCO, 1979, 258 p.

3. *Child-to-Child. Another path to learning* by Hugh Hawes. UNESCO:UIE, 1988, xii + 128 p. (UIE monographs, 13).
4. *Forms of pre-primary education appropriate to the socio-demographic conditions and cultural traditions – **Kenya*** by E.M. Mugiri. Paris, UNESCO, 1980, 34 p. ED-80/WS/98.
5. *Index of notes, comments. . . (child, family, community). Annotated list of Nos. 1-180 grouped into 13 substantive categories.* UNESCO-Unicef Co-operative Programme. Paris, UNESCO, 1987, 45 p.
6. *International consultation on pre-school education.* Paris, 23-27 November 1981. *Final report.* Paris, UNESCO, 1981, 29 p. ED-81/CONF.605/4.
7. *International meeting of experts on alternative low cost strategies for the development of early childhood education.* Paris, 3-7 November 1986. *Final report.* UNESCO, Paris, 1986, 13 p. + annexes ED-86/CONF.605/COL.3.
8. *The role of parents in the education of children of pre-school age in tropical Africa, India and the Maghreb countries.* Prepared by the International Federation for Parent Education. Paris, UNESCO, 1980, 48 p. ED-80/WS/97.
9. *Shareable experiences in early childhood care and education synthesis of case studies.* Prepared by the World Organization for Early Childhood Education. Paris, UNESCO, 1983, 141 p. ED-83/WS/94.
10. *A statistical overview of pre-school education in the world.* Paper prepared for the International Consultation on Pre-school Education, 23-27 November 1981. Paris, UNESCO, 1981, 141 p. ST-81/WS/13.

PRIMARY AND SECONDARY EDUCATION

1. *Allocation and management of national and international resources for universal primary education and literacy (UPEL) within the framework of a basic services strategy (BSS) : proposing some tools for analysis* by Hans Reiff. Paris UNESCO, 1985, 37 p. + annexes ED-85/WS/47.
2. *Asian regional seminar on access of girls to primary education.* Kathmandu, Nepal, 2-6 October 1978. *Final report.* Paris, UNESCO, 1978, 37 p.
3. *Bulletin. The major project in the field of education in Latin*

America and the Caribbean. UNESCO/OREALC. No. 1, April 1982+.

4. *Conspectus of documentation available in Latin America and the Caribbean regarding the adaptation of the content of primary education in areas of rapid urbanization and on the periphery of urban areas.* Seminar inter-regional operational on the relevance of primary education in zones of rapid urbanization. Santiago, Chile, 9-13 December 1985. UNESCO/OREALC, 1985, 18 p.
5. *Education for rural development, Republic of Liberia* by A.R. Chorlton. Paris, UNESCO, 1979, 50 p. FMR/ED/LAR/79/137.
6. *Education for rural development, Royal Government of Bhutan* by A. Muyeed. Paris, UNESCO, 1981, 21 p. FMR/ED/LAR/80/141.
7. *Formal and non-formal education in rural development* (A sample survey in the State of Karnataka, India). Paris, UNESCO in co-operation with the Asian Institute for Rural Development, Bangalore, 1980, 77 p. ED-80/WS/158.
8. *Gandhian basic education as a programme of interdisciplinary instruction at the elementary stage : some lessons of experience* by Veda Prakasha. Paris, UNESCO, 1985, 89 p. ED-85/WS/28.
9. *Interaction between adult education and universalization of primary education in the context of integrated rural development* (A research study conducted in Sri Lanka) published by UNESCO in co-operation with the Faculty of Education, University of Colombo, Sri Lanka. Paris, UNESCO, 1984, 131 p. ED-84/WS/69.
10. *Inter-regional operational seminar on the relevance of primary education in zones of rapidly growing urban areas.* Santiago, Chile, 9-13 December 1985. *Final report.* UNESCO/OREALC, 1985, 85 p. ED-86/WS/115.
11. *Inter-regional operational seminar to review the state of primary education with the aim of enhancing its relevance to rural areas.* Arusha, Tanzania, 17-22 June, 1985.
12. *Moving towards universal primary education and literacy.* A co-operative programme to forster universal primary education and literacy. UNESCO/Unicef, 1984, 43 p.
13. *Primary education on the threshold of the twenty-first century* by Jose Luis G. Garrido. (International yearbook of education). Vol. XXXVIII. Paris, UNESCO/IBE, 1986, 276 p.

14. *Rural-urban migration and the Jamaican child* by Erna Brodber. UNESCO/OREALC, 1986, 40 p. (PICPEMCE, Technical documents No. 5).
15. *School experiments in the Hungarian public education systems.* Case study prepared by Eva Zsadon-Mayer. Paris, UNESCO, 1987, 12 p. (CODIESEE Doc. 2/87).
16. *Seminar inter-regional operational on the relevance of primary education in zones of rapid urbanization.* Santiago, Chile, 9-13 December 1985. *Summaries of seminar documents published in Spanish.* UNESCO/OREALC, 1985, 37 p.
17. *Status of girls in primary education in some Asian countries and prospects.* Working documents of Asian regional seminar on access of girls to primary education. Paris, UNESCO, 1978, 37 p.
18. *Training modules on planning and management of universal primary education (UPE) programme.* UNESCO/PROAP, 1984.
19. *Universal primary education and its significance for rural development in China* published by UNESCO in co-operation with the Central Institute of Educational Research, Peking, People's Republic of China. Paris, UNESCO, 1984, 136 p. + appendix ED-34/WS/68.

PRIMARY HEALTH CARE AND NUTRITION EDUCATION

1. *Approaches to nonformal nutrition education.* Paris, UNESCO, 1983, 40 p. (NEDS No. 6) ED-83/WS/43.
2. *Easy-to-make teaching aids for nutrition teaching-learning.* Paris, UNESCO, 1984, 138 p. (Nutrition education document series (NEDS No. 10) ED-84/WS/89.
3. *Environmental education module on health, nutrition and the environment* (Environmental education series (EES), (EES No. 21).
4. *Health education intervention : annotated bibliography.* Paris, UNESCO, 1986, 103 p. (NEDS No. 13) ED-86/WS/83.
5. *Manual for developing a nutrition education curriculum* by Isobel R. Contento and Kathleen Morin. Paris, UNESCO, 1988, 174 p. (NEDS No. 16) ED-88/WS/42.
6. *Maternal and young child nutrition.* Paris, UNESCO, 1983, 120 p. (NEDS No. 3) ED-82/WS/3.

7. *New developments in nutrition education*. Paris, UNESCO, 1985, 232 p. (NEDS No. 11) ED-85/WS/7.
8. *Nutrition education: case study experiences in schools*. Paris, UNESCO, 1983, 95 p. (NEDS No. 1) ED-82/WS/112.
9. *Nutrition education : relevance and future*. Paris, UNESCO, 1983, 32 p. (NEDS No. 5) ED-83/WS/42.
10. *Nutrition education : role of colleges of education*. Paris, UNESCO, 1983, 84 p. (NEDS No. 2) ED-82/WS/119.
11. *Nutrition education : state-of-the-art. A review and analysis of the literature*. Paris, UNESCO, 1984, 115 p. (NEDS No. 7) ED-84/WS/27.
12. *Nutrition education : a state of the art review* by R.C. Hornick. United Nations Administrative Committee on Coordination, Sub-Committee on Nutrition State-of-the-Art Series. Rome, Food and Agricultural Organization of the United Nations (FAO), 1985 (Nutrition policy discussion paper No. 1).
13. *Nutrition and education achievement* by Ernesto Pollitt. Paris, UNESCO, 1984, 42 p. (NEDS no. 9) ED-84/WS/66.
14. *Operational guidelines for social marketing projects in public health and nutrition*. Paris, UNESCO, 1987, 68 p. (NEDS No. 14) ED-87/WS/52.
15. *Show and tell : a worldwide directory of nutrition teaching-learning resources* (NEDS special issue). Paris, UNESCO, 1985, 269 p. ED-85/WS/12.
16. *The UNESCO resource pack for nutrition teaching-learning : an introduction to volume I*. Paris, UNESCO, 1984, 74 p. + appendix (NEDS No. 8) ED-84/WS/65.

PSYCHOLOGY OF LEARNING

1. *The development of intelligence : hope and reality?* by Jose Luis Pinillos. Promotion of research on the educational process and applications in teaching practice. Report prepared for Venezuela. Paris, UNESCO, 1981, 68 p. FMR/ED/SCM/80/177F.
2. *European expert meeting on the forms of autodidactic learning*. Paris, 16-19 October, 1979. *Final report and recommendations* Paris, UNESCO, 1980, 179 p. ED-80/WS/64.
3. *Research on cognitive development and its facilitation. A state of the art report* by Milton Schwebel, Rutgers University. Paris,

UNESCO, 1983, 128 p. ED-83/WS/110.

REGIONAL AND INTER NATIONAL COOPERATION

1. *From goal to process concerns in education : a behavioural view of the role of experts in development* by F.L. Higginson and A.S. Hartwall. Paris, UNESCO, 1976, 21 p.
2. *International cooperation in education : the Burmese experience* by Dr.Nyi Nyi. Paris, UNESCO, 1979, 52 p.
3. *International cooperation in education in countries of Asia and the Pacific : objectives, statistical trends and prospects* by Peter Herold et al. Paris, UNESCO, 1983, 53 p.
4. *International cooperation in education : the Guatemala experience* by E. Castaneda. Paris, UNESCO, 1979, 48 p.

5A. *International cooperation in education in Sri Lanka/The Marga Institute*. Paris, UNESCO, 1979, 40 p.

5B. *Meeting of senior officials responsible for education in the Arab States*. Amman, Jordan, 22-26 June 1987, *Final report*. UNESCO/Mineduc Jordan. Paris, UNESCO, 1987, 41 p. ED-87/WS/39.

6. *Meeting of experts on cooperation in research and development of education in Europe*. Schloss Ottenstein, Austria, 11-13 May 1987. (i) *Final report*. Austrian Commission for UNESCO, 1987, 26 p. + appendices. (ii) *Information document* by Hans-Wolf Rissom, Paris, UNESCO, 1987, 8 p. + annexes.
7. *Regional conferences and educational development in Africa, Arab States, Asia and Latin America : Bombay 1952 - Mexico City 1979* by F.L. Bartels. Paris, UNESCO, 1983, 187 p.
8. *Regional conferences and educational development in Africa from the Addis Ababa conference 1961 to the Lagos conference 1976* by F.L. Bartels. Paris, UNESCO, 1983, 93 p.
9. *Technical co-operation in education in Africa - review and prospects*. Paris, UNESCO, 1984, 56 p. ED-84/WS/47.

SCHOOL ADMINISTRATORS, INSPECTORS AND OTHER PERSONNEL

1. *Case studies on professional, economic and social status of new categorsies of educators. Peru* by M.M. Pajuelo and F. Farro. Baris, UNESCO, 1977, 19 p. ED-77/WS/120.

2. *Case studies on professional, economic and social status of new categorsies of educators. The United States of America.* Washington D.C., International Council on Education for Teaching. Paris, UNESCO, 1977, 26 p. ED-77/WS/13.
3 *The Changing relationship between teachers and inspectors* by A. Bubtana. 15 p.
4. *Education in Malta : a look to the future.* Proceedings of a national workshop for further training of educational advisers and school principals in Malta, 12-23 October 1987. Paris, UNESCO, 1988, 184 p. + appendices.
5. *Education officer survey (Lesotho).* Contribution to Yaounde meeting, 5-17 December 1977. Paris, UNESCO, 1977, 17 p. ED-77/WS/139.
6. *The educational administrator and instructional materials.* Paris, UNESCO, 1984, 180 p.
7. *The educational leadership role of the primary school principal. Workshop guide.* Sections A, B, C. Paris, UNESCO, 1984, 4 fascicules.
8 *For a new approach to the problem of the training of inspectors* by G. Berger. Paris, UNESCO, 1977, 21 p. ED-77/WS/151.
9. *The Functions and training of non-teaching personnel contributing to school education* by Vladimir Hercík. Paris, UNESCO, 1978, 13 p.
10. *Manual for a workshop on the role of inspectors in the in-service training of teachers* by J. Porter. UNESCO/UNEDB/S, 1981, 61 p.
11. *Meeting of national directors and chief technical advisers of UNDP/UNESCO-assisted operational teacher-training projects in Africa.* Yaounde, 5-16 December 1977. *Conditions and stages for the implementation of a qualitative evaluation of teaching staff.* Paris, UNESCO, 1977, 45 p. ED-77/CONF.705/COL. *Final report.* Paris, UNESCO, 1977, 52 p. Ed-78/WS/133. *Working Paper.* Paris, UNESCO, 1977, 25 p. ED-77/WS/122.
12. *Methodological guide for case studies of participation of non-teaching staff in school education.* Paris, UNESCO, 1978, 3 p. ED-78/WS/14.
13. *On the roles of school inspectors as decision-making agents in education* by K. Leimu. Paris, UNESCO, 1979, 128 p.
14. *Proposal for the study of the role of school principals in in-*

service teacher training. Paris, UNESCO, 1979, 12 p. ED-79/WS/12.

15. *Regional seminar on the training of educational administrators and school inspectors*. Caracas, 28 November - 2 December, 1977. *Final report*. UNESCO/OREALC, 1978, 28 p.
16. *The role of the headteacher in in-service training* by J. Greenland. Paris, UNESCO, 1983, 83 p.
17. *The role of school director (headmaster/principal) in the professional and pedagogic in-service training of teachers in S.F.R. Yugoslavia*. A case study material for UNESCO. Skopje, 1981, 32 p.
18. *The role of school principals in in-service training in the Philippines*. Paris, UNESCO, 1980, 106 p.
19. *The role of teacher educators in the in-service training of teachers and other educational personnel through innovative measures* by A. Yousuf. 21 p.
20 *School administration - case studies in school administration*. Joint UNESCO/Unicef/UNDP/UWI report. Paris, UNESCO, 1977, 116 p. ED-77/WS/64.
21. *Seminar on the new profiles of inspectors and teacher educators*. Dakar, 17-21 December 1979. Paris, UNESCO, 1980, 55 p. ED-80/WS/147.
22. *Senior educational personnel: new function and training*. Vol. 1: *overview* by J.C. Pauvert, Paris, UNESCO, 1988, 51 p. (Educational studies and documents No. 52).
23. *Survey of non-teaching personnel involved in extra-curricular activities* prepared by the International Federation of Free Teachers' Unions, Brussels. Paris, UNESCO, 1978, 7 p. ED-78/WS/80.
24. *Survey of non-teaching personnel involved in school education programmes*. World Confederation of Organizations of the Teaching Professions (WCOTP). Paris, UNESCO, 1978, 10 p. ED-78/WS/79.
25. *The training of school administrators and supervisors* by E. Miklos. Paris, UNESCO, 1974, 140 p.

See also Education, Role, Service conditions and Status of Teachers (Chapter 8 *Bibliography*.)

TECHNICAL AND VOCATIONAL EDUCATION

1. *The application of computing in the teaching and learning process in technical and vocational education in Australia.* Paris, UNESCO, 1986, 119 p. (STVE No. 25) ED-86/WS/119.
2. *Computer sciences in vocational teacher education in Denmark.* Paris, UNESCO, 1986, 69 p. (STVE No. 10) ED-86/WS/3.
3. *Computers in technical teacher education in the United Kingdom.* Paris, UNESCO, 1984, 61 p. (Studies in technical and vocational education.
4. *Content of general education in programmes of agricultural, technical and vocational institutions in Ukranian SSR.* Paris, UNESCO, 1987, 49 p. (STVE No. 26) ED-87/WS/31.
5. *Content of general education in programmes of technical and vocational education - Finland.* Paris, UNESCO, 1986, 52 p. (STVE No. 21) ED-86/WS/67.
6. *Content of general education in technical and vocational schools - USSR.* Paris, UNESCO, 1986, 37 p. (STVE No. 14) ED-86/WS/32.
7. *The content of general education on technical and vocational education programmes in the United Kingdom.* Paris, UNESCO, 1986, 125 p. (STVE No. 17) ED-86/WS/43.
8. *Curriculum development in technical and vocational education.* Paris, UNESCO, 1982 (Info TVE series No. 8).
9. *Design and use of mobile units for technical and vocational education - Denmark.* Paris, UNESCO, 1986, 84 p. (STVE No. 19) ED-86/WS/54.
10. *Developments in commercial education.*.Paris, UNESCO, 1984, 62 p. (STVE No. 1) ED-84/WS/42.
11. *Distance learning for technical and vocational education at pre-university level establishments of open tech type* by D.A. Blackburn, R.C. Smith. Paris, UNESCO, 1987, 47 p. (STVE No. 27) ED-87/WS/34.
12. *Educational employment : speculations for the future.* Paris, UNESCO, 1978 (Info TVE series No. 4).
13. *Graphic communications. An introduction to technical drawing in primary education.* Paris, UNESCO, 1987.
14. *Graphic communication : a technical drawing course for general education.* (Consisting of a background paper, Teachers' Guide, 18 learning units). Paris, UNESCO, 1982,

reprinted 1988 (Info TVE series No. 6).

15. *Guide on the organization and the operation of documentation and information centers and services for technical and vocational education.* Paris, UNESCO, 1982 (Info TVE series No. 2).
16. *Information paper.* Paris, UNESCO (International Technical Illustration Bank (ITIB) series).
17. *Innovations in science and technology education.* Vol. II. ed. by Dr. David Layton, Paris, UNESCO, 1988, 299 p.
18. *Innovations in teacher straining in the field of agriculture - Federal Republic of Germany.* Paris, UNESCO, 1986, 118 p. (STVE No. 24) ED-86/WS/118.
19. *Innovations in technical teachers' training - Ukrainian SSR.* Paris, UNESCO, 1986, 50 p. (STVE No. 22) ED-86/WS/72.
20. *Integration of general and technical and vocational education.* Paris, UNESCO, 1986, 355 p. (Trends and issues in technical and vocational education No. 4).
21. *International annotated bibliography on technical teacher education.* Paris, UNESCO, 1986, 107 p. ED-86/WS/108.
22. *International congress on the development and improvement of technical and vocational education.* Berlin, German Democratic Republic, 22 June-1 July 1987. *Final report.* Paris, UNESCO, 1987, 28 p. + annexes ED-87/CONF.401/COL.15. *Major trends in technical and vocational education.* Paris, UNESCO, 1987, 24 p. + annexes ED-87/CONF.401/COL.II.
23. *International congress on the situation of women in technical and vocational education.* Bonn, Federal Republic of Germany, 9-12 June 1980. *Final document.* Paris, UNESCO, 1980, 5 p.
24. *A Long way . . . : a study on some activities implemented in the Netherlands to promote equality of opportunity for girls and women in scientific, technical and vocational education* by Ria Jaarsma. Paris, UNESCO, 1987, 95 p. ED-87/WS/42.
25. *Manual for the promotion of scientific and technological activities for young people.* UNESCO/OREALC, 1984, 108 p.
26. *Measures to provide the access of girls and women to secondary technical and vocational education in New Zealand* by Doris MacDonald. Paris, UNESCO, 1987, 47 p. + annexes ED-87/WS/40.
27. *Mobile units for vocational education - USSR.* Paris, UNESCO, 1986, 125 p. (STVE No. 18) ED-86/WS/45.

28. *Organisation of centralised workshops - USSR*. Paris, UNESCO, 1986, 51 p. (STVE No. 16) ED-86/WS/39.
29. *Organisation of educational and vocational guidance services* Paris, UNESCO, 1985, 98 p. (STVE No. 11) ED-86/WS/14.
30. *Organisation of productive work in secondary, technical and vocational education in the People's Republic of Bulgaria (The)*. Paris, UNESCO, 1984, 17 p. (STVENo. 3) ED/84/WS/43.
31. *The organisation of productive work in secondary technical and vocational education in the United Kingdom*. Paris, UNESCO, 1983, 78 p. (STVE No. 2) ED-84/WS/49.
32. *Organisation of productive work in technical and vocational education in the Republic of Kenya*. Paris, UNESCO, 1987, 101 p. (STEVE No. 28) ED-87/WS/33.
33. *Out-of-school scientific and technical education*. Journal published with UNESCO's assistance by the International Coordinating Committee for t;he presentation of science and the development of out-of-school scientific activities (ICC), Brussels.
34. *Policy, planning and administration of technical and vocational education in China*. Paris, UNESCO, 1987, 76 p. (STVE No. 29) ED-87/WS/48.
35. *Policy, planning and administration of technical and vocational education in Ghana*. Paris, UNESCO, 1984, 44 p. (STVE No. 4) ED-84/WS/44.
36. *Policy, planning and administration of technical and vocational education in India*. Paris, UNESCO, 1985, 172 p. (STVE No. 8) ED-85/WS/18.
37. *Policy, planning and administration of technical and vocational education in Netherlands*. Paris, UNESCO, 1984 (STVE No. 7) ED-84/WS/97.
38. *Policy, planning and management in technical and vocational education : a comparative study*. Paris, UNESCO, 1984 (Trends and issues in technical and vocational education No. 3).
39. *Policy, planning and management of technical and vocational education in the Hashemite Kingdom of Jordan*. Paris, UNESCO, 1986, 121 p. (STVE No. 12) ED-86/WS/12.
40. *Printed technical learning materials*. Paris, UNESCO, 1984 (Info TVE series No. 7).
41. *Production units and technical teacher education*. Paris,

UNESCO, 1982 (Info TVE series No. 10).

42. *Progress report on graphic communication course experiments conducted in Belgium, China, Cyprus, Finland, Hungary, India, Korea (Republic), Philippines, Sweden.* Paris, UNESCO, 1984 ED-84/WS/61.
43. *Prototype workshops and laboratories for technical and vocational education.* Paris, UNESCO, 1978 (Info TVE series No. 9).
44. *Science and technology in the primary school of tomorrow* by Graham Orpwood and Ingvar Werdelin, Paris UNESCO. 1988, 216 p. (IBE: Studies and surveys in comparative education).
45. *Study on the general educational requirements for access to vocational education in the Arab Republic of Egypt.* Paris, UNESCO, 1980, 39 p. (Surveys & studies in adult education) ED-80/WS/6.
46. *Study on the general educational requirements for access to vocational education in the Republic of Argentina.* Paris, UNESCO, 1980, 55 p. ED-80/WS/8.
47. *A Study on the general educational requirements for access to vocational education.* Progress report by Le Thanh Khoi. Paris, UNESCO, 1980, 33 p. (Surveys & studies in adult education) ED-79/WS/161.
48. *Technical and vocational education in the Arab Gulf countries.* Paris, UNESCO, 1986, 89 p. (STVE No. 20) ED-86/WS/66.
49. *Technical and vocational education information bulletin.* No. 1, + 1981 +.
50. *Technical education and vocational training in Egypt.* Paris, UNESCO, 1987, 111 p. (STVE No. 31) ED-87/WS/55.
51. *Technical teacher education course : a suggested one year curriculum.* Paris, UNESCO, 1978 (Info TVE series No. 5).
52. *Terminology of technical and vocational education.* IBEDATA series, UNESCO/IBE, 1984.
53. *Training apprentices in industrial training workshops - German Democratic Republic.* Paris, UNESCO, 1986, 120 p. (STVE No. 23) ED-85/WS/120.
54. *The Transition from technical and vocational schools to work.* Paris, UNESCO, 1983 (Trends and issues in technical and vocational education No. 2).
55. *UNESCO's revised recommendation concerning technical and vocational education* adopted by the General Conference at its

eighteenth session, Paris, 19 November 1974. Paris, UNESCO, 1983.

56. *Unit 22 : D.C. machines : bank unit.* Paris, UNESCO, 1982 (ITIB series).
57. *Unit 22 : D.C. machines : module.* Paris, UNESCO, 1982 (ITIB series)
58. *Unit 28 : electric machines selection, operation and servicing. Fault diagnosis : bank unit.* Paris, UNESCO, 1983 (ITIB series)
59. *Unit 28 : electric machines selection, operation and servicing. Fault diagnosis : module.* Paris, UNESCO, 1983 (ITIB series).
60. *World directory of selected research and teacher training institutions in the field of technical and vocational education.* paris, UNESCO, 1986.
61. *World-wide inventory of non traditional post-secondary institutions.* Paris, UNESCO, 1984.

WOMEN'S EDUCATION

1. *Analysis of some aspects of the action undertaken since 1975 by the section of equality of educational opportunity for girls and women to promote equality of educational opportunity for girls and women.* Paris, UNESCO, 1985, 51 p. ED-84/WS/24.
2. *Asian regional seminar on access of girls to primary education.* Kathmandu, Nepal, 2-6 October 1978. *final report.* Paris, UNESCO, 1978, 37 p.
3. *Comparative report on the role of working mothers in early childhood education in five countries.* Paris, UNESCO, 1978, 82 p. ED-78/WS/71.
4. *Education and training of professional women with a view to enabling them to resume their interrupted activities or to take up a new career* by Monica Langkau_Hermann. *Working document* of international seminar on women's education, training and employment in developed countries. Tokyo, Japan, 2-6 December 1980. Paris, UNESCO, 1980, 83 p.
5. *Education, training and employment opportunities for women in Sierra Leone*, Paris, UNESCO, 1974, 186 p.
6. *Eliminating sex stereotyping in schools.* A regional guide for educators in North America and Western Europe. Paris, UNESCO, 1984, 182 p. ED-84/WS/51.
7. *Equality of educational opportunity for girls and women.* Paris,

UNESCO, 1983, 62 p. ED-83/WS/55.

8. *Identification and elimination of sex stereotypes in and from school textbooks.* Some suggestions for action in the Arab world. Paris, UNESCO, 1983, 59 p. ED-84/WS/31.
9. *Identification and elimination of sex stereotypes in and from school textbooks.* Some suggestions for action in Asia and the Pacific, Paris, UNESCO, 1985, 37 p. ED-85/WS/58.
10. *International congress on the situation of women in technical and vocational education.* Bonn, Federal Republic of Germany, 9-12 June 1980. *Final document.* Paris, UNESCO, 1980, 5 p.
11. *International expert meeting on the rôle of women in the education of young people for peace, mutual understanding and respect for human rights.* New Delhi, India, 7-11 December 1981. *Summary record of discussions.* Paris, UNESCO, 1982, 35 p. + annexes ED-82/CONF.609/4.
12. *International seminar on opening-up to women of vocational training and jobs traditionally occupied by men.* Frankfurt, 11-13 November 1980. *Summary record of discussions.* Paris, UNESCO, 1981, 64 p. ED-80/CONF.708/COL.2.
13. *International seminar on women's education, training and employment, in developed countries.* Summary record of discussions. Tokyo, Japan, 2-6 December 1980. Paris, UNESCO, 1980, 83 p. ED-80/CONF.710/4.
14. *International symposium on the right of women to education with view to their access to employment*, Paris, UNESCO, 14-18 September 1987. *Final report.* Paris, UNESCO, 1987, 20 p. ED-87/CONF.809. *Reference document No. 1.* Paris, UNESCO, 1987, 56 p. ED-87/CONF.809/COL.2 *Women's right to education* by F. Besh. *Reference document No.* 2. Paris, UNESCO, 1987, 40 p. ED-87/CONF.809/COL.
15. *Inventory on the results of experience of Japan in developing successful approaches to improving the status of women.* Paris, UNESCO, 1976, 87 p.
16. *Jobs for women : a plea for equality of opportunity* by Germaine Borcelle. Paris, UNESCO, 1985, 165 p.
17. *Literacy for women : a development priority.* Paris, UNESCO
18. *A Long way... : a study on some activities implemented in the Netherlands to promote equality of opportunity for girls and women in scientific, technical and vocational education* by Ria Jaarsma. Paris, UNESCO, 1987, 95 p. ED-87/WS/42.

19. *Measures to promote the equality of opportunity for girls and women in vocational education in the German Democratic Republic* by W. Purgand with the co-operation of B. Gericke and G. Pogodda. Paris, UNESCO, 1987, 44 p. ED-87/WS/38.
20. *Measures to provide the access of girls and women to secondary technical and vocational education in New Zealand* by Doris MacDonald. A report on policies and selected activities. Paris, UNESCO, 1987, 47 p. + annexes ED-87/WS/40.
21. *National inventory on the status of women in Brazil.* Paris, UNESCO, 1977, 52 p.
22. *National inventory on nthe status of women in Ghana.* Paris, UNESCO 1977, 62 p.
23. *National inventory on the place of women in Tunisian society.* Paris, UNESCO, 1976, 80 p.
24. *National inventory on the status of women in the United Kingdom.* Paris, UNESCO, 1976, 51 p.
25. *National inventory on the status of women in the USA.* Paris, UNESCO, 1976, 78 p.
26. *National inventory on the status of women in the USSR.* Paris, UNESCO, 1977, 25 p.
27. *A National survey on sex biases in Zambian textbooks in primary and junior secondary schools and their implications for education in Zambia.* Paris, UNESCO, 1984, 43 p. ED-84/WS/25.
28. *Promotion of girls' and women's access to technical and vocational education : examples of action* by R. Begarra. Paris, UNESCO, 1986, 79 p. ED-86/WS/103.
29. *Report on the relationship between educational opportunities and employment opportunities for women.* Paris, UNESCO, 1975, 144 p. ED-74/WS/56.
30. *Review of studies on women in South-East Asia* by Leela Dube. Paris, UNESCO, 1980.
31. *The role of working mothers in early childhood education in Arab Republic of Egypt.* Paris, UNESCO, 1978, 31 p.
32. *The role of working mothers in early childhood education in Hungarian People's Republic.* Paris, UNESCO, 1977, 77 p.
33. *The role of working mothers in early childhood education in India* Paris, UNESCO, 1977, 200 p.
34. *The role of working mothers in early childhood education in Nigeria.* Paris, UNESCO, 1978, 68 p.

35. *The role of working mothers in early childhood education in Trinidad and Tobago*. Paris, UNESCO, 1978, 123 p.
36. *School curricula and standards of education and training in Madagascar*. Paris, UNESCO, 1978, 79 p.
37. *School curricula and standards of education and training in Portugal*. Paris, UNESCO, 1979, 77 p.
38. *School leavers in Australia* by Millicent Poole. Paris, UNESCO, 1978, 188 p.
39. *Standardization of education and curricula for boys and girls in general education, vocational and teacher-training schools in the Mongolian People's Republic*. Paris, UNESCO, 1979, 49 p.
40. *Status of girls in primary education in some Asian countries and prospects*. Working document of Asian regional seminar on access of girls to primary education. Paris, UNESCO, 1978, 37 p.
41. *A study on the portrayal of women and men in school textbooks and children's literature in France*. Paris, UNESCO, 1983, 66 p. ED-83/WS/118.
42. *Study on access of women to science education and training and associated careers in Malaysia*. Paris, UNESCO, 1983, 77 p. ED-83/WS/107.
43. *Study on curricula and standards of education and training for boys and girls in secondary schools and teacher-training institutes in Jamaica*. Paris, UNESCO, 1979, 99 p.
44. *Study on curricula and standards of education and training for boys and girls in secondary schools and teacher-training institutes in Jordan*. Paris, UNESCO, 1978, 63 p.
45. *A study on the differences between the educational programmes of young girls and young boys in Turkey*. Paris, UNESCO, 1979, 44 p.
46. *Study on the differences of curricula for girls and boys in Afghanistan*. Paris, UNESCO, 1978, 87 p.
47. *A study on educational opportunities and employment opportunities open to women in Sri Lanka*. Paris, UNESCO, 1974, 73 p.
48. *Study on portrayal of men and women in Chinese school textbooks and children's literature*. Paris, UNESCO, 1983, 69 p. ED/83/WS/22.
49. *Study on portrayal of men and women in school textbooks and children's literature in Norway*. Paris, UNESCO, 1983, 108 p.

ED-83/WS/45.

50. *Study on portrayal of men and women in school textbooks and children's literature in the Ukrainian Soviet Socialist Republic.* Paris, UNESCO, 1982, 56 p. ED-82/WS/109.
51. *A Study on some activities implemented in Sweden to promote equality of opportunity for girls in technical and vocational education* by Birgitta Aseskog. Paris, UNESCO, 1987, 55 p. ED-87/WS/30.
52. *Survey on the representation of women in higher education, research, educational planning, administration and management* carried out with the assistance of the INternational Federation of University Women. Paris, UNESCO, 1987, 173 p. ED-87/WS/8.
53. *UNESCO's contribution towards improving the status of women.* Report by the Director-General (20 C/17). Paris, UNESCO, 1978.
54. *Women's education in rural Thailand* (A survey of facilities, need and opportunities for basic scientific knowledge). Paris, UNESCO, in cooperation with the Faculty of Education, Chulalongkom University, Bangkok, 1980, 39 p. ED-80/WS/165.

APPENDIX M

REFERENCE SOURCES*

1. *1988 at UNESCO : New openings*, Paris, UNESCO, 1989.
2. *1990 International Literacy Year : A time for action*, Paris, UNESCO, 1989. (leaflet).
3. *APEID, 1986*. Bangkok, PROAP, 1986. (leaflet).

4A. *APPEAL 1986*, Bangkok, PROAP, 1986. (leaflet).

4B. *Adult education information notes*, Nos. 2, 3 & 4, 1988.

5. *Bulletin of the UNESCO Principal Regional Office for Asia and the Pacific* Vol. 1, No. 1, September, 1966 - to date.
6. *Catalogue of documents and publications : Education sector*, Paris, UNESCO, 1989.
7. *Consultative meeting on the incorporation of environmental education into technical and vocational education*, Singapore, 10-14 March, 1986, *Final report*, Singapore, UNESCO/UNEP, 1986, 65 p. + annexes.
8. *Current bibliographical sources in education*, 3rd ed., Bulletin of the IBE, Educational documentation and information, 1989, UNESCO/IBE, 1989, 89 p.
9. *Directory of educational documentation and information services*, 5th ed., UNESCO/IBE, 1988, 114 p. (IBEDATA series).
10. *Documents of the International Conferences on Education, 1979-1986 : Cumulative catalogue*, UNESCO/IBE, 1988, 147 p. (IBEDATA series).
11. *Education in Asia and the Pacific : Retrospect - prospect*, by Raja Roy Singh, Bangkok, PROAP, 1986, 187 p.
12. *Environmental education: Training of teacher educators, curriculum developers, educational planners and administrators*, by Usha Nayar, Anjana Mangalaguri, New Delhi, National Institute of Educational Planning and Administration, 1988,

* Consulted and extracts, where necessary, incorporated whith grateful thanks to authors/publishers of all these publications

327 p.

13. *Facts and figures*, Paris, UNESCO, 1987. *World Development:* Annual report, 1987, New York, UNDP, 1987.
14. *Fourth conference of ministers of education of member-states of the Europe region*, organised by UNESCO with the cooperation of United Nations Economic Commission for Europe, Paris, 21-27 September, 1988, *Final Report*, Paris, UNESCO, 1989, 41 p. + annexes, ED/MD/86.
15. *General Information Programme and UNISIST*, Paris, UNESCO, 1984.
16. *International conference on education*, 40th session, Geneva, 2-11 December, 1986, *Final report*, UNESCO-IBE, 1986.
17. *International conference on education*, 41st session, Geneva, 9-17 January 1989, *Final report*, UNESCO-IBE, 1989.
18. *International Institute for Educational Planning, 1986*, UNESCO/IIEP, 1986. (leaflet).
19. *International Literacy Year News*, No. 1, May 1989.
20. *International yearbook of education*, Vol. 40, UNESCO/IBE, 1988, 159 p.
21. *Manpower, employment and education in the rural economy of Tanzania*, by Guy Hunder, Paris, UNESCO/IIEP, 1966.
22. *Multiple class teaching in primary schools : A methodological guide*, Bangkok, UNESCO/APEID, 1988.
23. *Publication catalogue*, Paris, UNESCO, 1989.

24A. *Recent educational development in the world*, by J.C. Aggarwal, New Delhi, Arya Book Depot, 1989, 248 p.

24B. *Regional meeting of experts on new approaches to education of children of pre-school age*, Bangkok 4-12 September 1978, *Report*, Bangkok, PROAP, 1979.

25. *Regional operational seminar, Bangkok and Southern Thailand*, Bangkok, 1986, *Formal and non-formal education : Report*, Bangkok, PROAP, 1986.
26. *A review of education in the world : Statistical analysis*, Paris, UNESCO (ED/BIE/CONF/INTED/41/REF. 1).
27. *Role and functions of National Commissions*, by S.P. Agrawal, New Delhi, Indian National Commission to UNESCO, 1974, 46 p.
28. *Role of UNESCO in education*, by J.C. Aggarwal and S.P. Agrawal, New Delhi, Vikas Publishing House, 1982, 386 p.
29. *Second meeting of the intergovernmental regional committee*

for the major project in the field of education in Latin America and the Caribbean, Bagota - 24-28 March 1987, Paris, UNESCO, 1987.

30. *Sub-regional workshop on curriculum development*, Colombo, 1-30 October 1976, *Curriculum development : Analysis and review of progress, products and outcomes: Final report*, Bangkok, PROAP, 1976.
31. *Status of teachers.* Paris, UNESCO/ILO, 1967, 35 p. ED/WS/13A.
32. *Technical workinggroup meetings on learning needs and problems in primary education*, Bangkok, 1983, *Report*, Vol. 1 *Research issues* and *proposals*, Bangkok, PROAP, 1983.
33. *Towards universalization of primary education in Asia and the Pacific*, Bangkok, UNESCO/PROAP-APEID, 1985.
34. *UNESCO 1986-87*, Report of the Director-General of UNESCO, Paris, UNESCO.
35. *UNESCO activities in the field of education in European region since the conference held in Sofia in 1980*, Paris, UNESCO, ED-88/NINED/EUROPE/REF. 4.
36. *UNESCO and India.*, New Delhi, UNESCO Regional Office of Science and Technology for South and Central Asia, 1988.
37. *UNESCO and social sciences: Retrospect and prospect*, by S.P. Agrawal and J.C. Aggarwal, Delhi, Concept Publishing Company, 1988, 366 p.
38. *UNESCO chronicle*, 15(9) September 1969.
39. *UNESCO features*, July (II) 1967; February (II) 1968; January 1970.
40. *UNESCO sources*, No. 1, February 1989.
41. *UNESCO statistical yearbook 1988*, 25th ed., Paris, UNESCO, 1988, 1182 p.
42. *UNESCO's contribution towards world education.*, by J.C. Aggarwal, New Delhi, Arya Book Depot, 1986, 212 p.
43. *World development : Annual report, 1987*, New York, UNDP, 1987.
44. *Worldwide action in education: International Literacy Year*, Paris, UNESCO, 1990.
45. *Yearbook of Indian education 1988-89 : World overview*, by J.C. Aggarwal, Delhi, Doaba, 1989, 736 p.

Index